# Sustainable Enterprise

## A Macromarketing Approach

## Mark Peterson
*University of Wyoming*

Los Angeles | London | New Delhi
Singapore | Washington DC

Los Angeles | London | New Delhi
Singapore | Washington DC

FOR INFORMATION:

SAGE Publications, Inc.
2455 Teller Road
Thousand Oaks, California 91320
E-mail: order@sagepub.com

SAGE Publications Ltd.
1 Oliver's Yard
55 City Road
London EC1Y 1SP
United Kingdom

SAGE Publications India Pvt. Ltd.
B 1/I 1 Mohan Cooperative Industrial Area
Mathura Road, New Delhi 110 044
India

SAGE Publications Asia-Pacific Pte. Ltd.
3 Church Street
#10-04 Samsung Hub
Singapore 049483

Acquisitions Editor:   Patricia Quinlin
Associate Editor:   Maggie Stanley
Assistant Editor:   Theresa Accomazzo
Editorial Assistant:   Katie Guarino
Production Editor:   Libby Larson
Copy Editor:   Sheree Van Vreede
Typesetter:   C&M Digitals (P) Ltd.
Proofreader:   Stefanie Storholt
Indexer:   Sheila Bodell
Cover Designer:   Edgar Abarca
Marketing Manager:   Liz Thornton
Permissions Editor:   Adele Hutchinson

Printed in the United States of America

*Library of Congress Cataloging-in-Publication Data*

Peterson, Mark, 1956-

Sustainable enterprise : a macromarketing approach / Mark Peterson.

p. cm.
Includes bibliographical references and index.

ISBN 978-1-4129-9868-0 (pbk.)

1. Marketing—Social aspects. 2. Social responsibility of business. I. Title.

HF5415.P4419 2013
658.8'02—dc23          2012024976

This book is printed on acid-free paper.

SUSTAINABLE FORESTRY INITIATIVE
Certified Chain of Custody
Promoting Sustainable Forestry
www.sfiprogram.org
SFI-01268

SFI label applies to text stock

12 13 14 15 16 10 9 8 7 6 5 4 3 2 1

# Brief Contents

# Detailed Contents

# 4   Stakeholders in Marketing

**101**

# 5   The Role of Business in Society

**139**

## 6   The Role of the State in Society         173

## PART IV—ENTERPRISE WITH EQUITY IN MIND                     409

# 13   Developing Markets                                      411

# 14   Poverty Alleviation                                     453

# Preface

## A Macromarketing Approach

I wrote this book to explain how businesses can benefit by taking a more holistic approach to the marketplace. While attending the Macromarketing Conference in May 2005 in St. Petersburg, Florida, I was stunned when one of the panelists at the final session of the conference gave a simple response to the question: "What is the future of marketing?" This panelist, Cliff Shultz, who was then the editor of the *Journal of Macromarketing*, confidently asserted, "the future of marketing is macromarketing" (Shultz, 2005).

Macromarketing—taking a systems view of the interplay between marketing and society—had a rich history of scholarship with such accomplished scholars as Shelby Hunt, and Bill Wilkie contributing meaningfully to understanding the role of marketing in society. However, to my mind, macromarketers up to that time seemed to be satisfied with scholarship alone and had little interest in the practical aspects of market success for businesses. So when Cliff made his assertion, it struck me as a deep paradox—how could the ivory tower move to the mainstream of marketing practice? Yet, I instinctively knew he was right. Since then, business persons have increasingly sought answers for how to approach new complexities of the marketplace that macromarketers have studied over the years. This book is intended to help business persons tap into the wisdom accrued in macromarketing scholarship over three decades. In this way, the book is about managerial macromarketing—macromarketing for sustainable enterprise.

In 2009 and 2010, I taught a new marketing and society course to MBA students at the University of Wyoming. Unlike other schools, ALL students had to take the course because it was required. This experience proved uniquely valuable because with all students in the course, many doubts and reservations about "going green" were expressed by students. These students instinctively knew that profits had to be made for businesses to continue operations, and many sustainability-related issues about including stakeholders in planning and being mindful of equity issues did not come with explanations about how the bottom line would be affected. At the time, no books existed to address this issue of how to operate in the marketplace with a social conscience and achieve profits. I have written this book to help business persons, teachers, and students better understand how this can be done.

I believe most readers will find the contents of this book refreshingly different. Throughout the book, I have woven a theme of entrepreneurship—identifying and developing opportunities, regardless of the resources available. In this way, the book focuses on enterprise, rather than on "business as usual." Part 1 presents and explains macromarketing as a valuable frame for understanding what is occurring in marketplaces today. Part 2 explains factors contributing to market dynamism today, such as empowered consumers, collaborative relationships, and globalization. Part 3 gives special attention to issues related to the natural environment. Part 4 discusses issues related to equity, such as developing markets, and poverty alleviation. Part 5 sets a primary theme of the book—entrepreneurship—into perspective and includes an actual business plan from a sustainable entrepreneur as an appendix on the supporting website for the book, www.sagepub.com/peterson. The plan is not merely a checklist. It offers readers a more complete understanding of the thought and effort that goes into a successful business plan—especially the figures and tables.

Each chapter of the book begins with a vignette featuring a living protagonist facing a real-life challenge related to marketing and society. In this way, the human aspect of business emerges. Each chapter closes with a mini-case called Mavericks Who Made It featuring an entrepreneurial figure. Some of these come from history. Some come from realms other than modern business. However, each should lead readers to reflect more effectively on the content of the chapters. Questions follow both the opening vignette and the Mavericks Who Made It mini-cases.

Because this book addresses timely issues in the environment of the firm, it can be used in a variety of courses, including Marketing and Society, Business and Society, and a forward-looking Marketing Strategy course. However, this book will best match courses being fielded now with sustainability in the title. Such courses might be titled "Sustainable Enterprise," "Sustainable Business," and "Sustainable Marketing."

I wrote this book with my former MBA students in mind. However, my very capable reviewer/editor Laura Wespetal, a senior English major at the University of Wyoming and the university's Rhodes Scholar nominee in 2011, had never taken a business course. Through her attentiveness, the book should be accessible to all college students because she would not allow any business concepts or terms to be included without explanation.

Ancillary materials for instructors using this book will be posted at www.sagepub.com/peterson. These include (a) recommended Harvard Business School cases, (b) Microsoft PowerPoint slides, (c) additional short readings to supplement the book content, and (d) test bank questions with answers for each chapter, and (e) the author's blogging on sustainable enterprise.

My first thanks go to Costco Wholesale CFO Richard Galanti and Costco Wholesale Senior Vice President for E-Commerce & Publishing Ginnie Roeglin who were two of the first business persons to grasp what a book like this could contribute to the sustainable enterprise movement. As a result of Ginnie's willingness to advance sustainable business practices around the world, several Mavericks Who Made It mini-cases come directly from the pages of *The Costco Connection*. In this way, readers can gain a richer understanding about a sustainable enterprise, such as Costco, and its collaborative partners. During my research for the book, Costco's Director of Corporate Sustainability Karen Raines provided valuable perspective regarding the development of sustainable business practices at Costco.

Lisa Myers who heads Patagonia's environmental grant program was another business person who boosted the research involved in writing this book. Lisa willingly shared her time and perspectives on the environmental movement and stood ready to field questions from me any time. Patagonia's story is an important one among sustainable enterprises, and I appreciate Lisa's help in explaining key parts of it to me during a visit to Patagonia's headquarters in Ventura, California, in February 2011.

I would like to thank Dana Cushman, my first and only research assistant, whose two months of part-time work helped me launch this book project. Enormous thanks go to Laura Wespetal who applied her formidable writing skills as my reviewer/editor once the chapters came into existence. I look forward to reading Laura's books in the future. Finally, Richard Vann helped valuably with obtaining permissions for the many figures, tables, and photos of the book.

I have also appreciated the encouragement of the College of Business at the University of Wyoming and of my colleagues in the Management and Marketing Department. Special thanks go to John Mittlestaedt for doing the beta-testing of the first 10 chapters of the book in his Sustainable Marketing class in Fall 2011. As well, the thoughtful comments of each of the following reviewers for the chapters helped shape this book to be what you now hold in your hands:

Michael L. Bruce, Anderson University

Susan Dobscha, PhD, Associate Professor of Marketing, Bentley University

G. Scott Erickson, Ithaca College

Richard D. Hunley, Lindsey Wilson College

Dr. Michael R. Hyman, Stan Fulton Professor of Marketing, New Mexico State University

Stephanie Jue, Lecturer, University of Texas

Richard Kalish, JD, Adjunct Professor, School of Business and Leadership, Dominican University of California

Nada Kobeissi, Long Island University–C.W. Post

Gene R. Laczniak, Professor of Marketing, Marquette University

Roger D. Lee, PhD, Professor, Salt Lake Community College

Jill K. Maher, PhD, Robert Morris University

Michael J. Messina, PhD, Professor of Marketing, Gannon University

John D. Mittelstaedt, Clemson University

Nicholas Nugent, Jr., PhD, Florida Southern College

Lori D. Paris, PhD, California State University, Bakersfield

Mark J. Pate, King College

Gregory Portillo, School of Business, Holy Names University, Oakland, California

Nagarajan Ramamoorthy, PhD, University of Houston-Victoria

Mary Anne Raymond, Clemson University

Jose Rocha, Florida International University

Andy C. Saucedo, Professor, Business & Marketing, NMSU-Doña Ana Community College

Michael J. Scrivens, Professor, Rochester Institute of Technology

Cliff Shultz, Loyola University Chicago

Stanley J. Shapiro, Professor-Emeritus, Beedie School of Business, Simon Fraser University

Mr. Joaquin Tadeo, MBA, Assistant Professor, NMSU-Doña Ana Community College

Terrence Witkowski, California State University—Long Beach

I would also like to thank the team at SAGE Publications for helping to make this project come to life. I really enjoyed working with such pros as Pat Quinlin, Maggie Stanley, Katie Guarino, Liz Thornton, Lisa Shaw, Deya Saoud Jacob, Julie Nemer, Terri Accomazzo, as well as Libby Larson and the production team. You get things done in the finest tradition of SAGE's founder Sara Miller-McCune. I smile, but I know Sara's dog, Duke, wags his tail when thinking of you.

I thank my family for the time and encouraging gestures from my wife, Cindy, and daughters Emily, Angela, and Rachel over my years in academia. You have made me sustainable in all my endeavors.

Finally, this book is dedicated to all macromarketers—past, present, and future. Thank you for daring to take a "big-picture view" of the marketplace and for sharing it with others.

## REFERENCE

Shultz, C. J. II. (2005, May). *Panel on the future of macromarketing*. Macromarketing Conference, St. Petersburg, FL.

# PART I

# Macromarketing for Sustainable Enterprise

# 21st Century Micro and Macro Issues

## MID-COURSE CORRECTION FOR RAY ANDERSON

### Ray Anderson

In many ways, Ray Anderson represented the best of American entrepreneurship and business in 1994. A former football player at Georgia Tech and a veteran of the carpet-manufacturing industry, Anderson launched his own company Interface, Inc. in 1973 to manufacture carpet tile (modular carpet) in LaGrange, Georgia. Just over 20 years later, Interface had become the world leader in carpet tiles with annual revenues exceeding $1 billion.

However, in August 1994, at the age of 60, Anderson found himself in a crisis when the staff from Interface Research Corporation (the research arm of Interface) asked him to talk to them about his environmental vision for the company. Customers of Interface from all over the world had begun asking sales representatives about Interface's environmental position and their efforts to preserve and protect the environment. Leaders within Interface had formed a task force to begin framing a response to these questions; however, these difficult questions could not be answered without the input of the CEO, so Anderson was invited to speak to the task force.

This request distressed Anderson because Interface was so oil-dependent at the time that he later admitted Interface could be thought of as an extension of the petrochemical industry:

> Well, frankly, I didn't have a vision, except "obey the law, comply, comply, comply," and I was very reluctant to accept the invitation. The idea that, while in compliance, we might be hurting the environment simply hadn't occurred to me. (Anderson, 1998)

Anderson finally accepted the invitation to address the task force and then embarked on three weeks of reading and soul searching to prepare himself. During this time, Paul Hawken's *The Ecology of Commerce* serendipitously wound up on his desk. In reading Hawken's book, Anderson faced the haunting truth that environments could be ruined by industrial activity—the same industrial activity that Interface had pursued from its inception.

> I read it and it changed my life. It hit me right between the eyes. It was an epiphany. I wasn't halfway through it before I had the vision I was looking for . . . Hawken's message was a spear in my chest that is still there. (Anderson, 1998)

Hawken, who had founded the highly successful gardening supply store Smith & Hawken, was a business person whose ideas penetrated deeply into Anderson. Hawken departed from many environmentalists by asserting that the only institution on the planet capable of leading humankind out of its current mess and grim future was, in fact, business and industry. Government always seemed to follow, rather than lead. Religious institutions offered only criticism of society's problems, as did colleges and universities. The media also filled itself with criticism rather than solutions.

Anderson's entire outlook on business changed in preparing for the talk he gave about an environmental vision for Interface to representatives from all of Interface's businesses from around the world. He admitted to all in attendance the dire situation that would result from continuing with a traditional approach to business focusing only on the dyad of seller and customer. He called all 7,000 employees to contribute to what very likely would be a painful overhaul of the company and its processes in order to make the company environmentally conscious in all that it did. This internally focused effort would later be termed EcoSense. Anderson challenged Interface's suppliers to do the same. His mission was to first reach sustainability and then go beyond sustainability to convert Interface into a restorative company—one that simply does not do harm to the environment, but rather puts back more than it takes from the Earth.

For the first year, Anderson persistently urged his employees to catch the vision for Interface becoming a restorative enterprise by reducing, reusing, reclaiming, recycling, and importantly, redesigning. Beyond the core group who first heard Anderson's environmental vision for Interface, Anderson's urgings were barely heeded by the rest of the company, causing changes to be barely perceivable during the first year. However, after that first year, momentum began to gather among the employees, who, one by one, began to advocate for the redesign of the company. Eventually, so many accepted the mission and dedicated themselves to it that not only was the progress made in environmental stewardship remarkable, but also working at Interface became characterized by working not just for profit but for a higher purpose as well. Interface demonstrated to all firms that environmental stewardship could be realized in business and industry—even in what was once an energy-intensive, waste-producing industry.

The shared mission evolved into what is known as Mission Zero. Mission Zero is Interface's promise to eliminate completely the negative impact the company has on the environment by 2020. By the end of 2010, the results were astounding. Greenhouse gas emissions had so far been reduced by 44% in absolute terms (94% when factoring in offsets). Interface cut energy consumption by 43%, water consumption by 80%, and waste sent to landfills by 77% (Interface, 2011). Importantly, the culture of the company shifted to a new trajectory in pursuit of innovations for new machines, materials, and manufacturing processes that would help fulfill Mission Zero. During the same period since 1994, the company grew net sales by 32% (Anderson, 1998, p. 3; Interface, 2012). Figure 1.1 more completely depicts Interface's achievements in climbing what Anderson called "Mt. Sustainability."

## Your Thoughts?

- What do you make of Interface's redesign?
- What evidence have you seen that other companies around the world have begun to recognize their social and environmental impact?
- How and when did it become important for companies to start thinking about the impact they have on society?

**Figure 1.1**    Mount Sustainability at Interface Global

### MOUNT SUSTAINABILITY

Mission Zero Milestones

In 1994 founder Ray Anderson received a dramatic wake up call – something he describes as "a spear in the chest." He realized there was an urgent need to set a new direction for interface.

He challenged us to pursue a bold new vision:

"To be the first company that, by its deeds, shows the entire industrial world what sustainability is in all its dimensions; people, process, product, place and profits – and in doing so, become restorative through the power of influence."

From the beginning, we understood that sustainability had to be approached from a systems perspective or a "whole company" approach. Over the years as this commitment to sustainability reached all the parts of our business, it evolved into a shared mission; Mission Zero.

We're now sixteen years into our journey and a decade away from the date we predicted for achieving our vision – 2020. Company–wide commitment to Mission Zero has unleashed innovative thinking and connected us to a higher purpose. We're simultaneously pursuing sustainability along three paths – innovative solutions for reducing our footprint, new ways to design and make products, and an inspired and engaged culture.

#### FOOTPRINT

We have made great strides in reducing our footprint – those impacts that our company operations have on the planet.

- Installed solar PV arrays in the Netherlands, California, and Georgia
- Using landfill gas in our Georgia plant
- Eight of nine manufacturing facilities operate with 100% renewable electricity
- Reduced building footprints by adopting best in class green building standards, with six LEED certified facilities around the world, including the first LEED CI platinum space
- All global manufacturing facilities conform to ISO 14001
- Waste elimination programs achieved 42% reduction in waste cost since 1995
- Achieved $433 million in avoided waste cost since 1995
- Designed innovative TacTiles system to reduce the impact of installing our products

#### PRODUCTS

Mission Zero changed how we envision, design, and make products – away from a linear, take make waste industrial model toward a cyclical model based on nature.

- Biomimicry inspired us to create more sustainable and better performing products
- Developed Fairworks™ product line which considers social as well as environmental impacts
- Pioneered Life Cycle Assessment (LCA) to understand impacts of new materials and processes
- Launched first Environmental Product Declarations (EPDs) in our industry globally, providing transparency to our customers on product impacts

- Using recycled and biobased materials to move us closer to our end goal of closed loop products
- Pioneered the process of creating post consumer recycled nylon with our suppliers
- Diverted over 100,000 tons of material from landfills through our ReEntry program

**CULTURE**

Commitment to Mission Zero has created a culture of inspired thinkers who are finding innovative solutions and changing our business.

- By sharing his vision for sustainable business directly with associates, Ray Anderson inspired our employees and connected them to a higher purpose
- Empowered associates are presenting innovative new ideas like portable creels that reduce waste and save money
- Our Eco Dream Team of influential environmental thinkers brings fresh perspective and learning to our business
- Our changed culture is part of why we are consistently acknowledged as a global leader in the sustainable business movement – as evidenced by rankings in The Sustainability Survey from Globescan
- Our associates are taking Mission Zero into their local communities through volunteering and philanthropy

*Source:* Interface (2011).

## CHAPTER OVERVIEW AND LEARNING OBJECTIVES

This chapter will give a historical summary of how we have come to the place where using a macromarketing lens can reduce risk and help identify opportunities for entrepreneurially oriented firms. A macromarketing lens can be useful because it helps us understand the interplay between marketing and society. This chapter will specifically focus on the practice of sustainability and the seven reasons business is more mindful of society today, discuss what marketing and macromarketing are and why they are important, and conclude with a series of examples showing the implications of macromarketing for entrepreneurship.

The chapter concludes with FirstFruits of Washington featured as a maverick firm that made it.

FirstFruits demonstrates that applying spiritual values and a servant leadership model of business can result in capital gains for society. By making formerly unproductive land bloom with orchards and putting employees and the poor as beneficiaries of the firm's operations, FirstFruits of Washington exemplifies five-capital entrepreneurship as well as a mission and purpose that transcends a traditional two-capital approach to business.

After this chapter, you should be able to answer the following questions:

- What are the seven reasons businesses are more mindful of society today?
- What is the definition of markets? Marketing? Society?
- What is macromarketing, and why is it important?
- What is the emerging view of capitalism and its five types of capital (manufactured, financial, natural, human, and social)?
- What role do entrepreneurs play in moving the marketplace toward generating social and environmental gains?
- How can social responsibility be integrated into a sustainable enterprise?

# SUSTAINABILITY AND THE TRIPLE BOTTOM LINE: THE LESSON THAT SAVED INTERFACE

The story of Interface's redesign is one of the most encouraging from the early years of business' transition to more sustainable business practices. Anderson (2008) now credits the dramatic turn of Interface to sustainability, in hindsight, as saving the company from a soon-arriving demise in a mature cost-driven industry. Buffeted by cycles in the building industry, the stock price of Interface (NASDAQ: IFSIA) since 1990 suggests that Interface's redesign has not pushed the company into a disadvantageous position. Interface's continued financial viability suggests that it continues to be economically sustainable. See Figure 1.2 for Interface's 20-year stock-price record.

**Figure 1.2**   Interface's Twenty-Year Stock-Price Record (InvestorGuide.com, 2012)

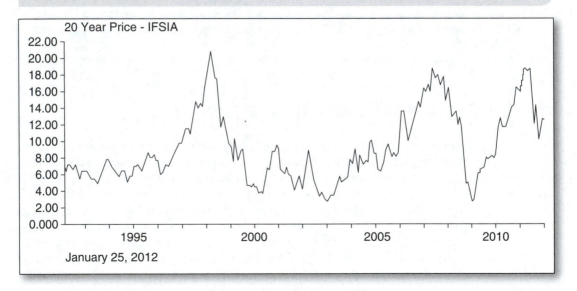

Many more businesses from around the world and across many sectors of the economy will be presented in *Sustainable Enterprise: A Macromarketing Approach*. More than 52,000 company web pages highlight the "triple bottom line" (people, planet, profit), signaling that these firms are beginning to account for their net social and environmental impact in addition to the traditional economic metric of economic profit (Hollender & Breen, 2010). Originally proposed by sustainability thought leader John Elkington, the triple bottom line, or balanced scorecard, is broader than economic results, and it includes measures of the firm's environmental effects (air quality, water quality, energy usage, and waste produced), as well as of social outcomes (labor practices, community impacts, human rights, and product responsibility) (Savitz & Weber, 2006). Are such cases merely outliers?

Is sustainability, preserving opportunities for future generations through care for social issues, environmental issues, as well as profits, a fad that will go away? More than 4,700 companies across 130 countries have signed the UN Global Compact pledging to follow its ten principles focused on 1) human rights, 2) labor, 3) the environment, and 4) anti-corruption (United Nations [UN], 2011). The next generation of business leaders will more than likely receive their business education at one of the 346 schools who have adopted the Principles for Responsible Management Education. These six principles focus on developing capabilities of students in the areas of sustainable value for business and society at large (Principles for Responsible Management Education, 2011).

The results for Interface suggest that sustainability is not only a morally relevant approach to business but also a smart way to approach business. Darrin Duber-Smith, President of the consulting firm Green Marketing, Inc. and a long-time observer of sustainability efforts, asserts that by 2020, what we now know as sustainable business practices will be known simply as "good business" (Duber-Smith, personal communication, October 2010). Duber-Smith also makes a point of informing audiences in industry and college classes that he votes Republican to make sure involvement with green initiatives is not perceived as exclusive to those voting Democrat.

In sum, it is likely that Interface's success will be replicated by other firms and by many start-up firms that will grow and prosper as the Industrial age ends and another comes into being. In this age of the Next Industrial Revolution, the purpose of the corporation must be redefined as creating shared value—not strictly economic profit (Porter & Kramer, 2011). The idea of shared value recognizes that societal needs—not just ordinary economic needs—define markets. Accordingly, expanding the total pool of economic and social value will need to be achieved by actors in 21$^{st}$ century markets. John Mackey, co-founder and co-CEO of Whole Foods Market, calls this "conscious capitalism."

## WHAT IS DRIVING THE TURN FOR BUSINESSES TO BE MINDFUL OF SOCIETY?

Although theories explaining the roots of conscious capitalism are only now emerging, several likely contributing factors can currently be identified (Hollender & Breen, 2010). The seven reasons business is more mindful of society are discussed below.

### Reason 1: Technological Improvements

Improvements in technology, especially telecommunications technology, increasingly gives power to individual consumers and citizens. In a networked world, accountability is more timely and powerful. Savitz and Weber (2006) call this the "Age of Accountability." Accordingly, externalities generated by firms, such as the variety and breath of pollutants produced, no longer go unrecognized. On the other hand, firms that embrace stewardship of the planet and concern for people in their pursuit of profits are more likely to be recognized and rewarded for such an approach to business. Some firms are going beyond separate reports for financial and nonfinancial results (e.g., corporate social responsibility or sustainability reports) and combining these into a single integrated report (Eccles & Krzus, 2010). At the same time, they are using the Internet to offer more detailed results to all of their stakeholders and to improve their level of dialogue and engagement with a wider set of stakeholders. Wall Street financial analysts have begun to take note because such integrated reporting adds noticeable value to the company. Contributions to sound business practices and a more sustainable society make enlightened firms more appealing to many stakeholders—including shareholders.

## Reason 2: Rising Prosperity and Environmental Values

Second, rising prosperity in countries of the world allows quality-of-life and environmental concerns to move higher in the priorities of consumers and citizens. This is happening all over the world. With higher income, individuals give higher priority to self-expression and to quality of life. There is a strong association between prosperity and environmental values (Inglehart & Welzel, 2005). The increased interest in environmentally friendly products can be seen in the demand for hybrid cars. Toyota anticipated this trend and introduced its Prius hybrid vehicle years before other competing firms (Bonini, Mendonca, & Oppenheim, 2006).

## Reason 3: Awareness of Earth's Limits

Rising awareness of the planet's limits suggest that new forms of production and consumption need to be developed. *New York Times* Foreign Affairs columnist and Pulitzer Prize winning author, Thomas L. Friedman (2008) characterizes the Earth as a hot, flat, and crowded planet. Friedman means that the Earth is characterized by (a) a changing global climate, (b) a developing world that is rapidly beginning to use many of the competitive capabilities of the developed world that were once thought to be nonexistent in a developing county, and (c) a developing world with a burgeoning population in urban areas. These all suggest that we are all more vulnerable to volatility and major social, economic, and political change than we previously perceived we were in the 20th century. The rise of China and India as economic powers suggests that demand for energy will continue to be pressed. As this happens, energy prices will move higher. Many of the sources for fossil fuels, such as Venezuela and Saudi Arabia, seem to be poised for difficult transitions in political leadership in the future. In sum, there is an increasing awareness that a take–make–waste approach within societies needs to be changed.

## Reason 4: Firms Can "Do the Right Thing"

Firms have gained increased ability to "do the right thing." The success of the voluntary standards movement in business has given businesses a way to improve process quality in both manufacturing and service businesses. Total Quality Management (TQM) has led to ISO 9000 certification in manufacturing, as well as to ISO 14000 in environmental protection. The ISO 9001:2008 standard provides a tested framework for taking a systematic approach to managing the organization's processes using satisfaction ratings of those inside the firm as well as of customers and partners outside the firm. This is done so the firm and its partners can consistently turn out a product that satisfies customers' expectations. Alternatively, the ISO 14000 family addresses various aspects of environmental management to identify and control the environmental impact of a firm's activities, products, or services, and to improve continually its environmental performance. Using these ISO frameworks for management practice, multinational enterprises have located factories and offices all over the world that can produce at world-class standards. Highly efficient processes have become synonymous with high-quality products and eco-efficiency. The increased power of firms to self-monitor is leading them to pursue eco-effective approaches to business where harm to the environment is avoided.

## Reason 5: Intangible Assets

Firms realize the increasing importance of intangible assets. *Fortune* estimates that 75% of the total value of the average U.S. corporation can be attributed to the patents, copyrights, employee knowledge and creativity, as well as customer goodwill they carry. In other words, physical stuff matters much less than what might have been previously thought. In such a world for business, having a purpose beyond earning a profit matters much. It enables a firm to attract the most talented and committed employees who will eventually make a difference in the competitive marketplace for the customers of the firm. It also attracts customers who will use their capabilities to make the firm a success through repeated purchase, involvement in new product development efforts of the firm, as well as word-of-mouth communication about the firm and its offerings.

## Reason 6: Nongovernmental Organizations

The rise of nongovernmental organizations (NGOs) bring a voice to those previously unheard in issues related to the citizenship of businesses. This is a powerful and new regulatory force. Those with concerns not adequately addressed by business or government increasingly establish an NGO to focus the attention of individuals, public institutions (local, national, and transnational), businesses, and other NGOs. A web presence also boosts fundraising and marshalling support from NGO constituents. Over the last 15 years, NGOs have proliferated to number in the millions and have grown to become the eighth largest economy in the world with operating budgets totaling more than $1 trillion (Hollender & Breen, 2010). During this time, trust in NGOs has steadily risen, while faith in business has declined as a result of debacles at Enron, WorldCom, and the Economic Meltdown of 2008 (Bonini et al., 2006).

Astute firms these days are working with select NGOs rather than resisting them. For example, global specialty coatings company AkzoNobel (the largest decorative coatings company in the world employing more than 24,000 with annual sales over $6 billion) collaborated with the U.K.-based NGO Forum for the Future to develop its successful Ecosure paints under the Dulux brand name. These Ecosure paints have a 30% lower carbon footprint than regular paints (AkzoNobel, 2011). AkzoNobel was then able to apply its new knowledge for producing lower carbon paints to its other brands of paint.

## Reason 7: Branding as a Social Phenomenon

Firms who consider branding to be much more of a phenomenon of society, culture, and politics—rather than one of the individual's mind—are better able to identify opportunities for innovation in branding (Holt & Cameron, 2011). Branding success for diverse firms such as Nike, Starbucks, Patagonia, Vitaminwater, Fat Tire, and the Freelancer's Union suggest that ideological opportunities emerge during major historical changes. Here, the brand can offer a superior cultural expression for consumers.

For example, Nike took the focus off of elite athletes succeeding in their chosen athletic domains (the typical advertising approach of its rivals) and put it on the human dimension of competition and life. In the 1970s and 1980s, diminished expectations for U.S. society was widespread as a result of the failure of the Vietnam War, the distrust of government resulting from the Watergate scandal, and the stagflation that plagued the economy for years. In such a milieu of anxiety, Nike articulated an anti-authoritarian theme in advertising by showing Nike athletes in ordinary training scenes showing their tenacious dedication in going it alone and embracing total responsibility for one's success. Nike led the trend for jogging by celebrating ordinary people pursuing their own training. Nike's "Just Do It" advertising theme developed a cultural mythology about Nike and showed women, people of poverty, and minority athletes succeeding on the level playing field of sport despite the societal discrimination they faced off the field. Here, Nike offered a broader view of competition that suggested that overcoming barriers, such as racism, sexism, and global poverty, are much more impressive than success in sport. This myth used the imperfections of society as a foil to boost Nike's association with those manifesting combative solo willpower and succeeding on their own terms in life.

**Table 1.1**   Reasons for Business Turning to Be More Mindful of Society

1. Technological improvements

2. Rising prosperity and environmental values

3. Awareness of Earth's limits

4. Firms can "do the right thing"

5. Increasing importance of intangible assets

6. Rise of nongovernmental organizations

7. Branding as a social phenomenon

## Implications

Although businesses have always been subject to sociopolitical forces, today these forces are more complex, and they can change more rapidly as a result of activists' ability to mobilize public opinion. Former Coca-Cola CEO Doug Ivester discovered this in a very painful way that cost him his job. In the summer of 1999, several dozen schoolchildren in Belgium reported feeling queasy. After treatment at clinics, the source of their illness was determined by health officials to be the Coca-Cola they had consumed that day. Ivester was initially slow in responding to this problem, and then he announced that the problem was a minor one—a bad batch of carbon dioxide. Meanwhile, with the backdrop of election campaigning in Belgium and its nonstop news coverage, the "minor problem" was rapidly perceived by many in Europe to be a major one about environmental contamination brought on by not just a business but a foreign one that has long been identified with American pop culture (Morris, Sellers, & Tarpley, 2000). It was a public relations disaster, and Ivester's efforts repeatedly seemed to be late and insufficient. Shortly afterward, two members of the board of directors, billionaire Warren Buffet and Herbert Allen, confronted Ivester and informed him that they had lost confidence in his leadership. Ivester subsequently submitted his resignation.

In sum, society might have been an afterthought for executive teams primarily focused on regulatory compliance in the 20th century. However, 21st century realities related to the seven reasons businesses have become more mindful of society have brought a heightened sensitivity to societal issues. Today, firms must recognize that society expects more from business; firms that act as if other people matter and protect and restore the ecosystem are more likely to achieve profits in a reliable way into the future (Werbach, 2009). Increasingly, firms are implementing a triple bottom-line or balanced scorecard that includes firms' economic, environmental, and social results (Savitz & Weber, 2006). Leaders of firms are giving more consideration to society not because these leaders are suddenly more moral in their approach, rather, because they are more pragmatic. If these leaders do not anticipate the changing landscape of societal issues, they will not be able to avoid problems that will damage their firms' reputations, and they will not be able to guide their firms to successful positioning relative to their competitors in the future.

# MARKETS

## Defining Markets

What comes to mind when you hear the word "markets?" A shopping center? A bazaar? A financial market like the floor of the New York Stock Exchange? eBay? Monster.com? All of these are examples of markets. A market is a social arena where firms, their suppliers, customers, workers, and governments interact (Fligstein & Dauter, 2007). Sociologists offer valuable perspectives on what are not markets. For example, unstructured, one-shot, anonymous social exchange is not a market. If you sell your laptop to a friend, a market was not part of this transaction. Sociologists give further definition to markets as being social arenas where repeated exchanges occur between buyers and sellers under a set of formal and informal rules. Importantly, markets depend on governments, laws, and social norms about activity in the marketplace.

Because human beings are self-oriented, distortions in the marketplace inevitably occur; often these issues are resolved with the assistance of the government, making it an integral part of the market system. For example, product failure raises problems for market actors. Determining responsibility among the set of suppliers, retailers, and customers can be problematic. Was the product misused by the customer, or was the product inherently flawed in manufacturing or damaged later in storage at the retailing store? The first aspect a sociology of markets (the study of marketing systems) suggests is that market actors will develop social structures to reconcile problems they encounter in exchange, competition, and production. Frequently, laws and government enforcement comprise these social structures, although mediation and arbitration can also be employed. However, if the actors involved cannot reach agreement, then the government must intervene—usually through a court system.

## The Role and Influence of Government on Markets

The debate over government's role in the market has long been debated. However, rather than get bogged down in the debate, this section will focus on the effect government has on the market. Specifically, this section will focus on the relationship between government market interaction and monopolies, the idea of the free market, and how changing markets demand a changing government role.

### Unfettered Markets and Monopolistic Market Actors

The self-orientation of humans can also lead to distortions in the structure of markets. Monopoly formation (one dominant actor, such as the Standard Oil Company for oil refining in the early 1900s) is an example of a market structure that has been deemed to be deleterious to the proper functioning of markets. The Sherman Anti-Trust Act of 1910 led to the breakup of Standard Oil into smaller competing firms (Peritz, 2008). Additionally, some actors in markets seek to restrain trade as when collusion among sellers in a market occurs. Scottish philosopher Adam Smith observed that in the 18th century, whenever rival merchants met, even for sharing a meal together, the interests of their customers were harmed. Higher prices to customers were one way such collusion might be manifested. Economists since Smith have generally agreed with his assertion. Today, governments define acceptable relations between producers or merchants so that competition will drive the activity of markets.

### Adam Smith and the Idea of a Free Market

Although buyers and sellers are the most salient actors in markets, history suggests that the self-orientation of humans will inevitably lead to disputes between actors in markets. This implies that in modern societies, governments will need to intervene so that markets can continue to function properly. In the time of Adam Smith, the British government sponsored companies in markets, such as the East India Company. Additionally, laws existed to forbid citizens from changing their jobs. Smith made the case that markets free of such government interventions would thrive and eventually perform a remarkable task for society—increasing the material well-being of society. In other words, if citizens and firms were allowed to own property, if labor were allowed to move freely in the job market, and if the rule of law prevailed, the market-based system for society would efficiently allocate the material resources (land, labor, and capital) (Smith, 2000). Buyers would be able to buy what they desired, while sellers would be able to sell what they desired. Today, China, still ruled by a Communist regime, struggles with the role of the government in markets because of its state-owned enterprises (almost always grossly inefficient entities). Even though the United States does not have China's state-owned enterprise system, U.S. society still struggles with the role of government in markets.

Today, "free market" is a portmanteau term that means different things to different people. To listen to some commentators in today's media, a free market means a market totally free and clear of any government intervention. No regulation and no taxes. But what about the government's role when market actors encounter problems? Because trust among market actors is so crucial to the proper functioning of markets, when such trust drops, social structures like the government are needed for conflict resolution, as well as for ensuring that safe products and services are provided in markets. So, in effect, a market totally free and clear of government intervention is like a unicorn—easy to draw on paper, but never actually seen walking around anywhere on Earth. No one has found fossil evidence for unicorns, either.

For those who propose strict and powerful regulation of markets, the accompanying increase in laws and licenses required to conduct business might slow market activity and increase the cost of doing business to levels that would render markets ineffective. If the issue is one of regulation of business, imagine if the World Cup soccer matches played every four years used no referees for the matches. It would not take long for the honor system to break down and chaos to reign on the field. On the other hand, if the World Cup organizers misguidedly saw the outcomes of matches as so important that they employed 1,000 referees and put them on the field for each match, it would be likely that the match would not succeed because of the interference of so many referees. An important decision for society is not whether there will or will not be involvement of the government in markets, since there will be government involvement for dispute resolution and for the regulation of safety in goods and services. Rather, the issue is to what degree governments will be involved in markets.

## Changing Markets, Changing Government Roles

The variety and dynamism of markets suggests that the role of government must be defined for markets and then redefined over time. For example, new markets are likely to be more fragile than stable established markets. This can be seen in the new markets for renewable energy where government involvement includes incentives (outright subsidies and tax exemptions to producers, as well as the government's support of university research into wind energy production). On the other hand, more established markets such as those for automobiles have attracted different forms of government involvement over the years. In World War II, the U.S. government steered production at auto plants toward the war effort. In the 1960s, the U.S. government imposed requirements for seat belts in cars. In the 1970s and 1980s, protectionist tariffs to protect the U.S. auto industry were endorsed by both the U.S. automakers and unions. Such calls were tempered later but still persist today. In sum, markets change, and the government's role in markets changes, as well. For example, if government regulation and programs cannot keep up with the rapidly changing market, a society will be at greater risk for harmful marketing distortions. More will be said about this in Chapter 2.

## MARKETING

### Changing Definitions of Marketing

Surprising to some, marketing's definition has changed twice since 1985. The American Marketing Association (AMA), the leading organization for marketers, includes a unit for marketing scholars. The AMA has committed to revisiting the definition of marketing every five years. In 2007, a task force led by Don Lehmann from Columbia University responded to widespread calls across academia to revise the definition of marketing. The 2004 revision had changed the 1985 definition of marketing and had focused exclusively on the firm, even to the extent of excluding the role of middlemen in marketing systems (such as channels of distribution), as well as institutions (such as retailers and wholesalers) (Hunt, 2010). After thorough reworking, Lehmann's task force agreed that the definition of marketing would be more inclusive and explicitly feature (a) the delivery of offerings, (b) institutions, and (c) society-at-large as a beneficiary of marketing. The current definition reads, "Marketing is the activity, institutions and set of processes for creating, communicating, delivering and exchanging offerings that have value for customers, clients, partners and society-at-large" (AMA, 2007, para. 2).

"Activity" implies that marketing can be done by individuals: entrepreneurs, as well as citizens (Hunt, 2010). "Institutions" means that manufacturers, wholesalers, retailers, advertising agencies, distributors, and marketing research agencies engage in marketing. Additionally, aggregated systems of institutions in a society participate in marketing, such as channels of distributions, networks, and supply chains. "Customers" refers to the exchange partners of for-profit firms. "Clients" refers to the exchange partners of nonprofit organizations (such as the American Cancer Society or Civil Air Patrol). "Partners" refers to those in collaborative networks and alliances that are increasingly evident in contemporary markets. Finally, "society-at-large" refers to the ultimate beneficiary of marketing—society. Marketing benefits society by contributing to increases in productivity and economic growth (Hunt, 2010). Here, society refers to the large-scale community that normally furnishes security and a national identity for its members (Dictionary.com, 2009).

### Understanding How Society Affects Marketing and Business Norms

Society is characterized by a distinctive culture and set of unique institutions. A distinctive culture is defined as the learned meaning system of a group. For example, U.S. culture is characterized by immigrants who support the idea that humans should rule themselves using representative democracy. Key institutions of U.S. society were established in the U.S. Constitution featuring a tripartite form of government with an executive, legislative, and judicial branch. The U.S. Constitution designed a manner for the institutions of the federal government to relate to each other.

This manner of inter-institutional relations ("checks and balances") across the three branches of government came out of the U.S. founders' deep concern about who would govern the one who governs (Prothero, 2007). Primarily as a result of the influence of the founders' Protestant Christian heritage (which views the nature of man to be corrupted), an executive branch with too much power was viewed as inevitably resulting in a king-like executive branch—the very thing that led to revolution and separation from Britain. For this reason, "checks and balances" were written into the U.S. Constitution. As the first modern democracy, the United States proved to be a pioneering culture in the realm of societal institutions.

The acceptance of checks and balances, on all levels of government, is a distinctive element of U.S. culture that characterizes the kind of self-rule embraced by U.S. society. The U.S. distain of a unipolar actor holding power also influences the business world, causing dominant marketplace actors to be viewed with suspicion by many citizens. As a result, anti-trust laws are part of the web of laws governing business, and monopolies are resisted by the U.S. society, which denies rule by any single entity, whether in government or in business. They are accepted by other societies and even ruled to be government run in sectors of the economy perceived to be sensitive ones, such as energy, telecommunications, banking, and military arms production. For example, the French utility Électricité de France (EDF) held a monopoly in the distribution, but not the production, of electricity in France until 1999 (EDF Group, 2012). With the coming of the European Union, EDF had to allow other distribution companies to enter the French market. However, EDF pursued a successful internationalization strategy and now produces power for other countries in Europe. It was entirely state-owned until 2004. The French government still owns 85% of the outstanding shares of EDF. In sum, heterogeneity characterizes the aggregate marketing systems in countries of the world.

**Table 1.2**   Defining Terms for Understanding Contemporary Markets and Marketing Approaches

1. **Markets**—social arenas where repeated exchanges occur between buyers and sellers under a set of formal and informal rules.

2. **Marketing**—the activity, institutions, and set of processes for creating, communicating, delivering, and exchanging offerings that have value for customers, clients, partners, and society-at-large.

3. **"Little m" approach**—the tactical aspects of marketing at the firm level, such as product development, promotion, distribution, and pricing.

4. **"Big m" approach**—how tactical marketing for a firm feeds into managerial decision making that affects other realms of the firm, such as operations, human resources, information systems, finance, and accounting.

5. **"Biggest M" approach**—macromarketing—taking a systems view of the interplay between marketing and society. Firms that take such an approach can be characterized as taking a five-capital marketing approach that articulates a firm's tactical marketing moves with the other functional areas of the firm in order to achieve triple bottom-line success.

# MACROMARKETING

## The "Biggest M"

A marketing management course at most universities strives to impart how firms would consider customers of the firm in their planning. This might be termed the "little m" approach (dealing with the tactical aspects of marketing, such as product development, promotion, distribution, and pricing).

In the first term at the Harvard Business School, MBA students take their first marketing course. The objectives of the course are to demonstrate the role of marketing in the company and to explore the relationship of marketing to other functions. Harvard marketing professor John Gourville reports that this marketing course takes a bigger view of marketing—how marketing feeds into managerial decision making that affects other realms of the firm, such as operations, human resources, information systems, finance, and accounting. Gourville calls this the "big m" approach (Datar, Garvin, & Cullen, 2010).

In contrast to limiting the focus of marketing to the firm and its customers, macromarketing has focused on a higher level of aggregation. According to Hunt (2010, p. 14), macromarketing refers to the study of (a) marketing systems, (b) the impact of marketing systems on society, and (c) the impact of society on marketing systems. In other words, macromarketers have taken a systems view of the interplay between marketing and society. In this way, macromarketing can be understood to be the "biggest M" approach.

## Early Macromarketing: Socialism and Capitalism

Macromarketing was the early focus of the marketing discipline in the years 1900–1920 (Wilkie & Moore, 2003). Here, marketing scholars took concern with the value of marketing's distribution activities as these contribute to economic and growth in society. For example, the distribution of harvested corn shows how one product can create a large economy of scale. First, the farmer grows the crop and places it in his grain silo. Next, a truck comes from the grain buyer and unloads the silo. Afterward, the corn could change hands and be processed up to five more times: (a) between the grain buyer and the regional buyer, (b) between the regional buyer and a corn syrup processor, (c) between a processor and the Pepsi-Cola Company, (d) between Pepsi-Cola and a franchised bottler of Pepsi-Cola, and (e) between a bottler and a local convenience store. This total chain of exchanges would comprise the distribution activities for the corn that later became a sweetener in Pepsi sold at a local convenience store. By each actor performing its role in the distribution system, enormous economies of scale are realized with time and money saved by all. Imagine if the farmer had to take his corn and sell it as an ingredient at thousands of convenience stores. The time and expense would exhaust anyone. However, the market system that evolved on its own coordinates and links the efforts of a diverse array of actors. In the end, much is accomplished for relatively little expense.

Although today there is general acceptance of the place for legal and culturally acceptable marketing practices, at the time of marketing's development, it was hard for scholars to understand why middlemen seemed to proliferate as economies grew. At the same time, a parallel effort was underway on the other side of the world to pursue a socialist approach to organizing the production and distribution of society's goods and services. The approach was led by Communists in the Soviet Union, and it proposed no private ownership of the means of production in society and central planning of all public activities in society.

In such a socialist system, independent middlemen were eliminated, and so were field sales people. Independent wholesalers, retailers, advertising agencies, distributors, and marketing research agencies were eliminated as well. These actors in the aggregate marketing systems of a free society such as the United States were the focus of the first marketing scholars who attempted to understand and explain the plusses and minuses of having such intermediaries in the aggregate marketing system.

Today, it is readily understandable that intermediaries do not just handle material goods. They move information about market conditions and possible wants and needs of customers in many directions in their respective marketing systems. In many ways, such information is more valuable than the goods moved today because it can be used to "create, communicate, deliver and exchange" streams of future offerings that will be valuable to customers. In general, socialism as instituted in the Soviet Union ignored the invisible flows needed to allow an aggregate system of provisioning for a society to work beyond a rudimentary level. For example, prices were not allowed to float in markets (what Friedrich Hayek termed socialism's "fatal conceit") (Hayek, 1988). Information about consumer demand was not detected, interpreted, organized, and moved to the right places in the system for timely action.

## Second-Wave Macromarketing Pioneers

After the first wave of interest in macromarketing in 1900–1920, a second wave of interest in macromarketing began in the 1970s. This was partly a reaction to many scholars' bedazzled interest in firm-centric marketing issues ("little m" for the most part). In the mid-20th century, marketing underwent a major refocus on managerial issues for the firm (Nason, 2006). With the success of a neoliberal approach in economics promoting the deregulation of state-regulated industries in the 1970s and 1980s, macromarketing and its concerns about externalities of operating businesses (such as environmental degradation and product safety) were less interesting to marketers and marketing scholars taking the firm as the focus of analysis.

Perhaps, as a result of their contrarian ways, a group of independently thinking scholars formed the *Journal of Macromarketing* in 1982 to encourage further research focused on the "biggest M." Over the course of its first 20 years, the *Journal of Macromarketing* adopted an eclectic style that more than anything else offered thinking about marketing set in context. The elements of such context and important questions macromarketing scholars have pursued since then include:

- *Quality of Life:* How does marketing affect material conditions of life, as well as happiness of individuals?
- *Marketing Ethics and Distributive Justice:* Why do marketers behave the way they do? Are the outcomes of marketing just and fair for all in society?

- *Global Policy and the Environment:* What role does marketing have in transnational phenomena, such as environmental degradation, financial crises, water and food shortages, and health problems?
- *Competition and Markets:* What happens in society when firms compete? What is fair competition?
- *Marketing and Development:* What does marketing mean for the current and future state of poor countries?

The traditional dimensions of macromarketing are recast as the acrostic "QUEENSHIP" in Figure 1.3. This acrostic suggests the versatility and ability to project power that the queen carries on the chess board. In military strategy, the infantry carries a similar designation as "the queen of battle." By seeking to understand the interplay of marketing and society (the "biggest M"), more sustainable approaches to conducting business come into view for the 21st century business.

When reviewing the contextual dimensions listed, these are increasingly influential matters for leaders of firms today. Times have changed. Now and in the future, firms seeking success in the marketplace must go beyond the "little m" and "the big m"—the highly controllable aspects of doing business for the firm. Globalization, instantaneous communication in a networked world, the new reality of risk in financial markets, planetary limits, and the imperative of firms to increase profits by marketing to the poorest consumers of the world make it critical for today's CEOs to understand the "biggest M."

**Figure 1.3** Traditional Dimensions of Macromarketing

**QUEENSHIP**

"A noble or regal quality as if a queen."
"The chess piece with the most moves."

| | |
|---|---|
| Qu– | Quality of life |
| E– | Ethics |
| En– | Environment |
| S– | Systems |
| Hi– | History |
| P– | Poor countries |

## The "Biggest M" & Business Acumen

According to Ram Charan, a long-time counselor to CEOs of major corporations around the world, business acumen is linking an insightful assessment of the external business landscape with the keen awareness of how money can be made (Charan, 2006). This managerial skill is the most important for the future success of a firm. If the firm's assessment of the external landscape—how patterns of converging and diverging trends fit together is not correct, then the firm's competitive positioning will be wrong. In short, if the firm's leaders do not do well in the "biggest M," the firm could be severely disadvantaged in the future.

Jeffrey Immelt became CEO of General Electric Company in 2001 with a challenging goal of increasing normal revenues of $130 billion each year by $10 billion each year (Charan, 2006). Immelt and his team stepped back and did serious thinking about GE's future and the "biggest M." They identified the forecasted growth of emerging-market economies (which are forecasted to exceed the growth of developed countries) as an opportunity. In the past, emerging-market countries were viewed by many business executives as too risky to pursue.

Immelt took another view on emerging markets—one that harmonized well with a macromarketing approach. Acknowledging the historical challenges of marketing in emerging markets made GE more sober about the challenges GE would face when entering emerging markets. GE knew that governments and citizens of emerging markets would need to make huge investments in basic services, such as reliable energy, clean water, and transportation systems. Because GE made equipment that would help improve such basic services, they calculated that the risk of investing in an emerging market would be worth it.

Although many emerging markets, such as China and India, desire economic growth to improve the economic prospects of their citizens, these same emerging-market countries also desire clean air and water. Again, GE's innovations in energy-efficient and low-emissions technologies could help these countries pursue growth while addressing important quality-of-life concerns related to avoiding environmental degradation. GE also had alternative energy technologies in development that would help emerging-market countries become more energy independent. At the time, GE's competitors had not aggressively pursued emerging markets, so GE faced lighter competition—another benefit for GE's strategy.

By 2011, GE had increased its operations overseas so that half of its revenues come from the more than 100 countries outside the United States. In hindsight, Immelt and his team took a macro approach, thought about the development needs of emerging-market countries, considered the political responses they would encounter in these counties, and then implemented their strategy in a highly effective way. In this way, GE's strategic thinking reflects the kind of business acumen that a macromarketing approach can lead a firm to adopt.

## A Wide-Angle Lens Is Needed to Perceive and Pursue the "Biggest M"

Amory Lovins is one of the leading proponents of properly valuing nature and people when doing business. He does not use the word "sustainability" because he believes it means many things to different people (Hopkins, 2009). Lovins uses a wide lens to view capitalism and does not only see capitalism as the productive use of financial and physical capital (money and goods), but he also sees two additional forms of valuable capital—people and nature. In firms across 30 sectors of the economy, Lovins and his team from the Rocky Mountain Institute (RMI) have seen that firms that use all four kinds of capital "make more money, do more good, and have more fun."

Despite some widespread (but dated) thought among business executives that taking an approach to business with the four types of capital in mind would result in higher costs, Lovins's RMI projects with industry (totaling more than $30 billion) for new facilities or for retrofitting of existing facilities typically save approximately 30% to 60% on energy consumption. This significant benefit comes with a two- to three-year payback—one of the highest return, lowest risk investments possible. Pursuing such a green course for a firm means that a firm turns waste into profit. Wastes and emissions are reduced because they are designed out of the systems of the firm. This quickly leads to enormous innovation and competitive advantage. Dow Chemical invested $1 billion to save $9 billion in energy expenses. United Technologies cut its energy intensity 45% in five years.

Similar to Lovins's view of capitalism, a five-capital view of capitalism partitions the "people" dimension in Lovins's view into two kinds of capital—human capital (talents, abilities, and focused interests of people) and social capital (the willingness and capability of people to cooperate with others). Firms pursuing a five-capital approach to capitalism become poised to take advantage of other benefits that increasingly elude firms with a two-capital approach to capitalism. Five-capital firms, which use a triple bottom-line or a balanced scorecard, are the kind of businesses that people want to do business with because people feel good about supporting such firms. More and more, environmental and social blunders lead to devastating setbacks for firms that are perceived as violating a tacit license agreed upon by the public and the firm (Rousseau's idea of the social contract). According to Lovins, networked activists today scare the leaders of two-capital firms more than regulators do.

**Table 1.3**    Comparison of the Two- and Five-Capital Views of Capitalism

| Two-Capital View of Capitalism | Five-Capital View of Capitalism |
|---|---|
| Financial capital (money) | Financial capital (money) |
| Physical capital (goods) | Physical capital (goods) |
| | Human capital (talents, abilities, and focused interests of people) |
| | Social capital (willingness and capability of people to cooperate) |
| | Natural capital (sum total of the ecological systems that support life and cannot be produced by human activity) |

In sum, five-capital firms see the landscape of business in a more complete way and are positioned to maneuver across the landscape of business in a more nimble fashion than two-capital firms. Firms that take such an approach can be characterized as taking a five-capital marketing approach that articulates a firm's tactical marketing moves with the other functional areas of the firm in order to achieve triple bottom-line success. Such success means earning profits while doing the best for the planet and people (and communities). In this way, five-capital firms manifest the broad view of markets and marketing characteristic of macromarketing—the "biggest M." Lovins points to the importance of the "biggest M" in the following way:

> If you are a company that sticks to its knitting, minds its own business and doesn't pay attention to what's happening in the world around you, you're probably riding for a fall and missing some big business opportunities, because in any business I can think of—30 sectors we've worked in so far—it's the hidden connections between your business and other opportunities that you think are well outside your boundaries that create extraordinary opportunity or risk, depending on the way you handle them. This is another way of saying that you need a really wide-angle lens. You can still have a sharp focus, but you sure need peripheral vision. (Hopkins, 2009, p. 40)

## Implications of the "Biggest M" for Entrepreneurship

The "biggest M" influences all areas of marketing—including entrepreneurship. Specifically, the "biggest M" has influenced entrepreneurs by causing them to focus on more than the two-capital approach, considering factors such as the environment. Through the following examples from both the for-profit and nonprofit sectors, we can see how the "biggest M" is influencing modern entrepreneurs.

### The Major Influencing Factor: A Focus on More Than Two Types of Capital

Using a two-capital approach, economists who have dared to consider entrepreneurship have defined entrepreneurship "as any entity, new or existing, that provides a new product or service or that develops and uses new methods to produce or deliver existing goods and services at lower cost" (Baumol, Litan, & Schramm, 2007, p. 3). As one can see, the focus in such a definition is on financial and physical capital. However, by using a wider lens and a five-capital approach, entrepreneurship can be seen as not just developing (a) new goods and services, or (b) using new methods for providing existing goods and services at lower cost, but also developing goods/services and methods of production and delivery that (c) improve the well-being of the environment or 4) society-at-large. In other words, entrepreneurs pursuing the accumulation of capital beyond the traditional two capitals (manufactured and financial capital) innovate to improve stocks of environmental, human, and social capital, as well as that of manufactured and financial capital.

For decades, Ray Anderson of Interface, Inc. was a two-capital entrepreneur. The story of the mid-course correction at Interface to try becoming an environmentally neutral company is one of primarily becoming a three-capital company (physical, financial, and natural). Along the way, Interface improved the human capital of its employees who worked in cleaner and less toxic industrial settings, as well as developed a transcendent purpose for the firm. This purpose is showing industry and business all over the world how a firm like Interface can transform itself to be a leader in sustainable business practices. In sharing its story and its knowledge with others, Interface accumulates social capital, which is the willingness of others (individuals and institutions) to cooperate with each other in productive endeavors. Interface's efforts also lift society, making individuals and institutions better able and more willing to cooperate in solving sustainability challenges for modern businesses. General Electric's strategic decision in 2003 to pursue opportunities in emerging markets with its more fuel-efficient and low-emission equipment shows signs of two-capital entrepreneurship possibly evolving into a five-capital one. Increasingly, though, new entrepreneurial ventures are emerging that pursue business with a five-capital approach instead of a two-capital one.

## Examples of Five-Capital Entrepreneurial Endeavors

### For-Profit Ventures

Canadian Tom Szaky dropped out of Princeton University in 2002 to lead TerraCycle, a company he founded to make useful products out of garbage (Szaky, 2009). Called by *Inc.* in 2006 the "coolest little start-up in America," TerraCycle is a privately owned small business headquartered in Trenton, New Jersey. TerraCycle began by producing organic fertilizer that was, in fact, worm castings (excrement) packaged in used soda bottles (Szaky, 2009). Since then, TerraCycle has grown into one of the fastest growing green companies in the world. TerraCycle's purpose is to eliminate the idea of waste. This is done by recycling (turning chip bags into a trash can) or upcycling (turning juice pouches into a pencil case). TerraCycle lists more than 280 products it has made and sold, which range from fashion accessories, like over-the-shoulder bags and backpacks made from juice packs stitched together, to toys, like kites made from Oreo packages. Many of these products are available at major retailers such as Wal-Mart and Whole Foods Market.

Called by some an "eco-capitalist company" (Szaky, 2009), TerraCycle has created national recycling systems for previously nonrecyclable items. The process starts by offering collect programs (many of them free) to gather waste and then converting the collected waste into a wide range of products and materials. More than 14 million people collect waste in 11 countries for TerraCycle, thereby diverting billions of pieces of waste from landfills.

With the exception of countries ruled by dictators, it would be difficult to find any countries today that do not truly desire to see more entrepreneurial activity in its society because of contributions to the economic growth of the country. As a result of the disruption entrepreneurs tend to engender as a result of introducing better ways of doing things, dictators instinctively oppose entrepreneurs and prefer the status quo. In open societies, successful entrepreneurship means more tax money for the government and less pressure to meet the well-being needs of members of society by income redistribution programs resented by many. Fueled by personal computers, mobile phones, and the Internet, the democratization of entrepreneurship is well under way in countries around the globe (The Economist, 2009). China and India have certainly awakened to traditional, two-capital entrepreneurship (Khanna, 2007).

*Not-for-Profit Ventures*

Through mostly not-for-profit and NGOs, social entrepreneurs build or transform institutions to advance solutions to social problems, such as poverty, disease, environmental degradation, illiteracy, human rights abuses, and corruption (Bornstein & Davis, 2010). In these ways, social entrepreneurs pursue a different kind of entrepreneurship that is typically focused on boosting human, social, or natural capital.

Previously known as humanitarians, social entrepreneurs such as Florence Nightingale used an analytical mind with unrelenting persistence to transform the care of wounded British soldiers in the Crimea War of the 19th century in Eastern Europe (Bornstein, 2004). She pioneered what would become known as the profession of nursing.

Today, social entrepreneurs like Fábio Rosa of Brazil have helped bring electricity to parts of Brazil that had never experienced life with electricity (Bornstein, 2004). Rosa's "Project Light" succeeded in its very first attempt to raise the living standards of low-income rural families by taking cheap electricity to their homes and farms. He did this by using steel wire, which is much cheaper than copper wire. The first experiment took place in Palmares do Sul, a rural community in the southernmost Brazilian state, Rio Grande do Sul. As many as a million rural residents of the state have no electricity, refrigeration, indoor plumbing, water pumps for irrigation, or other common household and farm electric appliances (Ashoka, 2011).

Rosa's pilot project from 1984 to 1988 boosted the living standards for 400 rural families in Palmares and brought results far beyond his expectations. His low-cost electrification not only stopped the flow of rural residents to cities, but also it reversed the flow. A study two years after the project's implementation showed that one in every three beneficiaries was someone who returned from the city to resume living in his former rural area. This was in large part because of the newly affordable electric service (Bornstein, 2004).

"The moment they have better living conditions in their native rural areas, people return from the cities," Rosa said. These results substantiate Rosa's contention that poor people are not lured to the city because it is better; rather, they are expelled from the countryside because it is unlivable. Given the means to live better, people stay near their rural roots. In the social change realized by Rosa's own engineering innovations related to simple electrification, and his effective work collaborating with government, business, and social institutions in Brazil, Rosa's story manifests some of the best qualities of social entrepreneurs today. As a result of his work, the quality of life for thousands of rural-dwelling Brazilians has improved dramatically.

More will be said about social entrepreneurs later (see Chapter 13), but what needs to be noted now about social entrepreneurs is (a) that their personal approach to business (which is often an extension of themselves) influences the business world and society's expectations of business, and (b) that an entrepreneur's success in creatively increasing capital stocks is usually ignored by traditional for-profit firms. As corporations increasingly seek profits in more challenging corners of a globalizing world, such as poor communities and those needing infrastructure improvements, they will increasingly learn from social entrepreneurs like Rosa who succeeded in these difficult settings first.

In the stories of their NGOs, social entrepreneurs often achieve a purpose for their endeavors that elude traditional two-capital firms. John Mackey, founder and Co-CEO of Whole Foods Market (one of the most profitable public food retailing business in the United

States), looks beyond the accumulation of two capitals in the success of his business. Mackey explains:

> I believe that business has a much greater purpose. Business, working through free markets, is possibly the greatest force for good on the planet today. When executed well, business increases prosperity, ends poverty, improves the quality of life, and promotes the health, and longevity of the world population at an unprecedented rate. (Elkington & Hartigan, 2008, p. 54)

## CONCLUSION

Businesses are more mindful of society today because of a changing environment for business. Technology improvements have shifted power to those in a knowledge economy who can harness the groundswell of information available on the Internet. As a result, businesses have more forces of accountability for their actions, such as empowered consumers and NGOs. At the same time, society has become more affluent, more brand aware, and more concerned about stewardship of the environment. Additionally, new competitors are emerging from unexpected corners of the planet and increasingly from countries such as China and India. As a result, the macromarketing imperative has emerged in marketing strategy.

Savvy firms of the 21st century will need to apply a wide-angle lens to issues outside of the firm, so that the firm's leaders can make sense of these issues in a timely way to navigate the firm successfully into the future. In short, business acumen increasingly means considering macromarketing dimensions. Macromarketing—the biggest M—traditionally has focused on the six QUEENSHIP dimensions of Figure 1.3 (quality of life, ethics, environment, systems, history, and poor countries). When applying a wide-angle lens to issues outside the firm, marketing strategists and entrepreneurs do not have to begin from scratch. Happily, they can draw on the accumulated knowledge of more than 30 years of macromarketing research about these QUEENSHIP dimensions that address marketing systems and the interplay between marketing and society.

Reconceptualizations of capitalism are emerging in this new day for businesses when sustainable business practices are of keen interest to business persons and scholars. One of these new views of capitalism features a five-capital view of business—instead of a traditional two-capital view (focused only on manufactured and financial capital). This view proposes that thriving businesses in the future will increasingly be characterized as seeking to accumulate five types of capital—(a) manufactured, (b) financial, (c) natural, (d) human, and (e) social.

## QUESTIONS

1. What were surprises you encountered in reading Chapter 1?

2. What are "little m," "big m," and the "biggest M?"

3. What is macromarketing?

4. What have been the interests of scholars during the first wave and second wave of macromarketing?

5. What are the six dimensions of current macromarketing thought?

6. What is business acumen? How does it relate to the "biggest M?"

7. What is the difference between two-capital firms and five-capital firms?

8. In your opinion, what would it take to reverse business becoming more mindful of society?

9. How have some entrepreneurs integrated the biggest M in their ventures? How have some industrialists?

## MAVERICKS WHO MADE IT

### Labor of Love—and Respect

### Family farm uses success to help others

### By Stephanie E. Ponder (2009)

GROWING UP ON a farm in Yakima, Washington, 15-year-old Ralph Broetje had a dream: to have his own apple orchard and to help starving children in India. And like a lot of dreams, it faded . . . but it didn't die. It simply lay dormant until it sprouted more than 20 years later.

Today Costco supplier Broetje (pronounced Bro-chee) and his wife, Cheryl, farm around 6,000 acres (including a few hundred organic acres) in southeast Washington, where they grow apples and cherries.

Their path to success included a few false starts, but by turning to their faith and the servant-leadership model of business (see sidebar), the couple created an $80 million business that packs around 5 million boxes of apples a year. (Cherries are packed elsewhere.)

Most of their fruit is packed under the label FirstFruits of Washington. The name comes from a Biblical passage in which God asks people to bring Him the first fruits of their harvest. True to the name, the Broetjes donate up to 75 percent of their annual earnings to needy groups around the world.

And while they work hard for a successful harvest, they are also dedicated to cultivating their employees. The result is a quadruple bottom line: profit, people, planet, and purpose.

"We're interested in bearing fruit that will last," Broetje tells *The Connection*. "We're working on the production of fruit and how it's doing in terms of people. It's our work, call and passion all in one."

*(Continued)*

(Continued)

## An Idea Takes Root

Ralph and Cheryl both come from farming families in Washington, so it's little surprise that shortly after they married in November 1967, they bought a few acres of cherries about an hour away from their Yakima home.

After seasons of bad weather, their crops and business thrived throughout the 1970s, and Broetje purchased more and more land. "I kind of lost track of why I was farming," he says.

And then came the 1980s. Between high interest rates and their bank's refusal to lend them operating funds, they had to sell everything. They moved with their three daughters to Prescott, Washington, where they started over, planting apple trees in land that until then had grown nothing but sagebrush.

## Leading by Serving

WHEN ASKED ABOUT their individual strengths, both Ralph and Cheryl Broetje hesitate before replying. Ralph finally says that he's "good at planting trees," and Cheryl says, "I'm into social justice."

The Broetjes took those strengths and combined them with Robert Greenleaf's servant-leadership approach (*www.greenleaf.org*) to define the family's business model.

In the 1970 essay, "The Servant as Leader," Greenleaf wrote, "The servant-leader is servant first. . . . It begins with the natural feeling that one wants to serve, to serve first. Then conscious choice brings one to aspire to lead."

The basic tenets of servant leadership call for leaders to

- Devote themselves to serving the needs of organization members
- Focus on meeting the needs of those they lead
- Facilitate personal growth in all who work with them
- Listen and build a sense of community

While Greenleaf created his model for the business world, the Broetjes recognize how it fits in with their Christian faith. Cheryl says they've always gone to church, and she realizes that business-people "haven't always been thought of as the best Christians."

Greenleaf also put forth the idea that people can lead from a for-profit business.

"We believe we're marketplace ministers," Cheryl adds, surprising herself with this new definition of their roles as servant leaders.

"We thought, 'We are our own business now, so we can do some stuff.' If we're not willing to see business as a possibility for helping, we're missing an opportunity."—*SEP*

The change in scenery served as a harbinger of the internal changes heading their way—and of the reawakening of 15-year-old Ralph's dream.

In addition to the apples, they planted more cherry trees—which weren't doing well. Ready to replace the cherries with more apples, Broetje decided to give the trees to the ministry. The next year they flourished. Since then, all of the profits from those trees has gone to ministries around the world.

## Sowing Seeds of Compassion

In 1984 the family went on a mission trip to an orphanage in Mexico.

"At this point in the story I like to say that at that time the labor market changed from white seasonal workers to young male Latinos," Cheryl Broetje says. "We went down [to Mexico] to see if we could understand what was going on. What we saw was that these people were economic refugees. When we returned it changed how we looked at employees and what our role was as employer."

"For me [the trip] was a wake-up call," says Broetje. "We were building more and more stuff. It made me realize that the dream was a vision for my life."

The first problem they set out to address was how to create sustainable work. Ralph began planting different varieties of apples—such as Fuji and Gala—which resulted in year-round work for his employees.

The next problem presented itself in 1987, when the Broetjes made the move to vertical integration by building a warehouse and packing line. The new building saved them the 100-mile drive to a packing facility, but it brought to light a new problem. The warehouse staff comprised mostly women, and the Broetjes learned that many of their employees were locking their children inside their homes all day or keeping older children out of school to watch their siblings.

So, the Broetjes built an affordable daycare. Today the daycare has 23 employees and has the capacity to take care of 77 children, from infants to 4-year-olds. Most of the Broetjes' nine grandchildren have spent their days there while their parents and grandparents worked a few hundred feet away in the main office.

Next, the Broetjes knew they needed to address the poor housing conditions their employees faced. "We learned that sustainable jobs, daycare and affordable housing were the keys to the workers showing up," says Cheryl. "Any one of those issues could run them out."

After hearing from employees who lived in cars, garages and other cramped quarters, more often than not paying bloated rents, the Broetjes invested $5 million of their own money to provide affordable housing.

Vista Hermosa, a community of 121 houses, opened in 1990. The residents named the community, which means "beautiful view." Just a few minutes' walk from the office and warehouse, the community is made up of mostly three- to four-bedroom homes. Rent, which has been raised only twice since the houses were built, costs around $485 for a four-bedroom home. In addition to the houses,

*(Continued)*

(Continued)

residents have access to an elementary school, public library branch, chapel, laundry facility and convenience store.

The Broetjes have kept on top of the issue by creating housing for seasonal workers and funding a community in nearby Pasco, Washington, that's designed to help their employees become home-owners.

"The housing piece is the one that's had the most influence," says Broetje. "It's an investment, so it has to be something you believe in."

One of the problems they have yet to solve is the ongoing issue of immigration. While the company follows all of the obligations that Social Security and the Internal Revenue Service place on any employer, they see beyond the paperwork. Their goal under comprehensive immigration reform is "for immigrants to be granted the legal process in order to secure short-term employment in this country, as well as a path of opportunity available for those who qualify and choose to go through the process of permanent citizenship," says Cheryl Broetje.

## Healthy Harvest

Broetje, trim and gray-haired, is soft-spoken and often defers to his wife with a point of a finger before answering a question. Cheryl, in turn, points back at him, encouraging him to speak. She offers a suggestion to understanding her quiet and unassuming husband: "Just remember, Ralph's into apples and kids."

Which leads to the realization of the second part of his dream. Not only have Broetje Orchards' charitable donations aided numerous people in India—and throughout the world—but the couple have adopted six kids from that country, bringing their total number of children to nine, ages 23 to 41.

Much the way the Broetjes have encouraged employees to explore their strengths, they have given their children the freedom to see where they best fit in with the business.

Suzanne Broetje, who heads the family's charitable-giving foundation (see next page), says her parents have created a solid management team that will one day run the business. She explains, "My parents always stressed that the orchard is *their* dream. 'We don't want to push it on you.'"

Six of the Broetje children—three boys and three girls—perform a variety of functions, doing everything from working in the orchards, warehouse and elementary school to processing payroll.

As for day-to-day operations, Cheryl has an office at their first nonprofit endeavor, the Center for Sharing (*www.centerforsharing.org*) in Pasco, where people are encouraged to explore God's call in their lives.

Ralph meets daily with crew leaders at 5:15 in the morning. His role is more teacher than farmer these days as he shares what he knows about planting, grafting and harvesting.

"I struggled to get through high school. It's not like I have any right being in management or business," says Ralph, who adds that he relied on shop and agriculture classes to get by. "But God had a plan; otherwise it wouldn't have happened."

## Vista Hermosa Foundation

GIBRAN ESCALERA just completed his master's degree in English at the University of Washington in Seattle. Since leaving for college he's returned every summer to spend time with the kids at Broetje Orchards' Camp Vista program and serve as an example of what's possible for those who grow up in the Vista Hermosa community. He volunteered at the on-site daycare, where his mother is the director. He went to the elementary school, and after graduating from high school received a scholarship for each year of his undergraduate studies. The common thread is that the Vista Hermosa Foundation funded each of those steps.

Begun in 1990 and now managed by Suzanne Broetje, Ralph and Cheryl Broetje's oldest daughter, the foundation has given away upwards of $50 million. In addition to funding the daycare and elementary school, the foundation also supports the following:

- **Camp Vista.** This summer-long program is for children entering first through sixth grades and is designed to offer a fun environment for improving or sustaining reading, writing and math skills. It's also meant to boost English reading, writing and comprehension skills in native Spanish speakers.

- **Scholarships.** Scholarships are awarded to children of Broetje employees, employees who want to further their professional development and low-income adults in several counties in southeast Washington.

- **Cherry Committee.** Each year the entire profit from the cherry harvest of 50 designated acres is given away. To foster a feeling of control and ownership, the Broetjes have removed themselves from the decision-making process and ask their employees to decide where the money will go. Past recipients have included communities in India, East Africa, the U.S. and Mexico.

- **Grants.** International grants are given out to faith-based, community-oriented initiatives. They've focused on Haiti, Kenya, Uganda, India, Mexico and Central America to help with issues of immigration, hunger and economic empowerment.

"We [Broetje Orchards] are successful; we make a profit. But it doesn't stop there," Suzanne says. "We're all for going the next step and looking at the whole person."

With Suzanne at the helm, the foundation not only tracks all of the projects and their progress, but also forges relationships with the groups and people they're helping.

"There are a number of things that we focus on, like education, leadership, agricultural training and empowering people to use the gifts and talents they have," she adds. "We don't want to just throw money at problems. We're in it for the long haul."  —SEP

(Continued)

(Continued)

## Supplier Profile

**Company**: Broetje Orchards

**Founders:** Ralph and Cheryl Broetje

**Employees:** 1,000 permanent employees; 2,800 during harvest

**Address:** 1111 Fishhook Park Road Prescott, WA 99348

**Phone:** (509) 749-2217

**Web site:** *www.firstfruits.com*

**Items at Costco:** Apples and cherries

**Comments about Costco:** "For years our desire to run a socially responsible business was considered quirky with partners like Costco, we can encourage each other as well as other businesses to pay attention to their people as well as their profits."—*Cheryl Broetje*
"For years they've been one of our top partners. We have similar models of management and codes of conduct. We're excited to be one of your suppliers."—*Ralph Broetje*

*Source: The Costco Connection*

## Questions

1. In your opinion, what are the factors for success for FirstFruits of Washington?

2. How would you describe the Broetje's business model?

3. What is a "quadruple bottom line" according to Ralph Broetje?

4. How important are the social values of the Broetjes to their approach to the design of the business model and their work in markets?

## REFERENCES

AMA Marketing Power. (2007). *Definition of marketing*. Retrieved from http://www.marketingpower
.com/AboutAMA/Pages/DefinitionofMarketing.aspx

Anderson, R. C. (1998). *Mid-course correction: Toward a sustainable enterprise: The interface model.* White River Junction, VT: Chelsea Green.

Ashoka: Innovators for the public. (2011). Retrieved from http://www.ashoka.org/node/3291

AzkoNobel. (2011). Coatings. Retrieved from http://www.akzonobel.com/

Baumol, W. J., Litan, R. E., & Schramm, C. J. (2007). *Good capitalism, bad capitalism, and the economics of growth and prosperity.* New Haven, CT: Yale University Press.

Big Charts. (2011). Chart generated by author at http://www.bigcharts.com

Bonini, S. M. J., Mendonca, L. T., & Oppenheim, J. M. (2006). When social issues become strategic. *The McKinsey Quarterly, 2,* 20–32.

Bornstein, D. (2004). *How to change the world: Social entrepreneurs and the power of new ideas.* New York, NY: Oxford University Press.

Bornstein, D., & Davis, S. (2010). *Social entrepreneurship: What everyone needs to know.* New York, NY: Oxford University Press.

Charan, R. (2006). Sharpening your business acumen: A six-step guide for incorporating external trends into your internal strategies. *Strategy and Business, 42.*

Datar, S. M., Garvin, D. A., & Cullen, P. G. (2010). *Rethinking the MBA: Business education at a crossroads.* Boston, MA: Harvard Business Press.

Dictionary.com. (2011). *Society.* Retrieved from http://dictionary.reference.com/browse/society

Eccles, R. G., & Krzus, M. P. (2010). *One report: Integrated reporting for a sustainable strategy.* Hoboken, NJ: Wiley.

EDF Group. (2012). Retrieved from http://www.edf.com/the-edf-group-42667.html

Elkington, J., & Hartigan, P. (2008). *The power of unreasonable people: How social entrepreneurs create markets that change the world.* Boston, MA: Harvard Business School.

Fligstein, N., & Dauter, L. (2007). The sociology of markets. *Annual Review of Sociology, 33,* 105–128.

Friedman, T. (2008). *Hot, flat, and crowded: Why we need a green revolution.* New York, NY: Farrar, Straus and Giroux.

Hayek, F. A. (1988). *The fatal conceit: The errors of socialism.* Chicago, IL: University of Chicago Press.

Hollender, J., & Breen, B. (2010). *The responsibility revolution: How the next generation of businesses will win.* San Francisco, CA: Jossey-Bass/Wiley.

Holt, D., & Cameron, D. (2010). *Cultural strategy: Using innovative ideologies to build breakthrough brands.* New York, NY: Oxford University Press.

Hopkins, M. S. (2009). What executives don't get about sustainability (and further notes on the profit motive). *MIT Sloan Management Review, 51*(1), 35–40.

Hunt, S. D. (2010). *Marketing theory: Foundations, controversy, strategy, resource-advantage theory.* Armonk, NY: M.E. Sharpe.

Inglehart, R.F., & Welzel, C. (2005). *Modernization, cultural change, and democracy: The human development sequence.* New York, NY: Cambridge University Press.

Interface. (2011). March 2012 Investor Report. Retrieved from http://www.interfaceglobal.com/Investor-Relations/Annual-Reports.aspx, slide 37.

Interface. (2012). Mission Zero milestones. Retrieved from http://www.interfaceglobal.com/ZazzSustainabilityAssetts/pdfs/Interface_pdf_summary_report.pdf

Investorguide.com. (2012). Chart built at http://www.investorguide.com

Khanna, T. (2007). *Billions of entrepreneurs: How China and India are reshaping their futures and yours.* Boston, MA: Harvard Business School Press.

Morris, B., Sellers, P., & Tarpley, N. A. (2000, January). What really happened at Coke Doug Ivester was a demon for information. But he couldn't see what was coming at the showdown in Chicago. *Fortune Magazine.* Retrieved from http://money.cnn.com/magazines/fortune/fortune_archive/2000/01/10/271736/index.htm

Nason, R. W. (2006). The macromarketing mosaic. *Journal of Macromarketing, 26*(2), 219–223. doi: 10.1177/0276146706291065.

Peritz, R. (2008, April 3). *The Sherman anti-trust act of 1890: A more dynamic and open American economic system.* Retrieved from http://www.america.gov/st/educ-english/2008/April/20080423212 813eaifas0.42149.html

Ponder, S. E. (2009). Labor of love—and respect. *Costco Connection, 24*(8), 22–25.

Porter, M. E., & Kramer, M. R. (2011). The big idea: Creating shared value. *Harvard Business Review.* Retrieved from http://hbr.org/2011/01/the-big-idea-creating-shared-value/ar/1

Principles for Responsible Management Education. (2011). Retrieved from http://www.unprme.org/

Prothero, S. (2007). *Religious literacy: What every American needs to know—and doesn't.* New York, NY: HarperCollins.

Savitz, A. W., & Weber, K. (2006). *The triple bottom line: How today's best-run companies are achieving economic, social, and environmental success—and how you can too.* San Francisco, CA: Jossey-Bass/Wiley.

Smith, A. (2000). *The wealth of nations.* New York, NY: The Modern Library Classics.

Szaky, T. (2009). *Revolution in a bottle.* New York, NY: Penguin.

The Economist. (2009 March). An idea whose time has come: Entrepreneurialism has become cool. *The Economist.* Retrieved from http://www.economist.com/node/13216053

TerraCycle. (2011). Available at http://www.terracycle.net

United Nations global compact: The ten principles. (2011). Retrieved from http://www.unglobal compact.org/AboutTheGC/TheTenPrinciples/index.html

Werbach, A. (2009). *Strategy for sustainability: A business manifesto.* Boston, MA: Harvard Business School.

Wilkie, W. L., & Moore, E. S. (2003). Scholarly research in marketing: Exploring the "4 eras" of thought development. *Journal of Public Policy & Marketing, 22*(2), 116–146.

## CHAPTER 2

# Markets—How Efficient and How Effective?

## "I FOUND A FLAW"

### Crashing Ideology

*The San Francisco Chronicle* described it as a remarkable moment (Zuckerman, 2008). On Thursday, October 23, 2008, Former Federal Reserve Chairman Alan Greenspan, once lionized as the greatest central banker of all time, sat before the U.S. House Committee on Oversight and Government Reform that had hastily convened to investigate the near collapse of the U.S. financial system. The meltdown began on September 15, 2008, after the investment bank Lehman Brothers declared bankruptcy. Despite having more than

$600 billion in assets and despite being a pillar of Wall Street, Lehman could not pay its creditors. It was the largest bankruptcy filing in U.S. history.

In 2006, Greenspan had stepped down as the Fed chief after more than 18 years as chairman, but now he was reluctantly back on the world's stage. A month after Lehman's bankruptcy and the near catastrophe to the financial systems of the world, the Congressional committee had summoned the 82-year-old Greenspan to testify.

With the glare of television lighting, Greenspan appeared uncharacteristically chastened and a bit bewildered by the sudden downturn in U.S. financial markets. Under hard questioning by committee Chairman Henry Waxman (D-Calif.), Greenspan admitted that in light of a "once-in-a-century financial tsunami," he had found a flaw in his market ideology.

As the television cameras of the world captured the historical reckoning in the committee room, Waxman pressed Greenspan, asking, "In other words, you found that your view of the world, your ideology was not right?"

"Absolutely, precisely," Greenspan said in reply, "That's precisely the reason I was shocked, because I have been going for forty years or more with very considerable evidence it was working exceptionally well." Later in testimony, Greenspan elaborated, saying, "Free markets did break down. That, as I said, shocked me. I still do not fully understand what happened" (Zuckerman, 2008, para. 14). Greenspan cited his mistake as believing that financial institutions would act in their own self-interest, therefore avoiding the risky lending that put them into so much trouble in the fall of 2008.

Betty Blecha, an economist at San Francisco State University, expressed pity for the once powerful Greenspan as she watched the testimony live on television. "When I watched him this morning, I actually found myself feeling a little bit sorry for him," Blecha said. She further commented, "When ideologues find their ideology crashing around them, it's something to see. He was intellectually honest about admitting the failings of an ideology he's believed in all his adult life. I think personally this has been a very difficult period for him" (Zuckerman, 2008, para. 12).

## The Great Recession Begins

In short order in 2008, titanic Wall Street firms were sold for pennies on the dollar (Bear Stearns) or filed for bankruptcy (Lehmann Brothers was the largest such filing in U.S. history at $600 billion) (Parloff, 2009). Fannie Mae and Freddie Mac were put into conservatorship by the federal government's $700 billion Troubled Assets Relief Program (TARP). A conservatorship occurs when an organization is subject to the legal control of an external entity, known as a conservator, such as the U.S. Department of Treasury. All major banks in the United States received cash infusions from the federal government, even if the banks did not need the infusions. This was supposed to protect the banks that actually did need the assistance so these needy banks would not see their stock prices ruined by investors shunning them. As a result of the haste in which the deal was consummated, the world's largest brokerage firm Merrill Lynch was sold to Bank of America at a price many investors perceived to be too high.

Committed to a logic of executive entitlement developed during previous years of prosperity, Merrill Lynch CEO John Thain pushed through $3.6 billion in executive bonuses, including a $10 million bonus for himself, as part of the deal to sell his company to Bank of America the day before the deal became final (Quelch, 2009). This came after Thain had spent $1.2 million of firm money that year to redecorate his office. Such narrow-minded actions emphasized the enormous gap in thinking between Wall Street and Main Street USA.

In the bygone days of investment banking, before deregulation of the finance industry in the 1980s, executives in investment banks use to call themselves "asset rich—but poor" (Sterbenz, personal communication, 2011). This was because of the vesting period for executive bonuses. The partnership of the investment bank would hold the bonus for five years before turning it over to the executive. In this way, if a firm did poorly in the subsequent five years, the bonus could be rescinded.

By comparison, when Wall Street firms perform well today, Wall Street executives receive millions in end-of-year bonuses. When they do not, they *still* receive end-of-year bonuses from TARP money given to major banks that will eventually come from taxes on ordinary citizens, such as long-haul, over-the-road, truck drivers based in Alabama or elementary school teachers in Kansas. Now, imagine if the economic crisis of 2008 resulted in these same truck drivers and school teachers losing their jobs; one can imagine the furor to be manifested in the political life of the United States. In fact, the first attempt to pass the TARP legislation was defeated in the U.S. House of Representatives on September 28th, because of representatives' anger about the arrogance of Wall Street and its disregard for Main Street.

Almost overnight, the U.S. government lent $85 billion to the world's largest insurance underwriter, AIG, and effectively took ownership of 79.9% of the firm. This move wiped out the existing shareholders and set the course for selling AIG's assets over the next two years (Karnitschnig, Solomon, Pleven, & Hilsenrath, 2008). Morgan Stanley and Goldman Sachs discarded their status as investment banks and chose to become bank-holding companies a classification that made them subject to more regulatory oversight but allowed them to seek government aid (New York Times, 2010). GMAC, the auto lender, and CIT, a lender to businesses, also chose to become bank-holding companies.

## Your Thoughts?

- What do you think about the events triggering the Great Recession?
- Would you be surprised that the eighth top firm on the Fortune 500 lists, Citigroup (bank), paid $5.3 billion in bonuses to its executives after posting losses of $27.7 billion in 2008 while taking $45 billion in TARP money from the U.S. government (Parloff, 2009)?
- What does Citigroup's 2008's actions say about market efficiency or about distributive justice, the just and equal allocation of goods and services, in society at this time?

## CHAPTER OVERVIEW AND LEARNING OBJECTIVES

This chapter will consider market efficiency in light of the subprime mortgage shock and the subsequent Economic Crisis of 2008. The sudden shift in the fortunes of financial markets in September 2008 suggests that new frameworks for understanding market behavior are now in order. In addition to former Federal Reserve Chairman Alan Greenspan's public admission that an important part of free-market ideology now appeared flawed to him, this chapter presents the implications of market inefficiency for society. Such implications include improved regulation of financial markets as well as developing deeper understanding for marketing systems characterized by complexity. Resource-advantage (RA) theory is one noteworthy effort to integrate the complexity of markets into thinking about marketing systems (Hunt & Morgan, 2004). RA theory offers an explanation of competition in markets that proposes that markets are inherently unstable because of the actions of marketers and entrepreneurs.

After this chapter, you should be able to answer the following questions:

- What are the three lessons from the Great Recession that go against much of what is implied by the efficient market hypothesis in finance and general equilibrium theory in neoclassical economics?
- Why should markets be conceived of as complex systems?
- Why is it valuable to view markets as complex systems that are poised for rapid and seemingly unpredictable change in an increasingly networked world?
- What does the resource advantage (RA) theory of competition say about the stability of markets?
- What does the resource advantage (RA) theory of competition say about the role of marketing in markets?

## DIZZYING UPHEAVAL IN FINANCIAL MARKETS

In the midst of this dizzying upheaval, the financial tsunami exposed Former NASDAQ Chairman Bernie Madoff of apparently running a $50 billion Ponzi scheme, in which early investors make handsome returns by being given part of the money of later investors who flock to make similar returns, but who are actually swindled (Lenzner, 2008). Soon Detroit automakers (and others, such as major banks including Bank of America) were queuing for bailout loans from the federal government. Some of those who had been captains of the U.S. economy now seemed to be confused by the very financial forces on which they were supposed to be experts. When in trouble, the "masters of the universe" on Wall Street eagerly sought government interventions in markets, which was a stance taken only out of desperate self-interest. A year before, they never would have advocated such government intervention.

Economists described the events of the fall of 2008 as the most remarkable period of government intervention into the financial system since the Great Depression (Levitt, 2008). As can be seen in Figure 2.1, the Dow-Jones Industrial Average of stock prices

**Figure 2.1**  Dow-Jones Industrial Weekly Average 2002–2012 (Investorguide.com, 2012)

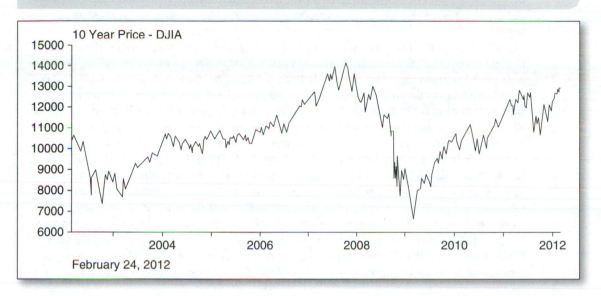

for 30 large U.S. companies went from 13,058.20 on April 28, 2008 to 6,626.94 on March 2, 2009—a drop of 49.24%.

Media newscasters began using the word "trillion" like never before in reference to the scale of proposed economic stimulus packages by the federal government. The Great Recession moved into its worst stages after September 2008, and soon it became the worst recession in U.S. economic history since the Great Depression (Mishel & Shierholtz, 2009). It extended into the winter and spring of 2009. From the peak, inflation-adjusted gross domestic product fell by 3.9% (Grant, 2009).

In the Great Recession, panic gripped every sector. Millions of workers lost their jobs as firms cut back on expenses. Real gross private domestic investment declined between second quarter and third quarter 2009 at an unprecedented annual rate of –41.6%, even faster than at any time during the Great Depression (Gordon, 2010). Swooning home prices reduced the equity U.S. households had in their homes (the value of their homes minus their debt on them) by $5.1 trillion, a 41% drop (Lahart, 2009). Americans also lost trillions of dollars in the stock market. No other episode of wealth destruction since the 1930s comes close to this.

## The Effects of the Market Upheaval

All of these events seem to have deeply affected the psyche of the American public and marketers. The effects of the current financial crisis shook 30 years of trust in minimally regulated markets that had accrued in the minds of American consumer-citizens. Almost overnight, a cloud of suspicion settled over free-market ideology. At once, calls for public policy changes for re-regulation—especially in the banking, finance, and real estate sectors began.

As a result of the increased connections between national markets today, the effects of the meltdown in U.S. financial markets began hitting other countries and their financial and goods markets (Reinhart & Rogoff, 2010, p. 242). The three banks of Iceland all failed (Forelle, 2008). Banks all over the world drastically cut back lending as the tumult unfolded. To generate cash flow, some marketers began making unprecedented offers. In the United Kingdom, car dealers began using pricing tactics from the grocery stores and the garment industry. For example, consumers could buy one Dodge Avenger sedan and receive a second for free—a two-for-one deal (U.S. News and World Report, 2008). Car dealers in Saudi Arabia daringly took another approach. Dealers there announced that they were "unaffected" by the crisis and sent the message to the public that prices will NOT go down (Muscatis, 2009). To the surprise of the dealers, Saudi consumers initiated a massive boycott campaign that spread like wildfire through Internet communication. The boycott campaign adopted the defiant slogan: "Let it Rust! (and let the model expire, so the price will have to come down when the new models arrive)." In Japan, Toyota, the world's largest selling auto manufacturer, stopped production in all of its factories in Japan because of declining sales.

## Who Is to Blame?

The earthquake in the financial and product markets around the world actually began in a market for goods in the United States—local real estate markets. Numerous parties contributed to the housing bubble in places like Los Angeles, Las Vegas, Phoenix, and throughout Florida. A housing bubble occurs in markets where home prices rise faster than wage levels in local real estate markets. Bankers, mortgage lenders, ratings agencies, and Wall Street innovators of standardized products (mortgages that are bundled together and resold to a larger company) did their part. Likewise, understaffed regulatory agencies of financial markets, government-backed mortgage buyers (Fannie Mae and Freddie Mac), as well as elected government officials (President George W. Bush to Rep. Barney Frank who were keen to see homeownership rise for all ethnic and income groups) also helped create and sustain a bubble in housing (Sowell, 2009). Consumers eager to move out of apartments into their own homes, as well as homeowners eager to use their homes as ATMs by refinancing as home prices rose, all contributed to the housing bubble as well. Additionally, speculators who would "flip" homes without occupying them contributed to inflated home prices.

The bubble can be seen in Figure 2.2, which depicts the S&P/Case-Shiller Home Price Index and its annual percentage change (S&P Indices, 2012). It is the leading measure of U.S. home prices and covers all nine U.S. census divisions. As shown, the index for both the 10-city and 20-city composite indices more than doubled from 2000 to its peak in 2006, but it returned to 2003 levels by early 2011.

With zeal, mortgage originators such as those from Quick Loan Funding (a now bankrupt company formerly based in Orange County, California) used the powerfully

**Figure 2.2**   S&P/Case Shiller U.S. National Home Price Index (S&P Indices, 2012)

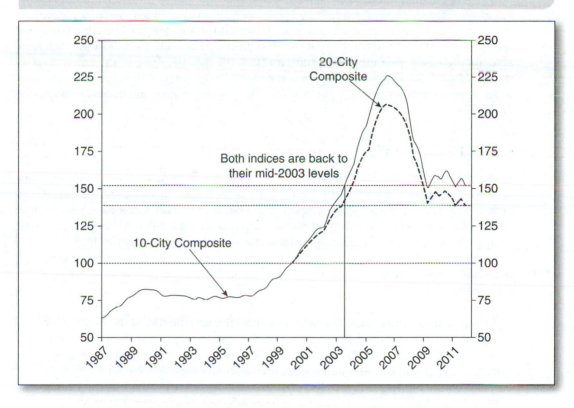

persuasive appeal "You can't wait, and we won't let you!" to lure those with limited ability to move into homes and begin paying monthly mortgages. Agents from Quick Loan Funding pushed "no income/no asset loans" (with "stated income" used instead of actual tax returns used to establish income) that Wall Street firms readily bought and then resold into mortgage-backed securities to cash-laden investors around the world (CNBC, 2009). Oversight proved to be insufficient. Cowardly rating agencies (such as Moody's, Standard & Poor's, and Fitch Ratings) avoided ruining the party thriving on the distorted pricing of risk for such loans that were bundled into securitized debt, such as collateralized debt obligations (CDOs). CDOs are the creation of pooled assets, such as thousands of mortgages that are later resold for investment purposes. As a result, an entire global financial system became poisoned as homeowners defaulted on their mortgage payments at higher rates than expected. However, by this time, the toxic loans had diffused through the blood stream of the financial system by way of the widespread securitization of loans. Ominously, no financial firm owning these toxic assets knew the degree of risk embedded deep within these CDOs.

In the run-up to the meltdown, Fed Chairman Alan Greenspan called for more alternatives to fixed-rate mortgages. To the surprise of many, even banks such as

Wachovia targeted first-time home-buyers on television with products such as "fixed-rate pick-a-payment mortgages" (CNBC, 2009). The "pay-option negative amortization adjustable rate mortgages" offered by some financial institutions allowed homeowners to pay whatever they could each month as the monthly balance would be added onto the mortgage amount with accompanying interest. In effect, the homeowner's mortgage loan actually increased each month. In sum, much of the damage done to the economies of the world's nations was accomplished in the mortgage industry of the United States using a "no questions asked" application of the marketing techniques taught in classrooms of universities.

## The Failure of Laissez-Faire

In conclusion, the housing bubble seduced market actors from across numerous sectors to pursue financial gains that came for a few but proved to be illusory or unsustainable for everyone else. Surprisingly to Greenspan and other free-market ideologues, self-interest and competition—the two pillars of laissez-faire economics—failed to keep the markets away from the precipice of disaster. Instead, the innovation and energy of financiers, the acquisitiveness of consumers, the persuasiveness of marketers, and a pro-market stance of regulators synergistically combined for a tsunami of toxic debt that washed over the economies of the world:

> In one sense, Greenspan had it right: nearly all the participants in the boom were acting "in their rational self-interest." The Mexican immigrant in Riverside County (LA area) looking to buy a new home; his mortgage broker searching the Internet and trying to find him an interest-only loan with an especially low teaser rate: the Vegas condo flipper starting to look farther afield, to Texas or Arizona; the Orange County mortgage lender sitting in his gleaming office building near John Wayne Airport and sending out for sushi lunch; the Wall Street banker rushing to put together a new CDO: the rating agency analyst staring at a pile of junky loans and pronouncing them as safe as T-bill; the Connecticut hedge fund manager reaching for the higher yield that subprime securities offered; the Chinese central banker diversifying out of Treasury bonds: the Florida newspaper publisher rushing out another glossy real estate supplement…all of these individuals were aping Adam Smith's butchers and bakers and pursuing their own ends. (Cassidy, 2009b, pp. 286–287)

Admissions of guilt in the subprime mortgage shock and the economic crisis of 2008 have been generally muted. However, in 2011, Len Berry, a distinguished marketing scholar at Texas A&M University, publicly decried what he termed the "mismarketing" of subprime mortgages and called the field of marketing scholars to do more to examine its role in the subprime mortgage debacle. "The marketing of subprime mortgages almost brought down the world economy," Berry said, "Our field [marketing] was directly involved in the creation and design of these new products and the selling of these instruments. But, I bet there is not a doctoral dissertation on this topic today" (Berry, 2011).

# RECONSIDERING MARKET EFFICIENCY

## A Milestone in Economic History

Alan Greenspan's testimony before Congress in October 2008 was a milestone in economic history because Greenspan had become an icon of free-market ideology. In brief, free-market ideology espoused a belief that markets could better accomplish society's need for allocation of resources, production, and employment. Additionally, free-market ideology carried a belief that lighter regulation of markets by government served society's interests better than heavier regulation of markets. Less regulation would result in better results than what could come from an activist government intervening in markets, because the market price would be determined without distortions from extra-market forces.

Before the near collapse of the world financial system in September 2008, increasingly deregulated markets were allowing the accumulation of financial capital in an unprecedented way. From 1992 to 2007, the GDP of the United States doubled from $6.58 trillion in 1984 to $13.23 trillion in 2007 (Bureau of Economic Analysis, 2011). During the same time, China was raising itself from abject poverty to one of the world's top three economies. China's economy now stands as the second largest economy with a GDP of $5.88 trillion in 2010 compared with the United States at $14.66 trillion (Dawson & Dean, 2011). While cautioning about the mistake of allowing market success to serve as the metric in the nonmaterial realms of life, author and social critic Paul Stiles (2005) asserts, "The market economy is the system of choice for providing for the material welfare of mankind, and for good reason: it works." (p. 15).

## The Unpredictability of Wall Street: A Lesson the World Learned Too Late

In the tumult of the financial crisis, what became clear was the unpredictability of a key sector of the U.S. economy—the financial services sector, especially the financial markets of Wall Street. It was as if many now realized they lived in an earthquake zone. Prior assumptions of stability and expectations for the future needed to be reconsidered beginning with important aspects of free-market ideology.

What economists term "moral hazard" had become part of the high-risk dealings of Wall Street financiers. Here, banks perceiving themselves as "too big to fail" behaved differently than if they perceived that they would have to pay the consequences for their sometimes risky actions. They took on enormous amounts of debt to amplify the gains they were making and misperceived that the federal government would provide a bailout for their firms if things turned out badly. For example, investment banks Bear Stearns and Lehman Brothers had leveraged up to 30 times their capital bases at the end of 2007 (Cassidy, 2009b, p. 313; Lewis, 2010). At such dizzying levels of debt, a mere 4% drop in the assets (loans) of an investment bank can wipe out its entire capital base. When this happens, recapitalization proves to be extremely difficult as investors shy away from putting good money into a bank with such known problems, as well as with perceived untold problems. Government intervention looms for such banks through either a bailout or bankruptcy declaration.

An important point to note here is the diverse nature of markets, which are social spaces where firms, their suppliers, customers, workers, and governments interact to exchange goods and services repeatedly. In hindsight, it can now be seen that the subprime mortgage crisis culminated in the summer of 2007 after years of low interest rates and overbuilding of homes in different regional markets of the United States. Here, one can see how markets influence other markets. Markets for real estate negatively influenced financial markets that, in turn, affected all markets in the United States and around the world once default rates on home mortgages increased and home prices began their downward turn.

This interconnectedness of markets suggests the complexity inherent in explanations about the health of the aggregate economy for a nation. Compounding this complexity is the now global scope for actors in markets. For example, German and Japanese financial institutions and others from as far away as Kazakhstan invested in the U.S. subprime market to obtain more attractive returns than what they could obtain investing in their own domestic real estate markets (Reinhart & Rogoff, 2009, p. 242). As of June 30, 2009, the Chinese government had invested heavily in asset-backed securities primarily backed by home mortgages sold by Fannie Mae and Freddie Mac (ChinaRealTimeReport, 2011). The Chinese government also invested more in U.S. Treasury bonds. By October 2010, China had become the top foreign investor in U.S. Treasuries by owning $1.175 trillion of U.S. Treasury securities, while Japan claimed second by owning $882.3 billion in December 2010 (Talley & Barkley, 2011). All of this suggests that foreign governments enabled interest rates in the United States to remain low in the United States, thereby partly fueling the housing bubble.

## Regulation and the Free Market

Although free-market ideology may not be dead, it certainly deserves reconsideration in light of its recurring blind spot for asset bubbles. Markets need effective regulation to avoid excessive lending that subsequently results in credit crunches in which banks cannot adequately judge the future business prospects for firms applying for loan—and therefore, wind up not making any loans. The challenge is figuring out the type and intensity of regulation. Some observers note that the patchwork of regulations that evolved over time in the United States proved to be effective in keeping financial markets from calamity from 1940 through 1990 (Sterbenz, personal communication, 2011).

Financial markets offer securities that are nothing more than promises to pay on future earnings of firms (Akerloff & Shiller, 2009). For the best functioning financial markets with innovations in financial instruments, such as derivatives (synthetic investment instruments based on the performance of actual investment instruments, such as options, futures contracts, or CDOs), regulation needs matching innovation. Markets, such as Wall Street, are evolving through regulation changes, as well as the ability to enforce these changes by government agencies. As will be discussed later, the United States currently uses a patchwork of agencies to regulate the financial markets. Without revisions in the system of regulating financial markets—and especially, the markets for financial derivates (synthetic instruments based on a set of underlying assets), a replication of the financial crisis of 2008 will very likely be seen in the future.

## Laissez-Faire Economics and the Efficient Market Hypothesis

Keeping in mind (a) the complex interconnectedness of markets, (b) the imperative for regulating markets efficiently, and (c) the changing nature of markets that today operate more rapidly and fluidly than at any previous time, one consequence emerges for proceeding with caution now after the economic meltdown of 2008. It seems that computer-driven financial markets do not have the harmony, stability, and predictability many had attributed to them.

When one returns to economic theory for insight into the nature of financial markets, several important starting assumptions are taken by economists that lead to highly formulaic outcomes. For example, people in markets are viewed essentially as *homo economicus*, rather than as *homo sapiens* (Bishop & Green, 2010). Based on this assumption of a market populated by people behaving as near automatons, economic orthodoxy brought forth the "efficient market hypothesis" (EMH) for the financial markets. The EMH is also commonly referred to as market efficiency. In the EMH, it is impossible for markets to be wrong because the price of any security represents all the information held by individuals in the market. In the buying and selling of the security by all interested actors in a market, the price of the security is determined by the information about the security available to all of the investors. Bajaj (2006) comments:

> The EMH has proven to be a powerful idea in explaining financial market behavior in good times. However, it is weak or even counter-productive when irrational behavior diffuses through markets leading to bubbles (in which asset prices no longer represent their enduring value), as well as in the inevitable crash that follows a bubble [Cassidy, 2009a]. In such cases, a microeconomist's downward sloping demand curve actually becomes upward sloping because of the speculative dimension buyers impart to such assets. Here, prospective home buyers actually desire homes with rapidly increasing prices, expecting they can re-finance them or re-sell them at a profit in the next few years. This happened in Phoenix, Arizona during the housing boom. Of course, these home prices were quickly absorbed into the mortgage-backed securities of the global financial system as solid prices for these assets. Until recently, this fast-growing area was a paradise on earth for home builders. Fulton Homes' developments, for example, were so popular last year that it was able to raise prices on its new homes by $1,000 to $10,000 almost every week. People were standing in line for lotteries," recalled Douglas S. Fulton, president of the company, one of the largest private builders in the Phoenix area. And they were "camping overnight begging to be the next number in the next lot in the next house." (p. A1)

In short, the EMH is blind to bubbles and crashes because of its assumptions. In good times of steady growth in the business cycle (a long-term pattern of growth and decline affecting production, inventories, and employment), the EMH seems to work very well. In such good times, buyers and sellers trust prices. It seems that assets are allocated efficiently and that all market players are disciplined promptly if they stray from prevailing prices. However, in the economic meltdown of 2008, bank stocks were driven to extremely low levels in a brief period by short selling that became like a shark feeding frenzy. Short sellers borrow shares of a stock and sell them immediately. They hope to reimburse the same amount of shares in the future by buying at a lower price and thereby capturing a profit between the original selling price and the later buying price. With "the up-tick rule" that had been in play in the stock markets up from the Great Depression up to the summer of 2007, short selling was only allowed after the security's price had gone up (Zandi, 2009). But without this "up-tick rule," it became rational to short sell bank stocks (Cassidy, 2009b).

Because the EMH provided such explanatory power for financial markets in good weather, biased reasoning crept in for market actors and regulators. The market conditions were perceived widely to be different this time because of (a) globalization, (b) the technology boom, (c) the superior U.S. financial system, (d) better understanding of monetary policy, and (e) innovation in markets (such as securitized debt). The efficiency of contemporary market operations made the bugaboos of the past (bubbles and crashes) things of the past (Reinhart & Rogoff, 2009, p. 20). In short, such biased reasoning led market actors and regulators to allow the market to venture into risky waters. The risk that the regulators and actors took was also heightened because the market conditions were not fully understood like previous market environments.

When the EMH dominated market thinking, three illusions came to life and intensified over time (Cassidy, 2009b) as presented in Table 2.1. First, the market always generates good outcomes. This is the illusion of harmony (among buyers and sellers). Second, the market is sturdy and well grounded. This is the illusion of stability. Third, putting a price on risk through exotic financial products (such as mortgage-backed securities [MBSs], collateralized debt obligations [CDOs], and credit default swaps [CDSs]) and distributing these to those willing to bear such risks greatly reduced the chances of a systemic crisis. This is the illusion of predictability. Played out over a period of months and years, the logic of perfection permeated the talking, reading, and thinking of market actors, regulators, and observers, such as the media. In this way, the culture of Wall Street changed with few ever recognizing it. A new kind of bull market emerged imputed with bulletproof, superhero capabilities by almost all.

**Table 2.1**   Illusions When the Efficient Market Hypothesis Has Dominated Market Thinking

1. The market always generates good outcomes.
2. The market is stable.
3. Markets are predictable.

In the good times, markets work and they seem to work efficiently. At the individual level, the idea of market efficiency becomes the dominant logic. In the later stages of the business cycle, cocky financiers emerge declaring that their losers/winners approach to investing is what makes markets efficient (removing the possibility of arbitrage where assets might be temporarily mispriced). Such unshakable confidence signals that hubris has arrived. Hubris is not part of rational economic behavior.

## The Consequences of Forgetting Past Financial Crises

Part of this hubris is the misperception that financial crises are only for developing countries. For example, a Latin American Debt Crisis involved many U.S. banks in the 1980s. It took years for these banks to unwind their positions in the debt of Latin American countries. The Asian Currency Crisis of 1997 rocked the currency values and economies of Thailand, Malaysia, the Philippines, and Indonesia. But the truth is that the U.S. economy has been wracked by financial crises throughout its history (Bishop & Green, 2010). In 1913, President Woodrow Wilson instituted a national system of banks known as the Federal Reserve Bank to bring more stability to the U.S. financial system. With the creation of the Federal Reserve, U.S. citizens were no longer subject to the volatility of bank notes created at banks of varying quality. Citizens accepting bank notes often had poor information about the financial viability of such banks in other states and frequently took losses on these bank notes.

In the Great Depression, bank runs in which depositors descended on a bank to demand their deposits happened so often that upon taking office, Franklin Delano Roosevelt closed banks for a week after his inauguration in March 1933. Only those banks judged to be financially sound were allowed to reopen (Bishop & Green, 2010, p. 133). In the early 1980s, Congress deregulated the operations of savings and loan banks in the United States. Many savings and loans (S&Ls) made long-term loans with fixed returns, while their short-term deposit-accounts had much volatility. This resulted in the Savings and Loan Crisis. The federal government had to take over more than 300 insolvent thrifts and had to institute the Resolution Trust Authority to dispose of the problem assets of these insolvent savings and loan institutions. The S&L Crisis was a harbinger of the Economic Crisis of 2008, as banking institutions again made long-term loans while investing in short-term markets with much volatility.

For the stock market, crashes have recently occurred. In 1999, the dot.com bubble crashed after investors displayed "irrational exuberance" for new dot.com companies. Many of these dot.coms were only notional entities and had made no actual sales to any customers.

Despite the history of periodic financial crises in the economy of the United States and its financial markets, memories of such events seem to weaken noticeably once they are passed and even seem to be forgotten by many. This has been termed "disaster myopia" (Cassidy, 2009b).

After 9/11, the United States was a country shaken by the first large-scale terrorism attack to hit the homeland. For two days after the attack, no one could see airplanes flying anywhere in the skies of the United States. For months afterward, National Guard troops with weapons greeted air travelers in airport concourses. In this way, the federal government took clearly visible steps to reduce citizen's fear regarding the security of the transportation system in the United States.

In this national security crisis, the Federal Reserve did its part in restoring confidence in the economy and the financial systems of the United States. However, unlike the National Guard troops that left airports in 2002, interest rates remained too low for too long. According to economist John Taylor of Stanford University, Greenspan's monetary policies from 2002 to 2005 restored confidence, but then the policies did not return to normal levels after a few months as they should have (Colvin, 2011). This resulted in plentiful money on easy terms for three years, and later it helped contribute to the financial crisis of 2008.

Much of this easy money flowed into the housing markets of Boston, Las Vegas, Los Angeles, Miami, Washington, DC, and elsewhere in the United States (Akerloff & Shiller, 2009, p. 36). The past financial disasters of the Great Depression and the S&L Crisis of the 1980s were faint memories by then. Furthermore, national financial crises were wrongly believed to be only for developing countries. In an important way, America's economic system itself was perceived to be "too big to fail." Sadly, this was not the case as housing prices nationally declined almost 30% from early 2006 to early 2008 (S&P Indices, 2011). The kind of problems injected into the financial system by the subprime mortgage shock takes years to dissolve.

In March 2011, more than two million American homes were in foreclosure, a third of which stood vacant (Schwartz & Streitfeld, 2011). Another two million households were behind on their payments and facing the prospect of foreclosure by the end of the year. Additionally, about a fifth of the nation's home loans exceeded the value of the underlying house, raising the risk that homeowners would simply walk away, thereby weakening the housing market further.

By reviewing the steps leading to the Great Recession, one can see the value of the "biggest M" in understanding large-scale phenomena related to markets. Here, marketing systems composed of lenders and mortgages brokers aggressively marketed loans for real estate acquisitions to willing consumers. Such acquisitions then served as the underlying assets for the synthetic investments instruments created by Wall Street banks in the form of CDOs and swaps that promised a higher rate of return than ordinary lending for these banks. The Wall Street banks and major banks bought and sold trillions of dollars of these CDOs and swaps among themselves in order to "manage risk." When the loans could not be repaid by consumers once their adjustable mortgage rates reset to a higher rate, the CDOs held by most all of the major financial institutions of the world that used home mortgages as the underlying assets lost enormous sums of money. Banks stopped lending because they could not assess their need for capital in the future, nor could they assess the credit-worthiness of other banks who likely held CDOs and swaps of an undetermined quality. As a result, the entire financial system of the world ground to a halt in the fall of 2008.

## LESSONS FROM THE GREAT RECESSION

### Lesson #1: The Complexity of Markets Can Overwhelm Elites

Although free-market ideologues previously admitted that markets were not perfect (Butler, 2008, p. 47), free-market ideologues' enthusiasm for lightly regulated markets tacitly sent the message that the extent of the imperfection of the securities markets was miniscule in pricing. This imperfection was purported to be so small that actively managed mutual funds did not outperform comparable benchmark indexes (Malkiel, 2005). Often the case for free markets consisted of comparing a free market to alternatives, such as socialism and communism—an extreme comparison. However, in actuality, a more useful comparison would be unfettered markets with more conservatively regulated markets. For example, it is useful to compare the conservatively regulated markets during the period of the Glass-Steagall Act (1933–1999) with the more unfettered markets after repeal of the Glass-Steagall Act. The Glass-Steagall Act's purpose was to control speculation by forbidding depository banks from investing in securities (Bhidé, 2010). In the future, legislation could transform the hodge-podge of agencies regulating banks at the state and federal level into an improved, unified system with a super-regulator that would articulate the coverage of the current set of regulatory agencies.

Effective regulation of the financial system will not be accomplished without political will to institute such reforms. Society must choose and back government leaders who will institute these reforms. In this way, the role of society in achieving improved market efficiency can be understood. Although the systemic risk for the financial system could be reduced through new forms of regulation, markets remain risky for individual actors in these financial markets. Consumers, investors, institutions, and businesses should realize that financial markets are likely to be anything but harmonious, stable, and predictable— even if seemingly major reforms occur.

## The Failure to Forecast Economic Crises

In April 2010, 18 months after his admission that self-interest in markets failed, Alan Greenspan noted that he was not alone in missing the housing bubble. "We all misjudged the risks involved," Greenspan said, "Everybody missed it—academia, the Federal Reserve, all regulators" (Miller & Zumbrun, 2010).

A Bloomberg survey of professional nongovernmental and governmental economists in May 2008 suggested the average forecast for growth in 2009 would be 2.0% with unemployment at 5.3%. In June 2008, despite knowledge of the subprime mortgage mess, Federal Reserve economists predicted economic growth in 2009 would be 2.4%, while unemployment would be 5.5% (Federal Open Market Committee [FOMC], 2008).

At the FOMC meeting on October 28 and 29, 2008, the members of the Board of Governors and the presidents of the Federal Reserve Banks provided projections for economic growth, unemployment, and inflation in 2008, 2009 (FOMC, 2008). Keep in mind that this meeting occurred *after* (a) the federal takeover of Fannie Mae and Freddie Mac, (b) the bankruptcy of Lehman Brothers, and (c) the announcement of the $700 billion Troubled Assets Relief Program (TARP) to rescue the financial system. Even then, elite economists failed to forecast the extent of the negative impact of the Economic Crisis of 2008 on the U.S. economy.

The dotted lines in Figure 2.3 represent the distribution of FOMC participants' projections for real GDP change in 2008 and 2009 given when the FOMC met in June 2008. Note the positive growth predictions. The solid line represents the distribution of participants' projections at the October 28th and 29th meeting. After the October meeting, there is much more variance in the projections for 2009. The worst projections called for a 1% contraction in real GDP. Instead, the economy showed no growth in 2008 and actually shrank by 2.6% in 2009 (Bureau of Economic Analysis [BEA], 2010). Unemployment went to more than 10%, and $50 trillion in wealth around the world evaporated (Brooks, 2010, p. 46).

**Figure 2.3** Distribution of Federal Open Market Committee Participants' Projections in June and October 2008 for the Change in Real GDP in 2008 and 2009

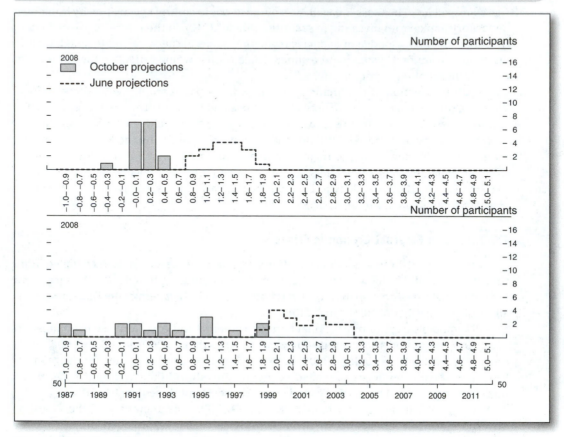

*Source:* www.federalreserve.gov

In reviewing these charts of the Federal Open Market Committee at a time in our nation's economic history when much was already known about the enormous setbacks in the financial markets and when much hung in the balance, it makes one better understand the *Fortune* columnist's assertion about the ability of elite economists in forecasting the future. He said, "It [economics] is not a science. It is not even an art. At best, it's a craft, like pottery" (Bing, 2009, para.1).

If the President of the United States, the best minds of the Federal Reserve Bank, the collective intelligence of economists, and highly paid bank CEOs do not see a crisis emerging before it is too late, how can anyone be sure modestly paid regulators charged with managing smaller pieces of the financial system will see a looming crisis and convince others of it as well? In the housing bubble, markets allocated capital in an awful way, but there is no current reason to believe governments could do better at this task:

Even if regulators somehow did design a perfect regulatory system, it would not last, simply because clever bankers would eventually find ways around it, just as people find ways to evade taxes, forcing tax law writers to constantly make changes. (Norris, 2011, p. 23)

This sentiment is echoed by Paul Romer, a senior fellow at the Institute for Economic Policy Research at Stanford, who asserts, "Every decade or so, any finite system of financial regulation will lead to systemic financial crisis" (Norris, 2011, p. 24).

### Is There a Solution?

Greenspan offers a simple solution to prevent financial crises. He proposes that financial institutions should hold much more capital than they have in the past, so that they can draw on that money in times of crisis (Miller & Zumbrun, 2010). Without adequate capital, any attempt at financial reform is likely to fail, he added.

"I think we're making this issue much too complex," Greenspan said. He further comments, "If you have adequate capital requirements, it almost doesn't matter what else you do with regulation" (Miller & Zumbrun, 2010, para.10).

Despite Greenspan's belief in a simple reform, the U.S. Congress passed the Dodd-Frank Finance Reform Law in the summer of 2010 (Dennis, 2010). This bill, encompassing more than 2,300 printed pages, established an independent consumer bureau called the Consumer Financial Protection Bureau within the Federal Reserve to protect borrowers against abuses in mortgages, credit cards, and some other types of lending. The law also gives the government new power to seize and shut down large, troubled financial companies, like Lehman Brothers, and sets up a council of federal regulators to watch for threats to the financial system. Under the law, the enormous market for derivatives and the complex financial instruments that helped fuel the crisis will be under government oversight (writing such legislation is proving to be a lengthy process.). Dodd-Frank also gives shareholders more say on how corporate executives are paid.

## Lesson #2: Develop Resilience in Complex Systems

If you have ever wondered why almost no one predicted such earth-shaking events as the collapse of the Soviet Union, or the economic meltdown of 2008, thinkers are now emerging to explain why experts failed to predict such pivotal events. In *The Age of the Unthinkable*, Joshua Cooper Ramo explains both the hazards and opportunities in an increasingly dynamic world subject to sudden and sometimes radical change (Ramo, 2009). In short, Ramo proposes that complex systems, despite their apparent stability, often become out of balance and become poised for sudden change. Some of these complex systems which Ramo discusses are marketing systems.

### Layton's Graphical Depiction of Complex Marketing Systems

In recent years, macromarketers have begun to focus on marketing systems (Layton, 2007, 2010). In this effort, Layton has defined marketing systems as a network of individuals, groups, and/or entities embedded in a social matrix that is focused on economic exchange. Notably, marketing systems are ubiquitous and have the primary role of putting in place assortments of goods, services, experiences, and ideas. Layton's mapping of marketing systems includes such patterns of systems as (a) autarchy/random, (b) emergent, (c) structured, and (d) purposeful (Layton, 2010). Autarchic systems are found in the early stages of market development where individuals or households are largely self-sufficient and use barter for exchange. Emergent marketing systems develop when competition is increasingly substituted for regulated or socially controlled outcomes. Trade within and between communities grows in emergent marketing systems. As corporate entities form from single firms to alliance or networks of firms (cooperating in production, distribution, or innovation), marketing systems become structured marketing systems.

As can be seen in the lower-left corner of Figure 2.4, traditional marketing has focused on the systems within the dotted rectangle, such as single firm offers to a market, distribution channels and vertical marketing systems (VMSs), and supply chains. Finally, purposeful marketing systems develop. These carry the distinguishing characteristic of the use of economic or political power to direct transaction flows toward the goals of the entity exercising such power. Layton maps these across three levels of aggregations: (a) micro (firm, household, or individual, (b) meso (loose aggregations of micro units), and (c) macro (societal in scope, composed of all micro and meso units). In this way, Layton plots 27 marketing systems in this matrix (2010).

Four of these 27 types of marketing systems are considered complex systems: (a) the aggregate marketing system for a country, (b) business networks, (c) commodity marketing systems, and (d) business ecosystems. Business ecosystems are typically composed of many loosely connected participants acting generally as a community and relying on each other for survival and effectiveness through a complex web of relationships. For example, Toyota and its constellation of financiers, suppliers, dealers, and service providers give an example of a business ecosystem. Business ecosystems compete against each other, but they can also simultaneously cooperate with each other in industry trade groups, lobbying efforts, and efforts to benefit both communities and societies in which they operate (Iansiti & Levien, 2004; Moore, 1996).

Layton plots these complex marketing systems in the meso- and macro-level systems. He also plots and characterizes these systems as being structured or purposeful. However intended, the terms "structured" and "purposeful" suggest durability. These terms also imply that an enormous force would be needed to destabilize a system, such as an aggregate marketing system. However, such complex marketing systems might decline or fail as a result of natural disasters, war, famine, blunders, criminal action, or competitive action from rivals. This raises the question of system sustainability. System sustainability depends on the adaptive capabilities of the system. Ramo (2009) notes how some systems manifest resilience in that when they are stressed, they learn and adapt. Accordingly, such resilient systems rebound or reform themselves to be stronger and more effective than they were before they experienced stress.

Ramo views stock markets and ecosystems as complex systems. In his view, such systems have internal dynamics that defy easy description and elude prediction. Change in such complex systems often takes place not in a smooth or gradual way, but as a

**Figure 2.4**   Mapping Marketing Systems

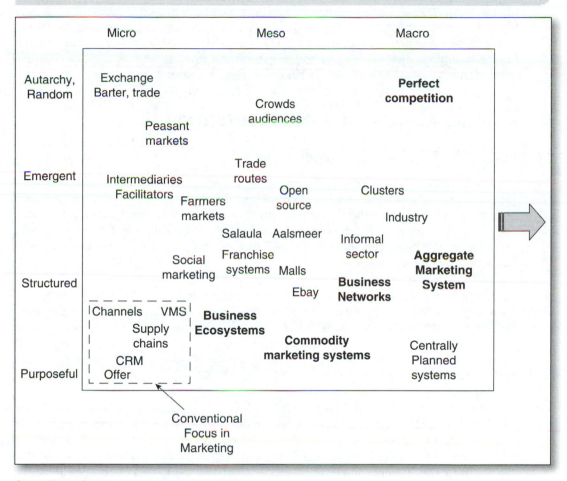

*Source:* Layton (2010).

sequence of fast, catastrophic events. By analogy, sometimes only a light force can induce an avalanche, while in other situations, only a major force can do this.

Consider the major earthquakes in Japan. In a few minutes, an advanced economy experienced significant and irreversible change. Additionally, these systems are very hard to manage or design from the outside. This is because they resist a Newtonian approach to physics in which the world can be reduced to building blocks that are assembled according to higher order systems built on linear relations.

While not stating it explicitly, Ramo endorses an interpretive approach to improving one's chances to sense that something is about to change in a complex system. In this case, a holistic understanding for complex systems is crucial. In addition, the observer must become extremely empathetic by connecting with the environment around oneself. Only by constantly probing and ceaselessly updating one's worldview can one do better at understanding complex systems. This is much in line with the thoughts of Watkins and Bazerman (2003), who believe firms can improve their ability to predict disasters. According to these authors, becoming more machine-like is not the way to understand the future. Instead, thinking about the future and likely threats in a systematic way should be done using qualitative analysis of information outside the firm, as well as employee inputs. Management must then synthesize what perils might be lurking in the future.

## THE RESOURCE-ADVANTAGE THEORY OF COMPETITION

### Challenging the Inherent Stability of Markets

In the midst of the housing bubble, economic theory proved to have a dangerous blind spot. Surprisingly to some, neoclassical economic theory either ignores the contributions of entrepreneurs and marketers or treats them as effervescent phenomena in a market economy that moves inexorably toward equilibrium. With this lens from neoclassical economics, the entrepreneur and marketer take on the role of nuisance factors in the destiny of a market economy.

In 1995, Shelby Hunt and Robert Morgan published their resource-advantage (RA) theory in the *Journal of Marketing* (Peterson, 2011). Briefly put, RA theory challenges neoclassical economics' view of general equilibrium and the inherent stability of market economies. While others such as Austrian economists and Keynesian economists have challenged such economic orthodoxy, Hunt and Morgan do this from the vantage point of marketing. As a result, RA theory imparts a dramatically different role to entrepreneurs and marketers as potentially valuable contributors to the life of a society with a sometimes roiling, but never steady market-economy.

RA theory (Hunt, 2000; Hunt & Morgan, 1995) challenges neoclassical economics' view of general equilibrium and the inherent stability of market economies. In such a hypothetical world of perfect competition, in which general equilibrium prevails across a market economy, not only do entrepreneurs and marketers have a transient role, but also so do profits as the inexorable self-corrections of the market displace entrepreneurs, marketers, and profits.

In the efficient market hypothesis (EMH), conceptually inspired by general equilibrium theory but focused on financial instruments, financial markets always generate the correct prices taking into account all of the available information (Cassidy, 2010b, p. 86). In the EMH, deviations from equilibrium values could not last for long because well-informed investors would buy or sell and make a killing (The Economist, 2009a). Bubbles do not exist in the EMH. In light of the dot.com crash in 2000, the volatility in oil prices in 2007 and 2008, and the housing crash in 2008 that triggered "The Great Recession," the EMH did not account for the irrational exuberance of investors including market veterans and hedge fund managers who tried to ride the bubble up further. Behavioral economist Richard Thaler summed things up as follows: "Those who denied that prices could get out of line, or ever have bubbles, look foolish" (The Economist, 2009a, p. 69). The idea that the market price is the rational or the right price had been badly dented.

In a recent lecture, Paul Krugman, winner of the Nobel Prize in economics in 2008, argued that much of the past 30 years of macroeconomics was "spectacularly useless at best, and positively harmful at worst." Barry Eichengreen, a prominent American economic historian, says the crisis has "cast into doubt much of what we thought we knew about economics" (The Economist, 2009b, p. 11).

Most scholars, market actors, and noncombatants (policy makers, regulators, and the media) had adopted the major premises of neoclassical economics about competition stabilizing the economy. Somehow, the thought of the American economy leading the global economy, which is based on rewarding firms that provided comparable quality in products just a few cents cheaper, seemed to imply that all sectors were close to "perfect competition." It was so innervating that it almost put one to sleep.

Such passivity bred by an inevitably stable market is the focus of Austrian economist Sherwin Rosen's question, "How many right-wing economists does it take to change a light bulb? None, because the free market will take care of everything" (Yeager, 1997, p. 160). At this point in time, the idea of laissez-faire reigned free—perhaps, a little too free.

## A Marketing Scholar's View on Competition: Shelby Hunt and RA Theory

As a scholar, Shelby Hunt has concerned himself with the "biggest M" for decades (Hunt, 1981). For contrarian thinkers such as Hunt, the market is a place where one must look out for one's self.

This is not caveat emptor in another guise, but with entrepreneurs and marketers continually introducing alternative offerings of possibly superior value, one must be alert for offerings that better suit one's real needs as a consumer and for offerings that might eclipse what your business currently offers. The autonomy and personal agency Hunt and Morgan (1995) impart to entrepreneurs and marketers in RA theory is in marked contrast to the passivity that inevitably is imparted about firms (price *takers*) in markets characterized by perfect competition as defined by neoclassical economics. By comparison, RA theory calls for a genuine appreciation for entrepreneurs and marketers.

### RA Theory's Three Tools

In presenting RA theory, Hunt and Lambe (2000) use three tools that appear in many explanations of the theory. First, a boxes-and-arrows diagram called, "A Schematic of RA Theory of Competition," features three boxes representing (a) resources, (b) market position, and (c) financial performance. As shown in Figure 2.5, these three constructs are influenced by societal resources, societal institutions, competitor-suppliers, consumers, and public policy. Here, the important idea is that competition is disequilibrating and ongoing. It is a constant struggle for a comparative advantage in resources that will yield a marketplace position of competitive advantage and, thus, superior financial performance.

The second tool Hunt and Morgan use is a nine-cell matrix called the "Competitive Position Matrix" (see Figure 2.6). This matrix features the vertical axis "relative resource costs" and the horizontal axis "relative resource-produced value." Using this matrix, one

**Figure 2.5**   Schematic of the Resource-Advantage Theory of Competition

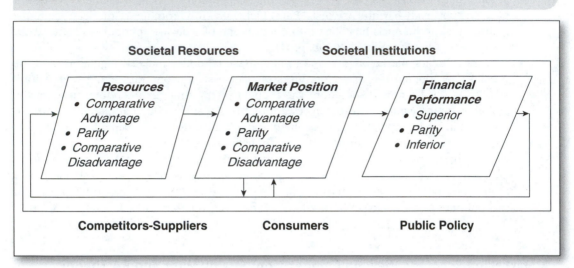

*Source:* Hunt and Morgan (1997).

can understand how firms with relative positions on both cost and produced value will fare in the marketplace. Firms and marketing systems gain competitive advantage through lower costs achieved through efficiency or through combining resources in a superior way, thereby achieving effective marketing. As other rivals develop their own efficiencies and effectiveness, the relative position of a firm or marketing system would move about the matrix. Again, the dynamic nature of markets is implied as RA theory describes the process of competition.

The third tool is a table composed of two columns that allows a comparison between neoclassical economic theory (perfect competition) and RA theory on the nine premises of RA theory (see Table 2.1). Notably, Layton positioned perfect competition in the upper-right of his matrix at the intersection of marketing systems characterized by atomized participants (autarchy, random) viewed from a macro (societal) perspective (see Figure 2.4). How many societal systems use highly atomized participants to accomplish the provisioning needed in society? None. Perhaps, grain production might take some of these perfect competition characteristics, but co-ops, buyer groups, and intermediaries render such competition as less than "perfect". In sum, perfect competition is a highly abstract concept that is useful to work out many theoretical economic issues, but it does not exist in reality—just like the unicorn.

## A Comparison of RA Theory and Neoclassical Economics

A comparison across the nine premises of RA theory brings some surprising realizations (see Table 2.1). First, neoclassical economics' premise that demand is homogenous in an industry does not square with the consumer segments well known to marketers. Such segments suggest that demand in industries is heterogeneous, as proposed by RA theory.

**Figure 2.6** Competitive Position Matrix

**Relative Resource-Produced Value**

| | | Lower | Parity | Superior |
|---|---|---|---|---|
| | **Lower** | **1**<br>Indeterminate Position | **2**<br>Competitive Advantage | **3**<br>Competitive Advantage |
| **Relative Resource Costs** | **Parity** | **4**<br>Competitive Disadvantage | **5**<br>Parity Position | **6**<br>Competitive Advantage |
| | **Higher** | **7**<br>Competitive Disadvantage | **8**<br>Competitive Disadvantage | **9**<br>Indeterminate Position |

*Source:* Hunt and Morgan (1997).

Second, the subprime mortgage shock suggests that the third and fifth premise of RA theory holds. Here, information was not perfect or costless for consumers getting over their heads in mortgage payments, or for mortgage lenders making loans to consumers with doubtful prospects of meeting their mortgage payments in an economic downturn. Information asymmetries characterized too many subprime mortgage transactions. Third, if human motivation was merely self-interest maximization, then more mortgage holders who owe more on their mortgages than their homes are worth would have defaulted on their loans. Many continue to make their payments and use their homes for shelter, rather than merely as a financial asset.

Returning to Interface, Inc. from Chapter 1, it is easy to see how the story of this revitalized carpet manufacturer illustrates the sixth through ninth premises of RA theory better than it does the corresponding premises of neoclassical economics. Here, a more holistic approach to the marketplace was taken that went beyond resources of land, labor, and capital to include many human dimensions, such as a focus on minimizing the firm's impact on the natural environment, giving a new purpose for the company, such as educating other firms how to orient and motivate themselves to climb "Mt. Sustainability." In this way, CEO Ray Anderson no longer only managed his company's production, but he also provided leadership by learning new approaches to develop his firm as a sustainable business.

**Table 2.1**    Comparison of Foundational Premises of Neoclassical Economic Theory and Resource-Advantage Theory (Hunt & Lambe, 2000, p. 35)

|    | Neoclassical Economics | Resource-Advantage Theory |
|----|------------------------|---------------------------|
| 1. | Homogenous demand in industries. | Demand is heterogeneous across industries, heterogeneous within industries. |
| 2. | Consumer information is perfect and costless. | Consumer information is imperfect and costly. |
| 3. | Self-interest maximization is goal of human motivation. | Human motivation is constrained self-interest seeking. |
| 4. | Profit maximization is the firm's objective. | The firm's objective is superior financial performance. |
| 5. | Firm information is perfect and costless. | The firm's information is imperfect and costly. |
| 6. | Firm's resources are capital, labor, and land. | The firm's resources are financial, physical, legal, human, organizational, informational, and relational. |
| 7. | Resource characteristics are homogenous and perfectly mobile. | Resource characteristics are heterogeneous and imperfectly mobile. |
| 8. | Role of management is to determine quantity and implement production function to adjust quantity produced. | Role of management is to recognize, understand, create, select, implement, and modify strategies. |
| 9. | Competition goes to equilibrium resulting in production of commodities. | Competitive dynamics are disequilibrium-provoking, with innovation endogenous. |

## The Importance of RA Theory

RA theory is an integrative theory of business strategy that brings together (a) industry-based, (b) resource-based, and (c) competence-based theories of business strategy. RA theory's relevance to market segmentation can be seen in the case of Black and Decker, Inc. This case illustrates how a global market segmentation strategy helped Black and Decker to reverse the performance of its power tools division in the 1990s (Hunt & Arnett, 2004a). It is important to understand the distinction between neoclassical economists. Neoclassical economists view market segments as artificial creations of suppliers. Market segments are subsets of the larger market containing certain people or organizations that a firm is targeting. In contrast, marketing researchers view the heterogeneity of demand as a naturally occurring phenomenon, rather than something that is created by a firm.

Neoclassical economics paints marketing practice in a dark way as market segmentation strategies are viewed as distorting consumer demand and providing lower value to consumers (Hunt & Arnett, 2004a, p. 20). Hunt and Arnett challenge this dark painting of marketing by declaring that such concerns about market segmentation strategies are unfounded when, in fact, such strategies deliver higher value to consumers and result in segment-by-segment competition leading to higher productivity and greater welfare for society.

Critics of RA theory have asserted that Hunt and Arnett (2004a) have rendered a straw man of neoclassical economics' implications for market segmentation (Cadeaux, 2004). Hunt and Arnett (2004b) note that such critics have never provided any evidence that their discussion of the neoclassical view of market segmentation is anything but accurate. To reinforce this point, Hunt and Arnett note that neoclassical perfect competition theory still dominates public policy discussions concerning antitrust laws and their enforcement—at least in the United States. As a result of neoclassical economic theory's influence, Hunt and Arnett wryly joke that it must be the most influential straw man ever.

It is valuable to see how Hunt and Morgan's (1995) RA theory now lines up with a new thrust in marketing scholarship. One of the most salient implications of Service-Dominant Logic (S-D Logic) is the move from a goods-dominant logic (which views marketers doing things *to* consumers and other businesses) to service-dominant logic (where marketers do things *with* consumers and other businesses). Hunt and Madhavaram (2006a) see this shift more broadly in terms of competition. Under an S-D Logic approach, firms become learning organizations as they begin to work together with consumers and competitors. As learning organizations, firms will likely learn more effectively by collaborating with consumers in new product development. By collaborating with other firms in a pro-competitive way (not in a collusive way to take advantage of consumers and other businesses), firms can gain more of a competitive advantage.

RA theory is heading toward a general theory of marketing (Hunt & Madhavaram, 2006b). Currently, a general marketing theory does not exist. RA theory's most valuable benefit may be showing how the micromarketing subjects of business and marketing strategy fit into the broader, macromarketing topic of competition.

## Thinking About RA Theory's Influence to Date

Judging from citation analysis, researchers in marketing, as well as strategy, seem to be the ones most influenced by RA Theory. However, citations for RA theory in economics journals are scant. Unfortunately, a theory without mathematical equations is not regarded as economics by economists. Briefly put, Hunt and Morgan were not speaking the language of neoclassical economists when they did not undergird RA theory with high-order mathematics. Because of the dynamic nature of competition that Hunt and Morgan propose, developing a set of equations to represent the precise amount of general disequilibrium across all sectors of the economy simultaneously would be inordinately difficult, if not impossible. (Hunt has even noted the impossibility of including a brand such as "Tide" in an equation.) Accepting the principal tenets of RA theory means the rules of the game would change dramatically in economics because general disequilibrium presents an intractable challenge in mathematically representing market phenomena. Global financier George Soros (2008) observes, "If prices aren't always right, it may be that they are always wrong" (p. 5). This presents a challenging problem for mathematically driven economics models and theories.

Previously, use of the EMH was done with abandon in financial economics because the financial markets were presumed to work perfectly:

> Few financial economists thought much about illiquidity or counterparty risk, for instance, because their standard models ignore it; and few worried about the effect on the overall economy of the markets for all asset classes seizing up simultaneously, since few believed that was possible. Macroeconomists also had a blind spot: their standard models assumed that capital markets work perfectly. (The Economist, 2009b, p. 11)

In RA theory, the illusion of stability in the marketplace is removed as innovation led by entrepreneurs and marketers continues to keep markets in disequilibrium. An entrepreneur's and a marketer's role in society is to innovate, and innovation results in an ever-changing, evolving marketplace. Accordingly, firm marketing executives would better spend their time by focusing on gaining a competitive advantage rather than on having mathematical models tell them that there is a linkage between marketing variables and the firm's stock price this quarter. Similarly, CEOs would do well to shift their focus now from efficiency to effectiveness (Hunt & Duhan, 2002).

By giving such focus to the entrepreneur and marketer, Hunt and his co-authors have given marketing and strategy scholars an alternative to neoclassical economics' view of businesses without business persons (Cassidy, 2009b, p. 102). Hunt and his co-authors have given not only a more realistic view of competition but also a view of businesses *with* business people, and potentially creative and adaptive business people, at that.

At this time, it can be said that RA theory stands to move scholars and students away from machine metaphors for the economy (along with all of the accompanying associations about precision, reliability, and stability) to metaphors related to living and evolving ecosystems (with accompanying associations of uncertainty in the environment, and the imperative that successful actors in the environment bring resourcefulness and creativity in order to survive). In this way, RA theory alerts marketers and strategists (as well as students and public policy makers) to the essential role that value creators, such as entrepreneurs and marketers, serve in economic ecosystems.

Interestingly, one emerging thrust in economics is the adaptive markets hypothesis (AMH) (*Economist,* 2009a). Based on evolutionary science, AMH views markets not as efficient in the way that EMH does, but as fiercely competitive. This very much matches the view of RA theory, which is also evolutionary in nature like AMH. Not surprisingly, the AMH focuses on a changing "ecology" of markets in which old strategies become obsolete as new ones emerge. Perhaps, in the future, researchers will connect the AMH with RA theory. This seems to be a very worthwhile direction to pursue.

And perhaps, in the not-too-distant future, economists (at least those pursuing development of the AMH) will begin integrating RA theory into their theories about markets. Time will tell. If this happens, it will be said that Hunt and his co-authors were ahead of their time. RA theory arrived before economics developed a replacement for neoclassical perfect competition theory.

## CONCLUSION

Markets are *not* perfect. They are not always rational. They are not always harmonious, stable, or predictable. Markets *are* dynamic and evolutionary. The actions of entrepreneurs, marketers, and policy makers contribute to the dynamism of markets. RA theory presents one explanation for a process of competition in dynamic and evolving markets. Governments *will* be involved in markets. The question is to what degree they will be and to what degree will they empower themselves to be effective. Markets are complex systems according to Ramo (2009) and Layton (2010). They can become poised critical systems that can rapidly collapse in a highly networked world similar to cities in seismic zones.

Rather than focusing on the efficiency of markets (the bailiwick of economics), those seeking to understand lessons related to the "biggest M" of marketing and society from the Economic Crisis of 2008 would do better now to refocus on how learning occurs in markets and how markets can become more effective. Neither of these topics is currently well developed in economics, but the work of behavioral economists developing the AMH suggests that a more human approach to understanding the nature of markets may soon prove beneficial.

Marketers and marketing scholars have knowledge to share regarding how market actors learn and how markets develop or devolve. Interestingly, a few maverick investors, such as Michael Burry or Kyle Bass, who recognized the bubble in the housing market in the mid-2000s, experienced first-hand the shady marketing practices of mortgage lenders as part of their field research. Such qualitative research proved to be the most convincing evidence for them to pursue their contrarian investing that later earned them hundreds of millions of earnings for their respective firms (Lewis, 2010). For these investors, a more human approach to researching financial markets has already proved enormously beneficial.

## QUESTIONS

1. What were surprises you encountered in reading Chapter 2?

2. In your opinion, how efficient are markets?

3. In your opinion, how harmonious, stable, and predictable are markets?

4. How sanguine are you about government intervention in financial markets? To what degree could government back out of financial markets without deleterious results?

5. To what degree do markets evolve in your opinion? How do they do it?

6. Compare and contrast the ideas of Ramo and Hunt regarding markets.

# MAVERICKS WHO MADE IT

## J. Kyle Bass

IN A TIME WHEN their own headlong pursuit of increasing profits led them to authorize the fielding of increasingly complex "risk management" instruments, such as collateralized debt obligations (CDOs) and synthetic CDOs, the masters of the universe of Wall Street were suddenly taking orders from Washington, DC. With hat in hand, they were bankrupt (like Lehman Brothers), acquired (like Bear Stearns and Merrill Lynch) or taking federal bail-out money through the TARP program (like insurance giant AIG and 770 troubled banks) in September 2008 (Lewis, 2010, p. 260). But one who saw things differently in 2006 and 2007 was investor J. Kyle Bass based in Dallas, Texas. Although home prices had been rising for the last five years at more than 10% annually, he had taken counter-positions in mortgage-backed securities to Wall Street investment banks because he believed housing prices would decline significantly for the first time since the Great Depression (Pittman, 2007). Bass wound up beating investment banks such as Bear Stearns at their own game, and he exited the markets in 2007 after netting more than $500 million in profits.

From his office in Dallas, one of the few "who saw it coming" in the subprime mortgage world was Bass and his Hayman Capital Partners. "The bottom line is that they (issuers of mortgage-backed securities) had tried to put lipstick on a pig to try to sell it to someone who didn't know what they were buying," Bass explained (CNBC, 2009). "When I sat down with them I asked them (investment banks dealing in exotic derivative contracts) what kind of home-price appreciation are you modeling in these things and they'd say 'six to eight percent a year.' They were modeling that into perpetuity like it was going to happen from now on. It was clear that wasn't going to happen. But nobody I met with (on Wall Street) even considered it was remotely possible that home prices might go down."

Bass foresaw a $27 trillion decline in U.S. home values that would take $6 trillion out of the home budgets of U.S. consumers, but he was met with denial when sharing his thesis with finance and real estate industry experts (Hanley, 2008). "Everywhere we went to raise money for our enterprise, people would say, 'Oh, we completely agree with you, but it's not going to happen here because of this, this, this, and this. Not just Dallas, everywhere I went. Portland, Seattle, Chicago."

Bass, a former salesman for Wall Street firms Bear Stearns and Legg Mason, had tried to short sell the housing market (borrowing shares, selling them in hopes of repurchasing the same amount of shares in the future at a lower price, thereby netting a profit), but he found that shorting major home-building companies did not work (Pittman, 2007). A leveraged-buyout firm would often bid for the home-building company, which would cause the stock to rise in price and would penalize Bass who had taken a short position expecting a price decline. However, Bass found that new standardized mortgage-bond derivative-contracts offered the chance to assume less risk with more profit potential.

Bass committed himself to learning and research. He visited Wall Street trading desks and mortgage servicers to learn about the contracts. He sat down with housing lenders and hedge fund analysts. He read *Collateralized Debt Obligations: Structures and Analysis* by Yale professor Frank Fabozzi. He read it twice.

"What I didn't understand was the synthetic marketplace," Bass says. "When someone explained to me that it was a synthetic CDO that takes the other side of my trade, it took me a month to understand what the hell was going on."

Bass teamed up with Mark Hart of Corriente Capital Management of Ft. Worth, Texas, and Alan Fournier of Pennant Capital in Chatham, New Jersey. As a salesman, Bass had sold securities to Fournier. Now, they researched bad loans together.

The two hired private detectives, searched news reports, queried Wall Street underwriters about which mortgage companies' loans were suspect, and then called those lenders directly. At one dubious mortgage company in California, Quick Loan Funding (now bankrupt), Bass called directly by phone to inquire about taking out a loan. The fast and loose manner in which his request was fielded convinced Bass to find out what CDOs contained loans from this company, and then to short the synthetic CDOs (sold as insurance against mortgage defaults) of these CDOs. Wall Street firms were making bets on other Wall Street firms' bets in the billions of dollars (Hanley, 2008).

A fear of Bass's was that the subprime problem would become understood before he was able to raise investment capital to take positions in the financial markets. He and his group had to travel feverishly to make pitches to potential investors and explain that they thought the housing market was about to collapse (Pittman, 2007). Beginning in August and September of 2006, Bass and his group used the leveraging power of derivatives to short sell $4 billion of subprime securities in the synthetic CDO market. For example, Bass and his team identified BBB-rated mortgage instruments, such as Nomura Home Equity Loan Inc. 2006-HE2M8, as an issue with 37% of its loans originated at Quick Loan Funding. In effect, Bass and his group developed their own ratings for what they viewed as risky CDO investment vehicles that had been rubber-stamped by the three ratings agencies (paid by the investment banks issuing these investment vehicles)—Standard & Poor's, Fitch's, and Moody's.

In January 2007, Bass extended his research effort to "meet the enemy"—the managers of the synthetic CDOs that took the other sides of his trades (Pittman, 2007). In pursuing what economists would describe as "counterparty surveillance" (a force to make markets more efficient), Bass attended the American Securitization Forum in Las Vegas to glean intelligence about the intentions of Wall Street investment banks regarding their exposure to risk in the mortgage markets. He discovered that his former employer Bear Stearns and its West Coast client Pimco were discussing a way to pay off bad mortgage loans early, so that short sellers like Bass would lose their money.

Alarmed, Bass enjoined other short sellers, such as New York-based Paulson & Co owned by John Paulson (no relation to former U.S. Treasury Secretary Hank Paulson. Likewise, Bass is no relation to the Bass family of wealthy investors based in Ft. Worth, Texas). Ten hedge funds or short sellers created a pressure group called the Asset Backed Securities Credit Derivatives Users Association (ACDUA) that petitioned the Securities and Exchange Commission to uphold its anti-manipulation provisions (Hanley, 2008). This tactic forced Bear Stearns to drop its threat to the short sellers.

In September 2007, Bass testified before a House subcommittee investigating these ratings agencies. He lambasted the agencies' sloppy valuation models and blamed their conflicts of interests with

*(Continued)*

(Continued)

the investment banks for undermining the soundness of the U.S. financial system. By December 2007, with foreclosures beginning to sweep the country, Bass had made a fortune for himself and his clients.

Bloomberg TV introduced Bass then as a man who had just made millions "basically betting against the subprime borrower" (Hanley, 2008). Bass disputed this portrayal. "We're not profiting off other people's demise," Bass said. "What we did is we made a very simple bet, and that very simple bet is that synthetic-CDO managers were over-levered, and they had no idea what they owned. It was two professional investors that made these bets. An individual can't come in and make these bets."

Although Bass contributed $15 million to a consumer rights group that seeks to have laws changed to allow distressed home-mortgage holders to be able to refinance their homes at more favorable lending rates when in bankruptcy, it would be hard to classify him as a consumer rights crusader. Critics contend that the success of such legal reforms would have depressed the bank stocks that he had already sold short.

Self-interest and risk-seeking seem to characterize Bass. He claims he has never voted in an election (and is not registered to vote). In 2002, he raced a $200,000 Porsche from Manhattan to Los Angeles in a road rally called the Gumball 3000. Ignoring posted speed limits and even employing a spotter helicopter at one point, he won the Gumball 3000's "Hottest Wheels" award for attaining 208 mph in a remote stretch of highway in Nevada.

In sum, although many individuals will find much appeal in Bass's story, he shares much in common with the Wall Street financiers he beat in a high-stakes bet about the nature of the real estate markets of the United States. But foremost, he succeeded by questioning the assumptions widely used by Wall Street, the Federal Reserve, and most actors in the housing market of the mid-2000s. He then did hands-on research and was cued by the questionable marketing practices of a firm, such as Quick Loan Funding. He and his team painstakingly found the CDOs that contained the BBB-rated loans for Quick Loan Funding, and then rapidly raised more than $100 million in investment capital to take a daring position against the investment banks of Wall Street. To keep his counterparties from manipulating the outcome of the deals they had struck with him, he lobbied the White House and Congress through the NGO he had formed—ACDUA. In addition to self-interest and risk-seeking, Bass took a broad approach to keep his deal on track by engaging the public sector and other NGOs. In these ways, Bass became a Maverick Who Made It.

## Questions

1. In your opinion, what were the factors of success for Kyle Bass?

2. Why do you think there weren't more investing success stories like Bass's as the housing bubble collapsed?

3. Regarding a five-capital approach to capitalism presented in Chapter 1, how many forms of capital accumulation can be evidenced in Bass's story for Hayman Capital Partners?

4. If Bass's comparative advantage can be described as "identifying over-levered entities," what other entities might be targets for Bass's short selling in the future? (Hint: If housing values decline, so will tax bases for the related municipalities. Another hint: If a country continues carrying a heavy debt-load and produces less because of an aging population, which countries might be targets for short selling by Bass?)

## REFERENCES

Akerloff, G. A., & Shiller, R. J. (2009). *Animal spirits: How human psychology drives the economy, and why it matters for global capitalism*. Princeton, NJ: Princeton University Press.

Bajaj, V. (2006, November 7). After Arizona's housing boom, 'For Sale' is a sign of the times. *The New York Times*, p. A1.

Bureau of Economic Analysis. (2010). [Graph illustration of annual growth in real GDP]. Industry Economic Accounts. Retrieved from http://www.bea.gov/newsreleases/industry/gdpindustry/gdpind_glance.htm

Bureau of Economic Analysis. (2011). [Table 1.16. Real Gross Domestic Product, Chained Dollars (Billions of chained (2005) dollars)]. Nation Income Accounts. Retrieved from http://www.bea.gov/national/nipaweb/SelectTable.asp?Popular = Y

Berry, L. (2011). *The future of the marketing discipline*. Presented at the American Marketing Association's Winter Educators' Conference, Austin, TX.

Bhidé, A. (2009). In praise of more primitive finance. *Economists' Voice, 6*(3), 1–7. doi: 10.2202/1553-3832.1534

Bing, S. (2009, April 2009). Nine things we'll probably forget when this is all over. [Web log post]. Retrieved from http://stanleybing.blogs.fortune.cnn.com/2009/04/27/9-things-well-probably-forget-when-this-is-all-over/

Bishop, M., & Green, M. (2010). *The road from ruin: How to revive capitalism and put America back on top*. New York, NY: Crown Business.

Brooks, A. (2010). *The battle: How the fight between free enterprise and big government will shape America's future*. New York, NY: Basic Books.

Butler, E. (2008). *The best book on the market: How to stop worrying and love the free economy*. New York, NY: Wiley.

Cadeaux, J. (2004). A commentary on Hunt and Arnett's paper market segmentation strategy, competitive advantage, and public policy: Grounding segmentation strategy in Resource-Advantage Theory. *Australasian Marketing Journal 12*(1), 26–29.

Cassidy, J. (2009a, October 5). Rational irrationality. *The New Yorker*. Retrieved from http://www.new yorker.com/

Cassidy, J. (2009b). *How markets fail: The logic of economic calamities*. New York, NY: Farrar, Straus and Giroux.

ChinaRealTimeReport. (2011, February 12). Much ado in China about Fannie and Freddie. *Wall Street Journal Online*. Retrieved from http://blogs.wsj.com/chinarealtime/

CNBC (producer). (2009, June 3). *House of cards.* [Television broadcast]. New York, NY: CNBC. Retrieved from http://www.cnbc.com/id/15840232?video = 1145392808&play = 1

Colvin, G. (2011, March 1). Alan Greenspan fights back. *Fortune*, pp. 82–90.

Dawson, C., & Dean, J. (2011, February 14). Rising China bests a shrinking Japan. *Wall Street Journal Online.* Retrieved from http://online.wsj.com/

Dennis, B. (2010, July 16). Congress passes financial reform bill. *Washington Post Online.* Retrieved from http://www.washingtonpost.com/

Federal Open Market Committee. (2008). Minutes of the Federal Open Market Committee, October 28 & 29th. Retrieved from http://www.federalreserve.gov/monetarypolicy/fomcminutes20081029ep .htm

Forelle, C. (2008, December 27). The isle that rattled the world. *The Wall Street Journal.* Retrieved from http://online.wsj.com/article/SB123032660060735767.html

Gordon, R. J. (2010, April 12). Guest contribution: NBER Panel Member Gordon says it is 'obvious' recession over. *Wall Street Journal Online.* Retrieved from http://blogs.wsj.com/

Grant, J. (2009, September 19). From bear to bull: James Grant argues the latest gloomy forecasts ignore an important lesson of history: The deeper the slump, the zippier the recovery. *Wall Street Journal Online.* Retrieved from http://online.wsj.com/

Hanley, C. (2008, April). Cashing in on subprime. *D Magazine.* Retrieved from http://www.dmagazine .com/Home/2008/03/13/Cashing_in_on_Subprime.aspx?p = 1

Hunt, S. (1981). Macromarketing as a multi-dimensional construct. *Journal of Macromarketing, 1*(1), 7–8.

Hunt, S. (2000). *A general theory of competition: Resources, competences, productivity, economic growth.* Thousand Oaks, CA: Sage.

Hunt, S., & Arnett, D. B. (2004a). Market segmentation, competitive advantage, and public policy: Grounding segmentation strategy in resource-advantage theory. *Australasian Marketing Journal 12*(1), 7–25.

Hunt, S., & Arnett, D. B. (2004b). Market segmentation strategy and resource-advantage theory: A response to Cadeaux and Dowling. *Australasian Marketing Journal, 12*(1), 32–36.

Hunt, S., & Duhan, D. F. (2002). Competition in the third millennium: Efficiency or effectiveness. *Journal of Business Research, 55*(1), 97–102.

Hunt, S., & Lambe, C. J. (2000). Marketing's contribution to business strategy: Market orientation, relationship marketing, and resource-advantage theory. *International Journal of Management Reviews 2*(1), 17–44.

Hunt, S., & Madhavaram, S. (2006a). The service-dominant logic of marketing: Theoretical foundations, pedagogy, and resource-advantage theory. In R. F. Lusch & S. L. Vargo (Eds.), *The service-dominant logic of marketing: Dialog, debate, and directions* (pp. 85-90). Armonk, NY: M.E. Sharpe.

Hunt, S., & Madhavaram, S. (2006b). Teaching marketing strategy: Using resource-advantage theory as an integrative theoretical foundation. *Journal of Marketing Education, 28*(2), 93–105.

Hunt, S., & Morgan, R. M. (1995). The comparative advantage theory of competition. *Journal of Marketing, 59*, 1–15.

Hunt, S., & Morgan, R. M. (2004). The resource-advantage theory of competition. In N. K. Malhotra (Ed.), *Review of Marketing Research, Vol. 1* (pp. 153-205). Armonk, NY: M. E. Sharpe.

Iansiti, M., & Levien, R. (2004). *The Keystone advantage: What the new dynamics of business ecosystems mean for strategy, innovation, and sustainability.* Boston, MA: Harvard Business School Press.

Investorguide.com. (2012). Chart built at http://www.investorguide.com

Karnitschnig, M., Solomon, D., Pleven, L., & Hilsenrath, J. E. (2008, September 18). U.S. to take over AIG in $85 billion bailout; Central banks inject cash as credit dries up. *The Wall Street Journal.* Retrieved from http://online.wsj.com

Lahart, J. (2009, July 28). The great recession: A downturn sized up. *Wall Street Journal Online*. Retrieved from http://online.wsj.com

Layton, R. A. (2007). Marketing systems: A core macromarketing concept. *Journal of Macromarketing, 27*(2), 193–213.

Layton, R. A. (2010). Marketing systems, macromarketing and the quality of life. In P. Maclaren, M. Saren, B. Stern, & M. Tadajewski (Eds.), *The SAGE handbook of marketing theory* (pp. 415-442). Thousand Oaks, CA: Sage.

Lenzner, R. (2008, December). Bernie Madoff's $50 billion Ponzi scheme. *Forbes*. Retrieved from http://www.forbes.com

Levitt, S. D. (2008, September 18). Freakonomics, Diamond and Kashyap on the recent financial upheavals. *New York Times*.

Lewis, M. M. (2010). *The big short: Inside the doomsday machine*. New York, NY: W.W. Norton.

Malkiel, B. G. (2005). Reflections on the efficient market hypothesis: 30 years later. *The Financial Review, 40*, 1–9.

Miller, R., & Zumbrun, J. (2010, March 27). Greenspan takes issue with Yellen on Fed's role in house bubble. Retrieved from http://www.bloomberg.com

Mishel, L., & Shierholz, H. (2009, June 2). The worst downturn since the Great Depression. *Economic Policy Institute*. *Retrieved from* http://www.epi.org/publications/entry/jobspict_200906_preview/

Moore, J. F. (1996). *The death of competition: Leadership & strategy in the age of business ecosystems*. New York, NY: HarperBusiness.

Muscatis. (2009). Let it rust. Retrieved from http://www.muscati.com/2009/01/let-it-rust.html

New York Times. (2010, October 14). Mortgages and the markets. *New York Times Online*. Retrieved from http://www.newyorktimes.com

Norris, F. (2011, March 10). Crisis is over, but where's the fix? *New York Times Online*. Retrieved from http://www.newyorktimes.com

Parloff, R. (2009, January 19). Wall street: It's payback time. *Fortune*, 57–69.

Peterson, M. (2011). RA theory moves entrepreneurs and marketers to center stage. *Legends of Marketing: Shelby Hunt, Vol. 7: Marketing Management and Strategy*. New Delhi, India: Sage.

Pittman, M. (2007, December 19). Bass shorted 'God I Hope You're Wrong' Wall Street (Update 2). *Bloomberg*. Retrieved form http://www.bloomberg.com/apps/news?pid = 21070001&sid = adp5U MQkZfwc

Quelch, J. (2009, May 4). What's next for the big financial brands. Working knowledge: A look at faculty research. *Harvard Business School, (87)*5.

Ramo, J. C. (2009). *The age of the unthinkable*. New York, NY: Little, Brown.

Reinhart, C. M., & Rogoff, K. S. (2009). *This time is different: Eight centuries of financial folly*. Princeton, NJ: Princeton University Press.

S&P Indices. (2012). Home prices continued to decline in November 2011 according to the S&P/Case-Shiller home price indices. January 31, 2012. Retrieved from http://www.standardandpoors.com/indices/sp-case-shiller-home-price-indices/en/us/?indexId = spusa-cashpidff--p-us----

Schwartz, N. D., & Streitfeld, D. (2011, March 2). Officials disagree on penalties for mortgage mess. *New York Times Online*. Retrieved from www.newyorktimes.com

Soros, G. (2008). *The crash of 2008 and what it means: The new paradigm for financial markets*. New York, NY: Public Affairs.

Sowell, T. (2009). *The housing boom and bust*. New York, NY: Basic Books.

Stiles, P. (2005). *Is the American dream killing you? How the market rules our lives*. New York, NY: Collins.

Talley, I., & Barkley, T. (2011, March 15). China sold treasuries for third month. *Wall Street Journal Online*. Retrieved from http://online.wsj.com

The Economist. (2009a, July 18). Efficiency and beyond. *The Economist, 392*(8640), pp. 68–69.

The Economist. (2009b, July 18). What went wrong with economics. *The Economist, 392*(8640), p. 12.

U.S. News and World Report. (2008, November 10). Car deal of the day: Buy one get one free Dodge Avengers. Retrieved from http://usnews.rankingsandreviews.com/cars-trucks/daily-news/081110-CarDeal-of-the-Day-Buy-One-Get-One-Free-Dodge-Avengers/

Watkins, M. D., & Bazerman, M. H. (2003). Predictable surprises: The disasters you should have seen coming. *Harvard Business Review, 81*(3), 72–80.

Yeager, L. (1997). Austrian economics, neoclassicism, and the market test. *Journal of Economic Perspectives, 11*(4), 153–165.

Zandi, M. (2009). *Financial shock: Global panic and government bailouts – How we got here and what must be done to fix it.* (updated edition). Upper Saddle River, NJ: Financial Times Press.

Zuckerman, S. (2008, October 24). Greenspan shocked at failure of free markets. *San Francisco Chronicle*, p. C1.

# Marketing and Society

## WHAT MARKETING CAN DO

### World-class Product + No Other Marketing = No Success

At 7:51 A.M. on Friday, January 12, 2007, a 30ish White man wearing a long-sleeved t-shirt and a baseball cap stationed himself against a wall next to a trash basket in Washington, DC's L'Enfant Plaza Metro station (Weingarten, 2007). He opened a violin case at his feet, took out the violin, shrewdly threw a few dollars into the case to cue those passing by to drop their change, and began playing for his audience in the subway station. The acoustics proved to be surprisingly suitable.

After 63 persons had passed by giving no notice to the violinist, a middle-aged man slowed his walk and turned his head but kept moving. Half a minute later, a woman tossed a dollar bill into the violinist's case as she walked past. After six minutes of playing, someone actually stopped against a wall and listened to the violinist. After almost 45 minutes of violin playing for commuters on their way to their government jobs, only seven people stopped and listened. The violinist played selections by Bach, Schubert, Massenet, and Ponce—some of the most compelling music written for the solo violin (Bix & Taylor, 2011). In all, almost 1,100 people passed the violinist. No crowd ever formed. By the time he ended, 27 people had thrown money into the violin case. There was no applause at the end. Total revenues for this performance came to $32.17.

As it turns out, a staff writer from *The Washington Post* had arranged the entire musical performance as part of a story on commuting to work (Weingarten, 2007). The violinist was none other than world-renowned violinist Joshua Bell playing a violin valued at $3.5 million—a 1713 Stradivarius. Two days prior to the Metro station performance, Bell had played the same violin before a sold-out concert in Boston where tickets averaged $100 each. At this stage of his career, Bell normally receives $1,000 per minute when he performs. However, Bell and his violin, both world-class products, are not worth $1,000 per minute by themselves:

> Behind every sold-out performance is the work of educators, market researchers and strategists, artistic directors, agents, advertisers, and ticket sellers—in short, all those helping Joshua Bell find and reach that middle-aged couple who is willing to pay $100 per seat at the Boston Symphony. Without them, the man whose talent can command $1,000 a minute walks away with $32 for almost an hour's worth of brilliant performance. (Bix & Taylor, 2011, p. 3)

In sum, the musician, who three months later received the Avery Fisher Prize as the best classical musician in America, could not command much of an audience without a complete marketing effort. In marketing management terms, Bell and his Stradivarius comprised only the product dimension of a marketing effort. At L'Enfant Plaza that January morning, the rest of a credible marketing effort (the promotion, the selection of a place for distributing the product, and the price) were either not done or done inappropriately. In the end, Bell remained almost invisible to those who passed him at L'Enfant Plaza. He received less than a thousandth of his normal take for performing. In this way, it is easy to see the impact of a complete and appropriate marketing effort.

Toward the end of his playing, Stacy Furukawa, a demographer at the Commerce Department, stopped her commute and positioned herself 3 m from the violinist. A huge grin came onto her face. She had been at Bell's free concert at the Library of Congress three weeks previously. She remained until the end of the performance:

"It was the most astonishing thing I've ever seen in Washington," Furukawa said, "Joshua Bell was standing there playing at rush hour and people were not stopping, and not even looking, and some were flipping quarters at him! Quarters!" (Weingarten, 2007)

**Your Thoughts?**

- You have probably heard the saying, "build a better mousetrap and the world will beat a path to your door." What did Joshua Bell's experience playing in the L'Enfant Plaza entrance to the Washington, DC Metro station suggest about this saying?
- If Joshua returned every day of the year and did the same thing, what do you think would happen?
- Say you met someone like Joshua playing violin in the L'Enfant Plaza entrance with the same proficiency. If you became this person's commercial consultant, and were paid on commission, what is the most important thing you could recommend for this person to do in order to develop this person's commercial performing career?

In this chapter, we will examine marketing's contributions to society. You will learn about flows in the aggregated marketing system, such as flows of physical goods, information, currency, as well as debt.

## CHAPTER OVERVIEW AND LEARNING OBJECTIVES

This chapter initially considers marketing's current contributions to society and then looks at flows of information and debt in the aggregate marketing system. Scholars and business practitioners have suggested that markets are people voting with their money (Dickinson & Hollander, 1991; Forbes & Ames, 2009, p. 14). As a result of such voting, preferences for certain products and services become known. Marketers then see to it that vote-winning products remain in the market. Some of these vote-winning products receive special enhancements and marketing efforts to make them more powerful when receiving votes at the cash register (where consumer votes are cast). With an absence of marketing capabilities in the aggregate marketing system, innovation and product flows are often restricted. Such limited choice for consumers has characterized socialist systems, such as those of North Korea, or societies ruled by corrupt autocratic regimes, such as Zimbabwe (Legatum Institute, 2012a). By comparison, the aggregate marketing system in developed economies can provide almost everything consumers want. However, adverse consequences can come with some consumption practices when consumers enjoy almost unrestricted market choices. Some of these practices include the consumption of tobacco products or attempting to carry heavy debt-loads for consumers. When such consumption practices continue for too long, societal costs emerge. These can emerge in the form of increased healthcare costs for the treatment and care of patients with debilitating illnesses, such as cancer or respiratory illnesses. These can also emerge in the form of macroeconomic problems, such as a sluggish or shrinking economy.

After this chapter, you should be able to answer the following questions:

- What can marketing do for enterprises and society?
- What does an absence or deficiency in marketing do to a society?
- What are the different flows in the aggregate marketing system for a society?
- Why do externalities (consequences for those not part of market exchanges) cause macromarketing to have a healthy skepticism toward markets?
- What are debt flows in the aggregate marketing system?
- Does a culture of debt prevail in the United States?
- Is it possible for a financial service firm or a bank to be a sustainable enterprise?

# MARKETING AND SOCIETY

## What Marketing Can Do for Societies

In the aggregate, marketing can be viewed as the provisioning system for a society (Fisk, 1974). In this way, marketing serves an economic function at the interface between supply and demand (Quelch & Jocz, 2007). Marketing adds value to goods and services by making them available to persons who want them, where they are wanted, when they are wanted, and at the price they are wanted. In Joshua Bell's foray into the Washington, DC Metro station, the right persons were not gathered in an appropriate concert hall at 7:30 P.M. at $100 per ticket to hear renditions of the classical masters, such as Bach or Schubert. If marketing had been done more effectively for Joshua Bell, he would have earned significantly more in profits for his performance.

From a societal perspective, marketing meets the consumption needs of those in society. In this way, marketing can be viewed as a social force. Although most marketing done by firms takes a "little m" approach by tactically applying elements of the marketing mix (product, place, promotion, and price) and does not overtly aim to create value for society, nevertheless, well-done marketing programs cumulatively have a positive impact on society by creating value for consumers.

Despite the social welfare contributions of marketing, not all of marketing's effects can be said to be positive for society. Legal enterprises, such as tobacco marketing, have a deleterious effect on the health of long-time users of tobacco products. Hundreds of years ago, the legal North Atlantic slave trade put millions of Africans into bondage in the United States and the Caribbean, while the Middle Eastern slave trade actually put more into bondage there (Lewis, 1994). Additionally, marketers lapse into deceit and fraud at times, and advertising remains controversial because of its ability to reinforce materialistic tendencies in individuals. In sum, misapplied marketing can reduce the quality of living in a society.

### Benefits of Marketing

Marketing provides many benefits to society. Specifically, consumer marketing offers benefits that are very much aligned with those of democracy (Quelch & Jocz, 2007).

*Benefit #1: Marketing facilitates free and fair voluntary transactions that occur as part of exchange.* Normally, both parties benefit as part of market exchanges. A broader view of exchange regards market exchanges as being part of a complex system of exchange between public, government, business, and other social institutions. More will be said about this later in this chapter.

*Benefit #2: As a result of marketing, consumers have control and choice over offerings presented in the marketplace.* Although an overabundance of choices might drive consumers to use experts to help them make purchases, competitive marketing has driven firms to satisfy smaller segments of consumers with increasingly differentiated products.

*Benefit #3: Consumers can actively participate in shaping the marketplace. This can be done by voting in the marketplace for products and services they prefer.* Consumers can also participate in formal marketing research programs conducted by firms, as well as co-creating new products with marketers. They also verbally endorse products to other consumers in a positive, negative, or neutral way, which influences potential consumers' decisions. If a product repeatedly gets bad reviews by consumers, demand will drop and the company will cease to make the product. Hence, the consumers shape the market.

*Benefit #4: The market facilitates communication between consumers and producers, allowing consumers to provide information to producers about the products they want.* Information is essential to a properly functioning market, and it moves buyers and sellers together while reducing uncertainties for both parties in a transaction. Persuasion is also integral to information exchange, as it creates two-way communication between consumers and producers. Through the marketplace, consumers can persuade producers by simply communicating their wants, such as, "If you the maker of this product would offer a smaller version of it, I would buy it immediately."

*Benefit #5: The market offers nearly universal inclusion.* By expanding the number of consumers in the market, marketers benefit through more profit opportunities. Marketing has brought similar brands and consumption experiences to all corners of the globe. In this way, marketing has given the world's cultures more common ground on which to meet.

*Benefit #6: Marketing can satisfy the wants and needs of consumers.* Marketing has democratized consumption by bringing goods and services to citizen consumers in ways that allow mass consumption. For example, Henry Ford's accomplishment 100 years ago was ingenious as he reduced the cost of production for autos, so that millions of autos could be sold to everyone, not only to the wealthy elite (although only in black). The resulting economic need for parts used in the production process, as well the need for an after-market consisting of car parts and repair services, has boosted employment and subsequently standards of living.

The benefits of marketing would correlate positively and strongly with dimensions of quality of life in a society directly involving markets, such as dimensions representing economic vitality and entrepreneurial activity. This can be seen in recent research published by the Legatum Institute—an independent, nonpartisan, public-policy group based in

London that produces an annual assessment of wealth and well-being of the world's countries (Legatum Institute, 2012b).

Figure 3.1 depicts a comparison of the rankings of Germany and Russia on the subindexes of the Legatum Prosperity Index (Legatum Institute, 2012b). Of particular interest here are the rankings for the subindexes representing the vitality of the economy, entrepreneurship, and opportunity. The rankings of these countries on the entrepreneurship and opportunity subindex are based on the view that low costs to starting a business and public perception of a good entrepreneurial environment are important to improving citizens' economic prospects and their overall quality of life. The subindex also assesses a country's ability to commercialize innovation, access to opportunity for different socioeconomic groups, and whether citizens believe hard work pays off in the future.

As shown in Figure 3.1, Germany ranks high relative to the other 109 countries in the Legatum Prosperity Index on the subindexes representing the economy, as well as entrepreneurship and opportunity (Legatum Institute, 2012c). By comparison, Russia (a relative late-comer to marketing in society) is average for entrepreneurship and opportunity and below average on the economy dimension.

**Figure 3.1**    Rankings of Germany and Russia on the Subindexes of the Legatum Prosperity Index

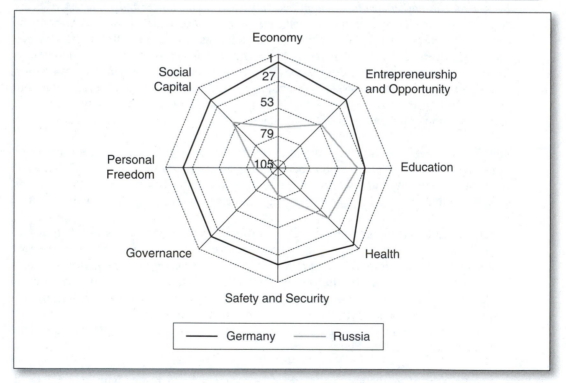

*Source:* Legatum Institute, 2012c

## What an Absence of Marketing Can Do to Societies

Some Western economists promised Russia that enormous increases in its standard of living could be realized "within a few years" once Russia became a "free-market economy" on January 1, 1992 (Murrell, 1993). Sadly, markets could not be imposed quickly in a top-down fashion. Despite shock therapy and the rapid transfer of the ownership of the means of production in the former Soviet Union, much was missing from the aggregate marketing system when Russia turned away from communism and central planning for the economy.

In the view of institutional economists, institutions comprise "the rules of the game" in societies (North, 1994). Specifically, institutions are the humanly devised constraints that structure human interaction. These include formal constraints (such as rules, laws, and constitutions), informal constraints (such as norms of behavior, conventions, self-imposed codes of conduct), and the inclination and ability to enforce such constraints. Such rules of the game influence individuals and organizations to pursue actions they perceive likely to fit their mental models of what should work in practice. For example, in 1992, plant managers in Russia had a network of relationships with state bureaucrats and other plant managers that enabled them to survive (Easterly, 2007, p. 62). Rather than execute exchanges in cash that would be subject to government taxation, many of these managers used barter and delivery of goods. In this way, these plant managers continued to produce goods nobody wanted. As a result, the Russian GDP shrank 40% in the four-year period from 1992 to 1995 (Holmes, 1997). The share of Russian firms that ran losses actually increased to 40% in the years after communism ended (Easterly, 2007).

One example of Russia's situation is the case of the Middle Volga Chemicals Plant in Samara Oblast. This plant found a "market" for ten tons of toxic chemicals it had produced. First, the plant passed the load of toxic chemicals to the Samara Oblast government, after bribing an official, in lieu of its required payment into the unemployment fund. The government was required to make transfers to relatively poor regional governments, and so it shipped the toxic chemicals to the unemployment compensation fund in the poor republic of Mari-El. No record of what eventually happened to the ten tons of toxic chemicals can be found today.

The invisible institutional framework in Russia in the years after communism continued to destroy value rather than to create it. For example, firm A would produce below-grade steel that was then used as input to firm B for its production of below-grade steel tubing. This weak steel tubing was used by firm C to make cheap bicycle frames soon to rust and break, which were then bartered with firm A as part of firm A's way to pay its employees in goods. All the while, firms A, B, and C used up valuable energy resources. The government authorities at the local and national level went along with such a loop of inferior production because these government officials did not want to confront large-scale unemployment. Without an appropriate conceptualization of what should be accomplished in business transactions, such as the imperative of delivering reliable and quality outputs that are beneficial to society, opportunity seekers in markets will likely become opportunists who benefit at others' expense.

# THE AGGREGATE MARKETING SYSTEM

## Physical Flows in the Aggregate Marketing System

The aggregate marketing system is the collection of all marketing systems in society (Wilkie & Moore, 1999). In the United States, more than 100 million households with more than 300 million consumers comprise the final nodes in the aggregate marketing system. More than 30 million Americans work directly within the AMS with the largest portion being sales persons. To convey some of the enormity of the AMS, William L. Wilkie and Elizabeth S. Moore (2002) focused on one series of exchanges occurring in the aggregate marketing system for a hypothetical consumer named Tiffany to have coffee and pastries one morning in her home. This story about breakfast at Tiffany's illustrates the scope and complexity of marketing and of marketing systems linked around the globe.

### AMS Example #1: Tiffany's Coffee Beans

The coffee beans in Tiffany's breakfast were grown on an eight-acre farm 1,000 meters above sea level in Colombia. The beans went from the farm to a de-pulping mill to separate the inner beans from their shell. They were then spread out to dry for several days in the sun, and then later, they were milled again to remove the parchment sheath covering the green beans. Buyers and the government coffee inspectors tested samples of the beans for grading. The beans were then put in 60-kilogram burlap bags marked with the grower's name and grade of beans. These bags were stored at a warehouse until purchased by a coffee buyer. Then, the beans were transported and later shipped by truck over the mountains to the port city where they were loaded into 20-ton corrugated steel containers for their four-day sea journey to the port of New Orleans in the United States.

Fortunately for those involved with coffee importing to the United States, the Harmonized Tariff Schedule of the United States lists coffee as a free import. After inspection by a team from the U.S. Customs and Border Protection Service, and after testing by the U.S. Department of Agriculture, the beans were driven to the coffee firm's silo facility. Here, the beans were loaded and blended with other similar beans and sent to a roasting plant. At such a plant, the roasted beans were again tested for quality and packaged into containers for consumers. These will then be sold to wholesalers or shipped directly to retailers. Finally, Tiffany made the purchase of the roasted beans, ground them herself in a grinder purchased two years ago at a Target store, and brewed her morning coffee.

### AMS Example #2: West African Onions

Physical flows in the AMS vary according to the geography, economic development, and culture of the countries involved for a particular product. In an ethnographic study of onion marketing in the West African countries of Niger, Benin, Burkina Faso, Ivory Coast, Ghana, and Togo in the early 1990s, research identified numerous challenges that dwarf the complexities of the physical flows highlighted in the story of Tiffany's breakfast coffee (Arnould, 2001). The extensive field work disclosed how the small roads in the farming regions restrict pick-ups from traveling them. Instead, small carts are used to collect the onions in the fields. Then, the carts take the loads of onions to small trucks. This leads to numerous exchanges of the easily bruised onions before the onions arrive at a regional bulking market serving dozens of villages.

Temporary storage must be found for the onions in adobe warehouses until sorting, sacking, and loading of onions can be done by temporary laborers. Nigerian export wholesalers, foreign importers' agents, and foreign exporters buy from the up-country bulking agents outside of Nigeria and then travel with the trucks to Niamey in Nigeria. Here, the onions are sold to retailers and shipped further south to coastal markets.

Tribal ties reinforced by political party membership keep the seemingly patchwork channel operations intact. Limited storage for the perishable crop, a long channel of distribution, poor telecommunications across the region, and rampant demands for illegal bribery, all contribute to depressing profitability in the onion trade in West Africa. For example, at the border crossing between Niger and Burkina Faso, the driver or wholesaler escorting the onions will pay around $150 to customs agents, $26 to the crop protection service, and $15 to the transit service. In addition, the driver or wholesaler might pay "respects" to the chief of the customs service ($40), and to the agent inspecting the truck ($20). From the border crossing at Kantchari to the capital of Burkina Faso, transporters encounter unauthorized roadblocks set up by rent-seeking customs agents, police, and gendarmes. Over the 204 kilometers, each of 15 roadblocks demands on average $8.50 to let an onion truck pass. Resistance to pay leads to delays or demands that the truck be unloaded to search for contraband weapons or drugs. There is one roadblock for every 13.6 kilometers of the journey, so the final tab for bribes paid on this part of the journey totals more than $127. Delays lead to increased amounts of spoilage for the onions (Arnould, 2001).

## Other Flows in the Aggregate Marketing System

An AMS would include all relevant aspects of business operations (both profit and not-for-profit), related centers of government operations, and all consuming units of a society—including NGOs as well as consumers. In encouraging researchers to focus on other levels of aggregation than the micro level, Wilkie (2001) notes the importance of the AMS for developing and transitional economies. In addition, he notes the need to go beyond the study of technology, economics, and the material side of a society's existence, and to study issues concerning society's softer "quality-of-life" dimensions.

The AMS is characterized by continuous flows in various forms, such as physical, monetary, persuasive, and informational flows (Wilkie & Moore, 2002). The objective of the persuasive and informational flows in the AMS is learning or teaching. An important outcome of learning would be better decisions for those involved in the AMS.

Figure 3.2 depicts some of these important intangible flows in the aggregate marketing system for societal development between marketers (including both for-profit and not-for-profit marketers), consumers, NGOs, and public policy makers (as representative of society's interests). Beginning on the left side, marketers send information to consumers (diagonally to the lower right of the figure) through promotional communication, public relations messages, and direct means through customer relationship management (CRM) programs. Consumers provide information to marketers through their participation in marketing research projects and co-creation participation. Additionally, "consumer voting," through patronage and purchasing, sends important behavioral signals to marketers (Dickinson & Hollander, 1991).

**Figure 3.2**   Information and Persuasive Flows in the Aggregate Marketing System

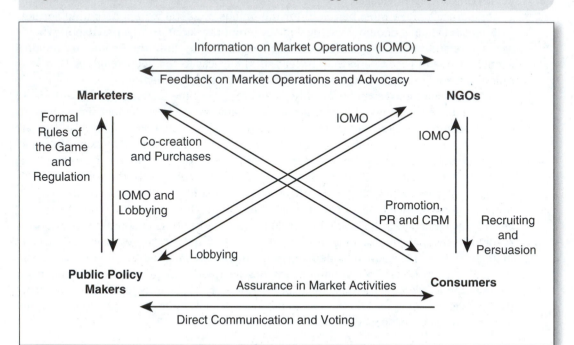

The role of NGOs captures both types of flows, information and persuasive, in the AMS. At the top right side of Figure 3.2, one can see how NGOs, such as Consumers Union (publisher of *Consumer Reports)* and FoodFirst Information and Action Network (www.fian.org, which advocates for humans' right to food worldwide), provide feedback on market operations to marketers. Additionally, NGOs often engage in advocacy with marketers attempting to encourage marketers to make changes voluntarily in their marketing operations. Marketers give information on their marketing operations directly or through other means, such as annual reports, and public relations messages. On the right side of Figure 3.2, it can be seen that NGOs try to recruit consumers and persuade them to support their causes, while consumers provide information on market operations to NGOs. From the top right corner of Figure 3.2 diagonally down to the lower left corner, it can be seen that public policy makers receive lobbying efforts from NGOs, while the public policy makers provide information on industries and sectors of the economy, as well as information of firms' compliance behavior with regulations and court rulings. Looking at the bottom of Figure 3.2, the flows of information between consumers and public policy makers are depicted. Assurance in market activities for consumers is important because trust is a crucial element in dealing with an uncertain and uncontrollable future (Ekici & Peterson, 2009). Institutional trust includes the public trust consumers direct at institutions (the specific structural arrangement within which actions and interactions take place) (Sztompka, 2000). With institutional trust, citizens consider the extent to which they trust the institution (the government or business) to fulfill its role in a satisfying manner. For example, a lack of trust in government regulators to ensure product safety may lead individuals to rely on nongovernmental sources for information about products (such as the Consumers Union in the United States), or to avoid consumption of the product altogether (as in the case of drops in demand for beef as a result of mad cow disease concerns). In this way, one can see that trust for institutions depends on the perceived performance of such institutions. In addition to trust of government regulators, consumers direct institutional trust at market-related institutions such as consumer groups, manufacturers and retailers, and the media (Ekici & Peterson, 2009). These market-related institutions function together as part of society's market ecosystem.

The left side of Figure 3.2 depicts the flow of information between public policy makers and marketers. Historically, this linkage has been characterized by tension between marketers and public policy makers, likely reflecting the unfortunate adversarial posture these two participants have traditionally taken in the AMS (Richie & LaBreque, 1975). Not surprisingly, mainstream scholars in the independent realms of public policy and marketing have missed what the other was saying over the years.

## Flows of Knowledge From the Public Sector to the Private Sector

In the flow of information of the AMS, the policy maker–marketer dyad represents how macro-level concepts are imparted to managers of firms at the micro level (see Figure 3.2). One important type of macro-level concept is related to fair trade in a society. Important cultural ideas about fair trade can be found in regulatory guidance on issues ranging from antitrust to consumer protection (Wilkie & Moore, 2002). In addition to regulatory guidance (and enforcement, when necessary), public policy makers can share development concepts with marketers. Not only can broad strategic goals for society be shared with marketers through policies to encourage and nurture small- and medium-sized enterprises (Storey, 2003), but also public policy initiatives can result in learning opportunities for marketers seeking to develop their own firms. In this way, knowledge would flow from the macro to the micro level of society.

Although the idea that policy makers have valuable insights for how marketers can be more effective might seem unusual, consider the following insights. First, many institutions of higher learning are publicly assisted, and research in the management disciplines (among others) conducted at these universities is used by many marketers to improve their own understanding of business phenomena and to improve their own firms. In this way, policy makers engender societal development through support of research endeavors that result in knowledge later used by marketers.

Second, conceptual approaches used by policy-making organizations to address daunting challenges in development can be instructive for marketers. For example, the World Bank has adopted a "four-capital approach" to sustainable development (Noll, 2002). These four types of capital include (a) natural, (b) produced, (c) human, and (d) social. Marketing scholars writing on development topics for policy makers have also used this framework (Kotler, Jatusripitak, & Maesincee, 1997). (In Chapter 1, this four-capital scheme was expanded to a five-capital one.)

Recently, scholars in mainstream marketing have proposed a new dominant logic for marketing by shifting focus from goods to services based on a distinction between resource types termed as operand (those on which an operation is performed) and operant (those that act on other resources to create a benefit) (Vargo & Lusch, 2004). Commenting on Vargo and Lusch's ideas, Hunt (2004) notes that operand resources are typically physical (machinery and raw materials), while operant resources are typically human (employee skills), organizational (routines and cultures), informational (knowledge about market segments), and relational (relationships with customers, suppliers, and competitors).

In sum, marketing scholars' operand resources correspond to natural and produced capital in the public policy realm, while marketing scholars' operant resources correspond to human and social capital. The leading thinking in marketing seems to have been adopted by policy scholars and policy makers years ago. Not only have policy researchers already embraced the theoretical significance of distinguishing between types of resources, but also these concepts have already moved into practice through progressive multinational policy organizations, such as the World Bank. The initial use of the concept of operand and operant resources by the World Bank and then later in marketing scholarship (and then to marketers) is an example of how knowledge has flowed (albeit belatedly) from the macro to the micro level.

## Flows of Knowledge From the Private Sector to the Public Sector

Looking at the other side of the information flow between marketers and policy makers, marketing scholars and practitioners do have theoretical concepts to share with policy makers. The foremost concept is marketing orientation, which is defined as "the organization-wide generation of market intelligence pertaining to current and future customer needs, dissemination of the intelligence across departments, and organization-wide responsiveness to it" (Kohli & Jaworski, 1999, p. 19). Public policy makers embracing the idea that government organizations need knowledge developed by marketers to improve the lives of their constituents could be said to take a market orientation to benefit citizens. In a similar way, Sheth and Sisodia (2005) have called public policy makers to adopt "citizen relationship marketing." Thus, these policy makers could initiate valuable micro- to macro-level flows of knowledge for societal development.

Wilkie and Moore (2002) have cited uncaring civil servants and the under-representation of consumer interest as being two of several types of possible economic imperfections of a country's AMS. Looking at one applied area of public policy, neither social-work scholars nor practitioners fully agree with the idea that users of public services should be regarded as "customers," as marketers would. Notably, this idea is receiving energetic discussion in the field of social work now (Estes, personal communication, 2004). However, all parties do agree that quality in publicly delivered services should be expected by those receiving such services.

In sum, it can be said that the two-way linkage between marketers and the public policy makers depicted in Figure 3.2 could be improved in terms of the effectiveness of information flows. Karla Hoff and Joseph Stiglitz (2001) have described information flows from governments to be an intervention because the information can change the behavior of participants. It seems that those in marketing and those in public policy have valuable concepts, frameworks, and research methods to share with the other. Scholars of macro-marketing, as well as marketing and society, are best situated to provide a bridge between these two realms and to improve the effectiveness of these information flows.

# BROADLY CONSIDERING MARKET EXCHANGES IN THE AMS

## A Closer Look at Macromarketing Systems

Macromarketing scholars traditionally have brought a healthy skepticism when considering market transactions by viewing market exchanges as creating both intended and unintended effects. This is a result of macromarketers' interest in the marketing systems embedded in the AMS, as well as of macromarketers awareness of the complex nature of the AMS as a provisioning system for society.

A macromarketer's systems perspective is a major point of difference between macro-marketing ("biggest M") and micromarketing ("little m") (Mittelstaedt, Kilbourne, & Mittelstaedt, 2006). Such a systems perspective leads macromarketers to regard systems as the whole being greater than the aggregation of its parts. To understand the "system-ness" of a set of elements, it is best to begin by removing elements and then observing the results. For example, if a person's organs are removed one at a time over an extended period, one can observe that digestion occurs in a much degraded way with difficulty, if at all.

In the opening vignette of the chapter, Joshua Bell was removed from the marketing system that gathers the right audience members in a favorable location, at an agreeable time, for the right price. Outside of this system, Bell's world-class performing talents had no value to those hearing him play (Weingarten, 2007). "I'm surprised at the number of people who don't pay attention at all, as if I'm invisible," Bell said, "Because you know what? I'm making a lot of noise!" (Weingarten, 2007, p. 10). The most awkward times for Bell were the times just after ending his playing of the compositions. The same people who had not noticed him playing did not notice he had finished. No applause. Nothing. Meadows (2008, p. 11) describes a system as "an interconnected set of elements that is coherently organized in a way that achieves something." Extracted from his marketing system, Bell achieved little.

Across the Atlantic, the popular mezzo-soprano Katherine Jenkins from Wales who sings a wide variety of songs (from classical, choral, traditional, musical theatre, to pop) replicated Joshua Bell's experience as a subway station performer. Disguising herself in less glamorous clothes and singing in public for the first time without high-heels, the 31-year-old Jenkins spent 45 minutes in Leicester Station of the London Underground on November 23, 2011 (Bryant, 2011). While enough commuters recognized Jenkins's distinctive voice to draw a small crowd (and some tears from listeners), she only earned about $15 for her performance. By comparison, promoters of Jenkins's concerts operating within a marketing system usually receive more than $150 per ticket for one of her concerts.

Fundamentally, a human system must have (a) elements, (b) interconnections, and (c) a purpose. The elements of a system are often visible and tangible entities. For example, in a shopping center, there are parking lots, buildings recognized as retail stores, back rooms inside the stores full of inventory in boxes, cash registers, and sales people out in the main area of the stores.

The interconnections in the shopping center are the relationships that connect the elements of the shopping center together and enable it to function as a place for commerce and social activity. For example, there are physical flows of goods into the stores (delivered by trucks), as well as physical flows out of the stores (taken away by consumers driving cars). The interconnections of the shopping center system would be harder to detect than the elements of the shopping center. These would include:

1. Regulations and standards that control the flow of electricity into the stores and into the electric signs by the highway leading to the shopping center.

2. Hiring practices that allow a trained set of workers to man the stores effectively.

3. Financial flows from retail outlets to the shopping center owner for renting their space in the shopping center, from the shopping center owner to a consortium of lenders for the mortgage on the shopping center, from the shopping center owner and retail outlets to local, state, and federal governments for tax payments.

4. Information flows that might include flow from the retailers to consumers about prices at the shopping center, promotions and advertisement from retail outlets, and featured brands at the shopping center. Such information flows might also include consumer-to-consumer verbal communication about the temperature of the retail stores during hot summer days, or the presence of teen groups at the shopping center parking lot on Friday nights.

Finally, the function of a nonhuman system or the purpose of a human system may have to be deduced from observation of the system's operation. This least obvious aspect of the system is often the most crucial determinant of the system's behavior. For example, the shopping center brings goods and services to consumers in a convenient and appealing manner. Accordingly, the purpose of the shopping center can be deduced to offering exchange opportunities between retailers and consumers. However, this purpose is likely an intermediate step to an improved quality of life for all who come to the shopping center for trade, employment, or pleasure.

## Externalities

Well-performing marketing systems can produce unexpected results for those not actively involved in the exchanges of markets (Mittelstaedt et al., 2006). Externalities are the uncalculated costs and/or benefits of exchange. In terms of macromarketing, these externalities are ways that marketing affects society. For example, when a shopping center becomes so popular that the surrounding road network is overwhelmed by traffic, then those not using the shopping center (but wanting to go someplace else) experience delays as a result of such traffic congestion. Those that drive these roads might become more aggressive in their driving in attempts to make up for lost time in transit because of the slower rates of traffic around the shopping center. Additionally, the extra use of the roads by shoppers, workers, and delivery trucks contributes to the accelerated wearing out of the road network, so that driving these roads might actually become more hazardous as a result of broken asphalt and pot holes. The externalities for the local community are (a) slower travel times and (b) more dangerous driving around the shopping center.

## Tobacco Marketing

Although it may be difficult to admit, the marketing of cigarettes might be the most successful marketing ever to occur—at least for the first half of the 20th century. In 1900, the cigarette was a little-used and stigmatized product in the United States (Brandt, 2007). But with the implementation of machines that could roll, cut, and package cigarettes at extremely cheap cost per unit, cigarette companies marshaled all the best of business practice to distribute effectively now low-priced cigarettes to American consumers. The American Tobacco Company used new forms of advertising and promotion, such as free matchbooks with advertising on the covers to make cigarette smoking appear to be fashionable and chic. As a result, the cigarette deeply penetrated American culture as a symbol of attractiveness, beauty, and power. Tobacco companies sold more than 416 billion cigarettes in their peak year, 1952 (Hilts, 1996). According to Gallup Polls, 45% of adults in the United States smoked by 1954 (Blizzard, 2004).

As a result of decades of opposition to cigarette smoking by public health officials, and health agencies, such as the American Cancer Society, cigarette smoking has declined in the United States. Today, 20% of Americans smoke regularly (Brandt, 2007). While the tobacco industry emphasized the individual choice of Americans to smoke in the highly successful Marlboro cigarette ads featuring the American cowboy on the frontier, the enormous health costs to society brought many in the United States to the realization that the externalities created by cigarette smoking were too much to bear. Each year, 435,000 U.S. citizens die from various diseases associated with their addiction to nicotine (Brandt, 2007). Former U.S. Surgeon General C. Everett Koop repeatedly told the public that tobacco deaths equaled three 747 aircraft crashing each day of the year with no survivors. However, smokers typically slowly die in hospitals one at a time, often after extended illnesses and suffering, ashamed they have brought this fate on themselves.

With such numbers of Americans entering the healthcare system each year for tobacco-related illnesses, healthcare insurance premiums increased to the point that the majority of Americans who did not smoke were contributing to the healthcare costs incurred by the minority of Americans who did smoke. In this way, cigarette smoking created negative externalities for nonsmokers, not just through the inhalation of secondary smoke. When the costs of these externalities were better realized, it became clear that the cost of cigarette smoking, like other externalities, was not fully reflected in prices paid in the marketplace for cigarettes.

# DEBT FLOWS IN THE AGGREGATE MARKETING SYSTEM

## Households Carrying Debt

As the externalities of cigarette marketing suggests, even those not directly involved in cigarette production or consumption wind up paying costs related to cigarette smoking.

This occurs primarily through higher healthcare insurance premiums, through the support of family members afflicted with tobacco-related diseases, and through higher taxes or government debt to fund Medicare (for the elderly) and Medicaid (for the poor) programs to assist those experiencing tobacco-related illnesses. However, increased household debt now affects millions in the United States. Early in 2010, more than 11 million households owed more on their mortgage than what their home was worth if they chose to sell it (McTevia, 2010). These homes were "under water."

After World War II, a credit revolution occurred in the United States and other industrialized countries (Geisst, 2009). This revolution became characterized by a general acceptance of credit cards and an extensive system set up to receive and process these consumer credit transactions. The United States moved to a "buy-now-pay-later" society, as opposed to the "save-now-buy-later" society it had been before the war. Usury laws were liberalized, and the marketing of "debt" was repositioned to be the marketing of "credit." A financial institution "extending credit" to someone carried the aura of giving a gift, as compared with a bank making a loan resulting in someone "going into debt." As a result, personal and indebtedness levels in the United States grew to levels never anticipated at the close of World War II:

> The approximately $2.5 trillion in consumer debt currently outstanding (mortgages excluded) represents $8,000 per person in addition to the $10 trillion displayed on the debt clock (at the corner of 43rd Street and Sixth Avenue in New York City representing US government debt), for $40,000 per person. Mortgages outstanding add another $15 trillion to the bill, for $88,000 per person. . . . If the consumer debt is charged at 10 per cent per year, mortgages at 6 per cent, and government debt at 4 per cent, the total annual interest bill is $1.55 trillion, and this does not include corporate or municipal debt payments. An individual's personal share of this debt service is about $5,200. (Geisst, 2009, p. 4)

Figure 3.3 depicts the debt load for households from 1999 to 2010. At the end of 2008, U.S. households owed almost three times more than they did at the beginning of 1999 (Gandel, 2011). Although households at the end of 2010 carried $1.1 trillion less than at the end of 2007, more than 63% of this decrease came from lenders foreclosing on homes, canceling credit cards, or otherwise giving up on trying to collect what they are owed.

### Effects of a Large Debt

One of the externalities of home foreclosures is that future borrowers now face more demands to obtain loans. For example, borrowers must place larger down payments when taking a loan than they would have in the recent past. In most cases, this will represent at least 10% of the purchase price of the home (Slife, 2011). Another externality can be seen in the bad loans guaranteed by federally owned secondary lenders Fannie Mae and Freddie Mac. This externality will cost taxpayers at least $169 billion through 2012.

The case could be made that individuals make the choice to take out loans, just as cigarette smokers are responsible for their own individual choices when engaging in highly addictive behaviors. However, when too many of people take on too much debt and default

**Figure 3.3**   U.S. Household Debt 1999–2010

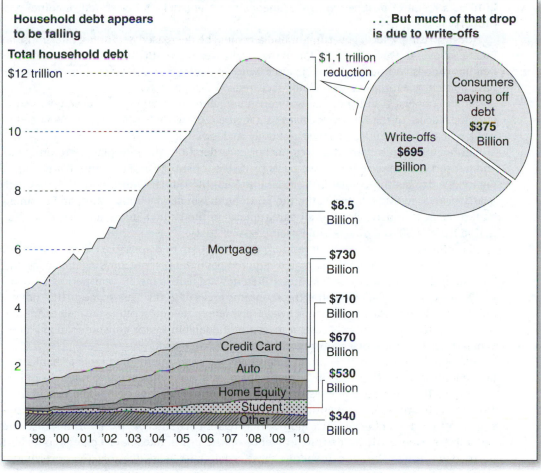

*Source:* Stephen Gandel, Not so frugal. Americans aren't paying off debt so much as banks are forgiving it. *Time,* March 14, 2011, p. 18.

on their loans or mortgages, an externality emerges as people who are not involved in these risky lending transactions end up facing higher hurdles to obtain loans for themselves.

At the local level, when multiple foreclosures occur in neighborhoods, the home values in neighborhoods decline. This likely leads to an unfortunate situation for a family who has always paid their mortgage on time but now must relocate for work reasons. Such a family now must sell their home for a lower price because home values in their neighborhood have declined.

Subsequently, when local governments downwardly reassess the property values in such neighborhoods, they receive fewer tax revenues. In February 2011, the National

Association of Counties (NAOC) conducted an economic status survey, which resulted in responses from 500 county governments in 44 states (Byers, 2011). Thirty-seven percent of respondents reported that their county government experienced a decrease in revenues in 2010 as a result of declines in miscellaneous revenue (such as investment income) and property taxes.

Not surprisingly, local government budgets must be decreased and/or tax rates must be increased over the entire jurisdiction of the local government. In this way, home owners in neighborhoods without such foreclosures wind up paying more in taxes than they would have if the home foreclosures had not occurred.

"It was not just Wall Street that was consumed with greed and misbehaved it was society," Joe Nocera of the *New York Times* said (CNBC, 2009). He further stated, "We need to call a recess, so our entire society is not built on debt."

Although Nocera's point deserves further consideration, the interplay between banks and consumers seems to follow the basic principles of supply and demand. For example, Figure 3.4 depicts three lines from Federal Reserve Board data representing the average yearly prime-lending rate for banks, the household debt service ratio (DSR), and business bankruptcies as a percentage of all bankruptcies in the United States across the 30-year period from 1980 to 2010 (Federal Reserve Board, 2011).

The DSR is an estimate of the ratio of debt payments to disposable personal income. Debt payments consist of the estimated required payments on outstanding mortgage and consumer debt. Although the DSR line drifted upward across the 30-year period, a downward turn in the line appears after the economic crisis of 2008. This suggests that households in the United States are turning away from debt in the midst of the difficult economic hard times they face. This suggests a measure of adaptability for consumers using debt. When times become worse, consumer debt service ratios decline.

A look at both lines representing the average-yearly prime-lending rates of banks and household debt service ratios in Figure 3.4 suggests that when lending rates drop, U.S. consumers have tended to increase their debt service ratio across the 30-year period from 1980 to 2010. Importantly, the prime rate and the DSR have a moderately inverse relationship (posting a Pearson product-moment correlation coefficient of −.60). Because the Federal Reserve Board has a strong influence on the prime rates banks charge to its best borrowers through the money supply, these results give evidence that the government influences the amount of debt households tend to carry in the United States.

A comparison of the line representing business bankruptcies as a percentage of all bankruptcies shows that this line trends downward similar to the way the prime rate moves across the period of study. However, when considering that the only other bankruptcies in this percentage computation are consumer bankruptcies, a dramatic story emerges: Businesses encounter a lower percentage of bankruptcies as the prime rate declines, which means that consumers account for an increasing share of bankruptcies as the prime rate declines. In other words, as prime lending rates decline, debt service ratios increase and, importantly, the percentage bankruptcies accounted for by consumers (the complement of business bankruptcies as a percentage of all bankruptcies). Importantly, the DSR and the percentage of bankruptcies accounted for by consumers (the complement of business bankruptcies as a percentage of all bankruptcies) have a markedly inverse relationship

**Figure 3.4**   The Prime Rate, Household Debt Service Ratio, and Business Bankruptcies as a Percentage of All Bankruptcies (all in %) 1980–2010

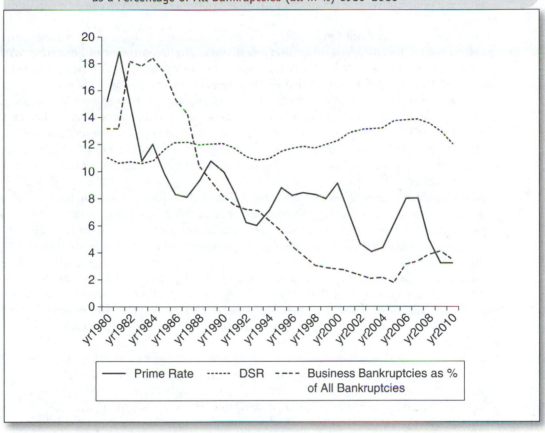

(posting a Pearson product-moment correlation coefficient of –.65). Because the Federal Reserve Board's intention of controlling the money supply and interest rates is to influence economic output (and therefore employment), it seems that an externality of this policy is that consumers take on increased debt loads and encounter a higher rate of personal bankruptcy.

## Students Carrying Debt

The federal government became the monopoly supplier of student loans in 2010 (Herszenhorn & Lewin, 2010). Instead of through a private bank, most students will now take out their loans through their college's financial aid office. Although the Department of Education will allow (for the first time) automatic increases tied to inflation in the maximum Pell grant award, the increase in the maximum Pell grant (to $5,900 in 2019–2020 from $5,550 for the 2010–2011 school year for individual students) is tiny, compared with the steep and relentless rise in tuition for public and private colleges alike. Because of this growing gap, the maximum Pell grant now covers only about a third of the average cost of attending a public university, compared with three quarters in the 1970s when the program began.

In economically difficult times, college students face a more demanding environment in which to pay their student loans after graduation. The Department of Education will require those who take out new loans after July 1, 2014 to devote 10% of their income to payments. This is down from 15% before the federal takeover of student loans.

Although the softening of terms will help students who borrowed money for their college educations repay their loans, these students have higher debt loads today, and they are entering a recovering economy without the abundant job prospects of recent years. The average debt load for those taking college loans in 2009 was $22,356 (Peter G. Peterson Foundation, 2011). These students accounted for almost 59% of all students attending college.

In this environment, aggressive marketing practices of for-profit colleges in lending have raised the concern of many. For-profit colleges raked in almost one fourth of the $89 billion available in U.S. government Title IV loans and grants, although they account for only 10% of the post-secondary students in the United States (Kroll, 2010). In award year 2008–2009, students at for-profit schools represented 26% of the borrower population and 43% of all defaulters (U.S. Department of Education, 2010). The median federal student loan debt carried by students earning associate degrees at for-profit institutions was $14,000. Steve Eisman, an outspoken investor whose contrarian wager against the subprime mortgage market paid off handsomely for him, harshly criticized the highly profitable for-profit college sector:

> Are we going to do this all over again? We just loaded up one generation of Americans with mortgage debt they can't afford to pay back. Are we going to load up a new generation with student load debt they can never afford to pay back? (Kroll, 2010, p. 3)

In the case of student loans, declaring personal bankruptcy will not absolve one of the responsibility to pay these loans. The debts are not dischargeable in bankruptcy, and graduates could lose eligibility for income-based repayment programs (Pilon & Korn, 2011). Those who keep up their payments will have their loans forgiven only after 20 years (Herszenhorn & Lewin, 2010). During the downturn, a record number of students have opted for these programs, delaying their debt responsibilities but prolonging their repayment time frame and amount (Pilon & Kroll, 2011). But by carrying the loans longer, such student borrowers will increase the likelihood debtors will declare bankruptcy and not pay their nonstudent loans.

## Governments Carrying Debt

The government also carries debt. As shown in Figure 3.5, the amount of debt as a percentage of GDP has fluctuated over the history of the United States (Congressional Budget

Office [CBO], 2010). Wars cause the government to increase its debt load markedly. The current public debt is so large (more than $14.6 trillion in April 2011) that it can only really be grasped by the ratio to the GDP of the United States. Here, the ratio of public debt to the GDP is 65.2% (Economist, 2010a).

**Figure 3.5**   Historical View of U.S. Government Debt as a Percentage of GDP

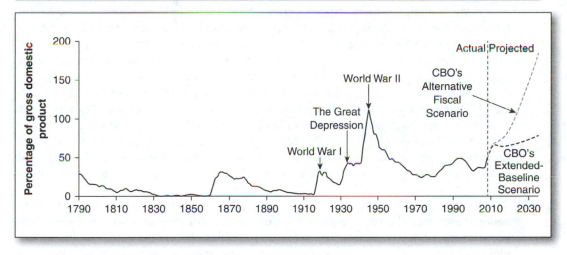

*Source:* Congressional Budget Office (2011, June).

The Peter G. Peterson Foundation notes that the public debt is the money actually borrowed, but this is dwarfed by unfunded promises to pay social security, Medicare, and other commitments that have been made. The total unfunded promises and liabilities total more than $62 trillion (Peter G. Peterson Foundation, 2011). This unfunded set of promises accounts for the Congressional Budget Office's surprisingly steep "alternative scenario" out to the year 2035.

## Sustainable Government Debt Levels

But what is a sustainable debt load for a country? This depends on factors such as (a) the development level of a country; (b) its recent fiscal, monetary, and economic history; (c) its currency's role in the global financial system; (d) the proclivity of its citizens (or foreigners) to buy the bonds of its government; (e) the ability of the citizens and governments to accept austerity; and (f) the ability of the marketing systems of a country to create increasingly valuable products and services. Developed countries have infrastructure in place that allows the reallocation of resources within the economy. For example, there has never been more college students than now in the United States, but these soon-to-be graduates will eventually need to find jobs and begin their careers. But they will do it in the context of a developed country. By comparison, the countries of the Middle East face an increasingly difficult task of not only educating those who desire college educations but also finding jobs for them after they graduate in the context of developing countries (McKinsey Quarterly, 2011).

Countries that have histories of economic turmoil, such as Argentina, find it more difficult to carry any more debt because such countries have spare financial reserves and creditors can impose increased interest charges of up to 5% on loans (Taylor, 2011). A country such as Japan has endured 20 years of no nominal economic growth, despite heavy government spending. Japan's current debt-to-GDP ratio is more than 100%—the highest such ratio in the world by far (Economist, 2010a). However, Japan has proven its ability to fund itself by issuing government debt to domestic investors. By comparison, 46% of the federal government debt in the United States is held by foreigners making it the most preferred choice among countries when risk aversion rises.

When interest rates rise, governments find it increasingly difficult to service the national debt. If the ratio of interest on the national debt to GDP (the interest coverage) rises above 5% with no sign of dropping (its current level is around 3%), then a financial crisis could be triggered (Taylor, 2011). The United States had an interest coverage ratio of around 2% for much of the 20th century (with the exception of during World War II). However, the interest coverage ratio rose above 5% in the 1980s and only drifted lower to about 4% through the end of the 1990s.

If the interest rate paid on public debt becomes larger than the growth rate of the national economy, then debt levels will rise for the country. Here, one can see the interplay between the vitality of marketing systems in the economy and the ability of the government to carry debt. A healthier economy can carry more debt. But excessive debt can crowd out investment into the marketing systems of the economy making lending more expensive (or not available) to private firms.

So what is a sustainable amount of debt for a government to carry? In a review of 31 emerging market countries, research suggests that a debt-to-GDP ratio of 30% was the median value for such an amount of debt (Abiad & Ostry, 2005). For developed countries, 60% is widely viewed as a prudent ratio of debt to GDP for a developed country (Economist, 2010b). For countries carrying a high debt load (above 90%), median growth rates fall by 1% and average growth is reduced even more according to research on 44 countries over a 200-year period (Reinhart & Rogoff, 2010). In emerging market countries, a high debt load (above 60%) led to median growth rates falling by 2% and average growth rates being cut in half.

### Who Pays the Debt?

The burden of government debt is carried by government employees, taxpayers, and bondholders (Taylor, 2011). Politics determines which of these stakeholders will pay the cost of running budget deficits. Argentina's fiscal crisis of 2000 and 2001 led it to cease paying its creditors. Ever since this time, the country has been unable to raise money in international markets (Congressional Budget Office, 2010). To avoid such a scenario, it is more likely that the United States will come to a political decision to accept austerity measures in the form of tax increases and spending cuts. But this decision may well pit the younger generation against the older generation (now positioned to consume an enormous amount of Medicare benefits through their retirement years).

"The failure to make the choice now about how to pay for the government we want and who will have to pay for it is to dump the choice on our kids," said Robert Bixby of the Concord Coalition (Peter G. Peterson Foundation, 2010). "So the calculation we need to make is this—is this OK? Are we comfortable doing this?"

## Reflections About a Culture of Debt in the United States

Capturing the important points about debt usage in the aggregate marketing system is a challenging task because of the disaggregated nature of debt use for consumers, businesses, nonprofits, and the government. A finding from reviewing Figure 3.3 was that Federal Reserve Policy seems to have an unintended consequence on consumers by creating a low-interest borrowing context for consumers. Some consumers end up taking on increased debt loads that later result in an increased number of consumer bankruptcies. One implication of this is that consumers would likely improve their ability to handle debt if they received more adequate education about prudent debt practices. No one plans to have a bankruptcy, but given that business cycles still exist, downturns in the economic life of the economy will be part of what consumers encounter over the course of their debt repayments. Conservatism should become a central element to the culture of debt that prevails in the United States.

## CONCLUSION

Consumer marketing offers benefits that are very much aligned with those of democracy. Through fair and voluntary exchanges, market participants can specialize their work and receive rewards for meeting the needs of others. The entire undertaking of the marketplace calls for the active participation of all. In this way, markets can be the provisioning system of society delivering what society values and can change the assortment of goods in the marketplace depending on consumer preferences and the information flows in the AMS. Rather than benefitting a small elite, a fully functioning market can benefit all in society.

Despite the successes of markets in provisioning for many societies, externalities (consequences for those not part of market exchanges) have led macromarketing scholars to have a healthy skepticism toward markets. The flow of financial capital is important to the success of the AMS. Debt flows in the AMS, while considered to be a normal part of activity for market actors, carry a degree of risk with them that must be well understood by market actors to avoid economic distress. Currently, consumers in many Western countries—as well as their governments—are attempting to pay down their debt levels from previous years when consumption levels ran high. This is part of the continuing story of how markets can allocate scarce resources for society and how risk remains endemic to activity in markets.

## QUESTIONS

1. What kind of things were unexpected for you to learn in Chapter 3?

2. What are your thoughts about marketing being the provisioning system for a society? Could there be better systems?

3. Why would it be said by some that cigarette marketing might be the most successful marketing ever done? What are the benefits and costs to society if this is true?

4. In your opinion, how valuable are the particular information flows in Figure 3.2 to each other? Which are the most important? The least important?

5. Looking at Figure 3.5's right side, a steeply rising dotted line can be seen representing a scenario for rising government debt. How likely do you think this scenario is to occur? If it does occur, what would be some of the implications for marketing in the aggregate marketing system with such a high level of government debt?

## MAVERICKS WHO MADE IT

### Arkadi Kuhlmann

### One man's mission to get you to save money

### By Tim Talevich (2010)

AT THIS TIME a decade ago, a large but relatively unknown Dutch-based company, ING, was weighing whether its successful online savings bank in Canada could work in a much bigger market, the United States. ING faced two daunting obstacles: People were leery of dot-coms after the big bust in 2000, and saving money seemed like a quaint, anachronistic idea at a time when major banks were heavily promoting spending, usually with their credit cards.

But ING Direct, approaching its 10th birthday, has succeeded, perhaps beyond the most optimistic expectations. With some 7.6 million customers and nearly $90 billion in assets, it is the largest online direct bank and the largest thrift in the U.S. The company, based in Wilmington, Delaware, prides itself on being an anti-bank—no physical branches—just a Web site, a network of call centers and seven ING cafes where customers sip coffee and do their ING banking.

ING Direct started out by offering basic savings accounts and gradually added checking plans, home loans and investment plans (Two ShareBuilder programs by ING Direct are available for Costco members. Go to Costco.com and click on "Services" for more information.) It succeeds by keeping costs low and offering service meant to assure customers that their banking needs can be met without actually seeing a bank teller.

Leading the company is CEO Arkadi Kuhlmann, a Harley-riding, palm-reading Canadian known as "the rebel banker" because, unlike traditional banks, his company disclaims fees and heavily promotes savings (the latter has earned Kuhlmann another moniker, "the CEO of savings"). His philosophy is to treat banking like a retail business, focusing on saving customers time and money.

Kuhlmann had a career in traditional banking before joining ING Direct. He worked for the Institute of Canadian Bankers and the Royal Bank of Canada, and also was CEO of Desk International, a foreign exchange and precious metals company, before being hired to launch ING Direct in Canada.

*The Connection* asked Costco member Kuhlmann about the challenges facing consumers and the banking industry as the new decade begins, why people should save more and what lessons his innovative company might offer for anybody running a business.

**The Costco Connection:** It's approaching a decade since ING Direct launched in the United States. What are the new challenges your company faces today?

**Arkadi Kuhlmann:** One new challenge today is that the federal government, through Fannie Mae and Freddie Mac, is heavily involved in the mortgage business to try to keep people in homes. These federal programs [let people get or keep] mortgages with no equity down. That challenges us because we sell mortgages, and the market is getting smaller for us.

Also, a lot of people are copying our advertising, our colors and what we say. So we have to continue to reinvent ourselves. Much like Costco, ING Direct has to keep finding ways to be more efficient and used technology to get our costs down so we can continue to offer a good value to our customers.

**CC:** It's been a tough couple of years for banks. Many either failed or needed government bailouts. Your thoughts on where all those banks went wrong—and how ING Direct avoided the mess.

**AK:** It's been a big financial crisis. A lot of the banks got caught up with pushing a lot of credit, which is all about growth and keeping the consumer buying. They reduced lending standards, such as not requiring equity in homes. People basically got a bit overextended. The banks pushed too much credit, but people also felt overconfident and took on too much credit.

ING Direct by its principle is always about leading Americans back to savings. So in the midst of this for the past nine years we have been building our business model of encouraging Americans to save for a rainy day and to save to be a bit independent. Our approach is that we can save you money, save you time. That has made us always more cautious on extending credit or giving mortgages, which we would only do with equity—for example, in a home. We always very strongly encourage consumers to balance their financial affairs.

We've grown to $90 billion in nine years and 7.6 million customers—that's about 100,000 new customers a month—basically on the platform of being savers. A lot of people are attracted to our simple products as a simple way of saving time and saving money. Our business is a bit self-selecting that way.

*(Continued)*

(Continued)

### Supplier Profile

**Name:** ING Direct

**Employees:** 2,200

**Phone:** 1-800-464-3473

**Web site:** www.ingdirect.com

**Products at Costco:** ShareBuilder online investing and ShareBuilder small business 401(k) plans

**Comments about Costco:**

"I think Costco's approach to the marketplace in terms of efficiency and value and being straightforward and transparent is identical to what we do. I think it's fair to say we are like the Costco of the banking industry."

—*Arkadi Kuhlmann*

*CC: You take pride in ING Direct acting more like a retailer than a traditional bank. How does a good retailer treat customers?*

**AK:** As a retailer, we try not to use "bank" in our name. We try to treat our customers in a way that when they leave us, whether on the phone or on the Internet or one of our cafes, they are happy. We want people to be happy and easily see they got a value deal.

The value deal is important because, when it comes to money, people get nervous about whether or not they got the right deal, whether they should have gotten something else or why they paid a fee for something. Being a retailer means making sure that every one of us serves the customer and that we stay connected with our customer base. We're in a high-volume, low-margin business. You succeed by executing extremely well and keeping your customer focus through the whole process.

*CC: Your way of doing business, the Orange Code, is about 10 years old. Has the recession prompted you to modify the code at all? Another way of asking the question is: How has the recession changed your company?*

**AK:** It's somewhat amazing that we haven't changed any of our business practices or our culture. In fact, since we were on the savings platform the market has come to us. We've had nothing to basically change or apologize for. Our conscience has been clear in terms of being able to look our customers in the face and say we have done right by you.

What the financial crisis has done is put a lot of constraints on our balance sheet and on our credit and our profit margin. People are not as creditworthy as they were before, so we have people with problems with their mortgages. But our view has been to aggressively work with people through the problem. If you can't stand with your customers in tough times, I'm not sure your reputation is worth a lot.

*CC: Leading people back to savings is more than a business pitch for ING Direct—it's a social mandate of sorts, a cause. Why is an ordinary Joe better off if he saves more?*

**AK:** The simple answer is Main Street America, which says we have to be a little like our grandparents: self-reliant, committed to having a buffer for a rainy day, able to help our neighbor out. You can't do that if you don't have any reserves. we got away from those values because we're very optimistic as a people. But we need to be more financially conservative because life is uncertain, and we can't always rely on government to solve all our problems. That's kind of a heartland America sentiment.

This isn't to say you can't live and spend money. But you must have a reserve, because it's the best way to improve the quality of your life. If you want to feel good about yourself, have a couple of thousand bucks in a savings account.

*CC: The recession blew many people's retirement plans out of the water. Give us some advice on what's the smartest strategy to recover.*

**AK:** Stick with the monthly program. The worst thing to do is to approach things by starting and stopping. If you have fixed allocations, stick through it. You do have to pay some attention to the transaction accounts. There's a lot of cost in mutual funds or in different programs, so you have to know what the fees are because they can take a bite out of the return.

Also, you should review the plans once or twice a year to see what your allocation is in terms of international exposure and large-cap exposure, and how much you want to keep in liquidity. This doesn't mean moving accounts around every month, but you can see where some of the bigger trends are.

You need to be active. Pay yourself first, save a bit every month, don't spend beyond your means and be a little more like our grandparents were.

*CC: This question might be of interest to anyone running a business: In this Internet age, customers are much more inclined to comparison-shop aggressively for products, whether it be a TV or a savings account. How do you retain customers who might find a better rate on the Internet—in your case, as high as a percentage point?*

> "And if you have a good reputation, as a retailer or a restaurant, it's that consistency
> at the end of the day that really pays off. You have to be good every day."
>
> —Arkadi Kuhlmann

**AK:** For us, it's all about the brand. We don't say we're going to be highest or lowest, depending on a savings or mortgage account, but we're going to offer good value. Rate is only part of the package.

*(Continued)*

(Continued)

I believe that people vote with their money. What does the company stand for? What are they all about? How does that basically reflect on me as a customer? For example. I believe people go to Costco for more than just buying stuff that's cheap. There's an experience there, an ongoing reputation, a consistency that people have some faith in. Faith is what they need. We spend a lot of time with those 25,000 moments of truth every day, reinforcing the faith that our customers have in the way we operate.

You have to put 10 out of 10 things together. It's the way you serve your customers. It's the offer you make and the way you execute it. And if you have a good reputation, as a retailer or a restaurant, it's that consistency at the end of the day that really pays off. You have to be good every day.

*CC: Do you still work occasionally in your call center? What are people saying these days?*

AK: The average call is about 2.5 minutes. People usually spend about 30 seconds talking about a balance or moving money: Can I open this account or make this payment? Then they spend the other minute and a half talking about the economy and money and whether they are budgeting right. You hear a lot of people having an opportunity to talk with somebody empathetic about the stress and trails they have with money.

That's a point where we as a retailer can make a huge difference by listening, giving a word of encouragement and a little support that they're on the right track by saving a bit of money. We tell them to not overextend and to keep doing what they're doing. We all just need a little encouragement now and then.

*CC: I always am curious what CEOs like to do in their time off. You? And what was that I heard about reading palms?*

AK: I enjoy painting, love to play tennis and sail. I love to ride a bicycle and a motorcycle. I do read palms—it's something I got from my grandmother. It's a great way to get to know someone. It's something you can use as a good thing over dinner or over a drink after dinner.

*CC: In your book [The Orange Code, John Wiley & Sons, 2009] you write, "It's strange, but the most dangerous challenges to our brand always come in the disguise of new products." Yet the business needs to grow. So what's next for ING Direct?*

AK: Sometimes size begins to gum up what you're doing. You start becoming too inwardly focused, you get set in your ways and it becomes a bit uninteresting. You get caught with the dilemma of wanting to be a change agent in the marketplace, but at the same time you get caught with this sense of "Well, don't fix it if it aint't broke."

But the smart guys will continue to break down things and rebuild them, because that's the only way you're going to keep moving forward and not get caught up with your own story and your own PR and your own issues from yesterday. Our customers always look up and want to see what's new. We have to create that bit of freshness, newness.

If you're a rebel and you're going against the grain, it's easy to do when you start out. But as you get bigger and bigger, it gets more difficult. You have to keep trying to break it down and make the organization as flat as possible and continue to be a bit irreverent. Because if you're not a bit irreverent, you're not anywhere near the edge.

## The Orange Code

AT THE HEART of ING Direct's operations is the Orange Code—a 12 point constitution for the company. Some of the code might be pertinent to your company.

1. **We are new here**. Every day is a new beginning a new set of challenges, a chance to reinvent ourselves.

2. **Our mission is to help people take care of the wealth they make**. Money is the fruit of work, and saving it is fundamental to freedom.

3. **We will be fair**. Everyone will be treated equally here.

4. **We will constantly learn**. Every experience we have will make us wiser and better at what we do.

5. **We will change and adapt and dwell only in the present and in the future**. We are nourished by thinking about what can be done.

6. **We will listen: we will invent: we will simplify**. Our customers can make us better if we let them. But we must first understand them.

7. **We will never stop asking why or why not.** Nothing can be sacred here except for our mission.

8. **We will create wealth for ourselves, too, but we will do this by creating value**. Profit is proof that were are fulfilling our mission.

9. **We will tell the truth.** We can't succeed without the trust of our customers.

10. **We will be for everyone**. To be our customer, people need only a dollar and the will to be independent.

11. **We aren't conquerors—we are pioneers. We are not here to destroy—we are here to create.** We have competitors, not enemies. We came here to offer people a choice.

12. **We will never be finished.**

*Source: The Costco Connection*

## Questions

1. Have you ever heard of ING Direct before? If so, what had you heard?

2. From what you have read, how does your current bank's services compare with those of ING Direct?

3. How different is the approach of ING Direct in encouraging customers to save as its primary focus?

4. Reviewing the Orange Code at the end of the article, which of the 12 points in this constitution for the company will be the most difficult to achieve? Would this be true of other banks, too?

## REFERENCES

Abiad, A., & Ostry, J. (2005). Primary surpluses and sustainable debt levels in emerging market countries. IMF Policy Discussion Paper, PDP/05/6.

Arnould, E. (2001). Ethnography, export marketing policy, and economic development in Niger. *Journal of Public Policy & Marketing, 20*(2), 151–169.

Bix, B., & Taylor, O. (2011, March 9). Just what do marketers do, anyway? *MarketingProfsToday*. Retrieved from http://www.marketingprofs.com/newsletters/marketing/

Blizzard, R. (2004, October 19). U.S. smoking habits have come a long way, baby. Retrieved from http://www.galluppoll.com

Brandt, A. M. (2007). *The cigarette century: The rise, fall and deadly persistence of the product that defined America*. New York, NY: Basic Books.

Bryant, M. (2011). Star Katherine Jenkins goes underground as a busker. *London Evening Standard*. Retrieved from http://www.thisislondon.co.uk/standard/article-24012980-opera-star-katherine-jenkins-goes-busking-on-the-tube.do

Byers, J. (2011). *The recession continues: An economic status survey of counties*. Washington, DC: National Association of Counties.

CNBC (producer). (2009, June 3). *House of cards*. [Television broadcast]. New York, NY: CNBC. Retrieved from http://www.cnbc.com/id/15840232?video = 1145392808&play = 1

Congressional Budget Office. (2011, June). *The long-term budget outlook*. Washington, DC: Congressional Budget Office.

Dickinson, R., & Hollander, S. (1991). Consumer votes. *Journal of Business Research, 22*, 335–346.

Easterly, R. (2007). *The white man's burden: Why the west's efforts to aid the rest have done so much ill and so little good*. New York, NY: Penguin Press.

Ekici, A., & Peterson, M. (2009). Consumer trust for market-related institutions and quality of life in a developing country: Comparing both sides of the poverty line. *Journal of Public Policy & Marketing, 28*(1), 56–70.

Federal Reserve Board. (2011). DSR ratio. Retrieved from http://www.federalreserve.gov

Fisk, G. (1974). *Marketing and the ecological crisis*. New York, NY: Harper & Row.

Forbes, S., & Ames, E. (2009). *How capitalism will save us: Why free people and free markets are the best answer in today's economy*. New York, NY: Crown Business.

Gandel, S. (2011, March 14). Not so frugal. Americans aren't paying off debt so much as banks are forgiving it. *Time*, p. 18.

Geisst, C. R. (2009). *Collateral damaged: The marketing of consumer debt to America*. New York, NY: Bloomberg.

Herzenhorn, D., & Lewin, T. (2010, March 26). Student loan overhaul approved by Congress. *New York Times*.

Hilts, P. (1996). *Smoke screen: The truth behind the tobacco industry cover-up*. Reading, MA: Addison-Wesley.

Hoff, K., & Stiglitz, J. (2001). *Modern economic theory and development*. In J. M. Meier & J. E. Stiglitz (Eds.), *Frontiers of development economics* (pp. 389–459). Oxford, UK: Oxford University Press.

Holmes, L. (1997). *Post-Communism: An introduction*. Durham, NC: Duke University Press.

Hunt, S. (2004). On the services-centered dominant logic for marketing. *Journal of Marketing, 68*(1), 21–22.

Kohli, A., & Jaworski, B. (1999). Market orientation: The construct, research propositions, and managerial implications. In R. Deshpande (Ed.), *Developing a market orientation*. (pp. 7–44). Thousand Oaks, CA: Sage.

Kotler, P., Jatusripitak, S., & Maesincee, S. (1997). *The marketing of nations: A strategic approach to building national wealth*. New York, NY: Free Press.

Kroll. (2010 May 27). Steve Eismen's next big short: For-profit colleges [Web log post]. Retrieved from www.motherjones.com

Legatum Institute. (2012a). The Legatum Prosperity Index—Zimbabwe. Retrieved from http://www.prosperity.com/country.aspx?id = ZW

Legatum Institute. (2012b). The Legatum Prosperity Index—Entrepreneurship & Opportunity Index. Retrieved from http://www.prosperity.com/entrepreneurship.aspx

Legatum Institute. (2012c). The Legatum Prosperity Index—Home. Retrieved from http://www.prosperity.com

Lewis, B. (1994). *Race and slavery in the Middle East*. Oxford, UK: Oxford University Press.

McKinsey Quarterly. (2011, April). Linking jobs and education in the Arab world. Retrieved from http://www.mckinseyquartly.com

McTevia, J. V. (2010). *The culture of debt: How a once-proud society mortgaged its future*. Ortonville, MI: MB Communications.

Meadows, D. H. (2008). *Thinking in systems*. White River Junction, VT: Chelsea Green.

Mittelstaedt, J. D., Kilbourne, W. E., & Mittelstaedt, R. A. (2006). Macromarketing as agorology: Macromarketing theory and the study of the agora. *Journal of Macromarketing, 26*(2), 131–142.

Murrell, P. (1993). "What is shock therapy" What did it do in Poland and Russia?" *Post Soviet Affairs, 9*(2) 111–140.

North, D. C. (1994, December 19). Economic performance through time. *The American Economic Review, 84*(3), 359–368.

Noll, H. H. (2002). Towards a European system of social indicators: Theoretical framework and system architecture. *Social Indicators Research, 58*(1-3), 47–87.

Peter G. Peterson Foundation. (2010). *IOUSA*. Documentary available at http://www.pgpf.org

Pilon, M., & Korn, M. (2010, February 4). Student-loan default rates worsen. *Wall Street Journal Online*. Retrieved from http://online.wsj.com/article/SB1000142405274870470930457612428047368414 2.html?KEYWORDS = Student-loan + default + rates + worsen

Quelch, J. A., & Jocz, K. E. (2007). *Greater good: How good marketing makes for better democracy*. Boston, MA: Harvard Business School Press.

Reinhart, C. M., & Rogoff, K. (2010, May). Growth in a time of debt. *American Economic Review 100*(2), 573–578.

Richie, J. R. B., & LaBreque, R. J. (1975). Marketing research and public policy: A functional perspective. *Journal of Marketing, 39*(3), 12–19.

Sheth, J. N., & Sisodia, R. J. (2005). A dangerous divergence: Marketing and society. *Journal of Public Policy & Marketing, 24*(1), 160–162.

Slife, J. (2011, March 12). Home runs? *World*, p. 76.

Storey, D. J. (2003). Entrepreneurship, small and medium sized enterprises and public policies. In Z. J. Acs & D. B. Audretsch (Eds.), *Handbook of Entrepreneurship Research* (pp. 473–511). Boston, MA: Kluwer Academic.

Sztompka, P. (2000*). Trust: A sociological theory*. Cambridge, UK: Cambridge University Press.

Talevich, T. (2010, February). Rebel with a cause. *The Costco Connection*, pp. 22–25.

Taylor, B. (2011, April 30). Paying off gov debt. Retrieved from www.globalfinancialdata.com

The Economist. (2010a, February 13). Not so risk-free. *The Economist, 394,* 74.

The Economist. (2010b, February 13). Withdrawing the drugs. *The Economist, 394,* 70–71.

U.S. Department of Education. (2010, September 13). Student loan default rates increase: Borrowers at for profit schools represent large and growing share of loan defaults. Retrieved from www.ed.gov.

Vargo, S. L., & Lusch, R. F. (2004). Evolving to a new dominant logic for marketing. *Journal of Marketing,68*(1), 1–17.

Weingarten, G. (2007, April 8). Pearls before breakfast. *The Washington Post*. Retrieved from http://www.washingtonpost.com/wpdyn/content/article/2007/04/04/AR2007040401721.html

Wilkie, W. (2001). Forward. In P. Bloom & G. Gundlach (Eds.), *Handbook of marketing and society* (pp. vii–xii). Thousand Oaks, CA: Sage.

Wilkie, W. L., & Moore, E. S. (1999). Marketing's contributions to society. *Journal of Marketing, 63*, 198–218.

Wilkie, W. L., & Moore, E. S. (2002). Marketing's relationship to society. In B. A. Weitz & R. Wensley (Eds.), *Handbook of marketing* (pp. 9–38). Thousand Oaks, CA: Sage.

CHAPTER 4

# Stakeholders in Marketing

## COMPLEXITIES OF BUSINESS

### To Whom Does a Business Person Owe Allegiance?

Max Keith (pronounced "Kite") stood more than six feet tall and always wore a short brush of a mustache. Working previously as a bookkeeper, he joined Coca-Cola's operations in Germany in 1933 at the age of 35 (Allen, 1994). Keith thought highly of himself, dressing with flair, and encouraged unswerving following to his strong leadership among employees.

At the time of Keith's hiring, there was hardly any soft drink business in the country. Most Germans regarded sweet drinks as being for children and the country and avoided them. Keith was determined to change this cultural attitude and worked tirelessly to win more distributors and customers to Coca-Cola consumption (Pendergrast, 1993). He would force his team to work 12-hour days and more sometimes collapsing at 2:00 A.M. only to

**101**

get up early and continue more work. Keith rose quickly to become the host-country deputy to the American director Ray Powers. In 1938, Powers died and Keith assumed the leading role for Coca-Cola in Germany.

In the winter of 1939, the CEO of Coca-Cola, Robert Woodruff, invited Keith to Coca-Cola's headquarters in Atlanta to discuss international operations and to get a "little better understanding" of his plans for the future (Allen, 1994). Woodruff let Keith know that he and the company were trusting him to look out for their interests in the uncertain days and years ahead. At the time, Woodruff had no other choice than to trust Keith.

The predicament Max Keith and Coca-Cola found each other in 1939 helps to understand the ethical complexities marketers can encounter with stakeholders of their firms, such as society, partners, investors, customers, and employees (SPICE). Sometimes, the ostensible interests of these stakeholders can come into conflict. Here, the original investors in an international subsidiary might be contributing significantly to a future war effort against Keith's own society. To complicate things, the government of Keith's society might confiscate the assets of the multinational corporation (MNC) in his country. Additionally, as a result of rationing and war's destruction, partner firms in Europe might no longer be able to meet the needs of Keith's business operations.

### Your Thoughts?

- To whom did a business person in war-time Germany owe allegiance, the original owners of the subsidiary or the possible owners of the firm, such as the German government or its agents (the directors of the rival soft drink firms)?
- What obligations does a firm in such circumstances have to partner firms, customers, and employees?

## CHAPTER OVERVIEW AND LEARNING OBJECTIVES

Stakeholders are groups that have a stake or interest in the activities that comprise a business. This chapter considers how firms and marketing systems in a society can consider stakeholders. This can be done by choice or by government direction.

Scholars generally define marketing strategy as the marketing behavior of firms when they compete in the markets (Varadarajan, 2011). Marketing strategy scholars have always taken keen interest in the context of competition. Today, major phenomena of interest for such scholars include (a) a changing competitive environment (which features new players—such as Google, Facebook, and state-owned enterprises—and an increased role for government in markets after 2008), (b) digital convergence (which makes industry boundaries more fuzzy—such as those among software, entertainment, research, the Internet, and telecom), (c) emerging markets, (d) the marketing of green technologies, and (e) impoverished subsistence marketplaces (such marketplaces account for more than five billion people on the planet) (Srinivasan, 2011). These phenomena are macromarketing in character because they concern the interplay of marketing and society.

In this setting of markets today, stakeholders are increasingly important for firms, as well as for scholars. Although researchers continue to investigate the impact of taking a stakeholder-orientation on firm profits (Bhattacharya & Korschun, 2008), scholars increasingly see that firms need to take a broadened and long-term view as part of developing their marketing strategy in the future. In this way, wisdom can be integrated into business decisions. In this chapter, Costco Wholesale serves as an exemplar of a stakeholder-oriented firm.

After this chapter, you should be able to answer the following questions:

- What is the stakeholder concept?
- What are primary stakeholders?
- What are secondary stakeholders?
- What is the special role of government as a stakeholder?
- What are reasons for firms to adopt a stakeholder orientation?

## STORM CLOUDS OF WAR OVERTAKE EUROPE IN 1939

Once World War II began in September 1939 with Germany's invasion of Poland and the subsequent response from Britain and France, the uncertain days envisioned by Woodruff arrived (Pendergrast, 1993). Soon, Germany placed Keith in charge of Coca-Cola properties in the occupied countries. Keith sent word through the Coca-Cola bottler in neutral Switzerland that he would try to keep the enterprises going. However, to everyone at Coca-Cola headquarters in Atlanta who received no other updates on life in Nazi-occupied countries during World War II, it seemed that Keith and the German lawyer for Coca-Cola Dr. Walter Oppenhoff had joined the Nazi Party and confiscated all the company's assets.

Doubts about Keith's loyalty persisted until after Allied troops came into Germany in the spring of 1945. After finding Keith outside a bombed-out city of Essen, where the Coca-Cola bottling plant had been destroyed by aerial bombing three times and rebuilt, Coca-Cola officials and U.S. Army personnel initially treated Keith as a Nazi collaborator. Keith was hurt and incensed by this treatment. However, the true story of Keith's exploits in German-occupied Europe during the war began to emerge in the months after the war.

Against improbable odds, Keith had succeeded at keeping Coca-Cola employees gainfully working across Europe and out of conscription, as well as out of concentration camps. This often meant intervening with German or local authorities when his employees violated wartime rules concerning use of contraband ingredients, such as sugar, in the soft drinks they made. Although sugar was rationed (on both sides of the conflict), Keith and his employees proved themselves savvy at contriving substitute ingredients for alternative products to Coca-Cola, which Keith only allowed to be placed in Coke's unique hour-glass bottle when all ingredients were available and real Coca-Cola could be put in such a bottle. The last such authentic Coke ran out in 1942 after being consumed at German hospitals for the military wounded.

Once war began, Keith moved to become part of the German bureaucracy. He and Dr. Oppenhoff managed to get themselves appointed to the Office of Enemy Property to supervise all soft drink plants wherever German forces took control. In this way, Keith and Oppenhoff took over Coca-Cola businesses in Italy, France, Holland, Luxembourg, Belgium, and Norway.

Keith then pursued developing alternative products with the limited set of ingredients he could obtain. His chemists concocted a fruit-flavored beverage not readily identifiable as orange, grape, berry, or lemon. This was because the ingredients came from whey and apple fiber left over from cider production. Keith challenged his employees to use their fantasy and name the fruit-flavored beverage in a contest. In this way, Fanta was christened. In 1943, Keith sold nearly three million cases of Fanta across war-torn Europe.

"Keith was strategic in his approach," retired Coca-Cola Japan executive Bob Broadwater observed more than 50 years after the war began (Broadwater, personal communication, 1990). Broadwater commented, "He really thought about things with a long-term perspective. That is why he didn't use the Coke bottles to bottle anything but Coca-Cola. Fanta and any other product went into any kind of bottle he could find. Importantly, he had concluded that someday ... the war would be over. And his consumers would want Coca-Cola the special way they enjoyed it before the war."

Keith honed his diplomacy during the war and adroitly navigated the hazards that emerged once war began. As a result, those with a stake in his success benefited. For example, German society benefited by a having an enjoyable consumer product available during a time of hardship and depravation. When the German military drafted his employees, Keith replaced them with ex-convicts unacceptable to the military (Pendergrast, 1993). His partner companies participated in a nonmilitary endeavor during war time that allowed them to continue in operation. Investors in the United States eventually received the profits earned by Keith and Coca-Cola's operations in Germany after the war. Customers of Coca-Cola across Europe enjoyed a small but important time of escape and refreshment during difficult days when they drank Coca-Cola and Fanta. Finally, his employees avoided forced labor elsewhere because they were already employed at a place of their choosing.

Throughout the war, Keith resisted all recruiting attempts by the Nazi Party as well as requests to merge his assets with those of Afri-Cola, which was controlled by Nazi Party members. Despite walking a fine line between collaboration and resistance throughout the war, in January 1945, he and Oppenhoff were summoned to the Ministry of Commerce. While there, a general angrily told the two Coke men to nationalize their company and to change the name within two days or be placed in a concentration camp (Pendergrast, 1993). Seeking help after receiving this ultimatum, Keith and Oppenhoff's friend at the Ministry of Justice told them that he could not intervene on their behalf in this situation because he was afraid that he, too, would be imprisoned if he did.

Keith and Oppenhoff prepared to return to the ministry the next day having not changed the name. Fortunately, the showdown with the general at the Ministry of Commerce never came because an Allied bombing raid killed him the night before the meeting was to take place. In this way, the business was providentially saved.

## The War Ends

After the war, Coca-Cola officials in Atlanta investigated European operations and concluded that Keith had conducted the business for Coca-Cola during the years of war. Although he could have produced Fanta for his own profit, he did not. Today, Fanta remains one of the successful brands in Coca-Cola's portfolio.

Keith and Oppenhoff had kept meticulous records safely hidden in an underground bank vault in Wurzburg in northern Bavaria that showed modest profits during each of the war years. Coca-Cola's trademark had survived in every occupied country in Europe, except Denmark (Allen, 1994). Keith had scrupulously protected the company's property. Although he could have merged his operations with Afri-Cola's, he did not. Although he could have joined the Nazi Party, he did not.

Although Keith's hard-driving and daring manner always made him stand out, Coca-Cola executives who doubted Keith's loyalty during the years of war were later embarrassed by these doubts. His collaboration with the wartime German government occurred when some degree of collaboration was demanded by all in German-occupied Europe (Pendergrast, 1993). In effect, the Coca-Cola Company concluded that Keith collaborated in ways to help the company and its stakeholders while going to great lengths to keep the Nazi Party at arm's length.

After some initial awkwardness in Coca-Cola's relationship with Keith after the war, the company arranged to have Keith named civilian administrator of Coca-Cola's bottling operations during the military occupation of Germany. In 1949, Keith resumed bottling Coca-Cola because CEO Woodruff decreed that bottling should return to those who bottled before the war. For his cleverness, daring, diplomacy, and loyalty, Keith became one of the favorite members of the Coca-Cola Company to CEO Woodruff (Broadwater, personal communication, 1990). To Woodruff, Keith had served the company as a steward during enormously difficult circumstances.

## STAKEHOLDER CONCEPTS

### Wisdom in Business

In Japanese society, businesses are expected to not only live in harmony with society but also to contribute to society in order to be accepted (Nonaka & Takeuchi, 2011). "The majority of companies that have failed did not maintain that balance," said Fast Retailing CEO Tadahi Yanai (Fast Retailing in Japan's fastest-growing apparel brand). "Everyone is, first, a member of society before one of the company. Thinking only about the company will undoubtedly result in failure." (Nonaka & Takeuchi, 2011, p. 62)

Macromarketing scholars propose that micromarketing decision making at the firm level has implications for society in terms of personal, social, and material welfare experienced by all (Mick, Bateman, & Lutz, 2009). In other words, the firm and society are inevitably and intimately linked. This linkage can be a positive one for society if firms pursue wisdom in their decision making. In such times for making decisions, wisdom involves taking a wide, long, and integrative viewpoint for forming evaluations, plans, and actions (Sternberg, 1998). Wisdom can be understood to be knowledge that is applied to attain a common good through the balancing of multiple interests, including oneself, others, and surroundings, over both short- and long-term horizons. Notably, wisdom considers long-term effects that transcend the individual as guidance toward the best good.

In the story of Coca-Cola's Max Keith, it can be seen that Keith took a wide, long, and integrative view on his precarious situation at the onset of World War II. He employed a practical wisdom that began with the crucial conclusion "that someday ... the war would be over." Keith also avoided what Kevin J. Clancy and Stephen C. Krieg (2000) term as "death-wish marketing," which would have (a) avoided ambiguous situations, (b) considered too few decision alternatives, (c) paid too much attention to competitors, (d) ignored real customers, and (e) rushed decisions. If he had wished to reduce tension in his work life immediately, he would have allowed the directors of Afri-Cola to become directors of Coca-Cola's subsidiary in Germany and dismantle Coca-Cola's operations. Instead, Keith responded fittingly to the complex and difficult circumstances he faced. He accepted the greater stress of balancing multiple interests of stakeholders during wartime to achieve better outcomes for an ensemble of stakeholders dependent on the success of Coca-Cola's European operations. Along the way, Keith achieved what his parent company resisted for the first 75 years of its existence—introducing a new product to the market. By doing so, he pioneered an enduring success—Fanta.

## Stakeholders

Stakeholder theorists view business as a set of relationships among groups that have a stake or interest in the activities that comprise a business (Freeman, Harrison, Wicks, Parmar, & De Colle, 2011, p. 24). In this way, business is about relationships between (a) society and communities, (b) partners (such as suppliers and lenders), (c) investors, (d) customers, and (e) employees. These classes of stakeholders comprise the SPICE set of stakeholders (Conscious Capitalism, 2011). A wide variety of stakeholders have been proposed for businesses, but these five comprise the set of primary stakeholders in this book. In 1963, the Stanford Research Institute (now SRI International) originally conceived of stakeholders as entities without whose support the organization would cease to exist. SRI Researchers have proposed a second set of stakeholders termed secondary stakeholders, including (a) government (local, regional, national, and transnational), (b) media, (c) competitors, (d) nongovernmental organizations (NGOs), and (e) future generations and the environment. There likely is no universal set of stakeholders that would apply to all businesses in all situations. However, these ten stakeholder groups depicted in Figure 4.1 represent a comprehensive set of stakeholders relevant to business today.

Remember that society was defined in Chapter 1 as being the large-scale community that normally furnished security and a national identity for its members. One can understand that society is another community—albeit one that is larger in scale than a local community. In a democracy, society and communities are the ultimate owners of commonly held assets such as (a) land (not owned by private citizens), (b) infrastructure

**Figure 4.1**  Primary Stakeholders (Inner Circle) and Secondary Stakeholders (Outer Ring) Primary Stakeholder: Society and Community

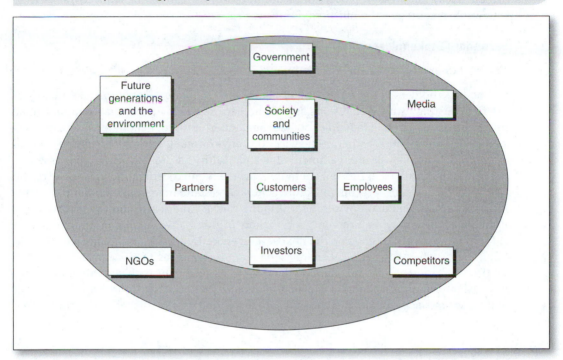

(such as public works projects including roads, highways, bridges, dams, canals, water and sewer systems, air terminals, Internet linkages, satellites, as well as ports and harbors), and (c) public institutions (with missions directed to the provision of the following: national defense, homeland security, local security, relations with other nations, management of the currency and facilitation of commerce, selected scientific research, public transportation, public health, education, and social welfare). In democracies, governments and their workers (both elected and nonelected) are the agents of societies that (a) establish laws, (b) run the judicial system, (c) manage public lands and the elements of publicly owned infrastructure, and (d) execute the operations of public institutions. More will be said about government as a stakeholder later in this chapter and in Chapter 6.

## Primary Stakeholders: Partners, Customers, Investors, and Employees

The other primary stakeholders in the inner circle of Figure 4.1, partners (suppliers and lenders), investors, customers, and employees, have a clear and direct impact on the conduct of a firm's business. Without these, the firm could not succeed and continue (Freeman et al., 2010). It should be noted that stakeholder theory's rival theory of management, emphasizes the preeminence of shareholders (investors or owners). More will be said about these two rival perspectives on business in the next chapter. The ethic of self-interest in competition sanctions aggressive firm behavior in markets to optimize the efficiency of their systems. As a result, the shareholder perspective often results in suppliers and customers becoming subcategories of competitors that are to be beaten or subdued (Green, 2009). Likewise, employees often became "costs" (to always be reduced) rather than renewable resources (to be nurtured) for firms.

## Secondary Stakeholders

### Future Generations and the Environment

The stakeholders in the outer ring of Figure 4.1 comprise secondary stakeholders of the firm. Listing future generations as stakeholders deserves further elaboration. Unlike the other stakeholders, it is hard to contact a member of future generations for a conversation that may concern them. Likewise, the environment, not being human, is also impossible to contact. Because a functioning and healthy natural environment is essential to sustaining human life, future generations have a highly overlapping interest with the natural environment. Accordingly, future generations stand in as a stakeholder representing a sustainable natural environment. Among Native Americans, the Great Law of the Iroquois Confederacy required decision makers of this Native American people to consider the impact of decisions on the next seven generations (Hollender & Breen, 2010). In industries, such as the electrical energy services industry, investment decisions are based on time horizons of 20 to 60 years (Rogers, 2011). Accordingly, with such time horizons, it is easier to see that the members of all stakeholder groups in the future will change over and be composed of those who currently are too young to take roles in such groups now.

### Media

The media has an interest in the marketing and operations of firms. Firms are targets of media interest because they are actors in society and communities that provide jobs, compete in markets, and interact with government entities, both legally and illegally. In short, firms do newsworthy things. Media also comprises "the fourth estate," or the informal branch of government that exposes corrupt government officials as well as harmful or unjust actions of government to society and communities.

### Nongovernmental Organizations

An NGO can be described as any nonprofit organization that is independent of government (Leverty, 2011). The United Nations (UN) Department of Public Information (DPI) describes an NGO as "a not-for profit, voluntary citizen's group that is organized on a local, national or international level to address issues in support of the public good. Task-oriented and made up of people with a common interest, NGOs perform a variety of services and humanitarian functions, bring citizen's concerns to governments, monitor policy and program implementation, and encourage participation of civil society stakeholders at the community level" (UNDPI, 2011).

NGOs have dramatically increased in number and activity in the last 50 years. In a 2002 survey conducted in 47 nations by GlobeScan and the Gallup Organization, 59% of respondents stated that they had a lot or some trust in NGOs, whereas only 39 % and 42 % stated they had similar trust for global corporations or large national companies (Argenti, 2004). In short, citizens often have more trust for NGOs than for big business.

U.S. President Barack Obama worked for the Developing Communities Project on the far south side of Chicago from 1985 to 1988 (York, 2008). This was an NGO set up by a consortium of churches to pursue job retraining for African Americans in a disadvantaged neighborhood. Obama wound up winning the expansion of a city summer-job program for teenagers and the removal of asbestos from one of the area's oldest housing projects.

NGOs have the flexibility to pressure governments and business and the ability to focus on one issue. NGO's interests that affect business range from hiring practices, wage and working conditions (topics of primary interest for labor unions), health issues, consumer advocacy, and education. After seven years of pressure on major businesses to end manufacturing operations in Myanmar because of its atrocious human rights record, the Free Burma Coalition won agreements from companies such as Adidas, Costco, Wal-Mart, and Levi-Strauss to end their operations in Myanmar (Spar & La Mure, 2003).

In May 2011, the watchdog group Corporate Accountability International began publishing a letter it had signed by 550 health professionals and organizations in six major metropolitan newspapers asking the McDonald's Corporation to stop marketing food high in salt, fat, sugar, and calories to kids and to retire Ronald McDonald (Jargon, 2011). NGOs have also influenced the Federal Trade Commission, the Food and Drug Administration, the Centers for Disease Control and Prevention, and the U.S. Department of Agriculture (to propose guidelines about increasing the amount of fruits, vegetables, and lean meats marketed to kids ages 2 to 17, as well as limiting the amount of junk food marketed).

### Competitors

Listing competitors as a stakeholder for a firm might surprise some. However, the way firms compete gives rival firms an interest in how their competitors market their goods and services, as well as in the way firms operate their businesses. For example, in the years prior to the subprime mortgage crisis in the United States, mortgage lenders reported that if they did not lend to questionable borrowers, their competitors would (CNBC, 2009). When such marketing practices are allowed to continue unabated, the result can be disastrous for an entire industry, as well as for society.

By comparison, some leaders of firms envision problems with current business practices and convince other firms in the industry that current ways of doing things are not sustainable. James Rogers, Duke Energy's CEO, joined with General Electric, 22 other firms (16 of which were on the Fortune 500 list), the World Resources Institute, and five leading environmental NGOs, to form the U.S. Climate Action Partnership (USCAP) (Rogers, 2011). The purpose of USCAP is to urge the federal government to enact strong legislation to reduce greenhouse gas emissions. Although this move received criticism from different quarters across the energy service industry, CEOs on the board of the Edison Electric Institute, the trade association for energy service companies, agreed that "if we didn't have a seat at the table, we would be on the menu" (Rogers, 2011, p. 53). Rogers's experience suggests that it pays to respect competitors and engage them in major issues of shared interest. However, in addressing such issues, firms must not violate antitrust laws prohibiting unfair collaboration across firms that would disadvantage consumers or other businesses in the industry.

### Government

As a stakeholder, government is unique in its ability to (a) set the rules of the game, (b) play umpire, (c) impose taxes, and (d) intervene directly and indirectly in markets. In establishing laws and policies, the government must move deftly and walk a fine line not to trigger unintended results. Rules, procedures for licensing, and standards must be adequate for protection but not so costly that innovation and entrepreneurship is discouraged or stopped (Beardsley & Farrell, 2005). For example, in the Philippines, it can take 13 to 25 years and almost 170 steps and signatures to acquire a piece of land legally (De Soto, 2000). Not surprisingly, between 60% and 70% of Philippinos do not have legal title to their land. The effect on the aggregate marketing system is that the main source of collateral for small-business owners and entrepreneurs is unavailable.

There are five areas of U.S. laws that regulate marketers' efforts to facilitate exchanges: (a) antitrust, (b) competitive torts (a competitive tort is an act that injures a competitor in some way, and for which the injured competitor may sue the wrongdoer for damages, such as false derogatory statements about the competitor's brand, or using below-cost pricing), (c) consumer protection (product safety and liability), (d) intellectual property, and (e) international trade (such as restrictions against dumping in which foreign companies must charge a market price in the United States of at least 8% above the cost of goods sold) (Petty, 2005).

In the United States, changes in tax laws have encouraged some businesses and professionals to file their income taxes as individuals. Accordingly, the corporate share of the nation's tax receipts have fallen from 30% in the mid-1950s to 6.6% in 2009 (Kocieniewski, 2011). But the government's current stance toward corporations paying income taxes seems favorable to businesses. The General Accounting Office has reported that 61% of U.S. corporations paid no federal income taxes from 1996 through 2000, a period of rapid economic growth and rising corporate profits (Veith, 2004). Nevertheless, it still makes the front pages of newspapers when GE reported earning $5.1 billion from its operations in the United States in 2010, but wound up paying no taxes (GE actually claimed a tax benefit of $3.2 billion that will carry over to future years and reduce any tax payments GE might have then) (Kocieniewski, 2011). GE's enormous tax department is led by a former Treasury Department official John Samuels and is often referred to as "the world's best tax law firm." Samuels's team includes former officials from the Treasury Department, the Internal Revenue Service, and almost all of the tax-writing committees in Congress. Although the corporate income tax rate is listed as 35%, companies like GE can reduce their effective tax burden by claiming a variety of deductions and credits, some of which they have actively and successfully lobbied the government to implement.

Direct intervention of government in markets can come through lending to businesses, providing loan guarantees for businesses, and even owning businesses. In September 2008, the U.S. Treasury did not intervene to rescue investment bank Lehman Brothers from bankruptcy in order to avoid reinforcing Lehman Brothers (and other investment banks in the future) for taking on too much risk (Bishop & Green, 2010). The Lehman Brothers bankruptcy triggered a sudden and wrenching reassessment of the viability of banks throughout the financial system. Because the extent of losses on other outstanding loans was unclear, banks ceased lending at a time when they would need to find additional cash reserves as more losses from outstanding loans. The survival of many major banks became questioned and the entire economy suffered a setback that threatened the economic life of the United States (and most other countries in the world).

In 2008, the federal government used Troubled Assets Relief Program (TARP) money to provide emergency loans to two U.S. automakers in distress, GM and Chrysler (Rattner, 2010). In the first half of 2009, a team from the U.S. Treasury Department guided these two firms through two of the most complex and sizable bankruptcies ever. Chrysler and GM emerged with much less debt on their balance sheets and new hope for better days ahead. With an improved outlook for GM and Chrysler, the two firms have resumed lobbying efforts in Washington, DC (Terlep & Mitchell, 2011). By exercising the right of political expression for firms upheld by the Supreme Court in its *Citizens United* ruling in January 2010, GM, which is still partly owned by U.S. taxpayers, spent more than $10 million in 2010 on its efforts to influence policy makers about issues, such as proposed emissions and fuel-mileage standards, the implementation of a new financial-overhaul law, and lifting limits on its executive pay. On its webpage, the U.S. Chamber of Commerce positions itself as the "biggest lobby in Washington consistently leading the pack in lobbying expenditures" (McKibben, 2011). A group called U.S. ChamberWatch used federal disclosure laws to examine the U.S. Chamber of Commerce's IRS 990 form and learned that 55% of the Chamber's funding came from just 16 firms that contributed more than $1 million each. Even local chambers of commerce have criticized the U.S. Chamber of Commerce for overemphasizing political action committees and business lobbyists, while holding little resemblance to the local chambers of commerce that have served as the cornerstones of their communities for generations. These examples illustrate the two-way connection and sometimes controversial influence among stakeholders (in this case, businesses and government).

## The Stakeholder Mindset

There is a linked aspect to stakeholder interests that can be understood to lie in a "harmony of interests" (Strong, 2009). Business and its set of stakeholder relationships must be viewed holistically as a marketing system in order to grasp that business is not the sum of its parts, but something greater that creates value for its stakeholders. In this way, one can grasp that the stakeholders' interests, while conflicting at times, are inherently linked to each other (Freeman et al., 2010). Accordingly, a stakeholder approach to business creates as much value as possible for stakeholders, without resorting to trade-offs. Such trade-offs might come in the form of benefitting one stakeholder at the expense of another. In the early stages of a venture, some stakeholders loom as more important than others. For example, listening to investors today might be more important than marshaling financial resources to make a tax payment several months in the future.

Matters of ethics routinely arise when taking a stakeholder approach to running a business. In this regard, the importance of stakeholders is a part of determining the overall utility or value that might result from a firm taking a certain course of action (Hunt & Vitell, 2006). Yankelovich (2006) terms a stakeholder approach as "stewardship ethics." With such ethics, managers remain committed to care for the firm and those it serves in a manner that responds to a higher level of expectations. If more firms upgrade their ethical norms to include a collective stance toward stakeholders, the ethical values of society will be reinforced resulting in more mutually beneficial stakeholder relationships.

In a complex and rapidly changing business environment, paying close attention to stakeholders will enable the alert and responsive firm to obtain important signals from the periphery of a firm's regular focus (Day & Schoemaker, 2006). Often, these signals first appear in a weak form and must be probed, interpreted, and compared with signals from other sources to prove advantageous for the firm in a timely way. Such signals often would come from the same stakeholders depicted in Figure 4.1, with the exception of future generations.

Importantly, it can be said that stakeholders can help the firm better envision future scenarios that seem unlikely now. For example, Google and Yahoo! have created their own blogs to communicate actively with customers and employees and to learn about emerging concerns at the periphery (Kirkpatrick, 2004). Attending a conference outside of a firm's own industry can provide valuable learning about the periphery. Such deliberate and active learning will likely prove more valuable for the firm than the continuance of focal vision targeting competitors along with attendance at industry conferences with the same competitors.

Vince Melchiorre, senior vice president and chief marketing officer for Philadelphia-based Tasty Baking, turned his firm to gain first-mover advantage in sugar-free pastries because he was regularly denounced by diabetics when he visited grocery stores twice a week for not allowing them to continue eating Tastykakes, an enjoyable consumption since childhood (Day & Schoemaker, 2006). By being out with stakeholders (partners in the retail trade and customers), he was able to receive signals for a new thrust for his firm in the midst of competitors developing low-carb pastries and internal product development personnel initially telling him that it was too difficult to produce a sugar-free pastry.

## Turning Toward a Stakeholder Orientation

Long-time leaders in marketing academia, such as David J. Reibstein, George Day, and Jerry Wind (2009), have called for a research agenda among marketing academics focusing on difficult problems facing firms and society. Again, the "biggest M," an orientation toward understanding the interplay of marketing and society, takes precedence as major societal concerns lead the list of pressing strategic issues. "How can marketing contribute to rebuilding confidence in the global financial system, finding a role for consumer choice in health care reform, reducing obesity, encouraging energy conservation, meeting the needs of consumers in developing countries and so forth?" (Reibstein et al., 2009, p. 2)

In light of the calls of leading scholars in marketing and marketing strategy to come to terms with issues related to the "biggest M," Robert Lusch and Fred Webster (2010) propose a revised view of the firm as a complex-network mechanism linking customer value and the value of the firm for all of its stakeholders. These leading thinkers in marketing propose that marketing's opportunity now and in the future will be as an integrator among stakeholders seeking value co-creation. Rather than book value (the price the firm could obtain for its assets upon liquidation), and market value (the number of outstanding shares multiplied by the firm's stock price), the value of the enterprise (the sum of the value derived from the firm by all the stakeholders) will become ascendant in the future. Instead of the traditional view of marketing as the advocate for the customer within the firm itself, this new view sees marketing as the advocate for the consumer with *all* resource providers within the networked enterprise.

In an era of business in which a firm like GM is viewed by government and many U.S. citizens as a resource that was not exclusively the property of its shareholders, GM was not allowed to go out of business because of the harm that would result to a wide set of stakeholders. Because the firm is no longer separate from its environment, Lusch and Webster propose that because the firm is integrated with the environment through networked relationships (as well as economic globalization and information technology), several new practices need to lead the firm into the future. First, leaders, managers, and employees need to bring empathy to fully understanding the preferences and ways of the firm's stakeholders. Second, streamlining the flows of communication and material with stakeholders must become the focus of planning because resources must be created and integrated across different stakeholders. Third, processes for working together to realize value must be accomplished by co-producing and co-creating value with customers, suppliers, and other stakeholders. Fourth, control must be integrated with learning as adaptive behavior in a network of stakeholders dedicated to value creation. Because the customer's calculus for value changes continuously, marketing must be a learning process for all in the network of stakeholders.

In sum, joint success across the firm's network of stakeholders should be the focus for stakeholder-oriented businesses in a networked world (Green, 2009). Connectivity, trust, and collaboration will be the watchwords in this new environment for firms because they must shift from traditional management to network orchestration (Wind, 2008). Companies such as Google seek to create a marketing ecosystem with partners and therefore have outmaneuvered rivals such as Yahoo!.

## The Importance of Employing Stakeholder Orientation

An important point here is that a business case for employing a stakeholder orientation is emerging now. Scholars in marketing and marketing strategy understand that the reasons for adopting a stakeholder orientation for the firm now go beyond the idea of being the "good guy." In industries attracting public review (such as forestry, energy, and mining), the government induces firms to consider stakeholders in the planning and conduct of their operations. Firms with high profiles in markets, such as Wal-Mart, receive continued scrutiny about its treatment of stakeholders from NGOs, government, and media. More and more, stakeholders compel these types of firms to listen when these stakeholders express concerns about firms' marketing and operations.

In an increasingly networked world, stakeholders also gain influence with firms not typically regulated in the past. Rather than reacting to stakeholder interests, these firms proactively seek to integrate stakeholders' views into their marketing and planning. Using a sample of 172 firms from a variety of industries in a database called SOCRATES (developed by the social investment research firm Kinder, Lydenberg, and Domini), Tracy L. Gonzalez-Padron and Robert W. Nason (2000) investigated firms' innovativeness. Firms were measured by their ability (a) to lead their industry in bringing notable innovations to market, (b) to derive their revenues from products and services related to environmental benefits, and (c) to seek nontraditional approaches to addressing social issues. In this way, these three dimensions of innovativeness correspond to the three dimensions of the triple bottom line. These researchers found evidence that the more innovative firms made a practice of internalizing the objectives of customers, employees, and community stakeholder groups, whereas the less innovative companies did not. Firms focused on being responsive to regulators were less innovative. In short, these researchers provided evidence of a positive relationship between voluntarily taking a strategic approach to collaborating with stakeholders and succeeding in innovation across the three dimensions of the triple bottom line.

## COSTCO WHOLESALE—A STAKEHOLDER-ORIENTED COMPANY

### An Advocate for the Consumer Within Its Enterprise Network

Jeff Brotman and Jim Sinegal founded Costco Wholesale in 1983 before the triple bottom line had been conceptualized. But today, Costco offers a glimpse at what a firm might look like if it views marketing as the advocate for the consumer with *all* resource providers within the networked enterprise, as recommended by Lusch and Webster (2010). A number of Costco's suppliers are featured in this book as examples of unique companies who understand a stakeholder orientation.

From its inception, Costco's leadership imparted to its employees an almost fanatical commitment to its customers who pay an annual fee to be members of its network (Costco, 2010a). More than 60 million people comprise Costco's membership (with Business, Gold,

**Figure 4.2**   Costco Logo

*Source:* http://media.corporate-ir.net/media_files/irol/83/83830/CostcoLogoStandards.pdf

and Executive membership levels from costing $50 to $100 per year). As an indicator of customer loyalty, 87% of Costco's members renew their membership each year. In 2010, Costco's revenue on its membership fee alone totaled $1.7 billion. When considering that Costco's profits amounted to $1.3 billion in the same year, one can see (a) how low the margins are for Costco customers and (b) how important customer loyalty and membership fees are to Costco's financial well-being.

For its members, Costco serves as a buying agent, preselecting popular products in sizes that offer the best value. Today, Costco operates an international chain of more than 550 membership warehouses (with an average store size of 143,000 square feet) that carry brand-name merchandise (including food and gasoline) at substantially lower prices than typically found at conventional wholesale or retail stores.

According to Jim Sinegal, the company's Chief Executive Officer:

> Costco is able to offer lower prices and better values by eliminating virtually all the frills and costs historically associated with conventional wholesalers and retailers, including salespeople, fancy buildings, delivery, billing and accounts receivable. We run a tight operation with extremely low overhead which enables us to pass on dramatic savings to our members. (Costco, 2011a)

Headquartered east of Seattle in Issaquah, Washington, Costco ranks number 28 in the Fortune 500 (Fortune, 2011) with revenues of almost $78 billion posting a razor-thin 1.7% profit margin. Although Wal-Mart Stores posts the largest revenues in the world atop the Fortune 500 (with $422 billion in sales in 2010), Costco is the leading specialty retailer in the United States (followed by Home Depot, Best Buy, and Lowe's). In 2011, Costco led all specialty retailers in Fortune's list of admired companies. In 2003, *Fortune* cited Costco as the only company feared by Wal-Mart (Helyar, 2003). Currently the third largest retailer in the United States, Costco is the eighth largest retailer in the world with 92% of its warehouses in the United States and Canada, and the rest in the United Kingdom, Taiwan, South Korea, Japan, Australia, and Mexico (Costco, 2010a).

Costco's mark-ups are capped at 14% (by comparison, department-store mark-ups can reach 40%), but across the store, the average mark-up is less than 11% (Costco, 2010a). What this means for the customer is that when Costco fortuitously comes across an unusual price on goods, the customer receives the benefit. For example, if Reebok manufactures too many running shoes one quarter, it might approach Costco about buying the excess run at a steep discount. If Costco buys this excess run of shoes, it would only add 14% on top of the price Costco would pay to Reebok, instead of taking a larger mark-up (putting the shoes on sale at a near normal price) and opportunistically capturing more profit for itself. Another way Costco cares for its customers is by extending them blanket permission for returns up to 90 days after purchase—no receipts, no questions.

Costco offers the best wages and benefits in retailing. As a result, Costco's employee turnover among its 147,000 employees is one third the average in retailing (Helyar, 2003). As a result, Costco enjoys lower training costs for employees because of the low turnover. Notably, the average tenure of store managers is more than 15 years (Helyar, 2003). Another benefit of attracting high-quality employees is minimal inventory shrinkage (as a result of theft and breakage). Costco's inventory shrinkage rate of less than two tenths of 1% is well below those of typical discount retail operations (Costco, 2010a).

A visit to Costco's headquarters will likely not lead to a visit with CEO Jim Sinegal who for years has spent more than 200 days each year traveling to Costco stores to inspire employees and question them about how their operations compare with those of its competitors (Helyar, 2003). Sinegal's office itself is transparent. The two interior sides of it have only waist-high walls. (If a private conversation is needed, Sinegal moves to a nearby conference room.) The wall behind Sinegal's desk is thick with curling photos pinned to the wall of Costco employees taken over the years.

While Costco's employees receive above average pay for the retailing industry, Sinegal is underpaid as a CEO relative to other CEOs in specialty retailing (Costco, 2010a). Since 1999, Sinegal receives $350,000 in annual pay (Costco 2011c). His cash bonus is limited to $200,000. But the bulk of his compensation can come in the way of restricted stock units (RSUs) that are part of a stock compensation arrangement where Sinegal receives a specified number of shares of the firm's stock (or an equivalent amount of cash) after a designated vesting period. This step ensures no opportunistic decisions have been made by Sinegal to boost company results artificially. For example, in November 2009, the Costco Board of Directors' Compensation Committee set criteria of a 3% increase (versus fiscal 2009) in total sales or pretax income for Costco in order for Sinegal to receive a grant of 50,000 shares of restricted stock. (This was valued later at $2,896,030.) In 2010, the company achieved this goal. In this way, Sinegal's interests are more closely aligned with the shareholders of Costco.

Figure 4.3 depicts the quarterly returns of the share price for Costco (the darker line) compared with the line representing the S&P 500 over the past 10 years (the lighter line). As shown, Costco's stock performance has exceeded the S&P 500 throughout most of the 2002–2012 year period.

## Costco's Mission and Code of Ethics

### Costco's Mission

The Costco Board of Directors, which has guided Costco to such success in the stock market, has 15 members (Costco, 2010a). These include Bill Gates, currently co-chair of the Bill and Melinda Gates Foundation; Susan Decker, former President of Yahoo! Inc.; and Charlie Munger, vice chairman of the board of Berkshire Hathaway, a hugely successful investment company chaired by Warren Buffet. The Costco Board meets quarterly. Costco proves to be an attractive entity for some of the best business minds today.

Costco's mission is "to continually provide our members with quality goods and services at the lowest possible prices" (Costco, 2010b, p. 1). Notably, this succinct statement can be readily understood by employees and stakeholders. "Our Mission" precedes "Our Code of Ethics" in a four-page document available on Costco's website for investor relations.

"'We're not doing brain surgery' as Jim Sinegal says," Costco Senior Vice President for Ecommerce and Publishing Ginnie Roeglin said. She emphasized that "trust with our members is extremely important to our success. We're fanatical about the things that go into

**Figure 4.3** Costco's Stock Performance 2002–2012 Compared With S&P 500 (Big Charts, 2012)

*Source:* www.bigcharts.com

this. We live and die with the Code of Ethics because there are no short cuts to providing true, honest value" (Roeglin, personal communication, 2011).

## Costco's Code of Ethics

Costco's Code of Ethics is included in its entirety in the appendix to this chapter and addresses the primary stakeholder groups of Figure 4.1. The code includes five points as depicted in Figure 4.4.

*Ethical Code #1: Obey the Law*

The first point in the code of ethics, obey the law, is a direct way Costco addresses the stakeholders of society and community. Costco's history plays an important role in shaping its first ethical code. Early inklings of Costco began with Sol Price, who was a pioneer in developing the warehouse club concept with his Fed-Mart in the 1950s (which he sold to a German company in 1975) (Helyar, 2003). He then launched Price Club stores in 1976. Sinegal worked in both operations for Price before launching Costco with current Costco

**Figure 4.4**   The Five Points of Costco's Code of Ethics

1. Obey the law.

2. Take care of our members.

3. Take care of our employees.

4. Respect our suppliers.

5. Reward our shareholders.

chairman Jeff Brotman in 1983. In 1993, Costco bought Price Club, further reinforcing the imprint of Price on the corporate DNA of Costco's culture.

When Fed-Mart began, competitors put government inspectors on Fed-Mart. As a response, Price and Fed-Mart had to be above reproach. As time went on, Price believed such an approach was good business. Retailers face multiple temptations to give local officials zoning bribes, to allow the retailer's buyers kickbacks from vendors, and to finagle health and safety requirements. None of these actions benefit customers or employees, and they were never tolerated by Price, or later Sinegal.

Another effect of Costco's first ethical code is that community stakeholders are better served when firms obey governmental regulations and laws. One way that Costco serves its community stakeholders is through price competition "In fact, our mere presence in a community makes pricing better throughout the area," Sinegal said, "Because when you have a tough competitor in the marketplace, prices come down" (Costco, 2009, p. 2). Price competition is helpful not only to consumers and communities themselves, but it also helps maintain a healthy market by encouraging competition and discouraging economic domination. Such domination leads to monopolistic behavior by firms in the form of higher prices to consumers or insensitivity to customer preferences.

### Ethical Code #2: Take Care of Our Members

The second point in the code of ethics, take care of our members, could be said by all retailers. However, Price early on came to view his role as a fiduciary for the customer. "We tried to look at everything from the standpoint of, 'Is it really being honest with the customer?'" Price said. He continued, "If you recognize you're really a fiduciary for the customer, you shouldn't make too much money. If you get something for a lower price, you pass on the savings" (Helyar, 2003, p. 164). Underscoring this point, Costco's profits in 2010 represented 1.7% of revenues (Costco, 2010a).

Costco managers who post average margins above 10% have to explain to Sinegal why they did not lower prices for the quarter (Helyar, 2003). For example, fresh foods buyer Jeff Lyons makes an allowance for product spoilage. Because his department had almost no spoilage one October, his profit margin widened by one-half percentage point (Helyar, 2003). "Our margin goal is 10 %, and there'd better be a very good reason you did better than that," Lyons said.

Costco gives an annual "Salmon Award" to Costco buyers who identify a supplier who improves quality, increases volume, and reduces the price of a product sold in Costco warehouses over time. This happened with a supplier of salmon for Costco who improved quality, saw the sales of salmon increase in Costco stores, and then responded by bringing down the price of salmon with the help of Costco managers. With the Salmon Award, Sinegal wants to reinforce its buyers in trying to create the next "salmon story" (Roeglin, personal communication, 2011).

Costco's vigilance for its customers' welfare translates into increased trust, which results in customers being more willing to try new products that appear in the stores. "With trust, customers know we've done our homework on products," Roeglin said, "So they will take a chance on an item" (Roeglin, personal communication, 2011).

One of the elements elaborated in the second point of the code of ethics is "giving back to our communities." This is done through employee volunteerism and both employee and corporate contributions to United Way and Children's Hospitals. In response to natural disasters, Costco has used its scope of operations to the advantage of those who have suffered. For example, in the major earthquake of March 11, 2011, in Japan, two people died as a result of the collapse of the parking ramp at the company's Tamasakai warehouse, which sustained significant damage (Costco, 2011b). To assist in the relief efforts, all Costco locations around the world began accepting donations at cash registers for the Red Cross/Red Crescent Relief Fund.

### Ethical Code #3: Take Care of Our Employees

The third point of the code of ethics, like the first two points, depends on Costco constraining itself to follow rules. Roeglin commented:

> There is an employee agreement or handbook. It says "here are the rules". A manager can't just fire a worker. It requires two levels of approval for those who have been with us more than two years. After the 90-day probationary period, they are *our* employees. The result is that you don't have to watch your back. This fosters a very productive environment without a lot of politics or passive/aggressive stuff. I know a fifteen-year employee who left ten years ago who still says "we" when referring to Costco. (Roeglin, personal communication, 2011).

### Ethical Code #4: Respect Our Suppliers

The fourth point in the code of ethics strives to find win–win opportunities for suppliers and Costco. "We want to be top-of-mind to our suppliers," Roeglin said, "We want them to send us their best concepts."

Because a Costco warehouse carries only 4,200 stock-keeping units (SKUs) compared with more than 100,000 for a Wal-Mart supercenter with dry goods and food (RetailingWorks, 2011), or 30,000 to 50,000 at a grocery store, such as Kroger (Berman, 2011), Costco limits the choice for its customer with its narrow product lines. Each SKU represents a differently packaged product in the store. For example, a 12-oz. shampoo and a 24-oz. size of the same brand represent two separate SKUs. However, the gain for suppliers whose products are sold at Costco's warehouses is dramatic. In 2009, the average sales per SKU at Costco was $18.4 million. By comparison, the average sales per SKU at Kroger was $1.5–$2.6 million (Berman, 2011, p. 68).

Suppliers that sell to Costco must abide by Costco's Supplier Code of Conduct, a six-page document that also is available on the investor relations website. This code addresses issues about the supplier's treatment of employees, compliance with labor and environmental laws, as well as encouraging suppliers to achieve "Above and Beyond Goals" (Costco, 2011d). Costco reserves the right to conduct audits of suppliers' facilities, its operations, and its books, as well as those of subcontractors the suppliers might use.

As with the other stakeholder relationships detailed in the Costco Code of Ethics, Costco imposes constraints upon itself with suppliers. "We are mindful of the percentage of business we account for with our suppliers," Roeglin said, "We can devastate a supplier if we suddenly walk away. So, we never let that be too large of a percentage" (Roeglin, personal communication 2011). Compared with the notoriously brusque treatment suppliers receive at Wal-Mart's headquarters in Bentonville, Arkansas, a supporting element for respecting suppliers is to "treat all suppliers and their representatives as we would expect to be treated if visiting their places of business" (Costco, 2010b).

### Ethical Code #5: Reward Our Shareholders

The fifth element in the code of ethics is written as follows: "If we do these four things throughout our organization, then we will achieve our ultimate goal, which is to reward our shareholders" (Costco, 2010b, p. 1). Costco has a website separate from its main website (www.costco.com) that presents a variety of documents and information to investors, such as earnings, conference call notices, legal settlements, and the annual report.

Costco's generous health benefits and above-average pay attracts criticism from some on Wall Street who follow its performance in the NASDAQ Stock Market. "Costco continues to be a company that is better at serving the club member and employee than the share holder," Deutsche Bank analysts Beil Dreher said (Helyar, 2003). In response, Sinegal gives a shrug, and comments:

> You have to take the shit with the sugar, I guess. . . . We think when you take care of your customer and your employees, your shareholders are going to be rewarded in the long run. And I'm one of them. I care about the stock price. But we're not going to do something for the sake of one quarter that's going to destroy the fabric of our company and what we stand for. (Helyar, 2003, p. 160)

## Costco and Its Secondary Stakeholders

Costco also addresses its secondary stakeholders: the government, the media, competitors, NGOs, as well as future generations and the environment (see Figure 4.1).

## Secondary Stakeholder #1: The Government

For the stakeholder of the government, unlike other major corporations, Costco pays taxes. In 2010, Costco's income tax expense was $731 million on income before taxes of $2.05 billion (Costco, 2010a). This amounts to an effective tax rate of 35.6%, a bit over the U.S. corporate income tax rate of 35%, second only to Japan's 39.5% (Kocieniewski, 2011).

As discussed in Chapter 3, the relationship between private firms and the public sector can be contentious and complex. Some of the criticisms aimed at Costco originate from Costco's activity in issues involving the public sector, such as the courts or the writing of laws.

The Institute for Justice has identified Costco as a corporate beneficiary of eminent-domain takings sites (Berliner, 2011). These occur when local developers use the courts to force land owners to sell their property for public or civic use (highways, utilities, or railroads) or, in some cases, economic development.

Costco does not have any registered Washington lobbyists, but it is not averse to petitioning the government for selected interests important to the firm. In late March 2009, Costco, Starbucks, and Whole Foods announced they had formed the Committee for a Level Playing Field to propose a "third way" be found to reform the nation's labor laws (Blumenthal, 2009). In this way, these firms, which are regarded to have some of the most progressive labor practices, jumped into the most contentious organized labor issue in decades. Later, they found themselves facing sharp criticism from all sides in a nasty fight over legislation that would make it easier for unions to organize under the Employee Free Choice Act currently stalled in Congress. The companies said they opposed ending secret-ballot elections for unionizing a workplace, replacing these with a public card check, and requiring binding arbitration for initial contracts.

"We saw this thing as a train wreck," Sinegal said of the bill, "We think card check is wrong. It's not fair to employers and workers and the arbitration requirement is crazy. But it's pretty tough to get both sides shooting at you, you either have to be a duck or inept" (Blumenthal, 2009). Despite a very favorable reputation in labor practices, some labor analysts say Costco, Starbucks, and Whole Foods could be among the first facing unionization if the Employee Free Choice Act, or EFCA, became law.

## Secondary Stakeholder #2: The Media

Regarding media as a stakeholder, Costco puts a wide array of information on its website for investor relations, such as Securities and Exchange Commission filings, audio recordings of CFO Richard Galanti's discussion of earnings reports, results of legal settlements, its Code of Ethics, and its Sustainability Report. Costco publishes its four-color *The Costco Connection* on glossy paper that is distributed to those who are Business or Executive Members. The monthly publication started as a piece for small business owners, but now, it has changed to more of a lifestyle magazine (Roeglin, personal communication, 2011). With a current circulation of more than 8.5 million, *The Costco Connection* reaches in excess of 1.6 million *more* readers each month than the worldwide circulation of *National Geographic* (National Geographic, 2011). Although officers of Costco are quick to point out that their public relations efforts are limited to store openings (Costco, 2010a), with *The*

*Costco Connection* and with its ecommerce presence on www.costco.com, it can be said that Costco actually owns two worldwide media outlets.

### Secondary Stakeholder #3: Competitors

Regarding competitors as stakeholders, Costco lists Wal-Mart, Sam's Club, and BJs Wholesale Club as presenting 800 competing warehouse stores in every major metropolitan area (Costco, 2010a). Among general merchandise retail competitors, Costco lists Wal-Mart, Target, Kohl's, and Amazon.com. Costco also competes against "category killers," focused on one or a narrow range of merchandise, including Lowe's, Home Depot, Office Depot, PetSmart, Staples, Trader Joe's, Best Buy, and Barnes & Noble. Sinegal uses such competitors and their merchandising and innovations to challenge his own troops, saying, "We need constant reminders to keep us on our game" (Helyar, 2003).

As the previous discussion about Costco's collaboration with Whole Foods and Starbucks on labor reform suggests, Costco is willing to join forces with competitors on certain occasions. Among leaders of retailing companies, there is evidence of respectful rapport at times, as the companies have to learn from the others' successes and failures to keep up in the industry.

One humorous episode illustrating retailers' respect for worthy competitors predates the founding of Costco in 1983. When Price Club opened in the 1970s, Sam Walton, founder of Wal-Mart, came out to investigate (Helyar, 2003). Price commented on Walton's visit, saying:

> He came out to look at a Price Club and he was very complimentary. He spent all his time telling me how impressed he'd been with Fed-Mart and how he'd never have all these Wal-marts and be worth $700 million without that model. "I owe it all to you," he said. I told him, "Then don't you think I'm entitled to a finder's fee?" (Helyar, 2003, p. 164)

### Secondary Stakeholders #4 and #5: NGOs, Future Generations, and the Environment

Costco encounters a wide array of NGO stakeholders. At the local level, employees give back to their communities not only through ongoing financial contributions through the United Way, but also through countless hours volunteered to local nonprofit agencies (Costco, 2009). Costco fosters a volunteer spirit among its employees by providing organizational help through the Costco Volunteer Center (CVC). The CVC serves as a clearinghouse for identifying local needs and then promoting and tracking volunteer opportunities (Volunteer Screening Blog, 2011). Each month, local charities can present their programs to the group, which finds ways to help.

In addition to boosting the volunteer efforts of its employees, Costco assists Children's Hospitals across North America with financial aid and personal support through the Children's Miracle Network.

In 2006, Costco began a collaborative relationship with the World Wildlife Fund, the world's largest private conservation organization, to identify sustainable fisheries for species designated as being at risk (Costco, 2011e). Costco also works with the Marine Stewardship Council (www.msc.org), the world's leading certification and ecolabeling program for sustainable seafood to identify which species of seafood should be discontinued for sales at Costco as a result of overfishing of the species.

Despite these efforts, the environmental activist organization Greenpeace targeted Costco in 2010 as one of seven food retailers in an effort to make their seafood purchasing and selling practices more sustainable (Lynch, 2010). Greenpeace's "Oh No Costco!" campaign highlighted Costco's practice of selling 15 out of Greenpeace's 22 red-listed species (destructively farmed seafood) (Schwartz, 2010). Members of Greenpeace picketed the company headquarters in Issaquah, Washington, the day before the appearance of a green blimp that carried the message, "Costco: wholesale ocean destruction" (Lynch, 2010). Representatives of Costco met with the activists and agreed to take their considerations under review. However, the two groups remained at odds over the definition of "sustainability" and whether Costco had taken enough steps to address overfishing of the oceans.

Later, Costco stopped sales of some of the species on Greenpeace's list. The "Oh No Costco!" website then became the "Oh Costco!" website with the following explanation headlined by "No Longer Wholesale Ocean Destruction":

> In a stunning win for the oceans, Costco has agreed to remove over half of its red list seafood items, pursue better practices in aquaculture and assume more of a leadership role in the ongoing global effort to develop a more sustainable tuna industry. Over the past eight months, Costco heard from environmental activists around the country – as well as from thousands of its own customers – on how the wholesale giant can and must do better to protect our precious ocean resources. (Greenpeace, 2011, para. 1)

In response to Greenpeace's concerns, Costco took action and actively worked to help protect the environment. Costco CFO Richard Galanti said:

> Greenpeace gave us a list of species of fish being overharvested. We reviewed the list, and said "OK, we agree" with these species on the list. So we stopped sales of these species. We are ready to admit it when we don't get it right, and we do it. But unless you are in 100% compliance with their demands, you are the enemy to such groups. You are never going to make the extreme ones happy. (Galanti, personal communication, 2011)

### Secondary Stakeholder #5: Future Generations

Regarding future generations as a stakeholder, Costco deploys sustainability and energy programs and supports education (Costco, 2010a). Because Costco's business model has always emphasized no-frills stores with low overhead costs, Costco did many things in a sustainable way before sustainability was widely pursued by businesses (more will be presented about Costco's green initiatives in later chapters). Costco Director of Corporate

Sustainability Karen Raines explained that Costco's business approach has always sought to eliminate needless expenses in operating the warehouses:

> Overhead skylights, reusing boxes at check-out (instead of using plastic bags) were done from the very beginning. Now we are reducing our wastes, such as food waste (after donations to local food banks), by using composting, worm farms, and animal feed farms. A lot of our lighting is on timers and sun sensors. We have solar panels being deployed in pilot programs to reduce our energy consumption and expense. (Raines, 2011)

Started in 1993, the Costco Backpack Program is a nationwide program (Volunteer Screening Blog, 2011). Each Costco warehouse identifies a local school to "adopt." Employees then distribute new backpacks filled with supplies to each student in a chosen grade. Since 2005, more than 225,000 backpacks have been given away in the United States each year by Costco. The Backpack Program is done concurrently with a company-wide Volunteer Reading Program that was launched in 1998. Interested staff members are trained to tutor children who need extra help developing better reading skills. They meet weekly with their students, who range from grade school to high school (Volunteer Screening Blog, 2011).

### Costco and Stakeholder Orientation

In summary, Costco offers a valuable case to consider how a large-scale, successful, international enterprise manifests important aspects of a stakeholder orientation. Although not perfect, Costco is importantly a learning organization. "Jim (Sinegal) says that 90% of every manager's job is to teach!" Roeglin (personal communication, 2011) said, "Everyone is in constant learning or teaching. We're not allowing complacency to settle in."

Although Roeglin asserts that Costco is not a marketing company, it may be more correct that Costco is not a 20th century marketing company (relying on promotion or information asymmetries with customers). Instead, Costco takes a wide-angle view on the marketplace, embraces the "biggest M," and strives to align the interests of its stakeholders on the way to creating value for customers, as well as other stakeholders in Costco's network of stakeholders.

Membership, in itself, brings accountability to Costco as every customer that walks in a Costco warehouse has a Costco card (and must update the information every year, actually paying to do so). "Members have a sense of entitlement like a shareholder would," Roeglin said (personal communication, 2011). "It's as if they were part owners." In these ways, Costco offers a valuable view of what more of marketing in the 21st century might become—networked value creation among stakeholders.

## CONCLUSION

The complexities of conducting successful business operations can be daunting. Nevertheless, firms that thrive and grow in the 21st century will most likely embrace a stakeholder orientation. By taking a broad view of markets, their actors, and stakeholders, firms can use the "biggest M" to integrate an understanding of the interplay of markets and society in strategic marketing for the firm. Firm leaders employing the biggest M will more likely identify the role of all stakeholders, such as government, as well as more aggregated marketing systems in the future success of the firm. Costco serves as a valuable example of a major corporation that manifests characteristics of a stakeholder orientation in many aspects of its operations.

## QUESTIONS

1. What were surprises you encountered in reading Chapter 4?

2. What does a stakeholder orientation have to do with the pursuit of wisdom in business decisions?

3. In your view, which stakeholder group would be the most challenging for a firm to integrate into its marketing and planning?

4. What factors are contributing to more marketing scholars embracing a marketing and society orientation (the "biggest M") today?

5. In what ways does Costco manifest a stakeholder orientation?

---

### MAVERICKS WHO MADE IT

#### Success at Sea

#### Trident Seafoods' Chuck Bundrant

#### Quality and sustainability are hallmarks of Trident Seafoods

#### By Stephanie E. Ponder

IF THERE'S ONE food that is consistently on consumers' minds for both its health benefits and environmental aspects, it's fish. The American Heart Association recommends at least two servings a week to do everything from increasing brain function to reducing the risk of heart disease. At the same time, it's impossible to avoid headlines about overfishing and matters of sustainability.

One company, Trident Seafoods, keeps working not only to bring customers the freshest and healthiest fish possible, but to help maintain the resource's long-term survival by staying well within catch limits.

*(Continued)*

(Continued)

## Netting Success

Trident Seafoods started with one boat, says founder and chairman Chuck Bundrant. Preceding the boat was a dream, one that Bundrant turned into a successful privately held and 100 percent American-owned seafood harvesting and processing company. While Trident processes fish from around the world, the company focuses on wild products from Alaska, including salmon, pollock, crab, halibut and cod.

Bundrant is modest about his success. "I've been blessed to be at the right spot at the right time with the right people," he tells *The Connection*.

In the fall of 1960, Bundrant was taking classes on a pre-veterinary track and working 40 hours a week. It was difficult to stay on top of both. The teen found inspiration in the film *North to Alaska,* and he and three friends set out from Tennessee on their own trek in January 1961. Bundrant laughs that "about the time we got to Seattle, my friends were ready to go back home."

Bundrant stuck it out, making $1.47 an hour working on a processing ship in Alaska's Aleutian Islands. He says the first few years were really tough, but he worked his way up from deckhand to captain and scraped together the funds to buy his own crab boat in 1965.

He built a second crab boat in 1967, but sold it two years later and headed back to Tennessee, where he considered becoming a farmer. But Alaska had gotten ahold of him, and three months later he returned, taking a job with Vita Food, a crab-processing business.

While working on a floating processor for Vita Food, Bundrant began to toy with the idea of catching and processing crab on the one vessel. At that time the combination was unheard of: Catching boats needed maneuverability, while processers needed space to handle and freeze the crab.

Ignoring the refrain of "it can't be done," Bundrant, along with his partners, Mike Jacobson and Kaare Ness, proved in 1973 that it could. Bundrant created a lay-out and had a naval architect draft the plans.

He called the resulting catcher processer the *Billikin*, after a Native American good-luck symbol. "That was the beginning of Trident Seafoods," says Bundrant. "The boat was an instant success."

The advantages of being able to catch and process at sea meant the *Billikin* could go to the most abundant areas and then process and freeze the crabmeat without heading back to shore.

As for Trident's success, Bundrant points to investing his profits back into the business and the decision around 1977 to diversify. It was what he calls "a three-legged stool" approach—fishing for crab, salmon and bottom fish.

Trident has grown to boast a fleet of more than 40 vessels, and through various mergers and acquisitions—and forging a relationship with Costco in 2000—its shore based presence has expanded to include 16 plants located throughout Alaska and the Pacific Northwest, plus one plant in Minnesota.

"The goal has always been to grow at a rate we could manage," says Bundrant.

## SUPPLIER PROFILE

**Company:** Trident Seafood

**Chairman:** Chuck Bundrant

**Employees:** 6,000 (at the height of the season)

**Address:** 5303 Shilshole Ave. N.W. Seattle, WA 98107

**Web site:** www.tridentseafoods.com

**Items at Costco:** 30 internationally—including fresh, frozen, deli, dry grocery & supplements

**Comments about Costco:** "The relationship with Costco has made us a better company. They continually pose challenges that help us improve our products to provide better value to the members."—*Joe Bundrant, Executive Vice President*

## Quality

From the beginning, Trident has taken pride in maintaining quality "from the source to the plate." It's a motto Bundrant is more than ready to back up.

"Quality control starts on the boats," he says. "We've incorporated checks and balances all the way."

The process starts with fishing the right varieties at the right time. Once caught, fish must pass through several stages of quality control, including everything from temperature monitoring to being x-rayed for bones. Everything is carefully weighed to make sure the weights are honest and accurate.

Trident employs a team of chefs and food scientists to create products that taste just as great at home as they do in the test kitchen at the company's seattle-based Innovation Center. Projects in the works include making their salmon burgers all natural, kosher and gluten free, and creating fish portions that won't turn rubbery in the microwave.

"Our customers are the ultimate quality-control monitors," says John van Amerongen. Trident's chief sustainability officer. "They tell us how we're doing and we pay very serious attention to all of their feedback. If you e-mail the address on our Ultimate Fish Sticks, *chucksfishsticks@tridentseafoods.com*. [Chuck Bundrant] will personally read [the] e-mail. Clearly it's very important to everyone here that the big boss gets positive feedback."

## Sustainability

Trident's quality-control measures go hand in hand with their efforts to address sustainability. The company works closely with the North Pacific Fishery Management Council, which regulates

*(Continued)*

(Continued)

groundfish management, and the Marine Stewardship Council, which promotes worldwide sustainable fishing practices.

"The key is matching input to output," explains van Amerongen. "Alaska has individual vessel quota management systems for pollock, king and snow crab, halibut and sablefish. Ending 'the race for fish' lets us concentrate full-time on product quality."

Another aspect of Trident's sustainability efforts is a commitment to using all parts of the fish. "Aside from the obvious products. Trident also makes fish oil and fish meal, and raw materials and byproducts are used in pet treats and fertilizer," explains Bundrant. "[Sustainability] is a long-term investment, and it's the right thing to do." He adds, "None of it's worth anything if there aren't any fish."

## A FEEL-GOOD FISH STORY

IT'S NOT JUST customers that Trident's founder Chuck Bundrant wants to make happy: He's committed to his independent fishermen, employees and the communities where the company has processing plants.

Take the plant in Akutan, Alaska, for example. Located near the end of the Aleutian Islands, it has 1,040 employees at the height of the season. It's very much a self-contained city, with Trident providing food and shelter for the employees. Bundrant built a church and recreation center between the plant and town so that everyone can enjoy it.

He's also reached out to the various communities where Trident has plants by supporting local sports teams, and in the summer of 2010 he brought three performers from Norway and one (a fisherman) from Sand Point, Alaska, to all of those communities on what was called the Great North Islands Gospel Tour.

Additionally, every summer he makes a stop at each of the plants. Bundrant, who has more than two dozen employees who've been with him for more than 30 years, likes to walk through the plants saying thank you to his crew. When he was unable to attend an employee's 20th-anniversary party, he was put on speakerphone to offer his congratulations.

"That's what keeps me going—my people," says Bundrant. "It's important to be sincere. Say thank you, and really mean it."

It was his father's commitment to employees that lured Bundrant's son. Joe, back to the family business in 1996 from a job in the food service industry. The younger Bundrant, who is the executive vice president, remembers talking with his dad about the three stages of running one's own business: First you're just out to prove you can do it; then fear takes over and you stay up nights worrying. Finally, you reach a place where you're doing what you're doing out of a sense of responsibility to the employees who helped you build your company. Bundrant told his son, "These people depend on us."

Joe remembers asking his dad. "What can I do to take pressure off of you?" Shortly after that conversation, Joe was working for Trident, committed to the business and especially to the people who make its success possible.

"You can't expect your people to take care of you if you're only looking at the bottom line," says Joe.—*SEP*

*Source: The Costco Connection* (February 2011)

## Questions

1. What role did innovation play in the initial success of Trident Seafoods?

2. How does Chuck Bundrant manifest a stakeholder orientation in leading Trident Seafoods?

3. Which of the stakeholders of Figure 4.1 appear in this "Mavericks Who Made It" piece?

4. Evaluate the importance of the different stakeholders to Trident Seafoods success.

# Appendix

## Costco's Mission Statement and Code of Ethics

## OUR MISSION

To continually provide our members with quality goods and services at the lowest possible prices.

In order to achieve our mission we will conduct our business with the following Code of Ethics in mind:

Our Code of Ethics

1. Obey the law.

2. Take care of our members.

3. Take care of our employees.

4. Respect our suppliers.

If we do these four things throughout our organization, then we will achieve our ultimate goal, which is to:

5. Reward our shareholders.

## Costco's Code of Ethics

1. Obey the law

The law is irrefutable! Absent a moral imperative to challenge a law, we must conduct our business in total compliance with the laws of every community where we do business. We pledge to:

- Comply with all laws and other legal requirements.
- Respect all public officials and their positions.
- Comply with safety and security standards for all products sold.
- Alert management if we observe illegal workplace misconduct by other employees.
- Exceed ecological standards required in every community where we do business.

- Comply with all applicable wage and hour laws.
- Comply with all applicable antitrust laws.
- Conduct business in and with foreign countries in a manner that is legal and proper under United States and foreign laws.
- Not offer or give any form of bribe or kickback or other thing of value to any person or pay to obtain or expedite government action or otherwise act in violation of the Foreign Corrupt Practices Act or the laws of other countries.
- Not request or receive any bribe or kickback.
- Promote fair, accurate, timely, and understandable disclosure in reports filed with the Securities and Exchange Commission and in other public communications by the Company.

### 2. Take care of our members

Costco membership is open to business owners, as well as individuals. Our members are our reason for being – the key to our success. If we don't keep our members happy, little else that we do will make a difference. There are plenty of shopping alternatives for our members and if they fail to show up, we cannot survive. Our members have extended a trust to Costco by virtue of paying a fee to shop with us. We will succeed only if we do not violate the trust they have extended to us, and that trust extends to every area of our business. To continue to earn their trust, we pledge to:

- Provide top-quality products at the best prices in the market.
- Provide high quality, safe and wholesome food products by requiring that both suppliers and employees be in compliance with the highest food safety standards in the industry.
- Provide our members with a 100% satisfaction guarantee on every product and service we sell, including their membership fee.
- Assure our members that every product we sell is authentic in make and in representation of performance.
- Make our shopping environment a pleasant experience by making our members feel welcome as our guests.
- Provide products to our members that will be ecologically sensitive.
- Provide our members with the best customer service in the retail industry.
- Give back to our communities through employee volunteerism and employee and corporate contributions to United Way and Children's Hospitals.

### 3. Take care of our employees

Our employees are our most important asset. We believe we have the very best employees in the warehouse club industry, and we are committed to providing them with rewarding challenges and ample opportunities for personal and career growth. We pledge to provide our employees with:

- Competitive wages
- Great benefits
- A safe and healthy work environment
- Challenging and fun work
- Career opportunities
- An atmosphere free from harassment or discrimination
- An Open Door Policy that allows access to ascending levels of management to resolve issues
- Opportunities to give back to their communities through volunteerism and fund-raising

## Career Opportunities at Costco:

- Costco is committed to promoting from within the Company. The majority of our current management team members (including Warehouse, Merchandise, Administrative, Membership, Front End and Receiving Managers) are "home grown."
- Our growth plans remain very aggressive and our need for qualified, experienced employees to fill supervisory and management positions remains great.
- Today we have Location Managers and Vice Presidents who were once Stockers and Callers or who started in clerical positions for Costco. We believe that Costco's future executive officers are currently working in our warehouses, depots and buying offices, as well as in our Home Office.

### 4. Respect our suppliers

Our suppliers are our partners in business and for us to prosper as a company, they must prosper with us. To that end, we strive to:

- Treat all suppliers and their representatives as we would expect to be treated if visiting their places of business.
- Honor all commitments.
- Protect all suppliers' property assigned to Costco as though it were our own.
- Not accept gratuities of any kind from a supplier.

These guidelines are exactly that – guidelines – some common sense rules for the conduct of our business. At the core of our philosophy as a company is the implicit understanding that all of us, employees and management alike, must conduct ourselves in an honest and ethical manner every day. Dishonest conduct will not be tolerated. To do any less would be unfair to the overwhelming majority of our employees who support and respect Costco's commitment to ethical business conduct. Our employees must avoid actual or apparent conflicts of interest, including creating a business in competition with the Company or working for or on behalf of another employer in competition with the Company. If you are ever in doubt as to what course of action to take on a business matter that is open to varying ethical interpretations, TAKE THE HIGH ROAD AND DO WHAT IS RIGHT.

If we follow the four principles of our Code of Ethics throughout our organization, then we will achieve our fifth principle and ultimate goal, which is to:

**5. Reward our shareholders**

- As a company with stock that is traded publicly on the NASDAQ Stock Market, our shareholders are our business partners.
- We can only be successful so long as we are providing them with a good return on the money they invest in our Company.
- This, too, involves the element of trust. They trust us to use their investment wisely and to operate our business in such a way that it is profitable.
- Over the years Costco has been in business, we have consistently followed an upward trend in the value of our stock. Yes, we have had our ups and our downs, but the overall trend has been consistently up.
- We believe Costco stock is a good investment, and we pledge to operate our Company in such a way that our present and future stockholders, as well as our employees, will be rewarded for our efforts.

## Reporting of Violations and Enforcement

1. The Code of Ethics applies to all directors, officers, and employees of the Company. Conduct that violates the Code of Ethics will constitute grounds for disciplinary actions ranging from reprimand to termination and possible criminal prosecution.

2. All employees are expected to promptly report actual or suspected violations of law or the Code of Ethics. Federal law, other laws and Costco policy protect employees from retaliation if complaints are made in good faith. *Violations involving employees* should be reported to the responsible Executive Vice President, who shall be responsible for taking prompt and appropriate action to investigate and respond. *Other violations (such as those involving suppliers) and those involving accounting, internal control and auditing* should be reported to the general Counsel or the Chief Compliance Officer (999 Lake Drive, Issaquah, WA 98027), who shall be responsible for taking prompt and appropriate action to investigate and respond. Reports or complaints can also be made, confidentially if you choose, through the Whistleblower Policy link on the Company's eNet or Intranet site.

**What do Costco's Mission Statement and Code of Ethics have to do with you?**

# EVERYTHING!

The continued success of our Company depends on how well each of Costco's employees adheres to the high standards mandated by our Code of Ethics. And a successful company means increased opportunities for success and advancement for each of you.

No matter what your current job, you can put Costco's Code of Ethics to work every day. It's reflected in the energy and enthusiasm you bring to work, in the relationships you build with your management, your co-workers, our suppliers and our members.

By always choosing to do the right thing, you will build your own self-esteem, increase your chances for success and make Costco more successful, too. It is the synergy of ideas and talents, each of us working together and contributing our best, which makes Costco the great company it is today and lays the groundwork for what we will be tomorrow.

# REFERENCES

Allen, F. (1994). *Secret formula: How brilliant marketing and relentless salesmanship made Coca-Cola the best-known product in the world*. New York, NY: Harper Business.

Argenti, P. A. (2004). Collaborating with activists: How Starbucks works with NGOs. *California Management Review, 47*(1), 91–116.

Beardsley, S., & Farrell, D. (2005, May). Regulation that is good for competition. *The McKinsey Quarterly*. Retrieved from http://www.mckinseyquarterly.com/

Berliner, D. (2011). Public power, private gain. *Institute for Justice*. Retrieved from http://www.ij.org/component/content/article/42-liberty/1828-ij-report-documents-10000-plus-eminent-domain-abuses-across-us-

Berman, B. (2011). *Competing in tough times: Business lessons from L.L. Bean, Trader Joe's, Costco, and other world-class retailers*. Upper Saddle River, NJ: FT Press.

Bhattacharya, C. B., & Korschun, D. (2008). Stakeholder marketing: Beyond the four Ps and the customer. *Journal of Public Policy & Marketing, 27*(1), 113–116.

Big Charts. (2012). Comparison graph generated by the author using data from http://www.BigCharts.com

Bishop, M., & Green, M. (2010). *The road from ruin: How to revive capitalism and put America back on top*. New York, NY: Crown Business.

Blumenthal, L. (2009, April 13). Starbucks, Costco fight "card check" union bill. *The News Tribune*. Retrieved from http://www.thenewstribune.com/2009/04/13/707521 starbuckscostco-fight-card-check.html

Clancy, K. J., & Krieg, P. C. (2000). *Counterintuitive marketing*. New York, NY: Free Press.

CNBC (producer). (2009, June 3). *House of cards*. [Television broadcast]. New York, NY: CNBC. Retrieved from http://www.cnbc.com/id/15840232?video = 1145392808&play = 1

Conscious Capitalism. (2011). Retrieved from http://www.consciouscapitalism.org

Costco. (2009). Costco Corporate Sustainability Report. January. Retrieved from http://phx.corporate-ir.net/phoenix.zhtml?c = 83830&p = irol-govhighlights

Costco. (2010a). Costco Wholesale Annual Report 2010. Available at http://media.corporate-ir.net/media_files/irol/83/83830/CostcoLogoStandards.pdf

Costco. (2010b). Costco Mission Statement and Code of Ethics (updated March 2010). Corporate Governance and Citizenship: Investor Relations, Code of Ethics. Retrieved from http://phx.corporate-ir.net/phoenix.zhtml?c = 83830&p = irol-govhighlights

Costco, (2011a). Costco Investor Relations, Company Profile. Retrieved rom http://phx.corporateir.net/phoenix.zhtml?c = 83830&p = irol-homeprofile

Costco. (2011b). Costco Wholesale Corporation Comments on Its Operations in Japan Following the Major Earthquake. Retrieved from http://phx.corporate-ir.net/phoenix.zhtml?c = 83830&p = irol-newsArticle_print&ID = 1539149&highlight =

Costco. (2011c). Costco 2010 Proxy Statement. Retrieved from http://phx.corporateir.net/phoenix.zhtml?c = 83830&p = irol-reportsannual

Costco. (2011d). Costco Wholesale Supplier Code of Conduct. Retrieved from http://phx.corporatecir.net/phoenix.zhtml?c – 83830&p = irol-govhighlights

Costco. (2011e). Costco Statement on Seafood and Sustainability. Retrieved from http://phx.corporateir.net/phoenix.zhtml?c = 83830&p = irol-govhighlights

Day, G. S., & Schoemaker, P. (2006). *Peripheral vision: Detecting weak signals that will make or break your company*. Boston, MA: Harvard Business School Press.

De Soto, H. (2000). *The mystery of capital*. New York, NY: Basic Books.

Fortune. (2011, May 23rd). The lists. *Fortune*, p. F-3.

Freeman, R. E., Harrison, J. S., Wicks, A. C., Parmar, B. L., & De Colle, S. (2010). *Stakeholder theory: The state of the art*. Cambridge, UK: Cambridge University Press.

Gonzalez-Padron, T. L., & Nason, R.W. (2009, December). Market responsiveness to societal interests. *Journal of Macromarketing, 29*(4), 392–405.

Green, C. H. (2009, October 2009). Wall street run amok: Why Harvard's to blame. *BusinessWeek*. Retrieved from http://www.businessweek.com/

Greenpeace. (2011). Activist ad hoc website opposing Costco's seafood practices. Retrieved from http://www.oh-no-costco.com/

Helyar, J. (2003, November 24). The only company Wal-Mart fears. *Fortune*, pp. 158–166.

Hollender, J., & Breen, B. (2010). *The responsibility revolution: How the next generation of businesses will win*. San Francisco, CA: Jossey-Bass.

Hunt, S. D., & Vitell. S. J. (2006, December). The general theory of marketing ethics: A revision and three questions. *Journal of Macromarketing, 26*(2), 143–153.

Jargon, J. (2011, May 17). Ronald McDonald called out by health groups. *The Wall Street Journal*. Retrieved from http://online.wsj.com/article/SB1000142405274870350910457632961034035839 4.html?mod = WSJ_business_LeftSecondHighlights

Kirkpatrick, D. (2004, October 4). It's hard to manage if you don't blog. *Fortune*, p. 46.

Kocieniewski, D. (2011, March 25). G.E. turns the tax man away empty-handed. *New York Times*, pp. A1, A17.

Leverty, S. (2011). NGOs, the UN, and APA. Retrieved from http://www.apa.org/international/united-nations/publications.aspx

Lusch, R., & Webster, F. (2010). *Marketing's responsibility for the value of the empire* (Report #10-111). Marketing Science Institute Working Paper Series.

Lynch, J. (2010, June 30). Green blimp launches Greenpeace campaign against Costco. *Issaquah Reporter*. Retrieved from http://www.pnwlocalnews.com/east_king/iss/news/97482194.html

McKibben, B. (2011, February 22). Money pollution: The U.S. Chamber of Commerce darkens the skies [Web log post]. Retrieved from www.huffingtonpost.com

Mick, D. G., Bateman, T. S., & Lutz, R. J. (2009, June). Wisdom: Exploring the pinnacle of human virtues as a central link from micromarketing to macromarketing. *Journal of Macromarketing, 29*(2), 98–118.

National Geographic. (2011). Advertising Opportunities. Retrieved from http://ngm.national geographic.com/ngm/advertising.html

Nonaka, I., & Takeuchi, H. (2011). The wise leader: How CEOs can learn practical wisdom to help them do what's right for their companies – and society. *Harvard Business Review, 89*(5), 58–67.

Pendergrast, M. (1993). *For God, country and Coca-Cola: The unauthorized history of the great American soft drink and the company that makes it*. New York, NY: Charles Scribner's Sons.

Petty, R. D. (2005). Societal regulation of the marketing function: Does the patchwork create a quilt? *Journal of Public Policy & Marketing, 24*(1), 63–74.

Ponder, S. E. (2011). Success at sea: Quality and sustainability are hallmarks of Trident Seafoods. *The Costco Connection, 26*(2), 26, 27, and 29.

Raines, K. (2011, May 6). Author's interview with Karen Raines, Costco's Director of Corporate Sustainability at Costco headquarters in Issaquah, WA.

Rattner, S. (2010). *Overhaul: An insider's account of the Obama administration's emergency rescue of the auto industry*. Boston, MA: Houghton Mifflin Harcourt.

Reibstein, D. J., Day, G., & Wind, J. (2009). Guest editorial: Is marketing academia losing its way? *Journal of Marketing, 73*, 1–3.

RetailingWorks. (2011). Why sell to Wal-Mart and Sam's Club? Retrieved from http://www.retailingworks.com/why.htm

Rogers, J. E. (2011). The CEO of Duke Energy on learning to work with Green Activists. *Harvard Business Review, 89*(5), 51–54.

Schwartz, A. (2010, June 30). Greenpeace launches aggressive campaign against Costco. *Fast Company*. Retrieved from http://www.fastcompany.com/1665470/greenpeace-launches-aggressive-campaign-against-costco

Spar, D. L., & La Mure, L. T. (2003). The power of activism: Assessing the impact of NGOs on global business. *California Management Review, 45*(3), 78–101.

Srinivasan, R. (2011). Comments shared as panelist in *Marketing Strategy 3.0*. Special session at the American Marketing Association's Winter Educators' Conference.

Sternberg, R. J. (1998). A balance theory of wisdom. *Review of General Psychology 2,* 347–365.

Strong, M. (2009). *Be the solution: How entrepreneurs and conscious capitalists can solve all the world's problems.* New York, NY: Wiley.

Terlep, S., & Mitchell, J. (2011, May 1). GM revs up its lobbying. *The Wall Street Journal.* Retrieved from http://online.wsj.com

United Nations Department of Public Information (UNDPI). (2011). Non Governmental Organizations. Retrieved from http://www.un.org/wcm/content/site/dpingorelations/index.html

Varadarajan, R. (2011, February). *Marketing Strategy 3.0*. Special session at the American Marketing Association's Winter Educators' Conference.

Vieth, W. (2004, April 11). Most US firms paid no income taxes in '90s. *The Boston Globe.* Retrieved from http://www.boston.com

Volunteer Screening Blog. (2011). Featured Corporate Volunteer Program: Costco. Retrieved from http://www.volunteerscreeningblog.com/corporate-volunteer-programs/featured-corporate-volunteer-program-costco/

Wind, Y. (2008). A plan to invent the marketing we need today. *MIT Sloan Management Review*, pp. 21–28.

Yankelovich, D. (2006). *Profit with honor: The new stage of market capitalism.* New Haven, CT: Yale University Press.

York, B. (2008, September 8). What did Obama do as a community organizer? *National Review Online*. Retrieved from http://www.nationalreview.com/articles/225564/what-did-obama-do-community-organizer/byron-york#

## CHAPTER 5

# The Role of Business in Society

## IT WAS STRICTLY BUSINESS

### Coca-Cola CEO Doug Ivester

Son of a textile-factory worker and raised in North Georgia, Doug Ivester capped a remarkable rise through the financial and operations ranks of Coca-Cola, Inc. by taking the reins of the company as CEO and chairman of the board at the age of 50. He was systematic in his approach to work and diligent, even being classified by some as rigid (Morris, Sellers, & Tarpley, 2000). He was big on discipline as CFO and later as president and chief operating officer. By all accounts, he was a brilliant No. 2.

"The highly disciplined organizations are the most creative," Ivester said, "If you can create high discipline, in effect you've created security and safety. . . . It's follow-up. It's returning phone calls. It's adhering to the control system. We operate with a rigid control system. It is an enabler, not a restricter" (Morris et al., 2000, para. 15).

As CEO, Ivester would schedule meetings with top aides at 30-day intervals—12 months in advance. His geographic group presidents from around the world would leave him voice mails almost every night. He had Coca-Cola invest heavily in information technology and used the resulting information to manage in an analytical and data-driven manner. Ivester commanded a vast number of details, but he seemed to lose sight of the big picture at times.

For example, in October 1994, as the new president and COO, Ivester delivered a principal address at a major industry trade show in which he described himself as a wolf—highly independent, nomadic, and territorial. "I want your customers," Ivester told the shocked audience comprising competitors and partner companies. "I want your space on the shelves. … I want every single bit of beverage growth potential that exists out there" (Morris et al., 2000, para. 30). In this way, Ivester signaled he would not be a statesman for the industry but a relentless adversary to those outside the Coca-Cola marketing system.

But inside the Coca-Cola marketing system, Ivester missed the diplomacy required to lead the marketing system of Coca-Cola, which comprises many powerful bottling companies. Almost 90% of Coca-Cola's business lies in the hands of bottlers. The largest bottler, Coca-Cola Enterprises (CCE), handles 70% of the bottles and cans in the United States and is nearly as large as Coca-Cola itself. In 1998, the stock price of CCE fell from $37 to $18, which eliminated more than half of the market capitalization of CCE. To make matters worse for CCE, Ivester raised the price of Coca-Cola concentrated syrup, the one material ingredient sold by Coca-Cola to its downstream bottlers.

"The perception on the Street [Wall Street] was that Ivester was running the Coca-cola Co. at our expense," one high-ranking bottling executive said. "Some had the view that he was raping the bottlers" (Morris et al., 2000, para. 26).

Facing simmering alienation across Coca-Cola's 11 major bottlers around the world, former president and COO, Donald R. Keough, wrote a six-page letter to Ivester with constructive suggestions on how to improve things. Ivester sent Keough a one-line response thanking him for his input. The gregarious Keough remained well regarded and well connected to current board members of Coca-Cola, such as Warren Buffet and Herbert Allen for whom he served as chairman of Allen & Co. (a successful Wall Street investment-firm focused on media and entertainment industries). Keough also served on the board of Coca-Cola's largest customer, the McDonald's Corporation.

Ivester's lack of political sensitivities to bottlers extended to customers as well. He made a comment to a Brazilian magazine about Coca-Cola devoting ten years to developing vending machines that could automatically raise prices in hot weather (the bottlers are the ones who actually own and operate the vending machines in the Coca-Cola system). Customers, meanwhile, looked at such plans as being opportunistic and insulting to their dignity (Fishman, 2003). Pepsi quickly announced that it would never exploit customers in hot weather. Later, the media declared Ivester's off-handed comment to the Brazilian magazine as one of the "great moments in the history of price foolishness" (Fishman, 2003, para. 2). Such vending machine technology might have been accepted by customers if it were presented as dropping the price in cold weather, rather than raising it in hot weather.

In addition to all of Ivester's consultative shortcomings, Coca-Cola's was about to face a colossal disaster that the company was not prepared to handle. This disaster further emphasized Ivester's faults.

## Your Thoughts?

- How would you describe Ivester's regard for vertical command and control within the hierarchy of Coca-Cola compared with his regard for horizontal diplomacy with those outside of Ivester's chain of command?
- Why do you think Ivester would regard the vertical and horizontal dimensions of organizational life in this way?
- What does this suggest about the development of leaders for major corporations?

## CHAPTER OVERVIEW AND LEARNING OBJECTIVES

This chapter will examine the role of business in society. Businesses provide employment and income for citizens. Businesses can also do more in society, and increasingly businesses are going beyond a two-capital approach focused on accumulating money and stuff. Still, a debate continues about the appropriateness of taking a five-capital approach that includes the first two types of capital plus human, social, and environmental capital (as discussed in Chapter 1). This chapter will examine emerging business trends, such as how corporate social responsibility has affected the business world. This chapter will also share more about the United Nations (UN) Global Compact (calling on businesses to address human rights, labor rights, and protection of the natural environment), as well as the Conscious Capitalism movement. Clif Bar, Inc.'s founder Gary Erickson is featured as a Maverick Who Made It by going against conventional thinking about selling his venture for millions of dollars and instead developing it as a distinctive nutrition-bar company with "mojo." After this chapter, you should be able to answer the following questions:

- Should a CEO regard his or her firm only as a profit-generating unit in an atomized universe of independent and competing businesses?
- Is the business of business simply business?
- How does corporate social responsibility (CSR) relate to taking a stakeholder orientation as presented in Chapter 4?
- What is the UN Global Compact?
- How are firms beginning to disclose nonfinancial reporting?
- What does Conscious Capitalism say about how to integrate concerns about environmental, social, and governance (ESG) into the life of the business?

# A CRISIS FOR COKE BEGINS IN BELGIUM

On June 8, 1999, an outbreak of health complaints in Belgium linked Coca-Cola to headaches and nausea experienced by some who had consumed Coca-Cola (Nemery, Fischler, Boogaerts, Lison, & Willems, 2002). These reports came less than two weeks after another food scare had begun. On May 25, Belgian and French media disclosed leaked reports about contamination of animal feed with dioxin—a cancer-causing substance. Subsequently, a major food scare ensued with a massive recall of eggs and chicken, followed by almost all meat and dairy products. As a result of this dioxin crisis in Belgium, the Ministers of Health and Agriculture were forced to resign.

Although Coca-Cola had a crisis management strategy, the complaints soon mushroomed into a crisis in Belgium beyond anything Coca-Cola had prepared as a worst-case scenario. The first reported victims of Coca-Cola were dozens of school children. With Belgian elections only two days away, the Health Minister took the most drastic action and ordered the recall and destruction of all Coca-Cola products. This amounted to 17 million cases at an estimated cost of $103 million. Health authorities in France asked Coca-Cola to shut down its Dunkirk plant near the Belgian border. The media repeatedly showed pictures of loads of dead chickens being dumped alongside loads of soft drinks being discarded.

Officials in Belgium and France complained repeatedly about Coca-Cola's inability to tell them in a timely manner what the company knew (Hays, 1999). Coca-Cola representatives sometimes appeared confused in their explanations about Coca-Cola's role in the crisis, and press conferences did not correspond to the brand's image of youth and energy (Nemery et al., 2002). On June 16, in a statement issued at 10:38 P.M. Brussels time, Ivester issued a terse apology from Atlanta saying, "We deeply regret any problems experienced by our European consumers" (Hays, 1999, p. 4).

Ten days after the first schoolboy became queasy after drinking a Coke, the top company officials arrived in Belgium. But when the Coca-Cola officials did respond, they tried to minimize the reports of illness. "It may make you feel sick, but it is not harmful," said Rob Baskin, a spokesman from Coca-Cola headquarters in Atlanta (Hays, 1999, p. 4).

By this time, governments in other countries in Europe, such as Germany and Spain, were recalling thousands of cases of Coca-Cola. On June 18, Ivester arrived in Belgium. Three days later, he issued a memo to all of this company's 28,000 employees about "the Belgian issue" in which the company's "quality control processes in Belgium faltered," adding, "I have personally tasted the products and held the packages involved with no adverse reaction" (Hays, 1999, p. 4). On June 23, the Belgian authorities allowed the sale of Coca-Cola products again. Coca-Cola ran a full-page ad in Belgian newspapers topped by a photo of a smiling Ivester. "I should have spoken to you earlier, and I apologize for that," the ad read. "Over the past several days in Belgium, we allowed two breakdowns to occur in fulfilling the promise of Coca-Cola" (Hays, 1999, p. 5).

Surprising to some, Coca-Cola's response to the incident in Belgium lacked regard for the central importance of customer's perceptions, even if these perceptions are divorced from the facts. Three years later in 2002, toxicology researchers described the incident as a "sociogenic or psychogenic illness . . . a constellation of symptoms suggestive of an organic illness, but without identifiable cause occurring between two or more persons who share beliefs related to those symptoms" (Nemery et al., 2002, p. 1662). In effect, these researchers said Coca-Cola found itself in a difficult situation in which media coverage distortedly conjured the notion among Europeans that a foreign multinational company not only poisoned Belgians but also began with poisoning Belgian children.

In the days after the first health complaints in Belgium, the delays and partial disclosures by Coca-Cola worsened things in the minds of Europeans. In a networked world connected by mass media and other communication technologies, a more immediate and decisive admission of a problem along with a proposal for its remedy to all stakeholders across a region—not just locally—would have been the more effective course of action to take. The Coca-Cola incident in Belgium highlights the hazard of viewing one's firm only as a profit-generating unit in an atomized universe of independent and competing businesses. In markets of the 21st century, it is not just "strictly business"—especially for corporations. Diplomacy must be included in the business leader's tool kit. The context of business matters, and the subtleties of the context can be understood by considering the history of events and the views of stakeholders in firm decision making.

In December of that year, Ivester resigned from Coca-Cola after receiving pressure to do so from key board members, such as Buffet and Allen (Morris et al., 2000). Observers noted that Ivester's replacement, Doug Daft, an Australian running Coca-Cola's Asian business, would need to repair relations on all fronts, "from bottlers to foreign governments to customers" (Morris et al., 2000, para. 7). The board made it clear it wanted no more one-man high-wire acts.

"It's a little like mountain climbing," a source close to the Coca-Cola board said. "Anyone can get to a certain level. But very few can function well in the really rare air. Doug [Ivester] was simply unable to give people a sense of purpose or direction" (Morris et al., 2000, para. 12).

To his credit, Ivester has found ways to benefit others from his experience. Ivester now imparts wisdom from his career in a brutally honest way with eight selected students from the University of Georgia's Terry College of Business twice each year on his 18,000-acre farm in south Georgia called Deer Run Plantation (McNair, 2011). "Tomorrow's business leaders will need to understand and embrace a diverse, complex and ever-changing world," Ivester said (Dodson, 2009).

## IS THE BUSINESS OF BUSINESS BUSINESS?

As a "brilliant No. 2," Doug Ivester could focus on the internal affairs of the Coca-Cola Company and impose his discipline and procedures for operations. As the No. 1 executive, Ivester extended his management style of command and control but lacked the ability for inclusive strategy development. Ivester did not have a collaborative vision of the future for Coca-Cola with other stakeholders, such as bottlers, investors, government officials, media, as well as society and communities. Ivester's view of business in society was one in which business conducts its operations with passing regard to other stakeholders.

Ivester operated under the agency view of management. In the agency view of management, the goals of business are predominately financial, and ethical actions by firms are often perceived as discretionary, if they are not required by law (Laczniak & Murphy, 2006). Also in the agency view, management acts solely as an agent of the stockholder and is responsible for maximizing investor returns—the supposed primary concern of shareholder groups. Ethics is seen as costly because it frequently requires the expenditure of organizational resources to conform to social norms. The agency view of management was crystallized in the writing of a famed economist of the 20th century Milton Friedman.

## Friedman: The Social Responsibility of Business Is to Make Profit

As a libertarian, Milton Friedman championed laissez-faire economics as a professor at the University of Chicago and at the Hoover Institution. As a leading monetarist economist, he opposed the existence of the Federal Reserve Bank. However, he argued that because the Fed did exist, the government should merely increase the money supply by 3% each year and only have contact with markets through the courts when businesses needed their civil disputes resolved. Friedman won a Nobel Prize in economics and commanded much intellectual authority before dying in 2006.

In 1970, Friedman wrote a provocative essay that appeared in *The New York Times Magazine* proposing that the social responsibility of business is to increase its profits (Friedman, 1970). It is important to remember that the publication of this piece by Friedman came at a time before either Margaret Thatcher in the United Kingdom or Ronald Reagan in the United States had taken office. These two leaders were proponents of scaling back the role of government in society (through deregulation of the economy and reducing taxes) and of encouraging more of a role for the private sector (through job creation with the accompanying benefits of wealth for citizens). Business education in the United States had not exploded as it did later in the next 20 years with a groundswell in MBA programs. In other words, Friedman was an intellectual leader.

In his essay, Friedman decried any other purpose for business other than increasing its profits. However, he did allow the "hypocritical window-dressing" of businesses spending to improve its image in the community by improving amenities in the community or improving the community's government. Through these ways, hiring and retaining employees might be done at lower costs. But Friedman denounced doing such actions as an exercise of "social responsibility" because doing so only strengthens the too prevalent view that pursuing profits is wicked and immoral. With such a view, the impulse to curb and control business through some external force persists. In this way, talk of social responsibility in business is pure and unadulterated socialism and undermines the basis of a free society:

> Once this view is adopted, the external forces that curb the market will not be the social conscience, however highly developed of the pontificating executives; it will be the iron fist of Government bureaucrats. . . . There is one and only one social responsibility of business – to use its resources and engage in activities designed to increase its profits so long as it stays within the rules of the game, which is to say, engages in open and free competition without deception or fraud. (Friedman, 1970, para. 29)

## The Debate Begins: Mackey Challenges Friedman

Thirty-five years after the publication of Friedman's piece, John Mackey, founder and CEO of Whole Foods Market, stepped up to do what other economists feared to do—debate Friedman. The debate focused on the topic of the social responsibility of business in the October 2005 issue of *Reason*. Mackey leads the world's largest retailer of natural and organic foods, with stores throughout North America and the United Kingdom. Like Friedman, Mackey identifies himself as a libertarian, but he says his ideas are neither left-wing or right-wing. Instead, he declares them to be "up-wing" (Mackey, 2009a).

Citing his 27-year-old company's sales of $4.6 billion in the previous year, as well as net profits of more than $160 million, and a market capitalization of more than $8 billion, Mackey asserted that Whole Foods measures success by "how much value we can create for all six of our most important stakeholders: customers, team members [employees], investors, vendors, communities and the environment" (Mackey, 2005, para. 5). In this way, Mackey adopted a stakeholder perspective (elaborated upon in Chapter 4) to debate Friedman.

Mackey explained that there was no magic formula to calculate how much value each stakeholder should receive from the company. "It is a dynamic process that evolves with the competitive marketplace," Mackey said. "No stakeholder remains satisfied for long. It is the function of the company leadership to develop solutions that continually work for the common good" (Mackey, 2005, para. 6).

Mackey also addressed one of Friedman's criticisms of corporate philanthropy as stealing from investors. He offered more detail about the philanthropy of Whole Foods that continues after 20 years. Five days each year, Whole Foods holds a "5 % Day" in which 5 % of a store's total sales are directed to a nonprofit organization. The stores select the beneficiary groups and tend to focus on groups with large membership lists. Those on the lists receive calls the week of the "5 % Day" to shop the store to support the organization. This usually brings in hundreds of new or lapsed customers. In this way, the "5 % Day" benefits a local group, but it is also an excellent marketing technique that has benefitted the investors of Whole Foods immensely over the years.

When Whole Foods drafted its mission statement in 1985, it announced that it would donate 5 % of the company's net profits to philanthropy. This predated the initial public offering of stock, and no investors have ever raised objections to the policy. Mackey pointedly asks, "How can Whole Foods' philanthropy be 'theft' from the current investors if the original owners of the company unanimously approved the policy and all subsequent investors made their investment after the policy was in effect and well publicized?"(Mackey, 2005, para. 11).

Not stopping there, Mackey asserts that shareholders of a public company own their stock voluntarily and can sell their shares if they do not agree with the philosophy of the business. Alternatively, shareholders can submit a resolution at the annual shareholders meeting to change any policy of the firm (a number of Whole Foods's policies have been changed this way):

> Corporate philanthropy is a good thing, but it requires the legitimacy of investor approval. In my experience, most investors understand that it can be beneficial to

both the corporation and to the larger society. That doesn't answer the question of *why* we give money to the community stakeholder. For that, you should turn to one of the fathers of free-market economics, Adam Smith. *The Wealth of Nations* was a tremendous achievement, but economists would be well served to read Smith's other great book, *The Theory of Moral Sentiments*. There he explains that human nature isn't just about self-interest. It also includes sympathy, empathy, friendship, love, and the desire for social approval. As motives for human behavior, these are at least as important as self-interest. For many people, they are more important. (Mackey, 2005, para. 14, emphasis in original)

In reply, Friedman (2005) surprisingly said, "The differences between John Mackey and me regarding the social responsibility of business are for the most part rhetorical. Strip off the camouflage, and it turns out we are in essential agreement" (para. 2). Friedman (2005) noted the success of Whole Foods in a competitive industry and observed, "had it devoted any significant fraction of its resources to exercising a social responsibility unrelated to the bottom line, it would be out of business by now or would have been taken over" (para. 2).

Friedman (2005) did assert that corporate philanthropy being a good thing is "flatly wrong" (para. 8). Friedman declared that outrageous tax laws contribute to this practice making sense because a stockholder can give more to charity if a corporation gives out of pre-tax earnings, rather than the stockholder's earnings, which would be double-taxed (taxes paid by the corporation, and then taxes paid by the stockholder on capital gains on the sale of the stock).

Finally, Friedman (2005) proposed that his statement, "the social responsibility of business is to increase profits," and Mackey's statement, "the enlightened corporation should try to create value for all of its constituencies," are equivalent (para. 15):

Note first that I refer to *social* responsibility, not financial, or accounting, or legal. It is social precisely to allow for the constituencies to which Mackey refers. Maximizing profits is an end from the private point of view; it is a means from the social point of view. A system based on private property and free markets is a sophisticated means of enabling people to cooperate in their economic activities without compulsion; it enables separated knowledge to assure that each resource is used for its most valued use, and is combined with other resources in the most efficient way. Of course, this is abstract and idealized. The world is not ideal. There are all sorts of deviations from the perfect market—many, if not most, I suspect, due to government interventions. But with all its defects, the current largely free-market, private-property world seems to me vastly preferable to a world in which a large fraction of resources is used and distributed by 501c(3)s and their corporate counterparts. (Friedman, 2005, paras. 15–16, emphasis in original)

In sum, Friedman acknowledges that incorporating stakeholder concerns in the marketing strategy of a business can prove effective in the less-than-perfect world in which business exists. However, he cautions that coercive plays by stakeholders could thwart the social good a business can provide, primarily through profit making. Of course, few stakeholders of a business hold coercive power over a business. Although Mother Nature would ultimately be one such stakeholder (through resource depletion or natural disaster), government would be the likeliest stakeholder to wield coercive power over the business. More will be presented on the role of the state in society in Chapter 6.

# CORPORATE SOCIAL RESPONSIBILITY

## What Does CSR Look Like in Business?

Zadek (2001) has asserted that the role of business in society is the 21st century's most important and contentious public policy issue. Business leaders recently have called for businesses to acknowledge the implicit social contract of obligations and mutual advantage between business and society (Davis, 2005; Yankelovich, 2007). Although the agency model or shareholder value model still holds sway in corporate board rooms throughout Anglo-Saxon countries (Davis, 2005), unenlightened self-interest seems to be giving way to enlightened self-interest (Mendonca & Miller, 2007). In a 2007 McKinsey Global Survey of 2,687 executives from around the world (36% of them CEOs or other C-level executives), only 16% reported believing that high returns to investors should be a corporation's sole focus (McKinsey, 2007).

As detailed in the previous section, government, acting as society's agent, has a variety of influences on business, even rescuing failed businesses (such as GM and Chrysler). Here, the costs to society by the liquidation of these firms were deemed to be too high by a Republican administration in 2008 and later a Democrat administration in 2009. In sum, the reported beliefs of executives that profits are not the sole purpose of business, and the actions of the U.S. government, suggest that support for a social contract of obligations and mutual advantage between business and society already exists in some form.

Although many agree that CSR refers to the duties of the firm to society (Smith, 2003), there is little consensus about the nature or scope of the firm's obligations to society (Berger, Cunningham, & Drumwright, 2007). Industry Canada, the department of the Canadian Government with responsibility for regional economic development, investment, and innovation, explains CSR in the following way:

> CSR is a concept that frequently overlaps with similar approaches such as corporate sustainability, corporate sustainable development, corporate responsibility, and corporate citizenship. While CSR does not have a universal definition, many see it as the private sector's way of integrating the economic, social, and environmental imperatives of their activities. As such, CSR closely resembles the business pursuit of sustainable development and the triple bottom line. In addition to integration into corporate structures and processes, CSR also frequently involves creating innovative and proactive solutions to societal and environmental challenges, as well as collaborating with both internal and external stakeholders to improve CSR performance. (Industry Canada, 2011)

Pursuing CSR from a desire to do good (the "normative case"), or from enlightened self-interest (the "business case"), has characterized firms' responses to societal obligations over time. Philanthropy has long been a mechanism for businesses and business persons to give back (Bishop & Green, 2008). But philanthropy might also allow monopolistic-prone businesses and industrialists to pillage first and then give back later to a few, as a means to forestall societal impatience with the deleterious business practices of monopolistic businesses (Edwards, 2010). Those who have ever experienced frustration with a Microsoft operating system for a PC, such as Windows Vista, might wonder whether the good works of the Bill and Melinda Gates Foundation (which address extreme poverty and poor health in developing countries, as well as the failures of America's education system) make up for the lack of choice in operating systems for PCs all consumers experience in a "competitive marketplace."

Additionally, "cause marketing" is increasingly observed despite claims by corporations that their philanthropic efforts are not marketing, per se. Pepsi chose not to spend $20 million on a handful of Super Bowl ads in early 2010, and instead, the company asked the public to vote online for charities and community groups to receive grants ranging from $5,000 to $250,000 (The Economist, 2010). This Pepsi Refresh campaign is an example of cause marketing in which firms try to win customers by ostentatiously doing good with products not inherently ethical (such as "fair trade" goods), but with boosted moral credentials through an association with a cause.

## The Benefits of CSR for Firms

Longtime senior-partner at consulting firm McKinsey and Company, Ian Davis sees both the shareholder value model of firm governance as well as many initial efforts in CSR (defensive in nature or merely for image enhancement) as missing the enormous opportunity when firms consider the relevance of social and environmental issues to their future strategy (Davis, 2005). Indeed, some assert that pursuing a purpose of increasing shareholder value means merely playing by the rules of the economic game and is a constraint, not a purpose, for a business (Campbell & Alexander, 1997). Defining a business' purpose in a well-articulated way is decisive in moving the firm toward an integration of the normative and businesses cases that would result in value creation for the firm and its stakeholders. The more focused and detailed a purpose is, the more likely the firm will be able to develop a winning strategy for itself. When The Body Shop, a global manufacturer and retailer of naturally inspired and ethically produced beauty and cosmetics products, declared one of its purposes to "make cosmetics that don't hurt animals," it limited itself (The Body Shop, n.d.). However, this self-imposed limit on its range of strategic choices helped to simplify its strategy development by focusing on customers who liked this position, as well as on finding suppliers who would agree to The Body Shop's stringent standards for ingredients and processes in production and logistics. The Body Shop is now owned by L'Oreal.

Davis (2005) proposes that "the ultimate purpose of business is the efficient provision of goods and services that society wants" (p. 75). In this view, profits are the reward of successfully delivering to society what it wants. Too often, firms have perceived social and environmental issues, such as animal rights, poverty alleviation, water conservation, energy resource depletion, obesity, healthcare, and climate change, in a defensive manner.

The contributions of business to society suggest how firms might actually effectively help address these and other issues in the future. For example, businesses not only provide employment, but they also harness physical and financial capital on a large scale to innovate and achieve productivity gains for society. In the immediate aftermath of Hurricane Katrina in 2005, Wal-Mart trucks delivered relief supplies to New Orleans before governments were able to do so. This suggests how a big business's innovations lead to acquiring the capacity and flexibility in its marketing systems to deliver needed supplies to a stricken area better than government can.

Firms treating CSR issues as tangential to their operations (relegating them to the public relations or corporate affairs departments) miss the opportunity for shifting the focus of the firms' leadership to important new areas of interest. Firms treating CSR as organic to their operations tend to shape public debate on issues relevant for society, and subsequently, to re-direct the firms' R&D efforts to rewarding areas of the future (Porter, 2006). In other words, these social and environmental issues offer opportunities for firms, not just threats or risks (Kanter, 2009). In short, value-creation opportunities come with these social and environmental issues.

Alert businesses can gain advantage over their competitors by identifying and developing effective and efficient ways to meet these needs before anyone else. For example, E. I. du Pont de Nemours and Company (DuPont), a major industrial company, has identified megatrends, and it has focused its R&D efforts as a chemical company on (a) increasing food production, (b) decreasing dependence on fossil fuels, (c) protecting lives and the environment, and (d) meeting emerging market demand for science-based solutions to problems there (Kullman, 2010). At the end of 2009, DuPont reported it has introduced 675 new products or services that make people safer. The firm intends to introduce 1,000 of these by 2015.

## Efforts to Develop Standards for CSR

### The UN Global Compact

In 2001, DuPont endorsed the UN Global Compact, which is a strategic policy initiative for businesses intended to align their operations and strategies with ten universally accepted principles in the areas of human rights, labor, environment, and anti-corruption (see Table 5.1). The UN realized that meaningful progress on the UN Millennium Development Goals to eradicate poverty and related social ills by 2015 would not be made without the participation of businesses. Some examples of social ills are women's inequality, poor education, health epidemics, environmental degradation, and exclusion from the global economy. In 1999, former UN Secretary-General of the United Nations Kofi Annan addressed the Davos World Economic Forum. Annan challenged business leaders to provide a human face for globalization by joining a global compact of shared values and principles (UN Global Compact, 2010). The resulting UN Global Compact resulted from principles contained in four existing declarations: (a) the Universal Declaration of Human Rights, (b) the International Labor Organization's Declaration on Fundamental Principles and Rights at Work, (c) the Rio Declaration on Environment and Development, and (d) the United Nations Convention Against Corruption.

Although UN Secretary-General Ban Ki-moon reported that almost 6,000 businesses across 130 countries (with about half of these having more than 250 employees) had signed the UN Global Compact by 2010 (Ki-moon, 2010), the majority of businesses in the world still have not signed the UN Global Compact. Because of requirements for businesses to post communications on progress (COPs) each year, more than 1,000 businesses have been de-listed as signatories as a result of lack of communication about their progress on adhering to the principles of the UN Global Compact (UN Global Compact, 2010). Among U.S. businesses, reasons for not signing the UN Global Compact relate to concerns about the implications of labor rights of the Compact, as well as to being involved in a UN endeavor (Williams, 2004).

**Table 5.1**   The Ten Principles of the UN Global Compact (UN Global Compact, 2010)

**Human Rights**

- Principle 1: Businesses should support and respect the protection of internationally proclaimed human rights; and

- Principle 2: make sure that they are not complicit in human rights abuses.

**Labor**

- Principle 3: Businesses should uphold the freedom of association and the effective recognition of the right to collective bargaining;

- Principle 4: the elimination of all forms of forced and compulsory labor;

- Principle 5: the effective abolition of child labor; and

- Principle 6: the elimination of discrimination in respect of employment and occupation.

**Environment**

- Principle 7: Businesses should support a precautionary approach to environmental challenges;

- Principle 8: undertake initiatives to promote greater environmental responsibility; and

- Principle 9: encourage the development and diffusion of environmentally friendly technologies.

**Anti-Corruption**

- Principle 10: Businesses should work against corruption in all its forms, including extortion and bribery.

Although the principles read as if they were drafted by regulators of business intent on constraining business operations, some nongovernmental organizations (NGOs) have criticized the Compact for lack of accountability for businesses signing the compact. In other words, the UN Global Compact is flawed because it is voluntary. Although these NGOs seek a binding legal framework for the transnational behavior of business in the realms of human rights, environment, and labor, they do recognize the UN Global Compact's intent to define expectations for businesses about their role in society.

## Principals for Responsible Management Education and Responsible Investment

The Compact has garnered attention around the world for the role of business in societies. While providing far-reaching aspirations with little implementation guidance, the Compact has spawned efforts such as the Principles for Responsible Management Education (PRME) in 2008, which now has more than 300 participating business schools agreeing to the principles and reporting on their progress annually (Woo, 2010). These six principles are included in the Appendix to this chapter. Additionally, the Compact has spawned the Principles for Responsible Investment, which encourages investors and investment groups, such as pension funds, to integrate ESG issues across their investment operations.

## The Global Reporting Initiative

Several voluntary reporting efforts are also enabling more businesses to embrace a stakeholder orientation and report more meaningfully on their ESG initiatives. The Global Reporting Initiative (GRI) is an independent, global organization whose purpose is to make reporting on ESG issues as commonplace as reporting on financial performance—and as important to firm success (Eccles & Krzus, 2010). In 2000, GRI released its first set of guidelines for sustainability reporting. These guidelines are developed in an ongoing way using a multi-stakeholder process. Currently, the third generation of guidelines, G3, is in use. These guidelines are now available in 25 different languages.

GRI and the UN Global Compact are collaborating about how to use the GRI guidelines for the COPs required by the Compact. In other words, the annual updates firms give on their progress in implementing the Compact would be done in a form similar to what GRI has established for reporting on ESG efforts by firms. Almost 1,400 businesses registered GRI reports in 2009 (GRI, 2011).

## The International Standards Organization: ISO 26000

ISO 26000 is a voluntary guidance standard for integrating businesses' responsibilities toward society into the fundamental expectations of business organizations (Bernhart & Maher, 2011). Emanating from the International Standards Organization based in Switzerland, ISO 26000 was developed by a global, multi-stakeholder group consisting of thousands of contributors and reviewers from more than 90 countries. The International Standards Organization is the same organization that fields voluntary standards for quality processes (ISO 9000), as well as for environmental management (ISO 14001), as previously discussed. The seven core subjects that comprise ISO 26000 are shown in Figure 5.1.

**Figure 5.1**   The Seven Core Subjects of ISO 26000 for Social Responsibility

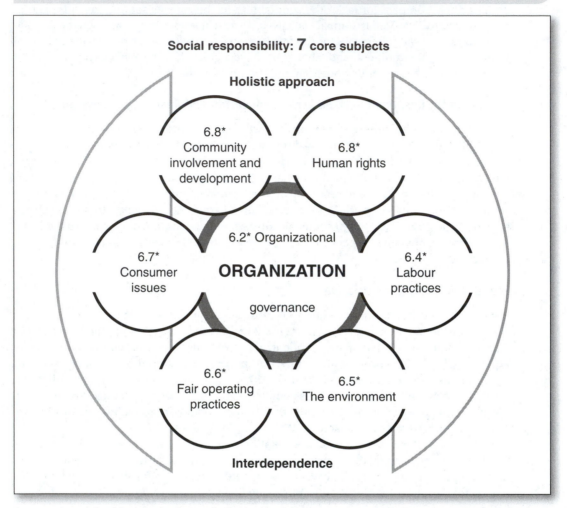

*Source:* © International Organization for Standardization. Available at http://www.iso.org/iso/sr_discovering_iso26000#std -graph1

Although the ISO emphatically asserts that ISO 26000 will not lead to certification, these standards will provide a framework for firms to develop and communicate their GSE endeavors to stakeholder groups. These guidance standards became finalized in December 2010, and as more businesses implement ISO 26000 standards, more firms will want to learn about the process of improving their firm's effectiveness in regard to ESG.

In sum, the UN Global Compact has won the attention of important actors in business as well as in civil society to give serious consideration for the role of business in the new economic circumstances of the 20th century. The successful fielding of voluntary standards, such as GRI's for sustainability reporting and ISO 26000 for integrating social responsibility across the organization, contributes valuably to making a stakeholder orientation a more meaningful approach to conducting business today and in the future.

## Lessons From Novo Nordisk

Novo Nordisk, a Danish-based pharmaceutical company, has focused on developing drugs for people with diabetes, hemophilia, and growth hormone deficiency for almost 90 years (Novo Nordisk, 2011). The firm has more than 30,000 employees working in 74 countries, and it markets its products in approximately 180 countries. In 2001, Novo Nordisk signed the UN Global Compact. Since 2004, Novo Nordisk has reported annually on its ESG performance (Eccles & Krzus, 2010) using GRI's G3 Sustainability Reporting Guidelines. This enables analysts and stakeholders to more readily grasp issues the firm encounters in the ESG realm but also to make comparisons of Novo Nordisk with other firms reporting on their ESG performance.

Although financial reporting is highly regulated, nonfinancial reporting is still in its infancy. For this reason, Novo Nordisk uses AccountAbility's AA1000 Assurance Standard in its ongoing effort to develop its sustainability reporting. The AA1000 Series of Standards is based on the principles of (a) *inclusivity:* people should have a say in the decisions that have an impact on them, (b) *materiality:* decision makers should identify and be clear about the issues that matter, and (c) *responsiveness:* organizations should be transparent about their actions.

Novo Nordisk has become a leader in sustainability reporting and now integrates financial and nonfinancial reporting. Such reporting is referred to as One Report and does not necessarily imply a single document but the collection of the material measures of financial and nonfinancial (ESG) performance. In this way, Novo Nordisk offers a glimpse of the future in ESG reporting. Figure 5.2 depicts the nonfinancial statement page from Novo Nordisk's 2011 annual report (Novo Nordisk, 2011). Note how this nonfinancial statement features social performance as well as environmental performance. Under social performance, patients, employees, and assurance comprise the three categories of reporting. Under assurance, the ethicality of Novo Nordisk is made more evident to stakeholders with information on (a) survey results focused on the company's reputation with key stakeholders, (b) the percentage of employees trained in ethics, (c) warning letters received and re-inspections required, and (d) audits performed on its suppliers. The company also puts an abundance of other ESG information on its website to allow different stakeholders the ability to create their own report on Novo Nordisk.

The continuing effort to improve corporate transparency can be seen in the story of Novo Nordisk. At least five U.S. companies, American Electric Power (an energy service company servicing more than 5 million customers in the Midwest), KKR (a Wall Street investment company), Pfizer (a pharmaceutical company), Southwest Airlines, and United Technologies declare that they practice integrated reporting (Eccles & Serafeim, 2011). Natura, a Brazilian cosmetics company, and Philips are acknowledged as leaders in integrative reporting and have been reporting this way since 2008.

**Figure 5.2**  Financial and Nonfinancial Reporting in Novo Nordisk's 2011 Annual Report

| | | 2011 | 2010 | Change |
|---|---|---|---|---|
| **Financial performance** | | | | |
| Sales total | DKK million | **66,346** | 60,776 | 9.2% |
| Diabetes care | DKK million | **50,425** | 45,710 | 10.3% |
| -of which modern insulins | DKK million | **28,765** | 26,601 | 8.1% |
| -of which Victoza® | DKK million | **5,991** | 2,317 | 158.6% |
| Biopharmaceuticals | DKK million | **15,921** | 15,066 | 5.7% |
| Gross profit | DKK million | **53,757** | 49,096 | 9.5% |
| Gross margin | % of sales | **81.0** | 80.8 | |
| Sales and distribution costs | % of sales | **28.6** | 29.9 | |
| Research and development costs | % of sales | **14.5** | 15.8 | |
| Administrative expenses | % of sales | **4.9** | 5.0 | |
| Operating profit | DKK million | **22,374** | 18,891 | 18.4% |
| Net profit | DKK million | **17,097** | 14,403 | 18.7% |
| Effective tax rate | % | **22.0** | 21.2 | |
| Capital expenditure, net | DKK million | **3,003** | 3,308 | (9.2%) |
| Free cash flow | DKK million | **18,112** | 17,013 | 6.5% |
| | | | | Long-term financial targets[1] |
| **Long-term financial targets** | | | | |
| Operating profit margin | % | **33.7** | 31.1 | 35% |
| Growth in operating profit | % | **18.4** | 26.5 | 15% |
| Operating profit after tax to net operating assets[1] | % | **77.9** | 63.6 | 90% |
| Cash to earnings (three-year average) | % | **112.8** | 115.6 | 90% |
| **Social performance** | | | | |
| Healthcare professionals trained or educated in diabetes | 1,000 | **835** | 373 | 123.9% |
| Donations | DKK million | **81** | 84 | (3.6%) |
| Employees (total) | Number | **32,632** | 30,483 | 7.0% |

| | | | | |
|---|---|---|---|---|
| Average of full-time employees | Number | **31,499** | 29,423 | 7.1% |
| Employee turnover | % | **9.8** | 9.1 | |
| Relevant employees trained in business ethics | % | **99** | 98 | |
| | | | | Long term social targets |
| **Long-term social targets** | | | | |
| Least developed countries where Novo Nordisk sells insulin according to the differential pricing policy | % | **75** | 67 | 100% |
| Engaging culture | Scale 1-5 | **4.3** | 4.3 | 4.0 |
| Diverse senior management teams | % | 62 | 54 | 100% by 2014 |
| **Environmental performance** | | | | |
| Energy consumption | 1,000 GI | **2,187** | 2,234 | (2.1%) |
| Water consumption | 1,000 m$^3$ | **2,136** | 2,047 | 4.3% |
| $CO_2$ emissions from energy consumption | 1,000 tons | **93** | 95 | (2.1%) |
| | | | | Long-term environmental targets |
| **Long-term environmental targets** | | | | |
| Energy consumption (change compared with 2007) | % | **(2.1)** | (20) | 11% reduction by 2011 |
| Water consumption (change compared with 2007) | % | **(34)** | (37) | 11% reduction by 2011 |
| $CO^2$ emissions from energy consumption (change compared with 2004) | | **(56)** | (55) | 11% reduction by 2014 |
| **Share performance** | | | | |
| Diluted earnings per share/ADR | DKK | **29.99** | 24.60 | 21.9% |
| Dividend per share (proposed) | DKK | **14.00** | 10.00 | 40.0% |
| Closing share price (B shares) | DKK | **660** | 629 | 4.9% |
| Market capitalisation (B shares)[2] | DKK billion | **296** | 292 | 1.4% |

*Source:* Novo Nordisk (2011, p. 2).

[1]The long-term financial targets were updated in February 2012. Please refer to p.6.
[2]Novo Nordisk B shares (excluding treasury shares).

**Table 5.2**   Multinational Company Philips's Report on Supplier Audits

| Location | Initial Audits 2010 | Continued Conformance Audits 2010 | Workers Employed at Sites Audited in 2010[1] | Average Number of Limited Tolerance Noncompliances 2010[2] | Average Number of Zero Tolerance Noncompliances 2010[2] |
|---|---|---|---|---|---|
| **China** | 113 | 94 | 174,431 | 13 | 4 |
| India | 15 | 11 | 7,770 | 15 | 3 |
| Indonesia | 6 | 4 | 4,657 | 7 | 1 |
| Philippines | 1 | — | 1,627 | 8 | 6 |
| Vietnam | 2 | — | 42 | 10 | — |
| **Asia excluding China** | 24 | 15 | 14,096 | 12 | 3 |
| Brazil | 14 | 4 | 3,978 | 13 | 4 |
| Mexico | 7 | — | 2,096 | 17 | 6 |
| **LATAM** | 21 | 4 | 6,074 | 14 | 4 |
| Ukraine | 2 | — | 240 | 3 | 2 |
| **EMEA** | 2 | — | 240 | 3 | 2 |
| **Total** | 160 | 113 | 194,841 | 13 | 4 |

[1]Based on information provided during audit.
[2]Average noncompliances per audit.

*Note:* LATAM = Latin America; EMEA = Europe, Middle East and Africa.

*Source:* Philips (2010).

Another example of a major company now measuring and reporting information on ESG factors is the Philips Corporation, which specializes in healthcare, lighting, and consumer products. Philips reports on its suppliers in its sustainability reporting, as shown in Table 5.2. The two right columns present evidence that not all suppliers pass the audits conducted by Philips, and the company shares this information with its stakeholders.

## The Effect of ESG and Sustainability Reporting

The picture emerging from these leaders in integrative reporting is an environment of accountability for businesses genuinely interested in ESG reporting. A more complete picture of the firm's operations and risks can be gained for stakeholders outside the firm. This richer flow of information would allow investors—particularly major investors, such as pension funds, mutual funds, and institutional endowment funds—to assess the long-term prospects for the focal company.

Some countries are now making sustainability reporting mandatory. Denmark, Sweden, France, and South Africa have some form of requirement for sustainability reporting (Iouannou & Serafeim, 2011). In a study of 58 countries, researchers found that after the adoption of mandatory sustainability reporting laws and regulations, the social responsibility of business leaders increases. According to the results of this study, sustainable development and employee training become a higher priority for companies when corporate sustainability reporting becomes required by law. Additionally, companies tend to implement more ethical practices, reduce bribery, and corruption. Not surprisingly, management credibility increases in such countries.

In January 2011, investors belonging to the UN Principles for Responsible Investment (UNPRI) sent a letter to the top 30 stock exchanges in the world and asked them to encourage better internal corporate governance by firms and to disclosure of how sustainability issues are addressed at the board level of publicly held firms. The investors sending the letter represent $1.6 trillion in assets. Such investors are increasingly seeking ESG performance data on companies. One indicator of this comes from a study by Robert G. Eccles and George Serafeim (2011) in which the research team investigated the number of times in two quarterly periods that investors accessed a long list of environmental and social performance metrics. Using Bloomberg's data, these researchers found 34 million hits for the items on the list and concluded they had a robust measure of investor interest in ESG performance metrics. In the United States, the Securities and Exchange Commission (SEC) clarified its existing rules in February 2010 to require companies to disclose material risks relating to climate change. In sum, stakeholders in the financial markets now view ESG information about companies as being relevant to a complete firm assessment. This suggests that ESG reporting already matters to an increasing number of those in the aggregate marketing system.

# CONSCIOUS CAPITALISM

## Defining Conscious Capitalism

Roy M. Spence and Haley Rushing (2009) propose that great leaders tend to be great practitioners of the Golden Rule: treating others as these leaders would like to be treated. A leader who has built a firm in a socially responsible manner is a leader who believes in the Golden Rule. This leader has likely viewed the firm from each stakeholder's perspective and has put himself or herself in the place of the stakeholder, asking, "Is this how I would want to be treated?"

Increasingly, successful organizations have to look at the whole system in which they operate. They can't just serve one stakeholder (e.g., the customer) and damn all others. In other words, you can't just live the Golden Rule with your customers, but not live by the Golden Rule with your employees or vendors or any other key stakeholder. It's not a pick-and-choose-when-you-want-to-live-by-it kind of principle. Universal principles are tricky that way. (Spence & Rushing, 2009, p. 141)

Rajendra Sisodia, Jaqdish Sheth, and David B. Wolfe (2007) have defined "firms of endearment" as companies that endear themselves to stakeholders by bringing the interests of all stakeholders groups into strategic alignment. No stakeholder group benefits at the expense of any other stakeholder group, and each prospers as the others prosper. In a study of 28 of these firms (such as Amazon, BMW, Costco, IKEA, and Patagonia; see Table 5.3), the publicly held firms in this group returned to investors more than nine times what the S&P 500 returned to its investors over a ten-year period ending June 30, 2006.

**Table 5.3** Firms of Endearment

| Amazon | Honda | Southwest |
|---|---|---|
| BMW | IDEO | Starbucks |
| CarMax | IKEA | Timberland |
| Caterpillar | JetBlue | Toyota |
| Commerce Bank | Johnson & Johnson | Trader Joe's |
| Container Store | Jordan's Furniture | UPS |
| Costco | LL Bean | Wegmans |
| eBay | New Balance | Whole Foods |
| Google | Patagonia | |
| Harley-Davidson | REI | |

*Source:* Sisodia, Sheth, & Wolfe (2007).

Today, firms of endearment that embrace a stakeholder orientation are said to be conscious businesses that have a higher purpose in mind rather than just maximizing profits (Conscious Capitalism Institute, 2011). The Conscious Capitalism movement challenges business leaders to re-think why their organizations exist and to go beyond superficial efforts in CSR so that their firms can thrive in a global marketplace comprising multiple stakeholders. The Caux Round Table details principles for stakeholder management in its Principles for Responsible Business that correspond to Conscious Capitalism (www .cauxroundtable.org) (Caux Round Table, 2011).

Whole Foods Market founder and Co-CEO John Mackey describes himself as a "conscious capitalist." According to Mackey, he and others joining the Conscious Capitalism movement are unapologetic advocates for free markets, entrepreneurship, competition, freedom to trade, property rights, freedom to contract, and the rule of law. However, unlike much of 20th century business thinking that did not grasp the interdependencies of systems (which so often lacks ecological consciousness or a sense of responsibility for other stakeholders than investors), conscious capitalists fundamentally view a business as a community of people working together to create value for other people and all the stakeholders (Mackey, 2009a).

## Conscious Capitalism at Work: Whole Foods Market

Whole Foods Market's value proposition is to sell organic, natural, and healthy food products to customers who are passionate about food and the environment (Porter, 2006, p. 90). Social issues and environmental issues are fundamental to Whole Foods Market's distinctiveness in retailing. It is also unique for commanding premium prices. The company emphasizes purchasing from local farmers, and its buyers screen out more than 100 common ingredients to food deemed by Whole Foods Market to distort taste or nutrition, such as artificial additives, sweeteners, colorings, and preservatives.

The purposes of Whole Foods Market lie in creating value for all of its major stakeholder groups and in earning profits for its investors (Mackey, 2007). The core values of Whole Foods Market represent a stakeholder orientation and very succinctly express these purposes:

- Selling the highest quality natural and organic products available;
- Satisfying and delighting our customers;
- Supporting team member happiness and excellence;
- Creating wealth through profits and growth;
- Caring about our communities and our environment;
- Creating ongoing win-win partnerships with our suppliers; and
- Promoting the health of our stakeholders through healthy eating education.
  (Whole Foods Market, 2010, p. 4)

Over the years, Whole Foods Markets has purchased more than 2.8 billion megawatt hours of wind-based renewable energy, earning six Environmental Protection Agency (EPA) Green Power awards from 2005 through 2010. It became the first retailer to offset 100% of its energy use with wind energy credits (Benett, Gobhai, O'Reilly, & Welch, 2009). Additionally, the company has made a commitment to reduce energy consumption at all stores by 25% per square foot by 2015. Stores are constructed using a minimum of virgin raw materials (Whole Foods Market, 2010).

In 2008, Whole Foods Market discontinued the use of disposable plastic grocery bags at the checkouts in all stores. Additionally, Whole Foods Market refunds each customer at least a nickel per reusable bag they use. Most stores participate in a composting program where food waste and compostable paper goods are regenerated into compost.

## Factors of Success for Whole Foods Market

An important factor in Whole Foods Market's success is its leadership and conscious culture. Mackey says that conscious leadership at the company is actually servant leadership (Fox, 2011). Here, leaders identify their own flourishing with the flourishing of the organization. In other words, leaders try to serve the organization and its purpose. More will be said about servant leadership in Chapter 8. Mackey emphasizes the importance of a higher purpose for the business because in fulfilling this higher purpose, the business will likely improve its viability in a competitive market. Conscious business is about becoming conscious of the business's higher purpose, which is not about maximizing stakeholder value in the short run. Conscious culture at Whole Foods Market allows the organization to fulfill its higher purpose, implement the stakeholder model, and enable conscious leadership to flourish.

Mackey asserts that it is absolutely essential to trust employees, which are called team members at Whole Foods Market. One way of reinforcing trust among team members is by disclosing information that might cause strife in other organizational contexts. For example, salary information is shared at Whole Foods Market. However, information that would leave Whole Foods Market vulnerable to competitors, such as future plans for developing its stores, is not shared.

Mackey shares salary information because he believes that by making this information public, he will prevent envy among team members. Mackey believes envy is part of human nature and every organization. Every three years, the employees prioritize and vote on the benefits that they most prefer. Teams in Whole Foods Market do their own hiring, work scheduling, and product procurement. Because team members have voted for the company, it has been named by *Fortune* as one of the 100 best companies to work for every year since 1997 (Whole Foods Market, 2011).

## The Whole Food Company: The Result of Mackey's Unique Leadership

According to Mackey, he resisted the heroic purpose of the company, trying to change and improve the world, for a long time because he thought the purpose of Whole Foods was to deliver excellent service. But employees of Whole Foods Market consistently told him he was wrong, and that Whole Foods Market's purpose was to impact the world in a positive way. This purpose now animates Mackey personally, as well as the company.

Mackey views his business as a complex adaptive system. In 1982, when Mackey had his first natural food store in Austin, Texas, he saw his dream turn into a nightmare when heavy rains produced floodwaters that came into his store (Sisodia, Sheth, & Wolfe, 2007). As he was beside himself considering the unfolding disaster, customers began flowing in to help him rebuild his store. In this way, Mackey's empathetic regard for his customers was reciprocated to him in this desperate situation.

When Michael Pollan, author of *The Ominvore's Dilemma*, criticized Whole Foods Market for not doing enough to promote local agriculture, or to market grass-fed beef, Mackey engaged him, rather than shunned him.

"When I read his book, of course I wasn't very happy about how Whole Foods was portrayed, and I began a dialogue with him," Mackey said (Fox, 2011, p. 122). "We ended up in a debate in Berkeley, California, back in February 2007, and a couple of thousand people showed up. That was a healthy exchange. And to give Michael credit, I think certain parts of his criticism ended up being true. . . . We had put way too much emphasis on organic and not enough on some of these other aspects, and it was good that Michael called us to task. That kind of criticism stings, but there was also an opportunity there. I actually think you should engage your critics and see them, too, as stakeholders who are helping you to improve" (Fox, 2011, p. 122).

Although Mackey has created a viable, competitive, business, the development of this business was not always smooth. In fact, Mackey even made some disastrous mistakes. In February 2007, controversy came to Mackey for writing a blog under an assumed name on a stock message board for seven years. Later that year in November, Mackey wrote a letter to his employees and declared that after limiting his pay to 14 times that of the average team member at Whole Foods Market, he was now taking it down to $1 per year, and having the board donate any future stock options for him to charity:

> The tremendous success of Whole Foods Market has provided me with far more money than I ever dreamed I'd have and far more than is necessary for either my financial security or personal happiness. . . . I am now 53 years old and I have reached a place in my life where I no longer want to work for money, but simply for the joy of the work itself and to better answer the call to service that I feel so clearly in my own heart. Beginning on January 1, 2007, my salary will be reduced to $1, and I will no longer take any other cash compensation. . . . The intention of the board of directors is for Whole Foods Market to donate all of the future stock options I would be eligible to receive to our two company foundations. (Mackey, 2007, para. 4)

In 2009, Mackey wrote an op-ed piece for *The Wall Street Journal* beginning with a brief statement of opposition to the Obama administration's healthcare entitlement program and then proposing eight alternative steps to reform healthcare (Mackey, 2009b). His opinions brought some protesters at some Whole Foods Markets, but Mackey points out that neither his blogging deception nor his views on healthcare hurt sales (Fox, 2011).

Figure 5.3 depicts ten years of returns on the stock prices for Whole Foods Market (WFM), and other food retailers, such as Kroger (KR) and Safeway (SWY). As shown, the economic crisis of 2008 caused the stock price of Whole Foods Market to dip below the other food retailers, but since then, the stock price of Whole Foods has recovered while the stock prices for the other food retailers have remained flat.

**Figure 5.3** Stock Returns of Food Retailers 2002–2012—Whole Foods Market, Kroger, and Safeway

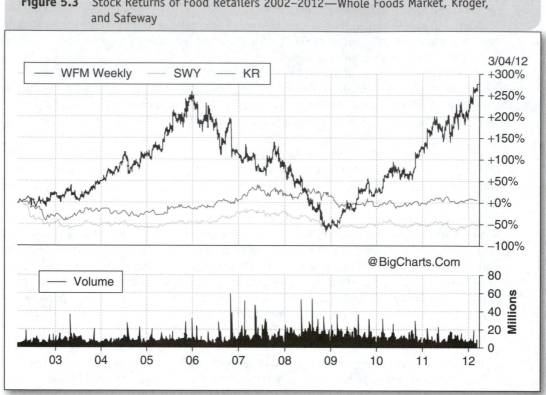

*Source:* www.bigcharts.com

## The Benefits of Conscious Capitalism

Jeffrey Hollender and Bill Breen (2010) view conscious capitalists like Mackey as pursuing a better form of capitalism, which is unfolding in a responsibility revolution. In such an age of responsibility, conscious capitalism proves to be profitable for two principal reasons. First, a company's most valuable asset, its reputation, provides "built-in insurance" in a time of general suspicion toward business. For example, 46% of respondents in a Edelman Trust Barometer survey in 2010 reported not trusting business to do what is right (Edelman Trust Barometer, 2010). At this time in the history of business, the intangibles of a firm (its patents, trademarks, knowledge, creativity, and consumer relationships) account for 75% of the value for the average U.S. firm (Hollender & Breen, 2010). In addition, a firm's reputation is under further scrutiny as a result of the availability of information via the Internet. Second, by aligning the interests of all the stakeholders, more harmony is produced, and greater numbers of satisfied stakeholders are willing to assist and contribute to the company. This provides the firm with access to a wider variety of people and their abilities than simply their employees, which in turn, increases firm success. In this way, socially and environmentally attuned employees, suppliers, NGOs, reporters, and customers can find ways to boost a purpose-driven company's success. In a global survey of individuals, 52% replied that all stakeholder groups are equally important (Edelman Trust Barometer, 2010).

## CONCLUSION

This chapter examined the role of business in society. Doug Ivester's short and turbulent term as Coca-Cola CEO highlighted the hazard of viewing one's firm only as a profit-generating unit in an atomized universe of independent and competing businesses. Milton Friedman's voice echoes from 1970 and resonates with many still in his argument that the "business of business is business." A debate between Friedman and Whole Foods Market CEO John Mackey, a leader in the Conscious Capitalism movement, sheds light on the legitimacy of some noneconomic aspects of business today. Corporate social responsibility (CSR) and a subcategory of CSR, Conscious Capitalism, were presented as approaches drawing heavily on a stakeholder orientation. Although some CSR initiatives of firms are defensive in nature and superficial, Conscious Capitalism proposes an integration of ways to address issues related to ESG into the life of the business.

## QUESTIONS

1. What new perspectives about the role of business in society did you gain from reading Chapter 6?

2. Based on the experience of Doug Ivester at Coca-Cola, why would corporate leadership be compared with mountain climbing with only a few performing really well in rarified air?

3. Thinking about the exchange between Whole Foods Market's John Mackey and economist Milton Friedman, what are your thoughts about the business of business being business? Had Friedman changed his views since 1970? Were his thoughts misconstrued in 1970? Explain.

4. In your view, how important is the development of standards for CSR to its continued success?

5. Which of the Firms of Endearment listed in Table 5.3 would you rate as your favorite? Explain. Which one would you like to learn more about?

6. In your view, to what degree is Conscious Capitalism a fad? Explain.

7. Would you like to join a firm pursuing Conscious Capitalism as an employee? What aspects of such a firm would make it appealing to you? Unappealing?

## MAVERICKS WHO MADE IT

### Raising the Bar at Clif Bar

### Gary Erickson

*Source:* http://www.clifbar.com/uploads/default/CBClogo.jpg

**T**WO EPIPHANIES DEFINE Gary Erickson's entrepreneurial saga in the life of the company he founded in Berkeley, California. The first came on a 175-mile bicycle ride with his buddy Jay (with whom he would cycle one or two thousand miles in Europe every summer) in the San Francisco area in 1990 (Erickson & Lorentzen, 2004). After eating another brand of energy bars all day, Erickson was famished but could not bring himself to eat another bite of the energy bars he was carrying with highly processed ingredients.

"It came to me: 'I could make a better bar than this,'" Erickson said. "I call that moment 'the epiphany.' Clif Bar exists because I wanted to make a better product for myself and for my friends. Two years later, after countless hours in Mom's kitchen, I had a recipe that worked."

The second epiphany for Erickson came on April 17, 2000, eight years after founding his company at the age of 33 and naming it after his father Cliff, who is his childhood hero and companion throughout the Sierra Nevada mountains (Clif Bar, 2011). Clif Bar, Inc., makes portable, convenient, nutritious energy bars for athletes and health-minded people. It had grown from a guy who lived in a garage with his dog, his skis, his climbing gear, bicycle, and two trumpets, to an energized company with $40 million in annual sales (Erickson & Lorentzen, 2004). Clif Bar's success had attracted Quaker Oats, a large retailer who wanted to buy the company from Erickson.

Erickson and his former business partner were minutes from selling their fast-growing nutrition bar company to Quaker Oats for $120 million. At the same time, other ventures were transitioning to corporate ownership. Kraft bought Balance Bar. Nestle had purchased PowerBar. All Erickson had to do was to sign the contract, and he would have netted $60 million. Instead, he went for a walk out in the Clif Bar parking lot.

Attorneys from Clif Bar and Quaker Oats had worked feverishly over the weekend to finalize the details of the sale. The company workforce had also put in extra hours over the previous months to prepare the company for the change in ownership. On his walk late in the morning, Erickson felt nauseated and attributed it to not sleeping well in the stressful weeks leading to the final transaction.

"I told my partner that I needed to walk around the block," Erickson said. "Outside, as I started across the parking lot, I began to weep, overwhelmed. 'How did I get here? Why am I doing this?' I kept walking. Halfway around the block I stopped dead in my tracks, hit by an epiphany. I felt in my gut, 'I'm not done,' and then 'I don't have to do this.' I began to laugh, feeling free, instantly. I turned around, went back to the office and told my partner, 'Send them home. I can't sell the company'" (Erickson & Lorentzen, 2004, p. 2).

Immediately, a weight was lifted from Erickson. None of his family or close friends gave him positive feedback about selling the company. Yet, Erickson stuck with his former business partner who feared that Clif Bar could not expand sufficiently without taking on enormous financing from outside the firm. But he realized that the sale of Clif Bar meant the end of his vision.

"I thought I was doing something good with Clif Bar," Erickson said. "I never thought of growing the company and selling. Why was that better than owning a company, employing people, creating great products, using the power of the company for philanthropic ends, and possibly making positive changes in the world?" (Erickson & Lorentzen, 2004, p. 23)

When the process of selling the company began, Erickson and his partner had stood before the employees of the company and made a promise not to sell the company to anyone who would not let them continue to run the company. Yet, a few weeks before the contract was to be signed, Quaker Oats let the two entrepreneurs know that their tenure as managers after the sale would be only a matter of months. Clif Bar would move to Quaker Oats headquarters, and the current employees of Clif Bar would be out of their jobs.

Erickson used his "gut" to make the decision not to sell and never looked back. However, his former business partner did and declared she was finished at Clif Bar and wanted to move on. She walked away with $62 million to be paid over the next five years. It would take Erickson five years to move from owning 67% of the shares of Clif Bar to become full owner. Instead of being up by $60 million, Erickson and his wife found their company now owing $62 million to his former business partner—a swing of $122 million!

When Erickson returned to Clif Bar, there were no cheers for him. The employee morale had plummeted over the term leading up to the intended sale of the company. Yet, Erickson set himself to turn around the company and pursue the path in business that would lead to mojo—the magic when he and his team of 65 employees were doing things the way they wanted, sensing the competitors squirm, and hearing the cash registers ring.

With the mojo of being good at what they did and knowing that everybody that mattered knew it, Clif Bar continued to pursue environmental and social goals.

The company set five bottom lines of (a) sustaining our planet, (b) sustaining our brands, (c) sustaining our people, (d) sustaining our community, and (e) sustaining our business. These "Five Aspirations" are promoted internally and provide a decision-making framework for employees (Choi & Gray, 2011). During annual reviews, employees receive feedback and bonuses based on their contributions to each of the five bottom lines and their abilities to balance their responsibilities.

Clif Bar can boast many successful bottom lines over the years since Erickson's second epiphany. These would include diverting 80% of their waste from landfills, providing sabbaticals to employees, expanding its brands to include Clif Shot (energy gel) and Luna (the top selling energy bar for women), paying employees for more than 20 hours of community service each year, and seeing sales move beyond $106 million in 2002. In this year, Erickson bought out his former business partner and became full owner of Clif Bar.

Erickson declared slow growth as a way for Clif Bar to retain its soul as well as mojo in the energy bar segment. Clif Bar had 65 employees when the near sale took place in 2000, but by 2006, it had 160 employees. At this time, Erickson named his successor as CEO—Sheryl O'Laughlin—and stepped out of day-to-day operations at Clif Bar.

In June 2010, Clif Bar initiated the Employee Stock Ownership Program (ESOP), which gave 20% ownership of the company to its more than 200 employees, with Erickson and his wife (Kit Crawford) retaining the rest. Upon the announcement of the ESOP, Erickson said, "by retaining private, employee ownership we will continue to have the freedom and flexibility to build a sustainable business with long-term focus for future generations" (Clif Blog, 2010, para. 3).

Clif Bar continues to reinforce the important dimensions of its unique company culture (being disciplined, entrepreneurial, and playful) in meaningful ways. The company facilities include a gym, rock climbing wall, yoga room, and massage rooms. Employees are allowed to bring their dogs to work, get 2.5 hours of paid exercise each week, and have access to free personal training (Roth, 2010). *Outside* magazine named Clif Bar, Inc. among its Best Places to Work in 2008, 2009, and 2010 (Outside, 2010).

## Questions

1. What were Gary Erickson's two epiphanies? How important do you think epiphanies are to leaders of established businesses? To entrepreneurs?

2. How important would you say the human dimension of emotion is to the life of established firms? To entrepreneurial firms?

3. What is mojo? Why was mojo so important to Gary Erickson?

4. What elements of Gary Erickson's story mark him as a maverick?

# Appendix

# Principles for Responsible Management Education (PRME, 2012)

## Principle 1

*Purpose:* We will develop the capabilities of students to be future generators of sustainable value for business and society at large and to work for an inclusive and sustainable global economy.

## Principle 2

*Values:* We will incorporate into our academic activities and curricula the values of global social responsibility as portrayed in international initiatives such as the United Nations Global Compact.

## Principle 3

*Method:* We will create educational frameworks, materials, processes and environments that enable effective learning experiences for responsible leadership.

## Principle 4

*Research:* We will engage in conceptual and empirical research that advances our understanding about the role, dynamics, and impact of corporations in the creation of sustainable social, environmental and economic value.

## Principle 5

*Partnership:* We will interact with managers of business corporations to extend our knowledge of their challenges in meeting social and environmental responsibilities and to explore jointly effective approaches to meeting these challenges.

## Principle 6

*Dialogue:* We will facilitate and support dialog and debate among educators, students, business, government, consumers, media, civil society organizations and other interested groups and stakeholders on critical issues related to global social responsibility and sustainability.

# REFERENCES

Benett, A., Gobhai, C., O'Reilly, A., & Welch, G. (2009). *Good for business: The rise of the conscious corporation*. New York, NY: Palgrave MacMillan.

Berger, I. E., Cunningham, P. E., & Drumwright, M. E. (2007, Summer). Mainstreaming corporate social responsibility: Developing markets for virtue. *California Management Review,49*(4), 132–157.

Bernhart, M. S., & Maher, F. J. (2011). *ISO 26000 in practice: A user guide*. Milwaukee, WI: ASQ Quality Press.

Bishop, M., & Green, M. (2008). *Philanthrocapitalism: How the rich can save the world*. New York, NY: Bloomsbury Press.

Campbell, A., & Alexander, M. (1997, November/December). What's wrong with strategy? *Harvard Business Review, 75*(5), 1–8.

Caux Round Table. (2011). The Caux Round Table: Moral capital at work. Retrieved from http://www .cauxroundtable.org/

Choi, D. Y., & Gray, E. (2011). *Values-Centered entrepreneurs and their companies*. New York, NY: Routledge.

Clif Bar. (2011). Retrieved from http://www.clifbar.com

Clif Blog. (2010, June 29). Clif Bar & Company Becomes 20 Percent Employee Owned [Web log post]. Retrieved from http://www.clifbar.com

Conscious Capitalism Institute. (2011). Stakeholders. Retrieved from http://www.consciouscapitalism .org

Davis, I. (2005, May 28). The biggest contract. *The Economist*, pp. 73–75.

Dodson, David. (2009). UGA alumnus Douglas Ivester to collaborate with the Terry College of Business on a unique educational initiative called the Deer Run Fellows Program. *News at the Terry College of Business*. Retrieved from http://www.terry.uga.edu/news/releases/2009/deer_run_fellows_ program.html

Eccles, R. G., & Serafeim, G. (2011). Leading and lagging countries in contributing to a sustainable society. *Harvard Business School Working Knowledge*. Retrieved from http://hbswk.hbs.edu/ item/6716.html.

Eccles, R. G., & Krzus, M. P. (2010). *One report: Integrated reporting for a sustainable strategy*. New York, NY: Wiley.

Edelman Trust Barometer. (2010). 2010 Edelman trust barometer. Retrieved from http://www.edelman .com/trust/2010/

Edwards, M. (2010). *Small change: Why business won't save the world*. San Francisco, CA: Berrett-Koehler.

Erickson, G., & Lorentzen, L. (2004). *Raising the bar: Integrity and passion in life and business*. San Francisco, CA: Jossey-Bass.

Fishman, C. (2003, February 28). Which price is right? *Fast Company*. Retrieved from http://www .fastcompany.com/magazine/68/pricing.html?page = 0 % 2C4

Friedman, M. (1970, September 13). The social responsibility of a business is to increase its profits. *The New York Times Magazine*. Retrieved from http://www.colorado.edu/studentgroups/ libertarians/issues/friedman-soc-resp-business.html

Friedman, M. (2005, October). Rethinking the social responsibility of business. *Reason*. Retrieved from http://reason.com/archives/2005/10/01/rethinking-the-social-responsi

Fox, J. (2011, January/February). What is it that only I can do? *Harvard Business Review*, *89*(1/2), 118–123

Global Reporting Initiative (GRI). (2011). *Year in review 2009/2010*. Retrieved from www.gri.org

Hays, C. L. (1999, June 30). A sputter in the Coke machine: When its customers fell ill, a master marketer faltered. *The New York Times*. Retrieved from http://www.nytimes.com/1999/06/30/business/sputter-coke-machine-when-its-customers-fell-ill-master-marketer-faltered.html

Hollender, J., & Breen, B. (2010). *The responsibility revolution: How the next generation of businesses will win*. San Francisco, CA: Jossey-Bass.

Industry Canada. (2011). Corporate social responsibility. Retrieved from http://www.ic.gc.ca/

Ioannou, I., & Serfeim, G. (2011). The consequences of mandatory corporate sustainability reporting. Harvard Business School Working Paper, 11-100.

Kanter, R. M. (2009). *Supercorp: How vanguard companies create innovation, profits, growth and social good*. New York, NY: Crown Business.

Ki-moon, B. (2010). Foreword. *United Nations Global Compact Annual Review—Anniversary Edition*. Retrieved from http://www.unglobalcompact.org/

Kullman, E. (2010). A message from our CEO. *DuPont 2010 Sustainability Progress Report*. Retrieved from http://www2.dupont.com/Sustainability/en_US/DuPont_2010_Sustainability_Progress_Report.pdf

Laczniak, G. R., & Murphy, P. (2006, December). Normative perspectives of ethical and socially responsible marketing. *Journal of Macromarketing*, *26*(2), 154–177.

Mackey, J. (2005, October). Rethinking the social responsibility of business. *Reason*. Retrieved from http://reason.com/archives/2005/10/01/rethinking-the-social-responsi

Mackey, J. (2007). I no longer want to work for money. *Fast Company.com*. Retrieved from http://www.fastcompany.com/node/58514/print

Mackey, J. (2009a). Creating a new paradigm for business. In *Be the solution: How entrepreneurs and conscious capitalists can solve all the world's problems* (pp. 73–113). New York, NY: Wiley.

Mackey, J. (2009b, August 11). The Whole Foods alternative to ObamaCare. *The Wall Street Journal*. Retrieved from http://online.wsj.com/article/SB10001424052970204251404574342170072865070.html

McKinsey. (2007). Assessing the impact of societal issues: A McKinsey global survey. Retrieved from https://www.mckinseyquarterly.com/Assessing_the_impact_of_societal_issues_A_McKinsey_Global_Survey_2077

McNair, C. (2011, Fall). Deer Run Fellowship: Rite of passage for the college's best and brightest. *Terry*, University of Georgia Terry College of Business Office of Marketing and Communications, pp. 22–31.

Mendonca, L. T., & Miller. M. (2007, May). Exploring business's social contract: An interview with Daniel Yankelovich. *McKinsey Quarterly*, *2*, 57–65.

Morris, B., Sellers, P., & Tarpley, N. A. (2000, January 10). What really happened at Coke: Doug Ivester was a demon for information. But he couldn't see what was coming at the showdown in Chicago. *Fortune*. Retrieved from http://money.cnn.com/magazines/fortune/fortune_archive/2000/01/10/271736/index.htm

Nemery, B., Fischler, B., Boogaerts, M., Lison, D., & Willems, J. (2002). The Coca-Cola incident in Belgium, June 1999. *Food and Chemical Toxicology*, *40*(11), 1657–1667.

Novo Nordisk. (2011). Novo Nordisk annual report 2011: Financial, social and environmental performance. Retrieved from http://www.novonordisk.com/

Outside. (2010 October). 50 best places to work in America. *Outside*. Retrieved from http://outsideblog.away.com/blog/2010/04/the-50-best-places-to-work-in-america.html

Philips. (2010). Philips annual report 2011. Retrieved from http://www.philips.com

Porter. (2006, December). Strategy & society. *Harvard Business Review, 84*(12), 78–92.

Porter, M. E., & Kramer, M. R. (2011, January/February). Creating shared value. *Harvard Business Review, 89*(1/2), 62–77.

PRME. (2012). Principles of responsible management education. The 6 principles. Retrieved from http://www.unprme.org/the-6-principles/index.php

Reason. (2005, October). Rethinking the social responsibility of business. Retrieved from http://reason.com/archives/2005/10/01/rethinking-the-social-responsi

Roth, M. (2010, May 12). Bay area's Clif Bar encourages biking and walking with 2-mile challenge [Web log post]. Retrieved from http://sf.streetsblog.org/2010/05/12/bay-areasclifbar-encourages-biking-and-walking-with-2-mile-challenge/

Sisodia, R., Sheth, J., & Wolfe, D. B. (2007). *Firms of endearment.* Upper Saddle River, NJ: Prentice-Hall.

Smith, N. C. (2003, Summer). Corporate social responsibility: Whether or how? *California Management Review, 45*(4), 52–76.

Spence, R. M., Jr., & Rushing, H. (2009). *It's not what you sell, it's what you stand for: Why every extraordinary business is driven by purpose.* New York, NY: Portfolio.

The Body Shop. (n.d.). Our Company. Retrieved from http://www.thebodyshop-usa.com/about-us/aboutus_company.aspx

The Economist. (2010, February 13). Give and take. *The Economist,* p. 68.

UN Global Compact. (2010, June). *United Nations Global Compact Annual Review – Anniversary Edition.* Retrieved from http://www.unglobalcompact.org/

Whole Foods Market. (2010). Annual stakeholders report 2010. Retrieved from http://www.wholefoodsmarket.com/company/investor-relations.php

Williams, O. F. (2004, October). The UN Global Compact: The challenge and the promise. *Leadership and Business Ethics, 14*(4), 755–774.

Woo, C. (2010). Implementing the United Nations Global Compact. In A. Rasche & G. Kell (Eds.), *The United Nations Global Compact: Achievements, Trends and Challenges* (pp. 115–143).Cambridge, UK: Cambridge University Press.

Yankelovich, D. (2006). *Profit with honor: The new stage of market capitalism.* New Haven, CT: Yale University Press.

Zadek, S. (2001). *The Civil Corporation.* London, UK: Earthscan.

## CHAPTER 6

# The Role of
# the State in Society

## MARCH 2011: NUCLEAR CRISIS IN JAPAN

### Prelude

Tokyo Electric Power Company, Inc. (TEPCO) traditionally relied on nuclear power for 40% of the electricity it generated (TEPCO, 2010). Established in 1951, TEPCO is a major industrial enterprise in Japan and currently serves more than 44% of the 127 million people of Japan including the world's largest metropolitan area of Tokyo with more than 32 million people (TEPCO, 2010).

But ominously, TEPCO had experienced problems in its safety record for nuclear power over the years. In 2002, TEPCO became mired in scandal when it came to light that leak inspectors found cracks found in the steel core-shroud of 11 reactors at its two nuclear power plants, but they reported no cracks in the final report. This led to shutdowns of these 11 nuclear reactors. In 2007, a 6.8 earthquake off the western coast of Japan near the Kashiwazaki-Kariwa nuclear plant of TEPCO disrupted operations at this nuclear power plant with the world's largest capacity and forced a shutdown of its seven nuclear reactors (McMurry, 2007). Yasuhisa Shiozaki, the government's top spokesman said, "Since there was such a huge earthquake that surpassed our expectations, we need to consider future measures for quake resistance." By March 2011, four of these reactors had resumed generating power, while the others remained idle awaiting governmental approval to return to operation.

## Catastrophe

On Friday, March 10, 2011, at 2:46 P.M. Tokyo time, an 8.9 magnitude earthquake, centered undersea off the northeastern coast of Japan 300 kilometers north of Tokyo near Sendai, began with a roar and rumble that shook skyscrapers on land and tossed furniture and wall decorations to the floors of homes and apartments (Fackler, 2011). But the real trouble came 15 minutes later when tsunami waves as high as 14 meters surged inland along the northeastern coast of Japan sweeping cars, trucks, and even burning buildings with them. Despite strict adherence to rigorous building codes by the Japanese, the tidal waves proved to be overwhelming along the sea coast with TEPCO's Fukushima Daiichi nuclear power plant.

In the confusing aftermath of the earthquake (which featured hundreds of aftershocks as strong as regular earthquakes), local governments and the federal government across Japan struggled with power outages as well as communication disruptions. Almost instantaneously, thousands of people were reported missing. But as the hours went on, the urgency of rescuing stranded citizens from bridges and flooded buildings gave way in the Japanese Prime Minister's office to concern about operations at the Fukushima Daiichi nuclear plant operated by TEPCO. The earthquake and tsunami had knocked out all the power supply and the cooling systems for reactor No. 1, bringing radiation to dangerous levels.

### Your Thoughts?

- Japan has no energy resources of which to speak, but it is a highly industrialized country with leading firms, such as Toyota, Nissan, Honda, Mitsubishi, and Fuji Heavy Industries. What do you think about Japan's society relying on 55 nuclear power plants to generate 30% of its electricity in this earthquake-prone region of the world?
- If nuclear power is terminated in Japan, what will this mean for (a) the economy of Japan, (b) the prices of consumer goods made in Japan, (c) and the worldwide operations of Japanese multinational companies, such as Toyota?

## CHAPTER OVERVIEW AND LEARNING OBJECTIVES

This chapter will examine the role of the state in helping determine the quality of life (QOL) in a society. In addition to guiding a society's response to natural disaster, the governments of modern societies have a broad influence across many realms of life. When government functions well, the quality of life for citizens usually increases. This chapter will review QOL research and recent approaches to measuring QOL across countries of the world. This chapter will also examine the influence of government in modern societies with a special focus on the influence of government on business. The U.S. government's bailout of auto manufacturers GM and Chrysler will be featured to illustrate some of the challenges of government intervening in a situation with multiple stakeholders. This chapter will also consider the concept of distributive justice and analyze possible reasons for political liberals and political conservatives to think differently when making moral judgments about economic and social issues. After this chapter, you should be able to answer the following questions:

- What are some challenges a society encounters that require the effort of both business and government to overcome?
- How semipermeable are the boundaries between business and government today?
- Is it possible for markets to exist without government?
- For societies embracing democracy and capitalism, what are some distortions that can emerge from government involvement in markets?
- What does recent research about the moral foundations for liberals and conservatives suggest about how citizens might think differently about economic and social issues?

## A HIGH-STAKES THRILLER

### Would Seawater Save Japan?

At 7 A.M. the next morning, Prime Minister Naoto Kan flew by helicopter directly to the Fukushima Daiichi plant desperately seeking an answer to one critical question: Why can't TEPCO still open valves to release rising steam inside reactor No. 1 to avoid a meltdown? (Yoshida, 2011). There, he met Masao Yoshida, director of the Fukushima No. 1 nuclear plant.

"Yoshida told Kan [TEPCO] would decide whether to open the valves manually within about one hour," said Manub Terada, a close aide to Kan who attended the meeting (Yoshida, 2011, para. 5). TEPCO had been unable to open the electric valves because of a blackout at the nuclear power plant. However, radiation in the reactor building had risen to levels so high that TEPCO hesitated to send in workers to open the valves manually.

When TEPCO finally did send in workers at 9:15 A.M., the high radiation levels in the darkened reactor building slowed the work, so the valves were not open until 2:30 P.M. Unfortunately, a disastrous scenario had already begun to unfold. Hydrogen, generated from the melting nuclear fuel, exploded and blew up the Unit 1 building at 3:36 P.M., severely disabling reactor 1.

That night, Prime Minister Kan asked aides about the risks and benefits of injecting seawater into the reactor to cool it (Onishi & Fackler, 2011). After weighing the possibilities, the decision was made to use seawater to cool the reactors. This decision would end up costing TEPCO $5.2 billion dollars because using cold seawater to cool the hot stainless steel reactors would cause irreparable damage to the reactors and render them useless (Tabuchi, 2011). The loss of the reactors represented about 25% of TEPCO's assets on its balance sheet and would likely bring power cuts to its service area.

At about 6:30 P.M., TEPCO ordered Yoshida to send in workers and start injecting seawater into reactor No. 1. However, 21 minutes later, TEPCO ordered Yoshida to stop. The TEPCO liaison to the prime minister reported that the prime minister seemed to be against it. Later, TEPCO's executive vice president Sakae Muto explained at a press conference, "Well, he said that was the atmosphere or mood" (Onishi & Fackler, 2011, p. 4).

However, Yoshida did the unexpected in the conformity-minded Japanese culture. He quietly ignored the order to stop pumping seawater onto the reactor. He had been bolstered by meeting Kan, a fellow alumnus of the Tokyo Institute of Technology, and knew he had the authority by International Atomic Energy Agency guidelines to make technical decisions at the plant. Later, this action to pump seawater onto the reactors was cited as the crucial step that averted a large-scale catastrophe (CNN, 2011a). However, TEPCO then erroneously informed the prime minister's office that the seawater cooling operation had stopped.

## Diplomacy During Disaster

During this unfolding crisis, the international dimensions soon became apparent. Leaders from neighboring countries, such as China and South Korea, became alarmed about the prospects of seawater with nuclear contamination flowing into their waters and fishing areas. The United States, with about 50,000 military personnel stationed in Japan, offered special technical help. Forty-eight hours after the earthquake, officials from the U.S. Nuclear Regulatory Commission arrived in Tokyo. However, these U.S. officials were unable to obtain information or even arrange meetings with their Japanese counterparts. Because Japanese government leaders did not strongly implement emergency response plans that had been developed long before the tsunami hit, the Japanese government was partially paralyzed in its response to the events that occurred after the tsunami hit.

Kan struggled to manage the nuclear crisis because he felt he could not rely on the protocols established by his predecessor to respond to such a crisis. Kan's distrust for business having unchecked influence on government officials ran deep. During his time as Japan's health minister in the mid-1990s, Kan became extremely popular after exposing his own ministry's use of blood tainted with HIV that led to the deaths of hundreds of hemophiliacs dying of AIDS. Kan had found the collusion between a pharmaceutical company and his own ministry, which had long known about the tainted blood.

At a crucial moment on the evening of March 12, Kan received a confusing risk analysis assessment from the chief nuclear regulator, a staunchly pro-nuclear academic (Onishi &

Fackler, 2011). Now, Kan was faced with what seemed to him a similarly collusive nuclear establishment consisting of politically connected utilities aided by bureaucrats in the Ministry of Economy, Trade and Industry, as well as compliant academics. "It's more of an emotional thing," later said Kenichi Mattsumoto, an adviser to Kan, "He never trusts bureaucrats" (Onishi & Fackler, 2011, p. 3).

As a result of Kan's lack of trust for the preestablished protocol for dealing with a nuclear crisis of this magnitude, Kan was forced to improvise the government's role in the crisis. In addition, obtaining accurate and timely information about what was happening in the nuclear plant proved to be elusive to Kan at critical times. In the unfolding drama at the Fukushima Daiichi nuclear plant, the problematic linkages between business and government in Japanese society led to confusion and delayed responses from both sides, as well as to sharing erroneous information with the public and leaders of other countries.

During the first three days of the crisis, the Kan administration left the handling of the crisis to TEPCO while it focused on relief efforts for hundreds of thousands of Japanese left homeless. But on March 14, a second explosion occurred at nearby reactor No. 3, and the TEPCO's president Masataka Shimizu asked the Kan administration to withdraw TEPCO's employees because of the dangers at the Fukushima nuclear plant.

When Kan heard about this request, his aids reported that he flew into a rage. Abandoning the plant would mean losing control of the four stricken reactors. At an emergency meeting early on March 15, Kan asked advisers what more could be done to save the reactors. Then he gave TEPCO two hours notice that he planned to visit the company.

At 5:30 A.M., Kan walked into TEPCO headquarters and posted a trusted aide, Goshi Hosono, to keep tabs on the company. Hosono's stationing at TEPCO headquarters was later seen as a turning point in helping the prime minister take over damage-control efforts at the plant. "For the first time, we knew what TEPCO was debating, and what they knew," said one adviser (Onishi & Fackler, 2011, p. 5).

However, the situation worsened at the Fukushima nuclear plant. The next day explosions occurred at reactors No. 2 and No. 4. In prior years, the government had allowed not only one reactor, but six, to be built at the Fukushima site on the seacoast above the Pacific Ocean. Two more reactors for Fukushima had been approved for the site (but rescinded in May 2011). The plant was designed to withstand a tsunami up to 5.7 meters. On March 25, TEPCO Senior Vice President Sakae Muto admitted the utility had never thought that waves the size of 14 meters were possible (Yoshida, 2011).

## The Crisis Ends—But Leaves Much to Be Discussed

Despite the sometimes ineffective response to the intensifying nuclear crisis by the Japanese government, the potentially calamitous situation at Fukushima was brought under control by the heroic efforts of workers at the plant. However, in the weeks that followed, TEPCO and the Japanese government revised important information related to the disaster. First, despite denials during the crisis, there actually had been core meltdowns in three of the afflicted reactors at Fukushima. If these had been allowed to continue, there would have been three complete meltdowns with resulting explosions spewing radioactive gas and debris similar to Chernobyl's single reactor in 1986. Second, the radiation levels had actually risen to levels twice than what was publicly admitted during the crisis. Finally, TEPCO earned additional derision for not praising Yoshida's actions, but rather giving him its lightest punishment of a verbal reprimand for defying the order to stop injecting seawater in reactor No. 1 (Onishi & Fackler, 2011). This merely added to Yoshida's sudden folk-hero status in Japanese culture because the continued use of seawater averted a nuclear catastrophe the world had never before witnessed.

"It came close to wiping out northern Japan as an area to be inhabited," nuclear physicist Michio Kaku said (CNN, 2011a). With regard to the spreading of misinformation during the crisis and the subsequent cover-up about how close Japan came to an unprecedented national and worldwide tragedy, television news-show host Elliot Spitzer made a comparison to the Economic Crisis of 2008. "It's even worse than what Wall Street did" (CNN, 2011b).

Japanese Prime Minister Naoto Kan resigned from office August 26, 2011 in the midst of widespread criticism of his handling of the aftermath of the March 11 tsunami and the crisis at the Fukushima Daiichi nuclear power plant (McCurry, 2011). One year after the disaster, plans to spend about $250 billion on reconstruction have stalled as a result of Prime Minister Yoshiko Noda's failure to offer a grand vision for such reconstruction, bureaucrats' aversion to take decisive action, and the economic stagnation that has persisted since the early 1990s (Pesek, 2012).

## Lessons From Fukushima

The Fukushima Daiichi disaster puts in high relief the social contract between society and business. Japanese society had granted TEPCO permission to build multiple nuclear reactors at Fukushima and to run them in a safe manner. As a result of an unexpected tsunami of epic proportion, power generation stopped, but the extremely hot nuclear core could not be cooled after the battery-powered back-up cooling system ran out of power eight hours after the blackout began at Fukushima Daiichi. Explosions of hot gasses occurred in four reactor buildings. The decision to pump seawater on hot reactors would cost TEPCO $30 billion in losses. However, with not one, but three, Chernobyl-like nuclear reactors about to erupt, market self-regulation would have been a delusional answer to the crisis in this case. Allowing TEPCO to walk away from the ruined Fukushima nuclear plant as the nuclear rods continued to melt and explode, and then go out of business sounds absurd given the danger of the company's damaged assets to the population of Japan.

Although it is hard to imagine the stress levels for government leaders at a time when they were contending with tens of thousands of deaths and hundreds of thousands of displaced people, a crisis developed at a business that soon eclipsed all other crises for these government leaders (and for the government leaders of other countries in the world). When the safety and security of a society come into risk, everyone's quality of life is threatened. "With nuclear power, there are lots of promises given about the ability to manage the risks," Royal Holloway of the University of London marketing professor Alex Reppel said. "And everything is done under the assumption that it will work. But what if it doesn't? What happens until we get it right? There is a transition period for technologies that change societal behavior and implications for society in this" (Reppel, personal communication, 2011).

In emergencies, but also in day-to-day life, government inevitably has an undeniable role in the quality of life experienced by the citizens of society. Businesses also contribute to quality of life, but as the disaster at Fukushima Daiichi highlighted, government carries a broader and heavier responsibility when natural disaster disrupts quality of life.

## RESEARCH IN QUALITY OF LIFE

In describing research in the marketing and society domain, William Wilkie (2001) has observed that such work implicitly rests on the question, "What type of society do we wish to create and inhabit?" Two subareas of research in this domain have emerged in the last 30 years: social marketing (intending to benefit the target audience directly) and QOL studies (focused more broadly on how well society or one group of society was faring, or focused on how well one aspect of life, such as work, was faring) (Wilkie & Moore, 1999).

In marketing thought, Philip Kotler (1986) has cited the choices for goods, the cultural environment, and the physical environment as fundamental dimensions of life quality. Joe Sirgy (2001, p. 10) has offered an expanded "contemporary view of QOL" with a starting set of dimensions for QOL being (a) economic, (b) work, (c) political, (d) leisure, (e) physical (health), (f) environmental, (g) social, (h) family, and (i) spiritual. Here, business can be said to be the dominant force in the first two dimensions, economic well-being and work well-being, while playing a significant role in delivering or providing the material conditions for the others.

The measurement of QOL has involved a broad set of contributors from across the social sciences. Scientific methods of measuring QOL have taken two approaches. The first "subjective" approach focuses on the measurement of subjective well-being (SWB), or individuals' subjective experience of their lives in terms of life satisfaction or happiness (Cummins, 2000). Subjective well-being refers to affective experiences and cognitive judgments about one's life (Larsen & Eid, 2008). In this vein, quality of life is the product of an overall appraisal of life that includes both good and bad experiences. The second "objective" approach has focused on social indicators or level of living measures (using quantitative statistics, such as economic output, crime rates, or political freedoms).

Table 6.1 presents the dimensions used across five measurement approaches to QOL. Ed Diener and Eunkook Suh (1997) performed correlation analysis using a 40-country dataset featuring a subjective well-being measure of the World Values Survey (Inglehart & Baker, 2000) and an objective QOL measure from *International Living* (Lears, 1996). Other researchers have used this set of seven objective QOL dimensions and found it to conform to extant theory of societal QOL with a comprehensive base in two domains: public policy and international marketing (Peterson & Malhotra, 1997).

The QOL dimensions used in four other approaches to QOL measurement complete Table 6.1. Here, the Legatum Institute's Prosperity Index from 2010 is aligned with the corresponding dimensions of not only Diener and Suh's study (1997) but also the recommended dimensions of French President Nicolas Sarkozy's Commission on the Measurement of Economic Performance and Social Progress (Stiglitz, Sen, & Fitoussi, 2010, p. 15), and two other QOL indexes. The New Economic Foundation's (NEF) Happy Planet Index (which gives emphasis to industrialized nations' negative impact on the environment), along with the United Nations's Human Development Index (HDI) are also presented in Table 6.1.

Presenting these different approaches to QOL measurement allows for important analysis. For example, how much influence do societies expect the state to have across these 13 unique dimensions? In thinking about this question, the two QOL dimensions for societies social capital and life satisfaction (The 12 and 13 dimensions of Table 6.1) would be viewed as the aggregation of individuals' successful engagement with others and completion of important life projects, respectively (Johansson, 2000). Accordingly, social capital and life satisfaction would not be the responsibility of the state. But for the rest of the dimensions, the state would be a primary stakeholder to boost these dimensions of QOL.

**Table 6.1**   Dimensions of Five QOL Measurement Approaches

| | QOL Dimensions (Diener & Suh, 1997) | Legatum Prosperity Index (Legatum, 2010) | Sarkozy's Commission on the Measurement of Economic Performance & Social Progress (Stiglitz, Sen, & Fitoussi, 2010) | Happy Planet Index 2.0 (NEF, 2009) | Human Development Index (UNDP, 2011) |
|---|---|---|---|---|---|
| 1 | cost of living (favorability) | | | | |
| 2 | health | health | health | life expectancy | life expectancy at birth |
| 3 | economy | economy | material living standards (income, consumption, & wealth) | | GNI per capita |
| 4 | infrastructure | | | | |
| 5 | freedom | personal freedom | political voice & governance | | |
| 6 | culture & recreation | | | | |
| 7 | environment | | environment (present & future) | ecological footprint | |
| 8 | | entrepreneurship & opportunity | | | |
| 9 | | governance | | | |
| 10 | | education | education | | mean years & expected years of schooling |

| | QOL Dimensions (Diener & Suh, 1997) | Legatum Prosperity Index (Legatum, 2010) | Sarkozy's Commission on the Measurement of Economic Performance & Social Progress (Stiglitz, Sen, & Fitoussi, 2010) | Happy Planet Index 2.0 (NEF, 2009) | Human Development Index (UNDP, 2011) |
|---|---|---|---|---|---|
| 11. | | safety & security | insecurity (economic & physical) | | |
| 12. | | social capital | social connections & relationships | | |
| 13. | | | personal activities including work | life satisfaction | |

## Government Services

The role of the state in modern societies based on democracy and capitalism is broad and extensive (Quelch & Jocz, 2007, pp. 231–232). The civilian employment for the federal government (excluding the U.S. Postal Service) tops 2 million people, making it the largest employer in the country (Bureau of Labor Statistics, 2011). Additionally, about 1 million people serve in the military.

The state establishes the laws and runs the courts, police, fire departments, and military forces. It collects taxes. Central banks in countries of the world contribute directly to the favorability of costs through monetary policy. The fiscal policy of the state also contributes to the cost of living for its citizens. The state runs Social Security and welfare programs, as well as housing programs. State-assisted or state-sponsored schools and institutions of higher learning develop knowledgeable and capable workers who can effectively run businesses, the public sector, and the civil sector, such as nongovernmental organizations (NGOs).

The state initiates public works projects, such as roads, highways, sea ports, airports, canals, as well as water and sewer systems. In many locales, the state provides sanitation services, and in some locales, it provides public utilities. The state operates regulatory agencies (such as the Federal Trade Commission), the Consumer Product Safety Commission, and the U.S. Department of Agriculture that, respectively, ensures fair competition in markets, product safety, and food safety. The state provides records of real estate titles and transactions. It also provides licensing bureaus. The state encourages development of railroad networks and communication networks. It also runs the mail system to link individuals and businesses throughout the country. Developing public policy regarding the cultural heritage of the country and the quality of the physical environment (air quality, water quality, and endangered species) comes under the authority of the state. Additionally, the conservation of natural resources on public lands is another important task of the state that also includes enforcement of public policy.

The government has created markets in the past. For example, in July 1994, the Federal Communication Commission (FCC) gathered leaders of the telecommunications industry at the Omni Shoreham Hotel in Washington, DC, for a week-long auction of licenses to use parts of the electromagnetic spectrum (McMillan, 2002). Previously, the FCC had held hearings to decide which applicants for licenses were to be allocated these licenses for free. The decision of who gets the right to use each piece of spectrum is a difficult one for government. Invariably, the process takes on aspects of a beauty contest where government officials use vague criteria for assigning such licenses. This inefficient process is also prone to favoritism. This was followed briefly by a lottery to allocate licenses that also proved inefficient. So when the first auction was held in 1994, no one knew how much these licenses would be worth in a market for them. As of 2008, the auctions have brought in more than $52 billion to the FCC. In this way, the FCC takes in more revenue than it spends each year. In 2000, the United Kingdom followed with an auction of part the spectrum there and earned $34 billion, while Germany's auction netted $46 billion. In Spain and France, the old beauty contest approach to granting spectrum licenses is still done.

Old habits die hard, even in the United States, as the government resumed the practice of giving away what the public owns. Congress voted to give spectrum for high-definition broadcasting to the television networks, instead of auctioning it. The FCC estimated the spectrum giveaway resulted in the government missing the opportunity to collect $70 billion. Senator John McCain called the spectrum giveaway "one of the great rip-offs in American history" (McMillan, 2002, p. 85). It is believed by some observers that the broadcast television's control of media coverage of election campaigns put them in a more powerful position to exert their will on Congress when compared to the telecommunications industry.

# THE SOCIAL RESPONSIBILITY OF GOVERNMENT REGARDING BUSINESS

## The U.S. Government Bails Out GM and Chrysler

During the economic crisis of 2008, a series of poor economic decisions made by Wall Street financiers and auto industry executives led to a social decision by the government to bail out firms that were previously thought of as highly sophisticated bankers and auto makers. At this time, the U.S. government quickly introduced the $700 billion Troubled Assets Relief Program (TARP) to bail out banks, insurers, and U.S. automakers (Rattner, 2010). The federal government wound up directing $82 billion to the automakers, their related finance companies, and even some auto industry suppliers. Two of the three major automakers in the United States, GM and Chrysler, accepted funds from TARP as part of a government bailout for these firms.

Shortly after the inauguration of Barack Obama as U.S. president in January 2009, an ad hoc group called the Presidential Task Force on the Auto Industry (comprising 14 U.S. Treasury or temporary government workers and calling itself "Team Auto") became the government's task force to guide these two automakers through restructuring and/or bankruptcy proceedings. The White House's director of the National Economic Council, Lawrence Summers, and the Secretary of the Treasury, Timothy Geithner, supervised Team

Auto under the leadership of former *New York Times* journalist and investment banker Steven Rattner. Within months, Rattner and his relatively young team of government workers had (a) fired the longtime CEO and Board Chairman of GM Rick Waggoner, (b) appointed replacements for Waggoner, (c) developed a $3 billion Cash for Clunkers Program to boost sales in the auto industry, (d) developed a restructuring plan for GM that included terminating four brands (Pontiac, Saturn, Saab, and Hummer), and (e) served as the midwife to a merger of Chrysler into the Italian auto maker Fiat (Rattner, 2010). Over the course of the bailout of GM and Chrysler, these firms used $82 billion dollars in TARP funds (including $1.5 billion for Chrysler Financial, $17.7 billion for GM's financial company General Motors Acceptance Company [GMAC, later renamed Ally], and $400 million for some auto parts suppliers) (Rattner, 2010).

Because of the dire future facing these two auto companies, and because of the flexibility offered to firms in working with their stakeholders in bankruptcy proceedings, much was accomplished in six months. In short, most stakeholders understood that sacrifice needed to be made or these automakers would need to cease operations and liquidate. Numerous stakeholders became apparent during the impending bankruptcy of these two U.S. auto giants. A glimpse of these stakeholders can be seen in the decision of the federal Judge Robert Gerber, who denied the petition of some of GM's bondholders to force a complete (and lengthy) restructuring under the supervision of the court. If such a conventional bankruptcy procedure were allowed, the bondholders would have saved a million dollars here and there, while GM would lose $100 million each day (Rattner, 2010). A passage of Judge Gerber's decision included in *Overhaul* by Steven Rattner follows:

> This case involves not just the ability of GM creditors to recover on their claims … it involves the interest of 225,000 employees, (91,000 in the U.S. alone); an estimated 500,000 retirees; 6,000 dealers and 11,500 suppliers. If GM were to have to liquidate, the injury to the public would be staggering. This case likewise raises the specter of systemic failure throughout the North American auto industry, and grievous damage to all of the communities in which GM operates. If GM goes under, the number of supplier bankruptcies which we already have…is likely to multiply exponentially. If employees lose their paychecks or their healthcare benefits, they will suffer great hardship. And states and municipalities would lose the tax revenues they get from GM and the people employed by GM, and the Government would be paying out more in unemployment insurance and other hardship benefits. Under these circumstances, I find it hardly surprising that the U.S., Canadian, and Ontario governments would not stand idly by and allow those consequences to happen. (p. 261)

Judge Gerber mentions all of the primary stakeholder groups of Figure 4.1 in Chapter 4 with the exception of GM customers. A lengthy bankruptcy would have harmed consumer confidence in GM regarding (a) the warranties currently in effect on their GM vehicles, (b) the resale value of their vehicles, and (c) the desirability of purchasing the same less-than-competitive vehicles from a company put in limbo by a long bankruptcy. Instead, the expedited bankruptcy of GM allowed its vast systems of stakeholders to begin afresh with

$65 billion less debt and the removal of annual structural costs from its North America operations totaling $8 billion (Rattner, 2010). Now, only four GM shareholders remained: (a) the U.S. government (initially 61% owner, reduced through a sale of shares after the initial public offering of stock in the new GM company to 33%), (b) the Canadian government, (c) the United Auto Workers retiree healthcare benefits trust, and (d) some of GM's old bondholders (Rattner, 2010).

Tables 6.2a and 6.2b present a snapshot of the GM bailout at the end of 2010. GM's restructuring using a rapid proceeding in section 363 of the U.S. bankruptcy code was enormously complex. These two tables offer an overview of the bankruptcy and emergence of the New GM, which had less in debt and fewer brands. As shown, shareholders lost their entire investment. With improving performance of the New GM, bondholders have kept doing better, as they make capital gains on the shares of their New GM stock. Although it seems that it lost $17 billion, the U.S. federal government fared well, considering that things could have become worse (Rattner, 2010). The Canadian government and the Ontario government took an 11.7% ownership stake in the New GM, as well as receiving a vitality agreement from the New GM to protect jobs remaining in Canada. Although the UAW took job cuts at plants to be closed, the union importantly funded the healthcare for their 500,000 retirees through the establishment of a healthcare trust called the Voluntary Employee Beneficiary Association (VEBA), which took ownership of 17.5% of the New GM (Rattner, 2010).

**Table 6.2a** Summary of Some Risks and Outcomes to Selected Stakeholders in GM Bailout

|  | *GM leaders* | *GM shareholder* | *GM bondholders* | *UAW* | *UAW retirees* | *Overseas workers* | *GM suppliers* |
|---|---|---|---|---|---|---|---|
| **Number of stakeholders** | 30 | 610 million trading shares | 100,000 held 20% of debt | 91,000 | 500,000 | 134,000 | 11,500 |
| **At risk** | survival | total investment | $27 billion | loss of 91,000 fully benefited jobs paying $28/hr avg. | healthcare benefits | 55 counties with jobs paying: Mexico—$7/ hr. China— $4.5/hr. India—$1/hr. | some 650,000 jobs |
| **Outcome** | CEO & Chairman fired but given $7 million severance Board shake-up | lost it all | $20 billion swapped for 10% stock in New GM $4.9 billion loss | 22,500 jobs cut no pay cut no benefit cut | VEBA—a new healthcare trust takes 17.5% stake in New GM | small dip in 2009 sales rebounded in 2010 | $450 million taken in federal support |

**Table 6.2b** Summary of Some Risks and Outcomes to Selected Stakeholders in GM Bailout

| | Dealers | GM car owners | Federal gov't | U.S. taxpayers | State gov't | Local gov'ts | Canadian gov't |
|---|---|---|---|---|---|---|---|
| **Number of stakeholders** | 6,000 | 10 million in U.S. with unexpired warranties | Congress plus 30 principals in executive branch | 100 million who paid taxes | 35 states with facilities | 140 cities with facilities | Congress plus 30 principals in executive branch |
| **At risk** | survival | warranties lower resale value for cars | $50 billion actually spent If GM liquidated $88.5 billion | $50 billion | tax revenues new jobless healthcare | tax revenues (Detroit-$20 million) | 20 plants 9,000 jobs 700 dealers |
| **Outcome** | 1,800 dealerships closed | no lapse in warranties | became owner of 61% of New GM | 61% owner of New GM (31% in 2012) | mixed results depending on plant closures | mixed results depending on plant closures | gave $9 billion for 11.7% New GM stake |
| | Survivors face less cannibalization | resale value still a market function | expected loss of $17 billion | owe $170 per taxpayer for GM bailout | | Double digit losses on land taxpayer | Vitality agreement protects jobs |

Although early estimates of the federal government's losses in the bailout of the auto industry came to $40 billion, the decisive and positive moves recommended by Team Auto and approved by President Obama in 2009, along with an upturn in auto sales, has led to a revised estimate of $17 billion of losses for the federal government (Shepardson, 2011). Car sales, rather than car financing, now accounts for GM's profits (Lutz, 2011). In 2010, all three automakers posted annual profits: GM $6.2 billion, Ford (which received no bailout) $6.6 billion, and Chrysler posted a slight profit.

The Congressional Oversight Panel (COP) noted in January 2011 that the bailout of GM and Chrysler may turn out to be one of the successes of the TARP program (Kroll, 2011). But while the automakers are all posting profits, the firms still owe the U.S. government billions of dollars as of February 2012 (Isidore, 2012). Taxpayers have fallen $1.3 billion short on the Chrysler bailout and are still waiting for $25.5 billion back on the GM deal. In total, the companies received about $60 billion between them. In the case of GM, the U.S.

Treasury still holds 500 million shares of GM stock that represent about one third of the company. If sold at prices in April 2012, they would be worth about $13 billion.

However, the COP asserted that a rescue by the U.S. Treasury of any large U.S. corporation that is considered to be "too big to fail" creates a moral hazard. As a result of this moral hazard, large corporations will make risky choices or fail to behave in a responsible manner. In such situations, leaders of "too big to fail" corporations would believe that a bailout from the federal government would eventually arrive. In this way, it can be seen how actions taken by a stakeholder (such as government) today might affect decisions by firms in the future.

## IMPERFECTIONS RESULTING FROM GOVERNMENT ACTIVITY IN MARKETS

### Setting the Rules of the Game

In setting the rules of the game, regulations and laws established by government to protect citizens might actually give preferential treatment to selected market participants. In some instances, a cartel of privileged sellers might result from imposed government standards and procedures. For example, the Benedictine monks at St. Joseph Abbey in Covington, Louisiana, began making and selling handmade funeral caskets priced between $1,500 and $2,000 to pay for food, healthcare, and the education of the monks at the abbey (Levitz, 2010). The abbey receives about 60 requests per year to make their simple caskets made of cypress. However, after the Louisiana State Board of Embalmers and Funeral Directors (eight of the nine board members are funeral industry professionals) delivered a cease-and-desist order to the monks in March 2010, and threatened them with fines from $500 to $2,500 per violation of illegal casket sales and jail time up to 180 days, only then did the monks learn that under state law in Louisiana, they needed a license to sell caskets—a high-margin item (no doubt, as a result of lack of competition). As it turns out, the monks would have to become licensed funeral directors to sell funeral merchandise. The monks tried twice to get the law changed, but the state legislature stalled in its response to their request (First Things, 2011). The Institute for Justice, a public-interest law firm, now represents the abbey in its federal lawsuit citing Louisiana's "casket cartel."

"The monks' story is just one example of a national problem in which industry cartels use government power to protect themselves from competition," Institute for Justice's president Chip Mellor said. "Protecting economic liberty and ending government-enforced cartels require … a willingness by the courts to confront what is often really going on when the government enacts licensing laws supposedly to protect the public" (Levitz, 2010).

### Playing Umpire

In playing the role of umpire in markets, government can make choices that are later seen to be incorrect. In the 1857 U.S. Supreme Court ruling known as the Dred Scott decision, the court ruled that slaves were the property of their owners (and could not be taken from their owners without due process) (Fehrenbacher, 2001). Furthermore, the court asserted that the U.S. Congress had no authority to prohibit slavery in territories of the

United States. The case was never overturned by the Supreme Court. However, the Civil War and the resulting 14th Amendment to the U.S. Constitution in 1868 established that all persons born or naturalized in the United States are citizens, and that the federal government did not have to reimburse anyone for the emancipation of slaves they once owned.

An important aspect of playing the umpire in markets is the even enforcement of regulations and laws. Because firms have the legal status of individuals in the United States (Mackey, 2009, p. 95), the rule of law must be applied equally to everyone. "If Whole Foods goes into a city and is told our cheese has to be refrigerated, it's fundamentally unjust if that rule isn't applied to our competitors as well—which, I might add, does sometimes happen in New York City," CEO of Whole Foods Market John Mackey said (Fox, 2011, p. 120).

Corruption is a challenge in all countries. But in countries without a free press that can criticize government officials and expose corrupt practices, it is much worse. In the past 15 years, the climate opposing corruption has improved in China, but a traditional way of receiving preferential treatment from government officials is to deliver gifts during the Chinese New Year (McGregor, 2005). In the past, cartons of cigarettes or bottles of expensive liquor were typical gifts. Now, laptops, golf clubs, home entertainment centers, and even automobiles might be on someone's holiday gift list. Financial centers such as Beijing and Shanghai are generally clean, said Ty Cobb, a partner at the law firm Hogan Lovells, but "the further you get away from those centers, the pressure mounts" to pay kickbacks and give gifts (Rubenfeld, 2011, para. 2). Although China might still be lax about even enforcement of anti-bribery statutes, in Russia "it's hard to tell … whether [an enforcement action is a] political purge or corruption" (Rubenfeld, 2011, para. 5).

## Imposing Taxes

Although it is rarely mentioned in the business press, the capability of the government to collect taxes is essential to having an effective government—which contributes enormously to societal QOL. Although this might be taken for granted in developed countries, developing countries, such as India, struggle to collect adequate amounts of tax revenues (Economic Times, 2011). With paltry tax collections, the state of Punjab in India has amassed $15.5 billion in debt (Sharma & Anand, 2011). The Punjabi government borrows about $1 billion more each year to pay debt servicing now running at $1.8 billion each year. Political will by lawmakers, the streamlining of laws to remove loopholes for tax evaders, and the development of a sufficiently paid corps of tax collectors are important elements in obtaining sufficient funds for government operations and avoiding excessive debt for governments.

## Direct and Indirect Interventions in Markets

### Direct Intervention

Intervention in markets by governments can be direct or indirect. In direct and sustained interventions in markets, some governments pursing what is termed "state capitalism" take ownership of businesses in key sectors (such as energy, transportation, and telecommunications) as well as in the operation of markets themselves. China, Russia, Saudi Arabia, Mexico, Brazil, and India are a few of the countries engaged in 21st century state capitalism where the state is the leading economic actor and uses markets primarily for political gain (Bremmer, 2010). Before the economic crisis of 2008, global financial institutions, such as major banks and the International Monetary Fund (which aims to keep countries solvent and trading with other nations), pressed developing countries to embrace the "Washington Consensus." This set of economic theories espoused (a) fiscal and budgetary discipline; (b) a market economy with property rights, competitive exchange rates, privatization of state-owned enterprises, and deregulation; as well as (c) openness to the global economy through trade liberalization and foreign direct investment. Such policies would be termed "economically liberal" because they would encourage individuals to control their own lives and make their own mistakes.

After the economic crisis of 2008, enthusiasm in developing countries for the Washington Consensus has weakened. The global audience is now increasingly skeptical of minimal involvement of governments in markets. Having a privately owned national champion firm like Cemex, now the third-largest cement maker, has much appeal in a country like Mexico (Bremmer, 2010). Cemex has close ties to the Mexican government that allows it to protect its position in the market through hostile takeovers of smaller Mexican competitors. Cemex has a market capitalization similar to Coca-Cola's and owns more foreign assets than Dow Chemical.

State-owned companies operating in global energy markets today include giants PetroChina, Brazil's Petrobras, Mexico's Pemex, and Russia's Rosneft and Gazprom. In 2008, China Mobile had more subscribers than any other cell phone company (with 488 million) (Bremmer, 2010). Importantly, those who run these state-owned companies answer first to those who wield political power in government or in a political party or in a royal family, rather than shareholders or other stakeholders. Those who wield political power want to accomplish political goals, such as solidifying their hold on power, rather than serving the public welfare. In China, the political leadership reserves the right to select the leaders of all major banks and large industrial companies. Would it be easier for a CEO to please shareholders concerned about profits or to please political bosses concerned about employment numbers and material support for other state-owned enterprises?

In India, the Agricultural Produce Marketing Committee (APMC) Act established in the 1950s required farmers to sell their produce in government-owned yards called *mandis* (Khanna, Tarun, Palepu, Knoop, & Lane, 2007). The original purpose of the mandis (meaning literally, markets) was to allow small farmers to avoid having to sell to buyers from higher castes with more money and power. In the mandis, buyers are not allowed to contact the farmers directly and the produce is auctioned. Unfortunately, the mandis did not preclude the exploitation of farmers. The yards are usually gridlocked with trucks unable to enter or leave. In the sun, the unsheltered produce ripens fast and often rots with waste up to 40% (Khanna et al., 2007).

At least 95% of agricultural produce reaches the end consumer through unorganized marketing channels like mandis, which many times leads to price fluctuations, wastage, and poor quality (Chaudhary, 2011). Farmers often transport produce to markets using carts and tractor trolleys, which not only delays the delivery process but also leads to wastage.

Importantly, information does not flow across the mandis, so inefficient pricing results. Additionally, access to the mandis by any buyer is not always a feature of the mandis. In sum, the mandis are a major hindrance to what the buyers and sellers would like. However, the government operators of the mandis and the political forces desiring the mandis to exist defend the place of the mandis in the Indian economy aggressively.

In the United States, the government bailouts of GM and Chrysler have been cited by some critics as not being efficient. For example, the COP gave criticism about the early sale of the government's interest in Chrysler Financial, saying the government lost $600 million in doing this (Shepardson, 2011). In a similar way, the Obama administration's strong preference to "get GM back on its feet, take a hands-off approach, and get out quickly" (Rattner, 2010) resulted in what some viewed as an early sale of troubled assets—$13.5 billion of the government's stake at $33 a share, instead of the $44.59 a share regarded as the "break-even price."

## Indirect Intervention

Although the GM bailout stands as a major intervention of the federal government in markets, intervention in markets can be indirect as well. In qualitative and observational research investigating the origin of materials and then the production, distribution, and recycling of a cotton t-shirt, Rivoli (2005) focuses first on cotton growers in the panhandle of Texas near Lubbock. In the flat, almost lunar landscape, these Texan farmers typically obtain about twice the world market price for their cotton. Although the farmers are entrepreneurial and resourceful, and their local and regional markets work well in matching buyers and sellers of cotton, a very favorable environment results from (a) government subsidies to cotton growers in the United States when world prices remain low, and (b) the government-assisted research programs in the science departments of universities, such as nearby Texas Tech University.

Here, the government subsidies ($3 billion a year to about 20,000 cotton farmers) (Grunwald, 2010) represent direct intervention in markets, whereas the support of scientific research benefitting the U.S. cotton growers represents indirect intervention in markets (Rivoli, 2005). The result of both kinds of intervention is that the cotton farmers in the United States have access to the latest science that allows them to improve their crop yields, and they know how to avoid competing when the risks are too high.

Brazil appealed to the World Trade Organization (WTO) about the subsidies given to U.S. cotton farmers for distorting trade and hurting farmers in developing countries. An Oxfam study found that eliminating these subsidies would boost world prices about 10%, which would be especially helpful to the 20,000 subsistence cotton growers in Africa (Grunwald, 2010).

Brazil won a WTO judgment against the United States for its cotton subsidies in March 2010 (Chan, 2010). The WTO gave Brazil permission to impose tariffs and other trade sanctions against U.S. products. The Brazilian sanctions were to include $591 million in tariffs on a wide array of goods, including autos, pharmaceuticals, medical equipment, electronics, textiles, and wheat. However, one day before these sanctions began, negotiators from the Office of the U.S. Trade Representative and the Agriculture Department reached a temporary deal with their Brazilian counterparts, putting the retaliation on hold (Grunwald, 2010). The United States agreed to subsidize Brazilian farmers (with subsidies totaling $147 million) to avoid ending subsidies to its own cotton farmers (Grunwald, 2010). In effect, the United States not only now subsidizes its own cotton farmers but also the cotton farmers of Brazil!

While the United States remains the second leading exporter of cotton (behind China with Brazil fifth [Klapper, 2009]), cotton crops have declined in recent years because farmers have chosen to grow corn because of the higher subsidies resulting from growing corn for ethanol production (Grunwald, 2010). Remember the Iowa caucuses are the first event in the U.S. presidential elections where corn subsidies are a leading topic and where opposition to such subsidies will likely spoil any presidential candidate's chances for later election. Up to 2006, the U.S. Department of Agriculture managed the Step-2 cotton-marketing program, which made payments to exporters and domestic mill users as compensation for buying higher priced American cotton (Klapper, 2009).

Thirty-eight percent of farmers in the United States received subsidies in 2009 (Cook, 2011). From 1995 to 2009, the U.S. government paid $246.7 billion in farm subsidies. In a bailout (such as for the financial services, insurance, and the auto industries), the government would receive much of its money back. With subsidies, there is no repayment.

## Summary

In summary, government serves as a unique stakeholder for firms and market operations. Unlike other stakeholders, government can (a) set the rules of the game, (b) play umpire, c) impose taxes, and (d) intervene directly as well as indirectly. Such interventions can be relatively brief as the bailout of the U.S. auto industry. By comparison, government interventions can be sustained for years as the farm subsidy programs of the USDA or the indirect interventions in agricultural markets through support for scientific research at universities. Government support for the educational system, in general, makes markets function better with educated buyers, sellers, and other stakeholders. The scale of direct interventions can run into the hundreds of billions of dollars, and the scope of such interventions can extend to supporting market actors in other countries.

Government intervention in markets receives criticism for distorting market prices and outcomes (Grunwald, 2010), but in countries pursuing state capitalism, such as China, such criticism is muted or unheard of because of the harsh political reality that does not allow freedom for the stakeholder of the media. State-owned enterprises, although many times ineffective in global markets as a result of bloated payrolls, enormous debt, and rigid bureaucracies, are increasingly becoming the largest competitors for multinational enterprises (Bremmer, 2010). In 2009, the Industrial and Commercial Bank of China (ICBC), China Mobile, and Petro China made *Forbes*'s list of the top five companies in the world based on market value.

Of course, firms and other stakeholders attempt to influence policy makers in government. According to records compiled by the nonpartisan CQ MoneyLine, firms legally lobbied such policy makers to the tune of a record $3.3 billion in 2008 (Schouten, 2009). This was up from $2.9 billion in 2007 and is more than double what was spent in 2004. "It's an arms race," the nonpartisan Center for Responsive Politics's Massie Ritsch said. "If your competitors are spending money on professional advocacy to play offense and defense in Washington, you feel you need to do the same" (Schouten, 2009, para. 3).

## Government and Distributive Justice

### The Development of Distributive Justice

When considering the fair allocation of limited resources, economist Adam Smith strongly opposed mercantilism—the conduct of markets to empower the state—and asserted that society would be much better off if individuals and businesses operated out of their self-interest. The end result would be allocation that would be done as if by "an invisible hand" and would be much more fair than what currently existed in 1776 when the Scotsman Smith published *The Wealth of Nations*. In recent years, some researchers have suggested that an overapplication of Smith's call to have markets free of government activity resulted in a false separation of the economic and social consequences of decision making of firm leaders and corporate boards in the 1990s (Mintzberg, Simons, & Basu, 2002). The authors further commented:

> As economists like Milton Friedman would have it, business attends to the eco-nomic, whereas government takes care of the social. ... Perfectly simple, except for one fatal flaw: Every economist readily recognizes that social decisions have economic consequences, in that they cost resources. So how can any economist or business executive fail to recognize that economic decisions have social conse-quences, in that they directly impact human beings? (p. 69)

Setbacks in stock markets of the world and subsequent policy mistakes by governments led to the Great Depression of the 1930s (Forbes & Ames, 2009). For example, after the stock market crash of 1929 that was fueled by borrowing to invest in speculative investments, the U.S. government reduced the flow of money in the financial system with high interest rates. Governments around the world invoked protectionist tariffs that further reduced trade and subsequently depressed business activity. Since this time, governments have seen business cycles as endemic to the private-property approach to society's provisioning through markets. As a result, governments have more intentionally addressed distributive justice through social programs as well as through citizens' participation in markets.

### Defining Distributive Justice

Distributive justice is a philosophy involving normative principles to determine fairness in the allocation of economic and social resources (Ferrell & Ferrell, 2008). Here, justice is defined as moral permissibility applied to the distribution of benefits and burdens. Rawls (1971) became a leader in thinking about distributive justice and asserted that inequalities in the distribution of goods and services could be allowed if the inequalities benefit the worst-off members of society. Government taxation and fiscal spending together combine as a primary means of such redistribution. Government entitlement programs, such as Medicaid, food stamps, and Temporary Assistance for Needy Families, are set up to benefit those with the least material resources in society. Federal Pell grants for attending college or university are also focused on financial need and do not require any repayment.

## The Controversy Over Distributive Justice

Distributive justice is a controversial topic and is addressed in democracies throughout the political system of the world. In this realm, countervailing pressure on elected officials is exerted from special interest groups, vocal constituents of elected officials, and voters in elections. Winners and losers emerge from political contests. A result of such struggle within the political system is a lingering unease with elected officials and diminished satisfaction with the political process of trade-offs and compromises.

The Edelman Trust Barometer manifests the phenomenon of mistrusting the political system (Edelman Trust Barometer, 2010). Figure 6.1a depicts the percentage of citizens across the United States, United Kingdom/France/Germany, and China who indicated *trust for government* by giving a response of 6 to 9 using a nine-point scale when responding to the following question: "How much do you trust government to do what is right?" Figure 6.1a depicts the time period 2001–2010. As shown, the European countries and the United States report the lowest trust, whereas China reports a high level of trust. The same question was posed about *trust for business* in the same countries. Figure 6.1b depicts these results. As shown, the Chinese express the most trust for business (and can be termed "optimists" about business), whereas those from the United Kingdom/France/Germany express the least trust (and can be termed "skeptics" about business). Those from the United States posted a moderate amount of trust and business (and can be termed "pragmatists").

In sum, there is much room for improvement in citizens' of Western democracies trust in either government or business to do the right thing. However, in a comparison of the U.S. respondents' level of trust for government with that of business, trust in business posts slightly higher levels in nine of the ten years of the study. Further research remains to be done regarding China, as global business is a relatively new phenomenon there, elections have not taken place since the Communist Party came to power in 1949, making timely information about the outside world difficult to obtain.

## The Ideas of Distributive Justice and the Size of Government

As a result of the active role the government has taken in addressing issues related to societal QOL (such as employment, inflation, education, healthcare, and pensions), the scale and scope of the government's role in regard to distributive justice continues to be debated. This debate commonly appears in the debate over whether a society should have a large government, which would emphasize more redistribution of wealth, or a small government, which would not emphasize distributive justice as heavily. For example, the ideas of Steve Forbes (publisher of *Forbes* business magazine) represent many of those advocating for a smaller role of government interaction in markets. Forbes proposes that government policies should be devoted to ensuring six conditions are present in the economy: (a) the rule of law, (b) respect for property rights, (c) stable money, (d) pro-growth tax system, (e) ease in starting a business, and (f) few barriers to doing business. Brooks (2010) echoes Forbes and calls for a turn away from big government and its expansive social programs, so that citizens can reap the rewards, as well as the consequences, of their own actions. He reports that across multiple studies, an average of 70% of those in the United States prefer free enterprise (similar to what Forbes proposes) as the core provisioning

**Figure 6.1a**    Trust in Government in the United States, United Kingdom/France/Germany, and China Over Ten Years

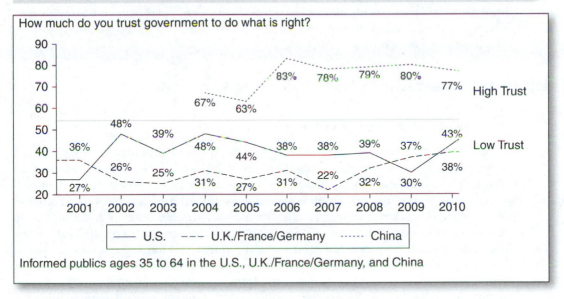

*Source:* Edelman Trust Barometer, 2010.

**Figure 6.1b**    Trust in Business in the United States, United Kingdom/France/Germany, and China Over Ten Years

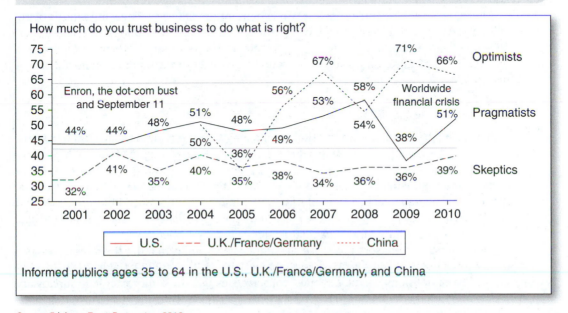

*Source:* Edelman Trust Barometer, 2010.

system for society to any alternative (that would be characterized by a more dominant role for government) (Brooks, 2010). However, since the outcomes of recent presidential elections in the United States have been fairly evenly split, this would suggest that the issue of big government more evenly divides the voting public. Democrats generally want the government to play a larger role in society, and Republicans generally want the government to play a smaller role in society.

## Liberal and Conservative Visions

### Constrained and Unconstrained Views

Researchers studying how social values affect political views have recently focused their thinking and research on individuals' political ideologies. Researchers are now studying how individuals who self-identify as liberal or conservative differ in their perspectives on (a) the inherent goodness of humans and (b) the breadth of psychological dimensions used to evaluate social and economic issues (Haidt, Graham, & Joseph, 2009). Regarding the nature of humans, Sowell (2007) has proposed that two visions about the nature of humans have characterized political thought and ideology in Western countries. One vision is the constrained vision, which views the nature of humans darkly and sees humans as being motivated primarily from self-interest. Economic philosophers such as Adam Smith and Hobbes are usually cited as being the leading expressionists for the constrained vision. These thinkers proposed that incentives are the most efficient means to motivate individuals to care and attend to the welfare of others. This is accomplished primarily through markets in modern societies, as individuals have to identify the needs of others and meet them in a competitive marketplace with superior products and services.

Alternatively, the unconstrained vision is more optimistic, and views humans as being willing to care for and attend to the welfare of others. Given the condition of modern societies filled with urban populations, the government is often seen as the institution that is most capable of fairly allocating the resources of society in a manner characteristic of distributive justice.

### Making Moral Judgments

Regarding the psychology of marking moral judgments, McAdams et al. (2008) has proposed that liberals primarily use two dimensions to make a moral judgment: (a) harm/care (is someone or something being harmed or in need of care?) and (b) fairness/reciprocity (is someone experiencing unfair treatment?). Since the Civil Rights Era in the United States, the focus of liberals has been on alleviating the injustice experienced by minorities and women in a society perceived to have racist and oppressive aspects to such groups (Jacobs, 2009). Ending discrimination became the rallying issue for liberals.

By comparison, conservatives use five dimensions when making their moral assessments about political and social issues (Graham, Haidt, & Nosek, 2009; Haidt, 2012). In addition to the dimensions used by liberals, conservatives use three more: (c) in-group/loyalty (is the proper allegiance being expressed to the group, tribe, or nation?), (d) authority/respect (is the social order and established hierarchies receiving due respect?), and (e) purity/sanctity (are unclean elements or practices being kept away from the group, tribe, or nation?).

The constrained/unconstrained visions of humans and man-made institutions, along with the two or five dimension used for making moral assessments, combine in influencing individuals toward liberal or conservative leanings regarding economic freedom and social freedom. This can be seen in Figure 6.2 where Haidt (2008) reports on a large-scale study of the importance of the five moral dimensions across those self-identifying as liberals, moderates, and conservatives. As shown, the liberals emphasize harm and fairness, while the conservatives use these (to a slightly lesser degree), as well as the other three dimensions. Results similar to these have been obtained by researchers in a variety of countries.

**Figure 6.2**    Five Dimensions of Moral Psychology for Political Groups in the United States

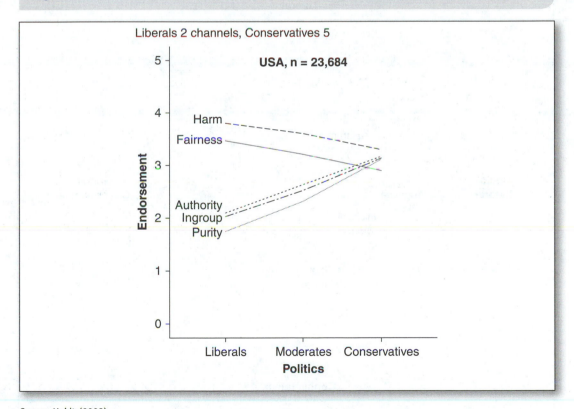

*Source:* Haidt (2008).

### Differences Between Liberals and Conservatives

Economic freedom would correspond to limited government involvement in markets, while social freedom would correspond to limited reliance on traditional social norms and traditional institutions of society, such as the family, schools, churches and businesses. In societies, liberals reflect a more atomized society where individuals pursue their own ends as long as they are not harming or being unfair to others. Conservatism reflects a society with more connecting tissue among individuals of the society and where societal structure, in the form of both institutions and social norms, is valued. In sum, liberalism implies more openness to new experiences and a veneration of tolerance and diversity. By comparison, conservatism implies that curbs are needed for human behavior or else excesses will result with sometimes deleterious consequences.

**Figure 6.3**  Social and Economic Freedom Diamond With Positioning of Some Well-Known Personalities

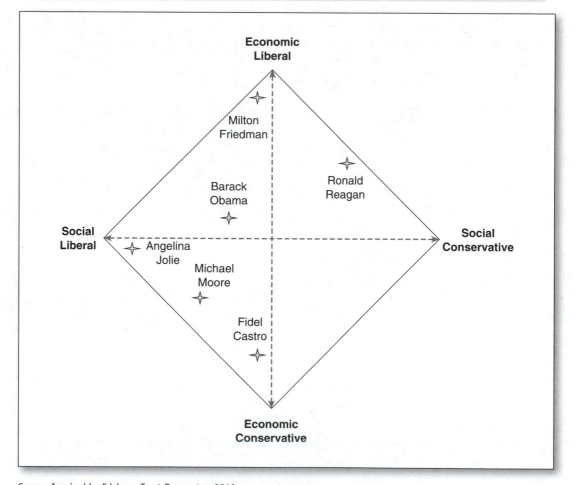

*Source:* Inspired by Edelman Trust Barometer, 2010.

Figure 6.3 depicts a four-section diamond with some possible positioning for well-known personalities, some of whom are featured in this book. At the top end, laissez-faire economist Milton Friedman (1970) would be placed. Opposite to this on the bottom end of the diamond would be Fidel Castro whose brand of communism seeks to restrict or eliminate markets in society. Ronald Reagan, an advocate of lower taxes and a smaller non-military public sector, anchors the upper right of the diamond. Opposite Reagan in the lower left sector of the diamond is documentary film-maker Michael Moore, a long-time critic of capitalism. Barack Obama occupies a place in the left of the intersection of the dotted lines. This is because of Obama's favor for an activist government but willingness to call on traditional norms and institutions to guide society. Hollywood's Angelina Jolie, a United Nations (UN) special envoy to refugees around the world occupies a position to the left corner. Although Jolie is willing to participate in the entertainment industry as a highly paid actress, her compassion for the hurting can be seen in her adoption of multiple children. But she remains unmarried to fellow star Brad Pitt as a live-in partner, thereby turning away from traditional norms.

In sum, the degree of distributive justice that permeates society is a political question in most societies today. Undergirding these ongoing debates about the size of government, the focus of social programs, and the perfectibility of man-made institutions are more assessments made by individuals. Liberals tend to emphasize the freedom of individuals in their decision making about social and economic issues while conservatives value preexisting structure in society, such as traditional institutions and norms.

## CONCLUSION

This chapter examined the role of the state in delivering QOL to a society. The opening story about the Japanese government's sudden immersion into simultaneous crises related to the March 2011 tsunami and the subsequent nuclear reactor meltdowns at TEPCO's Fukushima Daiichi power plant put in high relief society's mandate to have its government, rather than business, handle the most acute and threatening challenges to its existence. Quality of life is a primary concern for government and business, but modern government has a broader scope of operation in addressing societal QOL than businesses. The GM bailout of 2009 suggests how semipermeable the boundaries between business and government can be as the government decided the liquidation of GM and Chrysler would cause too much damage in society. By most accounts, the bailout of GM had many successful outcomes. However, other government activity in markets can have distorting effects on markets and those affected by these markets.

With many social and economic issues facing society, the role of the government in society is resolved through a political process. Distributive justice may be a driving concern for some of those involved in this political process. Research about the moral foundations of political views suggests that liberals and conservatives hold different views about the perfectibility of humans and man-made institutions with liberals more positive about these. Liberals' moral assessments are more influenced by concerns about harm and fairness, while conservatives use these two dimensions but also are influenced by concerns about the social order. Finally, the story of Arthur Guinness and the Guinness Brewery of Dublin, Ireland, shows how a business can operate for hundreds of years providing for the social welfare of its employees before government assumed this role in many countries of the world.

## QUESTIONS

1. What new perspectives about the role of the state in society did you gain from reading Chapter 6?

2. Of the 13 listed dimensions for QOL, which is most important to your QOL? Which is the least? Explain.

3. In your opinion, to what degree was the GM bailout a success? Explain.

4. Review Tables 6.2a and 6.2b, which present some risks and outcomes for stakeholders in the GM bailout. In your opinion, who lost the least? Who lost the most? Explain why you think this happened.

5. What imperfection that can result from government intervention in markets bothers you the most? Which bothers you the least?

6. Think about what you learned about distributive justice in this chapter. Can it be said that concepts of distributive justice focus on outcomes of the provisioning system of society? How do moral dimensions used in our psychological processing of issues related to distributive justice come into play in the political life of a society?

7. You can access the "shortest political survey" at www.theadvocates.org. Use this ten-question survey to gain one perspective on your possible political leanings. What do you lean? How would you improve this ten-question survey?

8. Haidt believes that understanding how those with different political views think can lead to increased productivity. For example, if conservatives used terms like "reciprocity" and "protecting the weak," they could more often find common ground with liberals and moderates. What terms or ideas could liberals use to find common ground with conservatives?

## MAVERICKS WHO MADE IT

### Arthur Guinness

**B**EFORE THE MODERN state began focusing on the health, education, and welfare of its citizens, urban areas remained cesspools of disease, ignorance, and misery. For example, Dublin, Ireland, had the highest rate of contagious disease, as well as the highest death rate of any city in Europe in the late 1800s (Mansfield, 2009).

Smallpox, measles, scarlet fever, whooping cough, dysentery, typhoid fever, and tuberculosis abounded in the squalid conditions brought on by overcrowding in such cities—similar to poverty-stricken cities of poor countries today. Ever since the famines of the 1840s, crowds of immigrants had relentlessly come into Dublin to escape their problems and to find a way to other lands via ship. However, the passage proved to be too expensive for most, and as a result, Dublin became swollen with the poor, diseased, and infirm.

One hundred years before these difficult times in Dublin, Arthur Guinness began brewing beer. At the time, most Europeans regarded water as being impure and drank beer instead. This even carried over to groups who left Europe for the New World, such as the Puritan Pilgrims who put ashore in Plymouth, Massachusetts, in order to begin brewing beer because their stocks of beer on board *The Mayflower* were running low (Mansfield, 2009).

Guinness experimented with roasting the barley sprouts longer in the first stage of brewing in order to refine the dark porter beer that was becoming popular in London. The result was the Guinness stout that has carried the family name since 1759 when Arthur signed the 9,000-year lease for property near St. James Gate in Dublin where he built his brewery. The brew he developed turned out not only to be very pleasing to many, but also because of the process Guinness used, he had to use the very best ingredients. The result was the Guinness stout retained its quality and favorable characteristics in shipping. This was unlike other beers, so Guinness gained a competitive advantage in exporting. Today, Guinness is brewed in 49 countries and sells the hearty, dark beer in 150 countries with sales totaling 2 billion pints each year (about 10 million per day.). It has become such an icon of Ireland that Queen Elizabeth II visited the Guinness brewery on her visit to Ireland in May 2011, and U.S. President Barack Obama drank a pint of Guinness in an Irish pub on his visit to Ireland in the same month.

As a maverick, Arthur developed quite a record of being an innovator in his approach to business. In addition to identifying the steps to make the unique Guinness beer, he once stood up to the local sheriff when the sheriff came to fill in a channel his men had dug from the River Liffey to St. James Gate. Arthur grabbed a pick-ax and furiously told the sheriff he would reopen the channel if the sheriff filled it in. After a lawsuit initiated by Arthur, the Guinness brewery struck a deal with the local

*(Continued)*

(Continued)

President Barack Obama holds a pint of Guinness and watches as First Lady Michelle Obama draws a pint at Ollie Hayes' Pub in Moneygall, Ireland, May 23, 2011.

government and obtained all the water it needed for ten pounds sterling per year. Today, the brewery obtains its water from the Wicklow Mountains south of Dublin.

Although Arthur attained upper middle-class status in Dublin, he viewed his business in a way inspired from his spiritual life. Arthur was a Protestant in Catholic Ireland. Evangelical Methodism taught by the renowned preacher and social reformer John Wesley who lived during Arthur's time had a strong influence on him. Methodism emphasized a transforming salvation for the individual as well as social outreach. It encouraged visiting prisoners and taking up collections for the poor. It also urged the rich to fulfill their Christian responsibilities to society. Toward this end, Wesley taught that Christians should gain wealth in order to give all they can to those in need.

Arthur's social conscience manifested itself through other innovations. He founded the first Sunday schools in Ireland at a time when these hardly existed anywhere else in the world. Surprisingly, he was opposed in this undertaking by Sabbatarians who perceived such Sunday schools as violating biblical injunctions against working on Sunday. He fought against dueling, and he chaired the board of a hospital for the poor. Arthur also promoted Irish arts and culture as a means to instill pride in his country-men, and he even spoke out against anti-Catholic laws. He became a champion for the rights of Roman Catholics in Ireland and treated his Catholic workers as if they were his social equals. Such nonconformist stands risked losing customers and standing in society, but Arthur pursued these unswervingly.

Arthur viewed his business success as a kind of mandate or calling to benefit not just his family, but to the broader good he could do in the world. In future generations, Guinness family members continued this legacy.

From 1860 to 1865, his grandson Benjamin Lee Guinness led the restoration of St. Patrick's Cathedral—a symbol of Christianity in Ireland—when the church established in 1192 had become dilapidated and had almost collapsed. In the late 1800s, the Guinness brewery hired a physician who visited workers' living quarters in what can only be described as one of the first public health cam-paigns. In this way, workers and their families were guided to better living conditions. Additionally, personal development programs ranging from hygiene, disease prevention, cooking, and infant feed-ing began to be fielded by the firm for the benefit of its workers.

By the 1920s, a Guinness worker enjoyed full medical and dental care, massage services, reading rooms, subsidized meals, a company-funded pension, subsidies for funeral expenses, educational benefits, sports facilities, fee concerts, lectures, and entertainment. They also were guaranteed two free pints of Guinness beer each day:

> The descriptions of Guinness benevolence—the buildings, institutions, trusts, parks, schools, and services that Guinness has left [in] its wake—could fill volumes. . . . Yet just as important as these monuments of stone and finance are the monuments that live in men's hearts. A hardened Dublin taxi driver tears up at the mention of the Guinness company. His grandmother . . . might have died in her youth had Guinness doctors not tended her so well. (Mansfield, 2009, p. 38).

In 1992, the Guinness family ceased to be directly involved in the management of the company, while retaining a financial interest (Griffiths, 2004). In 2007, the Guinness Company joined with Grand Metropolitan to create Diageo, the largest drinks company in the world. In 2009, Guinness celebrated its 250th anniversary of brewing.

## Questions

1. In what ways did Arthur Guinness demonstrate that he was willing to go his own way in leading his life and his business?

2. What contributed to Arthur Guinness becoming a maverick who made it, and not just another person who clashed with the status quo because of his different ideas?

3. If a company is merely a legal creation, why don't companies all behave the same when it comes to social issues?

4. Why were living conditions in cities like Dublin in the 1700s and the 1800s allowed to become so bad? What about living conditions in mega-cities of the third world, such as Nairobi, Kenya, or Calcutta, India?

## REFERENCES

Bremmer, I. (2010). *The end of the free market: Who wins the war between states and corporations?* New York, NY: Portfolio.

Brooks, A. C. (2010). *The battle: How the fight between free enterprise and big government will shape America's future.* New York, NY: Basic Books.

Bureau of Labor Statistics. (2011). Retrieved from http://www.bls.gov/

Chan, S. (2010, April 6). U.S. and Brazil reach agreement on cotton dispute. *New York Times.* Retrieved from http://www.nytimes.com/2010/04/07/business/07trade.html

Chaudhary, D. (2011, May 4). Produce supplier gets venture capital funding. *The Wall Street Journal.* Retrieved from http://online.wsj.com/article/SB100014240527487039371045763028322498757 92.html?KEYWORDS = mandis + india

CNN. (2011a, June 1). Physicist Michio Kaku: We came close to losing northern Japan. The Arena. Retrieved from http://inthearena.blogs.cnn.com/2011/06/10/michio-kaku-power-company-covered-up-level-of-nuclear-contamination-and-theres-a-rabbit-in-japan-born-without-ears-coincidence/

CNN. (2011b, June 1). Michio Kaku: Power company covered up level of nuclear contamination. Retrieved from http://inthearena.blogs.cnn.com/2011/06/10/michio-kaku-power-company-covered-up-level-of-nuclear-contamination-and-theres-a-rabbit-in-japan-born-without-ears-coincidence/

Cook, K. (2011). National summary analysis, farm subsidy database, environmental working group. Retrieved from http://farm.ewg.org/region?fips = 00000&regname = UnitedStatesFarmSubsidy Summary

Cummins, R. (2000). Objective and subjective quality of life: An interactive model. *Social Indicators Research, 52*(1), 55–72.

Diener, E., & Suh, E. (1997). Measuring quality of life: Economic, social, and subjective indicators. *Social Indicators Research, 40,* 189–216.

Economic Times. (2011). Union budget 2011: India needs to be more efficient in tax collection, says Robert Parker, credit suisse. Retrieved from http://articles.economictimes.indiatimes.com/2011-0228/news/28642390_1_inflation-forecast-fiscal-deficit-target-food-price-inflation

Edelman Trust Barometer. (2010). 2010 Edelman trust barometer. Retrieved from http://www.edelman .com/trust/2010/

Fackler. (2011, March 11). Powerful quake and tsunami devastate northern Japan. *The New York Times.* Retrieved from www.nytimes.com

First Things. (2010, February). While we're at it. *First Things,* pp. 69-70.

Fehrenbacher, D. E. (2001). *The Dred Scott case: Its significance in American law and politics.* New York, NY: Oxford University Press.

Ferrell, O. C., & Ferrell, L. (2008 March). A macromarketing ethics framework: Stakeholder orientation and distributive justice. *Journal of Macromarketing, 28*(1), 24–32.

Forbes, S. (2009). Capitalism: A true love story. *Forbes, 184*(7). Retrieved from http://www.forbes.com

Forbes, S., & Ames, E. (2009). *How capitalism will save us: Why free people and free markets are the best answer in today's economy.* New York, NY: Crown Business.

Fox, J. (2011, January/February). "What is it that only I can do?" *Harvard Business Review, 89*(1/2), 118–123.

Friedman, M. (1970 September 13). The social responsibility of a business is to increase its profits. *The New York Times Magazine.* Retrieved from http://www.colorado.edu/studentgroups/libertarians/ issues/friedman-soc-resp-business.html

Graham, J., Haidt, J., & Nosek, B. A. (2009). Liberals and conservatives relay on different sets of moral foundations. *Journal of Personality and Social Psychology, 96*(5), 1029–1046.

Griffiths, M. (2004). *Guinness is Guinness: The colorful story of a black and white brand.* London, UK: Cyan Communications.

Grunwald, M. (2010, April 9). Why the U.S. is also giving Brazilians farm subsidies. *Time.* Retrieved from http://www.time.com/time/nation/article/0,8599,1978963,00.html#ixzz1MiuQPxzr

Haidt, J. (2008, March). Jonathan Haidt on the moral roots of liberals and conservatives. Technology, Entertainment, Design (TED) Conference. Retrieved from http://www.ted.com/talks/jonathan_haidt_on_the_moral_mind.html

Haidt, J. (2012). *The righteous mind: Why good people are divided by politics and religion.* New York, NY: Pantheon.

Haidt, J., Graham, J., & Joseph, C. (2009). Above and below left-right: Ideological narratives and moral foundations. *Psychological Inquiry, 20*(2/3), 110–119.

Inglehart, R., & Baker, W. E. (2000, February). Modernization, cultural change and the persistence of traditional values. *American Sociological Review, 65,* 19–51.

Isidore, C. (2012, February 12). Still fighting over GM's bailout, *CNNMoney.* Retrieved from http://money.cnn.com/2012/02/16/news/companies/gm_bailout/index.htm

Jacobs, T. (2009, April). Morals authority. *Miller-McCune.* Retrieved from http://www.miller-mccune.com

Khanna, T., Palepu, H., Knoop, C. I., & Lane, D. (2007). *Metro cash & carry. Harvard Business School Case 9-707-505.* Boston, MA: Harvard Business School.

Klapper, B. S. (2009, September 1). WTO sanctions U.S. over cotton subsidies. *The Washington Post.* Retrieved from http://www.washingtonpost.com/wp-dyn/content/article/2009/08/31/AR2009083103679.html

Kotler, P. (1986). *Principles of marketing* (3 ed.). Englewood Cliffs, NJ: Prentice-Hall.

Kroll, A. (2011, January 13). Auto bailouts: A success story? *Mother Jones.* Retrieved from motherjones.com/mojo/2011/01/auto-bailouts-success-story

Larsen, R., & Eid, M. (2008). Ed Diener and the science of subjective well-being. In M. Eid & R.J. Larsen (Eds.), *The Science of Subjective Well-Being* (pp. 1–16). New York, NY: Gilford Press.

Lears, J. F. (1996). Quality of Life Index, *International Living, 15,* 1 and 9–18.

Legatum. (2010). *The 2010 Legatum Prosperity Index: An inquiry into global wealth and wellbeing.* Retrieved from http://www.prosperity.com

Levitz, J. (2010, August 25). Coffins made with brotherly love have undertakers throwing dirt. *The Wall Street Journal.* Retrieved from http://online.wsj.com/article/SB10001424052748703846604575448083489852328.html

Lutz, B. (2011). *Car guys vs. bean counters: The battle for the soul of American business.* New York, NY: Portfolio/Penguin.

Mackey, J. (2009). Creating a new paradigm for business. In M. Strong's (Ed.), *Be the solution: How entrepreneurs and conscious capitalists can solve all the world's problems* (pp. 78–113). New York, NY: Wiley.

Mansfield, S. (2009). *The search for God and Guinness: A biography of the beer that changed the world.* Nashville, TN: Thomas Nelson.

McAdams, D. P., Albaugh, M., Farber, E., Daniels, J., Logan, R., & Olson, L. (2008). Family metaphors and moral institutions: How conservatives and liberals narrate their lives. *Journal of Personality and Social Psychology, 95,* 978–990.

McCurry, J. (2011, August 26). Naoto Kan resigns as Japan's prime minister. *The Guardian.* Retrieved from http://www.guardian.co.uk

McGregor, J. (2005). *One billion Customers: Lessons from the front lines of doing business in China.* New York, NY: Wall Street Journal Books.

McMillian, J. (2002). *Reinventing the Bazar: A natural history of markets*. New York, NY: W.W. Norton.

McMurry, J. (2007). New leak identified at damaged Japanese nuclear plant. *guardian.co.uk*. Retrieved from http://www.guardian.co.uk/world/2007/jul/19/japan.justinmccurry/print

Mintzberg, H., Simons, R., & Basu, K. (2002, Fall). Beyond selfishness. *Sloan Management Review, 44(1),* 67–74.

NEF. (2009). *The Happy Planet Index 2.0: Why good lives don't have to cost the Earth.* New Economics Foundation. Retrieved from http://www.happyplanetindex.org

Onishi, N., & Fackler, M. (2011). In nuclear crisis, crippling mistrust. *The New York Times.* Retrieved from http://www.nytimes.com

Pesek, W. (2012, March 5–11). First disaster, then dysfunction. *Bloomberg Businessweek*, pp. 15–16.

Peterson, M., & Malhotra, N. K. (1997, Spring). Comparative marketing measures of societal quality of life: Substantive dimensions in 186 countries. *Journal of Macromarketing, 17*(1), 25–38.

Quelch, J., & Jocz, K. (2007). *Greater good: How good marketing makes for a better democracy.* Boston, MA: Harvard Business Press.

Rattner, S. (2010). *Overhaul: An insider's account of the Obama Administration's emergency rescue of the auto industry.* Boston, MA: Houghton Mifflin Harcourt.

Rawls, J. (1971). *A theory of justice.* Cambridge, MA: Harvard University Press.

Rivoli, P. (2005). *The travels of a T-Shirt in the global economy: An economist examines the markets, power, and politics of world trade.* New York, NY: Wiley.

Rubenfeld, S. (2011, April 1). Panel says provincial China presents compliance challenge. *The Wall Street Journal.* Retrieved from http://blogs.wsj.com/corruption-currents/2011/04/01/panel-says-provincial-china-presents-complianc-challenge/?KEYWORDS = uneven + enforcement

Schouten, F. (2009). Lobbying spending tops $3 billion in '08. *USA Today.* Retrieved from http://www.usatoday.com/news/washington/2009-01-26-lobbying_N.htm

Sharma, A., & Anand, G. (2011, May 15). Punjab, star of India's rise, faces steep fall. *The Wall Street Journal.* Retrieved from http://online.wsj.com

Shepardson, D. (2011, March 16). Panel says jury out on auto bailout. *The Detroit News.* Retrieved from http://detnews.com/article/20110316/AUTO01/103160328

Sirgy, M. J. (2001). *Handbook of quality-of-life research: An ethical marketing perspective.* Boston, MA: Kluwer Academic.

Sowell, T. (2007). *A conflict of visions: Ideological origins of political struggles*, revised edition. New York, NY: Basic Books.

Stiglitz, J. E., Sen, A., & Fitoussi, J. P. (2010). *Mismeasuring our lives: Why GDP doesn't add up.* New York, NY: The New Press.

Tabuchi, H. (2011, May 20). Head of Japanese utility steps down after nuclear crisis. *The New York Times.* Retrieved from http://www.nytimes.com

Tokyo Electric Power Company, Inc. (TEPCO). (2010). TEPCO. Retrieved from http://www.tepco.co.jp/en/index-e.html

UNDP. (2011). *Human development report: Sustainability and equity—A better future for all.* United Nations Development Program. Retrieved from http://hdr.undp.org/en/

Wilkie, W. (2001). Forward. In P. Bloom & G. Gundlach (Eds.), *Handbook of marketing and society* (pp. vii–xii). Thousand Oaks, CA: Sage.

Wilkie, W.L., & Moore, E.S. (1999). Marketing's contributions to society. *Journal of Marketing, 63,* 198–218.

Yoshida, R. (2011, June 7). Probe poised to take Tepco to task. *The Japan Times.* Retrieved from http://search.japantimes.co.jp/cgi-bin/nn20110607a3.html

# PART II

# Enterprise With Market Dynamism in Mind

## CHAPTER 7

# Contemporary Consumers

## VIDEO YOUR SHOPPING HAUL AND PUT IT ON YOUTUBE

### Shopping Haulers

Haul videos are homemade online videos in which shoppers (usually young women) show off what they purchased on their most recent shopping trip. Sharing their bargains and their enthusiasm for their selected brands has brought surprising results for some. There are hundreds of thousands of haul videos on YouTube with several posting millions of views. One of their appeals is providing a voyeuristic thrill about seeing how others spend money.

Since 2009, Elle and Blair Fowler, 24 and 19, respectively, have made plenty of money (ABC News Radio, 2011). So much that they moved from Tennessee to Los Angeles. The sisters started a website (www.elleandblair.com) with an active blog and are co-authoring a book. "Everything I do, everywhere I go, everything I taste, everything, I'm thinking of videos and blog ideas and I'm taking pictures so I can put it on a blog," Blair Fowler said.

After a day of chasing bargains at the mall and specialty stores, the sisters would return home and make videos of themselves cooing over their finds and explaining why they made their purchases. They would test cosmetics and discuss where they found good deals on these. They would also comment on the latest fashion trends. To date, millions have watched their videos.

"Companies would contact me and say, 'Our site crashed, the products sold out,'" Blair Fowler said. "I was like, 'Why?' and they were like, 'Well, you talked about it in your video'" (ABC News Radio, 2011, p. 1).

In one video that has received more than a million views in just a few months, Blair, the younger of the sisters and a brunette, sits on a bed and shows off a new dress. "And it's black, it's scoop neck and it has this really cute beaded design," Blair Fowler said (Harrison, 2011, p. 1). "But it's just a simple black dress and I got this because it's gonna be good especially with the holidays coming around – ex-specially, I know it's especially – I was raised to say especially, so that's what I'm gonna say."

With millions viewing the Fowler sisters, *Good Morning America* featured them on one of its shows. They are in talks about developing a reality show. Apparel chains, such as Forever 21 and TJ Maxx, have offered gift cards, video contests, and other rewards to the Fowlers and other haulers.

"Companies who do this – who provide gift cards or free merchandise to haulers – need to be aware of the potential downfalls, and what it could do to their image," Bryant University Marketing Professor Elaine Notarantonio said. "It could jeopardize their image" (Harrison, 2011, p. 1).

Maryapril Bautista of Los Angeles says she earns a 15% commission from a hair care company, Flat Iron Experts, on sales coming from her product reviews (Romano, 2010). "We talk about a product, and then we give a link to the Web site," Bautista said (ABC News Radio, 2011, p. 1). Using the screen name AprilAthena7, she makes less than $100 per month because her subscriber base is low. "But a lot of those girls probably have 50,000 and make a couple of thousand a month doing that," Bautista said (Romano, 2010, p. 1).

The Federal Trade Commission published guidelines about hauling in December 2008. If the haulers received free products, this must be disclosed. However, many haulers do not know this. Some haulers who pan products have received pressure from the negatively rated companies to take down the hauling videos.

A small clothing company Hot Miami Styles sent an e-mail asking Teresa Ulrich, a hairdresser from Vancouver, British Columbia, Canada, to review the free clothes they had sent her and to be "positive." Despite this, the 29-year-old Ulrich filmed her honest appraisal of the clothes. In her video, Ulrich held up a scrunched up blue garment that was supposed to be a dress. "It's so beyond bad, it's bad, bad, bad," Ulrich said. "It's car-wash bad – as in, I'll wash my car with it" (Romano, 2010, p. 2).

After the video was on YouTube for only a few hours and viewed 5,000 times, Hot Miami Styles e-mailed Ulrich and pressured her to take it down saying that two employees were terminated because of the "drop in sales." Ulrich declined the request. "I feel it's the integrity of the person, really," Ulrich said. "I feel like when people get stuff for free, they lie" (Romano, 2010, p. 2).

Ulrich is in talks about hosting a style program for a Canadian shopping website and thinks about hauling leading to a glamorous career. "That would really be amazing," Ulrich said. After reflecting, Ulrich posed a philosophical question. "When is it going to be enough stuff?" Ulrich asked. "When are we going to have enough?" (Romano, 2010, p. 3).

---

### Your Thoughts?

- What do hauling videos offer that paid advertisements do not?
- Would you be more likely to view a sponsored hauling video or an unsponsored one? What if the hauler received free merchandise to evaluate? What if the hauler just received a press release about a brand to alert the hauler to be looking for the brand during an upcoming shopping trip (instead of discovering the brand on his or her own like a typical shopper would do)?
- When are we going to have enough products?

---

## CHAPTER OVERVIEW AND LEARNING OBJECTIVES

This chapter will examine one of the driving factors of market dynamism—changing consumer preferences. Today, consumer behavior increasingly has not only a "me" dimension (What do I get?), but also a "we" dimension (What do I get to do with others?). The opening vignette about shopping haulers captures one version of such two-dimensional consumption—shopping for one's self and then telling the world about it online. The "Me" dimension of consumption raises an issue about materialism. Specifically, is more always better? Quality-of-life (QOL) researchers continue to debate at what level an increase in income results in no increase in subjective well-being (happiness). Despite the increased incomes in most countries of the world in recent years, many consumers remain vulnerable when receiving healthcare. Consumers also experience vulnerability as their incomes become uncertain during an economic downturn and as global climate change continues to unfold.

The "We" dimension of consumption has become more noticeable in the age of Facebook. Communication technology and emerging social media enable individuals and businesses to network themselves like never before. An increasingly networked world means that more than information can be shared more readily in the future. Consequently, collaborative consumption in the form of sharing, lending, renting, reselling, and volunteering all become more sensible. The folk-rock group The Grateful Dead is featured as the Mavericks Who Made It in this chapter. This group developed a strong community of fans because the band encouraged fans to record their concerts and share these recordings with their friends. As their music was shared, the band's following increased for their concerts. With widespread familiarity, the band made millions of dollars from touring and from sales of their merchandise sold at their concerts.

After this chapter, you should be able to answer the following questions:

- What elements compose a dominant social paradigm regarding material acquisition?
- What makes some in society "vulnerable consumers?"
- What is "voluntary simplicity?"
- What is it about collaborative consumption that could make it important for success in marketing in the future?
- In the future, could sharing play a prominent role in the economic system?

## THE "ME" IN MARKETS OF TODAY

### "Just a Little Bit More"

American industrialist John D. Rockefeller, whose overwhelming success in the oil refining led to his Standard Oil Company monopoly being broken up by the U.S. Supreme Court in 1910, was asked, "How much money is enough? Rockefeller, whose fortune exceeded $1.2 billion (one of the first billionaires ever), smiled at his questioner, leaned forward, and said, "Just a little bit more" (Kessel, 2008).

In his book, *Is the American Dream Killing You?: How the Market Rules Our Lives*, social critic Paul Stiles proposes that "the Market" is more than just an economic means of distribution, but it now constitutes a belief system in itself. According to Stiles, both the materialistic ethos of the Market (characterized by the assumption that "more is better") and the Market are actually innately opposed to the traditional foundation of American life that values opportunity and access for all citizens.

Stiles skewers baser pursuits in corporate life ("if it sells, it must be OK"), but he also does the same for baser pursuits in the lives of individuals. For example, he not only criticizes the production of vacuous or harmful media content, but also he criticizes the choices individuals make in consuming such media on a repetitive basis. In the end, Stiles's willingness to consider macromarketing phenomena broadly, and his incisive ability to identify the role of individuals who comprise society in accepting or contributing to each of these macro phenomena make his criticisms more powerful.

Additionally, the arguments in *Is the American Dream Killing You?* gain power through the comparisons Stiles sees possible when looking at phenomena with a broad lens. For example, in discussing The Market vs. the Nuclear Family, Stiles notes that the qualities the Market rewards, such as (a) the ability to look out for oneself and (b) opportunism, are deadly when applied in intimate relationships because such qualities are fundamentally based on a lack of trust. Stiles goes on to declare that love is not a market principle.

Stiles perceives a duality regarding the Market. According to Stiles, it carries aspects of Jekyll and Hyde. If the Market is surrounded with the right values, it is a good physician. However, if it is not, it is likely to become a predator. Stiles is clear about how the right moral sensibilities are developed outside the market. He is bold in pointing to the spiritual lives of humans as providing the source of such right values. Without these values, individuals can degrade themselves and their environment through their consumption.

In Stiles' view, this scenario is currently being played out. More and more individuals unthinkingly accept the market as the principal arbiter of life's decisions. To Stiles, society's hold on the right values is dangerously weakening. Stiles asserts that a deadly metaphysical conflict is under way driven by the Market's adoption of pure materialism, which regards the soul as nonexistent or irrelevant.

In many ways, Stiles's ideas resonate with macromarketing scholarship. For example, he applies systems theory to understand that the Market is not synonymous with society. In Stiles's view, the Market is a part of society. Stiles recognizes this as a critical distinction and then goes on to assert that the economy has two levels: individuals and the Market. Each influences the other as individuals engage in exchange, and prices inform individuals in markets about how goods and services are currently being valued. However, Stiles makes sure to mention that:

> While a human being is defined by his ability to distinguish between good and evil, to the Market good and evil are nothing but profit and loss—a very different standard. The Market may represent one side of human life—the collective judgment of people acting as traders—but it is not the voice of mankind. (Stiles, 2005, p. 27)

## Is "More Is Better" Correct?

Stiles's ideas also resonate with macromarketing scholarship about the Dominant Social Paradigm (DSP) (Kilbourne, McDonagh, & Prothero, 1997). The DSP is society's belief structure that organizes how people perceive and interpret the functioning of the world around them (Milbrath, 1989, p. 116). Similar to a worldview (which provides a model of the world and guides adherents in the world), the DSP of Western democracies after World War I became a materially focused ideology encouraging increased consumption for individuals (Bennett & O'Reilly, 2010, p. 6). In short, "more is better" became the driving ethos of society's members.

Governments have encouraged shopping and consuming beyond one's needs for a modest lifestyle. U.S. President Herbert Hoover articulated the notion that producing and consuming should be the great driving force of national life. In 1928, he told an audience of advertisers and public relations men, "You have taken over the job of creating desire and have transformed people into constantly moving happiness machines, machines which have become the key to economic progress" (Bennett & O'Reilly, 2010, p. 6).

The role of aspiration and the desire for incremental luxuries—things wanted, but not necessarily needed—is indispensable for productivity in the economic life of a society

(Ariely, 2011). However, sociologists such as Max Weber and Daniel Bell have expressed concern that the foundations of thrift and modesty on which capitalism rests are undermined by mass consumer pursuits, acquisitiveness, and widespread indebtedness in society (Kaufman, 2011).

For decades, researchers have grappled with the question of whether money can buy happiness. The Easterlin Paradox, which has been widely researched, suggests that there is no correlation between income and life satisfaction or between income and happiness over a threshold value of about $10,000 per year (Easterlin, 1974). Many researchers believed that once basic needs were covered, money did not buy happiness.

But recently, new large-scale studies have been conducted that suggest there is a positive relationship between income and life satisfaction, as well as between income and happiness. The income threshold for happiness saturation seems to be more like $75,000 per year (Kahneman & Deaton, 2010).

The results of the 2003 Gallup World Poll are depicted in Figure 7.1 (Deaton, 2010). Here each circle is a country, with a diameter proportional to population. The center of the circle marks the average life satisfaction and gross domestic product (GDP) for that country. Figure 7.1 suggests that life satisfaction is higher in countries with higher GDP per head. Notably, the slope is steepest among the poorest countries, where income gains are associated with the largest increases in life satisfaction, but it remains positive and substantial even among the rich countries.

Although scholars have debated the relationship between income and life satisfaction and between income and emotional well-being (experienced happiness), even more recent research using a later Gallup World Poll (the first representative sample of planet Earth using 136,839 respondents across 132 countries from 2005 to 2006) suggests that life satisfaction is, indeed, positively correlated with income (Diener, Ng, Harter, & Arora, 2010). More than 19% of the variance in life satisfaction was accounted for by income. However, only 3% of the variance in reported positive feelings on the previous day was accounted for by income. (Researchers measured feelings experienced during the previous day as a way to assess recent experienced happiness.)

## Is "More Is Better" the Complete Story?

The Gallup World Poll also studied social-psychological factors, which were measured using five standards: Did the respondent

- feel respected on the previous day
- have family or friends that could be counted on in an emergency
- learn something new yesterday
- do what he/she does best yesterday
- chose how his or her time was spent yesterday

These five items representing social-psychological wealth accounted for 20% of the variance in positive feelings experienced on the previous day.

**Figure 7.1** 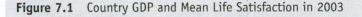 Country GDP and Mean Life Satisfaction in 2003

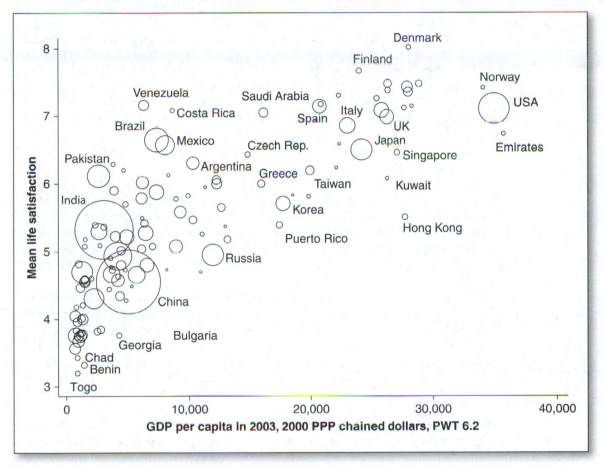

Source: "Life satisfaction and per capita GDP around the world" from Deaton, A. (2008 April 1). Income, health and wellbeing around the world: Evidence from the Gallup World Poll. *Journal of Economic Perspectives* 22(2), p. 56. American Economic Association (http://www.aeaweb.org/jep/index.php).

In sum, it seems that comforts increase life evaluations, whereas pleasures increase reports of positive feelings. In this way, money might have more to do with people having what they want, and social-psychological prosperity has more to do with feelings they like. Putting this together, both kinds of wealth—monetary and psychosocial wealth—likely contribute to lives characterized by fulfillment and happiness.

In another large-scale study conducted by the Gallup Organization in 2008 and 2009 called the Gallup-Healthways Well-Being Index (GHWBI), researchers analyzed the responses of 450,000 U.S. respondents (Kahneman & Deaton, 2010). Researchers found that most respondents reported being quite happy and satisfied with their lives. About 85%

experienced much positive affect (smiling enjoyment and happiness) each day. Twenty-four percent reported blue affect (sadness and worry), whereas 39% reported stress (participant could select more than one emotion). The average life satisfaction was 6.76 on 0 to 10 scale, with 10 representing the best possible life. Compared with other countries, the U.S. respondents rank high on life satisfaction (ninth after Scandinavian countries, Canada, the Netherlands, Switzerland, and New Zealand). The U.S. respondents ranked 5th for happiness, 33rd for smiling, and 10th for enjoyment. Alternatively, the U.S. group fared less well on worry (89th from best), sadness (69th from best), and anger (75th). The U.S. group reported very high levels of stress (5th in the set of 151 countries). In sum, the relatively high level of life satisfaction and positive affect for the U.S. respondents carries with it a corresponding cost—high levels of stress, anger, and sadness.

When examining relationships between income and measures of subjective well-being, researchers found that having low amounts of money led to reports of pain and unhappiness, but that the happiness saturation level was $75,000 per year (Rubin, 2011). With every doubling of income, respondents tended to report that they were more and more satisfied with their lives for household incomes well beyond $120,000. But when asked to assess the experienced happiness of the previous day (enjoyment, laughter, smiling, anger, stress, or worry), money mattered only up to about $75,000. After that, increased income did not buy more or less happiness. Notably, the average household income in the United States was $71,500 with about one third of households above this level.

Figure 7.2 depicts averages across eight household-income groups for three aspects of emotional well-being and one measure of life satisfaction (Kahneman & Deaton, 2010, p. 16491). The vertical axis on the left represents the fraction of the population experiencing a measure of happiness. A positive affect is the average reporting happiness, smiling, and enjoyment. "Not blue" is 1 minus the average of the fraction reporting worry and sadness. "Stress free" is the fraction of the population who did not report stress for the previous day. The vertical axis on the right represents the mean for the life satisfaction ladder on a scale of 0–10. The "Ladder" line in the graph represents life satisfaction.

"We suspect that this means in part, that when people have a lot more money, they can buy a lot more pleasures, but there are some indications that when you have a lot of money, you will savor each pleasure less," said Kahneman, who won the Nobel Prize for his research in behavioral economics. "Perhaps, $75,000 is a threshold beyond which further increases in income no longer improve individuals' ability to do what matters most to their emotional well-being, such as spending time with people they like, avoiding pain and disease, and enjoying leisure" (Sample, 2010, para. 7).

Interpreting these results, veteran QOL researcher Ed Diener said, "If you want to enjoy life, focus on relationships and health once you make more than $70,000 a year. If you are poor, it makes a great deal of sense to be concerned about higher income."

Research on these QOL issues are complex and will continue (Tierney, 2011). For example, researchers continue to reflect on the stability of subjective well-being in the United States for the last 50 years, despite rising income levels (Bok, 2010, pp. 13–14). Also, those that attach much importance to achieving wealth tend to suffer above-average unhappiness and disappointment. This is likely due to driven individuals neglecting human relationships, and later finding that financial success leads to fleeting happiness gains as adaptation occurs and satisfaction evaporates. Brooks (2010) argues that what is crucial in well-being is not how

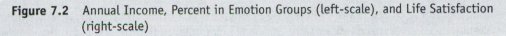

**Figure 7.2**    Annual Income, Percent in Emotion Groups (left-scale), and Life Satisfaction (right-scale)

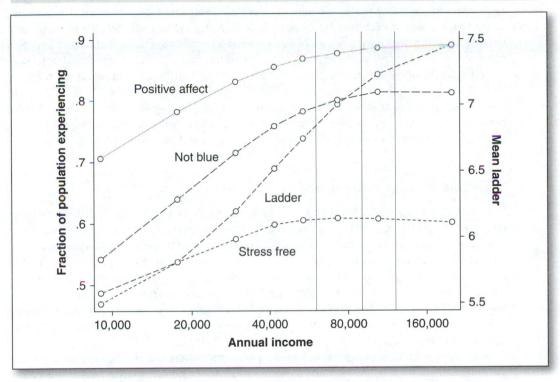

*Source:* Kahneman, D., & Deaton, A. (2010). High income improves evaluation of life but not emotional well-being. *Proceedings of the National Academy of Sciences, 107*(38), 16489–16493. http://www.pnas.org/content/early/2010/08/27/1011492107.full.pdf+html

happy one feels, or how much money is made, but rather the meaning found in life and one's sense of "earned success," the belief you have created value in your life or others' lives.

## VULNERABLE CONSUMERS

Although recent QOL research sheds light on some important questions regarding income and measures of subjective well-being, such research has consistently identified traps or troughs for individuals' QOL. For example, divorce, unemployment, disease, chronic pain, and being alone all contribute to reductions in life satisfaction and experienced happiness (Bok, 2010, p. 205). With lack of money, these setbacks in life have a more pronounced negative impact on subjective well-being. In other words, it is much worse to experience a life setback if one is poor than if one is not poor.

In research on consumer vulnerability, physical, psychological, and environmental factors contribute to consumers perceiving themselves at a power disadvantage in the marketplace (Baker, Gentry, & Rittenburg, 2005). For example, addiction, age, disability, gender, race/ethnicity, and cognitive deficiencies have all been cited as biophysical factors in degraded marketing exchanges. Likewise, fear of being victimized, social isolation, and socioeconomic status have been identified by researchers as psychological factors contributing to restricted access to the marketplace. Environmental factors include social upheaval or violence, the access to quality goods and services, the distribution of resources for trade, as well as transient states for individuals, such as grief or divorce.

The way markets are set up in societies might exclude many from full participation in some markets. Lack of access to goods and services offered in these markets would mean that significant portions of those living in a country would experience being "vulnerable consumers."

## Vulnerable Consumers: Healthcare

Healthcare is a service attracting much attention as costs continue to rise worldwide (Davis et al., 2007). Access to healthcare is a contentious issue, as many countries have healthcare resources, but access remains difficult for some. This issue is emerging at a time when lifestyle changes related to more sedentary work and to the overconsumption of food afflicts almost all countries. Ominously, the incidence for diabetes has risen 70% in the United States since 1990, but it is estimated that one third of those with diabetes do not know that they have it (Commonwealth Fund, 2011). In such ways, more people are becoming vulnerable healthcare consumers because they cannot access necessary medical services and diagnosis.

A Reuters poll of respondents across 22 countries conducted by Ipsos reports a near even split between respondents about access to quality and affordable healthcare being easy (48%) or difficult (52%) (Reuters/Ipsos, 2010). The United States places in the middle of the group of 22 countries with 52% of respondents reporting that access to quality and affordable healthcare would be easy to obtain. Sweden places first with 75% reporting that such access would be easy, while Japan reports the worst outlook with only 15% of respondents reporting that it would be easy to obtain access to quality healthcare.

Figure 7.3 reports on a study across seven developed countries regarding the quality, access, efficiency, and equity of the healthcare systems of these countries (Commonwealth Fund, 2010). Here, the $7,290 per capita healthcare costs in the United States are 87 % more than for Canada, the second most expensive country, but the United States places seventh among these seven developed countries. These results also underline how money may not purchase the best when it comes to healthcare for societies.

The issue then rises as to why the United States pays more than twice as much on average per person for healthcare rated lower in quality than the United Kingdom's. In fact, the United States spends more on average per capita healthcare than any other of the 30 Organisation for Economic Co-operation and Development (OECD) countries (Peterson & Burton, 2007). OECD countries are the developed countries of the world, as well as Mexico and Turkey.

**Figure 7.3**  The Commonwealth Fund's Comparison of Seven Societal Healthcare Systems

### Overall Ranking

| Country Rankings | |
|---|---|
| | 1.00–2.33 |
| | 2.34–4.66 |
| | 4.67–7.00 |

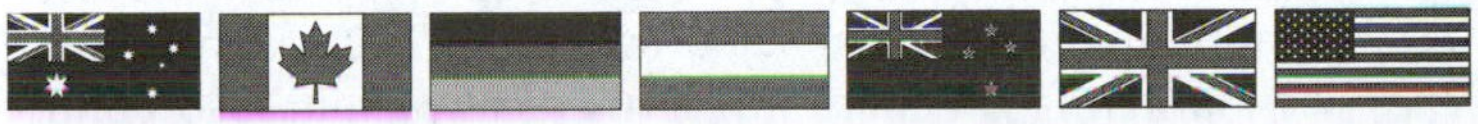

| | AUS | CAN | GER | NETH | NZ | UK | US |
|---|---|---|---|---|---|---|---|
| **Overall Ranking (2010)** | 3 | 6 | 4 | 1 | 5 | 2 | 7 |
| Quality Care | 4 | 7 | 5 | 2 | 1 | 3 | 6 |
| Effective Care | 2 | 7 | 6 | 3 | 5 | 1 | 4 |
| Safe Care | 6 | 5 | 3 | 1 | 4 | 2 | 7 |
| Coordinated Care | 4 | 5 | 7 | 2 | 1 | 3 | 6 |
| Patient-Centered Care | 2 | 5 | 3 | 6 | 1 | 7 | 4 |
| Access | 6.5 | 5 | 3 | 1 | 4 | 2 | 6.5 |
| Cost-Related Problem | 6 | 3.5 | 3.5 | 2 | 5 | 1 | 7 |
| Timeliness of Care | 6 | 7 | 2 | 1 | 3 | 4 | 5 |
| Efficiency | 2 | 6 | 5 | 3 | 4 | 1 | 7 |
| Equity | 4 | 5 | 3 | 1 | 6 | 2 | 7 |
| Long, Healthy, Productive Lives | 1 | 2 | 3 | 4 | 5 | 6 | 7 |
| Health Expenditures/Capita, 2007 | $3,357 | $3,895 | $3,588 | $3,837* | $2,454 | $2,992 | $7,290 |

*Source:* Commonwealth Fund (2010).

Economists evaluate healthcare in terms of the dollars spent on healthcare and the number of healthcare transactions made by individuals. Notably, the United States has fewer doctor visits per person than other OECD countries and a similar length of hospital stays. However, the intensity of service delivery at hospitals is greater in the United States as a result of the use of new medical technologies and the greater frequency of invasive procedures performed (such as coronary bypass and angioplasties). Other factors also contribute to higher spending per capita on healthcare in the United States. The United States has the highest incidence of cancer and has the highest incidence of obesity among the OECD countries.

With respect to price, U.S. prices for medical care commodities and services are significantly higher than in other countries. This serves as a key determinant of higher overall healthcare spending. In assessing what drives the difference between U.S. healthcare spending and the rest of the world, some leading health economists have responded this way: "It's the prices, stupid" (Anderson, Reinhardt, Hussey, & Petrosyan, 2003, p. 103).

In short, many of the same items and services cost more in the U.S. healthcare system than in other OECD countries. Part of this can be attributed to the United States using newer technology and the latest drugs in its hospitals, but at the final analysis, price is a function of market activity. It seems simply that the healthcare market in the United States is not as efficient as in other similar countries. Lack of competition among suppliers is one of the reasons for these high prices. For example, there are the same number of physicians graduating from U.S. medical schools in 1980 as there are now (Peterson & Burton, 2007).

Marketing practices in the medical system also contribute to distorted competition, which results in higher prices. For example, in 2009, the pharmaceutical company Pfizer agreed to the largest healthcare fraud settlement and largest fine for criminal fraud in history when it agreed to pay the $2.3 billion that the U.S. Justice Department's terms required (Harris, 2009). Pfizer had been accused of illegally marketing its painkiller Bextra (now withdrawn from the market) by using kickback schemes that paid doctors and clinics that prescribed the drug. It was the fourth time since 2002 that Pfizer had settled over accusations of illegal marketing.

On the market from 2001 to 2005, Bextra was approved for arthritis and menstrual cramps, but it was not approved for the treatment of acute pain. However, Pfizer told its sales reps to tell doctors that the drug could be used in the treatment of acute and surgical pain at doses above the approved level. Bextra's dangers, such as harm to the kidneys, skin, and the heart, increased with dosages. The drug was withdrawn in 2005 because of its risks to the heart and skin.

Pfizer is not alone in running afoul of the law. Almost every major drug maker has been accused in recent years of giving kickbacks to doctors or shortchanging federal programs. In the Bextra case, the U.S. Justice Department accused Pfizer of aggressive marketing tactics. For example, Pfizer would invite doctors to consultant meetings in posh resort locations. Doctors who attended had their expenses paid and received a fee for attending. Such weekend getaways for doctors are still common throughout the drug and medical device industries.

The implication here is that patients may be vulnerable consumers in a medical system with dubious prescription practices. Now more than ever, patients must ask their physician if the prescribed medicine is approved by the U.S. Food and Drug Administration (FDA) for the condition they face. If not approved, patients must press their physician to explain the reasoning for using the drug.

Figure 7.4 depicts life expectancy in OECD countries as a function of per-capita spending on healthcare using 2008 data (OECD, 2010). As can be seen, the United States far outspends other OECD countries, but most of the others post better results on an important outcome: life expectancy.

All actors in the U.S. healthcare system could do better to reduce the vulnerability of consumers in the healthcare marketplace. First, consumers can take better care of themselves by eating better and exercising more. Most of the diseases that kill people (heart disease, cancer, stroke, diabetes, and obesity) account for 70% of healthcare spending, but they are preventable through eating properly, exercising, choosing not to smoke, and

**Figure 7.4** Life Expectancy and Per-Capita Spending on Healthcare for OECD Countries

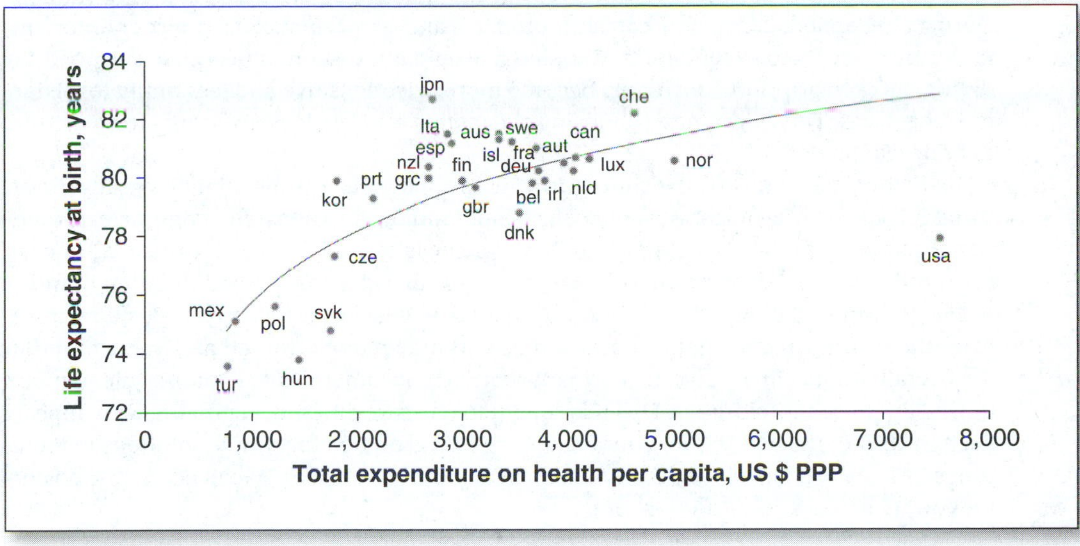

*Source:* OECD (2010).

minimizing alcohol consumption. The bad news is that two thirds of those in the United States are now overweight and one third are obese (Mackey, 2009).

Second, with an aging population burdened by chronic diseases (many resulting from lifestyle choices), it seems that demand for medical services will only go up in the future in developed countries, which will effect third-party payers. Some third-party payers are insurance companies and the government, and they will struggle with rising costs while pharmaceutical companies, medical institutions, and medical professionals pass on higher invoices than in other OECD countries. Changes need to be made in the healthcare marketplace or consumer vulnerability will only increase in the future.

Government-run healthcare will provide more access to healthcare in the United States. But how rising costs will be addressed is a question remaining to be answered. At Whole Foods Market, employees who achieve certain benchmarks for healthy living receive up to an additional 10% discount on purchases in the store (Golden, 2011). Many more employers will develop wellness incentive programs in the future. More will be said about employees in sustainable firms in Chapter 10.

## More Consumers Become Vulnerable in an Economic Downturn

An economic downturn also stresses consumers. John Quelch and Katherine Jocz (2009) prioritize products and services into four types: (a) essentials (food, shelter, clothing, transportation, and healthcare, (b) treats (indulgences whose immediate purchase is considered justifiable), (c) postponables (needed or desired items whose purchase can be reasonably put off), and (d) expendables (perceived as unnecessary or unjustifiable). The assignment of particular goods and services to the categories other than essentials is highly variable. During a recession, consumers can shift products and services, such as travel or entertainment, from treats to expendables. Cooking at home (an essential) becomes swapped for dining out (a treat). Most consumers become more price sensitive and less brand loyal during recessions. This might mean choosing cheaper private labels or switching from organic to nonorganic foods.

Marketers, too, tend to downshift during recessions. Where firms might have advertised using television, they might now choose cheaper radio campaigns. To economize, promotional campaigns might be extended and run longer. In terms of product, firms may choose to introduce low-cost versions of their more popular brands termed "fighter brands." Anheuser-Busch did this when it introduced Natural Pilsner in the early 1980s downturn. After the downturn, the fighter brand can be withdrawn or continued as a value brand in the overall product line. However, for many worried consumers, trusted brands mean much during tough economic times. Dell has sought to reassure different segments with appeals such as "Out of the box, within your means," "Depend on Dell for simple solutions in tough times," "The ideal laptop works anywhere, in any economy," and "Weak economy, powerful you" (Quelch & Jocz, 2009, p. 60).

## More Consumers Become Vulnerable on a Warming Planet

Researchers who have studied marketing in economic recessions note that consumers seem to return to their "normal" ways of consuming within two years of the recession's end (Quelch & Jocz, 2009). But what if a different way of consumption had to be undertaken by everyone worldwide? According to environmentalist-entrepreneur Paul Gilding, the modern world has caused the Earth to exceed its capacity of people, industry, and growth. While sounding as an alarmist to some, others, such as *New York Times* syndicated columnist Thomas L. Friedman, have used Gilding's words for reflection on the current times:

> You really do have to wonder whether a few years from now we'll look back at the first decade of the 21st century — when food prices spiked, energy prices soared, world population surged, tornados plowed through cities, floods and droughts set records, populations were displaced and governments were threatened by the confluence of it all—and ask ourselves: What were we thinking? How did we not panic when the evidence was so obvious that we'd crossed some growth/climate/ natural resource/population redlines all at once? (Friedman, 2011, p. 1)

Paul Gilding served as the head of Greenpeace International and started his own consulting company Ecos Corporation that advised major corporations on how to see sustainability issues as market forces and integrate them into business strategy. The clients of Ecos included a variety of firms, such as DuPont, Ford, Diageo, mining company BHP Billiton, China Light and Power, KPMG, and Zurich Financial Services. Gilding cites an alliance of scientists called the Global Footprint Network when asserting that current rates of economic growth suggest that the resources of the Earth are being depleted faster than they can be regenerated (Gliding, 2011). Such capacity constraints mean that a system collapse is underway.

Friedman says he has seen this first-hand in Sana, Yemen. With a population of 1,748,000 in 2010, Sana could be the first big city of the world to run out of water in the next ten years (Friedman, 2011). While in Sana, Friedman witnessed water being brought in by tanker truck.

The developing crisis about water in Sana is a commons problem. Here, short-run consumption of individuals depletes resources held in common for all and for future generations (Shultz & Holbrook, 1999). Such commons dilemmas have been encountered throughout history with the overgrazing of pasture lands, and now in the overfishing of fish beds around the world. Without regulation, taxes, or self-regulatory structures, a logic emerges among individuals to take from the commons without replenishing what is taken. More will be said about sharing as an antidote to the commons problem later in the chapter.

What Friedman observed in Yemen is occurring in other ways in other parts of the planet according to Gilding and it is a result of overconsumption. "If you cut down more trees than you grow, you run out of trees," Gilding said. "If you put additional nitrogen into a water system, you change the type and quantity of life that water can support. If you thicken the earth's $CO_2$ blanket, the earth gets warmer. If you do all these and many more things at once, you change the way the whole system of planet Earth behaves, with social, economic, and life support impacts. This is not speculation, this is high school science" (Gilding, 2011, p. 2).

## Voluntary Simplicity

Rather than wait for top-down solutions to the current commons problem, Gilding recommends widespread action be taken by individuals. In this way, the political landscape will change and government leaders will understand the imperative for legal and regulatory change. Toward this end, voluntary simplicity is an intentional movement to reduce individual consumption to free resources, particularly money and time, so that life satisfaction can be sought through nonmaterial aspects of life (Huneke, 2005).

There are different approaches to voluntary simplicity. Intending to improve the quality of their own lives, "Downshifters" seek less stressful ways of living and step out of the "earn and spend" cycle of living. High-paying, high-stress jobs are exchanged for lower paying jobs with more intrinsic value to the work and with more control given to pursue hobbies and relationships. By comparison, "Ethical simplifiers" move to simpler lifestyles for environmental and social justice reasons. They seek to minimize their part in environmental degradation and the exploitation of the poor around the world. Regardless of being motivated for self-centered reasons or social reasons, those pursuing voluntary simplicity seek to "shop less and live more."

Table 7.1 presents the results of Huneker's (2005) survey of 119 U.S. respondents who had chosen voluntary simplicity in their lifestyles. Like previous surveys of simplifiers, more than 75% of the respondents were female. Here a list of 21 practices derived from a search of the literature and prior studies was presented to respondents. The practices are presented in descending order of their mean importance. As shown, there are a variety of ways to pursue voluntary simplicity with the most important being avoiding impulse purchases, recycling, and eliminating clutter.

**Table 7.1** Voluntary Simplicity Practices Importance Ratings (9-point scale)

| | |
|---|---|
| Avoiding impulse purchases | 8.1 |
| Recycling | 7.6 |
| Eliminating clutter | 7.3 |
| Working at a satisfying job | 6.9 |
| Buying locally grown produce | 6.8 |
| Limiting exposure to ads | 6.8 |
| Buying environmentally friendly products | 6.7 |
| Limiting car use | 6.6 |
| Buying from socially responsible producers | 6.5 |
| Buying from local merchants | 6.5 |
| Limiting/eliminating TV | 6.4 |
| Limiting wage-earning work | 6.4 |
| Being active in the community | 6.0 |
| Being politically active | 5.7 |
| Composting | 5.7 |
| Making rather than buying gifts | 5.6 |
| Maintaining a spiritual life | 5.5 |
| Buying organic foods | 5.4 |
| Being friends with neighbors | 5.4 |
| Eating a vegetarian diet | 3.8 |
| Living in co-housing | 2.6 |

*Source:* Huneke (2005, p. 538).

Since its founding in 1997, the Center for a New American Dream has raised awareness about the negative impact of a hyper-consumer culture (The Center for a New American Dream, 2011). In addition to helping define conscious consuming and green living, the Center has focused on helping individuals downshift and find balance in life. The Center celebrates nonmaterial values and is an example of a new kind of environmentalism that puts people in the foreground, rather than spotted owls or other animals challenged by the economic activity of humans. Andrew Kirk, environmental history professor at the University of Nevada—Las Vegas said, "That's the thing about this current wave of environmentalism. It's not about, how do we protect some abstract pristine space? It's what can real people do in their home or office or whatever. It's also very urban. It's a critical twist in the old wilderness adage: Leave only footprints, take only photographs" (Green, 2007, para 11).

The turn to voluntary simplicity has brought out some high-profile endeavors to lead a different lifestyle. Colin Beavan became known as the "No Impact Man" when he embarked on a yearlong experiment to live with no impact on the environment. Unlike philosopher and social critic Henry David Thoreau who moved to Walden Pond in 1854 to live two years in a woodland cabin near Concord, Massachusetts, Beavan stayed in Manhattan and sought to scale down his consumption radically.

For an entire year, Beavan, his wife, and small daughter unplugged from the electrical grid, produced no trash, traveled only by self-propelled means, and bought only food that was grown within 250 miles (No Impact Project, 2011). By the end, Beavan and his family reported that not only was the "no impact" approach to living beneficial to the environment, but also it made them unexpectedly healthier, happier, and richer in ways they had not imagined.

## THE "WE" IN MARKETS OF TODAY

### Others as Enablers for the Consumer

Colin Beavan's consciousness-raising journey of "no impact" resulted in a book and a DVD both with the title *No Impact Man*. In a series of phases, Beavan goes further and eventually shuts off the electricity to his family's ninth-floor apartment (Jenkins, 2009). Because he could not blog without a computer, he erects a solar panel on his apartment building's roof to power it. At night, the apartment was lit with candlelight. Although such scenes added quirkiness and some spartan charm to the entire endeavor, what Beavan was attempting would not have appeared so silly if others in his apartment building had chosen to consume the same way as Beavan. If this had happened, the entire building could switch to solar panels or wind power. Then, the lights could come back and the refrigerator could be plugged in.

In sum, Beavan's solo journey was marked by deprivation, but it could have been a collective one with many of the amenities of modern life had his neighbors joined him. However, journeys like these do not necessarily need to be marked by deprivation. If Beaven's "others" (those who are connected to him through his apartment's hallways, stairways, elevators, utility lines, and plumbing) would have joined him in his process, there would have been fewer constraining forces. Rather, the apartment's collective pledge to be eco-friendly could have enabled everyone to live sustainably in a more hospitable way.

In a networked world of Internet and social media, the consumer-to-consumer, consumer-to-business, and business-to-business linkages bring a new potential for markedly different consumption experiences for all. Information sharing is the potential root for markedly different consumption experiences. For example, consumer-to-consumer linkages undergird what Pearson (2011a) calls "pre-commerce." In "pre-commerce," online consumers share ideas and product knowledge, as well as provide solutions for each other. To illustrate, consumers interested in the music of singer/guitarist Jack Johnson might go to www.jackjohnsonmusic.com, click on "community," join the discussion, trade tickets for an upcoming concert with others, arrange carpooling to the concert, and even leave suggestions for another children's CD. If Johnson ever delivered a disappointing live performance, this would be a place for fans to offer a critique. In a similar way, reading product reviews of Jack Johnson's latest CD at Amazon.com would help a consumer decide whether to make the purchase.

According to a July 2009 poll by Econsultancy, 90% of online consumers trust recommendations from people they know, but importantly 70% trust opinions from users they do not know (Pearson, 2011b). For someone interested in purchasing a GPS device for their car, she could go online to a high-tech product-review site, such as CNET (www.cnet.com), and examine product reviews for GPS navigation systems. If she liked the Motorola MotoNav TN765t, she could make a mental note about the click-through options to online retailers. Such online retailers would include Abe's of Maine (offering this brand and model at $279.00) and Amazon.com Marketplace (offering the same one at $135.99). She could also go to a site for other price comparisons, such as NextTag (www.nextag.com).

At NexTag, price comparisons can be made and maximum, minimum, and median prices over the last six months at online retailers can be examined. Graphs showing the number of online sellers each month, as well as the popularity of this brand and model each month, can also be reviewed. Customer reviews of the online retailers can also be read, along with final computations for price that would include shipping, handling, and sales tax based on the consumer's location. Before navigating away from NexTag, the site pops up a window inviting the shopper to put the Motorola MotoNav TN765t on a consumer's NexTag Radar for a selected price. Once this GPS appears online at that price, NexTag will send an e-mail alert to the shopper.

Preferring the price posted at CNET for Amazon.com Marketplace, a consumer could go to Amazon.com Marketplace and read reviews there from actual users ranging from five-star reviews to one-star reviews. Being risk averse, the one-star reviews might have the most immediate interest to the shopper. One of them points out that the latest map is two-years old (not good if someone lives in a rapidly growing metropolitan area), and the website provides no support. With these warnings in mind, a final examination of the selected brand and model of GPS device could be made at the local Best Buy store. But when the customer arrives at Best Buy, it would be likely that the customer knows more about the Motorola MotoNav TN765t than any salesperson in the Best Buy store.

This GPS-device shopping episode highlights the information-rich environment of pre-commerce in which consumers now move. Individual consumers are collaborating with other consumers, information providers, and businesses to empower themselves in the marketplace. But what would it look like if consumers used the Internet and social media for organized activity in the marketplace? Carrotmob gives a glimpse of what organized purchasing might look like in the future.

## Carrotmobbing

Brent Schulkin, a 20-something Stanford University grad living in San Francisco, is the creator of Carrotmob (www.carrotmob.org) whose motto is "We make it rain!". Carrotmobbing combines the idea of a "flash mob" with pro-social purposes. Instead of boycotting businesses for doing wrong, consumers organize online and through social media to reward a business that wins an auction among the other bidding businesses. The bids are composed of promised green or socially responsible improvements to their businesses. The business with the best promise wins the auction. The reward is a mob of several hundred customers—or thousands of customers—who arrive at the store on a designated day and make plentiful purchases.

**Figure 7.5**   Carrotmobbing

In a boycott, everyone loses.

In a Carrotmob, everyone wins.

In a Carrotmob campaign, a group of people offers to spend their money to support a business, and in return the business agrees to take action that the people care about. We are called Carrotmob because we use the "carrot" instead of the "stick." Traditionally, people who wanted to influence businesses would threaten or attack them. We believe people can have more influence on businesses by giving them a positive incentive to change: our money.

People want to "vote with their money" to advance their values and improve the world. There have already been hundreds of Carrotmobs in over 20 countries around the world. Join us.

*Source:* Carrotmob, http://www.carrotmob.org/about

Carrotmobbing began March 29, 2008, after Schulkin had approached 23 stores in his neighborhood of San Francisco and solicited bids for promising to spend revenues from Carrotmob patrons on energy-efficient improvements (Caplan, 2009). A small convenience store K & D Market won the auction with a promise to plow 22% of the day's revenue into greener lighting. During the Carrotmobbing, hundreds of green-minded customers descended on K & D Market lining up down the block outside at times and spending more than $9,200. Owner David Lee was delighted with the results and spent more than $2,000 on improved seals for refrigerators and energy-efficient lighting for the store.

Initially, observers thought that Carrotmobbing was a San Francisco phenomenon, but results in Canada, Germany, France, Australia, and New Zealand, as well as elsewhere, proves that reverse boycotts organized at the grassroots level are a global phenomenon. Schulkin now sees that instead of local retailers, Carrotmobbing could target major brands in the future pitting Nike, Adidas, and Reebok in the auctions for Carrotmobs:

> The idea of creating positive incentives for business to do good is not entirely new, but there are several recent developments that make now a good time for this approach to flourish: First, technology now allows us to easily connect and coordinate our activities like never before. Secondly, in the last couple years, environmentalism has gone mainstream. And third, we have a reputation economy, and companies are putting huge resources into protecting or improving their reputation. Moreover, these days bloggers and normal citizens have much more power over the reputation of businesses. In an age when companies are desperately trying to be seen as authentic and good, they have plenty of motivation to try and please an authentic grassroots network of consumers like us, since they know we have great power when it comes to defining their reputation. (Schulkin, 2008, para. 1)

## Reconsidering Ownership

Although carrotmobbing suggests the power available to consumers who organize other like-minded consumers to lead businesses toward greener and more socially responsible practices, technology and peer communities have given new meaning to sharing. *Time* calls "sharing" one of the "ten ideas that will change the world" (Walsh, 2011). Gansky (2010) notes that there are changing attitudes of consumers to ownership, particularly toward high-dollar products that are only necessary a few times a year. Networked-enabled sharing is now being done on the "Mesh" of mobile, location-based capabilities, as well as the Web and social networks. Finally, Rachel Botsman and Roo Rogers (2010) consider sharing more broadly in what they term "collaborative consumption," which includes sharing, bartering, lending, trading, renting, gifting, and swapping.

"We are relearning how to create value out of shared and open resources in ways that balance personal self-interest with the good of the larger community," *What's Mine is Yours* co-author Rachel Botsman said. "For the first time in history, the age of networks and mobile devices has created the efficiency and social glue to create innovative solutions, enabling the sharing and exchange of assets from cars, to bikes, to skills to spare space" (Rowan, 2011, para 5).

The story of Airbnb highlights the dizzying potential in what some term the "access economy," which goes against much of the logic of the "ownership economy." Airbnb founders Joe Gebbia and Brian Chesky knew each other from the Rhode Island School of Design and had moved to the South of Market or SoMa area of San Francisco where they were working as designers (Botsman & Rogers, 2010). When the annual industrial design conference came to San Francisco in October 2007, hotel rooms sold out. Gebbia and Chesky asked themselves why they shouldn't rent out their extra room by advertising it on the conference website. They did this and earned close to $1,000 in one week.

Their guests included a male designer from India who saw renting from Gebbia and Chesky as a great way to meet new people, a 35-year-old woman from Boston who wanted relief from a long commute and/or a high price for a hotel room, and a 45-year-old father of five from Utah. "It completely blew away our assumptions," Gebbia said. Surprisingly, Gebbia and Chesky did not feel like they were hosting strangers in their home. "They are strangers until you have a conversation with them," Chesky explained (Botsman & Rogers, 2010, p. ix).

**Figure 7.6**  Airbnb Lets People Find Accommodations Around the World

The pair recruited another friend Nathan Blecharczyk as a Web developer, and built a simple website in early 2008. The name Airbnb began as "air beds for conferences," but it now represents the idea that with the Internet and a spare room, just about anyone could become an innkeeper. By April 2010, Airbnb.com had 85,000 registered users and more than 12,000 properties in 3,234 cities across 126 countries of the world. But it has not stopped at conferences. "When we started, I never thought people would be renting out tree houses, igloos, boats, villas and designer apartments," Chesky said (Botsman & Rogers, 2010, p. xi). Castles in England rent for about $3,000 per night on Airbnb.com.

Travelers can search Airbnb listings and examine the profile of hosts along with the rat-ings given by past travelers, as well as photos of the room in which they would stay. The only fixed rules on Airbnb is that travelers must be able to ask questions of hosts prior to booking, and rooms cannot be a commodity, such as hotel or motel rooms. Both travelers and hosts rate each other after the stay, and these results accumulate to establish some-one's reputation on Airbnb. Through secure financial intermediaries, such as PayPal or credit card companies, the pre-payment made by a traveler does not become final until after the first 24 hours of a traveler's stay. The aspect of payment increases trust and puts both parties on their best behavior, making the entire process more reliable, but so does the online profile of host and traveler on Airbnb, which some refer to as "a trail of digital bread crumbs that makes it harder to pull off a scam" (Wortham, 2010, para. 30). Airbnb takes a standard 3% service fee from hosts, and a 6% to 12% service fee depending on the reservation price. The average New York City host with Airbnb makes $1,600 per month.

## Endless Possibilities for Collaborative Consumption

The possibilities for collaborative consumption seem endless. ZipCar has hundreds of thousands of members who pay an annual fee and can rent cars by the hour (The Economist, 2010). WhipCar is the United Kingdom's version in which car owners can rent out their cars in a way that does not affect the owner's insurance. Registering takes five minutes for lenders. Renters can go online and view all of the available cars nearby and the rates offered by lenders. After renters choose a car, lenders receive a cell phone text mes-sage that they can either accept or decline. Currently, lenders are taking in about $75 per rental. "Cars are 90 % under-utilized by their owners," Botsman said. "And 70 % of jour-neys are solo rides" (Hickman, 2011, para. 5). The variety offered to renters is another advantage of car sharing. "Today's a BMW day – or is it a Volvo day?" the ZipCar website asks (Rowan, 2011, para. 4).

Parkatmyhouse allows people to rent their driveways. SnapGoods lets users in a local setting share and rent physical products from mountain bikes to household tools. Zopa facilitates peer-to-peer money-lending, and so far the default rate is less than 1%. Kickstarter allows people to invest small sums in creative ventures. Bag Borrow or Steal applies the Netflix film-rental idea to expensive handbags, so that women can avoid the "emotional and financial sacrifices involved in the endless search for the 'right' accessory." Netflix, itself, earned $116 million in 2009. Rent-That-Toy facilitates rental of trikes.

Noncommercial forms of sharing are also abounding on the Internet now. Couchsurfing links people who have a spare sofa with travelers who would like to sleep on it (The Economist, 2010). Reciprocity is the key here as couchsurfers must do the same for some-one else in the network someday in the future. For exchanging children's clothes, there is thredUp. Freecycle facilitates giving things away so that one's stuff does not end up in a landfill. Hey, Neighbor! facilitates a network in a user's neighborhood where updates can be shared with other neighbors, such as "Felt the baby kick today," as well as requests for small favors like moving a couch or picking up mail while one is away (www.heyneighbor.com).

Consumers are setting up and executing their own "swishes," which are clothes swap-ping events (Hickman, 2011). Weekly swishes are now underway in Cornwall, United

Kingdom. An average of 35 attendees gather in unused corridors of commercial buildings for the exchanges. Entrance fees are charged consumers and points awarded for making exchanges. "Many women treat swishing like a clothes library," Cornwall swish-organizer Anna Dalziel said. "You sometimes see the same items rotating week to week. Some people come before they go on holiday just to stock up and I know some women who have swapped around 500 items over the past year. Facebook has been brilliant for us. I just announce to everyone who has signed up when the next event is and it goes from there" (Hickman, 2011, para. 18).

## CONCLUSION

This chapter offered a macromarketing perspective on a sacred cow of American culture—consumption. Social critic Paul Stiles's work in *Is the American Dream Killing You?* proposed that the economic system in which people exists works so well that hyper-consumption now threatens society. Other voices have echoed Stiles's views including macromarketing scholars who have asserted that the DSP holds powerful sway in society. This DSP is characterized by widespread acceptance of a "more is better" ethos characterized by material acquisitiveness for consumers and dominance of the natural environment by society. Business practitioners, such as Andrew Bennett and Ann O'Reilly, have reported that a majority in developed markets are concerned about a consumption-obsessed society. Consumption has always had limits to vulnerable consumers because of their lack of access to markets (Baker, Gentry, & Rittenburg, 2005) and to consumers in depressed times of business cycles (Quelch & Jocz, 2009). However, environmental degradation (Gilding's *The Great Disruption*) looms as a possible disruption to consumer culture and might force many to adopt lifestyles of less consumption. Taking a defiant stance toward mindless consumption, the voluntary simplicity movement encourages individuals to consume less to enjoy more.

Rising consumer choice in marketplaces helps firms realize that satisfying consumers increasingly is more difficult. A networked world implies the need for more market intelligence and more social capital. Collaboration becomes necessary as well. Firms adopting a service-dominant (S-D) logic will work with other firms, as well as consumers, to co-create products and services. A networked world also implies that consumers are increasingly obtaining what they want from other consumers, rather than from firms. With the rise of sharing, the role of community has come into focus. Sharing goes against a primary ethos of the market—competition. Nevertheless, forms of sharing are becoming more visible in exchange. Efforts to nurture the commons of society, and volunteering, are now becoming understood to be part of how society will care for its resources and people in the future. The implications of social media along with the rise of online communities suggest that preserving communities can be more valuable than short-term profits to both individuals and businesses. In the following section, the psychedelic band, the Grateful Dead, pioneered giving away recording rights to its concerts and as a result reinforced a community of devotees that sustained the band for 30 years.

## QUESTIONS

- What aspects of the "me" dimension of markets had you not considered before reading Chapter 7?
- What aspects of the "we" dimension of markets had you not considered before reading Chapter 7?
- To what degree do you agree with Paul Stiles's assessment that "the Market" actually poses a threat to the well-being of individuals, families, and other institutions in American society? How do you see evidence of hyper-consumption today?
- In what ways do you see consumers with limited access to fair or good exchanges in the marketplace today? At what times have you felt like a vulnerable consumer?
- What power do consumers have in markets today that they did not have 50 years ago? Five years ago?
- What practices of voluntary simplicity appeal to you in Table 7.1? Which do not appeal to you? Explain.
- In your opinion, what are the prospects for carrotmobbing in the future? What would it take for you to participate in a carrotmob? If you had a business, would you want to be carrotmobbed?
- What forms of collaborative consumption appeal most to you after reading Chapter 7? Which ones do you think will be around ten years from now?

## MAVERICKS WHO MADE IT

### The Grateful Dead

THE GRATEFUL DEAD emerged from San Francisco's 1960s rock-and-roll music scene. Initially, they seemed to have a brief fling with a modest degree of commercial success and then seemed to be headed to oblivion. However, "the Dead" proved to be one of the most enduring successes of the 1960s and continued to tour for more than 30 years—an eternity in the world of commercial music business. The band never had a top-selling album or single in the days when these were considered to be the staple of success in recording. But the band created and nurtured a community of "deadheads" that sustained them over three decades.

Today, the wisdom of the band can be seen in their different approach to the music business. First, the members of the band were accomplished musicians who really cared about the performance experience of their fans. To this end, no Grateful Dead concert was like another. The band performed over 2,300 live concerts from 1965 to 1995 establishing itself as the most popular touring act in rock history (Scott & Halligan, 2010). Of the 500 different songs performed in these concerts, 150 were original compositions that combined rock, country-western, improvisational jazz, gospel, and more. Relying on improvisation in the way of jazz musicians, the band members said they never knew what songs they would play in a concert. Unlike other acts, the Dead invested heavily in the best sound and light system, so that the experience of a Grateful Dead concert was unlike other bands.

Second, because the band chose to make money from touring, customers assumed primary importance for the band. The band established a mailing list and created a telephone hotline to alert its most loyal fans about its touring schedule ahead of any public announcement. Extending respect to these most loyal fans, the band reserved some of the best seats in the concerts for them. The band even capped the price of tickets for these fans, and distributed them through its own mail-order house. This meant that if you lived in Atlanta and wanted to see a show in Denver, you did not have to travel there to get tickets, and you did not have to camp out for really good tickets. What resulted from such customer focus was a community of enthusiasts for the Grateful Dead that fueled the band's success. Some Deadheads would attend all concerts during a year—usually about 100. With this business model, they were free to give away their music and even set up taper sections inviting concert-goers to plug in their recording devices at special tables with outlet cords in the concert halls in which they play. Today, the Dead are regarded as being masters of creating and delivering customer value.

The band consisted of guitarist Jerry Garcia (who is the namesake of "Cherry Garcia" ice cream at Ben and Jerry's), guitarist Bob Wier, bassist Phil Lesh, and two drummers Bill Kreutzmann and Mickey Hart as well as keyboardist Brent Mydland. These musicians and the others who constituted the Dead over the years were quite savvy about their organization. They incorporated early on. They also established a board of directors (featuring a rotating CEO position) composed of the band, road crew, and other members of the organization. They established a profitable merchandising division and were not bashful about suing those who violated their copyrights. The band's decision to allow taping at its concerts was an astute decision based on the belief that tape sharing would widen their audience and those taping would likely spend money on tickets or merchandise at the concerts. The band also licensed its logos to manufacturers—again, in the belief that their audience and base of fans would widen as a result. In the end, the Grateful Dead became one of the most profitable bands of all time.

The band's lyricist, John Perry Barlow, eventually became an Internet guru grasping the connection between the Dead's approach to business with what it took to succeed in the information economy. According to Barlow, the best way to increase demand for one's product is to give it away:

What people today are beginning to realize is what became obvious to us back then—the important correlation is the one between familiarity and value, not scarcity and value. Adam Smith taught that the scarcer you make something, the more valuable it becomes. In the physical world, that works beautifully. But we couldn't regulate [taping at] our shows, and you can't online. The Internet doesn't behave that way. But here's the thing: if I give my song away to 20 people, and they give it to 20

*(Continued)*

(Continued)

people, pretty soon everybody knows me, and my value as a creator is dramatically enhanced. That was the value proposition with the Dead. (Green, 2010, para. 13).

Strategic improvisation is what intrigues business scholars about the Grateful Dead's flexibility on stage, as well as over the years of business activity related to touring. On stage, the band members often made mistakes because they were always improvising. They simply shrugged it off and went on. In the end, they were authentic to their fans, and this was a key element of their appeal. Famed San Francisco rock-concert promoter Bill Graham once described the band by saying, "They're not the best at what they do, they're the only ones that do what they do" (Bjerklie, 1997).

## Questions

- What characterizes the Grateful Dead as a maverick?
- Is it surprising to you that putting the customer first was not part of a top-down firm-focused approach of businesses in the 1960s and 1970s? Despite what is taught in marketing courses about the need to take a customer-centric approach to business, what percentage of businesses use this approach instead of a firm-centric approach to business?
- What are your thoughts about the Dead's building of a powerful word-of-mouth fan network powered by free music? Do you know of other music groups that have built a similar network?
- How many Web-based businesses incorporate something similar to the Dead's "freemium" business model?

## REFERENCES

ABC News Radio. (2011). YouTube videos turn shopping sprees into potential profits. Retrieved from http://abcnewsradioonline.com/business-news/youtube-videos-turnshopping-sprees-into-potential-profits.html

Anderson, G. F., Reinhardt, U. W., Hussey, P. S., & Petrosyan, V. (May/June 2003). It's the prices, Stupid: Why the United States is so different from other countries. *Health Affairs, 22*(3), 89–105. Retrieved from http://content.healthaffairs.org/cgi/reprint/22/3/89.pdf

Ariely, D. (2011, May). The upside of useless stuff. *Harvard Business Review*. Retrieved from http://hbr.org/2011/05/column-the-upside-of-useless-stuff/ar/1

Baker, S. M., Gentry, J. W., & Rittenburg, T. L. (2005, December). Building understanding of the domain of consumer vulnerability. *Journal of Macromarketing, 25*, 128–139.

Bennett, A., & O'Reilly, A. (2010) *Consumed rethinking business in the era of mindful spending*. New York, NY: Palgrave McMillian.

Bjerklie, S. (1997, March). What are they worth? *Metropolitan*. Retrieved from http://www.metroactive.com/papers/sfmetro/03.97/rock-art-97-3.html

Bok, D. (2010). *The politics of happiness: What government can learn from the new research on well-being*. Princeton, NJ: Princeton University Press.

Botsman, R., & Rogers, R. (2010). *What's mine is yours: The rise of collaborative consumption*. New York, NY: HarperCollins.

Brooks, A. C. (2010). *The battle: How the fight between free enterprise and big government will shape America's future*. New York, NY: Basic Books.

Caplan, J. (2009, May 15). Shoppers, unite! Carrotmobs are cooler than boycotts. *Time*. Retrieved from http://www.time.com

Commonwealth Fund. (2011, March 29). Notable numbers: Purchasing high performance. Retrieved from http://www.commonwealthfund.org

Davis, K., Schoen, C., Schoenbaum, S. C., Dory, M. M., Holmgren, A. L., Kriss, J. L., & Shea, K. K. (2007). *Mirror, mirror on the wall: An international update on the comparative performance of American health care*. New York, NY: The Commonwealth Fund.

Deaton, A. (2008, April 1). Income, health and wellbeing around the world: Evidence from the Gallup World Poll. *Journal of Economic Perspectives, 22*(2), 53–72.

Diener, E., Ng, W., Harter, J., & Arora, R. (2010). Wealth and happiness across the world: Material prosperity predicts life evaluation, whereas psychosocial prosperity predicts positive feeling. *Journal of Personality and Social Psychology, 9*(1), 52–61.

Easterlin, R. A. (1974). Does economic growth improve the human lot?: Some empirical evidence. In P. A. David and W. R. Levin (Eds.), *Nations and households in economic growth Stanford* (98-135). Stanford, CA: Stanford University Press.

Friedman, T. L. (2011, June 7). The earth is full. *The New York Times*. Retrieved from http://www.nytimes.com

Gansky, L. (2010). *The Mesh: Why the future of business is sharing*. New York, NY: Portfolio.

Gilding, P. (2011). *The great disruption: Why the climate crisis will bring on the end of shopping and the birth of a new world*. New York, NY: Bloomsbury Press.

Golden, P. (2011). Whole Foods Market CEO John Mackey joins hundreds of senior health care leaders from U.S. and abroad as 8th Annual World Health Care Congress concludes in Washington, DC. *World Health Care Congress 2011*. Retrieved from http://www.worldcongress.com

Green, J. (2010, March). Management secrets of the Grateful Dead. *The Atlantic*. Retrieved from http://www.theatlantic.com

Green, P. (2007, March 22). The year without toilet paper. *The New York Times*. Retrieved from http://www.nytimes.com

Harris, G. (2009, September 3). Pfizer pays 2.3 billion on settle marketing case. *The New York Times*. Retrieved from http://www.newyorktimes.com

Harrison, A. (2011, January 5). From ordinary shopper to celebrity overnight. *National Public Radio*. Retrieved from http://www.npr.org/2011/01/05/132379365/from-ordinary-shopper-to-celebrity-overnight

Hickman, L. (2011, June 14). The end of consumerism. *The Guardian*. Retrieved from http://guardian.co.uk

Huneke, M. E. (2005, July). The face of the un-consumer: An empirical examination of the practice of voluntary simplicity in the United States. *Psychology & Marketing, 22*(7), 527–550.

Jenkins, M. (2009). Radical change writ small, for the planet's sake. Movie Review. Retrieved from http://www.npr.org

Kahneman, D., & Deaton, A. (2010 September 21). High income improves evaluation of life but not emotional well-being. *Proceedings of the National Academy of Sciences of the United States of America (PNAS), 107*(38), 16489–16493. Retrieved from http://www.pnas.org/content/early/2010/08/27/1011492107.full.pdf + html

Kaufman, M. T. (2011, January 26). Daniel Bell, ardent appraiser of politics, economics and culture, dies. *The New York Times*, p. A21.

Kessel, B. (2008). How much money is enough? *MSN.com*. Retrieved from http://articles.moneycentral.msn.com/Investing/StockInvestingTrading/HowMuchMoneyIsEnough.aspx

Kilbourne, W., McDonagh, P., & Prothero, A. (1997). Sustainable consumption and the quality of life: A macromarketing challenge to the dominant social paradigm. *Journal of Macromarketing, 17*(1), 4–24.

Mackey, J. (2009, August 11). The Whole Foods alternative to ObamaCare. *The Wall Street Journal*. Retrieved from http://www.wsj.com

Milbrath, L. (1989). *Envisioning a Sustainable Society*. Albany: State University of New York Press.

No Impact Project. (2011). Retrieved from http://www.noimpactproject.org

OECD. (2010). Health care systems: Getting more value for money: OECD Economics. Department Policy Notes, No. 2.

Pearson, B. (2011a). *Pre-commerce: How companies and customers are transforming business together*. San Francisco, CA: Jossey-Bass.

Pearson, B. (2011b May 31). Why pre-commerce is a game-changer. Retrieved from http://www.pre-commerce.com

Peterson, C. L., & Burton, R. (2007, September 17). U.S. health care spending: Comparison with other OECD countries. *CSR Report for Congress* (Order code RL34175). Washington, DC: Congressional Research Service.

Quelch, J., & Jocz, K. (2009, April). How to market in a downturn. *Harvard Business Review*. Retrieved from http://web.ebscohost.com/ehost/pdfviewer/pdfviewer?vid = 3&hid = 108&sid = 23ed06ec-40b1-4f25-9ea8-67171dac23a8 % 40sessionmgr110

Reuters/Ipsos (2010, April 17). Half (52 %) of global citizens would find it difficult for a very ill family member to get quality, affordable healthcare. Retrieved from http://www.ipsos-na.com

Romano, T. (2010, May 5). Look what I bought (or got free). *New York Times*. Retrieved from http://www.newyorktimes.com

Rowan, D. (2011, February 11). Rentalship is the new ownership in the networked age. *Wired*. Retrieved from http://www.wired.com

Rubin, C. (2011, September 7). At what price happiness? *Inc*. Retrieved from http://www.inc.com

Sample, I. (2010 September 10). The price of happiness? £50,000pa. *The Guardian*. Retrieved from: http://www.guardian.co.uk/science/2010/sep/06/earnings-pay-happiness-research

Schulkin, B. (2008 May 8). Interview with Carrotmob's creator, Brent Schulkin. *Green Girls Global*. Retrieved from http://www.greengirlsglobal.com

Scott, D. M., & Halligan, B. (2010). *Marketing lessons from the Grateful Dead: What every business can learn from the most iconic band in history*. Hoboken, NJ: Wiley.

Shultz, C. J. II, & Holbrook, M. B. (1999). Marketing and the tragedy of the commons: A synthesis, commentary, and analysis for action. *Journal of Public Policy & Marketing, 18*(2), 218–229.

Stiles, P. (2005). *Is the American Dream killing you?: How "the Market" rules our lives*. New York, NY: Collins.

The Center for a New American Dream. (2011). About. Retrieved from http://www.newdream.org

The Economist. (2010, October 14). The better business of sharing. What to do when you are green, broke and connected. You Share. *The Economist*. Retrieved from http://www.economist.com/node/17249322

Tierney, J. (2011, May 16). A new gauge to see what's beyond happiness. *The New York Times*. Retrieved from http://www.nytimes.com

Walsh, B. (2011, March 17). Today's smart choice: Don't own. Share. *Time*. Retrieved from http://www.time.com

Wortham, J. (2010, August 28). Neighborly borrowing, over the online fence. *New York Times*. Retrieved from http://www.nytimes.com/2010/08/29/business/29ping.html

## CHAPTER 8

# Collaborative Leadership

## "I'M LOVIN' IT"

### Jan Fields, CEO McDonald's USA

Jan Fields grew up in Vincennes, Indiana, the seventh of eight kids. In 1978, Jan Fields was 22 and wanted to attend community college but needed a job to help pay the bills. Her dream was to become a lawyer. "I walked into a McDonald's on my way to a job interview," Fields said. "I saw a sign that said 'Flexible Hours.' I had a child, my husband was in the Air Force and if I worked the night shift, I wouldn't have to hire a baby-sitter" (Shelby, 2011, p. 1). The McDonald's manager hired her on the spot. It was her first job.

Fields worked the night shift and earned $2.65 per hour and left each night with a blue polyester uniform smelling of French fries and hurting feet. "There were a lot of days I wanted to quit," Fields said. "But I learned never quit over one thing, one situation, one person. Come back, and the second day gets better" (Chen, 2011, p. 1).

The job with the cooking crew at the McDonald's eventually turned into a management job. One year turned into another, and Fields stayed with McDonald's but left the restaurant where she had her first job. After a succession of jobs with increasing responsibility over more than 30 years, Fields became President of McDonald's USA in January 2010 overseeing 14,000 U.S. restaurants with 700,000 workers (Sellers, 2011a). She is still a wife and mother, but she has added grandmother to her family roles. Her down-home and inspiring leadership style has led some to call her "the Oprah of McDonald's" (Sellers, 2011b).

"Although the early years were more challenging because there were fewer women in leadership positions, throughout my career at McDonald's I have received the support of colleagues," Fields said (QSR, 2011, p. 4). According to Fields, balancing work and life was the biggest challenge of her career. Fields sounds a theme with which many women working outside the home can relate. "I have a daughter who is grown now, but for much of her childhood I was juggling raising her and growing my career. Over the years, I learned that you can have it all—not just at the same time. I passed on some career-advancing opportunities while she was in high school so that she could complete all four years in one place—and I don't regret one minute of it. You have to make one thing a priority and achieve balance that way, rather than trying to do everything all at once" (Bennington, 2011, p. 2).

Although Fields never finished college, she can claim studying at the same tiny Catholic school, Old Cathedral in Vincennes, which has produced two other leaders in corporate America: (a) her brother, Jim Brocksmith, former deputy chairman and COO of accounting giant KPMG, and (b) former UPS CEO Mike Eskew who is now a director of IBM.

To succeed in the next phase of Fields's career in the highly competitive fast-food industry of the United States, Fields will need to win the support of franchisees for $1 million-refurbishing of each McDonald's restaurant. She will also have to complete McDonald's most ambitious menu innovation in 30 years—specialty drinks, such as cappuccinos, lattes, and smoothies.

"She is taking over at a time when it's getting tougher to grow sales in the U.S.," Chief Investment Officer at OakBrook Asset Management in the Chicago area Janna Sampson said (Sterrett, 2010, p. 1). Competition is fierce, and innovations are on the rise. For example, rivals Burger King and Subway have bolstered their breakfast menus.

To compete with rival businesses, McDonald's has begun to broaden its approach to marketing by focusing on becoming a better corporate citizen. After Justin Spurlock's criticism in his documentary "Super Size Me," McDonald's has focused on providing healthier options for its customers. It has revamped its menu to include more nutritious options such as oatmeal and chicken salads (Shelby, 2011). McDonald's has also partnered with environmental nongovernmental organizations (NGOS), such as Greenpeace and the World Wildlife Foundation, to save the Amazon Rainforest from being cleared. The scope of McDonald's operations multiply its green initiatives as thousands of suppliers have to change their processes to achieve green targets. Already 81 % of its packaging is made with renewable materials and 31 % from recycled fibers (Shelby, 2011).

One challenge Fields took on in early 2011 was to begin reimaging the role of McDonald's as a good employer. To help change public perceptions about its role as an employer, McDonald's announced that April 19th would be National Hiring Day and 50,000 workers would be hired across the United States in a single day. McDonald's had 62,000 applications for 13,000 restaurant worker positions in the Western United States in a 2010 large-scale hiring effort (Chicago Tribune, 2011). But would McDonald's be able to hire 50,000 workers in one day? According to Fields, this would mean $518 million more in wages for the coming year as well as $54 million in payroll taxes (Rohrlich, 2011).

Radio and TV ads for McDonald's National Hiring Day featured former workers, such as singer Macy Gray and track-and-field Olympian Carl Lewis, both who worked at McDonald's.

On National Hiring Day, bloggers and newspapers picked up on the press releases issued by McDonald's trumpeting its role in the economy and the upsides of working at McDonald's. Half of the owner-operators of the chain's franchises started as McDonald's restaurant employees, as did 40 % of the corporate staff and 30 % of its senior management (Chicago Tribune, 2011). Stores averaged $2.2 million in annual sales in 2007, but increased to $2.4 million in annual sales in 2010. Same-store sales (for those stores open more than one year) rose an average of 4 % over this period (The Economist, 2011). In this way, store managers run growing multi-million-dollar businesses.

Like Fields did years ago, many visited a McDonald's restaurant and completed a job application form on National Hiring Day. Fields's idea for winning national media attention for its recruiting effort—thereby boosting the effectiveness of the same recruiting—proved to be a winner. Remarkably to many, one million people applied for restaurant jobs at McDonald's that day. McDonald's did better than what they had promised and hired 62,000 workers. This is more than the net job increase for the entire U.S. economy in 2009 (Kroll, 2011). To put this in perspective, 938,000 people did not receive a job offer this day, giving McDonald's a 6.2 % acceptance rate for National Hiring Day. In this way, McDonald's proved to be more selective on National Hiring Day than the admission offices of Stanford, Princeton, and Yale universities.

## Your Thoughts?

- What did Jan Fields have against her making it in the corporate business world in 1978?
- What did she have going for her in 1978? Through her career?
- What does the McDonald's menu and restaurant overhaul suggest about firms like McDonald's?

*(Continued)*

(Continued)

- What kind of leadership is needed to convince franchisees who own 90% of McDonald's restaurants (Rexrode, 2011) that a menu change to specialty coffees implies an accompanying remodeling of stores to be more like cafes when the price tag on each remodeling for a franchisee is $1 million?
- What kind of leadership is needed to lead the public in reimaging McDonald's as a good employer? Has Fields succeeded in this task? How will we know she has?

## CHAPTER OVERVIEW AND LEARNING OBJECTIVES

One of the most important contributors to market dynamism today is the power consumers gain as a result of being networked. The implication for firms is that the days of controlling consumers or doing things to consumers is ending. The age of collaborating with consumers or doing things with consumers has arrived. In such a marketplace, firms must increasingly collaborate with other firms to meet the wants of empowered consumers with choices. In sum, authority—built on service and sacrifice to others—is rising in importance in today's marketplace, whereas coercion is receding.

This chapter will examine leadership in collaborative contexts. Knowing yourself and what is important to you is often cited as the first rule of leadership. Understanding others and the nature of leadership can be boosted by becoming familiar with widely held frameworks of leadership from scholars, such as those studying theories of human motivation and organizational leadership. In the increasingly networked 21st century, servant leadership rises to new importance. Servant-leaders obtain results for their organizations by giving priority attention to the needs of their colleagues and those they serve. Such an approach is particularly relevant for firms striving to apply the biggest M (macromarketing) and to take a stakeholder approach in the life of the firm.

More and more, co-creation is a major success factor for firms. Organizations find that it is too difficult to possess all of the resources needed to offer suitable products and services to demanding customers. This can also be seen in nonbusiness domains, such as K–12 education. The story of Seattle's former school superintendent John Stanford illustrates the importance of using the "biggest M" approach to organize a successful effort to revitalize a drifting school system.

After this chapter, you should be able to answer the following questions:

- What do many say is the first principle of leadership?
- How can understanding human values help one be a more effective leader in a firm considering adopting sustainable business practices?
- What characterizes a transformational leader?
- How does "N = 1, R = G" represent important aspects of a new age of innovation?

- What are four types of co-creation?
- What does service-dominant logic imply for the application of servant leadership?

# LEADERSHIP OVERVIEW

## The Importance of Knowing Yourself

Leadership is the art of inspiring action and guiding people in productive directions (Kanter, 2009, p. 257). It is very much about influencing people (Army, 2006, pp. 1–3). Despite the focus on others in definitions of leadership, scholars and long-time observers of leaders make a surprising assertion about success in leadership—self-awareness or knowing oneself comes first (Bennis, 2003, p. 48; George and Sims, 2007, p. 69; Goleman, 2004). In other words, to lead others well, leaders must know themselves because the first person leaders lead is themselves (Maxwell, 2007). "Before you set out to change the world and manage other people, you should look inside yourself and see whether you are ready to be a leader," Harvard Business School leadership teacher Joseph L Badaracco, Jr. said (Coutu, 2006, p. 55). "You should reflect on how well you can manage yourself. That takes time and it is an unnatural act for action-oriented people" (Coutu, 2006, p. 55).

Those who desire to lead must recognize and understand their emotions and motivations, and how these affect others. Those who understand themselves can anticipate their own behaviors in a variety of situations. Changes can be made accordingly. For example, if someone knows that they have a tendency to fall behind in completing projects, they can take adaptive measures to say "no" with a smile to requests of others that might cause them to lose focus at key times in a project.

Self-aware individuals can be recognized by their candor and the realistic self-assessments they can make. People generally admire and respect candor as a human trait. Leaders must frequently make candid assessments of their own capabilities, as well as of the capabilities of others. Ronald Heifitz who directs the Leadership Education Project at Harvard University's John F. Kennedy School of Government, asserts that the role of the leader in today's work world is to "help people face reality and to mobilize them to make change (Taylor, 2007, para. 2). This calls for a willingness to be radically honest with oneself regarding the reality at hand (Parks, 2005, p. 148). For example, leaders must assess whether goals can be achieved using the approach favored by the status quo or what has been done in the past. Alternatively, leaders must assess whether a new product should be launched or whether an acquisition of another firm should be undertaken. Making candid self-assessments comes from leaders' self-knowledge, which allows them to know their limits as well as their abilities. They are less likely to set themselves up for failure. Not surprisingly, such persons have self-confidence. Others are always watching leaders, and some have described being a leader as like living in a glass house (Integrated Leadership Concepts, 2011).

## Schwartz's Value Circumplex

Although leaders throughout a firm may always be in view of others, the personal values of leaders or their preferred ways of acting or being must be inferred by their behavior.

Psychologists have studied human values and regard them as learned beliefs that serve as guiding principles for a person or a social entity (Schwartz, 1994). Figure 8.1 depicts the Value Circumplex developed by psychologist Shalom Schwartz (these ten values are presented with more complete descriptors in Table 8.1). Here, the values are organized by motivational similarity, and dissimilar values are placed opposite each other in the circumplex. Values positioned next to each other in the circumplex are more similar to each other. Those across the circumplex from each other actually work in opposition to each other in a value system As one value rises, the other value opposite it tends to decline in influence in a person's value system. For example, universalism occupies the one o'clock position, which represents understanding, appreciation, tolerance, and protection for the welfare of all people and for nature. Opposite universalism is power at the seven o'clock position, which represents social status and prestige, as well as control or dominance over people and resources. Protecting the welfare of all people and nature opposes the value of dominating people and nature.

Researchers propose that attitudes and behaviors result from trade-offs within an integrated system of values, rather than the importance accorded to one value (Crompton, 2010). We can understand what this means in practice by looking at the four orientations outside the ring of ten "pie slices" representing the ten values in Schwartz's typology. Here, values of universalism and benevolence compose a self-transcendence orientation. Values of conformity, tradition, and security compose a conservatism or conservation orientation. Values of power, achievement, and (most of) hedonism compose a self-enhancement orientation, whereas (some) hedonism, stimulation, and self-direction compose an openness to change orientation.

In the cultural context of business today, the values below the broad black line in Figure 8.1 correspond to values aligned with traditional approaches to business focused on developing only two forms of capital—physical and financial. The values above the broad black line correspond to approaches to business seeking to develop more than physical and financial capital, such as environmental, human, and social capital (as discussed in Chapter 1).

## Implications of the Circumplex for Leaders

By using the circumplex, leaders can better understand where they give emphasis regarding these ten different values. For example, an entrepreneur talking about a new venture with another entrepreneur can go ahead and freely discuss the disruption and change that will likely result from the planned venture. Both entrepreneurs likely give high importance to values associated with openness to change. Alternatively, one of the same entrepreneurs talking about the same project with a city planning commission that highly values conservatism and conservation must highlight how the proposed project will preserve relevant parts of a historical neighborhood. While acknowledging the change the venture will bring to the community, the entrepreneur would do well to highlight the likely intentions of the founders of the community to someday have the community prosper. In this regard, ventures providing jobs and opportunities improve the security of the community, as well as help to preserve the traditional way of life in the community. In this way, the entrepreneur will be more likely to have a mutually beneficial exchange with the city planners. By comparison, if the entrepreneur disregards the conservativism of the city planners by immediately discussing needed changes in the community and how the venture will help bring about such changes, the entrepreneur will activate the fears of the conservative planners and thrust them immediately in the role of defenders of the status quo in the community.

**Figure 8.1**   Value Circumplex With 10 Values, 4 Orientations, and Correspondence to Types of Capital

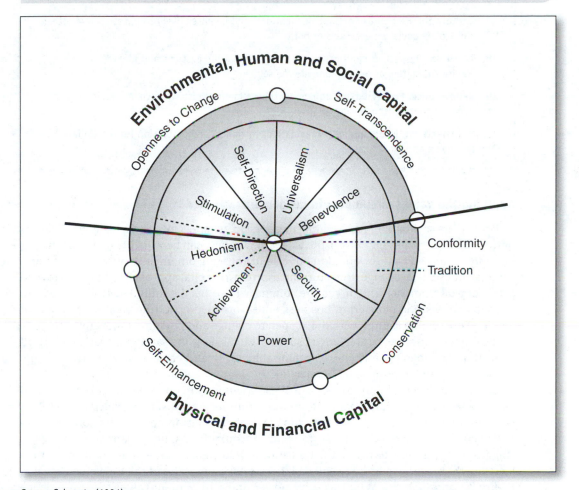

*Source:* Schwartz (1994)

**Table 8.1**   Basic Human Values of Schwartz (1994)

1. **Self-direction.** Independent thought and action; choosing, creating, exploring.

2. **Stimulation.** Excitement, novelty, and challenge in life.

3. **Hedonism.** Pleasure and sensuous gratification for oneself.

4. **Achievement.** Personal success through demonstrating competence according to social standards.

5. **Power.** Social status and prestige, control or dominance over people and resources.

6. **Security.** Safety, harmony, and stability or society, of relationships, and of self.

7. **Conformity.** Restraint of actions, inclinations, and impulses likely to upset or harm others and violate social expectations or norms.

8. **Tradition.** Respect, commitment, and acceptance of the customs and ideas that traditional culture or religion provide the self.

9. **Benevolence.** Preserving and enhancing the welfare of those with whom one is frequent personal contact (the "in-group").

10. **Universalism.** Understanding, appreciation, tolerance, and protection for the welfare of all people and for nature.

## Applying the Values Circumplex in Leadership

For leaders seeking change (and most leaders do, whereas managers likely prefer stasis or the status quo (Zaleznik, 1998)), the values circumplex can be valuable in understanding not only their own value orientation but also in engaging others in their quest for organizational and societal change. Here, turning from a two-capital approach to business toward a five-capital approach might require joining with other like-minded leaders open to change and desiring more from business endeavors than acquiring wealth. Such a turn would likely require staffing with those open to change and pursuing innovative solutions to customers' and society's challenges, such as water safety and sanitation, early childhood education, employment for people with disabilities, small business development, energy conservation, and disaster relief (Kanter, 2009).

But to establish coalitions and marketing systems toward these ends, those concerned with the status quo within organizations and within society must be engaged as well. This is the more demanding task of leadership in which persuasion needs to be done in effective ways—sometimes over years—to realize meaningful change. Leaders adopting the "biggest M" approach to the marketplace would do well to understand that those they lead and those with whom they will collaborate have a mixture of the ten values listed in Figure 8.1 and Table 8.1. When security, power, and achievement values take precedence in the value systems of others, the two-capital pay-offs for endeavors must be addressed. In time, with proper leadership and choice of projects, the appreciation and development of self-direction, universalism, and benevolence values will rise. Such humanistic values are positively correlated with interest and attitudes toward "bigger-than-self" issues, such as environmental protection, human development, and improving the lot of the disadvantaged (Crompton, 2010).

Wal-Mart's interest in "green" issues speaks to this. Attracted initially by the savings that can be obtained through lower cost ways to operate from reducing packaging materials, or working with suppliers to minimizing shipping costs, Wal-Mart has adopted many green process improvements (Wal-Mart, 2011a). For example, Wal-Mart set a goal of eliminating 20 million metric tons of greenhouse gas (GHG) emissions from its global supply chain by the end of 2015. Focusing first on 20 product categories, such as fabrics, Wal-Mart has helped dye mills in China eliminate from one to two tons of GHG emissions for every ton of colored fabric made. But along the way, Wal-Mart has discovered that it can be a powerful influence in society by selling healthier foods, selling LED lightbulbs, and sourcing from more local small- and medium-sized businesses.

On October 24, 2005, Wal-Mart boldly set three goals for itself: (a) to be supplied 100% by renewable energy, (b) to create zero waste, and (c) to sell products that sustain people and the environment. In making progress toward these goals, the culture of Wal-Mart has changed and, as a result, the culture of the marketplace is changing.

Others have noticed the change in Wal-Mart. Among its many awards in 2010, *BusinessWeek* named Wal-Mart as a Top 20 Firm for Leadership, and the World Environment Center awarded Wal-Mart its Gold Medal for International Corporate Achievement in Sustainable Development (Wal-Mart, 2011b).

## Know Others

Social psychologist Douglas McGregor proposed his X-Y theory in 1960 (McGregor, 2005). Here, Theory X and Theory Y represent two different views about human nature relevant to the practice of management. Theory X takes a negative view of human nature and assumes individuals generally dislike work, are inherently lazy, and require close supervision to do their jobs. Theory Y takes a positive view of human nature and assumes individuals are generally industrious, creative, and display abilities to self-organize and to exercise self-control in their jobs (enotes.com, 2011).

Although these tandem theories represent two highly divergent views of others' motivation and their interest in pursuing creativity, research results to support these theories have been mixed. Nevertheless, these tandem theories are widely taught in management courses because of the insights that can be gained for leaders when they enter new leadership contexts. For example, settings with much history and many rules or norms developed over a long period of time will likely have a well-developed sense of the way things have been done in the past—the status quo. In such a context, results can assume lesser importance than process—the way things get done. Because of the structure present in the form of established procedures, meetings of committees, and even a rank structure for employees, a directive or authoritarian management style would likely prevail. Communication is characterized by a top-to-bottom flow. Bureaucracies exemplify such contexts. The Dilbert cartoon strip by Scott Adams (an MBA grad from the University of California—Berkeley in 1986) lampoons work life in big business (Adams, 2011).

By comparison, a newer organization in the early stages of its development will likely have fewer elements of structure because of its size and the reliance on workers' self-control. In such a context, sanctioned protocols might even be repudiated by the ensemble of contributors gathered to pursue a compelling organizational outcome, such as being the first to obtain patent rights for a new cancer treatment. Rather than a judge, the manager will more likely act as a coach focused on how things can be improved in the future. Communication is characterized by a bottom-to-top flow or even a flow in all directions. New ventures in the high-tech realm exemplify such contexts.

Related to Theory X and Theory Y views of human nature is the issue of the inherent selfishness or cooperativeness of individuals. Although much of economics is based on the assumption of the rational self-interest of individuals (with markets mediating exchanges for homo economicus), a body of recent research in economics suggests that empathy and cooperation infuse the way humans seek to interact with each other (Benkler, 2011). When Microsoft introduced its encyclopedia Encarta in the encyclopedia market, it soon displaced the 32-volume print edition of Encyclopedia Britannica and other hefty encyclopedias. It seemed that digitization had triumphed over the printing press. However, in 2009, Microsoft stopped producing Encarta because of competition from a business model based on cooperation and collaboration, rather than on self-interested rationality. Wikipedia—the free encyclopedia that anyone can edit—had triumphed over a powerful business' digitization of an encyclopedia. Wikipedia weighs in as the seventh most trafficked website with more than 300 million visitors a month.

In today's networked world, Microsoft has taken a distant second place not only with Wikipedia but also in web server software (Benkler, 2011). More operators of mission-critical websites have chosen open-sourced Apache software over Microsoft's server software every year since 1999.

## Path-Goal Management and Transformational Leaders

### Path-Goal Management

A carrots-and-sticks approach to leadership in which the leader offers either rewards (carrots) or punishments (sticks) characterizes one of two popular models of leadership. This is the path-goal model of leadership, and it is termed a transaction model of leadership (House, 1996). Here transactional leaders perceive those they lead as being motivated by reward or punishment. Accordingly, these leaders try to explain clearly their expectations and then administer rewards and punishments based on the behaviors of their subordinates. They allocate work to subordinates whether resources are there or absent. The path-goal model is viewed as being widely deployed in business organizations today.

### Transformational Leadership

The other prominent leadership model is the transformational leadership model. The transformational leadership model features an engaging leader who collaborates with those being led to cast a vision for a future and then draws close to offer not only resources but also exhortation and encouragement to those pursuing the fulfillment of the vision

(Burns, 1978). Notably, transformational leaders are generally energetic, enthusiastic, and passionate. Not only are these leaders concerned and involved in the process, but also they are focused on helping every member of the group succeed as well. Importantly, transformational leaders can be identified by the change they impart to not only their organization, but also to individuals with whom they lead. The organization and the followers develop and improve their capabilities.

Transformational leadership is less frequently observed than path-goal leadership in business contexts. In corporations, Interface, Inc.'s CEO Ray Anderson exemplifies transformational leadership (see Chapter 1). His employees challenged him to articulate a vision about environmental stewardship of the company. After initially stumbling, Anderson recovered and together with his employees developed a vision for the firm called Ecosense. Along the way, a compelling purpose of the firm emerged—becoming a restorative company and teaching other industrial companies how to become sustainable ones. Innovations began cascading from Interface as individuals and teams within Interface engaged themselves in their new mission. Anderson exhorted not only his employees in this pursuit, but also he called other companies to go the way of sustainability.

In small- and medium-sized companies, Clif Bar's Gary Erickson exemplifies transformational leadership. He went millions of dollars into debt to preserve the community that he helped create. Erickson almost sold his company before he realized he would lose the transformational venue not only for having a positive impact on his sector of the market and his firm's customers, but also for bettering his firm and its employees.

In truth, transformational leaders will use techniques from the path-goal approach as leaders. For example, rewards and punishments will be used to structure and guide employees. However, because of the imperative of change that the transformational leader helps establish with the workers of the organization, timely exhortations for individuals will occur (as opposed to only in annual review sessions). Former NFL football coach Bill Parcells used to confront his players individually. "I've often said to a player, 'I don't think you're performing up to your potential; you can do better.' But I also made it clear that my goals were his goals: 'It's in your best interest that you succeed, and it's in my best interest that you succeed. We really want the same thing'" (Parcells, 2000, p. 181).

## Characteristics of Leaders

Organizations are systems with their own logics and the weight of tradition and inertia that oppose (fiercely) doing new things and taking risks (Rockefeller, 1973). Managers thrive in such contexts because they emphasize rationality and control, and they adopt an impersonal (if not passive) stance toward goals (Zaleznik, 1998). Committee work is comfortable for them and takes much of their time. By comparison, leaders working from high-risk positions are more willing to embrace risk and danger. They tend to feel separate from their environment. They may work in a firm, but they never belong to the firm and are never constricted by conventions of the firm. In this way, leaders are more like artists than managers because they are seeking change rather than preserving the status quo.

Looking again at the values circumplex of Figure 8.1, one can see how in a business context a transformational leader seeking change in the organization and in the individual workers would be more open to change (upper-left side of the outer-ring). With regard to the firm (the focal in-group or tribe for the managers), managers in the organization (particularly firms no longer classified as ventures after eight years of operations) would likely have values on the opposite side of the circumplex. This suggests that someone's value system will have to be altered when a leader proposes change for an established organization. Regarding the firm (the focal tribe here), leaders will likely have less conservative values and will be more open to change.

For those adaptive leaders intent on transforming their organizations and workers to adopt purposes related to developing environmental, human, and social capital, they must first know themselves and why they desire to see change. They must then evaluate the context (resources available, challenges faced, possible threats, stage in development of the team or firm, as well as talents and commitments of personnel). They must assess the system of values evident in the firm and gauge the gap between what the firm claims to stand for and how it behaves (Taylor, 2007). Afterward, they must then define reality regarding the goals of the firm and the resources and commitments of the workers to accomplish these goals (DePree, 2004). They do this by evaluating the gaps between the stated values of the firm and the recent performance of the organization.

## Servant Leadership

### A Pioneer of Servant-Leadership: Robert Greenleaf

Robert Greenleaf developed his theory of servant leadership as an executive of AT&T and finished his career as director of management research at AT&T (Beazley, 2003). Born in 1904, his working years spanned the era of the rise of corporate America. In his later life, he devoted himself to developing and promoting the idea of empowered employees. He wrote books on the topic and held teaching positions at MIT's Sloan School of Management and Harvard Business School. He also taught at Dartmouth College and the University of Virginia. The center he founded upon his retirement—the Robert K. Greenleaf Center for Servant Leadership located in Indianapolis—bears his name (www.greenleaf.org). Greenleaf died in 1990, but his ideas and teaching continue to inspire. Greenleaf believed that by improving leadership, social units (including families, businesses, and other institutions) would function better. As a result, society would improve and the ills afflicting society would subside (Greenleaf, 2003, p. 70).

The servant leadership model proposed and taught by Greenleaf seemed to be out of sync with the culture of command-and-control hierarchies characteristic of modern corporations. Here, power—the ability to force or coerce others to do one's will because of one's position or might—is frequently used to get things done because it works (Hunter, 2004). However, power also damages relationships over time.

Greenleaf studied research by sociologist Max Weber, as well as the lives of some of the great leaders from history, such as Jesus Christ, Martin Luther King, Jr., Mother Theresa, and Gandhi. Greenleaf noted the importance of authority—the skill of getting others willingly to do the will of the leader because of the leader's personal influence. Such authority is a function of who the leader is as a person, as well as of the character of the leader. The result of applying authority is a willing "I'll do it for *you*" from those with whom the leader works. This concept can commonly be seen in the relationship between mothers and children, since mothers have earned influence with their grown children as a result of their years of service and sacrifice for these children (Hunter, 2004).

## A Profile of a Servant-Leader

As a servant, the leader should extend himself or herself to identify the needs of subordinates and co-workers, and then meet those needs. In this way, those being served would be freed to solve problems they faced, achieve organizational goals, as well as improve themselves. The price for the leader pursuing servant leadership is sacrifice. A servant-leader's ego, a lust for power, pride, and other self-interests, will have to be set aside to serve effectively. This may be too high of a price to some. However, in highly competitive endeavors among firms, individuals must surrender their self-interest for the greater good, so that the whole adds up to more than the sum of its parts. Leadership trainer James C. Hunter said (2004):

> We may have to sacrifice our need to be liked, our bad habit of avoiding conflict, our desire to have all of the answers, to look good, to always be right. When we serve others, we will have to forgive, apologize, and give others credit even when we do not feel like it. When we extend ourselves for others, we will be rejected, underappreciated, and even taken advantage of at times. Indeed, we will have to sacrifice and subordinate anything that gets in the way of doing the right thing with and for people. (p. 78)

While taking a Theory Y approach to leadership believing the best about humans' motivation, servant leadership experts suggest that not every human can handle the responsibility required to function in servant-led organizations. "Ten percent or so of the people you lead will not only *not* respond to your authority but will try to sabotage you and everything you are trying to build," James C. Hunter said. "Get them out as soon as possible" (Hunter, 2004, pp. 75–76).

Although Greenleaf's ideas probably sounded naïve to hardened veterans of corporate life often characterized by in-fighting and turf wars, the changing nature of business now brings servant leadership into the mainstream. Because servant leaders listen to their employees, they learn from them. They tend to transfer this practice to listening to other stakeholders, such as their customers. This pays off in deploying the right programs, products, and services that make these customers happy (Keith, 2010).

Some prominent organizational behavior scholars now endorse a more humble approach to leadership and have begun speaking out against persistent myths about heroic leaders of firms that might be promulgated by the media, as well as schools of business. "Real leadership is often more quiet than heroic. It is connected, involved and engaged. It is about teamwork and taking the long-term perspective, building an organization slowly, carefully and collectively" (Mintzberg, Simons, & Basu, 2002, p. 71).

Examples of firms that have adopted servant leadership include Broetje Orchards (featured in Chapter 1; www.broetjeorchards.com), TD Industries (a mechanical construction and facility service company in the southwestern United States; www.tdindustries.com), Schneider Corporation (engineering and land development based in Indiana; www .schneidercorp.com), PPC Industries (one of the top electrical contracting firms in the United States with annual sales in the hundreds of millions of dollars; www.ppcpartnersinc. com), and Schmidt Associates (architectural firm; www.schmidt-arch.com).

### Remember the Situation

It should be noted that other theories of leadership feature the situation encountered by the leader as a key part of the leader's effectiveness. Fiedler's contingency theory is one of the most popular theories of management and suggests that the leader's effectiveness is based on the interaction of two factors: (a) leadership style and (b) situational favorableness (later called situational control) (Fiedler, 1967). When there is a good relationship between the leader and followers, a highly structured task, and the leader has a high degree of power, the situation is considered a "favorable situation."

Fiedler found that task-oriented leaders are more effective in extremely favorable situations (such as when the leader has a relatively high degree of control in leading the team to success or rewards, and when high trust exists between the leader and followers). Fiedler also found that task-oriented leaders are more effective in unfavorable situations characterized by the need for urgency (such as in responding to natural disasters). By comparison, Fiedler's research suggested that relationally oriented leaders who might be less willing to create discomfort for followers would perform best in situations with intermediate favorability (moderate levels of trust, task structure, and leader power).

The situational leadership model of Paul Hersey and Ken Blanchard suggests that instead of using just one style, successful leaders should change their leadership styles based on the ability and maturity of the people they are leading (Hersey, Blanchard, & Johnson, 2008). Using this theory, leaders should be able to adjust their emphasis on the task or their emphasis on the relationships with the people they are leading, depending on what is needed to get the job done successfully.

In sum, it would be wise to pursue servant leadership after considering the situation faced by the leader. Servant leadership might be most effective in improving relationships between the leader and followers. In this way, the team could develop itself, so that greater achievement could be attained.

## Corporate Good Citizenship Rising

Across businesses today, organizational structures are flattening and hierarchies are giving way to networks (Kanter, 2009). Organizations no longer work like machines that are cranked from those at the top. Firm leaders increasingly recognize they must be responsive to those outside the firm who have a voice and a choice. A social logic of good citizenship has emerged and continues to develop.

Firms such as Procter & Gamble, IBM, and Omron (a Japanese consumer electronics company) are responding to four forces in developing a social logic of good citizenship. Rosabeth Moss Kanter (2009), who chairs the Harvard Advanced Leadership Initiative, sees four forces influencing firms today:

1. Uncertainty and Volatility: system effects amplify small changes and sometimes multiply them. The Economic Crisis of 2008 began in the United States and almost instantaneously spread over the world.

2. Complexity: with loosened internal and external boundaries, firms now have increased flows of products, people, money, and ideas. The Internet makes all of these more accessible for firms. As a result, there are many variables now in play simultaneously. There are also more firms.

3. Diversity: there is more heterogeneity mostly resulting from an increased geographic scope for the operations of firms. Firms like China's Lenovo (personal computers) and Haier (durable goods like kitchen appliances) have leapt into leadership roles in their respective industries.

4. Transparency and Responsibility: as firms pursue global marketing, doing things as similarly as possible in different locales has a marked cost benefit for firms. It just does not make economic sense to run shoddy operations in one locale. NGOs have a global reach now. Trust has become paramount in a dynamic marketplace as firms must rapidly develop projects in new sectors of their operations with new collaborators.

With these forces now influencing firms, coercive power has decreased in importance while authority—built on service and sacrifice—has risen in importance. Relationship marketing has become feasible because of the accessibility for interaction with those outside of the firm (Rust & Espinoza, 2006). In short, relationships now eclipse control because relationships can adapt to changing circumstances for all, whereas control implies coercive power that eventually will be resisted by others. "A power culture in the new millennium is simply unable to compete with a culture of excellence, speed, quality, innovation—in short, with a culture in which people are playing with their heads in the game," James C. Hunter said (2004, p. 57).

Outside of the firm, it is hard to coerce other firms for long. Accordingly, firms tend to work with other firms on a volunteer basis. Within the firm, Max DePree, the chairman emeritus of Herman Miller, Inc., an innovative leader in the office furniture business for more than 60 years, asserts that workers should be treated as volunteers, rather than as assets owned by a company (DePree, 2004). (More will be said later about employees as stakeholders in Chapter 10).

"Healthy organizations consist of healthy relationships between customers, employees, owners (shareholders, taxpayers, etc.), and significant others such as vendors, suppliers, the community, unions, and the government," James C. Hunter said (2004, p.56). "Healthy relationships, healthy business; bad relationships, bad business" (Hunter, 2004, p. 56).

# A NEW ERA FOR INNOVATION

## A Networked World

As can be understood now, Greenleaf was ahead of his time in proposing servant leadership. Today, servant leadership fits well with many aspects of business. Networked customers have gained power relative to firms because these customers increasingly have rich information and many choices. To compete effectively, firms cannot possess all the resources needed to satisfy customers who increasingly demand customization. Prahalad and Krishnan (2008) characterize the situation firms now face as "N = 1, R = G." Here, "N = 1" represents the personalized co-created experiences customers want (sample size of 1), whereas "R = G" represents the global access to resources and talent needed to satisfy customers (Resources = the globe).

The Apple iPod represents what it takes to succeed with new products in this era. Instead of a vertically integrated firm designing components, manufacturing them, assembling them, and preloading content on the iPods, Apple only participates in the design and marketing of the iPod. It proudly puts in the iPod that it was "designed in California" (Prahalad & Krishnan, 2008, p. 23). Toshiba makes the disk drives. Matsushita and Toshiba make the displays. Samsung in Korea makes the SDRAM memory. Broadcom in the United States manufactures the video processors. Inventec from Taiwan does the final assembly at its plant in China. The customers themselves load the content that they want and, in this way, customize their iPod. A wide ensemble of contributors makes the iPod a multivendor and global product that results in a co-created personalized experience for customers.

In a world characterized by "N = 1," knowledge intensity must be increased from when the firm used the "invention model" where the innovation was principally developed within the four walls of the research and development group for the firm (Prahalad & Krishnan, 2008, p. 39). A multivendor approach now is needed to innovate because no firm has the requisite knowledge to succeed with increasingly complex products allowing the kind of quality demanded in customized co-created experiences. No firm can provide the speed in developing such innovations. As a result, the firm must accept "R = G."

## Procter & Gamble: An Example of the Networked World

At consumer products company Procter & Gamble (P&G), the multivendor model in new product development became more emphasized in a dramatic way early in the tenure of CEO A. G. Lafley who became CEO in June 2000. Lafley helped define the reality that in the 21st century, innovations require too many eyes, too many brains around the world, and too many man-hours for one firm to do what is needed to field innovation successes consistently. P&G abandoned the invention model because to have growth organic for the company of 5% per year, the firm must build the equivalent of a $4 billion business year after year (Huston & Sakkab, 2006). Like other firms its size, P&G found itself spending more and more for less and less top-line revenue growth from innovations.

In 2001, P&G adopted the goal of acquiring 50% of its innovations from outside the company. The purpose of this was not to replace the capabilities of the 7,500 researchers and staff contributing to innovation within P&G but to make better use of these resources. Half of these new products would come from the P&G labs, whereas the other half would come *through* them. P&G called this new approach to innovation Connect and Develop. In 2000, P&G had only 15% of its innovations come from outside the company, but in 2007, more than half came from outside P&G (Lafley & Charan, 2008).

In Connect and Develop, P&G collaborates with organizations and individuals around the world. It searches for proven technologies, packages, and products that can be improved on, scaled up, or marketed by P&G, or in partnership with other companies. P&G's research and development (R&D) productivity has increased 60% since implementing Connect and Develop (Huston & Sakkab, 2006, p. 61). P&G spends around $2 billion each year on R&D. Several success stories from the hundreds of new products P&G has developed with resources outside its R&D department include Olay Regenerist, Swiffer Dusters, and the Crest SpinBrush.

Importantly, Connect and Develop must be driven by the top leaders in a company to succeed. It cannot be merely an approach for the R&D group or an experiment in a corner of the company. P&G depends on a proprietary network of 70 technology entrepreneurs based around the world who serve as scouts for the company. They develop needs lists, and they examine the potential of adjacencies—potential products to those already successful for P&G, such as Crest whitening strips and flosses. What they are searching for are concepts with at least a working prototype developed.

P&G's technology entrepreneurs also meet with university and industry researchers, as well as form supplier networks that work on innovations. They actively promote these connections to decision makers in P&G's business units. Field observation is also important to the scouting of technology entrepreneurs. For example, a technology entrepreneur came on what later became the Mr. Clean Magic Eraser as a stain-removing sponge in a market in Osaka, Japan. The eraser has now been revised three times and has far exceeded its projected revenues.

P&G has found that of 100 ideas found on the outside, only 1 ends up on the market (Huston & Sakkab, 2006, p. 66, para. 1). But Connect and Develop has markedly improved P&G's performance in innovation. The success of Connect and Develop highlights what a former Procter & Gamble vice president for innovation and technology liked to say, "Creativity is really the process of making connections" (Lafley & Charan, 2008, p. 132).

## The Leader as Connector

Connecting workers inside the firm to ideas and entities outside is a way for leaders to add value to the firm. The ability to link people, ideas, and resources that those in the firm would not otherwise encounter takes on special value. For example, David Kenny is the president of Akamai Technologies, a firm headquartered in Cambridge, MA, which addresses problems associated with the Internet such as performance, security, and scalability. To serve its clients, such as the White House, Amazon.com, Hulu, and China Central Television, the company has created a globally distributed network of 100,000 servers deployed in 72 countries that are controlled by proprietary software.

Kenny spends much of his time traveling the world to meet with employees, partners, and customers. He spends time with media owners and leaders of firms like Microsoft and listens to what they say about digital platforms, Facebook, and cloud computing (Ibarra & Hansen, 2011). His clients tell him how they feel about macroeconomic issues, the G20, and how future generations will be affected by debt. Such conversations lead to new strategic insights, relationships, and external partnerships that prove indispensable to Akamai's future. Kenny uses several techniques to connect those inside Akamai with the world outside:

First, I check in on Foursquare often and post my location to Facebook and Twitter," Kenny said. "It lets employees in different Akamai locations know I'm in town so that anybody at any level can bring me suggestions or concerns. Second, every time I go to one of our locations, I have lunch or coffee with 20 to 40 people. We go around the room, and people ask questions on topics they most want to address. Often my answer is to connect with others in Akamai or even people at other companies who have expertise on the topic. Third, if I see a big opportunity when meeting with a customer or colleague, I will schedule a follow-up visit and bring along the right experts from Akamai. Fourth, whenever I travel, I try to make room to meet with two to three people I know in the location. Whenever possible, I bring someone else from Akamai with me to those meetings. (Ibarra & Hansen, 2011, p. 70, para. 11)

Such networking proved profitable for Akamai when the firm initiated an important strategic partnership with Swedish-based telecommunications company Ericsson. The partnership evolved out of a conversation Kenny had with a mid-level Ericsson executive in 2009 at the Monaco Media Forum. "It really changed my idea of what Ericsson could be, and I saw that we were both trying to solve a similar technical problem," Kenny said. "Then I worked through mutual friends to meet their CEO and arranged for the right people on his team to meet with their Akamai counterparts" (Ibarra & Hansen, 2011, p. 71).

A collaborative leadership style works well in dispersed, cross-organizational networks, as opposed to hierarchies (favoring a command-and-control style) (Ibarra & Hansen, 2011, p. 73). In such contexts, employees at all levels or a variety of external stakeholders may likely have relevant information needed by the firm. Performance is usually based on achieving shared goals. A collaborative leadership style fits well to cross-unit and cross-company work when innovation and creativity are essential to success.

Effective collaborative leaders take a strong role directing teams and will make sure insularity within groups is not allowed to persist. Although open disagreement with others is encouraged, politics should be kept to a minimum. A former Microsoft executive reported that the firm had developed a viable tablet computer more than ten years before Apple launched its smash hit iPad. However, competing Microsoft divisions conspired to kill the project (Ibarra & Hansen, 2011, p. 72).

## Co-Creation

Co-creation is a collaborative new product development (NPD) activity in which consumers actively contribute and select various elements of a new product offering (O'Hern & Rindfleisch, 2009). Customer co-creation would include firms engaging customers in the design and development of a new product offering, such as proactively encouraging customers to send product ideas to firms, or to offer opinions about new product concepts. Such co-creation would also include customer citizenship behaviors (extra-role behaviors, such as recommending the brand to other consumers) (Groth, 2005).

Open innovation is defined as moving outside the organization's own boundaries to develop new products and services (Norton, 2011). Open innovation includes four forms of co-creation. These are presented in Table 8.2. First, *collaboration* is defined as jointly developing a new product and improving it, such as Linux, Apache, or Firefox. Second, *tinkering* involves customers making modifications to commercially available products that will be used in future versions of the product. The computer game industry best illustrates tinkering. More than 90% of the content of the highly successful computer game, *The Sims*, has come from tinker-based modifications (O'Hern & Rindfleish, 2009).

**Table 8.2** Four Forms of Co-Creation

| | |
|---|---|
| 1. Collaboration | jointly developing a new product and improving it. |
| 2. Tinkering | customers making modifications to commercially available products that will be used in future versions of the product. |
| 3. Co-designing | small group of customers providing a firm with most of its new product content or designs. |
| 4. Submitting | actively soliciting designs from current or potential customers. |

*Source:* Adapted from O'Hern and Rindfleisch (2009).

Third, *co-designing* occurs when a small group of customers provide a firm with most of its new product content or designs. For example, Threadless.com uses co-designing by soliciting original t-shirt designs from current and potential customers and then invites its vast network of online customers to give evaluations of the designs. Designers develop a portfolio of successes while working with designer coaches in the Threadless community. Finally, *submitting* is a form of open innovation in which firms actively solicit designs from current or potential customers. Swedish appliance manufacturer Electrolux receives thousands of entries, and then it invites a small set of finalists to a six-day, company-sponsored retreat. Here, submitters participate in workshops, present their inventions, and compete for prizes (www.electrolux.com/designlab).

Adopting the co-creation concept can be considered a shift in the firms' perspective on customers. Customers are no longer considered as receivers of the values, products, and/or services provided by these firms; rather, customers are active partners in value creation (Prahalad & Ramaswamy, 2000). Increasingly, marketers are realizing the worth of viewing customers as co-creating collaborators (Lusch, Vargo, & O'Brien, 2007). One way marketers can collaborate with customers is through co-creation in the new product development process.

Although researchers have recently taken interest in the interactive orientation of firms with customers (Ramaswamy & Gouillart, 2010a), such interactivity remains broadly defined and includes new product development only as a small piece of such interactivity. Most of the research on consumer co-creation has been done in the context of B2B markets (business-to-business) (Hoyer, Chandy, Dorotic, Krafft, & Singh, 2010). However, firms today now find themselves facing a new type of consumer that is better educated, more collaborative, and tremendously more resourceful than at any time in the past (Bhalla, 2010).

There is much to be learned about how co-creation can be done in the future in business-to-consumer (B2C) exchanges, as well as in consumer-to-consumer (C2C) exchanges.

Venkat Ramaswamy and Francis Gouillart (2010b) have distilled four principles from their research of co-creation at dozens of companies. First, stakeholders will not wholeheartedly participate in customer co-creation unless it provides value for them. Second, the best way to co-create value is to focus on the experiences of all stakeholders. Third, stakeholders must be able to interact directly with one another. Of the four types of co-creation proposed by O'Hern and Rindfleisch (2009), only collaborating (as in the software development of Linux) really incorporates such cross-communication among stakeholders. Fourth, companies should provide platforms that allow stakeholders to interact and share their experiences. The following case focused on Nike + illustrates the value of this very well.

## Nike+

Nike + (pronounced NikePlus) offers insights into co-creation possibilities. Launched in 2006 as a partnership with Apple, Nike + offers a set of tools to engage runners and the running community at large more deeply than when Nike just sold shoes, and Apple just sold iPods (Ramaswamy & Gouillart, 2010a). Nike now includes a smart sensor in the shoe that can communicate with a built-in wireless receiver on the iPod Touch or iPhone. As one runs, music or news can be played in the iPod. The sensor keeps track of any records being set. If one is set, a voice-over by bicycling champion Lance Armstrong plays congratulating the runner on this new milestone. Once the run is completed, the runner can go to www. nikeplus.com and upload data from the run. Here, the data can be combined with the runner's database or the database of the runner's community. Charting and analysis can now be done. Challenges can be sent to other runners. Maps of past runs and upcoming runs can be captured—even as the runner travels.

Nike + provides the customer an engagement platform by which Nike can reach out to the customer on his or her terms. The platform invites the runner to connect with an enormous community of runners with more than 2 million from around the world registered as of 2009 (Ramaswamy & Gouillart, 2010a, p. 10). Not only can the runner's experience be co-created with Nike + in a customized way as C. K. Prahalad and M. S. Krishnan (2008) have described in this new age of innovation, but the engagement platform allows Nike to engage runners and their social networks in rich conversations that can generate deep insights into the running experience. For example, in 2009, Nike learned that the average run worldwide was 35 minutes, and that the most popular song played by runners was "Pump It Up" by the Black Eyed Peas.

The benefits of this co-creation effort for Nike are remarkable. First, Nike + has enabled Nike to reduce its traditional media spending from 60% of its advertising budget in 1997 to 33% in 2007, as Nike uses nontraditional forms of communicating with its customers, such as Nike + and social media (Ramaswamy & Gouillart, 2010a, p. 13). By 2007, Nike's $457.9 million nonmedia spending came to more than its $220.5 million of traditional media spending. Second, the risk of product/service development was shared with Apple. Third, future developments can be done with less risk because of the ability to experiment with new product and service ideas on Nike + .

The road to Nike's innovation success with Nike + was not always a smooth one. In 1987, Nike launched a clunky Nike Monitor about the size of a thick paperback book. Needless to say, runners did not take readily to the Nike Monitor. Developing Nike + involved collaborating across areas of the company that had never directly interacted before as well as with Apple. Bringing together jogging, music, social networking, and technological collaboration with Apple was no easy feat. It required managers from across the firm in areas such as apparel, technology, research, footwear design, and music to form a new kind of team. "The best teams get a little borderless," Michael Donaghu, Nike's director of footwear innovation said. "We got really borderless" (Ramaswamy & Gouillart, 2010a, p. 14).

## Service-Dominant Logic

Customers' demand for personalized co-created experiences now drives firms to create global networks of suppliers and resource providers to meet the demands of customers. In this world characterized by "N = 1, and R = G," a new shift in focus for marketers now becomes more apparent. This shift moves the focus of marketing activity from goods to service (Vargo & Lusch, 2008). Here, service is defined as the process of using one's resources for the benefit of another entity. Specifically, service is the application of knowledge and skills (operant resources) to benefit another entity. This new conceptual lens on marketing activity is called service-dominant logic (S-D logic):

> S-D logic is based on an understanding of the interwoven fabric of individuals and organizations, brought together into networks and societies, specializing in and exchanging the application of their competencies for the applied competences they need for their own well being. It is a logic that is philosophically grounded in a commitment to collaborative processes with customers, partners, and employees; a logic that challenges management at all levels to be of service to all the stakeholders; a logic or perspective that recognizes the firm and its exchange partners who are engaged in the co-creation of value through reciprocal service provision. It is about understanding, internalizing, and acting on this logic better rather than the competition. (Lusch, Vargo, & O'Brien, 2007, p. 5)

In the early 1900s, marketing was about taking goods and services "*to market*" (Lusch, Vargo, & O'Brien, 2007). The American Marketing Association defined marketing as the set of business activities that direct the flow of goods and services from producers to consumer. Accordingly, much of marketing thought was explaining the activities of middlemen in markets. After World War II, marketing thought in the United States moved to a "*market to*" orientation. Accordingly, customers were researched, segmented, targeted, promoted to, and distributed to.

With this goods-dominant logic from these previous eras of marketing, value creation was done by the producer or by the firm. The consumer, competition, and most other market variables remained independent of value creation. In fact, producers viewed consumers as contaminating or reducing the value they had put into the stuff they made. For example, the day after purchasing an automobile, its resale value dropped noticeably because it was "used." However, talented customers can actually increase the value of a car purchased new by installing special features and customization, such as stereo, radio, GPS systems, tinted windows, and custom painting not done at the factory.

In S-D logic, the orientation of marketing becomes "*marketing with.*" Accordingly, the customer is viewed as a collaborative partner who co-creates value with the firm. Service is understood to be the fundamental basis of exchange, whereas goods are viewed as a distribution mechanism for providing service (benefit to another entity). In S-D logic, service is the fundamental basis of exchange. Although often masked by complex combinations of goods, money, and institutions, this service basis of exchange is not always readily apparent. However, the implication of service being the fundamental basis of exchange is that service is always exchanged for service. In this regard, goods derive their value through use—the service they provide. In this vein, long-time Harvard Business School marketing professor Ted Levitt's assertion that "people want quarter-inch holes, not quarter inch drill bits" (Hunter, 2009, para. 8) makes much sense when applying S-D logic.

Nike + the running shoes with the smart sensors derive their value through use. Owners of the shoe use them for jogging and then upload data to the Internet. Once on the Internet, more value is created by interacting with the community of runners there to compare and learn about running trends from other users. Here, forces in the external environment for the firm can now be co-created as well, such as the social importance of being part of an online community of runners. In short, Nike used to sell shoes, but it now sells access to camaraderie. In this way, it can be seen that the firm does not create value but makes value propositions (that can be taken up and interactively developed by the customer, the firm, and other entities). In S-D logic, value is determined by the beneficiary—the one who benefits from the service rendered. Service is defined in terms of customer-determined benefit. As a result, value will be idiosyncratic, experiential, contextual, and meaning laden. Because value creation is interactional, it is inherently relational. Nike + illustrates these aspects of S-D logic well as one customer training for a marathon might prefer comparing her preparation for the London Marathon with others preparing for the same race (or who ran it last year). Such value would be different from an employee for IBM who wants to identify jogging trails in London on her next overseas trip there in order to maintain a healthy lifestyle.

With both the iPod and Nike + , Apple, Inc. served as a resource integrator. But so did others involved in the experience of using the iPod and Nike + . In S-D logic, all social and economic actors are resource integrators—not just firms, but individuals, households, firms, organizations, societies, and nations. In fact, service systems can be said to be any constellation of entities sharing information for the purpose of co-creating value (Vargo & Lusch, 2008, p. 5). These could include cities, city departments, businesses, business departments, nations, and national agencies. The smallest service system would be an individual, whereas the largest service system would be the global economy.

Lusch notes that as the division of labor has increased over the course of human history, another development occurred—the connectedness of individuals (Lush, 2006, p. 241). As each person specializes, more dependence and connectedness to others develops. In this way, the importance of the market and marketing can be understood in the way markets and marketing are primary drivers or creators of society. Society cannot exist without the exchange of the most fundamental resources for human existence, such as know-how. Accordingly, society can be understood to involve a complex web of service in both social and economic forms. Recognizing the mutual dependence of individuals in society, the purpose of commerce can be seen in a new light as not making and selling more stuff, but rather as mutually serving each other. In this way, the ethic of the servant leader seems to fit a new era of innovation characterized by networked collaboration.

## CONCLUSION

This chapter offered a macromarketing primer on leadership in the increasingly networked world of the 21st century. Leadership is learned, and leadership abilities evolve through life. Leaders come in all varieties of looks and backgrounds. When the situation is right, even the most shy or inwardly focused person can lead others—usually because of some knowledge of skill this person has acquired. Good leaders know how to contribute to team success when they do not have the trappings of command or the formal designation of "leader." The opening story of Jan Fields, the current CEO of McDonald's USA, illustrated this. Beginning as a cooking crew worker behind the counter of a local McDonald's restaurant, Fields has had a variety of leadership assignments at all levels of the McDonald's corporation. In her current position, she is responsible for the strategic direction and overall business results for 14,000 McDonald's restaurants in the United States. By comparison, she follows McDonald's CEO Jim Skinner who leads the world's largest food service company with more than 32,000 restaurants in 117 countries. In this way, one can understand how McDonald's USA is embedded in a larger worldwide organization.

The leadership overview in this chapter highlighted the need for leaders to know and understand themselves and what motivates them. The Schwarz values circumplex depicted in Figure 8.1 provided insights into the sometimes opposing values that compose the value systems of individuals, such as leaders themselves and those with whom they will work. Knowing others is also fundamental to being an effective leader. McGregor's Theory X and Theory Y suggests corresponding hard and soft approaches with those being led. Knowing the nature of leadership styles is also valuable for leaders. The path-goal model offers a version of the "carrot-and-stick" approach to leadership alluding to rewards and punishments given in an ongoing series of transactions between leaders and subordinates in organizations. By comparison, the transformational leader model sees the leader as a coach and exhorter who engages the organization as well as individuals in the organization to improve themselves. Servant leadership fits with the idea of a transformational leader.

The increasingly networked world of the early 21st century suggests that more collaboration will be done by firms outside of traditional firm boundaries. Accordingly, a service-dominant logic is more apparent in the conduct of commerce as it is better understood that service—the application of knowledge and skills to benefit another entity—is the foundation for all exchanges in society. With this S-D lens, the potential for leaders as servants and connectors can be seen only to increase in the future.

## QUESTIONS

- Given some of the new realities in business emerging from increased uncertainty, complexity, diversity, and the need for responsibility and transparency, how is McDonald's Inc. changing?
- What new ideas about leadership did you gain from reading Chapter 8?
- What values from the Schwarz values circumplex have business persons likely given greater importance in the past? Environmentalists? In your opinion, what would it take to change the importance accorded to these values in the values systems of representatives from each group?
- Have you ever worked in an organization where the leaders adopted many of the assumptions of Theory X? What was that experience like? Have you seen any movies depicting such a climate of leadership?
- What leaders have you read about or known that left the organization they led and the individuals in it better off after they left their leadership role?
- How do the iPod and Nike + represent a new age of innovation?
- Lusch asserts that, "Individuals without the exchange of service for service are anti-society. With the exchange of service comes society" (Lusch, 2006, p. 241). To what degree do you agree or disagree with Lusch?

## MAVERICKS WHO MADE IT

### John Stanford

SERVICE-DOMINANT (S-D) logic is now being used to understand the complex web of social and economic relations comprising society. In this regard, the purpose of all types of service systems can be said to be the exchange of mutual service (benefit). Because human knowledge and skills take such high importance in S-D logic, it is fitting to turn to the story of a leader of schools where the acquisition of knowledge should be the central focus.

John Stanford's last job before he died of leukemia in 1998 was as Superintendent of the Seattle Public School System. Before that he served four years as Manager of Fulton County, Georgia—the central county in the Greater Atlanta area. Before that, he served 30 years in the U.S. Army, and he retired as a Major General (two stars). In the Army, he was a logistician, so he understood supply chains and supporting the endeavors of other unit commanders. He also understood service—using one's abilities to benefit another entity.

But when he was hired to be superintendent of Seattle Public Schools in September 1995, many people in Seattle viewed him as a threat. Not understanding that a core dimension of Army life is learning and training, his initial critics saw that he had no formal experience as an educator. At his first open interview as part of the selection process to be the superintendent, the room was packed and Stanford could hear the murmuring. Many teachers supposed he would be inflexible and abrasive, unable to listen. Many parents feared he would try to bring excessive discipline to the schools that would squelch creativity. Stanford recalled his thoughts as he heard some of the principals of Seattle's schools whisper adamantly "Don't hire the general!" to the president of the school board as she introduced Stanford to the packed room:

> But I also knew how far from the mark that was. Thirty years of leading in the military had taught me that most leaders are the antithesis of those traits. Leading means inspiring, not commanding. Leading means loving the people you lead so they will give you their hearts as well as their minds. It means communicating a vision of where you can go together and inviting them to join. The community was right: a TV general could not have led the public schools. They didn't know me, but their stereotypes were different from my reality. Now I had two hours to change their minds. (Stanford, 1999, p. xi)

Stanford listened carefully to the concerns expressed in his first interview. He spoke with confidence when he said he would lead the schools to success, but that he could not run the schools alone. He would need help and would actively invite the participation of parents, businesses, and community groups to help raise the level of achievement in the schools. In this way, he signaled he would take a collaborative approach to the leadership task before him.

Stanford told those gathered for the open interview that despite the daunting problems facing the schools in Seattle, the children of Seattle could be reached and taught if a wide coalition of parents, teachers, staff, business people, and community leaders worked together. At the time, the problems for Seattle were similar to other urban school districts and included aging buildings, declining test scores, an inadequate budget, and racial tensions.

What Stanford did not disclose that first day was that he knew first-hand how students could be reached and put on the path toward excitement about learning and achievement. At the end of his sixth-grade year, his teacher Miss Greenstein visited his parents at their home in Yeadon, Pennsylvania, west of Philadelphia one afternoon to tell them that Stanford would have to repeat sixth grade. Stanford felt crushed and humiliated.

Later, Stanford would recall that Mrs. Greenstein showed courage and love for him because she had the courage to intervene:

> I say courage and love because that's exactly what it took. It took courage and love to look my parents in the eye and tell them - just as it takes courage and love to do the other things a school system must do if it wants to do what's best for its children. It takes courage and love to say to teachers, 'You must put aside your adult concerns.' (Stanford, 1999, p. xiii, para. 2)

His parents, both of whom had not completed elementary school, were shocked and disappointed. But Stanford's mother began a program of nightly reading with the young Stanford that eventually

*(Continued)*

(Continued)

led to him becoming energized about learning over a two-year period. In sum, Stanford himself was the embodiment of winning one of the most difficult challenges facing Seattle's Public Schools—reaching "unreachable" students so that they could lead productive lives.

The Seattle Public Schools took the risk and hired Stanford over two other candidates with superintendent experience and PhD's in education. Stanford took charge of the school district and immediately went out to schools to conduct his own qualitative research by observing, inquiring about teaching practices, and hearing from the community. Surprising to Stanford, capable principals and teachers had much to say about "adult issues," such as philosophies of education, or union contracts, but few actually talked about student achievement.

Early in his tenure, Stanford found the "true North" direction for the school district—student achievement. This became the central theme and the rallying cry for bringing together constituencies from across Seattle. Subprograms would be developed to emphasize parts of improving student achievement, such as calling all students to read more—a lot more.

Stanford believed that a love of reading was not just a schools issue. It was a cultural issue requiring community reinforcement (Stanford, 1999). Parents would need to read to their children every night and make sure their kids did their reading homework. Radio stations would need to broadcast messages encouraging children to read. Local sports celebrities would need to visit schools and talk about the importance of reading. Finally, thousands of volunteers would need to come to schools and tutor children one-on-one and read to them in small groups.

Fun things spiced the community-wide effort to emphasize reading. Students made chains of paper cars and airplanes and strung them through the hallways of the elementary schools as a way to claim the names of every book the kids had read. Principals fulfilled promises by sitting on the school roof for a day in a crazy costume because students at their school read to a certain level. Stanford fulfilled his own promise to be flown in by Army helicopter to one school if the students achieved the school's reading goal.

To Stanford, the pay-off of the reading program was student achievement. Teachers reported gains in reading comprehension, and the writing of students improved. Across Seattle, students adopted the superintendent's call to read 20 minutes each day. One mother said she thought she had heard every excuse for her child putting off doing household chores until one night her daughter declined to take out the garbage because she had to do her reading.

Stanford believed the school system would do better in boosting student achievement if it adopted a business approach. He regarded himself as "CEO of Destiny, Inc." leading a market-based school system. The school system began listening to its customers by systematically conducting community forums and surveys. Stanford and his team learned much. For example, they learned that parents wanted local schools that challenged students to attain their highest potential. In response, Stanford led an end to school busing. They also wanted arts and sports programs that were being cut as a result of budget shortfalls.

To include arts and sports programs, Stanford adopted university-style budgeting in which the city would provide a basic education while donors would contribute so that arts and sports programs and other program enhancements would be included in the curriculum of Seattle Public Schools. He brought in a professional fund-raising partner Alliance for Education. Together, they prepared a business prospectus for each potential donor detailing a comprehensive plan for how requested donations would be invested and what would be the measurable outcomes of each donation. For example, Microsoft would benefit from having a pool of highly literate job applicants in the future.

Businesses and foundations jumped into this first-of-its-kind philanthropy for public education by donating millions of dollars. Stanford and the school board adopted marketing practices too:

> The only way we'd generate the gargantuan amount of support we needed would be to market the schools constantly and deliberately. We'd need to communicate to the community over and over and over again the excitement we were feeling, the amount of change that was taking place, and the quality of what we were doing. We would need to sell the schools the way Nordstrom sells Nordstrom if we wanted to get investors excited enough to give. (Stanford, 1999, p. 158)

Inside the schools, the biggest change Stanford required of his principals was to become leaders rather than managers of their respective schools. He won a new union contract that would allow principals to hire the best teachers and to hold them accountable for student achievement. Instead of principals dealing with bus schedules and the operational aspects of their buildings and the discipline of students, Stanford wanted them to delegate these tasks to others, so that they could actually lead in their schools. In Stanford's view, the principals needed to set a vision for their school communities, and then inspire their teachers, students, and parents to achieve it:

> They needed to be setting goals for their teachers, helping the teachers set goals for students, and working with the teachers daily to make sure the students reached them. They needed to be observing their teachers, making sure they had the skills to do the job, and seeing that they got the support and training they needed. They needed to be meeting with parents, talking with them about their children and about the parents' role in education. They needed to build teamwork among the teachers, keep them focused on achievement, and rid their schools of the hundreds of other issues that got in the way. They needed to be "working" their communities, recruiting volunteers and resources for their teachers, getting the community excited about what was happening in their schools. Principals need to stop being the chief disciplinarians of their schools and become their chief education officers. (Stanford, 1999, p. 162)

Over a three-year period at the helm of the Seattle Public Schools, test scores for students rose, the performance gap between minority students and White students began closing, incidences of

*(Continued)*

(Continued)

violence declined, and the requirement for student graduation from high school changed from a 0.83 average on a 4.0 scale to a "C" average of 2.0. But importantly, the city of Seattle mobilized on behalf of children and education. Stanford's philosophy of "love 'em and lead 'em" connected with many across Seattle.

In 1998, leukemia came upon Stanford and overtook him nine months later. After his death, the entire city mourned for him in public gatherings. A Web tribute and excerpts from his book *Victory in Our Schools* are available at (http://seattletimes.nwsource.com/special/stanford/index.html). Stanford illustrated transformational leadership in a complex organization and embraced the "biggest M" in his engagement of stakeholders across Seattle for the transcendent purpose of serving the children of the city. The evidence of his transformational leadership is the changed public schools of Seattle and the improved performances of students, teachers, and staff.

## Questions

- In your opinion, what parts of Stanford's life story prior to moving to Seattle contributed to his success as a leader of the Seattle Public Schools? What is remarkable about his success in Seattle?
- How does Stanford's story of engaging Seattle for the benefit of children in Seattle illustrate concepts of leadership from Chapter 8?
- What role did a business approach play in the change in the Seattle Public Schools?
- What can be learned about collaborative leadership and co-creation from Stanford's experience as superintendent?

## REFERENCES

Adams, S. (2011). *How's that underling thing working out for you?* Riverside, NJ: Andrews McMeel.

Army. (2006). *Army leadership: Confident, competent, and agile* (FM 6-22). Department of the Army.

Beazley, H. (2003). Foreword. In H. Beazley, J. Beggs, & L. C. Spears (Eds.), *The servant-leader within: A transformative path*. New York, NY: Paulist Press.

Bennington, E. (2011). Lovin' it with McDonald's President Jan Fields. *Forbes*. Retrieved from http://www.forbes.com

Benkler, Y. (2011, July–August). The unselfish gene. *Harvard Business Review*, pp. 77–85.

Bennis, W. (2003). *On becoming a leader* (p. 48). New York, NY: Basic Books.

Bhalla, G. (2010). *Collaboration and co-creation: New platforms for marketing and innovation*. New York, NY: Springer.

Burns, J. M. (1978). *Leadership*. New York, NY: Harper & Row.

Chen, S. (2011). Cooking fries? Cleaning hospitals? Executives reflect on their first job. *CNN.com*. Retrieved from http://www.cnn.com

Chicago Tribune. (2011, April 10). Trying to alter 'McJob' image. *The Chicago Tribune*. Retrieved from http://www.vindy.com

Coutu, D. (2006, March). Leadership in literature: A conversation with business ethicist Joseph L. Badaracco, Jr. *Harvard Business Review*, pp. 47–55.

Crompton, T. (2010). Common cause: The case for working with our cultural values. World Wildlife Fund. Retrieved from http://www.wwf.org.uk/wwf_articles.cfm?unewsid = 4224

DePree, M. (2004). *Leadership is an art*. New York, NY: Currency Doubleday enotes.com. (2011). Encyclopedia of management: Theory X and Theory Y. Retrieved from http://www.enotes.com/management-encyclopedia/theory-x-theory-y

Fiedler, F. E. (1967). *A theory of leadership effectiveness*. New York, NY: Harper & Row.

George, B., with P. Sims (2007). *True north: Discover your authentic leadership*. San Francisco, CA: Jossey-Bass.

Goleman, D. (2004, January). What makes a leader? *Harvard Business Review*, pp. 83–91.

Greenleaf, R. K. (2003). The leader as servant *path*. In H. Beazley, J. Beggs, & L. C. Spears (Eds.), *The servant leader within: The transformative path*. New York, NY: Paulist Press.

Groth, M. (2005). Customers as good soldiers: Examining citizenship behaviors in internet service deliveries. *Journal of Management, 31*, 7–27.

Hersey, P., Blanchard, K., & Johnson, D. (2008). *Management of organizational behavior: Leading human resources* (9th ed.). Upper Saddle River, NJ: Pearson Education.

House, R. J. (1996). Path-goal theory of leadership: Lessons, legacy, and a reformulated theory. *Leadership Quarterly, 7*(3), 323–352.

Hoyer, W. D., Chandy, R., Dorotic, M., Krafft, M., & Singh, S. S. (2010). Consumer cocreation in new product development. *Journal of Service Research, 13*(3), 283–296.

Hunter, J. C. (2004). *The world's most powerful leadership principle: How to become a servant leader*. New York, NY: Crown Business.

Hunter, S. (2009, May 18). Customers buy holes not drill bits. *Lotta Guru*. Retrieved from http://lottaguru.com/customers-buy-holes-not-drill-bits/

Huston, L., & Sakkab, N. (2006, March). Connect and develop: Inside Procter & Gamble's new model for innovation. *Harvard Business Review*, pp. 58–66.

Ibarra, H, & Hansen, M. T. (2011, July–August). Are you a collaborative leader? *Harvard Business Review*, pp. 69–74.

Integrated Leadership Concepts. (2011). The first tenet of leadership: Know yourself. Retrieved from http://integratedleadershipconcepts.com/PDF/First_tenet.pdf

Kanter, R. M. (2009). *Supercorp: How vanguard companies create innovation, profits, growth, and social good*. New York, NY: Crown Business.

Keith, K. M. (2010, Summer). Servant leadership: Making the free enterprise system work better. *Diary of Alpha Kappa Psi*, pp. 32–35.

Kroll, A. (2011, May 9). Welcome to the McJobs recovery. *The Nation*. Retrieved from http://www.thenation.com

Lafley, A. G., & Charan, R. (2008). *The game-changer: How you can drive revenue and profit growth with innovation*. New York, NY: Crown Business.

Lusch, R. F. (2006). The small and long view. *Journal of Macromarketing, 26*(2), pp. 240–244.

Lusch, R. F., Vargo, S. L., & O'Brien, M. (2007). Competing through service: Insights from service-dominant logic. *Journal of Retailing, 83*(1), 5–18.

Maxwell, J. C. (2007, November 19). People do what people see. *Bloomberg Business Week*, Retrieved from http://www.businessweek.com

McGregor, D. (2005). *The human side of enterprise* (annot. ed.). New York, NY: McGraw-Hill.

Mintzberg, H., Simons, R., & Basu, K. (2002, Fall). Beyond selfishness. *MIT Sloan Management Review*, pp. 67–74.

Norton, R. (2011, May 24). The thought leader interview: Henry Chesbrough. *strategy + business, 63*. Retrieved from http://www.strategy-business.com

O'Hern, M. S., & Rindfleisch, A. (2009). A typology of customer co-creation. In N. K. Malhotra (Ed.), *Review of Marketing Research* (vol. 6, pp. 84–106). Armonk, NY: M.E. Sharpe.

Parcells, B. (2000, November–December). The tough work of turning around a team. *Harvard Business Review*, pp. 179–184.

Parks, S. D. (2005). *Leadership can be taught: A bold approach for a complex world*. Boston, MA: Harvard Business School Press.

Prahalad, C. K., & Krishnan, M. S. (2008). *The new age of innovation: Driving co-created value through global networks*. New York, NY: McGraw-Hill.

Prahalad, C. K., & Ramaswamy, V. (2000, January–February). Co-opting customer competence. *Harvard Business Review, 78*, 79–87.

QSR. (2011). Top women in quick service: Jan Fields, President of McDonald's USA. Retrieved from http://www.qsrmagazine.com

Ramaswamy, V., & Gouillart, F. (2010a). *The power of co-creation: Build it with them to boost growth, productivity, and profits*. New York, NY: Free Press.

Ramaswamy, V., & Gouillart, F. (2010b, October). Building the co-creative enterprise. *Harvard Business Review*, pp. 2–9.

Rexrode, C. (2011, April 19). McDonald's hiring day draws crowds, high hopes. *The Washington Times*. Retrieved from http://www.washingtontimes.com

Rockefeller, J. D. (1973). *The second American revolution: Some personal observations*. New York, NY: Harper & Row.

Rohrlich, J. (2011, April 13). Economists weigh in on McDonald's plan to hire 50,000 new employees. *The Daily Feed*. Retrieved from http://www.minyanville.com

Rust, R., & Espinoza, F. (2006). How technology advances influence business research and marketing strategy. *Journal of Business Research, 59*, 1072–1078.

Schwartz, S. (1994). Are there universal aspects in the structure and contents of human values?. *Journal of Social Issues, 50*(4), 19–45.

Sellers, P. (2011a, April 4). The woman behind McDonald's hiring blitz. *CNNMoney*. Retrieved from http://www.postcards.blogs.fortune.cnn.com

Sellers, P. (2011b, June 20). Fortune's most powerful women and Yahoo: Keys to success. *CNNMoney*. Retrieved from http://www.postcards.blogs.fortune.cnn.com

Shelby, D. (2011, April 12). McDonald's is very green—and now hiring. *MinnPost.com*. Retrieved from http://www.minnpost.com

Stanford, J. (1999). *Victory in our schools: We CAN give our children excellent public education*. New York, NY: Bantam Books.

Sterrett, D. (2010, May 3). McDonald's new US chief, Jan Fields, oversees re-imagining of décor, menu. *This Week's Crain's*. Retrieved from htpp://www.chicagobusiness.com

Taylor, W. C. (2007, December 19). The leader of the future. *Fast Company*. Retrieved from http://www.fastcompany.com/magazine/25/heifetz.html

The Economist. (2011, June 23). The bottom of the pyramid: Businesses are learning to serve the growing number of hard-up Americans. *The Economist*. Retrieved from www.economist.com

Vargo, S. L., & Lusch, R. F. (2008). Service-dominant logic: Continuing the evolution. *Journal of the Academy of Marketing Science, 36*, 1–10.

Wal-Mart. (2011a). Building the next generation Wal-Mart...Responsibly. 2011 Global Responsibility Report. Retrieved from http://www.walmartstores.com

Wal-Mart. (2011b). Wal-Mart corporate. Awards and recognitions. Retrieved from http://walmartstores.com/AboutUs/336.aspx

Wikipedia. (2011). File:Dilbert-20050910.png. Retrieved from http://en.wikipedia.org/wiki/File:Dilbert-20050910.png

Zaleznik, A. (1998). Managers and leaders: Are they different? *Harvard Business Review on leadership* (pp. 61–87). Boston, MA: Harvard Business School Press.

## CHAPTER 9

# Globalization

## ROCKIN' THE WORLD

### Bill Roedy—MTV Networks International

On September 22, 2010, Viacom Chairman and CEO Philippe Dauman sent a memo to all in Viacom informing them that one of the leaders of a Viacom subsidiary company, MTV Networks International's (MTVNI) CEO Bill Roedy, had decided to retire from 22 years as a relentless world-traveling executive focused on building MTV's audience around the world (Roedy, 2011). Beginning with a single channel in 1989, Roedy led MTVNI's effort to launch more channels and networks than any other entertainment company.

By the end of Roedy's run as leader of MTVNI, the company's operations included 175 locally programmed channels and 400 digital media properties across 165 countries. Upon his departure, the potential audience for MTVNI totaled more than 2 billion persons who speak 33 different languages. In 2010, MTVNI posted revenues of more than $1.3 billion (Andrews, 2011).

For many, it might be hard to imagine a career like Roedy's. In 1970, he graduated from the U.S. Military Academy, and then he served as a U.S. Army officer in the northern part of South Viet Nam for a year. He received the Bronze Star medal for his service:

> The lessons I learned during that time helped shape everything I did after that. I learned the importance of making quick and firm decisions, communicating those decisions clearly to my troops and then doing anything and everything necessary to implement them. I learned the importance of building morale, camaraderie, and a team spirit. I learned how to deal with the chain of command and how to get around it when necessary. And after living on the frontlines for a year, there isn't much that intimidates me. (Roedy, 2011, p. 11, para. 1)

Roedy later commanded nuclear missile sites in California for 18 months and in Italy for 3 years that offered a stressful existence but rich management experience. After seven years on active duty, Roedy chose to leave the Army and graduated two years later from the Harvard Business School. After graduating in 1979, he joined a startup cable channel Home Box Office (HBO) because his dream from his youth had been to work in television. Week by week, Roedy joined in making decisions about how the cable television would be built often house by house and neighborhood by neighborhood. The entrepreneurial atmosphere in the industry was incredibly exciting to Roedy.

Roedy traveled the entire country launching HBO—a commercial-free channel operating every hour of the day that had a perfectly symbiotic relationship with the cable television industry. HBO helped sell cable television subscriptions as one of the few attractive programming options in the early years of cable television:

> At HBO I practically lived on the road for 10 years. I was the cable industry's traveling salesman. In life as well as in business, the ability to sell is the foundation on which success is built. That is increasingly true as the world evolves. Some people are turned off by the concept of selling, but I think that's because they don't really understand it. Even in Vietnam I had to sell the mission. I had to inspire my troops. In the military, for example, even though I had the formal authority to force troops to obey my orders, I found that if people didn't believe in the mission, I never got a total effort from them. (Roedy, 2011, p. 25)

By the late 1980s, the frontier days of cable television were coming to an end as most of the United States had access to cable programming by wire or by satellite. Viacom recruited Roedy to become managing director of MTV Europe. Roedy moved to London and began his work of developing distribution across Europe for a new art form—music videos—on MTV. For MTVNI, Roedy blended the hard drive of a passionate entrepreneur with the nerve of a combat veteran. He told his young staff that the only rule was to break the rules:

We broke all the rules. We paid to get on the German cable system which no company had ever done before. We ran our programming on terrestrial systems, which cable channels didn't do; we transmitted our signal direct-to-home unencrypted so anyone with a dish could get it, we pushed cultural norms; we ran edgy programming. (Roedy, 2011, p. 48, para. 2)

Roedy would succeed in building in Europe. He assumed leadership of MTVNI and helped take MTV around the world. But in each country, often 85% of the programming came from the host nation talent with the balance coming from global sources. Such localization can lead to problems. For example, the local MTV channel in Taiwan began running nude, male wrestling. He shut it down. "You can lose control of the brand" (Jacobs, 2011, p. 1, para. 12). To prevent such programming lapses, MTV created brand police who would travel the world monitoring the channel's output.

As CEO, Roedy directed all of MTV Networks's global multimedia operations for the MTV brands, including Music Television, Nickelodeon, VH-1, VIVA, TMF: The Music Factory, Game One, Comedy Central, Paramount Comedy, Spike TV, and BET, which includes BET Hip Hop, BET Mobile, and BET.com. Roedy was honored as the UN Correspondents' 2009 Global Citizen of the Year for public service initiatives aired on MTV (mostly for HIV/AIDS prevention) that saved lives while building tremendous brand recognition and loyalty throughout the world. "The bottom line is that for the bottom line, doing good in the world is good for business," Roedy said. "I have little doubt that in many countries MTV's proven record of engagement without pushing a political agenda made it a lot easier for us to receive government approval" (Nichols, 2011, p. 1, para. 11).

## Your Thoughts?

- What did Bill Roedy have going for him when he began his business career in 1979?
- What did Bill Roedy have going against him when he began his business career in 1979?
- Leaving Harvard Business School, Roedy also had a job offer to join NBC—one of the three major broadcast networks—in a finance job overseeing programming. Walking the halls in Rockefeller Center in Manhattan, Roedy said later that it felt "very corporate." Instead, Roedy joined the startup cable channel HBO. How do you think Roedy's career would have progressed if he had chosen the conventional job at NBC rather than the unconventional one at HBO?
- Roedy once sang karaoke with Bono at 5 AM in a state-of-the-art karaoke club in Tokyo. (They sang Bruce Springsteen's *Born in the USA*.) Afterward, they were in Bono's specially equipped van listening as Bono sang along to tracks from his soon-to-be-released album. He said later that at times like these he was not the CEO of an international media corporation but a starstruck music fan. Is being a fan in this way acceptable for the CEO of an international media corporation?

## CHAPTER OVERVIEW AND LEARNING OBJECTIVES

This chapter will highlight some challenges for firms in a globalized world. MTV International's Bill Roedy made business rock through his years as he developed the world's largest entertainment network across a diverse range of cultures. In this context, Roedy had to develop partnering relationships with those who did not speak his language and who faced a wide range of challenges from Australia to Zambia. Roedy's one rule was to break all the rules.

On the frontier of building national media networks with all of the accompanying difficulties involved, MTVNI has had remarkable success. But global brands such as MTV are admired and feared as they build their markets around the world. For example, MTV can bring entertainment to many, but what cultural values in host countries might be undermined by its programming? What does a global brand like MTV give back to society wherever it goes? Why do boards of global firms allow their CEOs so much financial compensation?

Multinational enterprises (MNEs) are said to bring death to distance. Although the principal benefits of globalization to consumers in developed countries might be listed as (a) more choices and (b) lower prices, critics of globalization cite the inequities that often accompany globalization. According to these critics, workers face lower wages, while CEOs take home salaries higher than they have ever been. Additionally, globalization tends to promote diffusion of some negative outcomes of consumer culture, such as overconsumption, as well as criminal trafficking in contraband, such as illegal drugs and human slaves. Again, it seems that transparency is needed to stem the work of such trafficking networks. The story of Peter Eigen, founder of Transparency International, a nongovernmental organization (NGO) devoted to reducing corruption around the world, illustrates how one person can lead an effective movement to attack a malady of the business world said by many to be inevitable.

After this chapter, you should be able to answer the following questions:

- In what ways might it be a problem that CEOs of some global firms receive high pay?
- How can globalization be defined?
- What are some benefits of globalization?
- What are some criticisms of globalization?
- What are the seven wars related to globalization that societies now wage?
- What group in a society does bribe-paying hurt the most?

## BUILDING GLOBAL BRANDS

### Building the World's Largest Global Network

Wherever he went, Roedy wore sneakers. They became his trademark. He owned them in all colors. The sneakers made his back feel better, but they also encouraged the creative environment he wanted to instill at MTVNI. When he was the first private citizen to address the UN General Assembly, as a result of his work in fighting AIDS, he wore a dark suit and black sneakers. He also wore them to meet the Queen.

Roedy was in Berlin when the Berlin Wall fell in 1989. He believes television played a major role in bringing Eastern Europe to shake off communist rule. "I'm convinced it wasn't so much about the rock 'n' roll programming," Roedy said. "I think it was even more about the commercials. They saw how the other side lived" (Andrews, 2011, p. 1, para. 23).

### The Importance of International Travel

To build an international business, Bill Roedy did a remarkable amount of traveling. For example, in one month, Roedy visited 20 different countries (Roedy, 2011, p. 98). In another three-month period, he spent fewer than 10 days at home. Based out of London, Roedy went where the most important opportunity existed, which often meant going where problems had to be solved. He used to joke that there were times he went to China more often than to his office in the United Kingdom—only ten minutes from his home.

In launching MTV in different countries, Roedy discovered that what worked well in one market often had little application to the next market. Accordingly, he was not able to cut down on his travel because building an international business required being there— wherever *there* was. For example, it took nearly five years to put together a patchwork network of local and regional channels that allowed MTV Italy to send 13 hours of daily programming to 11 million households (Roedy, 2011, p. 105). Eventually, MTV obtained one of the eight national frequencies, but then the Italian government decided to reduce the number of frequencies to only six. Consequently, MTV, the only non-Italian broadcaster of the original eight, was cut. Roedy spent a year commuting back and forth between Milan and Rome meeting daily with lobbyists, government officials, and potential partners. It became apparent that Roedy and his team would not be able to reverse the government's decision, so MTV moved to purchase another national frequency. However, in the highly regulated environment, MTV had to form a joint venture with an Italian Company—Italian Telecom—and lose half of its business in Italy.

Over the years, MTV become the most distributed brand in the world (Nichols, 2011). However, it adapted its content in every country. "Everything was sensitized to the local audience and that was really the key factor I think to our success," Roedy said. We play rap in the Middle East … but the lyrics are not angry street culture, they're more about, I love my mother" (Nichols, 2011, para. 5). In the Middle East, Pakistan, and Indonesia, MTV airs the Muslim call to prayer five times each day.

Developing distribution agreements meant meeting with small cable operators in distant countries, powerful media moguls, as well as celebrities, such as Bono, Paul McCartney, and Will Smith. Roedy also met with leaders of governments to discuss distribution of MTVNI's programming, such as China's President Jiang Zemin, former Cuban President Fidel Castro, and former South African President Nelson Mandela.

### The Importance of Relationships in Business

With MTVNI, Roedy continued to travel extensively because of his belief in relationships, especially in Asia. Meeting one's audience in the media business and experiencing firsthand those things that made a difference to them mattered to Roedy. This allowed potential misunderstandings resulting from cultural differences or changing circumstances to be overcome. "It's important to look people in the eye," Roedy said. "When people travel, they often just do airport, conference room and a hotel. You've got to really experience the culture" (Jacobs, 2011, p. 1, para. 11).

For example, he traveled to China for 20 years to build relationships that eventually resulted in distribution of MTV in China. To protect its own media, and guard its culture, China severely restricts foreign media (Roedy, 2011, p. 153). In the end, the Chinese government agreed to allow a 24-hour, MTV-branded channel along the Pearl River Delta near Shanghai. In return, MTV would launch CCTV9, the English version of Chinese state TV, as a 24-hour news channel in U.S. hotels (Andrews, 2011, p. 1, para. 25). These negotiations were boosted by the managing director of the Chinese cable company Southern Media Corporation, Wang Keman. Because Wang had previously attended the Chinese military academy, Roedy arranged for Wang to receive a much-wanted tour of the U.S. Military Academy. Roedy claims he never thought his previous years in the U.S. military would directly influence his dealings in communist-led countries, but in this case, they did. They also helped in Russia as former Cold Warriors loved to discuss transitions in the former Soviet Union with Roedy.

He credits his physical fitness regimen for enabling him to endure his years of travel. During a series of vodka toasts upon launching MTV Europe in Leningrad in 1990, the Deputy Mayor of Leningrad Yuri Gerasimov ripped off his shirt and challenged Roedy to a wrestling match. Roedy soon found himself on the floor of the Winter Palace holding his host in a half-nelson wondering if he had gone too far this time (Roedy, 2011, p. 114, para. 6).

"I worked very hard to respect and reflect local cultures, which means every channel is different and that was quite unusual back then and it still is," Roedy said (Nichols, 2011, p. 1, para. 4). Roedy negotiated in dozens of languages, but he said he designed the MTVNI organization from lessons he learned in the military—keep the units small and close to the enemy. In MTVNI's case, this meant the competition.

Through MTVNI's *Staying Alive* campaign, Roedy led MTV's global efforts to promote HIV/AIDS awareness (Viacom, 2011). This campaign aimed to change behavior and reduce the stigma attached to the disease by producing award-winning documentaries, concerts, town halls, and public service announcements made available free and at no cost to all broadcasters. In describing Roedy, former U.S. President Bill Clinton once called Roedy "the best business man in the world" (The Literary Group, 2011).

## What the World's Consumers Expect From Global Brands

In 1983, Harvard Business School professor Ted Levitt declared that a global market for uniform products and services had arrived (Levitt, 1983). Many interpreted Levitt's words as a call to standardization across world markets. In this interpretation, marketing practices could be done the same way to achieve success as the world apparently wanted the elements of pop culture in Western markets, such as blue jeans, pop music, and fast food, as well as consumer durables like cars and refrigerators. In time, standardized global brands did not perform as well as predicted by Levitt. In their place, marketers used hybrid approaches to combine the best of global approaches in less visible areas, such as technology, manufacturing, and firm organization, with more local approaches in more visible areas, such as products, distribution, and promotion (Holt, Quelch, & Taylor, 2004). These "glocal" strategies have strongly influenced marketing ever since.

Toward the end of the 20th century, an antiglobalization movement became increasingly vociferous. It manifested itself at the annual World Economic Forum in Davos, Switzerland, with window smashing at McDonald's. Later, protests at the November 1999 World Trade Organization meeting in Seattle turned into "the battle in Seattle." Many protesters denounced the asymmetrical benefits to developed countries, as well as the externalities of global trade increasingly burdening countries in the developing world, such as exploitative wages, pollution, and cultural imperialism.

As popular culture became global and nations integrated themselves in the global economy, flows of tourists and laborers increasingly crossed borders. Television, movies, and music also flowed across borders. And more recently, the wide diffusion in the use of the Internet has further reinforced globalizing forces. Today, global brands are key symbols in an ongoing conversation people across the world have about what they like and who they are. Increasingly, global brands are viewed as having a powerful impact on people's lives, as well as on the well-being of communities, nations, and the planet.

## The Three Dimensions of Global Brands

Research about global brands suggests that people across the world associate three dimensions with global brands and base their purchase decisions on these (Holt, Quelch, & Taylor, 2004, p. 2, para. 5). First, a global brand signals quality. Global brands represent dynamism because many people believe that global brands are always upgrading themselves. By comparison, people perceived that local brands lack dynamism. Second, consumers see global brands as representing a global myth in which consumers can share a global identity with others on the planet. A self-transcendent aspect of this is an accompanying feeling that global brands make consumers feel part of something bigger than themselves or their national market. Global brands make consumers feel like citizens of the world.

Third, people expect global brands to act with social responsibility by addressing problems linked with what they sell and how they conduct business. In the past, there have been dark episodes for global brands, such as oil spills for petroleum giants Exxon and BP, and protests against Nike for not being vigilant in defending workers against abuse by Nike's contract manufacturers in developing countries. Increasingly, consumers will choose not to buy global brands that are perceived as not acting as stewards of the environment, worker rights, and public health. People have become convinced that global brands have a special duty to address social issues relevant to their operations. For example, people expect oil companies to address global warning, but they have much lower expectations for local firms to do so. Also, people across the world do not tend to become upset when local firms mistreat employees, but these same people will not accept global brands mistreating local workers. In effect, global brands are held to a higher standard likely because they are perceived to have extraordinary capabilities and power. An Australian reasoned this way: "McDonald's pays back locally, but it is their duty. They are making so much money, they should be giving back" (Holt, Quelch, & Taylor, 2004, p. 4, para. 2). To be credible, global brands' social responsibility efforts must demonstrate that the firms have directed their ample resources to benefit society.

## What Some CEOs Expect From Global Brands

### A Focus on Viacom

Bill Roedy's MTVNI is part of Viacom, Inc., an entertainment content company that provides programming for cable and satellite television, motion pictures, and digital products (New York Times, 2007). Its motion picture production and distribution division includes Paramount Pictures, Dream Works, MTV Films, and Nickelodeon Movies. When Equilar, a compensation benchmarking advisory company, released its 2011 report on CEO compensation, Philippe Dauman topped the list of 200 CEOs leading firms with annual revenues of $7 billion (Equilar, 2011). Dauman's compensation of $84.5 million actually only covered nine months because Viacom had changed its fiscal year from December to September within the last year.

As shown in Figure 9.1, four elements comprised Dauman's compensation: (a) base salary, (b) bonus, (c) stock, and (d) options. Dauman's 2010 compensation was 149% more than in 2009. The black dots on the bars on the right side of Figure 9.1 position the reported results among the set of 200 executives the report from Equilar covered. For example, Viacom's 30% return on investment was higher than about three fourths of those in the set of firms studied. According to Viacom's board, Dauman received the "significant one-time equity awards for several reasons including, Mr. Dauman's leadership and performance during his tenure (he's been CEO since 2006) at Viacom, and particularly during one of the most difficult economic environments in our history" (Krantz & Hansen, 2011). Dauman earned 11% more than Ray Irani of Occidental Petroleum, the CEO with the second most compensation in 2010. Irani retired in 2011, and his board has said it will be more difficult for the next CEO to receive such pay.

Figure 9.2 depicts Viacom's return on Viacom's stock during the term of Philippe Dauman as Viacom's CEO from September 5, 2006. The Walt Disney Company overtook Viacom's stock price in early 2008 and retained this advantage until spring 2011. Since this time, both firms have had comparable returns. Disney CEO Roger Iger earned $28 million in 2010.

### Did Viacom Make the Right Decision?

In sum, ambiguity surrounds the decision of the Viacom board to award the highest compensation of all CEOs in 2010. "The problem is, we're living in a world where .220 hitters make $10 million, so look at what you have to pay when you finally find a .300 hitter," said a leader of a Fortune 500 company with regard to overly generous pay packages for CEOs (Kirkland, 2006, p. 1, para. 5).

Some attribute the decision to factors such as Dauman signing a five-year employment contract with Viacom in 2010 and to the high-degree of ownership of Viacom (79% of

**Figure 9.1**  Equilar's Ranking of Top 5 in CEO Compensation for Firms with $7 Billion in Sales

| Company, Chief Executive | Compensation (In millions) ■ Salary ■ Bonus ■ Perks ■ Stock ■ Options | | Change in compensation '09 to '10 | 2010 company performance (Key) Revenue (mil.) | Profit chg. | Total return |
|---|---|---|---|---|---|---|
| **Viacom** Philippe P. Dauman | 2010 | 84.5 | +149% | N.A. | N.A. | +30% |
| | 2009 | 34.0 | | | | |
| **Occidental Petroleum** Ray R. Irani | 2010 | 76.1 | +142% | $19,157 | +45% | +22% |
| | 2009 | 31.4 | | | | |
| **Oracle** Lawrence J. Ellison | 2010 | 70.1 | −17% | $26,820 | +10% | +16% |
| | 2009 | 84.5 | | | | |
| **DirectTV** Michael D. White* | 2010 | 32.9 | NA | $24,102 | +133% | +20% |
| | 2009 | N.A. | | | | |
| **Stanley Black & Decker** John F. Lundgren | 2010 | 32.6 | +253% | $8,410 | −13% | +32% |
| | 2009 | 9.2 | | | | |

*Source:* Equilar (2011), http://www.equilar.com/ceo-compensation/2011/index.php

voting shares) held by Chairman Sumner Redstone. With such ownership of preferred voting stock, Redstone can run Viacom as he sees fit. (Redstone also is chairman at CBS and earned $35.3 million from each firm in 2010.) At the time of the award (September 2010), Viacom had underperformed its peer group of companies across five years and was only about even with the firms of the S&P 500. It seems the decision to award Dauman was based on forward-looking considerations, as opposed to backward-looking evaluations of Viacom's performance. In this way, Viacom's directors seem to have taken a long-term view on Dauman's development of Viacom. In an era of increased global interest by consumers in entertainment, Viacom's team anchored by MTVNI's Bill Roedy had accumulated many hard-won successes in establishing a formidable network of content and media companies spread across the globe. A question remains, though, about why Dauman's pay is triple that of Walt Disney Company CEO Roger Iger whose firm has posted similar results to Viacom since 2006.

## Star Effect and Other CEOs

Corporate governance experts also cite a "star effect" in media CEO compensation in which the chiefs do not want to make less than the talent they employ. For example, CBS pays "Judge Judy" Sheindlin more than $40 million per year (James, 2011, p. 1 para. 7). The 30 highest-paid media executives in the United States averaged nearly $22 million in 2010. This was more than twice the average of $10 million for CEOs leading Fortune 500 companies in the same year.

**Figure 9.2** Viacom's Stock Return During Tenure of CEO Philippe Dauman Compared with Time Warner, Inc., News Corporation, and the Walt Disney Company

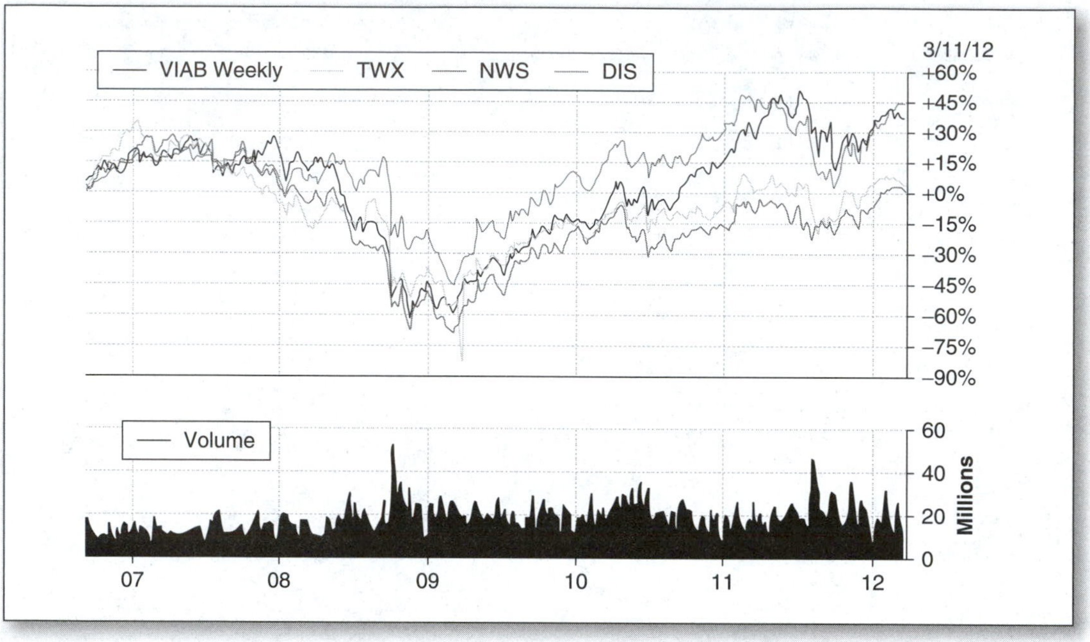

*Source:* http://www.bigcharts.com

A look at the bottom of the list of 200 CEOs tells another story about CEO pay. Here, these CEOs focus solely on improving the price of the stock they already own. The lowest paid CEOs in 2010 are a notable group including Apple, Inc.'s Steve Jobs, Whole Foods Market's John Mackey, and "the sage of Omaha" Warren Buffett. Vikram Pandit of Citigroup will receive $1.75 million in 2011 (PublicCitizen, 2011). These are depicted in Figure 9.3.

Since 1998, Apple's Steve Jobs received only $1 for his year's work that included no bonus or perks (Associated Press, 2011). Apple said it reimbursed Jobs $248,000 for company travel on his personal jet, a $90 million Gulfstream V he received as a bonus in 1999. Jobs, however, holds 5.5 million of Apple's shares. These shares gained about 60% in value during the 2010 fiscal year. In January 2011, Jobs's personal holdings of Apple shares totaled $1.84 billion in value. Notably, Jobs, 55, has not sold any shares since he rejoined the company in 1997 following a 12-year separation. He has not been awarded any new equity since 2003 and is currently its largest individual shareholder.

## Pay Inequity in Global Firms

The rising inequity in pay between CEOs and employees is cited by some as a flaw of the current form of globalization (Kirkland, 2006). In 1980, the average CEO made 42 times

**Figure 9.3**  Equilar's Ranking of Bottom 5 in CEO Compensation for Firms with $7 Billion in Sales

| Company, Chief Executive | Compensation (In millions) ■ Salary ■ Bonus ■ Perks ■ Stock ▨ Options | | Change in compensation '09 to '10 | 2010 company performance (Key) Revenue (mil.) | Profit chg. | Total return |
|---|---|---|---|---|---|---|
| **Citigroup** Vikram S. Pandit | 2010 | < 0.1 | −100% | $79,516 | −/+ | +43% |
| | 2009 | 0.1 | | | | |
| **Apple** Steven P. Jobs | 2010 | < 0.1 | 0% | $65,225 | +70% | +53% |
| | 2009 | < 0.1 | | | | |
| **Whole Foods Market** John P. Mackey | 2010 | < 0.1 | N.C | $9,006 | +102% | +22% |
| | 2009 | 0.7 | | | | |
| **Berkshire Hathaway** Warren E. Buffett | 2010 | 0.5 | +1% | $136,185 | +61% | +21% |
| | 2009 | 0.5 | | | | |

*Source:* Equilar (2011), http://www.equilar.com/ceo-compensation/2011/index.php

what the average worker made (AFL-CIO, 2011). In 2010, CEOs made on average 343 times the pay of the average worker. But between 1980 and 2003, average CEO pay at U.S. Fortune 500 companies rose by a factor of six—as did the average value of these firms adjusted for inflation (Reich, 2007, para. 11). By comparing CEO pay and the value of the firms they lead, it seems that investors are rewarding their CEOs in a way that corresponds to how firm value has grown. By comparison, real median household income in the United States increased from around $42,500 to $50,000 over the same period—an increase of 17.6%. In sum, the pay of CEOs at major corporations increased 34 times more than the median household income from 1980 to 2003.

In 2010, the median salary of CEOs rose markedly 27% from the previous year while overall worker pay increased by just 2.1% (Bloxham, 2011, p. 1). Viacom's Dauman made 2,546 times the median worker's pay in the United States of $33,190 (AFL-CIO, 2011). Put in another way, Dauman made 211 times more than U.S. President Barack Obama who earned $400,000 in 2010.

Others view unprecedented levels of CEO pay as to be expected. The competitive environment is intense with consumers ready to move to rival brands and investors primed to go to other investments when mediocrity takes hold at companies (Reich, 2007). Rival companies can use similar global supply chains and access low-cost suppliers from all over the world. Operations can be streamlined using the same software used at rival companies, while financing can be obtained from similar sources across the world as those of rivals. In this era of globalization, the CEO has become perceived by many as a more crucial factor in firm success than 40 years ago. "As the economy has shifted to supercapitalism, CEOs have become less like top bureaucrats and more like Hollywood celebrities who get a share of the house," former U.S. Labor Secretary in the Clinton administration Robert Reich said. "Today, Tom Hanks makes more than $20 million per film" (Reich, 2007, p. A13, para. 10). Given the choices consumers now have, movie studios willingly pay these sums for star power.

Today's big companies tend to pay their CEOs in a similar way for essentially the same reason as Hollywood studios. When CEOs used to be hired internally, the benchmarking was against the pay of all the executives below the CEO (Dillon, 2009). But with the trend to recruit outside "stars," the benchmarking became lateral.

In 1984, management guru Peter Drucker asserted that a CEO should not make more than 20 times what the average worker in the firm makes (Bloxham, 2011, p. 1, para. 3). Widening the pay gap much beyond that it makes it difficult to foster the kind of teamwork that most businesses require to succeed. This is especially true for midlevel management when CEO pay seems to have no bounds.

"The really important question is actually how do you motivate the guys below that top level," Fabrizio Ferri of the Harvard Business School said. "That's where you get into important issues around succession planning, sense of fairness, and balancing new ideas and taking global risks" (Dillon, 2009, p. 8, para. 2).

Allowing an enormous disparity in income to exist "corrodes" Drucker warned (Wartzman, 2008). "It destroys mutual trust between groups that have to live together and work together," Drucker said (Wartzman, 2008, p. 1, para. 8).

Notably, Drucker was not opposed to rewarding some extremely well. "There should, indeed there must, be exceptions," he wrote. "A 'star,' whether the super salesman in the insurance company or the scientist in the lab who comes up with a half-dozen highly profitable research breakthroughs, should be paid without any income limitation" (Wartzman, 2008, p. 1, para. 10).

But observers like Reich would counter Drucker's assertion by citing the super competitive environment of business in an era of globalization as making the 20:1 ratio proposed by Drucker as being suited for an era of much slower oligopolistic capitalism where bloated bureaucracies vied against each other. Today, Reich recommends a higher marginal tax-rate for those being paid like elite athletes or movie stars in the era of globalization.

CEO pay is now becoming a public policy issue. Under new rules included in the Dodd-Frank federal law, public companies must now give shareholders an advisory role in setting executive pay in what is termed "say on pay" (Costello, 2011). In March 2011, most shareholders voted against approving the generous executive pay packages for Hewlett-Packard senior executives. Carol Bowie, director of research at Institutional Shareholder services, believes executive compensation would probably keep going up and remain well above increases in the economy. However, CEO pay might be entering a new era of investor scrutiny. During the first year of the "say on pay" votes on executive compensation under the Dodd-Frank Act, investors have endorsed companies' pay programs in 91.2% of public firms (Allen, 2011).

For the firms receiving "no" votes to proposed executive compensation, pay-for-performance topped the list of concerns. Following this were concerns related to (a) paying taxes for CEOs (termed a "tax gross up"), (b) discretionary bonuses, (c) wrongful peer benchmarking, (d) excessive pay, and (e) failure to address significant opposition to compensation committee members in the past (Allen, 2011).

## A Global Firm With a Global Corporate Culture

United Kingdom–based Reckitt Benckiser (RB) gives a glimpse of what a highly global-ized company might look like (Reckitt Benckiser, 2011a). Focused on home, health, and personal care products, the firm has 41 manufacturing facilities around the world. Its 17 "Powerbrands" include the following brands that are tops in worldwide sales in their respective categories: (a) Vanish fabric treatment, (b) Calgon water softener, (c) Lysol multi-purpose cleaner, (d) Finish automatic dishwashing detergent, (e) Dettol antiseptic, and (f) French's mustard. RB's marketing investment is among the highest in the industry with RB's 2009 media investment accounting for 11.1% of net sales.

With a market capitalization of more than $38 billion, RB is one of the top 25 of the FTSE 100—the top 100 firms based in the United Kingdom as listed by *The Financial Times* and the London Stock Exchange. In 2010, its revenues were $13.86 billion (Reckitt Benckiser, 2011b, p. 30). The five-year comparison of the return on RB's share price with the return on the FTSE 100 from 2007 to 2012 is depicted in Figure 9.4 (Reckitt Benckiser, 2011c). As can be seen, RB has outperformed the FTSE over this term.

**Figure 9.4**   Five-Year Comparison of Reckitt Benckiser Stock Return with FTSE 100 (2007–2012)

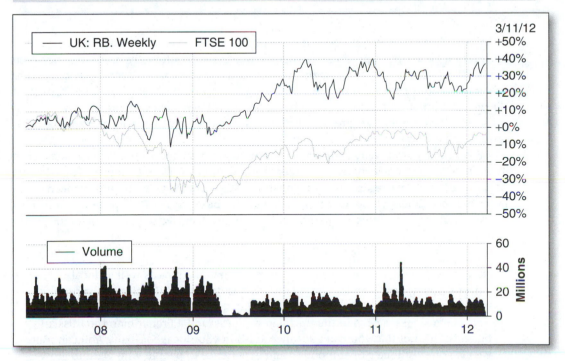

*Source:* http://www.bigcharts.com

With 29,400 employees worldwide, RB has a global workforce with 46% in Europe, 13.8% in North America and Australia, and 40.2% in the Developing World (Reckitt Benckiser, 2011b, p. 42). Fifty-three nationalities are represented in the top 400 leaders of RB (Becht, 2010). Most of these top managers regard themselves as being global citizens. Since 1999, RB has deliberately built a corporate culture based on global mobility because the leaders of the firm believe this is one of the best ways to generate new ideas and create global entrepreneurs. National diversity characterizes RB's senior team with two Dutch, two British, two Italian, one German, one South African, and one Indian. Such global diversity seems to work for RB. Since 2007, new products resulting from such cross-fertilization of managers account for 35% to 40% of RB's net revenues (Becht, 2010, p. 104, para. 2). From 1999 to 2010, net income at RB has grown 17% annually on average (Ibarra and Hansen, 2011, p. 72, para. 3).

Becht says:

> It doesn't matter whether I have a Pakistani, a Chinese person, a Brit, or a Turk, man or woman, sitting in the same room, or whether I have people from sales or something else, so long as I have people with different experiences – because the chance for new ideas is much greater when you have people with different backgrounds. The chance for conflict is also higher—and conflict is good per se, as long as it's constructive and gets us to the best idea. (Ibarra & Hansen, 2011, p. 72, para. 3)

In addition to national diversity, research on creative industries suggests that collaborations are most productive when firm leaders intentionally bring together both experienced people and newcomers, as well as those who have never worked together previously. More patents, financial returns, and critical praise tend to come from such diverse collaborative groups. Without being put together, people will choose to work with those who have similar backgrounds. Unfortunately, stasis and insularity characterize such groups and innovation usually declines.

RB resulted from a merger of British Reckitt & Colman and Dutch-listed Benckiser in 1999. Before the merger, many RB's units operated more or less independently of the rest of the world without regard to RB's global priorities. CEO Bart Becht and his leadership team began deliberately assigning managers who best carried RB's priorities into new markets. Subsequent to this, more moves of personnel occurred to become a multicountry company:

> Now in every country we have people of many nationalities as well as local citizens. Today, an Italian is running the UK business, and an American is running the German business. A Dutch-man is running the U.S. Business, an Indian the Chinese business, a Belgian the Brazilian business, and a Frenchman the Russian business. It's not that you can't advance at RB in your local company. You can. But we also offer unique global mobility and experience to people who want to grow their careers on a world stage. (Becht, 2010, p. 104)

To facilitate the culture of mobility, RB has streamlined its compensation for its top 400 managers across all of its markets. There is just one employment contract developed with global benchmarking. The annual cash bonus structure and long-term incentive plans are the same for everyone, as are the pension, medical, and other benefits. When employees take a job in another country, they are transferred as "local hires." With standard protocols, such as agreeing to pay for whatever school the employee chooses for his or her children, a transfer can happen to a new country in as little as two days.

The idea behind all of these elements is to encourage employees to focus primarily on the best job for them, regardless of the country. "Some people look at us and think they'd have to be nuts to work here. We're looking for people with a certain level of maturity, intensity, and competitiveness," Becht said. "I can tell in three minutes if someone would be a good fit for our company. We'd rather have a position open for a long time, if necessary, than put the wrong person in place. It's that important" (Becht, 2010, p. 106).

With so many languages in RB, the firm found it necessary to choose an official language of the firm—English. Admitting that the English is not always pretty, Becht said that expressing one's opinion is essential at RB:

You have to stand for something, no matter how bluntly you communicate it. That means our meetings are a bit chaotic. Everybody wants to be heard, so it's more like an Italian family dinner than a nicely organized board meeting. What takes over in our meeting is an intensity and a feeling that we have to fight for better ideas. Conflict is good. We don't care about consensus. Not having it doesn't slow us down and doesn't mean that people aren't aligned. We make decisions fast and then all stand behind them. What isn't tolerated is conflict that simply slows down decision making or is for political or personal gain. (Becht, 2010, p. 105)

## Building a Global Culture in a Global Firm

With the demands of competing in a globalizing world and with the outsourcing of functions formerly done by employees in the firm, the community aspect of firms has often weakened. Decades of short-term management—especially in the United States—along with the inflated importance of CEOs have reduced others in the corporation to commodities (Mintzberg, 2009, p. 140, para. 1). Not surprisingly, people's sense of community at the firm has eroded markedly.

Young successful companies usually have a sense of community in which workers have a sense of belonging to and caring for something larger than themselves. These companies are growing, energized, committed to their people, and look very much like a family. For example, Clif Bar's Gary Erickson (Chapter 5's Maverick Who Made It) went $60 million in debt to keep his connection to the work family he had helped create and to be part of a firm with "mojo" (Erickson & Lorentzen, 2004).

Part of the success of Reckitt Benckiser is the company's ability to engage its 29,400 employees. The culture of RB is dynamic, and almost every key decision is made in the meeting at which it is first discussed (Becht, 2010, p. 105, para. 4). "We expect people to come armed with facts, be prepared to argue their point of view, and be willing to live with the decision we ultimately make," Becht said. "Get 80 % alignment and 100 % agreement to implement. And move quickly" (Becht, 2010, p. 105).

Failure in such an environment is a huge incentive for the kind of people who fit well in the RB culture. Because of their competitiveness, they work faster for the next success. "Everyone wants to do something to get on the map," Becht said (Becht, 2010, p. 106, para. 6).

### Using Volunteerism and Philanthropy to Enhance a Corporate Culture

Despite the geographies covered by RB and the diversity of its people, the community aspect of RB can be seen in the way that this community extends itself to be engaged with constructive engagement with communities around it. For example, RB has emphasized the global aspect of the company's mission and culture through an annual "Global Challenge" (Reckitt Benckiser, 2011d). In June 2011, 65 employees from 34 countries teamed up in Brazil for the third global challenge. Half the group went on a rugged 71-km trek through the forested mesas and mountains of the Chapada Diamantina region of eastern Brazil, while the other half volunteered on a community project to renovate a children's nursery and play room used by young vulnerable kids in nearby Petrolina. The team raised $460,000 through sponsorships for Save the Children projects in Brazil, Angola, Tanzania, and India.

RB has chosen Save the Children as an ongoing beneficiary of RB employees' charitable endeavors. Like RB, Save the Children is based in the United Kingdom but has a global focus. Since 2003, RB and its employees have donated nearly $10 million to Save the Children in order to improve children's health, hygiene, and social development around the world.

In 2009, CEO Becht made headlines in the United Kingdom by exercising options for RB stock he had accumulated over his 15 years with RB. By exercising the options he held, Becht netted nearly $150 million and became the highest paid CEO in the United Kingdom nearly doubling the previous Financial Times/London Stock Exchange (FTSE) 100 pay record (Finch, 2010). Although critics howled about the astronomical payday for RB's CEO, Becht quietly transferred more than $180 million to a charitable trust he directs that supports organizations such as Save the Children (The Telegraph, 2011). In this way, praise for his giving eclipsed criticism of his high pay.

Becht's interest in philanthropy seems genuine. As the RB stock price has quadrupled over his 16-year term as CEO, he has earned more than $328 million since 2005 (Finch, 2010). But each year he would donate a "small fortune" to charities such as Save the Children and Médecins Sans Frontières (Daily Mail Reporter, 2010). By leading in philanthropy, employees at RB received encouragement for their own efforts to be engaged constructively with the communities around it.

# NAVIGATING GLOBALIZATION

## Globalist Views

Thomas L. Friedman is one of the most influential writers on the topic of globalization. Because his role as a syndicated columnist for *The New York Times* allowed him the scope of operation to travel the world and ponder the changes occurring in the ten years after the Berlin Wall fell in 1989, his book *The Lexus and the Olive Tree* explains the phenomenon of globalization in a holistic way (Friedman, 2000). Friedman saw globalization as the system that replaced the Cold War, and he believed the changes coming to the world would be led by the increased role of business in societies and would be generally positive. Because of this, some refer to his views as representing the most comprehensive, widely-read defense of neoliberal globalization (Ritzer, 2009, p. 119).

The title refers to the tension between striving for material gain (represented by the Lexus luxury automobile desired by many the world over) and holding onto cultural traditions that allow individuals to define themselves in a historical narrative (represented by the olive tree). Trade, technology, and finance bring consumers the Lexus, while geopolitics and ethnic and religious traditions nurture the olive tree. When out of balance, either the drive for prosperity or tribal ways have the power to eclipse or even harm the other. For example, the 9/11 attack on the World Trade Center is an example of a tribalistic backlash against the global commerce system. Alternatively, the current migration of millions of rural people to cities in China who are searching for jobs related to the global economy show how the drive for an improved standard of living can draw people away from places that used to define their cultural identities. Those in the city have access to global amenities, such as fashions, food, and entertainment, in addition to higher-waged jobs.

Friedman defined globalization as "inexorable integration of markets, nation-states and technologies to a degree never witnessed before" (Friedman, 2000, p. 9, para. 1). Such globalization enables individuals, corporations, and nation-states to extend their reach to places on the world "farther, faster, deeper and cheaper than ever before" (Friedman, 2000, p. 9, para. 1). According to Friedman, the driving idea behind globalization is free-market capitalism. With communication technology allowing instantaneous transmissions of data and voice signals and the elimination of the Cold War that justified protectionist legislation to restrict trade between countries, governments needed to reduce their interventionist ways in markets in order to allow globalization to provide the most benefits to consumers.

In *The World Is Flat: A Brief History of the Twenty-First Century*, Friedman updates his thinking about globalization by noting that while he was focused on the two-year aftermath of 9/11 to explain anti-American attitudes—particularly in the Middle East—developing countries such as India and China "caught up" in businesses processes (Friedman, 2006). Specifically, with computers and software now abundant in developing countries, skilled white-collar workers in such locales could now compete in the service economy of the globe. For example, an entrepreneurial businessman Jaithirth "Jerry" Rao that Friedman met in Bangalore, India, aggressively sought to win Friedman's approval to process Friedman's income taxes for a fee in the coming year. The business man had all of the appropriate forms needed and would fax, e-mail, or mail the completed tax documents to the United States from India. Although Friedman declined Rao's offer, it dawned on Friedman later that his own accounting firm might be outsourcing his own tax preparation to someone like Rao in India. Already hundreds of thousands of U.S. returns are outsourced to India and the number climbs every year (Friedman, 2006, p. 13). In examples similar to this, Friedman makes the argument for the global economic playing field being leveled.

"Flatteners" of the world according to Friedman include (a) the end of the Cold War; (b) the Internet-browser company Netscape's highly successful initial public offering (IPO) in 1995 that unleashed $1 trillion investment in fiber optic cable under the oceans in less than five years; (c) new forms of collaboration resulting from software integration;

(d) off-shoring of work to China and other developing countries; (e) large firms such as UPS taking over logistics for smaller firms; (f) setting up supply chains among suppliers, retailers, and customers to create value; and (g) Google for informing oneself about information and opportunities from all over the world.

Friedman delineates three great eras of globalization (Friedman, 2006, p. 9). Globalization 1.0 occurred from 1492 to 1820. Here, mercantilist countries and governments conducted globalization through their imperialistic conquests of the New World. The key agent of change was brawn or muscle and how cleverly it could be deployed. Globalization 2.0 occurred from 1800 to 2001. Here, multinational companies conducted globalization. The dynamic forces during this period of industrialization were breakthroughs in hardware, such as steamships and railroads and later telephones and mainframe computers. Globalization 3.0 now is unfolding. Here, individuals and small groups are globalizing themselves. They are collaborating and competing globally being connected through their personal computers that are connected through fiber-optic cable and work-flow software.

Friedman offers compelling descriptions about globalization and his predictions for increased competition at all levels—especially for individuals—are troubling to some. For example, he asserts that in a future globalized world, everything becomes commoditized—except imagination. Because the software tools and even education are now available to all around the world, what matters now is what one does with those tools and education.

In response to Friedman, some believe globalization has gone too far, while others believe it has not gone far enough. As one who sees that globalization could go further, Tufts University professor Amar Bhidé sees the venturesome culture in the United States as a reason more research and development for multinational enterprises can go off-shore (Bhidé, 2008). Conventional thinking among leaders of such firms remains that the creative part of developing new products must be kept in countries where intellectual property laws are rigorous and can be enforced, such as the United States or countries of Europe. Bhidé asserts that much of the current Apple iPhones and iPads were developed in Asia. In places like the United States, consumers willing to try the "latest and greatest" technology products are abundant relative to other locales on the planet. As a result, a system of taking ideas and inventions through the development process is stronger in the United States than anywhere else. In short, advances overseas in the research and development domain need not be feared by leaders of multinational enterprises, policy makers, or workers in the United States.

### Core-Gap Thesis

Like Friedman, former U.S. defense strategist Thomas P. Barnett believes that globalization has unstoppable momentum and that no one is in charge (Barnett, 2004). However, Barnett believes that globalization must be extended to all countries, but that it currently has far to go in this regard. Barnett believes that globalization is all about connectivity and will result in a peaceful "mutually-assured dependence." But globalization is weak in many parts of the world. Although China and India have connected to the globalization system, some regions of the developing world remain poorly integrated. Barnett proposes a Core-Gap Thesis in which countries in the gap that have had struggled to plug into globalization and join the functioning core of globalization (the developed countries plus the BRIC countries of Brazil, Russia, India, and China along with a few others). According to this thesis, problems in the Gap countries potentially can flare up and disrupt the ongoing process of economic integration that is dampening flames for violent confrontation. Again, the failed state of Afghanistan is an example of how a disconnected country can harbor extremists intent on disrupting globalization as seen in the terror attacks of 9/11. Figure 9.5 depicts the map of the world with Barnett's Core and Gap regions.

**Figure 9.5**   Barnett's Map of Globalization's Functioning Core and the Gap (inside the dotted line)

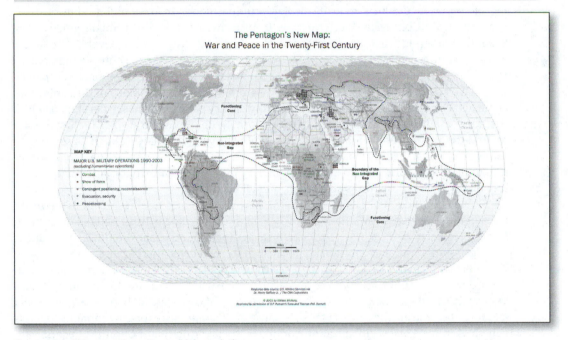

*Source:* http://thomaspmbarnett.com/high-resolution-map/

According to Barnett, political and social problems related to underdevelopment in Gap countries pose a threat not to countries in the Core but to the system of globalization. For this reason, the United States and other like-minded countries are in a long war against extremism in Gap countries through their military policing and political skills. Additionally, it is in the best interests of such leading countries in the Core to help Gap countries upgrade their capabilities to conduct business with the outside world. This means a focus on telecoms, banking, business, and investment exchanges, utilities, and border security. In fact, Barnett now works for an entrepreneurial venture Enterra Solutions that does that by offering to help in such market development. Enterra calls its approach "Development in a Box" (Barnett, 2009, p. 327).

## Antiglobalist Views

Counter to the pro-globalization view are those of antiglobalists. Kilbourne (2004) regards globalization as neoliberalism applied to the world. With such neoliberalism, the societal aspects of economic integration receive thin treatment while profit and efficiency become paramount. According to these critics, trade liberalization—the reduction or elimination of tariffs and other trade barriers—should not be the sole response of governments, but so too should promoting equity, employment, and a sensible pace for reforms related to trade (Stiglitz, 2007, p. 17).

Often, critics of globalization focus on injustices for those in the developing world resulting from global marketing of consumer products (Witkowski, 2005). First, the marketing of imported products tend to displace cultural goods in developing countries. For example, Coca-Cola leads West Africans to turn away from locally made ginger beer. Second, marketing places the protection of intellectual property for developed country inventions over the needs of local consumers. For example, pharmaceuticals may not be introduced in generic form in developing countries so that pharmaceutical companies from developed countries can seek out profits from the branded versions of these pharmaceuticals. Third, marketing promotes unhealthy dietary patterns from the developed world. Fast food and food containing high-fructose corn syrup are two examples fueling obesity around the world. Food with genetically modified organisms (GMOs), such as soy beans, remains under suspicion by some. Fourth, marketing promotes unsustainable consumption that is bad for the natural environment. As the world's platform for light manufacturing, China further despoils its soil, water, and air each year.

"Global markets undermine national sovereignty and create turmoil," Former International Society of Marketing and Development President Russ Belk said (Clifford, Rahtz, & Speece, 2003, p. 661). Protectionists in every country fear the flows of products, tourists, immigrants, and contraband because of the perceived threat these pose to society in its current form (Ritzer, 2009, p. 52). Government leaders opposing perceived oppression from developed countries, such as Cuba's Fidel Castro, North Korea's Kim Jung Il, and Venezuela's Hugo Chavez, roundly denounce globalization—especially because they see it as a force benefitting the United States. Because of the imperative for governments to intervene less in markets as globalization continues, social critic Noam Chomsky regards globalization as constraining democratic choice to trivial matters, such as what brands will be consumed. Finally, critics of globalization perceive that the "have" countries benefit more than the "have not" countries resulting in a wider gap both between and within countries (Stiglitz, 2007, p. 8).

Some who criticize globalization as a top-down phenomenon benefitting the developed world—particularly multinational enterprises—also see that an alter-globalization or bottom-up version of globalization could one day balance or outweigh the economic emphasis currently carried by globalization. In such a bottom-up globalization, grassroots networks in one country would connect with those in other countries. For example, students in California might financially support and protest on behalf of garment workers in Viet Nam, or religious groups in Europe would link to support Chinese artist and dissident Ai Weiwei. In short, globalization could bring greater solidarity for justice and more fully developed democracies around the world (Anderson, Cavanagh, & Lee, 2000, p. x).

## Semiglobalist Views

Strategy Professor Pankaj Ghemawat of Barcelona's IESE Business School takes issue with both globalists and antiglobalists for overreaching in making their claims about globalization (Ghemawat, 2011a). According to Ghemawat, the true state of the world today is semiglobalization. By "semi" he means partial as in 10% to 25%, rather than 50% (Ghemawat, 2011b, p. 23, para. 2). Although major multinational enterprises exhibit a high degree of internationalization, most other firms do not (Ghemawat, 2007). Ninety percent of all fixed investment that occurs is domestic (Ghemawat, 2011b, p. 29, para. 3). World Trade Organization director-general Pascal Lamy estimates that global exports account for only 20% of all the value produced in the world (GDP) (Ghemawat, 2011b, p. 28, para. 4).

Ghemawat says to ask oneself the following questions: (a) Why are major export deals involving private firms announced at meetings between heads of states? (b) Why do employees of foreign-owned companies often fear their career opportunities will be limited relative to their peers from the firm's home country? (c) Which governments do firms call to represent them at World Trade Organization disputes? (d) Why do foreign-ownership restrictions persist in industries such as media and airlines? (Ghemawat, 2011a).

Not only are firms and their business operations deeply rooted, but also according to Ghemawat, so are the people who staff these companies, invest in them, and buy their products. Ninety percent of the world's people will never travel abroad (Ghemawat, 2011a, p. 94, para. 8). Two percent of all telephone calls are international ones. In Europe, only 38% of news is international, while it is just 21% in the United States. Surprisingly, no more than 10% of charitable giving crosses national borders and foreign aid for most governments is only one thirty-thousandth of aid to domestic poor. In sum, as distances—geographic, cultural, political, and economic increase—cross-border interactions tend to decrease.

## Cosmopolitan Management

In a world requiring adaptation, the composition of the management team is the most critical ingredient. Most management teams are far from cosmopolitan—caring about and being aware of what is happening outside of the immediate region. For example, Ghemawat estimates that Americans comprise 80% of the top 200 managers at a global company, such as GE (Ghemawat, 2011a, p. 98, para. 4). For firm cosmopolitanism to take hold, a critical threshold of foreign-born managers need to be working in the company headquarters. Then, skillful leadership needs to be applied in order to allow this cultural diversity to be more of a benefit to the company rather than a detriment. "For many companies, the greatest challenge may be fostering the human capacity to connect and cooperate across distances and differences, internally and externally," Ghemawat said (2011b, p. 314, para. 3).

In light of such rootedness in corporate cultures, the examples of Bill Roedy's MTVNI and Bart Becht's Reckitt Benckiser discussed earlier in the chapter are more exceptional. When Bill Roedy took over MTV Europe, there was one American on the staff and he did not hire any more. He knew there were fears across Europe about the importation of American culture, and he wanted to build a European channel with European sensibilities

(Roedy, 2011, p. 44). Despite building one of the most international organizations in the world at MTVNI, Roedy only hired six Americans in his career there (despite being one himself). He now holds British and American dual citizenship.

Macromarketing researchers have considered whether firm capabilities and its home-country business ecosystem are the determining factor in firms' involvement in international marketing (Ellis & Pecotich, 2002). An alternative explanation proposed by these researchers was a cosmopolitan explanation for the firm's pursuit of a new market entry overseas. Given a capability and a motivation to go international, an awareness of foreign opportunities would then be the determining factor in pursuing international opportunities. Based on in-depth interviews with international and noninternational decision makers at small- to medium-sized firms based in Australia, researchers found support for the cosmopolitan explanation rather than for explanations based on other capabilities of the firm or its country business ecosystem.

Specifically, awareness of opportunities abroad proved to be the critical catalyst in the initiation process of market entry endeavors for the firms in the study. For example, an obstetrician who runs a medical products company, GoMedical, has links with a borderless community of fellow doctors and gives presentations at international conferences. Such appearances have reinforced his relationships with European doctors. Consequently, these apparently "weak ties" have provided entry points into markets such as Italy, Sweden, and Switzerland. In this regard, the "strong ties" this medical doctor has in his home country did not contribute to awareness of opportunities in markets of Europe. Although importantly, Australia provided a base for developing GoMedical as a business that could export medical products.

In light of these findings, the wisdom of MTVNI's Roedy to travel so frequently and incessantly over his career in building media networks makes much sense. He developed his own cosmopolitanism and therefore became aware of opportunities in a timely way in foreign locales. In this way, Roedy proved to be the connector for his firm in a world marked by distance and difference. MTVNI could not outsource this aspect of the firm to any other entity in a globalized world. The human dimensions of talent and commitment proved to be crucial for developing MTVNI's global network.

## The Wars of Globalization

Globalization entails not just economic flows across national borders, but also flows of every other kind, such as ideas, knowledge, technology, communications, workers, tourists, immigrants, culture, terrorism, pollution, waste, and pandemics, such as HIV/AIDS. In short, there is good, as well as bad coming across national borders. Societies today find themselves afflicted with illegal trafficking in (a) drugs, (b) arms, (c) intellectual property, (d) people, and (e) money to be laundered (Naím, 2003), as well as (f) terrorism and (g) corruption. To stand against these seven puts societies in seven wars related to globalization.

### Transparency International

Gains made in the war against corruption by an NGO called Transparency International may prove instructive for societies in their wars related to undesirable globalized flows.

The imperative for national governments to cooperate with each other and for transnational organizations to coordinate the efforts of national governments has never been greater.

Corruption is the abuse of entrusted power for private gain (Transparency International, 2011). At a minimum, it includes (a) bribery of public officials, (b) embezzlement, (c) trading in influence, (d) abuse of function and illicit enrichment by public officials, and (e) bribery of private sector employees. Bribery distorts market exchanges in favor of those who provide less value and hurts all whose life, livelihood or happiness depends on the integrity of those in authority.

When Peter Eigen from Germany served as the director of the World Bank's office for East Africa in Nairobi, Kenya, he noticed that systematic corruption in Kenya undermined everything his organization tried to do in helping with large infrastructure projects done for the purpose of developing needy countries (Eigen, 2009). When he began work on stopping such corruption, he received a notice from the legal department of the World Bank. He was told he was meddling in the affairs of partner countries, and this was forbidden in the charter of the World Bank.

Things worsened for Eigen as he chaired donor meetings where large corporations from the developed world would review projects proposed for development in Kenya. According to Eigen, the worst projects put forward were the ones realized first (Eigen, 2009). For example, a huge power project costing $300 million in West Kenya—in a beautiful area— would have no clients to buy the electricity, but it would be funded by an unholy alliance between powerful elites in the developing countries and suppliers from the North from such countries as France, United Kingdom, Canada, Japan, and Germany who were bribing these public officials. Eigen and his team knew such a project would destroy the environment as well as the land and streams for a surviving nomadic group of people in the proposed area. But it was not a useless project. It was going to be an absolutely damaging project for the future of Kenya. It would put a heavy debt on the society of Kenya and would siphon the scarce resources of the society away from much needed schools and hospitals. Transparency International (TI) veterans have concluded that the poor in countries are the ones hurt the most by corruption:

It was systematically driven by systematic, large-scale corruption with $10 million or $20 million going to Swiss bank accounts or accounts in Lichtenstein for the president and ministers of these countries. I saw not only one project like this during my years in Africa, but hundreds of projects like this. And so I became convinced that it is this systematic corruption that is perverting the economic policy-making in these countries. It is *the* main reason for the misery, for the poverty, for the violence, for the conflicts and for the desperation in these countries. It is why we have more than one billion people below the absolute poverty line. It is why we have more than one billion people without proper drinking water in the world. More than two billion without proper sanitation and the consequent illnesses this brings with 10 million children dying each year before the age of five. The cause of this to a great extent is grand corruption. (Eigen, 2009, 5 min, 30 s)

## The Early Years of Transparency International

Although stopped by the World Bank from opposing corruption, Eigen departed the World Bank in 1993 and founded TI an NGO dedicated to play a leading role in the anticorruption movement. At the time, only the United States had any strong legislation forbidding employees of U.S. companies from engaging in bribery overseas. The members of the World Bank thought foreign bribery was OK and just an aspect of the culture of business in foreign countries. In Germany, bribery was allowed and was even tax deductible.

Over the course of two years, TI convened representatives from major companies and another NGO, the Aspen Institute and asked them "what should be done about bribery?" (Eigen, 2009). Initially, the response was "it is what other cultures demand." Later, it became "if we stop it, companies from other countries will gain the business we now have." But Eigen and his TI team knew that deep down, these major companies detested bribery because it precluded such companies from selling their products made with quality at a low enough price that would benefit foreign societies. TI offered these major corporations an escape route from their dilemma of losing business. TI introduced concepts of collective action. Here, the competitors would go home and petition their respective governments to attend a convention held under the auspices of the Organisation of Economic Co-operation and Development (34 developed countries) in 1997 and sign a protocol obliging them to criminalize foreign bribery. The competitors did this, and the governments signed the protocol.

TI's actions in standing against corruption provides a valuable model for a three-way partnership among private firms, national governments, and NGOs. Surprising to some, the national governments at that time felt powerless to tell businesses how to conduct their operations outside of their home countries. TI and the Aspen Institute brought together competitors from a wide set of European countries and Japan for collective action. Then, the businesses returned to their home countries urging them to join with other countries to make foreign corruption illegal across these countries.

## The Work of Transparency International

Today, TI is a global network including more than 90 locally established national chapters. Other chapters continue to form and join this network. These chapters fight domestic corruption in several ways. They convene relevant players from government, civil society, business, and the media to promote transparency across society. For example, they seek increased transparency in elections, in public administration, in procurement, and in business. TI's global network of chapters and contacts also use advocacy campaigns to lobby governments to implement anticorruption reforms.

TI publishes an annual rating of perceptions for the amount and frequency of public sector corruption in countries of the world called the Corruption Perceptions Index (CPI) (Transparency International, 2012a). The CPI is based on surveys and assessments relating to the bribery of public officials, kickbacks in public procurement, embezzlement of public funds, as well as to the strength and effectiveness of public sector anti-corruption efforts. The results for the CPI in 2010 are depicted in Figure 9.6. As can be seen, Denmark, New Zealand, Singapore, Finland, and Sweden have the lowest perceptions for public sector corruption, while Somalia, Myanmar, Afghanistan, Iraq, and Uzbekistan have the worst. TI notes that three quarters of the world's countries have a problem with public sector corruption.

TI also periodically produces a Bribe Payers Index (BPI) (Transparency International, 2012b). Here, senior executives around the world were asked about the likelihood of foreign firms from countries they have business dealings with to engage in bribery when

**Figure 9.6**   Transparency International's 2010 Corruption Perceptions Index

*Source:* Transparency International, http://www.transparency.org/policy_research/surveys_indices/cpi/2010/results

doing business in the respondent's country. In short, the BPI assesses the supply of bribe money for 22 countries. In the 2008 report, Russia and China had the worst perceptions for paying bribes. They were followed by Mexico and India, respectively.

By doing the needed research on a murky topic, such as corruption, TI shines a light on the darker realms associated with globalization. TI's research and its widespread dissemination through its website (www.transparency.org) is another important ingredient in fueling the anticorruption movement. TI's approach based on establishing an extensive network of national chapters, imparting collective action concepts to businesses, working with governments, transnational organizations, and businesses could prove valuable in the other wars related to the other wars of globalization.

Although these wars have been going on for centuries (Naím, 2005), governments today find themselves unable to budget more for these wars. By comparison, globalization seems to have given more flexibility to drug traffickers, arms dealers, alien smugglers, counterfeiters, money launderers, as well as international terrorists. Without multisector-approaches to counter such traffickers, these wars seem to be tilted in favor of the bad guys and their networks (based on market forces of supply and demand) against an array of weakly connected bureaucracies around the world.

## CONCLUSION

This chapter offered a review of issues confronting companies and societies in this time of increased globalization. To put globalization in perspective, Ghemawat's four versions of the world from history will be used (Ghemawat, 2011b, p. 3). In the Wild World of World 0.0, no nations existed in the prehistoric times and only local borders mattered. In the Walled World of World 1.0 that emerged in the Age of Enlightenment (about 1700), the nation became the primary method of societal organization and national borders mattered most. In the One World of World 2.0 that emerged in the late 20th century, global markets and complete global integration seemed to be sweeping the planet. Finally, in the Workable World of World 3.0 that has emerged in the 21st century, markets can be seen to have a semiglobal character with partial global integration.

Using Ghemawat's framework for globalization, Bill Roedy's story can see beginning from World 1.0 where the nation and its borders mattered most. With Roedy's move to MTV Europe and his accompanying approach to establish a network with different programming in each country, Roedy leapt into World 3.0 where MTVNI acknowledged distance and difference across the world's countries in its programming. By comparison, Bart Becht's story at Reckitt Benckiser began in World 1.0 when nationally based companies from the United Kingdom and Holland merged. In the subsequent years, Reckitt Benckiser rapidly moved into World 2.0 as it developed a global company with a uniquely global culture in which the nationality of its managers received less and less emphasis.

Consumers around the world will inevitably decide which World version will predominate the 21st century. Research suggests that consumers see global brands (a) as signaling quality, (b) as bringing a myth to consumers of joining a global community defined by consuming common brands, and (c) as being obligated to be socially responsible to the locales where they do business. The social responsibility of multinational enterprises comes under more intense scrutiny when CEOs take enormous pay from their boards of directors representing the shareholders of these firms. With advisory "say on pay" votes on senior executive compensation now being conducted, attention to CEO pay in the era of increased globalization will continue.

Globalization involves the flows of the material and immaterial across national borders. Three views of globalization included those of (a) globalists carrying neoliberal ideas of restricted governmental action in markets, (b) antiglobalists who oppose neoliberalism and seek more direct government intervention primarily to preclude any lapses in protection of vulnerable populations and the environment, and (c) semiglobalists who see how much distance and differences across societies keep much of business focused on local concerns, but who nevertheless see regulation of markets as a important until societies figure out more of the dynamics of closer integration across national borders.

Finally, globalization also means that societies must now wage wars against what criminals increasingly send across national borders, such as drugs, arms, intellectual property, people, and money. Corruption in the form of bribery of foreign officials also crosses borders. Peter Eigen's founding of the Transparency International NGO and its contributions to the anticorruption movement highlight how a transnational approach to societal problems worsened by increased globalization, such as corruption, can be effectively addressed by a combination of NGOs, businesses, and national governments.

## QUESTIONS

- Based on what you learned about Bill Roedy, what made business rock for MTVNI during his time there?
- What are your thoughts about CEOs being paid like elite athletes or Hollywood stars?
- How do you see the stories of CEOs making $1 per year like Apple, Inc.'s Steve Jobs or Berkshire Hathaway's Warren Buffet say about CEO pay influencing society's tolerance of movie-star pay for CEOs in the future?
- What would appeal to you about joining Reckitt Benckiser as a manager? What would scare you a bit?
- In your view, how far has globalization gone—too far, not far enough, or just right? What will the next 20 years bring in terms of global integration of technology, commerce, finance, culture, people, and contraband?
- Does it surprise you that the United States was about 25 years ahead of the other developed countries in criminalizing foreign bribery? Why or why not?

## MAVERICKS WHO MADE IT

### Not Business as Usual

### Blake Mycoskie

### TOMS Shoes helps children in need, two shoes at a time

### By Will Fifield (2010)

**I**F YOU EVER TRY to visit TOMS Shoes headquarters, in Santa Monica, you might have trouble finding the 6,000-square-foot building, because, like the shoes the company sells, it's unusual. Tucked in between several other businesses, TOMS is more like a staging area than a corporate office. It has no

*(Continued)*

(Continued)

air conditioning and features a bare concrete floor, plain plywood cube walls and stacked cardboard boxes—yet the place emanates enthusiasm.

Blake Mycoskie, 34, founder of TOMS Shoes, calls himself the company's chief shoe giver because his company is a social enterprise—"Giving is TOMS' religion," Mycoskie explains. The company exists to supply children in need, all over the world, through what TOMS calls its "One for One" movement: For every pair of shoes TOMS sells, the company gives a pair away to a needy child.

Mycoskie, a Costco member in Marina del Rey, California, has started a string of successful businesses from scratch, beginning with EZ Laundry, a door-to-door laundry service, while he was a 19-year-old student at Southern Methodist University in Dallas. He's also established an advertising agency, a reality television network and a very successful online driver's education school for teens.

Mycoskie, who grew up the son of a doctor in Arlington, Texas, founded TOMS Shoes in 2006 after a visit to Argentina, where he saw scores of barefoot children with sores on their feet. Launching TOMS, whose name evolved from the company's original slogan, "Shoes for tomorrow," was his response to the glaring social need he observed. He says his trip to Argentina was the catalyst for him to combine his natural entrepreneurial bent with a strong desire to make the world a better place.

During its first year, supported by sales from the company website and retail stores that carry TOMS Shoes, the company gave 10,000 pairs of shoes to children in Argentina. As of September 2010 TOMS has given 1 million pairs of new shoes to children in 25 countries. (TOMS Shoes are not currently available at Costco because the company's production capabilities can't yet meet the demand Costco would likely require.)

In 2007, TOMS Shoes received the People's Design Award from the Cooper-Hewitt, National Design Museum, Smithsonian Institution. Two years later, Secretary of State Hillary Clinton presented Mycoskie and TOMS with the 2009 Award for Corporate Excellence, which recognizes companies' commitment to corporate social responsibility, innovation, exemplary practices and democratic values worldwide.

When I visit TOMS' headquarters in July, Mycoskie is sequestered somewhere in the earthy construct frantically dealing with a communications breakdown with partners in Ethiopia. When he emerges, he explains that podoconiosis—a debilitating ailment that causes extreme swelling, ulcers and deformity, especially in the legs—is prevalent there. It's caused by walking barefoot in silica-heavy volcanic soil, a common practice in rural farming regions of developing countries. However, the disease is preventable, and even reversible, by wearing shoes and practicing simple foot hygiene. That's why he's a little late for our interview: He's spent all morning trying to clarify TOMS' role in fighting this disease.

Mycoskie ushers me into a large room with a giant, dark wooden table that looks as if it were once a castle door, where we discuss the genesis of his company, its "One for One" business model and his thoughts on combining entrepreneurship and philanthropy.

**The Costco Connection:** *Your home office is different from most corporate headquarters.*

**Blake Mycoskie:** We try to use a lot of reclaimed and repurposed materials. Any time we can recycle and reuse, we try to, and that's why our [office] environment looks very organic and homemade.

*CC: During your time in Argentina, when you saw impoverished children with no shoes, was there a moment that was the impetus that became TOMS Shoes?*

**BM:** I met these volunteer workers helping children get shoes by going around getting donations. It was very obvious to me that these children needed shoes to go to school and to protect their feet, but I wanted to make sure the kids were going to get another pair of shoes when those shoes wore out, when they grew out of them.

I couldn't really get a good grasp on how that was going to happen. I don't know philanthropy. I don't have that background. But I know how to start a business because I'm an entrepreneur. I've started businesses since I was young. And so, I thought, if I can start a business that can sustain the giving, then I can feel comfortable that these kids will get the shoes that they need, over and over again.

## TO ARGENTINA (AND EVERYWHERE ELSE) WITH LOVE

TOMS' original line of shoes, now called Classics, is modeled after the *alpargata*, a rope-soled slipper that is common in the area of Argentina company founder Blake Mycoskie visited when he conceived the notion of TOMS Shoes. The product line has expanded since then to include Cordones, light-weight shoes that can be worn with or without laces; Botas, TOMS' version of high-tops; Stitchouts, a slip-on with stitching around the top of the sole; Wedges and Wrap Boots for women; and Youth and Tiny TOMS for children. The company offers many vegan-friendly material options in many styles that use no animal byproducts. The company also sells T-shirts, hats and other clothing items that are also matched with a pair of new shoes given to a child in need, one for one.—*WF*

That really was the aha moment for me. Most people look at problems in the Third World and one word comes to mind: charity. But for me the word "entrepreneurship" came to mind. And that's why I started TOMS as a for-profit business with our one-for-one model. I knew if we could get people to buy our shoes, and continue to buy our shoes, that I could sustain the giving and that would solve the issue that I saw there.

My advice to budding entrepreneurs is, don't try to be an entrepreneur, try to identify the problems in the world that you want to solve.

Blake Mycoskie

*(Continued)*

(Continued)

*CC: How did you get your "One for One" message across to customers in the beginning?*

BM: Just look at the box. Inside the shoe it says that with every pair of shoes you purchase you also give a new pair of shoes to a child in need, one for one. There's a picture of me giving shoes away on the box. It's all over our website. We just kept driving the message home: You're not just buying shoes; you're also helping another person get a pair of shoes, one for one.

I started TOMS as a spontaneous response to help kids. It wasn't like I had a shoe company and then decided to help kids. If that had been the case, our pricing would probably be very different. I said, "How much money do I need to charge so that I can give a pair of shoes away and have an office, hire people and grow this movement." And that's where I came up with the price. It's really that simple. Yes, they are more expensive because I want to give shoes away, but that was the whole model. If people can't buy into that idea, then they shouldn't buy our shoes in the first place.

*CC: What were some of the major obstacles when you were trying to launch TOMS Shoes?*

BM: Definitely production. And it continues to be a challenge. Because I didn't have any experience in shoes. Anyone who reads this article, I hope they get inspired by the fact that you don't need experience. Sometimes not having experience is the greatest thing in the world. If you have experience, you've already heard that you can't do it this way, and you can't do it that way, but with no experience you just do it your way.

For instance, with this shoe [Mycoskie reaches behind him and takes a shoe off a ledge on the wall behind him], anyone who is a real shoemaker would say this [he points to a seam in the front of the shoe] is a bad thing. You don't ever want to have a fold in the making of a shoe. But for us, this is the cheapest way and the only way we knew how to do it. Now it's become a huge part of our design.

People look at this and say, "Oh, that's a TOMS shoe," even if they just see this part. But that never would have happened if I were in the shoe business, because in the shoe business they say, "That's not good."

So the thing is, production has been a problem, it's been challenging, but having thrown myself and invested myself in it, I've learned a lot, and learned quickly, and we're continually improved our production and supply-chain management.

*CC: This kind of shoe,* alpargatas, *is based on the type of shoes you saw people wearing in Argentina when you conceived TOMS Shoes. Is it fair to say that was an unusual design in the shoe market?*

BM: Definitely in the U.S. and Europe, but farmers in Argentina have been wearing their version of this shoe for a very long time. So, I just took an existing shoe that they've been wearing and I created a better version of it. I put a rubber sole on it. I put arch support in the inside. I used softer materials. I only took something that existed and made it better, and I think that, from a design standpoint, is something for entrepreneurs to think about as well.

## A PASSION THAT INSPIRES

SHOES ARE ALMOST a side note of the TOMS Shoes business model. Company founder Blake Mycoskie says TOMS has inspired many other companies—some well established. some start-ups—to adopt their "One for One" business model, or a variation of it, into their operations. Twins for Peace (*www.twinsforpeace.com*), another shoe company, has adopted TOMS' "One for One" policy with its shoes. Booda Brand (*www.boodabrand.com*), a children's clothing company, donates one book to a child in need with every purchase through the organization Room to Read (*www.roomtoread.org*). Eyewear company Warby Parker (*www.warbyparker.com*) partners with renowned non-profits, such as RestoringVision.org, to deliver one pair of glasses to someone in need for every pair that it sells.

Mycoskie hopes this is just the beginning of a new way of doing business.

"As an entrepreneur, I always wanted to incorporate giving somehow in my business, but never could find the right way to do so," he explains. "TOMS allows me to mix my two passions, business and philanthropy, and prove that they are no longer mutually exclusive, I only hope to inspire others to do the same: find their passion and pursue it."

On April 8, 2008, TOMS launched its "One Day Without Shoes" event, an annual campaign during which TOMS asks people to go without shoes for one day in April to raise awareness of children growing up barefoot and the impact a pair of shoes can have on a child's life. The event gains momentum each year.

This year, actress Demi Moore appeared on *The Tonight Show* and explained what the event is about and took off her shoes to show support. Later in the show, Congressman Barney Frank walked onstage without his shoes to lend his support as well.

This year 250,000 people participated in the event. "It would be great if all the people reading this logged on to *www.onedaywithoutshoes.com* and registered for next year." Mycoskie says. "It will be held April 5, 2011. It's really encouraging to . . . that many people do the same thing on the same day."

---

Costco is a great example of that. I mean, they're not the first company to sell stuff in bulk, but they've taken something that existed and made it more efficient and added value to it. That's exactly what I've done. I took a shoe that's been around for a hundred years and I just built value into it.

*CC: Did you feel like it was a risk when you first put these shoes before the public, because they're so different?*

*(Continued)*

(Continued)

**BM:** Yeah, it was a risk, and it was also our greatest opportunity. Sometimes the biggest risk is the biggest opportunity, and that's a great lesson as well. No one [in the U.S.] was wearing a shoe like this when we started. There was a risk that no one wanted to wear a shoe like this [he laughs]. When people wear TOMS now they say, "Gosh, these are the most comfortable shoes in the world. They don't even feel like I'm wearing a shoe, they're so light." That, to me, was the opportunity. Now we have a style of shoe that we can own ourselves, that no one else has ever really done in the First World, because we took that risk.

*CC: What are some of the biggest obstacles TOMS faces right now?*

**BM:** Continuing to find really great giving partners. That's what I'm dealing with right now in Ethiopia. In order for us to help as many people in the most sustainable way we can, we've got to have great people on the ground. We partner with amazing organizations, nonprofits and NGOs [nongovernmental organizations] from around the world, and we've got to continue to find great partners.

If anyone reading this article is in the business of giving or is involved in an organization that provides aid, anywhere in the world, and you think you can also help the people whose lives they're working to improve by providing them with shoes, give us a call.

*CC: TOMS is dearly humanitarian. Did you also have a commitment to the environment?*

**BM:** Yes. Absolutely. It's something that's getting stronger and stronger every day, because it's becoming more and more of a personal passion for me. As a business owner and a CEO, I feel a responsibility to make sure we're being the best stewards of our environment that we can. So, besides adopting basic office principles, like not printing out e-mail and using the right kind of light bulbs, encouraging our employees to walk or ride bikes to work or to carpool, we're developing shoes made of post-recycled plastic bottles and hemp. A lot of our shoes are made of much more sustainable materials than when we first started.

*CC: What advice do you have for young people who are attracted to what you're doing through TOMS?*

**BM:** I don't think you can truly go out and start successful businesses and discover groundbreaking ideas by trying to do so. I think groundbreaking ideas and services and companies get started when someone sees something—that there's a problem, that something doesn't work, that there's a need in their life that's not being fulfilled.

My advice to budding entrepreneurs is, don't try to be an entrepreneur, try to identify the problems in the world that you want to solve. That, often, will lead to a great business idea. If you just go out and try to make money by starting a business, you're going to come up with something that's just like what everyone else has done. But if you look at the world and see opportunities that can be taken more seriously, then you come up with a great idea.

## MEMBER PROFILE

**Company name**: TOMS Shoes

**Founder:** Blake Mycoskie

**Products:** Shoes

**Address:** 3025 Olympic Blvd., Santa Monica, CA 90404

**Telephone:** (310) 566–3170

**Website:** www.toms.com

**E-mail:** info@tomsshoes.com

**Member at:** Marina del Ray, California

**Comments about Costco:** "We shop at Costco a lot as a company because we have 80-plus employees now. We try to do things like Fun Friday, where we offer snacks, and we celebrate company birthdays with parties and things like that. Personally, I love wine. So I buy a lot of wine at Costco."

—*Blake Mycoskie*

*CC: A lot of people say TOMS is changing the way people think about business. How has TOMS changed you?*

**BM:** The greatest thing that has happened in my life since starting TOMS is that I've learned that you need very little to be happy. And I've learned that from the people that I've given shoes to. I'd say they've given more to me than I have to them. When I started TOMS I had a lot of stuff. I had a big loft with art and furniture and all this, and I live on a boat right now. One of the choices I made three years ago, in doing that, was I wanted to simplify my life and get rid of all the stuff. The more time I spend working in the field, giving and running this company, the less I need and the happier I am. TOMS has taught me to cherish experiences and enjoy the simplicity of life, and has brought me so much more happiness. When you give someone something like a pair of shoes, you're saying. "You matter." That message is as important as the shoes.

*Source: The Costco Connection* (September, 2010).

*(Continued)*

(Continued)

## Questions

- How would Blake Mycoskie's venture have developed differently if he had put off philanthropy until he retired from the business?
- To what degree would you say TOMS Shoes is a charity?
- Blake Mycoskie majored in business at SMU's Cox School of Business in Dallas, TX. How do you think his involvement in meeting the needs of poor children around the world would have been different if he had majored in social work, instead of business? (He launched his first venture EZ Laundry in the fall of 1997 as a student. It grew quickly thanks to a marketing campaign in which sorority members wore company-branded t-shirts and actively recruited other student clients in exchange for free dry cleaning. The company soon expanded across seven universities and Mycoskie found himself managing 40 employees and eight trucks before he sold the business for a profit (SMU, 2011)).
- If you could ask Blake one question, what would it be?

## REFERENCES

AFL-CIO. (2011). Executive paywatch. Retrieved from http://www.aflcio.org/corporatewatch/paywatch/ceou/database.cfm?tkr = VIA.B&pg = 6

Allen, T. (2011, June 28). US proxy season review: 'Say on Pay' votes. *ISS Specialty Research*. Retrieved from http://blog.riskmetrics.com

Anderson, S., Cavanagh, J., & Lee, T. (2000). *Field guide to the global economy*. New York, NY: The New Press.

Andrews, A. (2011, January 29). MTV president Bill Roedy has taken his music channel from the Berlin Wall to SpongeBob SquarePants. *The Telegraph*. Retrieved from http://www.telegraph.co.uk

Associated Press. (2011, January 7). Apple CEO Steve Jobs' 2010 salary remains $1. *Fox News*. Retrieved from http://www.foxnews.com/scitech/2011/01/07/apple-ceo-steve-jobs-compensation-remains/

Barnett, T. P. M. (2004). *The Pentagon's new map: War and peace in the twenty-first century*. New York, NY: G. P. Putnam's Sons.

Barnett, T. P. M. (2009). *Great powers: America and the world after Bush*. New York, NY: G. P. Putnam's Sons.

Bhidé, A. (2008). *The venturesome economy: How innovation sustains prosperity in a more connected world*. Princeton, NJ: Princeton University Press.

Becht, B. (2010, April). Building a company without borders. *Harvard Business Review*, 88(4), 103–106.

Bloxham, E. (2011, April 13). How can we address excessive CEO pay? *Fortune Management*. Retrieved from http://management.fortune.cnn.com

Clifford J. S. II, Rahtz, D. R., & Speece, M. (Eds.). (2003). The proceedings of the 8th international conference on marketing and development. In Belk, R. (Ed.), *What's wrong with globalism and what's to be done about it? In Globalization, transformation, and quality of life*. Rijeka, Croatia: Faculty of Economics, University of Rijeka, pp. 661–670.

Costello, D. (2011, April 9). The drought is over (at least for C.E.O.'s). *The New York Times*. Retrieved from www.nytimes.com

Daily Mail Reporter. (2010, March 2). £17m charity gift from Reckitt boss. *This Is Money*. Retrieved from http://www.thisismoney.co.uk

Dillon, K. (2009, September). The coming battle over executive pay. *Harvard Business Review*, 87(9), 1–8.

Eigen, P. (2009, November). Peter Eigen: How to expose the corrupt. *TED*. Retrieved from http://www.ted.com/talks/peter_eigen_how_to_expose_the_corrupt.html

Ellis, P., & Pecotich, A. (2002, June). Macromarketing and international trade: Comparative advantage versus cosmopolitan considerations. *Journal of Macromarketing*, 22(1), 32–56.

Equilar. (2011). Top 200 US CEOs. Retrieved from http://www.equilar.com/ceocompensation/2011/index.php

Erickson, G., & Lorentzen, L. (2004). *Raising the bar: Integrity and passion in life and business*. San Francisco, CA: Jossey-Bass.

Fifield, W. (2010). Sole man: TOMS Shoes tries on a different model. *The Costco Connection, 25*(9), 24–25.

Finch, J. (2010, April 7). Bart Becht's £90m pay packet. I need a lie-down. *The Guardian*. Retrieved from http://www.guardian.co.uk/business/2010/apr/07/viewpoint-bart-becht

Friedman, T. L. (2000). *The Lexus and the olive tree: Understanding globalization*. New York, NY: Anchor Books.

Friedman, T. L. (2006). *The world is flat: A brief history of the twenty-first century, release 2.0*. New York, NY: Farrar, Straus and Giroux.

Ghemawat, P. (2007, March). Managing differences. *Harvard Business Review. 85*(3), 58–68.

Ghemawat, P. (2011a, May). The cosmopolitan corporation. *Harvard Business Review*, pp. 92–99.

Ghemawat, P. (2011b). *World 3.0: Global Prosperity and How to Achieve It*. Boston, MA: Harvard Business Press.

Holt, D. B., Quelch, J. A., & Taylor, E. L. (2004, September). How global brands compete. *Harvard Business Review, 82*(9), 1–8.

Ibarra, H., & Hansen, M. T. (2011, July–August). Are you a collaborative leader? *Harvard Business Review, 89*(7/8), 69–74.

Jacobs, E. (2011, June 5). Rock, hard work and hard places. *Financial Times*. Retrieved from http://www.ft.com

James, M. (2011, May 29). Viacom execs at top in media pay. *Los Angeles Times*. Retrieved from http://articles.latimes.com

Kilbourne, W. E. (2004, December). Globalization and development: An expanded macromarketing view. *Journal of Macromarketing*, 24(2),122–135.

Kirkland, R. (2006, June 30). The real CEO pay problem. *Fortune*. Retrieved from http://cnnmoney.com

Krantz, M., & Hansen, B. (2011, April 4). CEO pay soars while workers' pay stalls. *USA Today*. Retrieved from www.usatoday.com

Levitt, T. (1983, May/June). Globalization and markets. *Harvard Business Review, 61*(3), 92–103.

Mintzberg, H. (2009, July–August). Rebuilding companies as communities. *Harvard Business Review*, 87(7/8), 140–143.

Naím, M. (2003, January/February). The five wars of globalization. *Foreign Policy*, pp. 29–36.

Naím, M. (2005). *Illicit: How smugglers, traffickers, and copycats are hijacking the global economy*. New York, NY: Anchor Books.

New York Times. (2007, July 19). Viacom, Inc. Retrieved from http://topics.nytimes.com/top/news/business/companies/viacom_inc/index.html?inline = nyt-org

Nichols, M. (2011, May 12). Bill Roedy reflects on military and MTV in new book. *Reuters*. Retrieved from www.reuters.com

PublicCitizen. (2011, February 8). Executive compensation: Taking Stock. Retrieved from http://www.citizen.org

Reckitt Benckiser. (2011a). US Corporate Factsheet. Retrieved from http://www.rb.com/Investors-media/Investor-information

Reckitt Benckiser. (2011b). *Driving innovative growth: Annual report and financial statements 2010*. Retrieved from http://www.rb.com/Investors-media/Investor-information

Reckitt Benckiser. (2011c). Share price graph. Retrieved from http://www.rb.com/Media-investors/Share-price-information/Share-price-graph

Reckitt Benckiser. (2011d). Community. Retrieved from http://www.rb.com/Our-responsibility/A-Million-Brighter-Futures/Global-Challenge

Reich, R. (2007 September 14). CEOs deserve their pay. *The Wall Street Journal Online*. Retrieved from http://www2.econ.iastate.edu/classes/econ101/orazem/LAS125/CEOs%20Deserve%20Their%20Pay%20-%20WSJ.pdf

Ritzer, G. (2009). *Globalization: A basic text*. Malden, MA: Wiley-Blackwell.

Roedy, B. (2011). *What makes business rock: Building the world's largest global networks*. Hoboken, NJ: Wiley.

SMU. (2011). Blake Mycoskie. Retrieved from http://cox.smu.edu/web/guest/blake-mycoskie

Stiglitz, J. E. (2007). *Making globalization work*. New York, NY: W. W. Norton.

The Literary Group. (2011). Bill Roedy. Retrieved from http://www.theliterarygroup.com

The Telegraph. (2011, March 29). Reckitt Benckiser chief Bart Becht paid £18m on back of 18pc profit rise. Retrieved from www.telegraph.co.uk

Transparency International. (2011). *About Us*. Retrieved from http://www.transparency.org/

Transparency International. (2012a). What is the corruption perceptions index? Retrieved from http://cpi.transparency.org/cpi2011/in_detail/

Transparency International (2012b). Bribe payers index 2011. Retrieved from http://bpi.transparency.org/

Viacom. (2010). Viacom's 2010 Form10-K Report. Retrieved from http://phx.corporateir.net/phoenix.zhtml?c=85242&p=irol-IRHome

Viacom. (2011). Viacom's announcement of Roedy's retirement. Retrieved at http://www.billroedy.com

Wartzman, R. (2008, September 12). Put a cap on CEO pay. *BusinessWeek*. Retrieved from www.businessweek.com

Witkowski, T. H. (2005). Antiglobal challenges to marketing in developing countries: Exploring the ideological divide. *Journal of Public Policy & Marketing, 24*(1), 7–23.

# PART III

# Enterprise With the Environment in Mind

## CHAPTER 10

# The Environmental Imperative

## "TURNING THE TANKER AROUND"

### The Greening of Brazil's Petrobras

In the late 1990s, Petrobras began its transformation from a state-owned enterprise with a national monopoly on oil exploration and production to a quasi-governmental entity with 60% of its equity traded on the Bovespa and the New York Stock Exchange (Gabrielli, 2009, p. 44). Petrobras began facing new competitive forces, new stakeholders, and a new emphasis on profits and growth. It also set out to double oil production within ten years and to expand operations into 27 countries.

But shoddy operations in the form of corroded pipes and faulty leak detectors led to a string of oil spills for Brazil's largest company Petrobras from 1997 to 2001. After an oil spill dumped 350,000 gallons of crude oil into Guanabara Bay—a tourist destination, fishing community, and wildlife habitat near Rio de Janeiro in 1997—another one occurred in January 2000 because a Petrobras pipe did not have modern sensors. Oil poured out for two hours before the leak was detected. Environmental groups were furious. Local fisherman protested outside of the firm's headquarters in Rio. Activists from Greenpeace chained themselves to the railings outside Petrobras headquarters and left oil-soaked birds that had died as a result of the spill.

Six months later in 2000, Petrobras had a larger oil leak at a refinery near Curitiba in southern Brazil as more than 1 million gallons of oil flowed into two rivers. This time, critics cited inadequate staffing and emergency plans. The media ran streams of derisive commentaries about the firm. The BBC described Petrobras as demonstrating "an embarrassing level of incompetence" (Gabrielli, 2009, p. 43, para. 2). The company had to pay millions of dollars in fines for these and other mishaps. In addition to harming the environment, the mishaps raised questions among investors, reduced profits, damaged the firm's image, and demoralized employees. Because the government of Brazil owned a majority of the shares of the firm, all Brazilians felt a sense of betrayal and disappointment for Petrobras's performance. Accidents and oil spills increasingly stained the reputation of Petrobras and adversely affected its ability to market its brands effectively.

Then, an even worse mishap occurred for Petrobras as two explosions occurred on its P-36 oil platform on March 15, 2001, killing 11 employees. The $350 million rig had been the world's largest floating production platform and served as a symbol of pride for both the firm and the nation of Brazil. The P-36 sank five days later and leaked 300,000 gallons of oil (Gabrielli, 2009).

The company had become a danger not only to the environment also but to its employees because of its operational deficiencies. Petrobras realized it had to change itself fundamentally. It began reforming itself by revitalizing leadership, and by having leadership focus on meeting or exceeding health and safety standards, as well as environmental stewardship.

Petrobras has not had a major accident since the P-36 disaster. It is acknowledged as a global leader in sustainable business practices and the world's third-largest energy company (Petrobras, 2011). Petrobras operates in 28 countries and has become widely respected for its deep and ultra-deep ocean operations. A year after the infamous BP Deepwater

Horizon oil spill that put 4.9 million barrels of oil into the Gulf of Mexico from April to July 2010, the U.S. Bureau of Ocean Energy Management, Regulation, and Enforcement (BOEMRE) gave permission to Petrobras to begin oil production in the Gulf at depths of 2,500 meters (OffshoreEnergyToday.com, 2011).

The firm is a member of the World Business Council for Sustainable Development and is a signatory of the UN Global Compact (a social and environmental policy program discussed in Chapter 5.) Petrobras is now listed on the Dow Jones Sustainability Index, which tracks the financial performance of the leading sustainability-driven companies around the world (Dow Jones, 2011). In 2009, the Global Reporting Initiative gave Petrobras its highest rating for transparency, while the research and rating firm Management & Excellence ranked Petrobras number one among the world's oil and gas companies for sustainability.

"There's a metaphor in business about turning the tanker around," current Petrobras CEO José Sergio Gabrielli said, "We did it with an entire oil company" (Gabrielli, 2009, p. 44).

Petrobras's CEO during the tumultuous period of 1999–2001 created a new director-level position for health, safety, and environment, as well as launched the Program for Excellence in Environmental and Operational Safety Management (PEGASO). This program represented a $4 billion investment and encompassed more than 4,000 individual projects designed to prevent accidents. PEGASO was not just another risk management program, but rather it served as the centerpiece for transforming the company into an industry leader for environmental performance. PEGASO had an immediate impact and markedly improved Petrobras's safety record.

## Your Thoughts?

- Why do you think Petrobras began racking up operational mishaps in the late 1990s?
- What factors led Petrobras to begin changing its ways?
- What aspects of the P-36 disaster compelled Petrobras to transform its corporate culture? Why couldn't this disaster be shrugged off as "just what happens in the oil and gas industry?"
- What changes helped Petrobras "turn the tanker around?"
- How green can Petrobras ever be if it produces and refines a product with many negative environmental externalities, such as air pollutants and carbon?

## CHAPTER OVERVIEW AND LEARNING OBJECTIVES

This chapter will discuss what Philip Kotler—a leading thinker in marketing—calls "the environmental imperative" (Kotler, 2011b). Macromarketing scholars have long focused on environmental degradation as an externality of marketing. In fact, "environment" is the third of the six core dimensions in macromarketing's QuEEnSHiP acronym presented in Chapter 1. The question emerging from such research was, "can anything be done about this externality?" Now, managerially oriented scholars like Kotler are suggesting that the some of the assumptions of marketing practice, such as limitless resources of the Earth and unconstrained carrying capacity for waste on the planet, are wrong. At this juncture when such fundamental assumptions of marketing are being rethought, macromarketing offers valuable insights into crucial societal issues regarding the environment. Many of these issues have already received treatment over the years by two schools within macromarketing—the developmental school and the critical school of thought.

This chapter also presents the importance of the ethical concepts of citizenship (being responsible to society at large) and stewardship (being responsible to another stakeholder) in responding to the environmental imperative. For firms pursuing environmental stewardship, employees will lead this effort. In this pursuit, the values and principles of employees help firms discover new products, new markets, and new internal processes for conducting operations.

Not surprisingly, firms that treat the physical environment with respect tend to do the same with other stakeholders, beginning with their own employees. In other words, stewardship is not limited to environmental stewardship. Stewardship of resources also applies to human resources—within the firm first, and then outside the firm. Transparency is a core dimension of firms marked by stewardship ethics. This can be extended to an "open books" atmosphere where just about all information in the company is made available to employees in the firm.

Firms responding to the environmental imperative are likely to find a receptive audience to their actions. Notably, many environmentalists who took an adversarial stance toward business are now seeking to work with businesses because of the recognition of the importance of jobs and employment to society (Nordhaus & Shellenberger, 2007). Here, a recognition that profits must be made by businesses is an important aspect of this revised way of regarding business persons and their endeavors.

Values-driven firms, such as New Belgium Brewing Company based in Fort Collins, Colorado, pursue profits and draw on a more humanistic approach to stakeholders to obtain these profits. The results of taking a triple-bottom-line approach can be seen in the firm being able to make its Belgium-style brown ale more distinctive and appealing to a wider set of customers. New Belgium accomplished this by using its community of pastoral amateurs to call consumers to this movement that pursued a less materialistic but higher quality of life.

Finally, the story of Wilcox Family Farms—a 100-year-old farm that sits on 1,500 acres of sustainable farmland along the Nisqually River near Roy, Washington—will be featured under the Mavericks Who Made It section. Today, the fourth generation of Wilcox Family Farms continues the tradition of sustainable farming to supply families and businesses such as Costco with quality, organic, cage-free eggs and products.

After this chapter, you should be able to answer the following questions:

- What is the environmental imperative?
- How did the developmental school and the critical school differ in their views regarding the role of marketing systems in environmental stewardship?

- How are citizenship and stewardship similar? Different?
- Why are employees endemic to success in shifting to sustainable business practices?
- How can sustainable enterprises choose to identify and reinforce their values and principles for a far-flung workforce?
- What advantages do values-driven companies gain regarding branding?
- How can sustainable enterprises reinforce a high-involvement culture of the firm?
- How can sustainable enterprises reinforce sustainable suppliers around the world?

# FROM BAD BUSINESS TO GOOD BUSINESS

## Petrobras Transforms Itself

"From a purely financial perspective, environmental mismanagement was just bad business," Gabrielli said. "From an investor relations perspective, ignoring the growing demand for transparency and sustainability was also clearly bad business. And, from a personal perspective, the company's new sustainability strategies mirrored my own beliefs, rooted in my political and academic past" (Gabrielli, 2009, p. 44).

During his student days in the 1960s, Gabrielli became a prominent activist in the student movement challenging Brazil's dictatorship. He was prominent enough to be jailed by the army in 1970. After his release, Gabrielli helped found the Workers' Party. He later received a PhD in economics from Boston University in 1987 and began an academic career at the Federal University of Bahia in northeastern Brazil. Gabrielli joined Petrobras in 2003 as director of finance and investor relations when Petrobras's environmental initiatives were rapidly expanding in importance in the company.

Gabrielli's progressive, leftist, political orientation from his student days colors the way he thinks about Petrobras's role in Brazilian society and in the world. He views the legitimacy of business—its social license to operate—as coming from business's power to drive social improvement. As an economics researcher, his views crystallized about the responsibility of business toward society. "Private enterprise, of course, is responsible to shareholders, but supporting sustainability goals is not at odds with that," Gabrielli said. "It's complementary—and necessary" (Gabrielli, 2009, p. 45, para. 1).

Since its inception in 1953 as a state-run monopoly, Petrobras and the development of Brazil intertwined themselves. In 2011, the government held 64% of the voting shares of the company (Gall, 2011). Gabrielli sees himself as a steward of the spirit of the Petrobras employees, who collectively see their firm as an integral part of Brazil's development. This national pride explains in part how the company culture embraced the audacious goal of becoming a leader in environmental stewardship, despite an awful record in environmental stewardship.

"As CEO, I approach environmental performance issues in three broad ways: improving our own culture and operations, influencing—indeed, pressuring the companies that do business with us, and championing renewable-energy development," Gabrielli said (Gabrielli, 2009, p. 45).

A core element of Petrobras's internal strategy is its health, safety, and environment (HSE) program. This huge operation called for a $2.5 billion investment by Petrobras in

2009. The framework for the program consists of guidelines in 15 areas, such as leadership, regulatory compliance, risk evaluation and management, training, and accident analysis. Senior, executive, and general managers have participated in more than 1,000 audits, field trips to refineries, off-shore platforms, and pipelines. Gabrielli or one of the board members of Petrobras has joined 28 of these site visits. Petrobras is close to having its units achieve the highest standard for environmental management, ISO 14001 from the International Standards Organization. Petrobras's near achievement of this standard sends a strong message about environmental stewardship to their network of 4,000 suppliers—70 % of whom were from Brazil in 2007:

> Like companies anywhere, Brazilian suppliers often won't go beyond minimum legal requirements unless they have clear incentives to do so. Given our size and clout, we realized that we could promote improved social and environmental performance in companies throughout Brazil by giving the highest performers our business. (Gabrielli, 2009, p. 46)

Petrobras's clout is likely to increase. In October 2010, it had the largest ever public stock offering, which raised $70 billion for the company (Mason, 2011). It aims to triple oil production to six million barrels per day by 2020 from its 2011 production of two million per day. Currently, Petrobras is growing faster than any other oil company in the world, and this will likely enable it to become the largest company based on market value by 2016.

Petrobras acknowledges that its products put a lot of carbon into the atmosphere when they are consumed. While not intending to stop producing oil, Petrobras's long-term plan is to become a driver of renewable energy development. The firm has contracts to do joint projects, research, and technology exchanges with 170 Brazilian universities and research centers and more than 70 international institutions (Gabrielli, 2009, p. 47, para. 1).

"The arc of our narrative is so clear from the catastrophes at the start of the decade to our recovery and now, leadership," Gabrielli said. "But in actuality, we don't compartmentalize environmental stewardship—and I think any company would be unwise to do so. It's integrated into our broader CSR and sustainability strategy, which includes good corporate governance, transparency, and investments in social development, particularly in Brazil" (Gabrielli, 2009, p. 47, para. 2).

## Commerce in the Age of Transparency

### Kotler's Environmental Imperative

Northwestern University's Philip Kotler is one of the most respected scholars of marketing today. His popular textbooks have influenced business culture around the world to the point that terms in his book (such as consumer orientation, segmentation, targeting, and positioning) are known by those who have never studied marketing formally (Hackley, 2009, p. 2).

Today, Kotler cites not one, but a set of environmental challenges that compose an environmental imperative for society, such as (a) climate change, (b) depletion of the ozone layer that protects the Earth from ultraviolet radiation, (c) soil degradation and increased desertification, (d) increased air and water pollution, (e) reduction in the availability of fresh water, and (f) increasing depletion of physical and natural resources, such as oil, copper, timber, and ocean fisheries. Kotler sees that companies now need to make drastic changes in their product development, manufacturing, financial, and marketing practices if sustainability is to be achieved. This is the environmental imperative.

In this era of the environmental imperative, firms will not want to appear indifferent to larger economic, social, and environmental concerns (Kotler, 2011b). With consumers e-mailing, blogging, and tweeting both the good and bad aspects of firms and their activities, firms are now "swimming in a highly transparent fishbowl" (Kotler, 2011b, p. 134). As a result, accountability has increased markedly for firms in society (Meyer & Kirby, 2010).

## The Influence of the Internet

When asked if there would be a widespread conversation in society about a "green economy" if the Internet did not exist, *The New York Times* Environment Correspondent Felicity Barringer, said, "No" (Barringer, 2008, personal communication). With the Internet, entrepreneurs with green innovations can keep these in front of possible consumers and investors much longer as a result of new communication technologies. Using social media, corporate-sized nongovernmental organizations (NGOs), such as the Environmental Defense Fund and the Natural Resources Defense Council (1.3 million supporters), can mobilize its supporters on legal and scientific issues regarding the environment (NRDC, 2011). Online communities, such as SustainLane—billing itself as a people-powered green guide—serve as a way people interested in living healthy lives on a green planet can discuss local green news and share information and tips (SustainLane.com, n.d.). The members of SustainLane.com have written reviews on more than 30,000 green products and businesses across the country.

By going to www.scorecard.org, one can quickly find the largest polluters where one lives or works. Figure 10.1 depicts one of the results from entering the zip code for Hollywood in Los Angeles County in Southern California. As shown, Los Angeles County is one of the worst/dirtiest counties in the United States.

Even pollution from far away can be traced back to its source. For example, the North American Commission for Environmental Cooperation released a study showing that three quarters of the dioxin in the breast milk of Inuit women in Nunavut, Canada's northernmost territory, came from municipal waste incinerators in the Midwest and Eastern parts of the United States (Weaver-Zercher, 2010).

In April 2006, a dense cloud of soot, toxic chemicals, and gases from smokestacks of coal-burning plants in northern China along with dust and desert left China and swept over Seoul, Korea. A U.S. satellite spotted the cloud as it came across the Pacific. As a result of such weather-born exports from the developing world, air filters in places such as Lake Tahoe and eastern California become dark (Bradsher & Barboza, 2006). Particles of sulfur, carbon, and other compounds can work their way deep into the lungs contributing to respiratory damage, heart disease, and cancer. A conservative estimate of deaths from air pollution alone in the United States each year is 130,000 (Diamond, 2005, p. 492). In China, sulfur dioxide from burning coal results in 400,000 premature deaths each year (Bradsher & Barboza, 2006, p. 1). In sum, as scientific measurements have become more

**Figure 10.1**   Results From Scorecard.org Suggest Pollution Is the Unglamorous Side of Hollywood

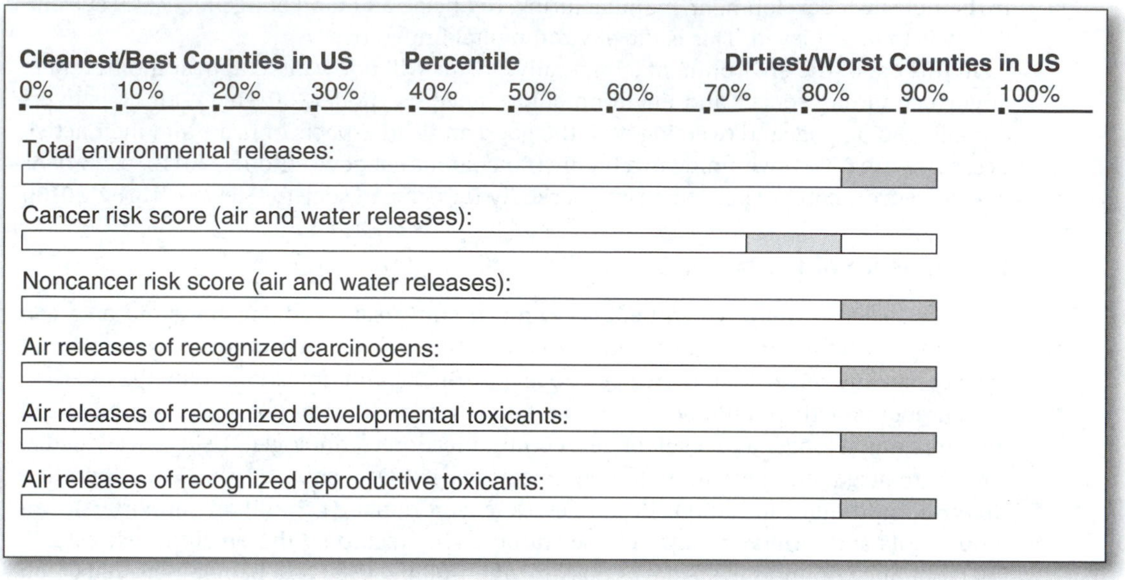

**Cleanest/Best Counties in US**      **Percentile**                      **Dirtiest/Worst Counties in US**
0%      10%     20%     30%     40%     50%     60%     70%     80%     90%     100%

Total environmental releases:

Cancer risk score (air and water releases):

Noncancer risk score (air and water releases):

Air releases of recognized carcinogens:

Air releases of recognized developmental toxicants:

Air releases of recognized reproductive toxicants:

*Source:* Scorecard, http://scorecard.goodguide.com/env-releases/county.tcl?fips_county_code=06037#major_chemical_releases

sophisticated, the global aspect of air pollution has become undeniable. China's problems are now the world's problems. Much of the particulate pollution in Los Angeles originates in China according the *Journal of Geophysical Research* (Kahn & Yardley, 2007, p. 1).

## Can Marketing Be Reinvented?

However, air pollution is just one of the maladies afflicting countries today—especially in the developing world. The long list of other environmental problems include the following: biodiversity losses, cropland losses, desertification, disappearing wetlands, grassland degradation, invasive species, overgrazing, river flow cessation, salinization, soil erosion, trash accumulation, water pollution, and shortages (Diamond, 2005, p. 358).

Despite decades of disseminating marketing principles and techniques focused on finding out what customers want and giving it to them (the "little m"), Kotler now emphasizes a new turn for marketing in which marketers need to replace a narrow view of meeting one need for the customer with a more complete view of the customer (similar to the "biggest M") (Kotler, 2011a):

People today have a lot of concerns about the future. They hear about water shortages, air pollution, fat in their diet, rising healthcare costs. Most manufacturers don't address these concerns. Each focuses on a slice of the customer's life. A toothpaste manufacturer only thinks of the person's teeth and a washing machine manufacturer only thinks of a person's need to clean clothes. Marketers need to replace their vertical perspective of a customer with a horizontal perspective where they see the customer's full humanity. Companies need to show that they share the same concerns as customers and that they are acting on these concerns." (p. 34, para. 5)

Kotler singles out companies that care about the planet as those likely to win larger followings in the future. This is because largely unexamined assumptions of marketers about marketing are now being reconsidered. Kotler predicts that the environmental agenda emerging from this reconsideration of marketing's fundamental assumptions will have a profound effect on marketing theory and practice (Kotler, 2011b, p. 132).

Previously, marketers assumed that unlimited consumption was good, the planet's resources and its carrying capacity for waste and pollution were infinite, and that quality of life increased as consumption increased. In short, resource limitations and externality costs were abstract notions reserved for academic debates. However, these constraints are more clearly evident. High market prices for commodities, such as oil, iron, and precious metals, reflect resource limits related to the development of countries such as China and India. Food prices reached a 20-year high in 2011 (Associated Press, 2011).

## Macromarketing Perspectives on Sustainability

Sustainable development refers to "meeting the needs of the present without compromising the ability of future generations to meet their own needs" according to the UN's Brundtland Commission formerly known as the UN's World Commission on Environment and Development (WCED, 1987, chapt. 2, sect. 4). An emerging consensus is that the three pillars of sustainability are social, environmental, and economic sustainability (Haugh & Talwar, 2010, p. 385). These correspond to the "triple bottom line" of people, planet, and profit discussed in Chapter 1.

### Schools of Macromarketing Sustainability Thought

Among macromarketing scholars, two schools of thought have emerged about sustainability—the developmental school and the critical school (Mittelstaedt & Kilbourne, 2009). The developmental school views markets as the most efficient provisioning mechanism for economic growth, human development, and quality of life. Accordingly, questions about sustainability would focus on how existing marketing systems can be improved to provide sustainability to societies. The critical school offers a critique of marketing and what it sees as marketing's inherent dependence on neo-liberal ideas of competition in markets as allocating society's resources. Those in the critical school regard exchange as being based too much on the materialism and status needs of consumers. In sum, the developmental school sees markets and marketing as part of the solution for moving toward sustainability, while the critical school sees markets and marketing as part of the problem—moving societies away from sustainability.

The developmental school views marketing systems as improving people's lives. Sustainable consumption can be initiated by consumers because consumers vote with their money in markets. Consequently, the favored versions of their products succeed in markets. This means that producers change their behavior to survive. Also, governments can intervene in markets to provide incentives that would advance the interests of consumers, such as providing tax breaks for renewable energy companies, or corporate average fuel economy targets (CAFÉ) standards for automobile emissions. If the developmental school had a theme song written by the Beatles, it would be "We Can Work It Out" because this school believes that marketing systems can change and evolve.

By comparison, the critical school views marketing systems as inherently unstable. According to the critical school, markets are inherently unstable because an underlying Dominant Social Paradigm (DSP) influenced the development of marketing systems. In short, the DSP can be characterized by a materialism of "more is good," as well as a pragmatic stance toward competitive markets that "if it works, it must be good." If the critical school had a theme song written by the Beatles, it would be "Revolution" because this school believes that nothing short of a radical overhaul of the DSP and its implied goal of wealth accumulation would be needed to change the course of societies.

Currently, consumers in developed countries consume resources well beyond their real needs as part of the materialistic lifestyle, and consumers in lesser developed countries aspire to consume beyond their needs (Ger & Belk, 1996). Longtime macromarketing scholar George Fisk was known to repeat the following question to stir reflection on the implications of the materialistic lifestyle being passed to those in developing countries: "What are we going to do in twenty years when 500 million Chinese start their cars in the morning to drive to work?" (Fisk, 1997, personal communication).

Fisk's rhetorical question implies an endorsement of the critical school's indictment of the ideology that the meaning of life is to be found in buying things. which undergirds the DSP (Ger, 1997; Kilbourne, McDonagh, & Prothero, 1997). If the DSP does not radically change, marketing systems will ruin the environment. Kotler cites the current CEO of Unilever Paul Polman as a very strong advocate of sustainability in business (Kotler, 2011b, p. 133). However, when Polman, who has been CEO for 18 months, declares that his consumer products company Unilever will double sales and do this while reducing Unilever's environmental impact and footprint (Stern 2010), Kotler asserts that this does not make sense:

> This poses a difficult challenge, however. If every company such as Unilever was to succeed in doubling its business, sustainability will be impossible to achieve. We have heard many times that if less developed countries would by some miracle achieve the living standards of more advanced countries, pollution, road and air traffic, and energy power outages would smother our quality of life. Something between a zero-growth goal and a modest-growth goal would make more sense. (Kotler, 2011b, p. 133, para. 3)

Kotler envisions stakeholders will have to accept many difficult changes if companies are to attain sustainability. Environmental sustainability considers the impact of business on (a) the quality and quantity of natural resources, (b) the environment, (c) global warming, (d) ecological concerns, (e) waste management, (f) lowering energy and resource use,

(g) renewable energy production, and (h) improved pollution and emissions management (Townsend, 2008). Kotler envisions CEO and senior executive compensation packages as having to change. For example, senior executives must not only have to show economic success but also success in achieving predetermined goals for the company in the eight areas of environmental sustainability.

## Can the DSP Be Changed?

The critical school asserts that a radical change needs to be made in the DSP. Although this suggests that a catastrophic climate event might be the precipitating event leading to such a de-valuing of wealth accumulation (Gilding, 2011), another way could be less sudden and more gradual over time. Prothero is one scholar from the critical school who sees the way forward as marketing environmental stewardship as a commodity (Prothero & Fitchett, 2000). In other words, can green become "cool?" This would imply deemphasizing consumption while emphasizing citizenship (Prothero, McDonagh and Dobscha, 2010).

The existence of a consumer segment termed "lifestyles of health and sustainability" (LOHAS, for short) implies that there is a chance that the DSP could be radically changed over time. One estimate of the LOHAS segment suggests that 19% of adults in the United States fall into this category or the "cultural creatives" category (those whose consumption is strongly influenced by values related to environmental concern). Current distinctive consumption for this segment includes organic foods, energy-efficient appliances, alternative medicines, and eco-tourism (Kotler, 2011b, p. 134).

Recent research suggests that a sustainability discourse in the marketplace and in the media might be moving many toward a more holistic and global perspective (Prothero et al., 2010). The global economic meltdown that began in 2008 brought questioning of key assumptions for the DSP that the institutions of the economy were rationally configured and resistant to volatility. Al Gore's *An Inconvenient Truth* was seen by millions around the world. Television shows focused on helping viewers lead greener lives have taken the airwaves in the United Kingdom and the United States. Businesses have begun embracing the idea of green. The concept of buying local to avoid the carbon emissions incurred in long-distance transportation has begun to be part of consumer thinking. It now is even green and chic to many.

The rise of these elements as part of a green commodity discourse suggests that social marketing of an idea, cause, or behavior, might prove to weaken the current DSP and possibly shift cultural norms to a sustainability mindset (Kotler, 2011b, p. 135). In this way, a convergence of the views of the developmental and critical schools of macromarketing might occur. The positive aspect of marketing (the social marketing of environmental stewardship and the demarketing of overconsumption) might save marketing from destroying the very foundation on which it exists for "without a habitable natural environment, there will be no quality of life" (Kilbourne et al., 1997, p. 19).

## Doing the Right Thing

While Kotler wonders about how sustainability can be made to boost the business prospects for firms, individual actors continue to "do the right thing" regardless of the short-term economic consequences. No doubt, the emerging discourse favoring environmental stewardship reinforces individual decision-makers to behave more like citizens, rather than like traders of goods and services when confronting environmental issues for the firm. For example, Jay and Jacki Givens have owned Givens Collision Repair Center in Frederick, Maryland, since 1998 (van Schagen, 2011). From the beginning, the Givens's have always been as green as possible, reusing everything they could. They installed special equipment to spray Waterborne products (high-quality, water-based paints that release half the toxins of solvent-based paint products), but they knew they could do more. They recently built a new facility, and eco-minded upgrades, such as strategically placing windows and skylights, and installing high-efficiency heat pumps and insulation, led to remarkable savings.

However, the Givens's were not just motivated by savings of greening their new building. They installed a BaySaver filtration system underground to clean and filter any groundwater leaving their property before it reached the Chesapeake Bay. It was a $185,000 undertaking that will never see a monetary return for the Givens (van Schagen, 2011, p. 66).

"There has definitely been a lot of good that has come out of it that I don't think we'll ever be able to put a dollar figure on," Jacki said. "But you've got to lay your head down at night and know that you're doing things the right way—that means a lot to us" (van Schagen, 2011, p. 66).

One of their employees, manager Rex Ransom, explained what installing the water filtration system means to the workers this way: "I think it's pretty neat ... to know that they care enough to make sure that the water that's getting down to the water treatment plant isn't going to affect my kids," Ransom said. "They're responsible for 18 people and 18 people's families, and they really take that seriously" (van Schagen, 2011, p. 66).

"We're proud of what we're doing," Jacki said. "and we're going to continue to do what we can—not just for us, but for our kids and our grandkids—to move not just our facility but our industry into a greener and cleaner arena" (van Schagen, 2011, p. 66).

The Givens's approach to their business illustrates the three ethical norms in the American Marketing Association's (AMA's) statement of ethics (AMA, 2011). First, Givens Collision and Repair Center seeks to do no harm. In this they deliberately choose to avoid harmful actions, such as releasing unfiltered groundwater leaving their property. This "beyond compliance" ethic is similar to other firms that have dedicated themselves to stewardship and citizenship. Second, the Givens foster trust in the marketing system. Toward this end, the firm strives for fair dealing and the avoidance of deception in the delivery of the services the firm provides. The savings realized through green processes of their business and the green aspects of their new building relieve the firm from financial pressure that might lead to opportunistic behavior with stakeholders. Finally, the Givens embrace ethical values that nurture relationships with their employees as well as other stakeholders. The six ethical values highlighted in the AMA Statement of Ethics and Norms include (a) honesty, (b) responsibility, (c) fairness, (d) respect, (e) transparency, and (f) citizenship. These are presented in Table 10.1. Such values can serve as a ready starting point for firms intent on identifying dimensions of their approach to business.

**Table 10.1**   Ethical Values for Marketers from the AMA Statement of Ethics

| | |
|---|---|
| **Honesty** | – to be forthright in dealings with customers and stakeholders. |
| **Responsibility** | – to accept the consequences of our marketing decisions and strategies. |
| **Fairness** | – to balance justly the needs of the buyer with the interests of the seller. |
| **Respect** | – to acknowledge the basic human dignity of all stakeholders. |
| **Transparency** | – to create a spirit of openness in marketing operations. |
| **Citizenship** | – to fulfill the economic, legal, philanthropic, and societal responsibilities that serve stakeholders. |

*Source:* AMA (2011).

Importantly, codes of ethics can become meaningless if the leaders of the firm treat such codes and their underlying ethical values as mere ornaments for a ruthless culture focused on the material success of the firm. Enron, based in Houston, Texas, began as an energy-trading and services firm that rapidly rose to post sales of more than $101 billion in 2000 (McLean & Elkind, 2004). It was cited by *Fortune* as America's Most Innovative Company six times. However, it collapsed and declared bankruptcy in late 2001 because it engaged in purposeful and systematic accounting fraud. More than 20,000 employees lost their jobs. Those employees who had focused their 401k retirement plans on Enron stock lost their retirement savings, too.

The ethical values of Enron displayed in its code of ethics were "respect, integrity, communication and excellence." Although such values are admirable to readers outside the firm, many inside the firm likely interpreted these values to be applicable only for how the employees should treat each other and not necessarily applicable for how the employees should treat those not in the firm. The Enron leadership reinforced a shallow approach to business by posting up-to-the-minute updates of the Enron stock price not only in the lobby of Enron's headquarters but also in the elevators. Such cues made the point that raising the stock price of Enron was to be the unswerving pursuit of all employees in the firm. In the end, the firm's "profit uber alles" culture—the understanding that profit was more important than anything else—led firm leaders and some Enron employees to commit crimes for the purpose of attaining more success in the marketplace than what Enron had rightfully earned (Wee, 2002).

## Citizenship and Stewardship

Several action steps accompany each value in the AMA Statement of Ethics. The first point for action listed under the citizenship value is "to protect the ecological environment in the execution of marketing campaigns" (AMA, 2011, p. 2, para. 4). Citizenship in this regard is similar to the principle of stewardship as part of enlightened marketing (Laczniak

& Murphy, 2006). While citizens have rights, they also have obligations to the wider society (Prothero et al., 2010, p. 153). Stewardship embraces a duty to the common good and responsibility to act for the betterment of the host environment and community. Such duty and responsibility obligates marketers not to impose external costs on society and future generations—especially the physical environment—that would result from marketing operations. McDonald's decision in the early 1990s to eliminate non-biodegradable polystyrene containers and return to more ecologically friendly—but more expensive—paper packaging is one example of citizenship and stewardship.

The word "steward" comes from the old English word "stigweard," which means "guardian of the house and more specifically, of the farm animals" (Audebrand, 2010, p. 420). The traditional responsibility of the steward to an owner is important, but so are wider obligations to the general public, to future generations, to other species, and to all of the natural world. Stewardship involves not only carefully tending the environment, but guarding and protecting it from harm. Phrases such as "looking after something," "being accountable for something," and "doing something on behalf of someone," are all heard when people discuss stewardship. Stewardship does not imply ownership or final authority regarding what is guarded and protected. In this way, stewards recognize they are embedded in a system and are responsible to someone, to some others, or to something else.

In a recent study of firms committed to triple-bottom-line achievement, the citizenship and stewardship aspects of stakeholder marketing became apparent (Mish & Scammon, 2010). These private firms in the United States have a commitment to simultaneous social, environmental, and economic objectives. Each of these firms had operated for at least two bottom lines (profit and either planet or people) for 15 years and at least three bottom lines for at least 5 years (profit, planet, and people). Eight of the nine firms claimed membership in the Green Business Network (http://greenbusinessnetwork.org), a network of more than 5,000 U.S. businesses that are "green" in the sense of operating to solve—rather than to cause—social and environmental problems (Green Business Network, 2011). In short, these firms had operated as stewards for many years, so they give a valuable perspective on stewardship.

The leaders of these firms viewed the marketplace as unified in the sense that all actors in the marketplace are interconnected peers. Additionally, these leaders interpret the actions of their firms in relation to all players throughout the entire system. These firms carried a moral stance that their actions should in no way harm the weakest-link stakeholders in the market system, such as the environment or future generations.

Although each firm regarded itself as doing marketing differently from others (such as unilaterally disclosing all nontoxic ingredients on product labels rather than hiding them as "trade secrets"), each firm committed itself to the interconnectedness of the market system in order to help transform industries and institutional norms. The perception about the interconnectedness of the actors in the market system allowed these firms to generate intelligence about all stakeholders and diffuse this intelligence through the organizational structure of these firms. By viewing their stakeholders as partners or potential partners, these stakeholders became sources of value for the customers of these firms. With this view, stakeholder needs hold implications for system well-being, as well as for the well-being of each actor in the system.

Other research calls firms to recognize that the same stakeholder might be represented in multiple stakeholder groups for the firm (Smith, Drumwright, & Gentile, 2010). For example, a customer might also be a citizen, parent, employee, community member, or person who may one day be healed of a major illness because of a treatment derived from a rare plant in an endangered forest. To avoid a myopic view of the marketplace where only customers or competitors would be in focus (and other stakeholders perceived only in a fuzzy way), firms must move from a market orientation to a stakeholder orientation (Ferrell, Gonzalez-Padron, Hult, & Maignan, 2010). This research suggests that marketers must first map the stakeholders of their firms. Although this can be more difficult than it first appears, stakeholders must be identified beyond generic categories as real people with names and faces. The importance of these stakeholders must be rated, as well as their interconnections.

## The Role of Employees

The easiest stakeholders to list with names and faces should be the employees of the firm.

For firms pursuing environmental stewardship, the employees' values and principles are like a compass that enables these firms to find their way to new products, new markets, and new internal processes for conducting operations. In a McKinsey survey, CEOs rated employees as the group that has the greatest impact on the way companies manage their societal expectations (Bielak, Bonini, & Oppenheim, 2007). These employees represent an enormous reservoir of talent and energy for building a firm with stewardship ethics of caring for the social, environmental, and economic outcomes of business operations (Yankelovich, 2006).

In most firms that view the environment and future generations as stakeholders, employees are the ones who prove to be instrumental in the process of changing organizational culture. In Chapter 1, Interface, Inc.'s employees asked Ray Anderson to address them on his environmental vision for the company. At that time, Anderson had no vision at all. But the encounter with his employees set him on a course of deep reflection that eventually led to Anderson's "mid-course correction" to join his employees in leading his company to climb "Mt. Sustainability" (Anderson, 2009).

When IBM's Sam Palmisano sought to refresh his firm's values when he became chairman and CEO, he conducted a 72-hour Web chat in July 2003 about what IBM stood for. This showed his regard for the 350,000 IBM employees in 170 countries (Kanter, 2009, p. 63). Using IBM technology and innovation technologies, this interactive forum became known as the ValuesJam. More than 140,000 participated in the voluntary session for the company. When Palmisano proposed the ValuesJam idea to the IBM board, he was asked if this were "socialism." Palmisano explained that the ValuesJam would enable employees to establish their own values and embrace them. If employees could contribute to IBM's value system, they would feel more connected to the company and this would help IBM build a long-lasting institution. "When you are working for the same company for twenty years, you need to be proud of it," an IBM sector director in Latin America said. He continued:

The reason I wake up early every day to come to IBM is because this company has values that we really believe in. This is the reason I'm here, because I really believe in this company. I know we are doing good things for society. Of course we are a business, and we have our targets, but we can give other things. And we do it. (Kanter, 2009, p. 64)

A team took all of the inputs collected from the ValuesJam and combined them to three core values: (a) dedication to every client's success; (b) innovation that matters, for our company and the world; and (c) trust and personal responsibility in all relationships (Kanter, 2009, p. 64). After these values were announced, Palmisano received a surprising number of thoughtful messages from employees that amounted to three feet of paper printouts—which he carried into a staff meeting.

Some IBM managers use the values in training new hires and in developing leaders. In thinking about the three overarching values for IBM (client success, innovation, and relationships), these are likely to be similar to other firms' values. Importantly, IBM's values have vitality because employees use them in discussions with each other and management when they discuss the company. When a firm discusses and identifies its values, then the values and principles can serve as a guidance system for self and peer control, as well as for business decisions (Kanter, 2009, p. 3).

Values typically become more important for the firm in uncertain times because they orient employees on all levels to the firm's abiding priorities, such as its social purpose. Research on small firms in the technology sector suggests that when uncertainty in the external environment increases, owner-managers increase their engagement with employees. This, in turn, results in improved performance (Sawyerr, McGee, & Peterson, 2003). Notably, this study found no such role for external networking as it did for internal networking of the owner-managers of these firms.

## New Belgium Brewing Company's Employees

Values-centered entrepreneurs who embrace a mission of being socially responsible in the manner of Conscious Capitalism (discussed in Chapter 5), tend to work with employees in a more egalitarian way than traditional firms. For example, New Belgium Brewery, which makes Fat Tire Beer, practices open-book management and trains all employees in financial literacy so that they can read the firm's financial books in a more meaningful manner (Choi & Gray, 2011). Although salary information for employees is aggregated so individuals' salaries cannot be directly known, all other financial information can be accessed by any employee through the accounting department. New Belgium also includes all of its employees in strategy development, budgeting, and departmental planning. It takes time, but integration of employees in the management life of the company results in a high-involvement culture.

Founded in 1991 in the basement of founders Jeff Lebesch and Kim Jordan, New Belgium employees can participate in its Employee Stock Ownership Plan, which has resulted in 43% of the firm being employed by its employees (Moses, 2011). Citing environmental activist Guy Dauncey (www.earthfuture.com), the leaders of the firm believe that "if it's not fun, it's not sustainable" (Moses, 2011, p. 1). New Belgium's original Belgian-type beer is called Fat Tire, which refers to a wide-tired bicycle used by Lebesch when he traveled through Belgium to research beer formulas. Bonding between the firm and its employees is reinforced by the firm presenting each employee with a cruiser bicycle after one year of service. After five years of service, employees celebrate with a company-funded trip to Belgium. In these ways, New Belgium provides meaningful ways to connect emotionally with New Belgium as the core element of a brand community (Sartain & Schumann, 2006).

The firm cites its organizational culture as the most important and transferrable tool to drive sustainability. "We have tried to make our relationship with our co-workers—in terms of running the business—very transparent," co-founder and CEO Kim Jordan said. "I think that's a foundational piece of who we are" (Choi & Gray, 2011, p. 74). To Jordan, transparency means shining a light on the firm's successes as well as on its shortcomings, so that stakeholders can be the judge of New Belgium's authenticity—how its actions match the things the firm says about itself (Jordan, 2007). In its 2007 Sustainability Report, New Belgium's sustainability director admitted that an aggrieved ex-employee rightly accused the firm of incorrectly using the phrase "100% wind-powered" when natural gas provided over half the energy needed to make beer at the firm (Orgolini, 2007).

New Belgium's transparency is also evident in the four-page Annual Summary of New Belgium's Sustainable Business Story included as an appendix at the end of this chapter (New Belgium, 2010). This summary presents (a) New Belgium's values-driven commerce, (b) its high-involvement culture, (c) its philanthropy, (d) its environmental impact, and (e) its recent accomplishments in sustainability. Although including technical detail (similar to the nonfinancial reporting of Denmark-based healthcare company Novo Nordisk in Figure 5.2 of Chapter 5), the summary is made "fun" by the graphic design and tone of the writing.

The founders of New Belgium sought to make profits not despite their triple-bottom-line approach (people, planet, and profits), but because of it. Integrating servant leadership concepts (see Chapter 8) into the conduct of operations at "the Mothership"—the employees' term for the brewery in Fort Collins, Colorado—managers strive to empower employees to make the very best product. Together, everyone "figures out the future" (New Belgium, 2007). For example, one worker suggested using the water used to rinse the inside of beer bottles to be captured and used to rinse the outside of bottles (Wallace, 2009). In this way, the company became a better water steward using what had been regarded as "waste" in another way.

The firm captures waste methane from its process water treatment plant and burns this to generate electricity for running its brewery and offices, resulting in saving $60,000 in electricity expenses in 2009 (New Belgium, 2010). This closed-loop approach is one aspect of New Belgium's operation. Using this approach, the firm pursues a "cradle-to-cradle" route to eco-effectiveness by designing things intelligently so they are not useless at the end of their lives (McDonough & Braungart, 2002). Their products and their components can be used again and again with zero waste.

New Belgium offers a rich example of a values-driven enterprise that celebrates the community aspect of working for a common purpose in business (Yankelovich, 2006). With its high-involvement culture, New Belgium attracts employees that do not want to be hired from the neck down. Such employees become "highly empowered and resourceful operatives: HEROs for short" (Bernoff & Schadler, 2010, p. 10). In other words, such employees are ready for more of a Theory Y workplace (discussed in Chapter 8), where they can join a collaborative community according the highest value to people who look beyond their specific roles to make marginal contributions that boost the common purpose of the firm (Adler, Heckscher, & Prusak, 2011). At New Belgium, Don Rich and Marc Finer figured out that the cardboard dividers between bottles were not needed in 12-unit packages of Fat Tire beer. The triple-bottom-line savings were (a) more than $280,000 for the cost of the dividers, (b) 150 tons of paperboard for the dividers, and (c) eliminating the leading cause of downtime in packing the product—the dividers. In the Annual Summary of New Belgium's Sustainable Business Story, it was noted that "Marc and Don got at least a few high fives in the hallway for this one" (New Belgium, 2010, p. 1).

Today, jobs at any firm require increasingly higher levels of discretionary effort. Such effort takes an extra degree of initiative, and this depends on employee commitment. Before World War II, only 18% of jobs could be classified as high-discretion jobs (Yankelovich, 2006, p. 112). The rest were characterized by routine. By 1982, discretionary jobs accounted for 43% of jobs, and in 2000 they accounted for 62% of jobs. For jobs that cannot be outsourced or automated, many of the remaining jobs call for high levels of commitment. Values-driven firms such as New Belgium position themselves well for the future. In 2008, a *National Geographic* survey of more than 80% of U.S. workers polled agreed that it was important to work for a company or organization that makes the environment a top priority (Kaufield, Malhotra, & Higgins, 2009).

**Figure 10.2**    Tour de Fat

*Source:* http://www.newbelgium.com

## Branding New Belgium From the Inside Out

In *Cultural Strategy: Using Innovative Ideologies to Build Breakthrough Brands*, authors Douglas Holt and Douglas Cameron featured New Belgium as a case study in how brands are more of a phenomena of society and culture than they are of the mind's conception of tangible and emotional benefits (Holt & Cameron, 2010). Holt and Cameron served as consultants to the firm during the development of the firm's first (and probably last, according to the authors) television advertising campaign.

After spending an enormous time at the brewery, the pair of consultants noted that few of the brewery employees were active participants in the mountain outdoor adventure subculture, even though *Outdoor* magazine had included New Belgium as one of the best places to work in 2010 (Roberts, 2010). New Belgium's founders were both professionals (Jeff an electrical engineer and Kim a social worker) who had given up their careers to pursue an avocation they loved regardless of where it took them (Holt & Cameron, 2010). To Jeff and Kim, much fun came from experimenting with beer styles and improvising beer equipment. Very few of the staff were trained professionally for their jobs, and the founders liked it this way. For example, the COO joined the company as a graduate student in philosophy. In sum, the cultural assets of the company were (a) a company of creative amateurs, (b) pastoral organization of a family, and (c) the single-speed cruiser that represented human-scaled technology that had not been overpowered by other technology.

Kim Jordan, one of New Belgium's founders and current CEO, describes her experience with the firm in the following way:

> What could be greater than a job where you get to think about and talk about and co-create a brand with people. And for me, brand is absolutely everything we are. It's the people here. It's how we interact with one another. And then there's the other piece of that creativity, obviously—designing beers. Not only do I get to play with scissors and crayons, but I get to sit with a group of incredibly creative people and talk about what kind of beers do we want to make that please us and will please our customers. (Jordan, 2010)

Holt and Cameron steered New Belgium's advertising campaign toward presenting the essence of New Belgium—amateurs who brewed beer for the joy of doing it. Such amateurs worked in a place where new things happened most days and everyone was encouraged to create some fun during the day. For example, the firm has a mountain biking course on site and employees are encouraged to use it before and after work, as well as during lunchtime. By comparison, the target group for the advertising campaign were beer drinkers on the West Coast whose work lives were typical of many working in office cubicles where the technology of e-mail and voice mail had intensified the pace of the day and kept them from what they yearned to do—constructing the self through creative acts:

> Our creative challenge was to devise a pastoral call to arms, calling out to [trapped white collar workers] in Seattle, Silicon Valley, Santa Monica, San Diego, and points beyond, allowing them to dream a bit that they too might someday have a chance to give it all for their avocation rather than their 8-to-8 job. (Holt & Cameron, 2010, p. 237)

In the end, Holt and Cameron came up with a call-to-arms declaration of "Follow Your Folly: Ours Is Beer." In this way, the campaign proposed that the community of New Belgium were part of a movement of fellow travelers who were enjoying a quality of life very appealing to what David Brooks terms "Bourgeois Bohemians" (or Bobos—the knowledge workers of today's educated class) (Brooks, 2000). The two ads focused on an engineer who dropped out of the rat race to make single-speed bicycles by hand in a mountain town.

In this way, the downshifting to a higher quality of life became the crucial association for New Belgium beer. The ad campaign was run for 14 weeks as an experiment in five markets of the Western United States where sales results were later compared with five markets where the ad campaign did not run. Sales increased 37% where the ad campaign ran compared with 2% where it did not (Holt & Cameron, 2010, p. 242). In short, the campaign inspired by the organizational culture of New Belgium proved to be a major success as a result of customers who wanted an accessible way to connect with the cultural expression represented by the New Belgium brand.

In the end, New Belgium's story represents a firm push away from the materialistic, "more-growth" ideology of the DSP. "What is wealth?" New Belgium sustainability specialist Katie Wallace said. "Is it bling or is it being outdoors in a clear environment, organic food from farmers you know and having lower obesity in schools? We are not just here for more cash and bigger houses. We are here for quality of life" (Wallace, 2009).

## CONCLUSION

This chapter discussed some of the major issues related to the environmental imperative for societies. Because of an absorption with "little m" issues regarding more profitable marketing practices for the firm without regard to externalities, marketing scholars are just now beginning to give attention to the profoundly important topic of the environmental imperative.

Two schools in macromarketing have debated important questions related to the environmental imperative over the years. Those in the developmental school of macromarketing believed marketing systems could be changed. Opposing this view were scholars in the critical school who believed the culture of consumption must be radically altered if environmental degradation were to cease. A crucial question of this dialectic of opposing schools of thought is as follows: "Can societies shift to a less materialistic and less status-seeking foundation and accept less consumption?" This question persists today, although there are signs that the culture of consumption can be changed by none other than marketing itself—in the form of social marketing and the desirability of "going green."

In the course of business operations, decisions must be made that have ethical aspects. In fact, ethical issues dominate board meetings, but most of them come back to the notion of corporate culture (Mendonca & Miller, 2007). Although the firm might meet legal compliance on an issue, those in the firm must answer whether the courses of action being considered are honorable and whether they serve the public good. Ethics of citizenship and stewardship orient those in the firm to consider obligations to others and to society that go beyond self-interest. In this way, enlightened self-interest can be pursued.

Employees form the fabric from which the firm is woven. Engaged employees who bring their best to the enterprise and commit themselves to solve the problems entailed in "figuring out the future" are increasingly indispensable to success. Values-driven firms pursing a triple bottom line not only attract talented workers but also can become committed employees to the purpose of these firms. New Belgium Brewing Company's story highlights how branding can be done from the inside with employees defining the organizational culture and then the values of this culture infusing advertising for the brand.

## QUESTIONS

- Explain what is meant by "the Age of Transparency."
- Go to www.scorecard.org and find out how two places you have lived rate on air and water quality. Who are the major polluters for these places?
- Regarding marketing systems and the environment, do you tend to agree more with the developmental school of macromarketing or the critical school? Explain.
- To what extent do you believe companies, firms, and consumer/citizens can voluntarily downshift from a highly materialistic quantity-of-life approach to living to one focused more on quality of life?
- What would it take to see a noticeable shift?
- What aspects of New Belgium's story appeal to you? What aspects of working for New Belgium would you want to know more about before going to work there?
- What is the most notable learning you gained from reading New Belgium Brewing Company's Summary of Annual Summary of New Belgium Brewery's Sustainable Business Story in Appendix 1? In what areas would you say the firm could improve in the future?
- After reading New Belgium Brewing Company's Employee Benefits in Appendix 2, which benefits are the most distinctive to you?
- In your own life, if you really "followed your folly" as suggested by New Belgium's advertising, what would you do? What would it take to continue pursuing this as your long-term vocation or avocation?

## MAVERICKS WHO MADE IT

### The Chicken, the Egg and the Future

### Family Farms and Organic Farming

### Seeking sustainable supplies for a growing planet

#### By Tim Talevich (2011)

THREE YEARS AGO, Wilcox Farms, a family-run business that had raised cows, chickens and crops in rural Washington since 1909, was in big trouble. Competition, market fluctuations and a spate of other modern problems had pushed the farm to the brink of closure.

*(Continued)*

(Continued)

"It was bad-real bad," recalls Barrie Wilcox, 71, whose grandfather started the farm at the turn of the century. "On one Tuesday, we were told the bank would close us down the next Sunday."

Today, Wilcox Farms [i]s healthier than ever. The company, now run by fourth-generation family members, is one of the leading egg producers in the Pacific Northwest (and a supplier for Costco warehouses in the region). Oddly, it's operated more like the Wilcox Farms of early years. Feed comes from the farm itself or from a few local suppliers, chickens can run free, products are sold locally, and as much as possible is recycled—including tons of chicken manure for fertilizer.

The Wilcox Farms story is one of sustainability. Costco worked closely with the company to develop an organic egg program to supply Pacific Northwest warehouses, and is applying the same business model to nine other egg producers in regions throughout the country (see "It's all in the family" on page 25). The goal, explains Teresa Noonan, a Costco buyer who oversees the program, is to ensure a local, sustainable supply of high-quality organic eggs to meet a growing demand among Costco members.

But the story has much broader implications. If these sustainable production methods work for these farmers and their eggs, what about for other farm-raised foods? And can similar sustainable programs be established for limited commodities such as nuts, vanilla, coffee and fish, which come from developing corners of the world? Costco and other companies are looking for the answers to these questions as they face the challenges of shrinking global resources and growing demand.

## A New Business Model

Costco started working with the 10 chicken farms about three years ago as it sought reliable supplies to meet a growing demand for organic eggs, which are sold under the Kirkland Signature label. Most of the farms had long histories of producing conventional eggs. Organic eggs represented a new business opportunity—but also brought new challenges.

Reliable sources of organic feed were needed for the chickens. Accommodations had to be made to allow the birds to roam and forage outside their roosts—one of the stipulations for organic certification. Also, the producers had to meet a long list of other regulations for their farms to be certified as organic.

Some of the farms had chicken houses and pasture available for the new operations. At Wilcox Farms, for example, a dozen empty chicken houses were available on the property, along with adequate pasture areas next to the houses. In other cases, the farmers started from scratch to build new facilities. That's the case at L&R Farms in Pendergrass, Georgia, where four new buildings for organic operations are under construction.

Another issue concerned packaging. At Costco, conventional eggs have typically been shipped in steel racks that hold 240 cartons, each with 18 eggs. But a better system was needed to reduce truck trips from the farms to Costco's warehouses and make stocking the eggs easier and safer in the warehouses. The solution was new, stronger packaging made from recycled water bottles. Now, 300 cartons, each with 24 eggs, fit on a pallet. The farmers had to adapt their processing machinery to handle the new packaging.

For the farmers, this has all taken time, money and new thinking. But they believe there's a future in organic eggs—and it's the right thing to do.

"From a farmer's standpoint, our business is to look after the consumer and look after our animals," says David Lathem, whose father started L&R Farms in 1957. "Organic and cage free are an important part of our industry that's growing. I feel like it's a worthwhile investment because it will be a growing part of our business in the future and we need to be involved."

"People want to know where their food is coming from and what quality it is," adds Andy Wilcox, 39. He, his brother, Brent, 42, and their cousin Chris, 46, now run the farm. "The combination of wanting local food and knowing its quality is really driving the future for our family."

## Defining Sustainability

In its simplest interpretation, a sustainable program is one that ensures an adequate ongoing supply of a product. But it's not quite so simple.

The Sustainable Food Lab (*www. sustainablefoodlab.org*), an organization that promotes sustainable practices in the food industry, says these practices cover several areas, from the environment to social issues. With sustainable food programs, the soil's health is maintained and improved, nearby rivers and streams are kept clean and greenhouse gas emissions are minimized. Economically, the businesses involved must be able to thrive. And the people in every step of the process—farmers, workers, processors and others—must enjoy livable incomes.

Hal Hamilton, of the Sustainable Food Lab, says there's no universal label that certifies a product as "sustainable" as there is for, say, organic products. "In general we think of sustainability as a path rather than a destination," explains Hamilton. "So the products we buy from responsible production are becoming more and more sustainable over time."

For farmers, one indicator of sustainable practices is their carbon footprint. A convenient way of measuring this footprint is through an innovative software program called the Cool Farm Tool, developed at the University of Aberdeen in Scotland. With this program, farmers can enter details about their crops, fertilizers, soil composition, pesticides and so on, and the tool instantly calculates their greenhouse gas emissions.

The tool's goal, Hamilton says, is to reveal best farming practices for any farmer, from egg producers to wheat growers.

*(Continued)*

(Continued)

## CASE STUDY: VANILLA

Ugandan vanilla farmers have made great strides in improving their farming techniques and growing high-quality beans.

FOR MANY YEARS, Madagascar has been the leading producer of fine vanilla beans, supplying some 70 percent of the world's supply. But storms and political unrest have often disrupted production—leaving supplies unreliable, driving up prices for the vanilla extract and putting money in the hands of traders, not farmers.

Seeking another source of high-quality vanilla, Costco turned to Uganda, which has excellent conditions for growing vanilla beans. Through an ambitious program that involved Costco, UVAN, a Uganda-based vanilla bean processor, a Danish flavor company and the Danish government, the Ugandan vanilla Industry today has become a key player in the world's vanilla industry. And its success is based on sustainability.

The development program, initiated five years ago, focuses on educating the farmers about the best vanilla growing and harvesting methods, and on improvements in the communities. Vanilla bean farming wasn't new in Uganda: Farmers had tried it before, but the industry had never brought fair returns because of poor production practices and limited access to world markets.

One early step under the development program was to show the farmers the value of allowing the beans to mature on the vine. Traditionally, farmers picked the beans early for quick cash—and to avoid having them stolen. Beans that are allowed to mature have higher vanillin content—thus a richer vanilla extract and significantly higher value on the market, explains Kristen Hayes. Costco's buyer of vanilla products.

Also, UVAN established a curing station so the beans could be cured to high standards, consistently. This eliminated a system of middlemen and enables the farmers to get premium prices for high-quality beans.

But perhaps the program offering the biggest long-term impact is new village savings and loans that offer families access to loans.

Many of the families live in remote areas without any banks. The savings and loans offer them cash to diversify their businesses and increase their incomes. For example, Kristen says, a family could borrow money to buy chickens for eggs—which they could eat or sell—or seeds to grow and sell vegetables.

"In a country where financing is difficult to get, these small loans make an incredibly big difference for these families," says Kristen.

And Costco's role? The company is partnering with the farmers to create a reliable supply of high-quality vanilla. This partnership offers a steady market for the farmers and helps them plan for the future. The vanilla is blended and sold as Kirkland Signature™ Pure vanilla and is also used to flavor Kirkland Signature Vanilla Ice Cream. It all translates into huge savings for members: The price for a 16-ounce bottle of Kirkland Signature Pure Vanilla is below $7.

Today, about 9,500 Ugandan farmers are involved in the program.

"We are essentially partnering with these families to produce the best vanilla in the world," sums up Kristen. "It's a system where everybody wins. That's sustainability."—TT

"Farming systems around the world are using the same greenhouse gas calculator to estimate their current greenhouse footprint and identify those practices that would be the most likely to reduce the footprint in a pragmatic way," he says.

All 10 farms supplying Costco's organic eggs used the Cool Farm Tool during the past year to examine their carbon footprint and develop more environmentally friendly procedures. In late June, the group convened near Portland, Oregon, to share findings and swap ideas on improvements. Discussion ranged from smarter ways of transporting feed to their farms to potential uses of chicken manure for biochar, a type of charcoal that might be profitable as a soil amendment.

All these topics might offer insights for other farmers, Hamilton says.

"Some of the things about transport, feed production, the handling of manure, different places where energy consumption could be reduced—those are all interesting and useful for other kinds of producers," says Hamilton. "For example, some of the feed sources for chickens are similar to feed sources for dairy cows. So there are some lessons that can be shared."

## Looking Beyond Chickens and Eggs

If the push for sustainability works for eggs, what about other foods? That's an increasingly critical question, says Sheri Flies, an assistant general merchandising manager in Costco's corporate food department. A growing demand for food from emerging countries such as China and India, shrinking resources, political instability and other factors make it more important than ever to find ways for the Earth and its farmers to provide for its habitants, perpetually.

Many foods, known as limited-resource commodities, are part of our daily diets. They include all kinds of nuts, coffee, organic milk, fish and shrimp, vanilla, spices, cocoa, olive oil and maple syrup, and they are grown or produced everywhere from Africa to Central America to Southeast Asia.

"Everything is a limited resource commodity or relies upon a limited resource for its production," says Sheri. "Demand is out-stripping current supply, and as Costco continues to grow, we need to make sure that we are sourcing our products in a responsible way so that our members continue to receive high-quality products and everyone in the supply chain receives a fair return."

*(Continued)*

(Continued)

This means going to the source to understand the process from the beginning to the end, developing long-term partnerships with the people in the supply chain and helping to improve the yields and quality, Sheri says. Costco can do all of this most directly with the products it creates under its Kirkland Signature label.

## IT'S ALL IN THE FAMILY

COSTCO HAS ESTABLISHED regional organic egg programs with egg producers around the country who supply their local Costco warehouses with organic eggs. Many of those producers are third- or fourth-generation farmers who have adapted their operations to specialize in organic, cage-free chickens.

Here's the list of suppliers

**Utah:** Oakdell Egg Farms, Lewiston, Utah (www.oakdell.com). The Woodward and Wright families have operated this farm since 1908, when Cecil and Bertha Woodward received 10 chickens as a wedding gift.

**Bay Area:** Den Dulk Poultry Farms (www.dendulkpoultry.com) and NuCal Foods (www.nucalfoods.com), both in Ripon, California. The Jenkins family has operated Den Dulk Poultry Farms for more than 50 years. NuCal Foods, led by the Gemperle family, is an agricultural cooperative of family-owned farms.

**San Diego:** Chino Valley Ranchers, Arcadia, California (www.chinovalleyranchers.com). The Nichols family is the fourth generation to operate the farm, which has been in business since 1953.

**Texas:** Soncrest Egg Co., Gonzales, Texas. The Baker family is a third-generation husband, wife and daughter team. Many employees on the farm have been there for 20 years.

**Northeast:** Pete and Gerry's Organic eggs, Monroe, New Hampshire (www.peteandgerrys.com). Current operators include Jesse Laflamme and Peter Stanton and others who are the extended family of farm founder Robert Ward. The farm began in the early 1900s and now partners with some 20 small family farms to provide sustainably produced organic eggs.

**Midwest:** Herbruck's Poultry Ranch, Saranac, Michigan (www.goodeggproject.org), and Nature Pure LLC, Raymond, Ohio. The Herbruck family established their farm in 1958. Nature Pure operated by the Lausecker family, which has owned the farm for 23 years.

**Southeast:** L&R Farms, Pendergrass, Georgia (www.landrfarmsinc.com). The Lathem family founded the farm in 1957 with 25,000 laying hens. They are adding an organic program to their operations.—*TT*

"The issue of sustainability is something we think about for every Kirkland Signature item: How can we make it better for the member, how can we make it better for the people or animals that produce it and how can we make it better for the environment?" Sheri says. "Our dream is that our Kirkland Signature guarantee will become synonymous not only with quality and value but with sustainability."

To that end, Costco has supported sustainable programs in several areas, working either directly with producers or in cooperation with other organizations. This ranges from working with farmers in Guatemala to grow green beans and sugar snap peas to helping develop a robust vanilla farming industry in Uganda (see "Case study: vanilla").

At Wilcox Farms, adopting sustainable farming practices is a matter of economics—and more. The rolling farmland lies in the shadow of majestic Mount Rainier, whose melting snows feed the Nisqually River, which winds through the farm. A healthy salmon run populates the river. The family sees itself not as owners of the picturesque land, but as caretakers.

"From my generation's standpoint, we have a legacy," says Chris Wilcox. "We are not going to be the generation that sells the farm. We are going to pass it on to the next generation and then the next. This is our legacy."

*Source: The Costco Connection* (August, 2011).

## Questions

- What consumer phenomenon is driving the growth of locally grown, organic food these days?
- What does it mean to have a sustainable program as a farmer?
- How is a retailer like Costco involved in developing sustainable food production in the United States? In overseas locations?
- What are examples of collaboration evident in the sustainable food production movement?

# Appendix 1

## Annual Summary of New Belgium Brewery's Sustainable Business Story

### Greetings, friends!

Welcome to the Annual Summary of New Belgium's Sustainable Business Story. We are honored that you are taking a moment to familiarize yourself with our heart-felt approach to business at this Colorado-based brewery. This report highlights the content of our larger report available online at www.newbelgium.com/sustainability and strives to communicate our commitment to honoring the triple bottom line planet, people and profit.

At New Belgium, we both follow and lead in a global movement to create values driven commerce which preserves our ability to flourish as human beings. This is truly a collaborative process. If you have feedback or suggestions, we welcome you to contribute to our effort by dropping us a line at sustainability@newbelgium.com.

At New Belgium to be environmental stewards we believe we need to:
Lovingly care for the planet that sustains us.

Honor natural resources by closing the loops between waste and input.

Minimize the environmental impact of shipping our beer.

Reduce our dependence on coal-fired electricity.

Protect our precious Rooky Mountain water resources.

Support innovative technology.

Focus our efforts on conservation and efficiency.

Advocate for policies which enable restorative practices.

Share our wealth with non-profits working to protect natural resources.

Model joyful environmentalism through our commitment to relationships, continuous improvement, and the camaraderie and cheer of best.

Remember that if it's not fun, it's not sustainable!

### High Involvement Culture

New Belgium is regularly approached by other businesses, students, and curious beer drinkers who want to know how we have implemented sustainability initiatives. Though solar panels and recycling programs are exciting, our company culture is the most important and transferrable tool we've employed to drive sustainability.

While High Involvement Culture is a foundation for our sustainability efforts, its purpose is much larger in scope. The value of consciously creating culture was recognized early on at New Belgium which allowed us to become a living example of research that shows high performing companies push decision making and accountability throughout the organization. When you share the risks and rewards of ownership, people have a passion for what they do and love to come to work.

A high involvement culture is conductive to a triple bottom line approach to business. Coworkers are actively participating in the reducing waste, increasing efficiency, all while having fun and feeling empowered.

## Triple Bottom Line + High Involvement Culture =

In 2009, coworkers Don Rich and Marc Finer implemented an idea of theirs to remove the cardboard dividers in our 12 packs. The results to the triple bottom line were outstanding! Check out these annual savings:

- $280.000 + for the cost of dividers.
- 150 tons of divider material (paperboard).
- Boost in efficiency by eliminating one of the leading causes of downtime during 12-pack production in packaging.

Marc & Don got at least a few high fives in the hallway for this one.

Every year, we donate to hundreds of non-profits in every state we sell beer. Find the list and application at newbelgium.com/Community/local-grants.

Over 30 million people in the Western United States depend on the Colorado River for food, water and power. In fact, nearly 40 percent of the water we drink here in Fort Collins comes from the it. Currently, numerous diversions siphon water from the river's headwaters making it possible to inhabit this highly populated, arid region of Colorado.

From the majestic Rocky Mountain National Park where the headwaters originate, the Colorado River begins a journey that it hasn't finished in almost 20 years. What was once a massive water rich wildlife estuary where the river should meet the Sea of Cortez, is now an expansive swath of parched and lifeless desert devastated by over-allocation and unsustainable development.

Working to address the threats that the Colorado River currently faces, a coalition of seven sustainably-driven corporations and foundations has united to raise funding and awareness. Save the Colorado, initiated by New Belgium Brewing and the Clean Water Fund, will donate over $500K to environmental non-profits in the Colorado River basin working to protect, restore and conserve.

You can help support the stewardship, donate funds, and better understand the flight of this threatened river at www.savethecolorado.org.

## DID YOU KNOW?

After working here for one year, our coworkers are gifted a custom New Belgium cruiser bicycle!

New Belgium is employee owned.

New Belgium started in our founders' basement in 1991.

All interior wood in our packaging hall is beetle kill pine.

Alternatively Empowered means making business decisions based on minimizing environmental impact, encouraging the growth of our employee owners, and being a socially responsible contributor to our community. It's rewarding, challenging, and educational. It's what makes us New Belgium.

## Renewable and Distributed Systems Integration (Department of Energy Grant)

When we collaborate with other talented organizations and institutions in our community, we find we can reach heights impossible to achieve on our own.

New Belgium is partnering with the City of Fort Collins, Colorado State University and other energy focused companies in a grant from the Department of Energy (DOE) to demonstrate 20–30 percent peak electric load reduction. The collaborative project will be the first phase of implementing FortZED, a long term vision for a zero energy district in downtown Fort Collins. Learn more at www.fortzed.com.

Using the grant funds, we commissioned a 200 KW photovoltaic array on top of our Packaging Hall in January 2010. It is the largest privately owned array in Colorado to date, and will produce almost 264,000 kWh each year, contributing over 3% of our total electricity. Our current effort under this project is the implementation of Smart Grid technology. Keep an eye on our website for updates!

## Closing a Loop: Power From Waste Water

14% of New Belgium's electricity comes from our own waste! At our on-site Process Water Treatment Plant, New Belgium uses microbec to clean all of our production wastewater through a series of anaerobic (without air) and aerobic (with air) basins. A byproduct of this process, methane gas, is harvested and piped back to the brewery, where it powers a 292kW combined heat and power (CHP or co-gen) engine. A beautiful example of closed-loop system!

Every year, we donate to hundreds of non-profits in every state we sell beer. Find the list and application at www.newbelgium.com/local grants

## RECENT ACCOMPLISHMENTS

Energy

- Installed a 200 kWh photovoltsia solar energy above the Packaging Hall that will replace almost 264,000 kWh of cool-powered electricity each year.
- 39 hybrid vehicles in our company fleet 2 company bicycles for Beer Rangers.
- Revamped server room to use virtualization technology. Consolidated renewal physical servers into one, saving energy.

- Optimized operation of our CHP engine that burns waste biogas from our Process Water Treatment Plant. In 2009 we generated 857,000 KWH from this waste source & saved almost $80,000 in electricity costs.

### Waste

- Achieved our highest landfill diversion rate to date: 99.99%
- Removed cardboard dividers from our 12 packs. Saving cardboard and money.
- Removed 14 bottled water stations reducing energy and transportation for water.
- Made process improvements to our work cooler and whirlpool that save 2.9 ml of work lost per brew, saving water, energy and raw materials.
- Implemented electronic billing—significantly reducing paper use in accounting.
- Installed a new recycling center in our community kitchen, removing more compost and recyclables from the landfill bin.

### Sustainable Agriculture

- Purchased the first crop of Colorado Organic Hope.

### Philanthropy

- Donated 1% of our revenue to environmental non-profits. Member of 1% For The Planet.

### Culture

- Voted "Best Place to Work" by Outside Magazine in 2008 and #2 in 2009.
- Included in Wall Street Journal's Best Small Workplaces in 2008.
- Crested a comprehensive, multi-faceted INreach program to further engage coworkers in sustainability efforts at home and at work.

### Carbon Accounting

- [2008] Measured & published the carbon footprint of a 6-pack of Fat Tire. The study can be found at newbelgium.com/sustainability.
- [2009] Measured corporate GHG emissions following GHG Protocol.
- [2010] Piloted the WRI/WBCSD draft protocol for Scope 3 and Lifecycle emissions.

### Bike Advocacy

- Named one of only two platinum-level Bicycle Friendly Business by the League of American Bicyclists.
- As of 2009 our Tour de Fat festival has raised over $125 million for bike-related non-profits.

### Purchasing

- Implementing Sustainable Purchasing Guidelines, quarrying all significant vendors about their environmental and social practices.
- Worked with paperboard supplier to double the recycled content in our 12 packs and 24 packs (from 44% to 88% recycled content.) The rest of our cardboard packaging contains 100% recycled content.
- Worked with vendors to reduce packaging on point of sale items.

*Source:* New Belgium Brewing Company.

# Appendix 2

# New Belgium Brewing Company's Employee Benefits

Employee Perks

## What You Get

New Belgium offers co-workers a Total Benefits package, that includes stock ownership in an ESOP, 401k, excellent health benefits, an outstanding work environment and career development opportunities. Through these comprehensive offerings, every individual has the chance to achieve personal growth as well as financial and professional growth.

## Skinny Dipping Season

One of the cornerstones of New Belgium's benefits program is comprehensive, affordable health care coverage. We offer medical insurance with no copay for yearly wellness visits, dental, prescription drug, and vision coverage. Also available are two Flex plans you contribute to with pretaxed dollars; a Medical flex program and a Dependent Care program for those co-workers with DayCare needs. With wellness playing an ever increasing role in ou[r] work/life balance, New Belgium offers it's co-workers the use of four free memberships to the Fort Collins Athletic Club or a Corporate discount to any 24 Hr Fitness Club nationwide. We also sponsor Yoga classes on site and discounted massages once a month with a free massage during your Anniversary month.

## Derailleur

New Belgium provides co-workers and their families some protection from the unexpected. We offer health coverage long term disability benefits and basic life insurance. Individuals can also opt to participate in voluntary options, such as short term disability insurance, AFLAC or voluntary life and accidental death and dismemberment insurance. New Belgium also offers their co-workers access to an Employee Assistance Program (EAP) which gives each co-worker confidential access to legal advice and balancing work/life issues.

## Double Track

New Belgium knows it can be challenging to balance commitments and priorities so we offer our co-workers generous Paid Time Off (PTO). PTO starts accruing from your first work day as a percentage of hours worked. For example, after working a year at new Belgium a full-time co-worker will accrue over 13 days of PTO to be used for vacations, sick days, well days, etc. Your accrual rate rises from there! We also have 10 paid holidays annually as well as adoption assistance and a paid sabbatical program.

## Blere de Mars Season

New Belgium encourages our co-workers to save for the future. The company's 401k match is 100% of the first 3% a co-worker contributes and 50% of the next 4th and 5th percent. Company contributions, as well as co-worker contributions, are immediately 100 percent vested. After 12 months of employment and 1000 hours worked, co-workers become eligible to participate in New Belgium's Employees Stock Ownership Program (ESOP).

## Times 'o Whimsy

New Belgium believes that having fun and enjoying life is as important as working hard. That is why we give our co-workers a free, limited release Fat Tire bike for their First Anniversary with New Belgium. We sponsor and participate in numerous extracurricular team sports such as volleyball, Rolle Bolle, basketball, softball, soccer, bicycle races, a Cyclocross course on site and individual runner's endurance races. We hold annual activities including barbeques, Compass breakfasts. Tour de Fat festivals, Employee Art Shows. Bowling nights and St. Arnold's Day (patron saint of beer) celebrations. We also celebrate each month's employee Birthdays and Anniversaries by catering a free lunch. New Belgium also encourages our co-workers to give back to the community by reimbursing them one hour of PTO (paid time off) for every two hours of volunteer work they contribute.

## The Gravy

All New Belgium co-workers receive a discount on merchandise in our retail (Liquid) centers, as well as discounts on all our beers. Co-workers also receive a 12-pack of Employee beer a week and an opportunity to enjoy one (1) shift beer after clocking out after their shift. Co-workers have access to a complete kitchen with free condiments, coffee, tea, milk, fruit infused seltzer water and newspapers, along with a Recycling Center. Compost Handling and shower facilities. Because of New Belgium's relationship with like-minded companies, co-workers have access to our vendor's Pro-deals. To help our co-workers "Follow Their Folly": our dress code is casual!

## High Involvement Culture

We believe that our dedication to high involvement culture and a loving, high performing workforce sets us apart. We believe that the collective is stronger than the individual and that informed co-workers will make responsible decisions. We practice open book management, which also includes access to financials and we facilitate a monthly meeting where co-workers are informed on the latest and greatest New Belgium news. We also meet annually with all co-workers to gather input and make decisions about the upcoming year's business plan. This opportunity for input and involvement helps align individual performance to New Belgium performance. We believe in community social and environmental responsibility and dedication to modeling our care values and beliefs.

## Beer Wrangling

Our Beer Rangers (Sales Force) will receive Relocation Assistance when needed support with establishing a home office styled out with the latest and greatest New Belgium attire, the use of a hybrid company car and a company credit card for job related expenses and entertainment.

*Source:* New Belgium Brewing Company.

## REFERENCES

Adler, P., Heckscher, C., & Prusak, L. (2011, July–August). Building a collaborative enterprise. *Harvard Business Review,* pp. 95–101.

American Marketing Association (AMA). (2011). Statement of ethics. Retrieved from http://www .marketingpower.com

Anderson, R. C. (2009). *Confessions of a radical industrialist: Profits, people, purpose—doing business by respecting the earth.* New York, NY: St. Martin's Press.

Associated Press. (2011). Food prices hit 20-year high in February, U.N. says. *Denverpost.com.* Retrieved from http://www.denverpost.com/business/ci_17535513

Audebrand, L. K. (2010). Sustainability in strategic management education: The quest for new root metaphors. *Academy of Management Learning & Business, 9*(5), 413–428.

Bernoff, J., & Schadler, T. (2010). *Empowered: Unleash your employees, energize your customers and transform your business.* Boston, MA: Harvard Business School Press.

Bielak, D., Bonini, S.M.J., & Oppenheim, J.M. (2007, October). CEOs on strategy and social issues. *The McKinsey Quarterly,* 1–8.

Bradsher, K., & Barboza, D. (2006, June 6). Pollution from Chinese coal casts a global shadow. *The New York Times.* Retrieved from http://www.nytimes.com

Brooks, D. (2000). *Bobos in paradise: The new upper class and how they got there.* New York, NY: Simon & Schuster Paperbacks.

Choi, D. Y., & Gray, E. R. (2011). *Values-centered entrepreneurs and their companies.* New York, NY: Routledge.

Diamond, J. (2005). *Collapse: How societies choose to fail or succeed.* New York, NY: Penguin Books.

Dow Jones. (2011). Dow Jones Sustainability Index. Retrieved from http://www.sustainability-index. com/

Ferrell, O. C., Gonzalez-Padron, T. L., Hult, T. M., & Maignan, I. (2010). From market orientation to stakeholder orientation. *Journal of Public Policy & Marketing, 29*(1), 93–96.

Gabrielli, J. S. (2009, March). The greening of Petrobras. *Harvard Business Review,* pp. 43–47.

Gall, N. (2011, June 21). Brazil's risky energy play. *Brazil in Focus.* Retrieved from http://www .brazilinfocus.com

Ger, G. (1997). Human development and humane consumption: Well-being beyond the "good life." *Journal of Public Policy & Marketing, 16(1),* 110–125.

Ger, G., & Belk, R. W. (1996). Cross-cultural differences in materialism. *Journal of Economic Psychology, 17*(1), 55–77.

Gilding, P. (2011). *The great disruption: Why the climate crisis will bring on the end of shopping and the birth of a new world.* New York, NY: Bloomsbury Press.

Green Business Network. (2011). Green Business Network. Retrieved from http://greenbusiness network.org/

Hackley, C. (2009). *Marketing: A critical introduction.* Thousand Oaks, CA: Sage.

Haugh, H. M., & Talwar, A. (2010). How do corporations embed sustainability across the organization? *Academy of Management Learning & Education, 9*(3), 384–396.

Holt, D., & Cameron, D. (2010). *Cultural strategy: Using innovative ideologies to build breakthrough brands.* Oxford, UK: Oxford University Press.

Kahn, J., & Yardley, J. (2007, August 26). As China roars, pollution reaches deadly extremes. *The New York Times.* Retrieved from http://www.nytimes.com

Kanter, R. M. (2009). *Supercorp: How vanguard companies create innovation, profits, growth and social good.* New York, NY: Crown Business.

Kaufield, R., Malhotra, A., & Higgins, S. (2009, December 21). Green is a strategy. *strategy + business.* Retrieved from http://www.strategy-business.com

Kilbourne, W., McDonagh, P., & Prothero, A. (1997, Spring). Sustainable consumption and the quality of life: A macromarketing challenge to the dominant social paradigm. *Journal of Macromarketing,* pp. 4–24.

Kotler, P. (2011a, April 30). How I do it. *Marketing News,* p. 34.

Kotler, P. (2011b). Reinventing marketing to manage the environmental imperative. *Journal of Marketing, 75,* 132–135.

Jordan, K. (2007). Letter from the CEO. New Belgium Brewing Company 2007 Sustainability Report. Retrieved from http://www.newbelgium.com

Jordan, K. (2010). Our joy ride – Kim (video). Retrieved from http://www.newbelgium.com/culture/jobs .aspx

Laczniak, G., & Murphy, P. (2006). Normative perspectives for ethical and socially responsible marketing. *Journal of Macromarketing, 26*(2), 154–177.

Mason, R. (2011, August 2). Petrobras will soon overtake Exxon as world's biggest listed oil company. *The Telegraph.* Retrieved from http://www.telegraph.co.uk/finance/newsbysector/energy/oilandgas/ 8675640/Petrobras-will-soon-overtake-Exxon-as-worlds-biggest-listed-oil-company.html

McDonough, W., & Braungart, M. (2002). *Cradle to cradle: Remaking the way we make things.* New York, NY: North Point Press.

McLean, B., & Elkind, P. (2004). *The smartest guys in the room: The amazing rise and scandalous fall of Enron.* New York, NY: Portfolio Trade.

Mendonca, L. T., & Miller, M. (2007). Exploring business's social contract: An interview with Daniel Yankelovich, *The McKinsey Quarterly.* Retrieved from http://www.mckinseyquarterly.com

Meyer, C., & Kirby, J. (2010, April). Leadership in the age of transparency. *Harvard Business Review,* pp. 38–46.

Mish, J., & Scammon, D. L. (2010). Principle-based stakeholder marketing: Insights from private triple-bottom-line firms. *Journal of Public Policy & Marketing, 29*(1), 12–26.

Mittelstaedt, J., & Kilbourne, W. (2009). Macromarketing perspectives on sustainable consumption. *Proceedings from Sustainable Consumption and Production: Framework for action. Conference of the Sustainable Consumption Research Exchange (SCORE!) Network* (pp. 17–26). Brussels, Belgium.

Moses, S. (2011). New Belgium Brewery: If it's not fun, it's not sustainable. *Commute by Bike.* Retrieved from http://www.commutebybike.com/2011/07/15/new-belgium-brewery-if-its-not-fun-its-not -sustainable/

New Belgium. (2007). 2007 Sustainability Report: New Belgium Brewing Company. Retrieved from http://www.newbelgium.com

New Belgium. (2010). Annual Summary of New Belgium's Sustainable Business Story. Retrieved from http://www.newbelgium.com

Nordhaus, T., & Shellenberger, M. (2007). *Breakthrough: From the death of environmentalism to the politics of possibility.* Boston, MA: Houghton Mifflin.

NRDC. (2011). Natural Resources Defense Council. Retrieved from http://www.nrdc.org

OffshoreEnergyToday.com. (2011, March 21). Petrobras first to use FPSO in U.S. Gulf of Mexico. *Offshore EnergyToday.com.* Retrieved from http://www.offshoreenergytoday.com

Orgolini, J. (2007). Letter from the sustainability director. New Belgium Brewing Company 2007 Sustainability Report. Retrieved from http://www.newbelgium.com

Petrobras. (2011). About us/profile. Retrieved from http://www.petrobras.com/en/about-us/profile/

Prothero, A., & Fitchett, J. A. (2000). Greening capitalism: Opportunities for a green community. *Journal of Macromarketing, 20*(1), 46–55.

Prothero, A., McDonagh, P., & Dobscha, S. (2010). Is green the new black? Reflections on a green commodity discourse. *Journal of Macromarketing, 30*(2), 147–159.

Roberts, M. (2010). Outdoor's 2010 best places to work. Retrieved from http://www.outsidetelevision.com/shows/outside-today/new-belgium-brewing

Sartain, L., & Schumann, M. (2006). *Brand from the inside: Eight essentials to emotionally connect your employees to your business.* San Francisco, CA: Jossey-Bass.

Sawyerr, O., McGee, J., & Peterson, M. (2003). Perceived uncertainty and firm performance in SMEs: The role of personal networking activities. *International Small Business Journal, 21*(3), 269–290.

Smith, N. C., Drumwright, M. E., & Gentile, M. C. (2010, Spring). The new marketing myopia. *Journal of Public Policy & Marketing, 29*(1), 4–11.

Stern, S. (2010, April 4). Outsider in a hurry to shake up Unilever. *Financial Times.* Retrieved from http://www.ft.com

SustainLane.com. (n.d.). Home Page. Retrieved from http://www.sustainlane.com/

Talevich, T. (2011). The Chicken, the egg and the future. *The Costco Connection, 26*(8), 22–25.

Townsend, C. R. (2008). *Ecological applications: Towards a sustainable world.* Oxford, UK: Blackwell.

van Schagen, S. (2011, April). Driving change: Family-owned collision repair shop going green. *The Costco Connection*, p. 66.

Wallace, K. (2009, April 9). Presentation at Sustainable Business Practices Forum. University of Wyoming.

WCED. (1987). *Our common future.* UN Commission on Environment and Development. Retrieved from http://www.un-documents.net/ocf-02.htm#I

Weaver-Zercher, V. (2010, January). The afterlife of trash. *Sojourners*, pp. 30–32.

Wee, H. (2002, April 11). Corporate ethics: Right makes might. *BusinessWeek.* Retrieved from http://www.businessweek.com

Yankelovich, D. (2006). *Profit with honor: The next stage of market capitalism.* New Haven, CT: Yale University Press.

## CHAPTER 11

# Environmentally Oriented Business

# USING BUSINESS TO BENEFIT THE ENVIRONMENT—IS IT POSSIBLE?

## "Dirtbag" Yvon Chouinard's Patagonia

When told he could pursue an initial public offering (IPO) to sell shares in his privately owned company, Yvon Chouinard (pronounced "shun ARD"), owner of Patagonia (a designer, marketer, and distributor of high-performance outdoor wear based in Ventura, California), shook his head. "That would be the end of everything I've wanted to do," Chouinard said. "It would destroy everything that I believe in" (Casey, 2007, para. 39).

According to Chouinard's environmentalist friend Tom Brokaw (former NBC Nightly News anchor), Chouinard uses more colorful language to explain his aversion to cashing in his company: "He (Chouinard) says, 'I don't want a Wall Street greaseball running my company,'" Brokaw said. "That is a direct quote" (Casey, 2007, para. 40).

Chouinard is a successful entrepreneur whose story inspires his devoted contrarian employees (where 900 apply for every job opening) (Casey, 2007). Today, leaders of other businesses, such as Wal-Mart, seek Chouinard's counsel in seeking solutions to what Chouinard describes as the environmental crisis.

Chouinard readily expresses irreverence for traditional business and a reverence for nature. In the introduction to his book *Let My People Go Surfing: The Education of a Reluctant Businessman* (2005), Chouinard begins with brutal honesty:

> I've been a businessman for almost fifty years. It's as difficult for me to say those words as it is for someone to admit being an alcoholic or a lawyer. I've never respected the profession. It's business that has to take the majority of the blame for being the enemy of nature, for destroying native cultures, for taking from the poor and giving to the rich, and for poisoning the earth with the effluent from its factories.
>
> Yet business can produce food, cure disease, control population, employ people, and generally enrich our lives. And it can do these good things and make a profit without losing its soul. (p. 3)

Chouinard describes Patagonia (www.patagonia.com) as an experiment to challenge conventional wisdom and present a new style of responsible business (Chouinard, 2005, p. 5). In this way, Chouinard intends to present an alternative to the endless growth implied by capitalism that deserves the blame for the destruction of nature. He declares that he and his employees have the means and the will to prove that doing the right thing leads to a good and profitable business.

Patagonia is the second business Chouinard started. The first, Chouinard Equipment Company, emerged from his passion for mountaineering and rock climbing. He bought a coal forge for his parent's garage in Burbank, California, and taught himself how to do blacksmithing in the early 1960s. He sold specially made steel pitons (three-inch strips of steel with a hole for threading rope or clipping in a carabiner) that climbers used to pound into cracks in the rock for securing themselves from falling. Later, he made chocks, which are quarter-sized hexagonal steel-nuts that could be wedged in a crack in the rock for anchoring a climbing rope. In this way, Chouinard began manufacturing gear for the outdoors.

Selling pitons and chocks out of the back of his car to other climbers at $1.50 each did not leave much cash on which to live. But at the time, climbing the 3,000-foot faces of granite in California's Yosemite National Park was Chouinard's true love. Dumpster diving or living for weeks on cat food was part of what Chouinard describes as "the dirtbag way— living as close to the wild as possible with as little as possible" (Casey, 2007, para. 13).

Chouinard managed to keep climbing even after being drafted in the U.S. Army in the mid-1960s and being sent to South Korea for two years. When he returned to the United States, he made several big-wall ascents that marked him as one of the best rock climbers of his day (Casey, 2007). Over the years, his business changed but existed primarily to allow him and his wife, Malinda, to pursue their wilderness adventures, such as climbing El Capitan in Yosemite, surfing Baja in Mexico, or skiing in the Tetons.

In 1972, they moved into clothing by launching Patagonia. Then, they sold rugby shirts, corduroy knickers, and boiled-wool mittens. The Chouinards threw themselves into their work, but were clear that they would pursue business on their terms: (a) making products of high quality manufactured in the most responsible way and (b) allowing employees enough flexibility to enjoy the outdoors or be at home when their children became ill. They intended to keep Patagonia private and say no to anything that might compromise their values. They believed that if they focused on doing things right (just as in rock climbing), that profits would come (just as making the summit would in rock climbing). They were right.

In 1985, Patagonia began giving 10% of its annual profits to environmental groups (Reinhardt, Casadesus-Mananell, & Freier, 2004, p. 18). Patagonia's catalog attracted many because of its dramatic photography of rock climbers, surfers, kayakers, or trail runners in the majesty of nature, as well as its off-beat text celebrating the "dirtbag way" of thriving in the wilderness with very little material support. At this time, there was also a rise of more affluent city-workers craving for a challenge in the wild (Holt & Cameron, 2010). This attractive customer segment embraced the idea of vicariously living a life of adventure in rugged and exotic locales like those featured in Patagonia's catalog. Happily for Patagonia, these customers were willing to pay 25% more for outdoor gear that reinforced their tie to sophisticated adventure.

The year 1991 proved to be a crucial one for the firm. An economic recession pinched Patagonia's drive for growth and resulted in the laying off of 20% of its workforce (Reinhardt et al., 2004). To stabilize the firm, previous CEO Kris McDivitt Tompkins, described in Chouinard's book as a beach girl, returned to serve as CEO after a three-year retirement (Chouinard, 2005, p. 42). Such tumult led Chouinard to go deeper with the real reason for the firm's existence—healing the environment. Patagonia began looking at what it could control with regard to its own role in environmental degradation. It commissioned its first life-cycle review of the major fibers used in its apparel. This eventually led to pioneering sustainable textiles, such as organic cotton and polar fleece jackets made from recycled plastic bottles (Holt & Cameron, 2010, p. 118). The firm also stepped up its funding of environmental groups, and it began to share what it was learning about making the firm sustainable. In this way, Patagonia became more intentional about being a role model for other companies so that other firms would adopt more environmentally friendly ways.

In Patagonia's Fall 1991 catalog, Chouinard published an essay titled "Reality Check" in which he admitted that everything Patagonia makes pollutes. As a result, Patagonia alerted its retail distributors that it intended to pursue a no-growth strategy. This was later amended to a slow-growth strategy as Chouinard and his executive team sought ways to resolve the tension between their business and Patagonia's commitment to the environment.

Today, Patagonia is organized around environmental activism (Holt & Cameron, 2010). In 1996, the firm articulated its statement of purpose that sets the firm on a course to "build the best product, do no unnecessary harm, use business to inspire and implement solutions to the environmental crisis" (Patagonia, 2011).

## Your Thoughts?

- What is a dirtbag?
- What do linkages with the dirtbag subculture do for the branding of Patagonia?
- Regarding the critical school and the developmental school of macromarketing presented in the previous chapter, how would you classify Yvon Chouinard?
- How important are Patagonia's customers to its influence on businesses today?
- What do you think of Patagonia's statement of purpose?

## CHAPTER OVERVIEW AND LEARNING OBJECTIVES

Through a presentation of exemplars, this chapter will showcase some of today's most important topics in environmentally oriented business. Among these are (a) the background for environmentally oriented business, and (b) the roles of government, big business, and entrepreneurial ventures in greening the marketplace. The Patagonia story suggests how a firm might emphasize environmental activism in its endeavors. Firms such as Patagonia are on a mission to make money, serve humanity, and help the planet (Lovins, 2010). These are triple-bottom-line firms who meaningfully integrate people, planet, and profits into their marketing and operations.

Conservation is a foundational concept of environmental stewardship, which is embraced by companies such as outdoor retailer REI, Inc. Today, conservation of the atmosphere's ability to regulate our climate is emerging as an important issue. National governments continue to debate what can be done while the provincial government of British Columbia has enacted a carbon tax in order to reduce greenhouse gas emissions that are harmful of the atmosphere. In 2005, Wal-Mart changed course and declared itself as pursuing an environmental orientation. By 2009, Wal-Mart's CEO had appeared twice before Congressional committees asking for limits on greenhouse gas emissions.

Finally, this chapter will look at Neiman Enterprises CEO Jim Neiman, who explains what it took to transform his business into one that is more environmentally oriented. This forest-products company based in Northeast Wyoming took 10 years to obtain certification from the Sustainable Forest Institute because Neiman wanted his employees to understand the value of adopting sustainable business practices rather than have them imposed on them by his decision. Neiman will be featured as a Maverick Who Made It.

After this chapter, you should be able to answer the following questions:

- Why is entrepreneurship controversial to those of macromarketing's critical school?
- What does it mean to become an environmentally oriented business?
- How important is the concept of conservation to environmental stewardship?
- What are the six natural resource systems the Environmental Protection Agency (EPA) has proposed to be the focus of environmental stewardship?
- How do common goods differ from public goods?
- Is the atmosphere surrounding our planet a public good or a common good?
- If the natural infrastructure that supports civilization becomes degraded and incapable of reliably performing services to humans, can national governments be expected to work together to repair this natural infrastructure?
- What role is the U.S. government now taking to reduce greenhouse gas emissions?
- What other actors are taking action to reduce greenhouse gas emissions?
- How can established firms become more environmentally oriented?

## PATAGONIA AND THE ENVIRONMENT

### Patagonia and Philanthropy

The third part of Patagonia's mission statement is to "use business to inspire and implement solutions to the environmental crisis" (Patagonia, 2011). Through philanthropy, Patagonia has created organizations that allow other firms to direct their philanthropy to environmental causes. For example, the firm co-founded the Conservation Alliance in 1989 with other outdoor companies, such as REI, The North Face, and Kelty (Patagonia, 2010). Since its founding in 1989, the Alliance has contributed more than $9.5 million to conservation projects throughout North America (Conservation Alliance, 2011). These projects have resulted in protecting more than 50.5 million acres of land, stopping or removing 28 dams, and preserving access to thousands of miles of rivers and several climbing areas. Patagonia is a Pinnacle Member as one of seven firms (among the 177 active firms) that contribute more than $100,000 annually to the Alliance.

In 2001, Yvon Chouinard also founded 1% for the Planet with Craig Mathews, owner of Blue Ribbon Flies outfitter and guide service for fly fishing based in West Yellowstone, Montana (1% for the Plant, 2011). Chouinard and Mathews hatched a plan to encourage more businesses to donate 1% of sales to environmental groups. Chouinard called it an "Earth Tax." Mathews suggested that it be named "1% for the Planet." Mathews's idea eventually won over Chouinard. Since 2002, 1% for the Planet has signed up more than 1,200 members in 38 countries. In 2010, its members gave more than $15 million to campaigns for clean air, pure water, safe food, and wild places. Since its inception, the members have directed more than $50 million toward environmental groups as part of its mission to "Keep Earth in Business" (1% for the Plant, 2011).

Every member company of 1% for the Planet has the opportunity to engage in a dialogue with the rest of the 1% for the Planet membership to foster new business relationships and to connect for sharing ideas and resources. "Companies like Clif Bar, and New Belgium are members of 1% for the Planet," Lisa Myers Patagonia's Director of Environmental Grants said. "These more than 1,200 members of One Percent for the Planet are our peers" (Myers, 2011, personal communication).

## Patagonia Helps Wal-Mart

Although inspiring a movement among businesses to direct philanthropy toward organizations that defend or improve the natural environment is a major accomplishment by itself, Patagonia's most significant accomplishment to date might be winning over business leaders of firms that will never join 1% for the Planet to recognize that industry and ecology are inherently connected. By working with one firm, Wal-Mart, Chouinard might more favorably impact the marketplace than in any other way.

Chouinard has visited Wal-Mart's headquarters in Bentonville, Arkansas, to explain the operating principles of Patagonia to Wal-Mart's leaders, as well as to a gathering of 1,200 buyers for Wal-Mart (Ridgeway, 2010). Chouinard told the audience to lead "an examined life" so you know the consequences of your actions, and once you know them "clean up your act" (Ridgeway, 2010, p. 44). Afterward, Wal-Mart CEO Lee Scott went to the podium with his closing remarks:

"There's a third of you out there who know what we're doing and why we're doing it," Scott said. "There's another third who don't quite understand but you're getting there. And there's a final third telling yourselves this isn't the company that Sam Walton founded, and you don't understand and you may not be willing to learn. In the future, there may not be a place for you at Wal-Mart." (Ridgeway, 2010, p. 44)

"The revolution really has started," Chouinard later remarked about his work with Wal-Mart. "I'm blown away by Wal-Mart. If Wal-Mart does one-tenth of what they say they are going to do, it will be incredible" (Casey, 2007, p. 5).

The enormous scale of Wal-Mart's operations is what excites others about Patagonia's consultative relationship with Wal-Mart's leadership. Rick Ridgeway, Patagonia's Vice-President of Environmental Initiatives, recalled one of the first phone conversations with Wal-Mart's executives. "We wondered how sincere are they?" Ridgeway said. "In a subsequent phone call, the Wal-Mart folks must have sensed our hesitation because they said, 'If we do start using organic cotton, we have a lot of influence on our supply chain. Maybe we could do something like persuade the entire country of Pakistan to switch to organic cotton farming'" (Ridgeway, 2010, p. 44).

It is remarkable that Patagonia serves as a role model for environmental stewardship not only for like-minded members of 1% for the Planet but also for the largest company in the world. Wal-Mart's leaders did not need to hear about philanthropy from Chouinard. They needed to understand better how to integrate environmentally oriented principles into their operations. (More will be shared about Wal-Mart's sustainable business practices later in this chapter.)

## Patagonia's Environmental Wisdom

Much of Patagonia's environmental wisdom came in costly ways. In 1991, the firm was growing at 50% a year but became derailed during the savings-and-loan crisis (Patagonia, 2010). "The bank reduced our credit line twice in several months and the company ended up borrowing from friends to meet payroll and laying off 20 % of its workforce on July 31," Chouinard recalled. "That's a day I still refer to as Black Wednesday" (Chouinard, 2010, p. 5).

"We had become dependent, like the world economy, on growth we could not sustain," Chouinard said. "If I hadn't stayed in business, I never would have realized—the hard way— the parallel between Patagonia's unsustainable push for growth and that of our whole industrial economy" (Chouinard, 2010, p. 5).

After this near-death experience for his firm, Chouinard and those who remained over-hauled the company mission statement and began asking questions. Growth for the firm was questioned. Soon, the employees of the firm were asking about the environmental harm caused by manufacturing and distributing clothes. "That's the problem with questions," Chouinard said. "Once you start, you can't stop" (Chouinard, 2010, p. 5).

After opening a brand new store in Boston, almost everyone who worked there had a headache. It turned out that the clothing shipped to the store—made of cotton—was finished using too much formaldehyde. Fixing the ventilation at the new store would not fix this problem. Accordingly, Patagonia's employees asked how cotton is grown. After getting answers, the firm switched over to organically grown cotton for its clothes made of cotton.

Afterward, questions came about conditions inside factories where Patagonia's clothes were stitched together. Many of these were in the Far East. What goes into dyes and finishes on clothing that would make them more water repellant? How about shipping and carbon footprints? "It was expensive, time-consuming and deeply complex," Chouinard recalled. "As I said recently at Patagonia's Tools for Grassroots Activists Conference, a gathering of environmental activists at a camp in the Sierra Nevada, 'Leading the examined life is a pain in the ass'. But it's worth it" (Chouinard, 2010, p. 5).

Chouinard believes he learned the hard way to stop growing at an unsustainable rate and still stay in business. He and his team at Patagonia admit they do not have all the answers, but they take confidence when realizing that they have been asking the questions longer than anyone else. Today, Patagonia is a thriving firm posting more than $400 million a year in sales (LeBarre, 2010).

## The Footprint Chronicles

Patagonia's leaders are not shy about disclosing the damage their own company does to the natural environment. The firm's spirit of total disclosure can be seen in their launching of *The Footprint Chronicles*, an interactive minisite on its website, which details what the company makes and how it makes it in minute detail. For example, one of the more than

150 products in The Footprint Chronicles is Patagonia's Nano Puff Pullover. After clicking on this product, the webpage featured in Figure 11.1 appears. Here, the trail of the Nano Puff Pullover is presented on the map of the world with six accompanying videos activated when the viewer clicks on one of the photos in the middle of Figure 11.1. These videos focus on (a) design done in Ventura, California; (b) the recycling of polyester fibers done at the Teijin factory in Matsuyama, Japan; (c) the making of the polyester fabric at Fukui, Japan; (d) the making of the Prima Loft insulation in Rudong, China; (e) the sewing of the garment at the Taiwanese-owned Quang Viet Enterprise Co. (Ltd.) located outside of Ho Chi Minh City, Viet Nam; and (f) the quality check done at Patagonia's Distribution Center located in Reno, Nevada.

The symbols in squares to the right of the Nano Puff Pullover are depicted in the Figure 11.1 balloon when a viewer's mouse is scrolled over them. These report on manufacturing and shipping the garment to the Reno distributions center for the following dimensions: (a) energy used (11 kW—similar to burning an 18-kW bulb for 25 days), (b) the distance traveled (12,545 miles or 20,189 km), (c) $CO_2$ emitted (5.5 pounds—or ten times the weight of the garment), (d) waste generated (2.7 oz. or 76.5 grams—about one third the weight of a woman's Nano Puff Pullover), and (e) water consumed (63 liters of water—enough to provide 21 persons with drinking water for a day).

**Figure 11.1**    The Footprint Chronicles at www.patagonia.com

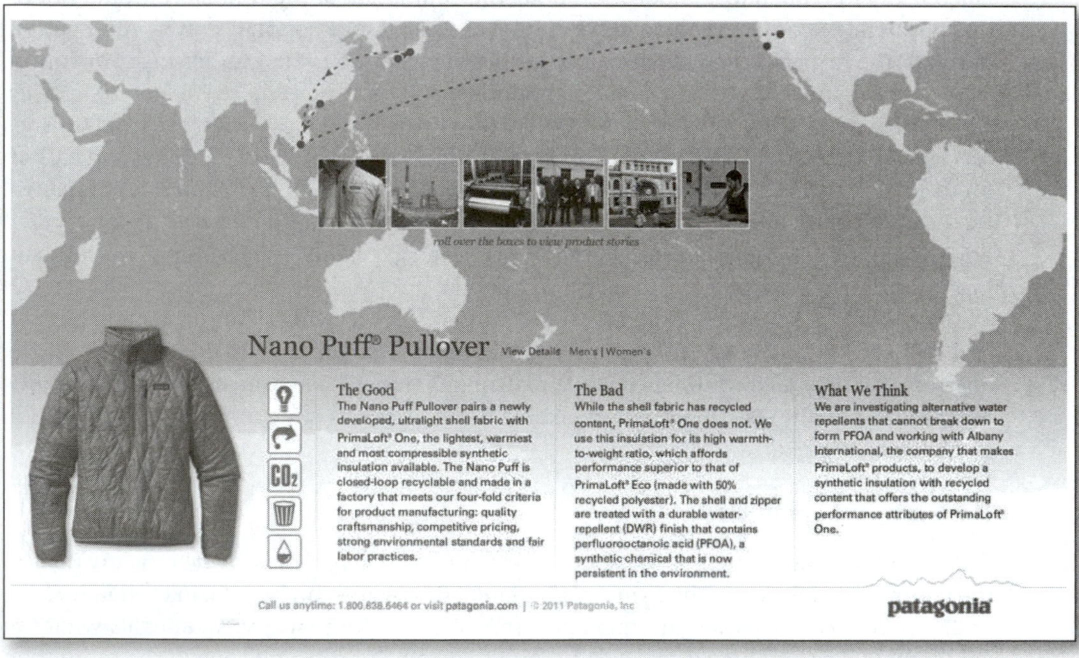

*Source:* Property of Patagonia, Inc. Used with permission.

Highlights of the footprint of the Nano Puff Pullover are described on the webpage featured in Figure 11.1 with headings such as "The Good," "The Bad," and "What We Think."

Patagonia takes the opportunity to detail why the garment has some worthy features with regard to strong environmental standards and fair labor practices. It acknowledges that although the polyester shell is made of recycled polyester, the Prima Loft insulation is not. Additionally, the shell and zipper are treated with a water-repellant finish that contains a synthetic ingredient that persists in the environment. Patagonia also reports here that it is seeking alternative finishes that will not persist in the environment like the current finish does, and that it is working with the maker of Prima Loft insulation to develop ways to use recycled polyester in the manufacturing of this insulation.

## Reactions and Implications of the Footprint Chronicles

Becoming broadly transparent about the manufacturing and sourcing of its products was scary to Patagonia's leaders, at first. Casey Sheahan, Patagonia's current CEO, worried that the firm would get "filleted," but the firm went ahead anyway (LaBarre, 2010).

The reaction was universal applause. With this, the firm pushed to develop The Footprint Chronicles website to be a model of how to tell a firm's story in a way that connects and engages persons across wide constituencies in the cause of the firm. This is done even when the news is bad.

"We're honest about it," Sheahan said. "We're dirty. Everything we make pollutes. There is no such thing as a sustainable company. We're just doing the best we can" (LaBarre, 2010, p. 1).

Sheahan notes that shrinking a firm's environmental impact is not an area for obtaining a competitive advantage. He asserts that it is everybody's business. However, when a firm shares, it learns. "There are no secrets at Patagonia," Sheahan said (LaBarre, 2010, p. 2). The result of this transparency is employee commitment to the values of the firm. Patagonia employees regard themselves as stewards of these company values. When confronted with bad news, they tend to make an effort to understand why it occurred. Then they share the lesson and hear from others on ways to improve even more.

Chouinard's story highlights the possibilities of how entrepreneurship can change not only the marketplace, but society as well. Patagonia has become a magnet for every kind of institution desiring to learn how to pursue a path toward sustainability (LaBarre, 2010). Over the course of more than 30 years, Chouinard built a recognized brand that symbolized appealing ways for customers to experience nature equipped with Patagonia's outdoor gear and to support the idea of wilderness conservation at the same time (Holt & Cameron, 2010). As his venture grew, his financial resources for environmentally oriented philanthropy increased, as well. His firm attracted environmentally conscious employees (300 at the headquarters today, 700 more in the United States, and 500 overseas), and together they pioneered many environmentally innovative practices, such as using organic cotton, developing green buildings, and beginning a successful on-site day-care center at Patagonia's headquarters (Choi & Gray, 2011, p. 25). He also has inspired other businesses to commit themselves more deeply to environmental stewardship and has served as a teacher to many seeking his assistance in this regard. It is hard to imagine Chouinard having such a similarly positive effect on society's stewardship for the environment in any other role than as an entrepreneur.

# BACKGROUND FOR ENVIRONMENTALLY ORIENTED BUSINESS

## Conservation

REI is a national outdoor retail co-op, based in Seattle, Washington, that began as a way for 21 mountain climbing buddies to obtain the outdoor gear they needed (REI, 2011). In 2010, REI boasted more than 4 million members who pay a one-time $20 fee and most years received a REI dividend of 10% on purchases made. REI offers its own line of award-winning gear and apparel, in addition to products from the top brands for camping, climbing, cycling, fitness, hiking, paddling, snow sports, and travel. These other brands include Patagonia, The North Face, and Columbia.

REI declares itself to be passionate about the outdoors and committed to promoting environmental stewardship. Those who take responsibility for how their actions affect environmental quality can be called environmental stewards (EPA, 2005).

Environmental stewardship is not new. Influenced by naturalists such as John Muir who petitioned the U.S. Congress to pass the National Parks bill passed in 1899, Republican Teddy Roosevelt championed conservation during his U.S. presidency from 1901 to 1909 (Gingrich & Maple, 2007, p. 28). It has been said that perhaps Roosevelt's greatest and most enduring contribution as president was instilling an ethos of natural resource conservation in Americans (Lallanilla, 2011). He also preserved some 230 million acres—about the size of *two* Californias and one Ohio—as national parks, national forests, game preserves, national monuments, and other federal reservations. He created the Forest Service and appointed renowned conservationist *Gifford Pinchot* as its head. On the way to these accomplishments, he showed future presidents and environmentalists how to achieve legislative success.

"The conservation of natural resources is the fundamental problem," Roosevelt once said. "Unless we solve that problem it will avail us little to solve all others" (Lallanilla, 2011, p. 1).

Conservatives, such as Paul Weyrich (founder of the Heritage Foundation think-tank), William Lind (an expert on military affairs), as well as former U.S. Speaker of the House Newt Gingrich, give ringing endorsement to conserving natural resources. "As conservatives," Weyrich and Lind said:

> We believe in conserving many things: traditions, morals and culture, but also clean air and water, farms and countryside, energy [much of which must now be imported] and the soil itself, on which we all depend for our daily bread. Conservatives do not like waste. Reckless, frivolous, thoughtless consumption was never a conservative virtue. A society's real strength comes from production, saving and investment, not consumption. Earlier generations of Americans understood this and lived accordingly. (Weyrich & Lind, 2009, pp. 50–51)

Renowned Harvard biologist E. O. Wilson theorized that an innate bond exists between humanity and nature. He termed this love of life or living systems as biophilia (Gingrich & Maple, 2007, p. 26). With this in mind, the move to preserve nature from human use or to conserve nature (so that it can be used wisely for future availability or productivity) can be seen to be part of environmental stewardship. In other words, a moral imperative to protect and manage nature based on love for it is shared by many today across the entire political spectrum (Gingrich & Maple, 2007).

## Natural Infrastructure—Could It Break Down?

The EPA believes that environmental stewardship is indispensable for becoming a more sustainable society (EPA, 2005). Toward this end, the EPA proposes that environmental stewardship can focus on the following natural resource systems: (a) air, (b) ecosystems, (c) energy, (d) land, (e) materials, and (f) water. Increasingly, however, the capability of humans to control environmental systems seems to be in question. For example, although plants and animals comprise part of nature, the atmosphere and weather systems are another part of nature. With increased awareness about global climate change (recorded temperatures across the Earth have increased 1 degree Fahrenheit over the last century), it seems that the planet might be on the verge of shifting to a new equilibrium with a higher overall temperature (Thorne, Ferrell, & Ferrell, 2008, p. 320). The propensity for this shift is likely being exacerbated by the greenhouse gasses pumped into the atmosphere each day by humans and animals. Concentrations of carbon dioxide—an otherwise harmless gas that plants use in photosynthesis—are growing at a rate that plant life cannot adequately process. As a result, the blanket of greenhouse gasses in the atmosphere is thickening with the effect that temperatures and weather are changing.

The specter of global climate change puts Teddy Roosevelt's words about the depletion of natural resources as the fundamental problem in a new light. Rather than caring for nature for aesthetic or moral reasons that may be optional to humans, the environment must be cared for because it actually serves as infrastructure for human civilization. Natural resource systems such as the six serving as the focus for environmental stewardship according to the EPA can be damaged beyond repair or degraded in their ability to provide service to humankind.

Stewart Brand, the founder and editor of *The Whole Earth Catalog* and an ecologist, calls himself an "ecopragmatist" (Brand, 2009). Brand asserts that civilization requires a tranquil climate to prosper. In this way, the climate provides ecosystem services to humans. Brand makes the observation that modern humans are trained to overlook infrastructure. Humans seem to notice infrastructure only when it does not work. Brand states:

> There are some exceptions. People like the romanticism of railroads and admire bridges and ships. Small towns decorate their water towers. But working mines, containership ports, power plants, power lines, cell-phone towers, refineries, dumps, sewerage—all bear one sign: KEEP OUT. Those places are left to the workers, who are low-status. One might say exactly the same about ecosystem infrastructure, such as watersheds, wetlands, fisheries, soil, and climate. (p. 16)

Brand proposes that a deep bow of thanks is due to environmentalists who have been drawing attention to dangerous breakdowns of natural infrastructure and setting about the protection and restoration of it:

A bridge is infrastructure, and so is the river under it. Both support our life, and both require maintenance, which has to be paid for somehow. Radio spectrum is infrastructure, and so is an intact ozone layer. Both support our life, and both require international agreements to avert a 'tragedy of the commons.' (p. 16).

A common dilemma occurs when a shared resource is degraded or consumed for short-term gain by those sharing the resource, rather than managing the resource for the long-term benefit of all.

### Common Goods Dilemma

Elinor Ostrom, the first woman to win the Nobel Prize in economics (in 2009) for her research about cooperative ownership, points out that a "common" actually means that agreements or institutions are in place for the successful sharing of a common good. For example, farmers in some Swiss villages share a communal meadow to graze cows. No overgrazing occurs because there is a common agreement among villagers that no one is allowed to graze more cows than they can care for over the winter—a rule in effect since 1517 (Walljasper, 2010). According to Ostrom, "the commons" more accurately refers to the wide and diverse set of common-pool resources or common goods (such as forests, grazing lands, irrigation waters, and fisheries) and public goods (such as knowledge and national defense). So, what many refer to as a "commons dilemma" would be better termed a "common goods dilemma."

**Figure 11.2**  A Typology of Goods Based on Excludability and Rivalrousness

|  | Excludable | Nonexcludable |
|---|---|---|
| Rivalrous | **Private goods**<br>food, clothes, autos, iPods | **Common goods (Common-pool resources)**<br>grazing lands, forests, irrigation waters, fisheries |
| Nonrivalrous | **Club goods**<br>movie theaters, private parks, satellite television | **Public goods**<br>air, broadcast television, national defense |

*Source*: Varian (1992).

Figure 11.2 depicts a typology of goods based on the excludability and rivalrousness of the goods (Varian, 1992). Excludability refers to whether some people can be excluded from using the good. The rivalrousness of goods is based on the degree to which the consumption of the good by one person reduces the availability of the good to others for similar consumption.

As shown in the upper-left quadrant of Figure 11.2, food for one person is a private good because it is excludable and rivalrous. It can be owned by one person, and when a person eats a lunch, it cannot be eaten by others. Common goods can be found in the upper-right quadrant of the matrix. Here, irrigation waters are shared by many farmers (making them nonexcludable), but they are rivalrous (because the consumption of any portion of the irrigation waters renders that portion unusable by other farmers). In the lower-left quadrant, club goods are those that are excludable and nonrivalrous. For example, tickets can be sold to a cinema screening of a movie (making the movie screening excludable), and many patrons can view the movie simultaneously without reducing the movie consumption of others (making the movie screening nonrivalrous). Finally, in the lower-right quadrant, public goods are those that are nonexcludable and nonrivalrous. The air we breathe is an example. The air is shared by all (making it nonexcludable), and one person's breathing does not reduce the amount another person can breathe (making it nonrivalrous).

Although the air we breathe is a public good, the atmosphere surrounding the Earth turns out to be a common good whose overuse by all humans can degrade the services it provides humankind. Specifically, the production of greenhouse gasses by humans is increasing the heat-insulating property of the atmosphere. In this way, a dilemma concerning an important common-pool resource—the atmosphere—is now emerging because the infrastructure service of a tranquil climate provided by the atmosphere seems to be at risk of degradation (Cohen & Winn, 2010).

## A Challenge Unprecedented in Scale and Scope

Because no country controls the atmosphere surrounding the planet, addressing global climate change effectively seems to be a challenge on a scale that humankind has never before faced. The Kyoto Protocol, signed by 192 countries in 1997, set binding limits for developed countries to reduce their greenhouse gas emissions (Friedman, 2008). According to the Kyoto Protocol, these developed countries (excluding the United States and Australia who did not sign the protocol) would reduce their overall $CO_2$ emissions from 2008 to 2012 by 20% (Lomborg, 2007). Carbon dioxide accounts for 80% of the world's emissions of global warming gases from human-made sources (Bradsher, 2006). Other gases from industrial processes, plus methane from landfills and coal mines, account for the rest of these emissions.

Although Kyoto's backers hailed it as a small first step, it is widely seen as mostly symbolic because the impact on rising global temperatures (even if the United States and Australia had signed the protocol and adhered to it) would be only slight in the face of surging development in Third World countries such as China and India. This can be seen in Table 11.1's tabular depiction of carbon dioxide emissions for 2009. As shown, carbon emissions for China and India rose while those for developed countries declined in North America and Europe. China now ranks number one in carbon dioxide emissions (Rogers & Evans, 2011).

In 2006, when confronted with the forecast that China would overtake the United States in carbon emissions by 2009, the Chinese government's response was to blame the developed countries for their leading role in greenhouse gas emissions during the history of the Industrial Age. "You cannot tell people who are struggling to earn enough to eat that they

**Table 11.1** The U.S. Energy Information Administration's 2009 Data on $CO_2$ Emissions (Millions of Metric Tons)

| Locale | Amount | Percentage Change from 2005 |
|---|---|---|
| **North America** | **6,411** | **−9%** |
| United States | 5,425 | −9% |
| Canada | 541 | −13% |
| Mexico | 444 | 12% |
| **Central & South America** | **1,212** | **10%** |
| Brazil | 425 | 15% |
| Argentina | 166 | 9% |
| Venezuela | 159 | 9% |
| **Europe** | **4,307** | **−8%** |
| Germany | 766 | −10% |
| Italy | 408 | −14% |
| France | 397 | −4% |
| **Eurasia** | **2,338** | **−7%** |
| Russia | 1,557 | −6% |
| Ukraine | 252 | −29% |
| Kazakhstan | 184 | 10% |
| **Middle East** | **1,688** | **16%** |
| Iran | 529 | 18% |
| Saudi Arabia | 438 | 8% |
| United Arab Emirates | 193 | 38% |
| **Africa** | **1,119** | **6%** |
| South Africa | 451 | 4% |
| Egypt | 190 | 18% |
| Algeria | 113 | 26% |
| **Asia & Oceania** | **13,238** | **26%** |
| China | 7,707 | 40% |
| India | 1,591 | 34% |
| Japan | 1,098 | −12% |
| **World** | **30,313** | **7%** |

*Source:* U.S. Energy Information Administration (2012). International Energy Statistics: $CO_2$ Emissions. http://205.254.135.7/cfapps/ipdbproject/IEDIndex3.cfm?tid=90&pid=44&aid=8

need to reduce their emissions," said Lu Xuedu, the deputy director general of Chinese Office of Global Environmental Affairs (Bradsher, 2006).

Unregulated emissions from China, India, and other developing countries are likely to account for most of the global increase in carbon dioxide emissions through 2021 (Bradsher, 2006). Leading environmentalists see the need for the four energy-using governments (the European Union [EU], the United States, China, and India) to get tough in setting rules and enforcing them (Brand, 2009). However, skeptics declare that although a cosmopolitan approach is needed, the likelihood of international agreement is poor:

> The likelihood of the EU, the US, China, India, and others all coming to a global understanding of the distribution of responsibility and allowing their sovereignty to be thereby compromised is so close to nil that major international treaties cannot be the starting point for addressing the issue. (O'Hara, 2011, p. 282)

In sum, the atmosphere could be a common good with rules for protecting its climate regulating properties, but because of the inability of governments to agree on how to do this, a dilemma regarding this common-pool resource exists. No doubt, government leaders in Beijing who can only see 400 meters horizontally into the haze on a cloudless day with their eyes burning know instinctively that a problem exists. Much of China's jump in carbon emissions can be attributed to increased burning of coal. According to U.S. government statistics, China's coal consumption doubled over the two decades from 1980. But from 2002 to 2007, it doubled again (Black, 2011). As the world's burning of coal increased as much from 2003 to 2006 as it had in the previous 23 years, China has accounted for 90% of this increase (mostly for electricity generation) (Bradsher, 2006). (India accounted for 8% of the increase, whereas the United States accounted for the rest.)

## Public Sector Entrepreneurship to Reduce $CO_2$ Emissions

Carbon capture and storage (CCS) is an emerging technology that might allow the vast coal reserves of the planet to be used while reducing carbon dioxide emissions that would protect the climate (Pew Center on Global Climate Change, 2011). CCS involves separating the $CO_2$ from other gases emitted in the process of burning coal and liquefying the resulting gas. The liquefied $CO_2$ can be transported for several hundred miles and then injected deep underground, miles below the surface of the Earth, in suitable geological formations, deep underground saline aquifers, or disused oil fields (Jha, 2008). The last method is often used in a process called "enhanced oil recovery," where $CO_2$ is pumped into an oil field to force out the remaining pockets of oil that would otherwise prove difficult to extract. The United States has the capacity for underground storage of current levels of domestic $CO_2$ emissions from its coal-fired electricity-generation plants for more than 300 years (Pew Center on Global Climate Change, 2011).

The U.S. government's CCS efforts took an important step in August 2011 when construction began on the government's first industrial-scale CCS project in Decatur, Illinois, that received $141 million in government funds and $66.5 million from the private sector (Business Green, 2011a). When the CCS facility commences operations in 2013, it will capture and store 1 million tons of $CO_2$ each year generated from ethanol production at a nearby Archer Daniels Midland biofuels plant. The gas will be held 7,000 feet beneath the surface in the saline Mount Simon Sandstone formation that has the capacity to sequester all of the 250 million tons of $CO_2$ produced each year by industry in Illinois.

The Obama administration intends to field 16 demonstration projects across 13 states by 2016. Toward this end, it has provided $41 million over three years for these demonstration projects to share. "Charting a path toward clean coal is essential to achieving our goals of providing clean energy, creating American jobs and reducing greenhouse gas emissions," U.S. Secretary of Energy Steven Chu said. "It will also help position the United States as a leader in the global clean energy race" (Business Green, 2011a, para. 11). In this way, the government's entrepreneurship will combine two things a well-run government can do effectively: fund research and initiate programs.

Such public sector entrepreneurship comes at a time when the Great Recession (discussed in Chapter 2) has reduced government tax receipts, as well as private sector funds for participating in such CCS projects. "We're seeing a decline in new projects due to a softening global economy and uncertain carbon price," said Brad Page, head of the Australia-based Global CCS Institute (Watts, 2011, para. 9). No government has come to terms with what might be the cost of putting carbon into the atmosphere in the future. Currently, Australia's government is expected to set a level of about $23 per ton of carbon, but U.S. Secretary of Energy Steven Chu believes the price needs to be $80 a ton for CCS to be economically viable with the current technology being used (Watts, 2011). "The US needs a price on carbon sooner rather than later," Chu said. "This is something where we are losing time. It is very important that we get moving" (Watts, 2011, para. 13).

The U.S. Congress would have to approve new climate regulation that would include pricing schemes for carbon, but this seems to be unlikely in the next few years. Without a price set for carbon, American Electric Power abandoned its plans to build its $668 million CCS facility at its Mountaineer coal-fired power plant in New Haven, West Virginia. "At this time it doesn't make economic sense to continue work on the commercial-scale CCS project beyond the current engineering phase," said Michael G. Morris, AEP chairman and chief executive. "It is impossible to gain regulatory approval to recover our share of the costs for validating and deploying the technology without federal requirements to reduce greenhouse gas emissions already in place" (Business Green, 2011b, para. 5).

## Prospects for a Low-Carbon Future

In sum, government can entrepreneurially build demonstration projects to validate CCS technologies, but it seems more is needed or a tragedy of the commons will result as the atmosphere accumulates $CO_2$ and forecasted climate disruption accelerates in a nonlinear manner (Shultz & Holbrook, 1999). Without the externality of greenhouse gas emissions being included in the price for energy, private firms do not find CCS to be financially viable with current technologies. Richard Jones, deputy executive director of the International Energy Agency (IEA), warned that with current polices, CCS will have a hard time being deployed.

### British Columbia's Carbon Tax

Newer policies might focus on including the full cost of emitting carbon in market pricing with a carbon tax placed on $CO_2$ used in business operations. Despite the reluctance of national governments to raise any taxes in a time of economic uncertainty, the provincial government of British Columbia went ahead and imposed its own carbon tax of about C$20 per ton of $CO_2$ in 2008 (Marshall, 2011). (At the time of writing, U.S. dollars and Canadian dollars were about equal in value.) The tax is revenue-neutral in that the government lowers the taxes of corporations and individuals at a rate comparable with the carbon tax they pay.

The carbon tax first required British Columbians to pay C$.18 more for a gallon of gasoline (Marshall, 2011). In July 2012, the next phase of the carbon tax requires British Columbians to pay C$.27 more for a gallon of gasoline when the tax rises to C$30 a ton of $CO_2$-equivalent. Because 85% of British Columbia's electricity comes from hydropower, the tax has little effect on electricity users. Instead, the most of the tax is being paid by drivers and by businesses, as well as by individuals using natural gas, propane, or coal. The cost for other fuels, such as natural gas or coal, varies by their carbon content. Combustion accounts for three fourths of the province's $CO_2$ emissions, and the tax applies to these. The rest of the province's emissions have other sources, such as methane seeping from landfills.

As a result of the carbon tax, public institutions have sought to include more energy-efficient technologies (Marshall, 2011). For example, in the Resort Municipality of Whistler, community manager Ted Battiston says the tax played a role in changing from propane tanks to solar panels and geothermal pumps in the heating unit of the local swimming pool. Heavy emitters of greenhouse gases, such as cement manufacturers, complain loudly about how imported cement is now threatening the vitality of their businesses. Alternatively, businesses with a small carbon footprint are not complaining much about the tax. This brings the heavy emitters to call for a different way of recycling the carbon-tax revenue. According to these heavy emitters, instead of the tax proceeds going to every business, more of the cash should help carbon-intensive companies improve their energy efficiency.

After its first years, economists now say the tax is too small for a full economic assessment. Another reason for increasing the tax comes from the Pembina Institute, a Canadian nonprofit think-tank working to advance sustainable energy solutions. According to the Pembina Institute, British Columbia's carbon tax needs to rise to C$200 a ton for British Columbia to meet its emission reduction targets by 2020. Yet, even at its initial rate, there are early signs that the tax is changing behavior—the true goal of the tax.

So what does British Columbia's example mean for national governments? Paul Bledsoe, a senior adviser at the Bipartisan Policy Center, believes that a tax on energy is one of the few ways that the U.S. government could obtain new sources of revenue if tax reform is done to reduce the federal deficit. One goal of reform would be to reduce taxes for corporations and individuals—exactly what a carbon or energy tax could finance.

"The enormous political appeal of cutting corporate and individual tax rates as part of debt reduction has the potential to more than offset the political push back on a consumption tax, at the right moment," Bledsoe said (Marshall, 2011, p. 6).

## EPA and Emissions Regulation

In April 2007, the U.S. Supreme Court declared that Massachusetts had standing to bring a legal suit against the EPA for not regulating greenhouse gases—specifically $CO_2$—emitted from automobile tailpipes. Previously, $CO_2$ had not been considered a "pollutant" under the Clean Air Act. In a 5-4 decision, the Supreme Court asserted that Massachusetts faced harm that was both actual and imminent because of the risk of harm from costly storms and the loss of coastal shore that would result from climate change (Yergin, 2011, p. 502). Some called the ruling the most important environmental ruling of all time. In addition to classifying $CO_2$ as a pollutant, it termed the EPA's current stance of nonregulation as being not in accordance with the law. If Congress did not legislate the regulation of carbon, the EPA was supposed to.

The EPA's subsequent move to regulate emissions from stationary sources, such as coal-fired electricity-generating plants, drew a backlash from Congress and more than a dozen states, such as Texas (Galbraith, 2010). It seems that the battle over $CO_2$ regulation will depend on the composition of the Congress in the coming years. The stance of Congress will also be crucial in determining whether an international regime for climate change emerges.

Although the Kyoto Protocol did not achieve its major objective of reducing greenhouse gas emissions from developing countries, and although carbon legislation is side-tracked in the U.S. Congress, businesses have already begun to address this issue in their move to more sustainable business practices. For example, GE CEO Jeffrey Immelt kept hearing from his senior executives throughout 2003 that customers were talking more about wanting "clean" or environmentally friendly solutions in the gas turbines, locomotives, and light bulbs they were buying from GE (Yergin, 2011, p. 499). Immelt convened a meeting of electric-utility executives and environmentalists to discuss major energy issues in 2004. At this meeting, climate moved to the front of the discussions. GE later fielded its Eco-Imagination program that represents GE's commitment to pursue innovations to environmental challenges (www.ecomagination.com).

In addition to the opportunities businesses now recognize as accompanying concern about environmental issues, such as global climate change and loss of biodiversity, businesses have begun to realize that sustainable business practices can contribute to their increased competitiveness. Wal-Mart is a case in point. In 2005, CEO Lee Scott declared that climate change was at the top of his list of environmental challenges that had to be addressed (Humes, 2011, p. 103). Air and water pollution, water shortages, destruction of critical habitats, and the reduction of biodiversity rounded out his list of environmental challenges. Later, Scott would testify before Congress twice in 2009 advocating for reduction of greenhouse gas emissions. In these ways and in a myriad of operational changes, Wal-Mart began turning away from a ruthless approach to business that disregarded the environment and communities. Other businesses could no longer say that sustainable business practices were too risky if Wal-Mart had adopted them. How strange could environmentally friendly business leaders be if Wal-Mart now wanted a low-carbon future?

## Wal-Mart Sets Sail to Harness Winds of Change for Sustainable Business Practices

Rather than continuing to view corporate social responsibility as an ethical veneer to shield the firm from criticism in society, Wal-Mart realized that the most sustainable business, the cleanest, and the least wasteful would gain a competitive advantage (Humes, 2011,

p. 3). Costs would be lowered (meaning profits would likely rise accordingly), and customers would be pleased with better products and services (and other stakeholders would be pleased, as well). This advantage would not accrue in some abstract future time, but now—during the watch of the company's current leaders. Accepting this premise, then, led to understanding that the pivotal question facing this era of business would be not if business will obey the laws of nature but when and how and on whose terms? Would Wal-Mart be an innovator and lead sustainability—thereby obtaining the valuable knowledge acquisition first-movers can obtain—or would it wait for its competition, the courts, or Congress to bring compelling force for Wal-Mart to do this?

Since 2005, Wal-Mart has accepted that sustainable business practices represent a better way to do business (Humes, 2011). The firm turned away from ingrained thinking that such business practices meant extra costs, and instead, it saw these sustainable business practices as ways to eliminate waste and the costs that go with such waste. The firm had noticed the operational efficiencies obtained by Patagonia and Nike. Wal-Mart had also struggled with persistent criticism of its operations. In 2004, the firm had attained immense size with a 12,000-mile, computer-controlled supply chain moving goods to more than 7,000 stores. Its truck fleet of 7,200 trucks was the largest in the world. With operations on such a scale, a slight reduction in costs for heating or cooling the stores, or for running the trucks that were continually on the move, would mean millions of dollars more in profits to the firm. Unlike most corporate social responsibility efforts that might pursue good works of philanthropy to enhance a firm's image and "give back" to communities or society, sustainable business practices would actually impact company performance in a positive way.

Wal-Mart's leaders also recognized that no retailer had ever retained its dominance for more than one generation (Humes, 2011, p. 10). A study the firm had done by McKinsey & Company consultants disclosed that 8% of Wal-Mart's customer base had stopped shopping there because of Wal-Mart's poor image as a corporate citizen regarding the environment and labor practices. With 176 million customers around the world, this meant that Wal-Mart would have 14 million more customers if the firm was not repeatedly in the news for business practices many viewed as too aggressive. Such aggressiveness manifested itself in not supervising its factory suppliers' egregious use of child labor in places like Pakistan, and in trying to force a supercenter into places like Inglewood, California, through a voter referendum intended to bypass opposition in the Inglewood City Council. (Voters rejected Wal-Mart's bid with 60% voting against allowing the supercenter to be built.)

Under the leadership of CEO Lee Scott, the company looked at their operations with a new lens and recognized that waste in any form meant a process could be made more efficient. For example, customers could obtain the benefits of a gallon-sized plastic container of laundry detergent from a concentrated form of the detergent without the water content of the gallon-sized container of detergent. Why would an otherwise savvy retailer like Wal-Mart stay with the larger size and incur all of the shipping costs and lost shelf space this would mean? The answer was clear: The more environmentally friendly version of the laundry detergent would be Wal-Mart's choice. By multiplying such a decision by the number of laundry detergent buyers in Wal-Mart stores, and then by multiplying this by the number of times each year these customers buy laundry detergent, one can understand the enormous savings in costs Wal-Mart can capture by changing its view of sustainable business practices in just one product category. The reduction in carbon emissions accompanying such a change is likewise staggeringly enormous. Wal-Mart's sales would make it the 20th largest economy on the planet if it were a country—the size of Poland's GDP (Scott, 2005).

Wal-Mart's move to sustainable business practices came through a confluence of factors. Chairman of the Wal-Mart board Rob Walton, son of founder Sam Walton, had become involved with Peter Seligman of Conservation International and had even gone scuba diving in Costa Rica with Seligman and Stone Gossard, guitarist for Pearl Jam. Seligman introduced Walton to a former river-guide-turned-consultant Jib Ellison from California and his BluSky consultancy for sustainable business practices. Procter & Gamble had already taken major steps to develop and adapt sustainable business practices as a major supplier of Wal-Mart. Other influences on Wal-Mart's move to sustainability included an inner change in CEO Lee Scott who had spent more than a year in field locations understanding the effects of environmental degradation. By this time, Scott had become exhausted by responding to relentless criticism of its hard-driving push for low prices with its usual reply that low prices benefitted families struggling to make ends meet.

By 2004, customers had come to expect Wal-Mart to serve as a role model for other businesses. Not only this, but the younger generation of consumers seemed to understand the environmental imperative for businesses and would increasingly demand businesses behave as good citizens in the future. Lee Scott saw the future for Wal-Mart as a green one, if it were to retain its prominence as a business.

## Green Light for Sustainable Business Practices at Wal-Mart

In 2005, Scott, through the use of a live video feed, gave a major address carried to his employees at every one of its 6,000 stores and to its (then) more than 62,000 suppliers. To the surprise of almost everyone, Scott asked in an emotional tone what if Wal-Mart performed at its best everyday—just as it had done in the aftermath of Hurricane Katrina when Wal-Mart trucks did what the governments could not do by bringing relief supplies to devastated communities along the Gulf Coast of Louisiana and Mississippi:

> During Katrina, I was reminded of the vision and innovation of Sam Walton. We became who we are by serving the underserved. The smart folks predicted we'd lose our shirt with a discount store in a small town. There is another crowd of smart people who think that if a company addresses the environment, it will lose its shirt. I believe they are wrong. I believe, in fact, that being a good steward of the environment and in our communities and being an efficient and profitable business are not mutually exclusive. In fact they are one in the same. And I can show you why. (Scott, 2005, p. 103)

Despite early skepticism that Wal-Mart's interest in sustainable business practices was just a passing fad or greenwashing (deceptively performing some green activities to continue with environmentally harmful business practices), Wal-Mart continued to focus on integrating sustainable business practices into its operations. For example, its move to small detergent bottles was done over the objections of suppliers such as Unilever who had tried the small bottles before but watched sorrowfully as customers continued to buy the larger bottles that simply contained more water in them (Humes, 2011, p. 147).

Wal-Mart pressed manufacturers such as Unilever and Procter & Gamble to revise the packaging so that customers would clearly see that the small bottle equaled the big bottle. Scott went to television shows such as Ellen Degeneres and promoted Small & Mighty All detergent. Degeneres's show featured a mock game called "Lighten Your Load" in which contestants brought in their dirty laundry to demonstrate how the contents of one bottle of the concentrated detergent was enough to wash clothes in the 32 washing machines set up in the parking lot behind the studio.

With such changes in marketing the concentrated detergents, the customers began buying the concentrated detergents. After three years, the laundry detergent industry had been transformed with every detergent maker promoting its eco-friendly concentrated formulations not only in the United States but also around the world. Wal-Mart estimated that over these three years, the move to concentrated detergent saved 125 million pounds of cardboard, 500,000 gallons of diesel fuel (used to ship the detergent), 95 million pounds of plastic resin (used in manufacturing the bottles), and 400 million gallons of water (formerly used to dilute the detergent when it came in the larger sized bottles) (Humes, 2011, p. 23).

Wal-Mart took steps toward becoming a more sustainable firm after Scott's pivotal address in 2005. These continued after long-time Wal-Mart executive Mike Duke took over as CEO upon the retirement of Scott in early 2009. Later that year, the firm announced its plans to develop a worldwide sustainable product index that would establish a single source of data for evaluating the sustainability of its products (Herrera, 2009). Eventually, products would have tags reporting on the sustainability grade the product earned, and apps for smart phones would be developed to enable shoppers to do their own quick research on product sustainability.

## "The Index"

The first step in this project to develop "The Index" was to notify Wal-Mart's suppliers of its intentions (and what this would mean for them). Accordingly, the firm sent a letter to its suppliers in 2009 posing 15 questions to them about their own processes and operations (Wal-Mart, 2011). These are depicted in Figure 11.3.

The second step in developing The Index was the formation of an independently governed Sustainability Consortium that would construct the product database—the essential ingredient to The Index. Duke intended this product database to be open, composed from many sources, reviewed by peers, and carrying no hype for brands included in the database (Humes, 2011, p. 192). Founding members of this consortium included the green household cleaning products company Seventh Generation; agribusiness giants Monsanto, Cargill, and Tyson Foods; cleaning products company Clorox; Dairy Management, Inc.; Waste Management; Disney; SC Johnson; Procter & Gamble; Pepsico; computer manufacturers Hewlett-Packard and Dell; and a dozen others. Wal-Mart competitors, Best Buy and Safeway, joined after a few months. These member companies paid up to $100,000 to join the consortium and form the steering committee for setting policy for the consortium. Despite the lower rate for nonprofits ($10,000), only one joined—the environmental group World Wildlife Fund.

**Figure 11.3** Fifteen Questions Wal-Mart Proposed to its Suppliers in 2009 as Part of Its Supplier Sustainability Assessment

|  | **Sustainability Supplier Assessment Questions** |
|---|---|
| **Energy and Climate**<br><br>Reduce energy costs and greenhouse emissions | 1. Have you measured and taken steps to reduce your corporate greenhouse gas emissions? (Y/N)<br><br>2. Have you opted to report your greenhouse gas emissions and climate change strategy to the Carbon Disclosure Project (CDP)? (Y/N)<br><br>3. What are your total annual greenhouse gas emissions in the most recent year measured? (Enter total metric tons $CO_2e$, e.g. CDP 2009 Questionnaire, Questions 7-11 Scope 1 and 2 emissions)<br><br>4. Have you set publicly available greenhouse gas reduction targets? If yes, what are those targets? (Enter total metric tons and target date, e.g. CDP 2009 Questionnaire, Question 23) |
| **Material Efficiency**<br><br>Reduce waste and enhance quality | Scores will be automatically calculated based on participation in the Packaging Scorecard in addition to the following:<br><br>5. If measured, please report total amount of solid waste generated from the facilities that produce your products for Walmart for the most recent year measured. (Enter total lbs)<br><br>6. Have you set publicly available solid waste reduction targets? If yes, what are those targets? (Enter total lbs and target date)<br><br>7. If measured, please report total water use from the facilities that produce your product(s) for Walmart for the most recent year measured. (Enter total gallons)<br><br>8. Have you set publically available water use reduction targets? If yes, what are those targets? (Enter total gallons and target date) |
| **Nature and Resources**<br><br>High-quality, responsibly sourced raw materials | 9. Have you established publicly available sustainability purchasing guidelines for your direct suppliers that address issues such as environmental compliance, employment practices, and product/ingredient safety? (Y/N)<br><br>10. Have you obtained 3rd party certifications for any of the products that you sell to Walmart? If so, from the list of certifications below, please select those for which any of your products are or utilize materials that are, currently certified. |

| | Sustainability Supplier Assessment Questions |
|---|---|
| **People and Community**<br><br>Vibrant, productive workplaces and communities | 11. Do you know the location of 100% of the facilities that produce your product(s)? (Y/N) |
| | 12. Before beginning a business relationship with a manufacturing facility, do you evaluate their quality of production and capacity for production? (Y/N) |
| | 13. Do you have a process for managing social compliance at the manufacturing level? (Y/N) |
| | 14. Do you work with your supply base to resolve issues found during social compliance evaluations and also document specific corrections and improvements? (Y/N) |
| | 15. Do you invest in community development activities in the markets you source from and/or operate within? (Y/N) |

*Source:* Wal-Mart. Supplier Sustainability Assessment. Page 4 of 32. www.walmartstores.com/download/4055.pdf

The third step for The Index would be the creation of the tags and apps that would allow The Index to be readily used by consumers in their shopping. Upon the formation of the consortium, not every firm in the consortium wanted a big red tag for nonsustainability attached to their products in stores, so the idea of a red (not sustainable) or green tag (sustainable) for products did not initially receive unanimous support within the consortium (Humes, 2011, p. 194). By comparison, other firms in the consortium felt confident that they would receive favorable ratings for sustainability and wanted to have their sustainability scores known by the public as soon as possible.

## GoodGuide to the Rescue?

Despite the challenges Wal-Mart has encountered in developing The Index, a nonprofit GoodGuide (www.goodguide.com) seems to be making inroads on offering credible sustainability ratings for products on three dimensions: (a) health, (b) the environment, and (c) society (labor and human rights). The company founded in 2007 by Dara O'Rourke, a supply-chain expert and professor at the University of California—Berkeley, now rates more than 100,000 consumer items on these three dimensions on a scale from 1 to 10. GoodGuide also offers a mobile app that allows the user to swipe a product's bar code at the store to receive GoodGuide's rating (see Figure 11.4). For shopping online, GoodGuide has developed a toolbar situated at the bottom of a computer screen that automatically shows its ratings for products that one might view at shopping sites, such as Amazon.com (Keegan, 2011, p. 134).

O'Rourke believes GoodGuide is about halfway to ironclad ratings. It has put together a team of life-cycle specialists, engineers, chemists, and nutritionists who comb through data from more than 1,000 sources, such as company-issued information, government agencies, research firms, environmental groups, academia, and the media. "It can take you five years to do a risk assessment of one chemical," O'Rourke said. "We're taking what we believe is the best available science and getting it out to consumers right away" (Keegan, 2011, p. 134).

**Figure 11.4**   Comparison of Two Companies at GoodGuide.com

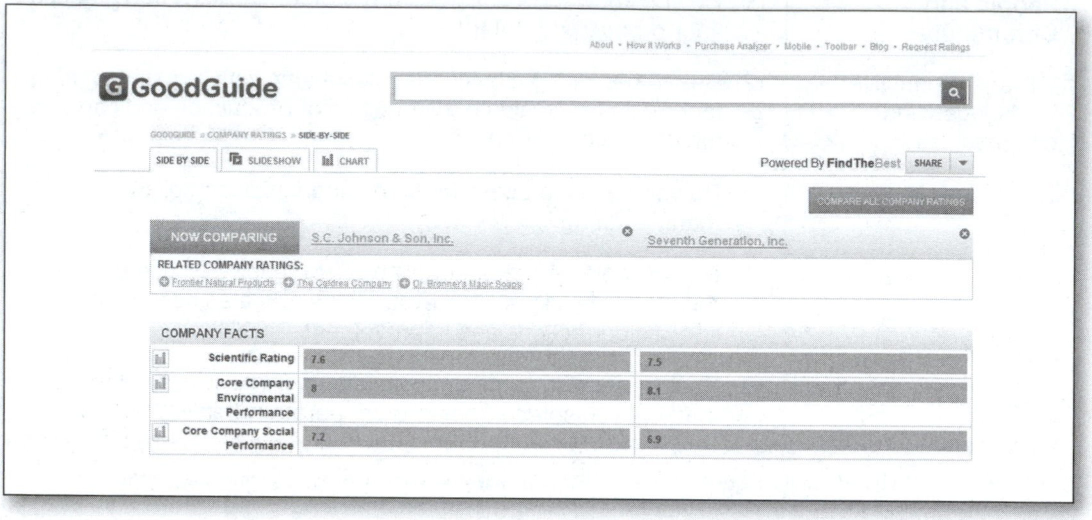

*Source:* http://www.goodguide.com

## Measuring a Product's Carbon Footprint

A product's carbon footprint represents the amount of carbon dioxide and other greenhouse gases that are emitted into the atmosphere when products are made, shipped, stored, and then used by consumers. According to Nic Marks, founder of the New Economic Foundation's Center for Well-Being based in London, the introduction of the carbon footprint concept has been the most important development in recent years for the environmental movement (Marks, 2007, personal communication). Calculators for business and individual carbon footprints are now easily accessible at websites such as www.carbonfootprint.com. By using such calculators, citizens can understand their own possible contribution to global climate change. In this way, carbon emissions are no longer clear, odorless, and tasteless; instead they take on a more concrete form in the minds of individuals. With such measurement comes responsibility and accountability, where before there was none or very little.

However, it turns out that measuring a product's carbon footprint requires a standardized approach that still needs to be refined. For example, when carbon footprint measurement began, firms focused on the product ingredients. But this told little about upstream processing (before the manufacturer received the inputs used in manufacturing), as well as about downstream activities (such as shipping of the product and the use and disposal of the product by consumers). In sum, a product's carbon footprint often depends on the breadth of the lens used to compute the carbon footprint. For example, the biggest contributor to a laundry detergent's carbon footprint is the clothes dryer—a downstream process not directly related to the ingredients of the detergent (Ball, 2008a). With this in mind, it is easier to understand that the simplest way to cut carbon emissions may be to use less of a product, or to use it in a way that is less convenient—such as washing one's clothes by hand. Drying laundry outside on a clothes line will result in 4.4 pounds less carbon dioxide per load being emitted into the atmosphere (Ball, 2008a).

As a benchmark, the average person in the United States is responsible for the emission of 118 pounds of carbon dioxide each day (Ball, 2008a). This is almost 20 metric tons per year—about five times the average of those who do not live in the United States. The simplest statistic about the carbon footprint is that for every mile a car drives, it emits about one pound of carbon dioxide. The average car in the United States emits five tons of carbon dioxide every year.

But as firms calculated the carbon footprints of their products, they discovered some amazing things. For example, Stonyfield Farm, the leading U.S. producer of organic yogurt and a major supplier to Wal-Mart, believed that energy used in making the yogurt was the biggest piece of the carbon footprint for its yogurt (Humes, 2011, p. 194). Stonyfield's leaders were stunned to learn that energy was a distant fourth in determining the size of its carbon footprint. The milk used to make the yogurt was first, followed by packaging and distribution. Stonyfield's leaders learned that cows burp regularly to digest their food (moving it across four stomachs). With these burps, the cows emit methane—a greenhouse gas. Methane gas is 25 times more harmful as a greenhouse gas than carbon dioxide. As a result, a cow's carbon footprint is 80% of a car's (Ball, 2008a). This means that in terms of contribution to global climate change, a cattle herd represents a fleet of cars about 80% the size of the number of cows in the herd.

What is a firm like Stonyfield to do when faced with thousands of cows belching the equivalent of 4 tons of carbon dioxide into the atmosphere every year? In 2009, Stonyfield worked with its organic dairy farmers who began to feed its cows with flax and other feed rich in omega-3 fatty acids to reduce methane from cow burps (Humes, 2011, p. 195). In such ways, Stonyfield hopes to score far above the industry average on The Index when it finally emerges.

To bring firms to a common approach for measuring the carbon footprints of their products, the International Standards Organization (ISO) issued guidance in ISO 14064-1 in Spring 2006; companies around the world are now using it and the related GHG (greenhouse gas) Protocol to calculate emissions consistently (Carbon Clear, 2009). Firms announcing their carbon footprint should be following these guidelines or major pieces of their carbon footprint will be ignored. For example, Dell Computers received criticism for not including the carbon emissions of its suppliers and consumers when the firm announced it was "carbon neutral" in 2008 because it had purchased carbon off-sets for a narrowly defined carbon footprint the firm had calculated for itself (Ball, 2008b). In fact, Dell's suppliers and consumers each had carbon footprints 10 times the size Dell had computed for itself. In effect, Dell had only neutralized about 5% of the greenhouse gases that go into making and using its products.

## CONCLUSION

This chapter began by posing the following question: "Is it possible to use business for the benefit of the environment?" A review of Yvon Chouinard's outdoor clothing company Patagonia highlighted how the firm has not only directed millions of dollars to nonprofits supporting environmental conservation and activism, but also it has inspired legions of customers and other businesses to pursue more environmentally friendly ways to conduct their affairs.

For "no-growth" proponents of macromarketing's critical school, the reality of operating a business remains unpalatable. Chouinard once told an audience of Wal-Mart employees that if a company were going to make anything, it had to acknowledge that it would damage the world (Humes, 2011, p. 204). For those who focus on the environment as the prime source of value for human living, Chouinard's words mean that business in its current form and with its objective of growth is an enemy of the environment. In this view, the atmosphere would be regarded as a public good, that no one human or one business has the right to appropriate for its own purposes. Alternatively, for the "some-growth" proponents of macromarketing's developmental school, managing the environment is acceptable. In this view, the atmosphere would be regarded as a common good—if humans could just agree on the rules for managing it as a common good.

This chapter's review of the public sector's potential for managing the atmosphere as a common good suggests that the likelihood of this happening soon is weak. However, it seems that increasingly individuals think that greenhouse gas emissions matter in global climate change. For this reason, businesses have begun to take note and to follow environmentally oriented, trail-blazing businesses, such as Patagonia. In 2005, Wal-Mart's leaders recognized that the next generation of consumers perceived that environmental issues mattered and that these future consumers would punish firms that ignored environmental issues. Investors would soon care. Insurance companies setting rates in an era of climate disruption would assess risk according to these developments. As a result, Wal-Mart decided to go "all in" and pursue sustainable business practices for itself and its suppliers, so that its customers would benefit from safer, more reliable, and more efficiently made products. In sum, no business will receive the sustainability equivalent of a 4.0 grade point average (Humes, 2011, p. 204). However, the actions of businesses such as Wal-Mart and its now 100,000 suppliers worldwide suggest that a movement has begun in the business world to pursue sustainability business practices.

Although Wal-Mart initiated an effort to develop The Index for product sustainability in 2009 envisioning a number from 1 to 10 or a color-coding scheme, it has found this undertaking more daunting than it first seemed. Andrea Thomas, Wal-Mart's Senior VP for Sustainability, promises less. "By 2014, consumers will have more information about the sustainability of products they buy," Thomas said (Keegan, 2011).

One part of this challenge arises from trade-offs that firms make to be more green. For example, Patagonia adopted organic cotton as the input for its clothes—thereby avoiding harmful pesticides in the growing of cotton. However, even organic cotton uses a surprising amount of water—increasingly in short supply (Keegan, 2011). One estimate asserts that a pair of jeans requires 1,200 gallons of water to manufacture. Another part of the challenge stems from overseas manufacturers having little information about the inputs and coatings they currently use. For example, when former U.S. Treasury Secretary Hank Paulson was touring a Chinese factory during his term in the cabinet of President George W. Bush, he asked the factory manager about pollution controls at the plant that was pouring out thick smoke from its smokestack at the time. The manager pointed to a nearby field. "See those two camels and a goat?" the manager asked Paulson. "When they fall over from the pollution, we turn off the factory" (Keegan, 2011, p. 133).

In sum, it seems that although it is not possible to conduct business without changing the environment, it is possible to conduct business so that the environment benefits. In other words, business can be done not just in an eco-efficient way (doing less bad) but also in an eco-effective way (that replenishes, restores, and nourishes the rest of the world) (McDonough & Braungart, 2002). However, businesses are in the early stages of developing sustainable business practices that would be termed eco-effective. More will be said about this in the next chapter.

With the population of the world expected to grow from 7 billion today to 9 billion by 2050 (it is forecast to decline slowly after this), firms like Wal-Mart will be poised to engage many more customers around the world. However, Wal-Mart CEO Duke explains, "[I]f our environmental demands continue at the same rate, we will need the equivalent of two planets to maintain our standard of living in another 25 years" (Keegan, 2011, p. 134). With this in mind, the solution offered by the critical school of macromarketing that calls for less consumption seems to be an important element in future approaches to doing business in a way that benefits the environment. In short, demarketing consumption will likely be a social marketing effort that will take a broad and enduring effort to make it cool to consume less in the future.

## QUESTIONS

- In what ways does Patagonia benefit the environment?
- To what extent can other firms benefit the environment like Patagonia?
- What are controversies about sustainable entrepreneurship?
- Is the atmosphere that surrounds the Earth a public good, a common good, or something else? What might it become in the future at some time?
- What role do you envision governments taking with regard to global climate change in the future? Explain. What would it take for government to take a different role than the one you envision?
- Compare and contrast the environmental stewardship of Patagonia and Wal-Mart.
- Using a 1 to 10 scale with "1" representing "enemy of the environment" and 10 representing "replenishing and restoring the environment," how would you rate Patagonia? Wal-Mart? How would you expect to rate them in 10 years? What does this mean for society and societies?

# MAVERICKS WHO MADE IT

## Jim Neiman

IN 1906, PRESIDENT Theodore Roosevelt established Devils Tower—a flat-topped tower of gray, igneous rock rising more than 280 meters above the surrounding forest and grasslands of the Black Hills in far-northeastern Wyoming—as the first national monument protected area in the United States (National Park Service, 2011). About six miles from Devil's Tower, in the exposed-red clay hillsides of the Black Hills, lies Hulett, Wyoming (population 500), headquarters for Neiman Enterprises, Inc. (NEI).

Jim Neiman's grandfather, A. C. Neiman, built a saw mill in the Black Hills to process Ponderosa pine timber. Today, NEI owns the last saw mill operating in Wyoming, as well as two other mills 60 miles from Hulett in the South Dakota Black Hills.

In 2000, Neiman decided to integrate sustainable business practices into the operations of the firm he inherited from his father. Rather than force his firm to embrace these sustainable business practices rapidly and earn the Sustainable Forestry Initiative's (SFI) certification, Neiman chose to educate his employees and allow them to embrace the principles of sustainability over a ten-year period. He wanted a more sustainable approach to business baked into the culture of his firm. In 2010, Neiman Enterprises operations received SFI certification. Neiman commented:

> It took time so people could buy into it," Neiman said. "It was about culture change. It was about bringing them along, rather than ruling by edict. We wanted to pass decision-making to the lowest level, so the new philosophy of the company would actually permeate the culture. (Neiman, 2011, personal communication)

The SFI promotes sustainable forest management, and certification indicates the firm sources its wood fiber legally from noncontroversial forests. Certification also indicates the firm employs sustainable forestry practices to protect water quality, biodiversity, wildlife habitat, species at risk, and

Forests with Exceptional Conservation (SFI, 2011). The firm's employees, as well as independent contractors working for the firm, must be trained in sustainable forestry practices. In short, SFI-certified forest-products companies value the long-term productivity and health of forests. This includes soil productivity and protection from wildfire, insects, disease, and invasive plants and animals.

*Neiman explains:*

Certification is expensive. I spend between $150,000 to $250,000 per year to accomplish all that certification requires and I don't get a penny back. Our employees ask 'why are you doing this when you don't get any financial incentive?' My answer is that you have to believe in it. I want to have the right thing done on the ground—not just doing what a customer might want. (Neiman, 2011, personal communication)

Rather than tightly focusing on delivering the grades of wood that a customer at Home Depot might want when they want it, Neiman wants his 450 employees and 250 contract workers to follow the firm's sustainability philosophy whose first principle is integrity.

"How do you really get the right thing done out there where our people work?" Neiman asked:

It means convincing 28 logging crews who are independent, 75 logging truckers who are independent, that they have to follow our philosophy. For example, in the Spring the ground is wet, and we might be almost out of logs in the mill. Yet, somebody wants to pull out a truck and go out on the wet ground to retrieve some logs in the forest. But our philosophy would say it is of a higher importance to run out of logs in the mill, rather than risk our equipment and people in precarious situations in the forest, then. You'd be surprised how employees can be more forward-thinking before Spring and figure out how to put more logs down in retrievable places. (Neiman, 2011, personal communication)

Complexity characterizes forestry today. For example, Neiman spends one to two days each week on "bug issues." Most of the Rocky Mountain region from British Columbia in Canada to New Mexico has experienced drought conditions that have weakened trees' ability to fend off the pine bark beetle that bores under the bark of the tree carrying a fungus with it. The spreading fungus stops the flow of sap up the tree killing infested trees in 48 hours. British Columbia has lost 33 million acres of pine trees, while Colorado has lost 5 million acres (Robbins, 2008). The U.S. National Park Service allowed thinning of the forest near Mount Rushmore in the Black Hills as a step to allow the remaining trees better access to water in order to improve their chances of surviving infestation. (These thinned trees were not approved for merchantable timber.)

*(Continued)*

(Continued)

Humans have controlled fires in forests in the last century. Forest fires used to contribute to a diversity of tree ages in the forest. However, today most forests in the United States are old:

> We don't tolerate fires, but our forests here are 120 years old," Neiman said. "That is way, way too old. We need a diverse-age population of trees. I have walked the Medicine Bow Forest [in southeast Wyoming]. The younger trees are surviving, because the bugs are only hitting down to 5-inch diameter trees. (Neiman, 2011, personal communication)

With broader canopies, the trees keep snow in the winter from accumulating on the ground where it would later melt and soak deep into the ground. Instead, the snow evaporates up in the boughs of the pine trees. "Eighty percent of water is not getting to aquifers these days," Neiman said. "At the base of the trees, there is just a bed of pine needles, no other growth. The trees are their own worst enemy because they are so old and so large."

The first leases for logging on U.S. National Forest Service lands were written for the Black Hills National Forest in western South Dakota and northeastern Wyoming, covering an area 125 miles long and 65 miles wide. Neiman and his firm must abide by the rules and regulations of the U.S. Forest Service. Accordingly, only selective cutting is done in which a mixture of trees from one stand would be harvested (as compared with clear-cutting).

Controversy continues to haunt the forest products industry. Currently, there are two certifications for sustainable forestry: the environmentalists' certification group the Forest Stewardship Council (FSC) and the forest products and paper association certification group SFI. ForestEthics, an environmental group, has denounced the SFI as a greenwashing effort mainly because the SFI was launched by the American Forest & Paper Association (ForestEthics, 2010).

"For the FSC, there is no certification if you log on federal lands," Neiman explained. "We can't even begin the FSC process because we work with the U.S. Forest Service."

Two different environmental groups have eyed Neiman Enterprises warily over the years: the Biodiversity Conservation Alliance based in Laramie, Wyoming (www.voiceforthewild.org) and the Sierra Club (http://southdakota.sierraclub.org/BlackHills). Neiman said:

> They want to stop logging in these forests. They don't believe man should be there. They don't want hunting and mining either. They would let only a few backpackers in there. On the other hand, the Nature Conservancy is a group that accepts managing the land and encourages being a good steward of the earth. (Neiman, 2011, personal communication)

The specter of a ban on logging in the Black Hills someday lingers:

> When the spotted owl issue wiped out 325 saw mills in the West in the 80s and 90s, we had to diversify Hulett so that if an endangered species was identified in the Black Hills, Hulett could survive. The town is basically a ranching, timber and tourism locale. To broaden our tourism appeal,

we built a golf course, and an airport. This was a sustainability issue. In an ongoing way, I give employees time for family and time to do their civic work. I helped start the ambulance service in Hulett. I was the first certified emergency medical technician here. (Neiman, 2011, personal communication)

Jim Neiman's story illustrates some of the complexity and controversy that comes with working in an industry so deeply involved with the environment. Integrating sustainable business practices into his firm took time and still requires hundreds of thousands of dollars each year to maintain. Neiman consults regularly with foresters, and he serves on four land-use planning boards at the local, Black Hills, regional, and national levels.

Taking a holistic approach to his business led him to not be satisfied with leading an enterprise providing jobs for 700 employees and contract workers. He helped make Hulett a more sustainable community through the development of ambulance services, as well as building infrastructure to support tourism in the future. Since 2001, he has also served as a member of the University of Wyoming Board of Trustees.

"Sustainability—it goes way deep," Neiman said. "How do you sustain the family business? How do you keep the community healthy?"

## Questions

- Why did Neiman choose to take the slow approach in obtaining certification by the Sustainable Forest Initiative?
- What are the costs to Neiman for pursuing sustainability at Neiman Enterprises? In the community?
- How would those from macromarketing's critical school assess Neiman's performance in sustainability? How would those from macromarketing's developmental school make the same assessment?
- What does Neiman's story say about living one's life with an environmental-orientation in a rural community, as opposed to a suburban locale or a city?

## REFERENCES

1 % for the Planet. (2011). *1 % for the Planet*. Retrieved from http://www.onepercentfortheplanet.org

Ball, J. (2008a, October 6). Six products, six carbon footprints. *The Wall Street Journal*. Retrieved from http://www.online.wsj.com

Ball, J. (2008b, December 30). Green goal of 'carbon neutrality' hits limit. *The Wall Street Journal*. Retrieved from http://www.online.wsj.com

Black, R. (2011, July 5). Global warming lull down to China's coal growth. *BBC News*. Retrieved from http://www.bbc.co.uk

Bradsher, K. (2006, November 7). China to pass U.S. in 2009 in emissions. *The New York Times*. Retrieved from http://www.nytimes.com

Brand, S. (2009). *Whole earth discipline: An ecopragmatist manifesto*. New York, NY: Viking.

Business Green. (2011a, August 26). US breaks ground on first industrial-scale carbon capture project. *The Guardian*. Retrieved from http://www.guardian.co.uk

Business Green. (2011b, July 1). AEP: Lack of climate regulation killed $668 m CCS project. *The Guardian*. Retrieved from http://www.guardian.co.uk

Carbon Clear. (2009, February 2). Dell, carbon footprints and boundaries. *Carbon Clear Blog*. Retrieved from http://carbonclear.blogspot.com

Casey, S. (2007, May 29). Patagonia: Blueprint for green business. *Fortune*. Retrieved from http://cnnmoney.com

Choi, D. Y., & Gray, E. R. (2011). *Values-centered entrepreneurs and their companies*. New York, NY: Routledge.

Chouinard, Y. (2005). *Let my people go surfing: The education of a reluctant businessman*. New York, NY: Penguin Books.

Chouinard, Y. (2010). Leading the examined life is a pain in the ass. *Patagonia environmental initiatives 2010* (p. 5). Ventura, CA: Patagonia.

Cohen, B., & Winn, M. I. (2007). Market imperfections, opportunity and sustainable entrepreneurship. *Journal of Business Venturing*, 22, 29–49.

Conservation Alliance. (2011). *About Us*. Retrieved from http://www.conservationalliance.com/about

EPA. (November 2005). *Everyday choices: Opportunities for environmental stewardship*. Report to Stephen L. Johnson, Administrator, US Environmental Protection Agency. EPA Innovation Action Council. Washington, DC.

ForestEthics. (2010, November). *SFI: Certified greenwash*. Retrieved from http://forestethics.org/down loads/SFI-Certified-Greenwash_Report_ForestEthics.pdf

Friedman, T. (2008) *The world is hot, flat, and crowded: Why we need a green revolution*. New York, NY: Farrar, Straus and Giroux.

Galbraith, K. (2010, December 16). Politics at two levels in fight with the EPA. *The New York Times*. Retrieved from http://www.nytimes.com

Gingrich, N., & Maple, T. L. (2007). *A contract with the earth*. Baltimore, MD: Johns Hopkins Press.

Herrera, T. (2009 September 24). Wal-mart Sustainability Index means big business. *Green Biz.com*. Retrieved from http://www.greenbiz.com/blog/2009/09/24/walmart-sustainability-index-means -big-business

Holt, D., & Cameron, D. (2010). *Cultural strategy: Using innovative ideologies to build breakthrough brands*. Oxford, UK: Oxford University Press.

Humes, E. (2011). *Force of nature: The unlikely story of Wal-Mart's green revolution*. New York, NY: Harper Business.

Jha, A. (2008, September 5). Explainer: How carbon is captured and stored. *The Guardian*. Retrieved from http://www.guardian.co.uk

Keegan, P. (2011, July 25). The trouble with green product ratings. *Fortune*, pp. 130–134.

Lallanilla, M. (2011, May 21). Theodore Roosevelt and the environment: Was Teddy Roosevelt a true environmentalist? *About.com*. Retrieved from http://greenliving.about.com

LaBarre, P. (2010, December 30). Moving past austerity: Business leadership principles for 2011. *Fortune*. Retrieved from http://www.fortune.cnn.com

Lomborg, B. (2007). *Cool it: The skeptical environmentalist's guide to global warming*. New York, NY: Alfred A. Knopf

Lovins, L. H. (2010). Foreword. In M. Russo (Ed.), *Companies on a mission: Entrepreneurial strategies for growing sustainability, responsibly, and profitably* (pp. x–xii). Stanford, CA: Stanford University Press.

Marshall, C. (2011, March 22). British Columbia survives 3 years and $848 million worth of carbon taxes. *The New York Times*. Retrieved from http://www.nytimes.com

McDonough, W., & Braungart, M. (2002). *Cradle to cradle*. New York, NY: North Point Press.

National Park Service. (2011). *Devil's tower*. Retrieved from http://www.nps.gov/deto/index.htm

O'Hara, K. (2011). *Conservatism*. London, UK: Reaktion Books.

Patagonia. (2010). *Patagonia environmental initiatives 2010*. Ventura, CA: Patagonia.

Patagonia. (2011). Patagonia's Mission Statement. Retrieved from http://www.patagonia.com

Pew Center on Global Climate Change. (2011). Coal and climate change facts. Retrieved from http://www.pewclimate.org

REI (2011). About REI. Retrieved from http://www.rei.com/aboutrei/about_rei.html

Reinhard, F., Casadesus-Mansanell, R., & Freier, D. (2004 December 14). Patagonia. *Harvard Business School*.

Ridgeway, R. (2010). Use business to inspire and implement solutions to the environmental crisis. *Patagonia environmental initiatives 2010* (p. 44). Ventura, CA: Patagonia.

Robbins, J. (2008, November 18). Bark beetles kill millions of acres of trees in West. *The New York Times*. Retrieved from http://www.nytimes.com

Rogers, S., & Evans, L. (2011, January 31). World carbon dioxide emissions data by country: China speeds ahead of the rest. *The Guardian*. Retrieved from www.guardian.co.uk

Scott, L. (2005). Address to Wal-Mart employees and suppliers, October 24th. In E. Humes (Ed.), *Force of nature: The unlikely story of Wal-Mart's green revolution* (p. 103). New York, NY: Harper Business.

SFI. (2011). Sustainable Forestry Initiative. Retrieved from http://www.sfiprogram.org

Shultz, C. J., & Holbrook, M. B. (1999). Marketing and the tragedy of the commons: A synthesis, commentary, and analysis for action. *Journal of Public Policy & Marketing*, *18*(2), 218–229.

Throne, D. M., Ferrell, O.C., & Ferrell, L. (2008). *Business and society: A strategic approach to social responsibility* (3rd ed.). Boston, MA: Houghton Mifflin.

Varian, H. R. (1992). *Microeconomic analysis* (3rd ed.). New York, NY: W. W. Norton.

Walljasper, J. (2010). *All that we share: A field guide to the commons*. New York, NY: The New Press.

Wal-Mart. (2011). Sustainability Index. Retrieved from http://walmartstores.com/sustainability/9292.aspx

Watts, J. (2011, September 22). Carbon capture progress has lost momentum, says energy agency. *The Guardian*. Retrieved from http://www.guardian.co.uk

Weyrich, P. M., & Lind, W. S. (2009). *The next conservatism*. South Bend, IN: St. Augustine's Press.

Yergin, D. (2011). *The quest: Energy, security, and the remaking of the modern world*. New York, NY: The Penguin Press.

## CHAPTER 12

# Sustainable Entrepreneurship

## SEEING OPPORTUNITIES IN SOCIETAL IMPERFECTIONS

### Mia Birk—President and Co-Owner of Alta Planning + Design

New Yorkers had not seen this before, but it might change city life for good. It was a kiosk with a rack of wide-tire bikes set up in a pedestrian plaza in the middle of Manhattan. According to the announcement made in front of the kiosk and bikes on September 14, 2011, New York City's government had named Alta Bicycle Share to initiate an ambitious bike-share program to feature 10,000 bicycles available at 600 stations in Manhattan. For a yearly membership of less than $100, members will have unlimited access to the bicycles for trips less than 45 minutes.

Although the idea of New Yorkers donning bicycle helmets and riding about Manhattan and Brooklyn might make some wonder if hallucinogens had been mixed into a city planner's granola, similar bike-sharing programs have been launched in recent years in cities such as Washington, DC; Boston; Minneapolis; Chicago; Denver; Montreal; Toronto; and Melbourne, Australia. Important to New York Mayor Michael R. Bloomberg, bicycle usage has helped unclog other global cities from traffic congestion, such as London and Paris, and has made these cities more hospitable to pedestrians and bicyclists. Bloomberg wanted to see this happen in New York. To accomplish this, he had already rolled out 250 miles of bike lanes and now had announced the bike-sharing program to help make New York City's transit system greener.

The bicycle and pedestrian movement gaining momentum now has developed over many years through the sometimes patient and sometimes daring efforts of bicycle activists, city planners, policy makers, and bicycle commuters in thousands of communities around the world. Today, Mia Birk is one of the most high-profile leaders of this movement as President and Co-Owner of Alta Planning + Design based in Portland, Oregon.

Birk obtained a bachelor's degree in government and French from the University of Texas at Austin. When she went from her suburban home in Dallas to continue her studies in Washington, DC, car parking loomed as a problem. Her brother gave her his 10-speed bicycle to use. Despite being a self-described "couch potato" at the time, she used his bicycle and liked the by-products of bicycle commuting. She lost weight and felt better.

"Within a few weeks, I was in the best shape of my life, and a lifelong love affair had begun," Birk said. "Since then, I have been a dedicated bicyclist for recreation, touring, exercise, and daily utilitarian trips. I have two children—ages 13 and 9 and see bicycling as a win-win strategy for maintaining my family's health, safety, budget, and community connection" (Szczepanski, 2010, p. 1).

In her international environmental studies major at Johns Hopkins University that she began in 1988, she looked at transportation and "how where we live affects how we get around" (Moon, 2010, p. 1).

She realized that the bicycled offered at a win–win proposition to relieve congestion in cities of the world, reduce air pollution, and reduce obesity for individuals:

My first job out of grad school was researching international transportation issues. In growing Asian and Latin American cities, massive investment was poured into road building. The results? Thick congestion, horrific air quality, health and safety problems. In European and Japanese cities where the emphasis was on compact development with bicycling and walking, congestion went down while health, air quality and safety improved. Light bulbs were going off in my head. At the crossroads of my personal transformation and sustainable transportation stood a win-win solution—the bicycle. And with this epiphany came clarity. I wanted to transform American cities into bike-friendly places. (Birk, 2011, 2 min, 20 sec)

Birk was in Washington, DC, in 1991 when the federal transportation bill first included funding for trails, bike lanes, and sidewalks. Because she was working with a coalition focused on energy conservation, she became aware that jobs would soon be available in the bicycle and pedestrian field (Moon, 2010).

Birk's credibility in the bicycle and pedestrian movement originated from her accomplishments as a public sector worker in Portland from 1993 to 1999 during the city's rise to become the top bicycling city in the United States (Moon, 2010). During this time, Birk served as Portland's bicycle program manager.

From 1994 to 2010, Portland topped *Bicycling* magazine's list of "America's Top 50 Bike-Friendly Cities" (Moon, 2010). By 2000, Portland (with a population of more than 500,000) had 300 miles of bike trails and thousands of bike parking spaces. But more importantly, the car-centric culture of Portland shifted from regarding bicycling as a fringe activity to a point of civic pride. Bike safety is now taught in Portland schools, and many children ride their bicycles to school each day. More than 4,000 rides, races, and bike events occur each year, such as a free breakfast in the public square to celebrate "Bike to Work" month. Busses have bike racks. The mayor rides, and businesses have embraced the opportunities of a bicycling culture. For example, realizing that one car parking space (allowing one customer to park) can be replaced with a bike rack that allows 20 customers to park, businesses have begun to swap one parking space so that more bicycle-riding customers can park near their stores. More than 100 car spaces have been replaced with 61 bike "corrals," creating 1,098 on-street spaces (Dulken, 2010, p. 2).

All of the infrastructure improvements in Portland to boost bicycling cost $60 million, according to Birk (2011). "That might sound like a lot," Birk said. "But that's less than 1% of the transportation budget for the city. That amount would buy us only one mile of urban freeway. That is one heck of a bang-for-a-buck investment."

"In the early 1990's only 1% in Portland regularly commuted," Birk said. "Today, 8% do. Fifteen per cent use their bikes some of the time and this is 30% in some neighborhoods. As the bike usage rate rose, the crash rate went down. In addition to improved health and air quality, the city gained a $100 million dollar industry with 1,500 green jobs" (Birk, 2011, 11 min, 40 sec).

Bike parking is now an art form in Portland. Bike racks can be found in the shape of salmon, coffee cups, lotuses, and other whimsical shapes. Such art racks share the joy and delight of cycling with those who see them. Other cities, such as New York and Nashville, Tennessee, have copied these designs.

Recognizing that not all bicycle rides are for vigorous exercise in spandex, clothing companies now offer designs in stretch silks and merino wools. Some commuters hit the streets in Italian suits and ties, or with floral print dresses flowing behind them. Even water spray from a wet road can't keep these commuters from their bicycle riding. "A good suit sheds the water," architect Rick Potestio said. "And even if you're a little damp, you look better than you would showing up in some geek attire" (McInerny, 2008, p. D1).

"People think Portlanders just drank some microbrew one night and started riding bikes in the morning," Birk said. "Not the case at all" (Dundas, 2011, p. 11). The truth is that, despite some forward-looking funding for beginning bike trails as a reaction to the 1973 Arab Oil Embargo, Birk often endured bitter public meetings in Portland. Portland's culture and transportation system, like many other U.S. cities, focused on the automobile. But Birk proved skillful in creating change inside the system of city government, regional planning organizations, citizen groups, and businesses (Dundas, 2011, p. 11). Early in her time as Portland's bike program manager, she mobilized citizen support that led to the city council adopting a bike-network plan. She later helped this plan come into reality by resolving thousands of ugly, traffic-engineering prob-lems. Along the way, she had to fight federal regulators, explain her actions to the skeptical journalists of *The Oregonian* newspaper, and cajole reluctant city maintenance workers to finish the planned work for colored bike lanes, bike bridges, and a trail along the Willamette River (Birk & Kurmanskie, 2010). "There are political battles behind every single piece of infrastructure that exists," Birk said. "To succeed in that arena, you have to build teams" (Dundas, 2011, p. 12).

Birk left her job after giving birth to her son. It wasn't long after that she received a phone call from Michael J. Jones, a former city planner from the East Bay of San Francisco. Jones had recently launched a two-person planning and design consultancy focused on biking and walking. He asked if she would like to open an office for him in Portland. Birk jumped at the chance.

"I am happy to say that the lessons learned transcend Portland," Birk said. "Our nation-wide staff is working in hundreds of communities across North America and beyond giving millions the opportunities to live healthier lives" (Birk, 2011, 10 min, 50 sec). With Jones as CEO, Birk now serves as president of Alta Planning & Design, and she leads a 75-person staff of engineers, planners, and landscape architects who execute similar plans for cities large and small—even in Dubai. "It seems like, again and again, I've worked to take some-thing that's really small and make it into something larger," Birk says. "I'm trying to teach people to look at their cities' landscape and imagine what might be possible" (Dundas, 2011, p. 12).

"If we plan and build our cities around driving, then that's what we will do," Birk said. "But if we plan and build around bicycling and walking, and then encourage people to do so in ways that are meaningful to their lives, then that's what we'll do. We have only begun to scratch the surface, because 60 % of the population is interested in cycling and 40 % of trips in the US are less than two miles—a ten-minute bike ride" (Birk, 2011, 12 min, 44 sec).

## Your Thoughts?

- Why did New York City pursue such an ambitious bike-sharing program?
- How did Birk's studies help her envision a transportation future for cities and then go help invent it?
- Why would *Bicycling* magazine name Portland as its top bike-friendly city for 17 consecutive years?
- How would Birk's story likely have turned out differently if she had been athletically inclined from an early age and became an elite, professional bicycle road-racer?
- In what ways would you say Birk is an innovator?

## CHAPTER OVERVIEW AND LEARNING OBJECTIVES

This chapter will highlight some of today's most important topics in environmental entrepreneurship. The "planet" dimension of sustainable entrepreneurship will be considered from the perspectives of both macromarketing's critical school and the developmental school (which were discussed in the previous chapter). A crucial question these schools of thought address is whether growth-oriented entrepreneurial firms can be good for the environment. In addition to the controversy surrounding growth (and how this contributes to environmental degradation itself), environmentally oriented businesses are also controversial because of (a) their involvement in political action and (b) the potential of other worthy social causes being eclipsed by the attention environmental issues might receive from the media and in public discourse. More will be said about these controversies in Chapter 15.

A set of contributing factors to the recent turn by some firms toward sustainability can be understood by considering the context in which business is now conducted. Specifically, social, technological, and resource changes comprise the "STaR" elements of the context for business and must now be considered (Werbach, 2009). A brief examination of what fuels environmentally oriented firms—consumers purchasing "green" brands—will give insight into the possible future of such firms.

Firm responses to the environmental imperative are diverse. As sustainability consultant Darren Duber-Smith observes, no firm has ever attained 100% sustainable status (Duber-Smith, 2009). A "cradle-to-cradle" approach to turn waste for firms into food for other entities is at the core of architect William McDonough's emphasis on reusing and recycling to be more environmentally effective. As a consultant, McDonough and his partner Michael Braungart have developed the McDonough-Braungart Protocol to assist firms such as the Ford Motor Company and furniture-maker Herman Miller to improve the environmental stewardship of their operations. The McDonough-Braungart Protocol represents one way for firms to self-regulate themselves. Voluntary compliance to internationally respected standards is one avenue for firms to pursue self-regulation. The International Standards Organization based in Switzerland offers an ISO 14001 certification program for environmental management similar to the quality standards in manufacturing, such as ISO 9000, or the most recently developed standards for social responsibility—ISO 2600 (see Chapter 5). Other formalized approaches include CERES, and the Natural Step (Mager & Sibilia, 2010).

As part of self-regulation, metrics for environmental stewardship are important for environmentally oriented firms. The carbon footprint is one metric that enables firms to gauge their contribution to increasing the amount of carbon in the atmosphere—a key factor in global climate change. Such metrics often lead firms to realize that their supply chain accounts for a major portion of the carbon footprint for their products and services. The elusive pursuit of carbon neutrality raises questions about how carbon neutral a firm can become.

Any product, service, or process that delivers value using limited or zero nonrenewable resources and/or creates significantly less waste than conventional offerings can be classified as "clean tech." Three main sectors of clean tech include (a) transportation, (b) water, and (c) energy. Examples of ventures from each of these sectors will be featured in this chapter's Mavericks Who Made It. This chapter concludes with not one but four Mavericks in Markets to illustrate how four types of market imperfections hold opportunities for entrepreneurs to create profit-making solutions for environmental problems (Cohen & Winn, 2007, p. 31). These market imperfections to which ventures can be targeted follow: (a) inefficient systems, (b) externalities, (c) flawed pricing mechanisms, and (d) imperfectly distributed information.

After this chapter, you should be able to answer the following questions:

- What are the four stages of entrepreneurship?
- What is sustainable entrepreneurship?
- What are three reasons macromarketing scholars believe consumers are changing their attitudes and lifestyles to reflect more concern for the planet and communities today?
- What is ISO 14001? CERES? The Natural Step?
- What is the LOHAS segment of consumers?
- What is meant by "cradle-to-cradle" design?
- What are the five stages characterizing businesses' move toward the integration of sustainable business practices?
- What is clean tech? What are types of clean tech?

## UNDERSTANDING SUSTAINABLE ENTREPRENEURSHIP

Entrepreneurs are those who provide a new product or service. Entrepreneurs are also those who develop and use new ways to produce or deliver existing goods and services at lower cost (Baumol, Litan, & Schramm, 2007). "Entrepreneurs innovate. Innovation is the specific instrument of entrepreneurship" (Drucker, 1985, p. 30). The effect of innovation is the creative destruction (old forms of business being made obsolete by new forms) cited by the 20th century economist Joseph Schumpeter who celebrated the entrepreneur.

Mia Birk's story highlights important aspects of taking an entrepreneurial orientation. First, entrepreneurship does not begin with a product or service but with an opportunity that is rooted in the external environment (Morris, 1998). From her work in promoting energy conservation policy in Washington, DC, she recognized that the federal transportation legislation's inclusion of funding for bicycle and pedestrian travel would create many opportunities for transforming urban landscapes into communities aggressive about including such travel in their transportation systems. She took the opportunity to go to Portland as the city's bicycle program manager recognizing that Oregon was forward-thinking in developing alternatives to automobile travel. Oregon was already using a portion of the state budget to enhance roadways for bicycle travel. This illustrates how the opportunity—public funding of bicycle and pedestrian transportation infrastructure—existed in the external environment outside of any one firm.

Then, over a period of seven years in the 1990s, Birk provided community-wide leadership to change the culture of Portland to be more bicycle friendly (Mapes, 2009). Importantly, she learned what it took to win approval for infrastructure improvements for alternative means of transportation so that many constituencies were pleased with the outcome. This illustrates how entrepreneurs are not born, but they develop over time through learning.

When Michael J. Jones contacted her after she had left her position with city government, she was ready to join him by opening the Portland office of his new firm. In this way, she would develop the opportunities for planning and designing bicycle and pedestrian transportation into the plans of cities across the United States and beyond. The bike-sharing program of Alta in New York City was not its first. Alta Bicycle Share had already successfully launched bike-sharing programs in Boston and Washington, DC.

**Figure 12.1**   There Are Over 175 Capital Bikeshare Stations in the Washington, D.C. Area

In all of its bike-sharing programs, Alta Bicycle Share does not control all aspects of the bike-sharing program but relies on its other partners, such as Public Bike Systems of Montreal, which provides the bicycles and kiosks with solar-powered docking stations, theft-resistant locking devices, and credit-card processing technology. Alta Planning +

Design serves as a "big brother" to Alta Bicycle Share by joining in when pitching new business and giving depth when Alta Bicycle Share interacts with governmental agencies unwilling to work with startups (Coster, 2011).

## Stages of Entrepreneurship

Entrepreneurship does not only occur at a particular point in time. Rather, a dynamic process of entrepreneurship takes time to unfold (Morris, 1998). Across identifiable stages, the entrepreneurship process can be managed. Results of research suggest that the process of entrepreneurship can be characterized by four phases (see Table 12.1): (a) searching, (b) planning, (c) marshaling, and (d) implementing (McGee, Peterson, Mueller, & Sequiera, 2009).

The *searching* phase involves the development by the entrepreneur of a unique idea and/or identification of a special opportunity. This phase draws on the entrepreneur's creative talents and the ability to innovate. Entrepreneurs, as compared with managers, are particularly adept at perceiving and exploiting opportunities before these opportunities are recognized by others (Hisrich & Peters, 1998). Birk and her colleagues were not the first company to field a bike-sharing program. In Washington, DC, Clear Channel Communications, provider of advertisements and signage at subway and bus stops, launched SmartBike in 2008 (Martinez, 2010). However, marketing problems plagued SmartBike. Without enough bikes and bike stations and too little promotion, SmartBike never fared well. Its pricing was only targeted to commuters with an annual $40 subscription fee. Tourists had no cheaper option. However, Capital Bikeshare, launched by Alta Bicycle Share, had more bikes and plenty of promotion.

**Table 12.1**   Stages of Entrepreneurship

Searching—developing a unique idea or identifying a special opportunity.

Planning—converting the idea/opportunity into a workable business plan.

Marshaling—assembling resources to bring the venture into existence.

Implementing—growing the business.

*Source:* McGee, Peterson, and Sequiera (2009).

The *planning* phase consists of activities by which the entrepreneur converts the idea into a workable business plan (McGee et al., 2009). Here, the entrepreneur may or may not actually write a formal business plan. However, he or she must evaluate the idea or business concept and give it meaning as a business. The plan addresses questions such as follows: What is the size of the market? Where will the business establishment be located? What are the product specifications? How and by whom will the product be manufactured? What are the start-up costs? What are the recurring operating costs of doing business? Will the venture be able to make a profit, and if so, how soon after founding? How rapidly will the business grow, and what resources are required to sustain its growth?

The *marshaling* phase involves assembling resources to bring the venture into existence (McGee et al., 2009). At the end of the planning phase, the business is only "on paper" or in the mind of the entrepreneur. To bring the business into existence, the entrepreneur gathers (marshals) necessary resources such as capital, labor, customers, and suppliers without which the venture cannot exist or sustain itself.

Capital Bikeshare is based on a public–private partnership with capital expenditures for kiosks and bicycles provided by public funding, while user fees coving the operations run by private companies, such as Alta Bicycle Share (Martinez, 2010). The city retains any advertising revenue at the kiosks or on the bicycles. Additionally, the city controls the colors of the bicycles (Whitford, 2011).

The final phase is *implementing* (McGee et al., 2009). The entrepreneur is responsible for growing the business and sustaining the business past its infancy. To this end, the successful entrepreneur applies good management skills and principles. As an executive-level manager, the entrepreneur engages in strategic planning and manages a variety of business relationships with suppliers, customers, employees, and providers of capital. Growing an enterprise requires vision and the ability to solve problems quickly and efficiently. Not unique to entrepreneurship, these tasks are also required of effective managers. However, the entrepreneur is the primary risk-bearer of the enterprise with a financial stake in its long-term growth and success.

Operational risk for launching a bike-sharing program emerges from having the venture's property stolen or damaged. Alta Bicycle Share knows that the moment bikes and stations are established, they will be challenged by thieves or vandals. "The first thing people do—mostly teenagers—is try to steal the bikes. They'll jerk them up and down and side to side," Alta Bicycle Share CEO Alison Cohen said. "In Montreal they have a picture of a Ford F-150 with a rope connected to a bike, but the truck couldn't get the bike out of the dock. With a system that's secure like that, theft and vandalism are very minimal. The only real theft we've seen in the US has been people using a stolen credit card to take a bike and not return it" (Whitford, 2011, p. 1).

Entrepreneurs are calculated risk-takers (Morris, 1998). They are not wild-eyed risk takers; as research suggests, their propensity to accept risk is not very different than society at large. They will thoroughly analyze and evaluate the prospects for ventures and deals based on the risks evident for financial returns, technical success, and sufficient numbers of customers paying for their products or services.

In addition to the risk-taking inherent in pursuing innovation, entrepreneurs must bring proactiveness to the implementation of the plan to bring their focal concept into a viable product or service and an ongoing business enterprise (Covin & Slevin, 1989). In other words, they must put their plan into action. This almost always requires perseverance, adaptability, and a willingness to accept some responsibility for failure of the venture (Morris, 1998).

## Sustainable Entrepreneurship Defined

Sustainable entrepreneurship is the process through which individuals and teams create value by focusing on the well-being of the natural environment and communities in the pursuit of opportunities (Shepherd & Patzelt, 2011). As in all entrepreneurship, such opportunities represent a favorable set of circumstances that create a need or an opening for a new business concept (Morris, 1998). It can occur in any organizational context and results in new products, services, or processes that bring benefit to individuals, organizations, and society.

In the case of Alta Bicycle Share, entrepreneurs such as Mia Birk and Michael J. Jones had advanced awareness of how city leaders all over the world were increasingly turning to firms like theirs for designing more livable urban areas with bicycle and pedestrian travel as part of the transportation systems of these cities. Most city planners did not have the focused ability to design and win support across multiple constituencies for bicycle and pedestrian infrastructure in urban areas as Alta Planning + Design did. Along with this narrow expertise, Alta Planning + Design's leaders had a cosmopolitan awareness of what was happening in other places regarding business development systems that would boost bicycle and pedestrian usage.

Macromarketing researchers have found evidence suggesting that entrepreneurs with contacts in foreign countries are more likely to pursue international trade because these entrepreneurs are aware of opportunities abroad (Ellis & Pecotich, 2002). For example, Montreal based its bike-sharing program on the successful programs of Lyon, France (never before considered a bike-friendly city), and Paris (which has more than 20,000 bicycles positioned across the city (Martinez, 2010). A key innovation in the Montreal program was the theft-resistant docking device for the bicycles and the credit card processing technology for the kiosks. Both of these innovations became key features of Alta's ventures as Montreal Public Bike System Co.—that only began in 2008—became a supplier.

In addition to reconsidering assumptions or thinking in unconventional ways to perceive opportunities, entrepreneurs must move in a timely way to take action on their plans. Otherwise, rival firms may move and gain a competitive advantage. In other words, a window of opportunity exists for entrepreneurs. For example, Alta Bicycle Share's principal rival in the early stages of its existence is B-Cycle—a joint venture of the major healthcare insurance company Humana, ad-agency Crispin Porter & Bogusky, and Trek Bicycle—operating in 11 cities including Chicago and Denver.

Birk and Jones of Alta Planning + Design had to persuade a nascent entrepreneur, Alison Cohen, who was moving toward launching her own venture, to become the first CEO of Alta Bicycle Share. Alta Bicycle Share's current CEO Cohen (who lives in Philadelphia and works out of her apartment) had thought firms would provide a stable of bikes for their employees to use freely and that she could manage bike-sharing programs for these firms.

However, Birk and Jones of Alta Planning + Design recruited Cohen to lead Alta Bicycle Share before she was able to execute her own venture. "My approach was to do a mini market test that required a limited amount of capital investment," Cohen said. "Then I would write a business plan" (Coster, 2011, p. 1). Three years later, Cohen still has not written a plan, and Alta Bicycle Share is now posting $3 million in revenues and already making a profit.

In sum, sustainable entrepreneurship is similar to traditional entrepreneurship with the exception that the sustainable ventures focus primarily on improving the well-being of the natural environment and communities. For Alta Bicycle Share, the natural environment is improved as fewer energy resources are depleted by bicyclists and little $CO_2$ is emitted by bicyclers into the atmosphere. Communities are enhanced by bicycle sharing as congestion in downtown areas declines, the air becomes cleaner, and individuals become physically fitter. Successful sustainable entrepreneurship in the private sector creates jobs and rewards investors.

## GREEN OPPORTUNITIES FOR SUSTAINABLE ENTERPRISES

### Concern for the Planet and Communities on the Rise

Opportunities always reside outside of the firm and not in product or service concepts themselves. For example, "better mousetraps that nobody wants" can describe the largest category of new product failures (Morris, 1998, p. 26). In other words, a new product can be technologically sophisticated, but when it is introduced into the marketplace, its sales lag and it fails. Such failure could occur because (a) customers are already satisfied, (b) the concept is too difficult to comprehend, (c) the perceived switching costs are too painful, or (d) customers simply do not have a need for such a product or service.

Some macromarketing scholars believe consumers are changing their attitudes and life-styles to reflect more concern for the planet and communities today (Prothero, McDonaugh, & Dobscha, 2010; see Table 12.2). First, the global economic meltdown of 2008 has brought many consumers to rethink the promises of endless economic growth. As discussed in Chapter 2, leaders of important institutions in societies (such as major depository banks, investment banks, and central banks) appeared misguided and even naïve regarding their own perceptions of risk for their operations. Although new regulations followed, such as the 2,319-page Dodd-Frank Wall Street Reform and Consumer Protection Act of 2010 Act, it will take years to prove how effective this legislation will be in reducing risk for the financial system (Acharya, Cooley, Richardson, Sylla, & Walter, 2011).

**Table 12.2**   Reasons Macromarketing Scholars Offer for Changing Consumer Attitudes Toward the Environment and Communities

1. The idea of endless economic growth is now being rethought after the economic meltdown of 2008.
2. The emergence of environmentally oriented media programming has reinforced nurturing attitudes toward care of the Earth.
3. Institutions, such as the United Nations and nongovernmental organizations (NGOs), have proposed goals, standards, and approaches to better the environment and communities.

*Source:* Prothero, McDonagh, and Dobscha (2010).

Meanwhile, higher unemployment continues to plague economies of the world. In the midst of such setbacks, individuals are reconsidering the latitude society had previously accorded to the conduct of business by large corporations and financial institutions. Disillusionment for improved functioning of the economy and for the prospects of individuals has fueled protest movements, such as Occupy Wall Street. It seems as if many more realized they had underappreciated what matters more than wealth accumulation—the natural environment and community life.

Second, the emergence of environmentally oriented media programming has reinforced nurturing attitudes toward care of the Earth (Prothero et al., 2010). Al Gore's 2006 documentary-movie *An Inconvenient Truth* proved to be very influential in raising awareness of global climate change and the role of humans in this change. Planet Green is a cable channel in the United States that provides programs related to green issues, such as "World's Greenest Homes," and Science Guy Bill Nye's show "Stuff Happens," which explains where stuff goes after we use it and what impact it has on the environment. Additionally, magazines that promote simple living, such as *Mother Earth News*, and others that focus on environmental issues, such as *E – the Environmental Magazine*, are now abundant. Finally, books continue to be published about sustainability, such as *Hot, Flat and Crowded* by Thomas L. Friedman (2008a). These books help raise awareness for environmental issues and what can be done about them.

Third, institutions have proposed goals, standards, and approaches to better the environment and communities. These include initiatives of the United Nations (UN), such as the Millennium Development Goals and the Global Compact for businesses (established in 2001). The Millennium Development Goals call for the eradication of poverty and related social ills by 2015, and the UN Global Compact asks companies to support a set of core values in the areas of human rights, labor standards, the environment, and anticorruption (these were discussed in Chapter 5). Other institutions and NGOs have made contributions to raising awareness of issues related to sustainability. For example, in 2000, the U.S. Green Building Council developed an internationally recognized certification system for the design, construction, and operation of environmentally friendly buildings called the Leadership in Energy and Environmental Design (LEED) Green Building Rating Systems™ (USGBC, 2011). Receiving one of the top LEED certifications, such as Silver, Gold, or Platinum, translates into understandable advantages for owning and maintaining these certified buildings—if for no other reasons than the reduced expense of operating them.

NGOs such as the International Standards Organization based in Geneva, Switzerland, developed a suite of standards for environmental quality management—ISO 14000—which today is the most widely implemented environmental management system (Mager & Sibilia, 2010). ISO 14000 first asks a business to create an environmental policy. The next step is to determine the environmental impacts of all the products, services, and activities done by the firm. Then, the firm plans its environmental objectives and measurable targets. Finally, the firm implements its plan, checks it in an ongoing way, makes corrections, and engages in management review of its progress.

Similar sets of principles for environmental management include the CERES principles, which mandate that results of reports on the environmental impact of the firm be made public, and the Natural Step Framework, developed by Swedish oncologist and karate-champion Dr. Karl-Henrik Robèrt (Mager & Sibilia, 2010). The Natural Step was adopted and made popular by Interface, Inc.'s founder and CEO Ray Anderson (featured in Chapter 1).

The principles of the Natural Step to become a sustainable society are reducing (a) the progressive buildup of substances extracted from the Earth's crust (such as heavy metals and fossil fuels), (b) the chemicals and compounds produced by industrial processes (dioxins, DDT, PVC), (c) the progressive physical degradation of nature and natural processes (over-harvesting of forests), and (d) conditions that undermine individuals' capacities to their basic human needs (such as unsafe working conditions and meager wages).

In working with hundreds of companies, municipalities, academic institutions, and not-for-profit organizations all over the world, the nonprofit The Natural Step has found that sustainable decision-making does not lead to negative outcomes for firms. But, rather, adopting sustainable business practices leads to new opportunities, reduced costs, and dramatically reduced ecological and social impacts.

## Consumers Notice Changes in Business Operations

Consumers have watched businesses become more environmentally oriented in recent years. Wal-Mart's transition is still in progress, but it typifies some of the most earnest efforts to adopt sustainable business practices that will not be missed by consumers over the world. In choosing to emphasize energy conservation, Wal-Mart put compact fluorescent light bulbs (CFLs) at eye level for consumers instead of on the top three shelves (Bonini & Oppenheim, 2008). To increase comfort for the spiral shapes of the CFLs, Wal-Mart installed them in displays of ceiling fans in the stores (Humes, 2011, p. 149). In the face of manufacturer resistance (incandescent bulbs wore out quicker than CFLs), Wal-Mart pressed its case for CFLs suggesting that it could create its own private label brand of CFLs if light bulb manufacturers did not meet its orders for the CFLs. The results were astounding: Wal-Mart exceeded its sales goals, and Wal-Mart customers saved an estimated $40 on electricity over the life of each CFL. For all of the 137 million bulbs sold, $10 billion in electric bills would be saved over the life of the bulbs.

A very visible business in the United States, NASCAR, the automobile racing organization owned by the France family, has now embraced an environmental orientation (Belson, 2011). NASCAR is similar to many for-profit businesses today in that it is focused on cutting costs by recycling, conserving, and generating its own energy. Accordingly, NASCAR's teams, track operators, and sponsors have adopted an ambitious set of green initiatives that includes planting trees to offset carbon emissions and deploying sheep to keep the infield grass short.

Going green not only saves money, but it has also created new revenue by attracting sponsors to NASCAR that want to trumpet their eco-friendliness to the millions of fans who watch races on television and at the track. NASCAR also claims to have the largest recycling program in all of sports because of two NASCAR sponsors—Coca-Cola and Coors Light— that will recycle about 12 million bottles during the 2011 season. Hundreds of tons of cardboard are also collected each season.

NASCAR has also supported other projects like the installation in 2010 of 40,000 solar panels over 25 acres at Pocono Raceway in Long Pond, Pennsylvania. After spending about $15 million to build the three-megawatt solar farm, the track now saves about $500,000 a year in energy costs and has produced electricity equal to 324,000 gallons of gasoline.

"We gained a lot of fans because of it," said Brandon Igdalsky, Pocono Raceway's president. "Our generation is trying to clean up the things that our grandparents and great-grandparents did." (Belson, 2011, para. 15)

The Roush Fenway team, a joint venture between Roush Racing and Fenway Sports Group (owners of the Boston Red Sox), builds race cars and fields race teams. It recycles 96% of each car it produces. It has also eliminated Styrofoam cups from its operations and has bought bicycles for workers to get around its facility in North Carolina. All of these steps for NASCAR are only the beginning of a long process to clean up the sport.

"We're realists and we race cars that burn a fossil fuel that get four to five miles per gallon, and we can't change that," said Ian Prince, the chief sustainability officer at Roush Fenway. "But we can change the other 99 percent of it" (Belson, 2011, para. 23).

Businesses and environmentalists have increasingly been working together. For example, McDonald's and Greenpeace have combined efforts to avoid further destruction of the Amazon Rainforest (Prothero et al., 2010). After initially criticizing McDonald's in 2006 for buying chickens raised on soybeans grown on illegal farms carved out of the Amazon Rainforest in Brazil, the following year Greenpeace joined forces with McDonald's to pressure the major soy traders in Brazil into placing an unprecedented two-year moratorium on the purchase of any soy from newly deforested areas (Butler, 2009).

New brands have entered the marketplace positioned as delivering sustainable benefits. For example, Tom's of Maine entered as a manufacturer of natural-ingredients-only personal care products in 1970 (Tom's of Maine, 2011a). Tom and Kate Chappell moved from Philadelphia where Tom worked for an insurance company to Kennebunk, Maine, in 1968. Because of their goal to simplify their lives, they sought out natural, unprocessed foods, as well as unadulterated products. As they were unable to find natural personal care products for themselves and their children, Tom and Kate decided to create and sell their own. They launched their venture with a $5,000 loan from a friend and the philosophy that their products would not harm the environment.

Over the years, the product line of Tom's of Maine moved from nonphosphate laundry detergent to natural personal care products, such as the first natural toothpaste (1975) and deodorant (1976). Recognizing the future value of an established brand with an authentic commitment to sustainable business practices in the fast-growing natural, personal-care-products category, Colgate-Palmolive purchased 84% of Tom's of Maine in 2006 for $100 million (Wohl, 2006). The Chappells hold the remaining stock in their business that now boasts 90 products that are distributed in more than 40,000 retail outlets where millions of consumers encounter them in their shopping.

"When we first started out, this brand-new idea of natural products and sustainable companies seemed a little crazy to some," Tom Chappell said. "In the years since, though, more and more people have begun to believe, like we do, that nature can provide many of the health benefits we need — and that companies should minimize their environmental impact while working towards positive change in our communities. Together, we've really started to make a difference" (Tom's of Maine, 2011a, para. 1).

## Consumers Turn Toward Green

Segmentation studies on U.S. consumers in recent years have identified a Lifestyles of Health and Sustainability (LOHAS) segment that is the most interested in green products

**Figure 12.2**   Good Business at Tom's of Maine Focuses on Environmental Stewardship

*Source:* http://www.tomsofmaine.com

and services (Ottman, 2011). Approximately 19 % of U.S. consumers (43 million adults) would be assigned to the LOHAS segment in 2009. These consumers are the most environmentally conscious and physically active of the consumer segments. Demographically, these consumers tend to be married, educated, middle-aged, and female. LOHAS consumers have the second highest income level, so they have the means needed to buy a variety of products and services—and perhaps paying a premium for some of these.

LOHAS consumers are active in their communities and support environmental and social causes. They are conscious stewards of the environment as evidenced by their energy and water conservation, their use of cloth shopping bags, and their advocacy for environmental causes. They will use the Internet to investigate new green brands, and 71 % of them report a willingness to boycott brands that offend their values (this is twice as high as any other segment).

Importantly, they are early adopters of green technologies, and they are vocal in recommending green products and services to friends. This means that they have an impact (positive or negative) in the diffusion of innovations for any green product of which they form an opinion. In other words, they would play the role of a valued expert on green products and services in their social network. Considering that the growing market in the United States for goods and services focused on health, the environment, social justice, personal development, and sustainable living totals an estimated $290 billion (LOHAS, 2011), the role of LOHAS consumers is a crucial one for brands positioning themselves as promoting sustainable living. In research conducted by the Natural Marketing Institute, other segments express varying degrees of interest in sustainable living (Ottman, 2011). However, no segment is as committed to green purchasing as the LOHAS segment.

Research about consumers' perceptions of products promoted as green or sustainable is emerging. For example, one set of studies found evidence that consumers may not always view sustainability as an asset for companies or products. Consumers' want for sustainability depends on the type of benefit consumers most value for the product category. In these studies, consumers associated higher product ethicality with gentleness-related attributes and lower product ethicality with strength-related attributes (Luchs, Naylor, Irwin, & Raghunathan, 2010). In categories such as shampoo, tires, and liquid hand-sanitizer, sustainability is a liability for product choice when strength is especially valued. Here, a lack of ethicality is associated with being especially concerned with "getting the job done," even if it comes at a price to others. By comparison, ethicality carries an association of being "gentle" and perhaps even "weak."

An analysis of these results is in order. For example, the study did not perform subgroup analysis on consumers with pro-sustainability attitudes. By focusing on this subgroup, the researchers could have understood how consumers, who are the most likely to purchase green products, made associations between the ethicality of companies or products with terms such as "gentle" or "strong."

Another set of studies found evidence that altruism—in the form of buying green products that cost more—signals one's willingness and ability to incur costs for others' benefit (Griskevicius, Tybur, & Van den Bergh, 2010). These results suggest that such altruism is a "costly signal" associated with status. In other words, in addition to signaling that a person is prosocial (doing things for others), altruism can demonstrate that one has the resources (time, energy, money, relationships, or other) and the ability to incur the costs of self-sacrifice for public welfare. Interestingly, eliciting status motives for respondents increased the desire for green products when shopping in public (but not private) and when green products cost more (but not less) than nongreen products.

These results may help explain a surprising phenomenon in the marketplace. When tax credits for hybrid cars expired in late 2006, sales actually went up by 68.9%. Although this sales spike might have occurred if the tax credits remained in place, industry observers were similarly bewildered when Lexus introduced a conspicuously pro-environmental and ultra-expensive Lexus LS600h priced at more than $100,000 in 2007. Sales for this Lexus exceeded projections by more than 300%. The costly signaling framework would explain these results by suggesting that the higher price allows the buyer to signal to others that the buyer has the resources to afford such a car. By comparison, other studies have found evidence that lower-priced conservation behaviors, such as taking public transportation, signals that a person does not have the resources to afford more expensive means of transportation (Sadall & Krull, 1995). Consequently, such behavior is accorded lower status.

Again, without performing a subgroup analysis on respondents with higher attitudes toward sustainability, it is not known how those who regularly perform these behaviors regard them. For example, a person like Interface's Ray Anderson had an aversion to green behaviors before he learned more about the environmental imperative and understood his role in it (Anderson, 1998). Subsequently, he changed his mind about things in what he termed a "mid-course correction." Someone like Anderson after his mid-course correction would likely accord more respect to the self-sacrificing behaviors done to improve the environment than someone from the general public.

It seems that the key question about green consumption is "how rapidly is it being adopted by consumers around the world?" Studies have now identified LOHAS consumer segments of substantial size in 23 countries (LOHAS, 2011). With Wal-Mart's decision to promote green products, such as CFLs, it is likely that green consumption will become part of mainstream consumption in the future. With the accountability mechanisms of the Web and social media in the 21st century, which firms want to be known for providing products and services that are more harmful to the natural environment and communities?

## Businesses Turn Toward Green

### Using Nature's Principles

Naturalists define sustainability as the capacity of healthy ecosystems to continue functioning indefinitely (Unruh, 2008). One can perceive the idea of ecosystem sustainability in the United Nations's Bruntland Commission report as the commission defined sustainable development as meeting "the needs of the present without compromising the ability of future generations to meet their own needs" (World Commission on Environment and Development, 1987). Because of the usefulness of the sustainability framework for improving the efficiency and effectiveness of businesses and society, further consideration of how nature can inform approaches to human activities is warranted.

In recent years, researchers and thinkers have investigated how the principles of nature and Earth's complex and self-regulating biosphere can be applied to the operations of businesses (Unruh, 2008). In nature, cycles characterize living organisms and ecosystems. Dead animals and plants become food for other animals and plants. Using a life-cycle approach, firms have analyzed their operations using a "cradle-to-grave" approach of all steps from material extraction to disposal to understand the energy, resources, and emissions associated with the production and marketing of their brands (Ottman, 2011). An outcome of such an approach was that firms pursuing sustainable business practices emphasized "reduce, reuse, and recycle" (Unruh, 2008, p. 113). However, if firms still included synthetically derived materials in their products, such as polyvinylchloride (PVC), their efforts to reduce, reuse, and recycle would remain problem-ridden for the environment. Synthetic compounds, such as PVC, are "monstrous hybrids" in which biological and technical ingredients are mixed together in a way that makes it infeasible to separate them at the end of the product's life (Lee & Bony, 2008).

Going beyond this "cradle-to-grave" approach in which products (made of monstrous hybrids) go to a landfill after their useful life, architect William McDonough and his chemist business-partner Michael Braungart have become leading advocates for a "cradle-to-cradle" approach for firms. Using the McDonough Braungart Design Chemistry (MBDC) consulting firm's cradle-to-cradle (C2C) design protocol, the concept of waste goes away. Using C2C, firms design products, packaging, and systems from the very beginning to be fully recyclable (McDonough & Braungart, 2002a). The C2C concept also designs monstrous hybrids out of products. McDonough & Braungart compared the C2C approach to traditional practice in the following way:

> The characteristic design approach of the last century was "cradle to grave" It involved digging up, cutting down, or burning natural resources—releasing toxic material into the environment in the process—to make products that became useless waste at the end of their useful lives. By contrast, [the] cradle-to-cradle approach mirrors nature's regenerative cycles so that at the end of its useful life, a product and its component materials are used to make equally valuable products. C2C thinking does not just focus on minimizing toxic pollution and reducing natural resources waste. It goes one step further, demanding that companies redesign industrial processes so that they don't generate pollution and waste in the first place. (Lee & Bony, 2008, p. 5)

Using as few raw materials as possible in the design of products mimics nature's ways. This makes recycling easier than using many or making a common mistake of the industrial age by including many synthetic materials in the manufacture of modern products. For example, MBDC examined the composition of the Aeron desk chair made by furniture manufacturer Herman Miller based in Zeeland, Michigan, and operating in more than 40 countries (Miller, 2011). MBDC found that more than 200 components made from more than 800 chemical compounds were used in the manufacture of the Aeron. Herman Miller used the analysis conducted by MBDC to design its award-winning Mirra desk chair whose dramatically simplified set of materials allows the Mirra to be 96% recyclable (Unruh, 2008, p. 115). Instructions for disassembling the Mirra for recycling are included with each chair.

Figure 12.3 depicts the ecoScorecard webpage for the Mirra chair made by the Herman Miller subsidiary Geiger. The ecoScorecard system is a Web-based tool that helps architects and designers measure the environmental impact of available products and materials using the major environmental rating systems. Recyclable materials comprise 33% of the content of the Mirra chair. As can be seen on the ecoScorecard, postconsumer recycled-materials make up 27% of the Mirra chair, while preconsumer recycled-content makes up 6% of the Mirra chair (Mirra Chair, 2011). Importantly, the ecoScorecard presents the certifications for the Mirra chair, such as those from the Greenguard Environmental Institute (focused on improved indoor air quality), the Business and Institutional Furniture Manufacturers' Association (BIFMA), and MBDC's Cradle-to-Cradle certification.

## Benefits From Using Nature's Principles in Business

Architects and building developers striving to obtain LEED certification for the environmental sustainability of their buildings would use inputs such as the ecoScorecard information depicted in Figure 12.3 in choosing the materials and office equipment for their buildings. Points toward LEED certification would be gained by using environmentally certified products in a building being considered for LEED certification. Products with high ratings not only contribute to the sustainability of the building, but also they make such buildings less costly to maintain. Importantly, such green buildings are more productive

**Figure 12.3** Geiger's ecoScorecard for the Mirra Chair

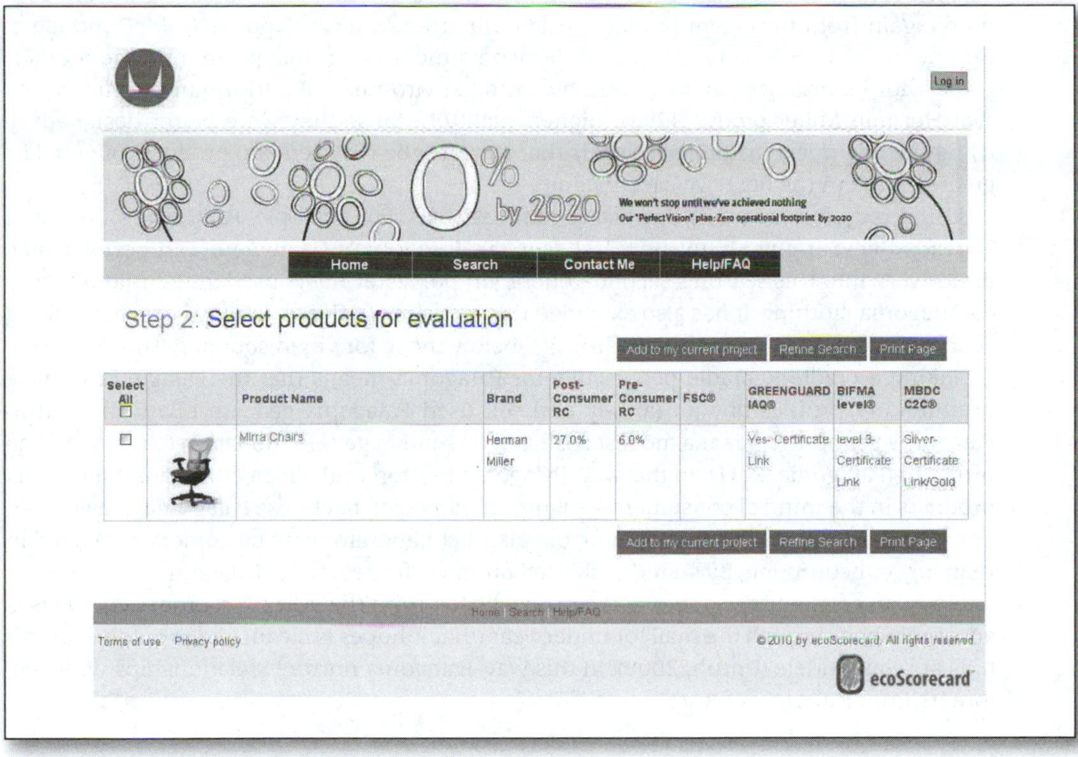

*Source:* Mirra Chair (2011), http://hermanmiller.ecoscorecard.com/catalogs/new_search

places for employees as a result of better indoor air quality, lighting, and toxin-free furniture. Such products can qualify for the U.S. EPA Environmentally Preferable Purchase Program (www.epa.gov/epp) and for sale on eBay's site for socially and environmentally just products (www.worldofgood.ebay.com). In these ways, environmental certification can give access to buyers and marketplaces where green has added value.

Firms such as Herman Miller have gained numerous advantages from adopting closed-loop recycling principles of nature's ways in pursuing sustainability for their products. For example, Herman Miller has become a more flexible market player because its procurement process seeks materials that will not be regulated or restricted in the future (MBDC, 2011). Herman Miller stopped producing the paneled exterior of its iconic Eames chairs out of rosewood because it recognized rosewood was an endangered species (Michler & Fehrenbacher, 2011). By switching to walnut for the Eames chair, Herman Miller avoided a more expensive material (and one likely to be regulated or restricted in the future).

In the manufacturing process, Herman Miller gained financial benefits by avoiding employee exposure to harmful chemicals and reducing regulatory costs. In the design process, Herman Miller created a source of more readily accessible raw-materials by designing products for end-of-life material recovery. It seems now that this ability to forecast the return of materials to the industry for future use will be the most significant economic gain from intelligent product design imparted by a C2C approach (McDonough & Braungart, 2002b). Finally, Herman Miller won a more defensible position in the marketplace with its products characterized by strong environmental performance. This means that Herman Miller products have higher quality because they were better designed by using the healthiest materials for users that can later be recycled into products of equal or greater value in the next cycle (upcycling).

Using recycled materials drastically reduces costs. For example, Patagonia's Common Threads Recycling program turns last season's Patagonia's Capilene brand performance underwear into this season's second-generation polyester fibers used in the manufacture of Patagonia clothing. It has also extended this recycling to fleece. Energy costs for making such second-generation polyester are 76% below those for virgin sourcing (Unruh, 2008).

Taking a cradle-to-cradle perspective for Patagonia means that the Patagonia website prominently profiles how to (a) buy and sell used Patagonia gear on eBay, (b) send in Patagonia gear for repair at a modest cost, and (c) send in gear for donation to the recycling program (Patagonia, 2011). In this way, Patagonia reinforces the idea of the durability of its products in the mind of consumers—an important reason to choose Patagonia. It also positions itself as not only a manufacturer, but also a collaborator with customers interested in reducing consumption. By taking back used products for recycling, Patagonia also assumes a role in reverse logistics—getting the product back from the user for reprocessing. This is accomplished through the mail for underwear (that it hopes is clean) and through drop-off bins at retail outlets (Unruh, 2008). In this way, Patagonia nurtures relationships with customers important to its future.

## The Pathway to a More Sustainable Business

A green marketer for more than 20 years, Jacquelyn Ottman now lists "green is mainstream" as her first of The 20 New Rules of Green Marketing (Ottman, 2011, p. xiii). Although many firms have not taken the leadership roles in the movement of sustainable business practices, such as Herman Miller and Patagonia, increasingly the good sense of seeking virtuous closed-loop cycles is being adopted by businesses around the world. Figure 12.4 depicts the percentages of respondents indicating the adoption of sustainable business practices in different domains of business operations in the 2011 McKinsey Global Survey. As shown, most respondents indicate sustainability integration across eight of the ten domains. This suggests that businesses have moved a long way toward sustainability since McDonough and Braungart first introduced cradle-to-cradle principles in the 1990s. These results also suggest that many more firms will likely move to integrate sustainability concepts into their operations in the coming years.

A pathway these firms will likely travel toward integration of sustainable business practices will likely be characterized by five stages (Nidumolu, Prahalad, & Rangaswami, 2009). Compliance with the law captures the essence of the first stage. In another form, compliance

**Figure 12.4**   Percent of 2,956 Business Executives From Around the World Reporting on the Adoption of Sustainable Business Practices

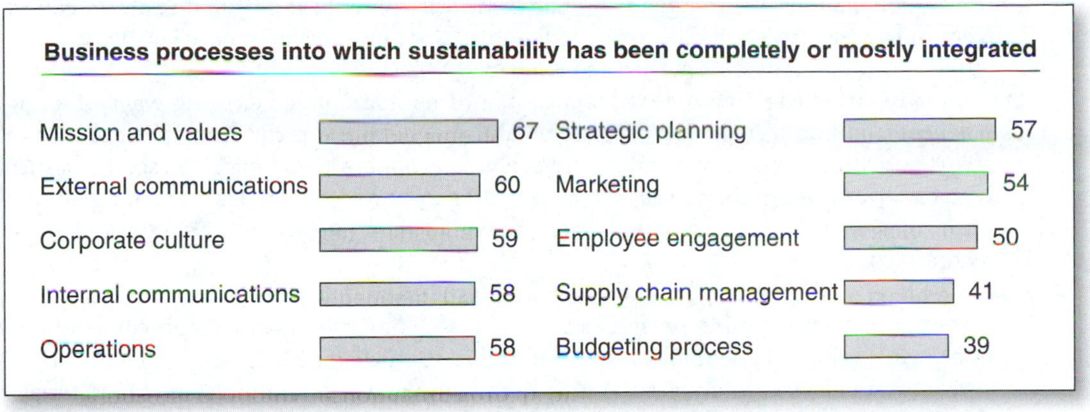

**Business processes into which sustainability has been completely or mostly integrated**

| Process | % | Process | % |
|---|---|---|---|
| Mission and values | 67 | Strategic planning | 57 |
| External communications | 60 | Marketing | 54 |
| Corporate culture | 59 | Employee engagement | 50 |
| Internal communications | 58 | Supply chain management | 41 |
| Operations | 58 | Budgeting process | 39 |

*Source:* Exhibit from "The business of sustainability: McKinsey Global Survey results," October 2011, McKinsey Quarterly, www.mckinseyquarterly.com. Copyright © McKinsey & Company. All rights reserved. Reprinted by permission.

with voluntary codes developed by NGOs can be done, such as general ones like the Greenhouse Gas Protocol or sector-specific ones like the Forest Stewardship Council code. Such standards are often more demanding than most countries' laws.

Driving toward efficiencies is the second stage for firms moving beyond compliance (Nidumolu et al., 2009). In 1999, chemical manufacturer DuPont estimated that every ton of carbon it did not emit saved its shareholders $6 (Lovins & Cohen, 2011, pp. 6–7). By 2007, DuPont's waste reduction efforts saved the firm $2.2 billion a year. Notably, the company's profits that year came in at $2.2 billion. In short, DuPont solved its waste problems at a profit. Toxins and waste represent inefficient design and production processes. Such inefficiencies can be identified by performing life-cycle assessment on a firm's products. The furniture company Herman Miller illustrates this. Once, MBDC analyzed the chemistry of its products, Herman Miller had to require its suppliers to provide less toxic materials, if Herman Miller would succeed in fielding healthier furniture.

Once firms and their leaders begin to realize that a sizable number of customers prefer eco-friendly products and services, firms will begin designing products to be eco-friendly in the third stage (Nidumolu et al., 2009). For example, when Procter & Gamble conducted life-cycle assessments on laundry detergent, the firm realized that U.S. households spend 3% of their annual electricity budget on heat for washing clothes. Consequently, the firm made the development of cold-water detergents a priority. In 2005, the firm introduced Tide Coldwater in the United States and Arial Cool Clean in Europe. By 2008, 21% of British households washed their clothes in cold water—up from 2% in 2002.

In the fourth stage, firms develop new business models by finding novel ways of capturing revenues and delivering services in tandem with other companies (Nidumolu et al., 2009). For example, Waste Management merely used to haul garbage from businesses to landfills. Its annual sales of $14 billion made Waste Management the market leader in garbage disposal. However, in 2007, the firm realized that $9 billion worth of reusable materials might be recovered from the garbage it carried to landfills each year. The firm set up a unit called the Green Squad and partnered with Sony in the United States to collect electronic waste from what it carried to landfills. Not only is value recovered, but waste is reduced through the effort of the Green Squad.

Finally, firms can create next-practice platforms that change existing ways of doing business (Nidumolu et al., 2009). These breakthroughs would result from questioning the status quo. In terms of environmentally-oriented products, these might be solving issues with electric batteries for cars, developing hydrogen-powered vehicles, or turning impure water into drinkable water. These products would integrate what is being called clean technology.

Clean tech refers to any product, service, or process that delivers its value by using limited or zero nonrenewable resources and/or creates much less waste than conventional offerings (Pernick & Wilder, 2007, p. 2). Opportunities for clean tech breakthroughs currently appear fruitful in (a) solar energy, (b) wind power, (c) biofuels and biomaterials, (d) green buildings, (e) personal transportation, (f) batteries for mobile power, (g) the smart grid, and (h) water filtration.

## CONCLUSION

This chapter examined sustainable entrepreneurship. Researchers have identified a process for entrepreneurship that features four stages: (a) searching, (b) planning, (c) marshaling, and (d) implementation. Entrepreneurs come in many forms, but most are motivated by achievement—accomplishing what they set out to do (Morris, 1998). Money, while necessary to fund the venture and help grow it, often becomes more of a scorecard for intrinsically motivated entrepreneurs. Sustainable entrepreneurs create value by focusing on the well-being of the natural environment and communities in the pursuit of opportunities (Shepherd & Patzelt, 2011).

Sustainable entrepreneurs, like all entrepreneurs, are agents of change. Not surprisingly, sustainable entrepreneurs find themselves embroiled in controversy because (a) opponents of growth see them as bringing more consumption and material depletion of the Earth's resources, (b) political action is part of what some of them do, and (c) their successes with their own causes sometimes move other causes lower in priority in public discourse.

Macromarketing scholars have noted that more consumers are changing their attitudes and lifestyles to reflect more concern for the planet and communities today. This is likely a result of (a) the global economic meltdown of 2008 that brought many consumers to rethink the promises of endless economic growth, (b) the emergence of environmentally oriented media programming that reinforced nurturing attitudes toward care of the Earth, and (c) institutions that developed frameworks for activities to better the environment and communities, such as the UN Millennium Development Goals, the UN

Global Compact for businesses, LEED certification for buildings, ISO 14000, CERES, and the Natural Step.

To what degree consumers and businesses go "green" remains to be seen. Consumers in the segment Lifestyles of Health and Sustainability (LOHAS) already represent millions who will prioritize what firms, their products, and services contribute to sustainability in their purchase decisions. Longtime green-sector consultant Jacquelyn Ottman has recently declared that green has become mainstream because 83% of consumers identify themselves to some degree as preferring green products and services (Ottman, 2011, p. xiii). Other research suggests that making green purchases can win status for consumers (Griskevicius et al., 2010). Despite such an advance for green purchasing, some consumers still interpret sustainable positioning of brands as indicative that the brands will not get the job done as well as conventional brands (Luchs et al., 2010).

Cradle-to-cradle design pursues biomimicry in applying nature's principles to the operation of business. Here, recycling takes a central role with the "waste" of one process becoming the "food" for another. Research suggests that firms typically go through five stages in integrating sustainable business practices into their operations: (a) complying with the law, (b) driving toward efficiencies, (c) designing eco-friendly products, (d) developing new business models, and (e) creating next-practice platforms that change existing ways of doing things (Nidumolu et al., 2009).

This chapter also considered clean tech, which refers to delivering value by using limited or zero nonrenewable resources and/or creating much less waste than conventional offerings (Pernick & Wilder, p. 2). The chapter concludes with a look at four Mavericks in Markets. The stories of these mavericks illustrate how each addressed a market imperfection to help solve an environmental problem that became the opportunity to earn rewards in the marketplace.

## QUESTIONS

- How would you compare your assessment of the viability of sustainable ventures before you read the chapter with your assessment now? What is one thing you learned that puts into perspective how a business could help solve environmental problems?
- Thinking about the sustainable entrepreneurs you encountered in the chapter, what is a theme that unifies many of the elements of their stories? Elaborate why you see this theme.
- What makes sustainable entrepreneurs distinct from conventional entrepreneurs?
- To what degree do you think sustainability is a fad? What does NASCAR's adoption of sustainable business practices say about sustainable business practices being a fad?
- What aspect of sustainable entrepreneurship in the chapter encourages you to consider joining a sustainable venture or starting your own?
- What are some ways society could encourage and reinforce sustainable entrepreneurship?

# MAVERICKS WHO MADE IT

## Clean-Tech Opportunities Emerge From Four Market Imperfections

Market imperfections have contributed to environmental degradation (Cohen & Winn, 2007, p. 35). However, these same imperfections offer rich opportunities for entrepreneurially oriented firms to develop new technologies and business models that can not only reduce environmental harm but also actually reverse the effects of environmental degradation.

Four types of market imperfections can be identified that offer sustainable entrepreneurs the chance to create profit-making solutions (Cohen & Winn, 2007, p. 31). These are (a) inefficient systems, (b) externalities, (c) flawed pricing mechanisms, and (d) imperfectly distributed information. If entrepreneurs can successfully introduce environmental innovations into the marketplace, a more sustainable future will likely develop for all.

### Market Imperfection 1: Inefficient Systems— Shai Agassi of Better Place

Despite neoclassical economics' assumption that firms are perfectly efficient in their resource allocation, perfect resource utilization is unlikely in practice (Cohen & Winn, 2007). Similarly, consumers likely only meet a fraction of the potential efficiencies from natural resources. Markets would perform better if firms and consumers would improve their efficiencies.

Today, entrepreneurial opportunities abound for implementing recycling systems. Biomimicry is one such approach in which industrial systems imitate nature where one creature's waste is another's food. In the cradle-to-cradle approach, if biodegradable materials compose products, these can become food for biological cycles. DesignTex, a U.S. designer of fabrics for furniture and upholstery, combined with Swiss textile-manufacturer Rohner to create a compostable upholstery fabric (McDonough & Braungart, 2002a, p. 106). The cradle-to-cradle approach also proposes that technical materials can stay in technical cycles in which they continually circulate as valuable nutrients for industry.

Better Place came into existence in 2007 to become the world's leading electric vehicle services provider. In this way, the firm intends to help move the world from oil-based to sustainable transportation. It plans to do this by setting up battery-switching stations for electric automobiles. It will use the cradle-to-cradle approach by keeping the technical materials (batteries) in the technical cycle for recharging and reuse.

Shai Agassi is the founder and CEO of Better Place. An Israeli citizen, Agassi graduated from Technion, the Israel Institute of Technology, in 1990 and went into software programming. He founded TopTier software in 1992 and later moved it to California (Shai Agassi—Wikipedia, 2011). Later, he became president of the Products and Technology Group at German-based software firm SAP AG in his thirties. By many accounts, he was in line to become CEO, but he left to pursue a larger scale challenge—making zero-emission vehicles a reality in countries around the world.

In 2008, Israel became the first country—and Renault the first carmaker—to implement the Better Place model of building open-network infrastructure to enable mass adoption of electric vehicles (Better Place, 2011). Denmark, Australia, California, Hawaii, and Ontario have followed suit. Better Place customers buy the electric vehicle (EV) at a reduced cost of about $20,000, although the first electric vehicles sold in Denmark were more than $38,000 (and included a home-battery charger that pushed the price to about $40,000) (Taylor, 2011). The battery packs are leased for a fixed subscription fee of about $350 a month (Berman, 2011). That fee includes access to the batteries, swap stations, and charge points.

At Better Place battery switch stations that look like drive-through car washes with gleaming white exteriors, drivers enter a lane where automated operations take over (Better Place, 2011). The car moves along a conveyor while the switch platform below the vehicle aligns under the battery, washes the underbody, initiates the battery release process, and lowers the 600-pound lithium-ion battery from the vehicle. The depleted battery is placed onto a storage rack for later servicing. A fully charged battery is then lifted into the waiting car. The switch process takes less time than a stop at the gas station, and the driver and passengers may remain in the car throughout.

Syndicated columnist Thomas L. Friedman is an enthusiastic endorser of Agassi and his venture describing Agassi as someone who could "sell camels to Saudi Arabia" (Friedman, 2008b). Such sales skills have helped in winning hundreds of millions of dollars in funding for Better Place. In 2010, London-based bank HSBC invested $125 million after 12 months of research on Better Place and the requirements for its economic viability (Taylor, 2011).

"Think about the (San Francisco) Bay Area, even at $4 a gallon," Agassi said. "It costs $150 million to put a [battery swapping/charging] network across the Bay Area. [We will offer] a car that will be sub-$20,000 and about $300-and-change to drive all you want" (Berman, 2011, p. 2).

The eventual success of Better Place will depend in part on other firms developing the technology EVs consumers will own and the batteries Better Place will own, so that the price for these continues to decline. Although Agassi is driving his firm to supply 3-minute battery changes in order to compete with the refueling time required for gasoline-fueled autos, the possibility of queues for these 3-minute battery changes exists. The company counters that the EVs for Better Place will have smart devices installed that will inform drivers of the wait times at nearby battery-switching stations.

"The impact of this shift towards electric will be felt first in Europe, where gasoline is heavily taxed, and in China, which is actively incentivizing electric car through central government planning and directed development guidance to its car industry aiming to leapfrog gas-burning vehicles," Agassi said (Agassi, 2011, para. 11).

## Market Imperfection 2: Externalities—Bruce Kania of Floating Island International

For the past two centuries, industrialization and population growth have served as the focus of progress in many societies (Floating Island International, 2011a). A cost for such progress has been

*(Continued)*

(Continued)

the widespread contamination and destruction of wetlands and waterways. Such costs represent negative externalities because a downstream third party incurs these costs without receiving equivalent benefits as those in the original set of exchanges (Cohen & Winn, 2007). In addition to the environment and future generations experiencing degraded ecosystems, those depending on waterways for safe drinking water and for recreational opportunities in the current generation also experience this externality of development.

In 2000, inventor and outdoorsman Bruce Kania bought a farm east of Billings, Montana, near the Yellowstone River. Roaming his farmland with his dog, he experienced an externality related to water contamination resulting from modern methods of farming and ranching. Every time his black dog Rufus jumped into a pond, the dog came out red and reeked of a foul odor (Stark, 2006).

Kania soon realized that his farm was at the end of a 60-mile irrigation ditch that carried nitrogen and phosphorous from fertilizers that had run off into the ditch and been carried downstream by the water in the irrigation ditch (Stark, 2006). Too many nutrients like these in water led to too much algae. Such an overabundance of algae restricted other tiny species upon which insects, birds, and fish depended. The result was foul water and a damaged eco-system.

Concerned for his dog, Kania instinctively felt "we could do better" and sensed a genuine opportunity for invention (Floating Island International, 2011b). Kania had become intrigued with biomimicry as a way of solving human problems using solutions modeled on nature. He asked himself whether a new and natural stewardship tool could be developed that could clean water and, in the process, improve life for all the creatures who live in it. (Floating Island International, 2011b).

To answer this question, Kania brought together a team of engineers and plant specialists who turned to the floating peat bogs of Northern Wisconsin for inspiration (Floating Island International, 2011b). Kania had grown up among these floating islands, where world-record fish are to be found within crystal-clear waters. The team set about "biomimicking" these floating riparian structures.

They created an island capable of supporting the weight of plants and soil. Layers of a flexible, matrix material made from postconsumer materials (recycled plastic drink bottles) form the floating island. Plants are then inserted into precut pockets. The matrix material serves as a cushiony batting that is porous and allows the plants' roots to reach the water.

Figure 12.5 depicts how the floating islands clean water. Circulation carries particulates including nitrates, phosphates, and ammonia across the roots of the plants on the underside of the floating water. As the plants grow, tiny microbes begin clinging to the island. These microbes take excess nutrients out of the water.

Microbes are responsible for breaking down nutrients and other water-borne pollutants, but to be effective, they need a surface to stick to. The floating island matrix, with its dense fibers and porous texture, is the perfect surface area for growing large amounts of microbes (in the form of biofilm) in a short time. Nutrients circulating in the water come into contact with these biofilms and are consumed by them, while a smaller fraction is taken up by plant roots. The team called the breakthrough technology BioHaven® floating islands.

**Figure 12.5** Floating Island Wetlands (FTW) Process for Cleaning Water

*Source:* http://www.floatingislandinternational.com/products/biohaven-technology/

The unique design of these floating islands means that 250 square feet of island can clean and restore an acre's worth of wetland surface area. In testing, 22 persons crammed onto a 250-square-foot island and stayed afloat (Stark, 2006, p. 2). These floating islands can be launched in either shallow or deep water, and they can be securely anchored or tethered to ensure that they remain in a specific location. They are almost infinitely customizable, and they can be configured in a variety of ways. Wildlife, such as water fowl and turtles, are attracted to the floating islands.

By 2010, more than 4,000 islands had been launched by Floating Island International for cleaning not only lakes and streams but also for wastewater lagoons, farm effluent ponds, and any other waterway impacted by sewage or landfill effluent (Floating Island International, 2011b). Floating islands are being deployed along the steel bulkheads that line the final one mile of the shipping channel of Cleveland, Ohio's Cuyahoga River (the same one that caught fire in 1969) that runs into Lake Erie (Scott, 2011). The floating islands replicate the once green-leafy banks of the river that hosted insects upon which fish fed (Scott, 2011).

Floating Island International's successes help one understand how externalities can become opportunities for eco-entrepreneurs oriented to solving problems in the natural environment. In the case of Floating Island International, an entrepreneurial achievement in solving smaller environmental problems can make enormous environmental challenges now seem like opportunities for the ambitious entrepreneur.

*(Continued)*

(Continued)

Kania envisions floating islands restoring "dead zones" such as the pollution-laden mouth of the Mississippi River, or the Chesapeake Bay near Washington, DC. "How do you cure a dead zone?" Kania asked. "One island at a time" (Stark, 2006, p. 2). Kania also envisions floating islands that would buffer the effects of hurricanes in coastal areas, and take in excess carbon dioxide contributing to global climate change.

## Market Imperfection 3: Flawed Pricing Mechanisms— Karl Ulrich and TerraPass

Conventional theories of economics assume natural resources are plentiful and that their market value accurately reflects supply and demand. Many ecosystem services (such as clean air and water, renewable energy, and a regulated climate) are undervalued or not priced at all (Cohen & Winn, 2007). A more sustainable economic system would price natural capital appropriately. Research published in *Nature* that was conducted by a team comprising ecologists, economists, and geologists from a variety of universities estimated the current value of ecological services that allow the Earth to be inhabited would be $33 trillion each year (Costanza et al., 1997). This was nearly double the combined output of the world's nations when the study was conducted.

Although nonrenewable energy resources currently remain cheaper than most renewable alternatives, a persisting issue for the use of these nonrenewables is their underpricing in the marketplace (Yergin, 2011). Renewable energy resources (solar, wind, wave, tidal, geothermal, landfill gas, and biomass sources, such as wood, fiber, ethanol, butanol, and biodiesel) are now emerging, but they struggle to be economically competitive with nonrenewable energy with its established infrastructure for extraction, processing, and distribution (and all of the cost efficiencies related to these).

Renewables have done well in states and countries (such as California and Germany) where the government has mandated quotas for renewable energy in the portfolio of energy sources. In California, the renewable portfolio standard (RPS) is set to be 20% by the end of 2013, 25% by the end of 2016, and 33% by the end of 2020 (DSIRE, 2011). Renewables have also thrived where the resource exists in abundance and prices for rival uses of the renewable have declined. This happened with ethanol made from sugar cane in Brazil in the first part of the 21st century (Orsato, 2009, p. 131). Nevertheless, about $100 billion is still needed to overhaul the distribution system as well as to improve the efficiency of the sugar mills in Brazil for global export.

To help renewable energy projects obtain funding, inventor and Wharton Business School Professor Karl Ulrich and his class of 41 MBA students launched a venture called TerraPass in 2004 that sells carbon offsets (TerraPass, 2011a). A carbon offset is a certificate representing the reduction of one metric ton (2,205 lbs) of carbon dioxide emissions, the principal cause of global warming (TerraPass, 2011b). Although complex in practice, carbon offsets represent a fairly simple idea. Consumers and businesses can determine how much carbon dioxide their activities generate and then pay TerraPass money to counterbalance the environmental damage they have caused. Figure 12.6 depicts this process.

**Figure 12.6** How Carbon Offsets Work

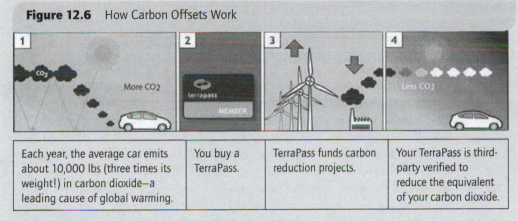

| Each year, the average car emits about 10,000 lbs (three times its weight!) in carbon dioxide—a leading cause of global warming. | You buy a TerraPass. | TerraPass funds carbon reduction projects. | Your TerraPass is third-party verified to reduce the equivalent of your carbon dioxide. |
| --- | --- | --- | --- |

*Source:* Terra Pass (2011b), http://www.terrapass.com/about/how-carbon-offsets-work.html

For every ton of carbon emissions reduced through renewable energy projects, one carbon offset would be created. Renewable energy project developers can then sell these offsets to finance their projects. For example, a wind farm generates clean energy, which reduces carbon emissions from coal-burning power plants. To finance its operations, a wind farm can sell these reductions in the form of carbon offsets. TerraPass, which is a for-profit company, invests in things like wind power, landfill gas reclamation, and biomass energy production.

The *New York Times* named TerraPass one of 2005's most noteworthy ideas. Today, the company is not alone in its field with dozens of competitors—but it has excelled by packaging its product well. For example, a family of four can offset its carbon consumption for $369 (TerraPass, 2011b). Alternatively, a one-year offset for a dorm room on a college campus runs $41.65.

Within its first year, TerraPass registered over 2,400 members, reduced 36 million pounds of $CO_2$, and earned countless national press and blog articles. TerraPass has grown steadily (Terrapass, 2011a, para. 2). The firm has a small staff in an office near the Bay Bridge in downtown San Francisco. The firm works directly with carbon reduction projects, providing revenue to dairy farms, landfill gas installations, and other projects that yield carbon credits. Importantly, TerraPass has helped individuals and businesses to reduce over 1 billion pounds of carbon dioxide. In concrete terms, the enduring value of the work of TerraPass will likely be operating as a major player in the funding of the infrastructure for renewable energy resources that otherwise would have not made the grade as a result of conventional market pricing. Not bad for what was once an MBA course project.

"I look around and I think we've had an impact," Ulrich said (Pompilio, 2008, para. 40).

*(Continued)*

(Continued)

## Market Imperfection 4: Imperfectly Distributed Information—Janice Cheam of Energy Aware

Information asymmetry is a primary cause of market distortion. It occurs when individuals hold different information about resources, markets, and opportunities (Cohen & Winn, 2007). For example, very few consumers know how much energy they use in their homes. This lack of knowledge on the part of the consumer reinforces inertia in the consumers' buying habits, so that the consumer likely consumes more energy than is needed. This has adverse effects on both the environment and the financial resources of consumers.

Yet, this imperfect information generates entrepreneurial opportunities. Start-up firm Energy Aware offers a potential solution for eliminating imperfect information for the consumption of energy in the home, as well as in businesses. Based in Vancouver, British Columbia, Energy Aware produces the PowerTab—a smart wireless display that can be used around the home to provide utility customers wireless real-time information on power consumption and electricity rates (Energy Aware, 2011; see Figure 12.7). Research has shown that instantaneous feedback can reduce energy consumption by up to 20%.

**Figure 12.7** The PowerTab In-Home Display

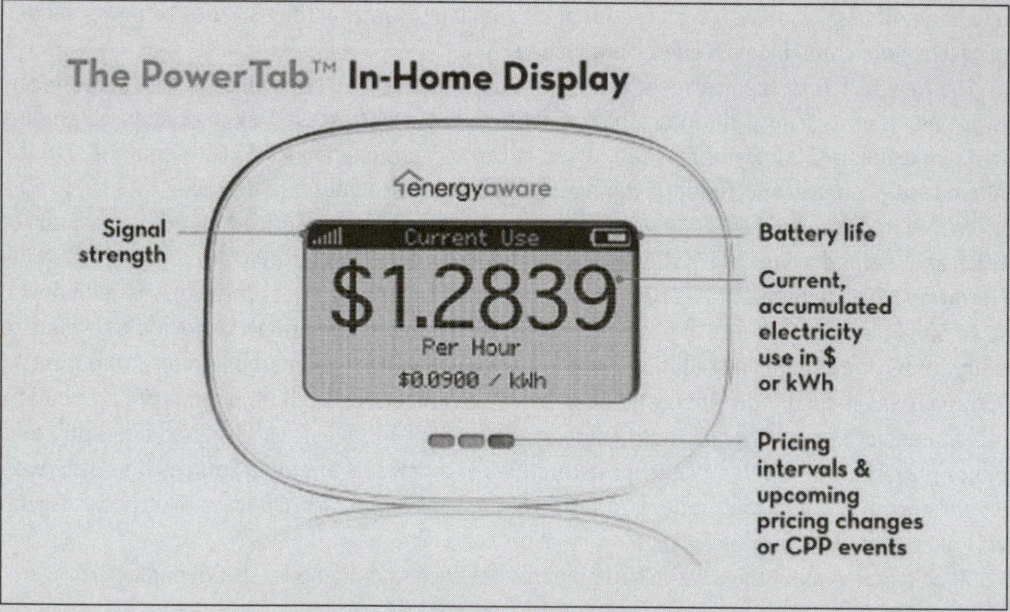

*Source:* http://www.energy-aware.com/our-products/ihd/

Energy Aware has won numerous start-up competitions around the world. In 2009, the B.C. Technology Industry Association named the firm "most promising start-up" (Severinson, 2011). The firm has development partnerships with several smart-grid developers, and it has sold more than 5,000 PowerTabs around the world.

CEO and founder Janice Cheam began Energy Aware as part of an entrepreneurship course at the University of British Columbia in 2005. She admits now she never intended to turn the idea of Energy Aware into a real company. But later, when interviewing at some of Vancouver's most influential consulting firms after graduating in 2006, an interviewer told her she would not encounter such a rich experience in consulting as she would developing Energy Aware. Stunned, Cheam recognized the truth of her interviewer's perspective and subsequently decided to act. She called up her old class-mates and persuaded them to continue developing Energy Aware.

Cheam faced two challenges most new entrepreneurs encounter: (a) being unknown and (b) need-ing money (Severinson, 2011). Family members, angel investors, and a single venture capital firm, Renewal Partners Co., together contributed about $600,000 for Energy Aware's launch. But raising the funds needed to continue improving the product and developing the business remain two formi-dable challenges.

Although told by some potential investors to move to California, Cheam kept Energy Aware in Vancouver. The Canadian government provides assistance through its Industrial Research Assistance Program that has helped pay salaries associated with Energy Aware's research projects, and its Scientific Research and Experimental Development Tax Incentive Program, which gives a tax credit for money spent on R&D.

Cheam's firm seems to be on the verge of a breakthrough in the marketplace. Energy Aware has sold the PowerTab to energy service companies in Australia, Finland, and North America for pilot projects (Severinson, 2011). The company's goal is to win a major contract and outfit millions of homes, instead of thousands. If this happens, then Energy Aware will become one part of the devel-opment of the "smart grid." The grid would use smart metering infrastructure (SMI) to provide two-way, real-time communications between energy suppliers and consumers (Energy Aware, 2011). With up-to-the-minute data transmitting between homes and supplier, consumers would then be able to make choices about their energy consumption, while suppliers would be better able to manage load distribution on the electrical grid.

Some envision the reworking of the massive infrastructure that allows the transmission and dis-tribution of electrons to result in something like the Internet (Pernick & Wilder, 2007). Such a grid would operate in a flexible, secure, and redundant manner. Not only would rooftop-based solar modules on millions of homes pump energy into the grid during the day, but also the solar-generated energy could be stored in fuel cells for use at night and whenever unexpected power outages occurred. Additionally, smart refrigerators and washing machines would power up and power down to achieve peak efficiency for households, as well as for the grid itself. Today, Energy Aware is striving to succeed with an idea and technology that would help consumers realize the benefits of improved household energy consumption that a smart grid would provide in the future.

*(Continued)*

(Continued)

## Questions

- Which story of the four Mavericks in Markets featured in this chapter appeals to you most?
- Into which venture would you *most* like to make a $50,000 stock investment, if this were possible? Explain.
- Into which venture would you *least* like to make a $50,000 stock investment, if this were possible? Explain.
- Which venture do you believe will result in having the most positive impact on the natural environment? The least? Explain.
- How are these four ventures similar?
- How are they different?
- Which market imperfection would you like to address if you launched an environmentally oriented venture? Explain.
- Considering all the sustainable entrepreneurs featured in this chapter from Mia Birk to Janice Cheam, what role did higher education play in identifying the venture idea for these sustainable entrepreneurs? Do environmental problems targeted by sustainable entrepreneurs require more technical or intellectual skills as part of the entrepreneurs' tool kit?

## REFERENCES

Acharya, V. V., Cooley, T., Richardson, M., Sylla, R., & Walter, I. (2011). Prologue: A bird's-eye view, The Dodd-Frank Wall Street Reform and Consumer Protection Act. In V. charya, T. Cooley, M. Richardson, R. Sylla, & I. Walter (Eds.), *Regulating Wall Street: The Dodd-Frank Act and the new architecture of global finance* (pp. 1–32). New York, NY: Wiley.

Agassi, S. (2011, March 18). Shai Agassi's plan to make buying an electric car easy. *The Atlantic*. Retrieved from http://www.theatlantic.com

Anderson, R. C. (1998). *Mid-Course correction: Toward a sustainable enterprise: The Interface model*. White River Junction, VT: Chelsea Green.

Baumol, W. J., Litan, R. E., & Schramm, C. J. (2007). *Good capitalism, bad capitalism and the economics of growth and prosperity*. New Haven, CT: Yale University Press.

Belson, K. (2011, September 13). Gentlemen, start conserving. *The New York Times*. Retrieved from http://www.nytimes.com

Berman, B. (2011, September 29). Better Place's Shai Agassi: To succeed, electric cars must beat 3-minute gas fill-up. *Plugincars*. Retrieved from http://www.plugincars.com

Better Place. (2011). The solution. Retrieved from http://www.betterplace.com

Birk, M. (2011, April 30). Pedaling towards a healthier planet. *TEDxPortland Mia Birk*. Retrieved from http://www.miabirk.com

Birk, M., & Kurmanskie, J. (2010). *Joyride: Pedaling toward a healthier planet*. Portland, OR: Cadence Press.

Bonini, S, M. J., & Oppenheim, J. M. (2008, October). Helping 'green' products grow. *The McKinsey Quarterly*. Retrieved from http://www.mckinseyquarterly.com

Butler, K. (2009, August 18). Greenpeace: Lovin' McDonald's. *Mother Jones*. Retrieved from http://motherjones.com

Cohen, B., & Winn, M. I. (2007). Market imperfections, opportunity and sustainable entrepreneurship. *Journal of Business Venturing, 22*(1), 29–49.

Costanza, R., d'Arge, R. de Groot, R., Farber, S., Grasso, M., Hannon, B., Limburg, K., Naeem, S., O'Neil, R. V., Raruelo, J., Raskin, R. G., Sutton, R., and van den Belt, M. (1997). The value of the world's ecosystem services and natural capital. *Nature, 237*, 253–260.

Coster, H. (2011, June 27). Beating a new path for commuters. *Forbes*. Retrieved from http://www.forbes.com

Covin, J. G., & Slevin, D. P. (1989, January). Strategic management of small firms in hostile and benign environments. *Strategic Management Journal, 10*(1), 75–87.

DSIRE. (2011). Renewable portfolio standard. Database of state incentives for renewables & efficiencies. Retrieved from http://www.dsireusa.org/incentives/incentive.cfm?Incentive_Code = CA25R

Duber-Smith, D. (2009, March–April). Sustainability: The green imperative. *ICOSA*, pp. 92-94.

Dulken, D. (2010, October 8). Joyride: Bicycling our way to safe and splendid communities. *The Huffington Post*. Retrieved from http://www.huffingtonpost.com

Dundas, Z. (2011, October). Brainstorm: Explore the genesis of innovation: 12 Oregonians changing our world. *Portland Monthly*, Retrieved from http://www.portlandmonthlymag.com

Drucker, P. (1985). *Innovation and entrepreneurship*. New York, NY: Harper Business.

Ellis, P. D., & Pecotich, A. (2002). Macromarketing and international trade: Comparative advantage versus cosmopolitan considerations. *Journal of Macromarketing, 22*(1), 32–56.

Energy Aware. (2011). The smart grid: How it works. Retrieved from http://www.energy-aware.com

Floating Island International. (2011a). Our vision. Retrieved from http://www.floatingislandinternational.com

Floating Island International. (2011b). Company profile. Retrieved from http://www.floatingislandinternational.com

Friedman, T. L. (2008a). *Hot, flat and crowded: Why we need a green revolution—and how it can renew America*. New York, NY: Farrar, Straus and Giroux.

Friedman, T. L. (2008b, September 28). Texas to Tel-Aviv. *The New York Times*. Retrieved from http://www.nytimes.com/2008/07/27/opinion/27friedman.html

Gingrich, N., & Maple, T. L. (2007). *A contract with the earth*. Baltimore, MD: Johns Hopkins University Press.

Griskevicius, V., Tybur, J. M., & Van den Bergh, B. (2010). Going green to be seen: Status, reputation, and conspicuous conservation. *Journal of Personality and Social Psychology, 98*(3), 392–404.

Hisrich, R. D., & Peters, M. P. (1998). *Entrepreneurship*. Boston, MA: Irwin McGraw-Hill.

Humes, E. (2011). *Force of nature: The unlikely story of Wal-Mart's green revolution*. New York, NY: Harper Business.

Lee, D., & Bony, L. (2008). *Cradle-to-Cradle design at Herman Miller: Moving toward environmental sustainability*. Case number 9-607-003. Boston, MA: Harvard Business School Press.

LOHAS. (2011). LOHAS online. Retrieved from http://www.lohas.com

Lovins, L. H., & Cohen, B. (2011). *Climate capitalism: Capitalism in the age of climate change*. New York, NY: Hill & Wang.

Lovins, L. H. (2010). Foreword. In M. Russuo (Ed.) *Companies on a mission: Entrepreneurial strategies for growing sustainability, responsibly, and profitably* (p. xi). Stanford, CA: Stanford University Press.

Luchs, M. G., Naylor, R. W., Irwin, J. R., & Raghunathan, R. (2010, September).The sustainability liability: Potential negative effects of ethicality on product preference. *Journal of Marketing, 74*(5), 18–31.

Mager, D., & Sibilia, J. (2010). *Street smart sustainability: The entrepreneur's guide to profitably greening your organization's DNA.* San Francisco, CA: Berrett-Koehler.

Mapes, J. (2009). *Pedaling revolution: How cyclists are changing American cities.* Corvallis: Oregon State University Press.

Martinez, M. (2010, September 20). Washington, D.C., launches the nation's largest bike share program. *Grist.* Retrieved from http://www.grist.org

MBDC. (2011). Value of certification. Retrieved from http://www.mbdc.com

McDonough, W., & Braungart, M. (2002a). *Cradle to cradle.* New York, NY: North Point Press.

McDonough, W., & Braungart, M. (2002b). The anatomy of transformation: Herman Miller's journey to sustainability. Retrieved from http://www.mcdonough.com/writings/anatomy_transformation.htm

McGee, J., Peterson, M., Mueller, S., & Sequiera, J. (2009). Entrepreneurial self efficacy: Refining the measure. *Entrepreneurship Theory and Practice, 33*(4), 965–988.

McInerny, V. (2008, May 6). Spandex yielding to new cycling styles. *The Oregonian,* pp. D1–D2.

McKinsey Global Survey. (2011, September). The business of sustainability. *McKinsey Quarterly.* Retrieved from http://www.mckinseyquarterly.com

Michler, A., & Fehrenbacher, J. (2011, April 24). Inhabit interview: Green Architect & Cradle to Cradle Founder William McDonough. *Inhabit.* Retrieved from http://inhabitat.com/inhabitat-interview -green-architect-cradle-to-cradle-founder-william-mcdonough/

Miller, H. (2011). Where we are. Retrieved from http://www.hermanmiller.com

Mirra Chair. (2011). Environmental product summary. Retrieved from http://hermanmiller.ecoscore card.com/catalogs/new_search

Moon, D. (2010, October 8). Bicycle guru shares passion in new book. *The Jewish Review.* Retrieved from http://www.jewishreview.org

Morris, M. H. (1998). *Entrepreneurial intensity: Sustainable advantages for individuals, organizations, and societies.* Westport, CT: Quorum Books.

Nidumolu, R. Prahalad, C. K., and Rangaswami, M. R. (2009). Why sustainability is now the key driver of innovation. *Harvard Business Review, 87*(9), 56–64.

Orsato, R. J. (2009). *Sustainable strategies: When does it pay to be green?* New York, NY: Palgrave Macmillan.

Ottman, J. A. (2011). *The new rules of green marketing: Strategies, tools, and inspiration for sustainable branding.* London, UK: Berrett Koehler.

Patagonia. (2011). Patagonia's Mission Statement. Retrieved from http://www.patagonia.com

Pernick, R., & Wilder, C. (2007). *The clean tech revolution: The next big growth and investment opportunity.* New York, NY: Collins.

Pompilio, N. (2008, November). Practicing what he preaches. *Wharton Alumni Magazine.* Retrieved from http://whartonmagazine.com/issues/summer-2008/practicing-what-he-preaches/

Prothero, A., McDonagh, P., & Dobscha, S. (2010, June). Is green the new black? Reflections on a green commodity discourse. *Journal of Macromarketing, 30*(2), 147–159.

Sadall, A. E., & Krull, J. L. (1995). Self-presentational barriers to resource conservation. *Journal of Consumer Research, 35,* 257–267.

Scott, M. (2011, September 3). Greening the Cuyahoga River: Man-made floating plant islands the latest scheme in recovery efforts. *The Plain Dealer.* Retrieved from http://blog.cleveland.com/ metro/2011/09/greening_the_cuyahoga_river_ma.html

Severinson, P. (2011, August). Is small business bad for B.C.? *BCBusiness*. Retrieved from http://www.bcbusinessonline.ca

Shai Agassi—Wikipedia. (2011). Shai Agassi. Retrieved from http://en.wikipedia.org/wiki/Shai_Agassi.

Shepherd, D. A., & Patzelt, H. (2011, January). The new field of sustainable entrepreneurship: Studying entrepreneurial action linking "what is to be sustained" with "what is to be developed." *Entrepreneurship Theory & Practice, 35*(1), 137–163.

Stark, M. (2006, July 9). Man claims his floating island invention can clean pollution. *Napa Valley Register*. Retrieved from http://napavalleyregister.com/business

Szczepanski, C. (2010, November 3). Up close and personal with Mia Birk. *Momentum*. Retrieved from http://momentumplanet.com

Taylor, A. III. (2011, March 16). Researcher changes tune on Better Place. *Fortune*. Retrieved from http://money.cnn.com

TerraPass. (2011a). About TerraPass. http://www.terrapass.com/about/

TerraPass. (2011b). How carbon offsets work. Retrieved from http://www.terrapass.com/about/how-carbon-offsets-work.html

Tom's of Maine. (2011a). Good business: *Heritage*. Retrieved from http://www.tomsofmaine.com

Tom's of Maine. (2011b). Good business: Environmental Practices. Retrieved from http://www.tomsofmaine.com

Unruh, G. C. (2008, February). The biosphere rules. *Harvard Business Review*. Retrieved from http://hbr.org/2008/02/the-biosphere-rules/ar/1

USGBC. (2011). An introduction to LEED. Retrieved from http://www.usgbc.org

Werbach, A. (2009). *Strategy of sustainability A business manifesto*. Boston, MA: Harvard Business Press.

Whitford, D. (2011, May 17). The technology behind bike sharing systems. *Fortune Tech*. Retrieved from http://tech.fortune.cnn.com

Wohl, J. (2006, March 22). Colgate to buy majority stake in Tom's of Maine. *Environmental News Network*. Retrieved from http://www.enn.com

World Commission on Environment and Development. (1987). *Our common future*. New York, NY: Oxford University Press USA.

Yergin, D. (2011). *The quest: Energy, security, and the remaking of the modern world*. New York, NY: Penguin Press.

# PART IV

# Enterprise With Equity in Mind

## CHAPTER 13

# Developing Markets

## ATTEMPTING TO EXPLAIN DEVELOPING MARKETS

### Charles C. Slater—A Pioneer of Macromarketing

#### Graduate of the School of "Hard Knocks"

Although Charles C. "Chuck" Slater was born and raised in the United States, his life before the age of 21 led him to experience first-hand economic deprivation, family stress,

411

human misery, and warfare (Nason, 2010). Later in life, when he became a pioneering leader in the field of macromarketing, Slater focused his research and others' on explaining how marketing could improve the lives of those living in developing countries where many contend with challenges Slater faced in his own childhood.

Slater was born in Denver, Colorado, on July 29, 1924. When he was five, his mother suddenly died. At the same time, the Great Depression descended on the country and most of the world. Six months after his mother died, lenders foreclosed on the Slater family home in their attractive Denver neighborhood. With these events, harsh reality drove out childhood innocence from the lives of Slater and his brother Robert (who was 15 months older).

For the rest of their years growing up, instability characterized the lives of the Slater boys. A chronic bone disease (osteomyelitis) hampered Slater's father throughout his life. The disease repeatedly sent Slater's father to the hospital, thereby disrupting his startups and his ability to earn money as an employee. As a result, the boys moved in and out of foster homes in Denver, Chicago, and Indianapolis, while their father tried to earn enough money to provide for them all. To keep the boys from being sent to the public orphanage in Chicago, Slater's brother dropped out of school to help support the family by working in a series of low-level jobs doing delivery, clerking, and assembly-line work. (Despite this disruption in his education, Robert Slater eventually served as a U.S. Air Force Colonel and became a successful New York City attorney.)

Overcoming the uncertainty in their lives, Slater blossomed as a student in high school and graduated a year early. He accepted a scholarship from the University of Chicago and attended there his freshman year. However, World War II had begun, and the Army was drafting many of his peers. In response, Slater enlisted in an Army program promising two years of college followed by officer training. After one year at Iowa's Grinnell College, the Army terminated this program and called Slater to accelerated basic infantry training.

One month after "D" Day, June 4, 1944, Slater and his 320th Infantry Regiment of the 35th Infantry Division entered combat operations in Normandy, France. The 35th Division stayed in daily combat for 11 months fighting 1,600 miles across five countries (35th Infantry Division, 2011). When his infantry company met the Russians in Northern Germany at the Elbe River, Slater and five others (out of 250) were the only original soldiers who had landed with the company in Normandy. The others who began with them had died or had been gravely wounded. Slater left the completed war in Europe as a Second Lieutenant in the reorganized 320th Infantry Regiment. The war ended with Slater standing on the wharf in San Francisco waiting to board a ship for the invasion of Japan. He narrowly missed joining the Pacific war effort.

## Graduate of Northwestern University

After the war, Slater enrolled at Northwestern University, and by 1956, he had completed a bachelor's in business administration and both a master's and a PhD degree in economics (Nason, 2010). After receiving these degrees, Slater worked as a marketer for Omar Inc.'s supermarket division based in Omaha, Nebraska. After three years, he joined Arthur D. Little's consulting firm and worked as head of the consumer marketing section for five years. However, Slater increasingly felt a need to explain ways in which business could contribute to an increased quality of life for societies of the world. Toward this end, he felt he would have more latitude in academia to pursue research related to business' contribution to the common good of society. Therefore, Slater joined the marketing faculty of Michigan State University in 1963.

As a professor, Slater visualized marketing as a means of achieving humanistic goals, such as poverty alleviation—especially in developing markets (Nason, 2010). Although scholars at this time gave attention to marketing and society issues, the field of marketing scholarship was beginning a turn away from macro-level issues (the "biggest M") toward micro-level issues ("little m"). When considering moving marketing management issues to the focus of his research, Slater took the attitude that he had already "been there and done that" as a marketer and as a consultant. Instead, he chose to focus on the biggest M and dove into the study of marketing systems in developing countries.

## Field Research in Developing Countries

By 1964, Slater had won two sizable grants from the United States Agency for International Development (USAID) for studying the role of marketing in the economic development of Latin America (Nason & White, 1981). In Puerto Rico, Bolivia, and Brazil, he conducted field research with eclectic teams of social science researchers that focused on the food supply systems for a region of the countries involved. Because he was focused on explaining macro-level phenomenon, Slater drew on the technical expertise of economists, agronomists, agricultural economists, communication and attitude specialists, systems and model builders, industry analysts, as well as marketers to build an understanding of the development process and define the role of marketing in it (Peterson, 2006). For 12 years, Slater led teams of researchers to complete similar studies in the Cauca Valley region in Colombia, Costa Rica, Kenya, Lesotho (a country in Africa surrounded by South Africa), and Rhodesia (which would later become Zimbabwe) (Layton & Grossbart, 2006).

Slater's research in northeastern Brazil is typical. He took focus on the food supply for an area of about one fourth of the area of Brazil with per capita income of $100 per year (Nason, 2010). In this same region, 7% of people living there earned 50% of the income. His team used a channel mapping method it had developed to measure the flow of agricultural products from farms to urban consumption. Along the way, the team surveyed all kinds of channel participants and measured their literacy, their psychological traits (such as achievement orientation, cooperativeness, fatalism, and innovativeness), and their use of mass media. Slater and his team then created a model of the region with its behavioral characteristics. In this way, the model could identify where the greatest physical and psychological barriers existed that prevented increased market participation. The models also allowed trade-off analysis to show what might happen if different interventions were taken.

Slater's research in Brazil discovered two startling findings. First, up to 50% of perishable and semiperishable agricultural goods became inedible before they reached consumers because they had spoiled (Nason, 2010). Second, each actor in the marketing system from farmers to channel members acted rationally—given their limited knowledge and their appraisal of the risks and barriers facing them.

The knowledge resulting from the work of Slater's teams allowed researchers, policy makers, and businessmen to understand where innovation should be tried and what the likely outcome might be. For example, flood and drought insurance could be offered in some situations to improve results in the marketing system. In other situations, changes in the channel could be implemented, such as the introduction of refrigeration at certain places, coordination of purchasing at fair-like supermarkets, and the introduction of different modes of transportation. Slater's theory of market process proposed that farmers and channel members were key actors in a marketing system for society that could provide food in cities at lower costs while providing more income to farmers. However, Slater's recommended changes would have to be implemented before such productivity increases would be realized.

Slater moved to the University of Colorado—Boulder in 1968 (Nason, 2010). Before succumbing to cancer in 1978, he continued his field research and launched the first Macromarketing Seminar at the University of Colorado—Boulder in 1976, which many regard as his greatest achievement.

Slater approached life with confidence and self-assuredness as many entrepreneurs might. Slater's last doctoral student, Lee Dahringer, described him as "proud, sure of self, willing to put it on the line, and a bit of an ego" (Nason, 2010, p. 290). Dahringer elaborated on Slater's leadership ability in this way:

> As a doctoral student at U of Colorado, I was walking down the hall when Chuck, whom I barely knew and had no courses with, came up and asked 'would you like to go to Africa?' Thinking he was joking I said 'sure.' Six months later, I was on a plane with Chuck to Lesotho, Africa! Simply put, without his leadership in organization, and his leadership in developing new scholars in the area, the area of Macromarketing would not exist today. (Nason, 2010, pp. 290–291)

---

### Your Thoughts?

- How did the adversity Chuck Slater experienced during his childhood contribute to what he did later in life?
- How did Slater's war-time experiences influence the way he approached his scholarly research?
- What knowledge did Slater's team create when doing their work in places like northeastern Brazil?
- Of all the things Slater accomplished in his life, why would some say that his greatest achievement was being a founder of macromarketing?

---

## CHAPTER OVERVIEW AND LEARNING OBJECTIVES

This chapter will focus on the nature of developing markets and will give a special examination of the poor in developing countries. The World Bank (2010) classifies 210 countries as low-, middle-, or high-income countries based on gross national income (GNI) per capita. The low-income (GNI/capita of $975 or less) and middle-income countries (GNI/capita from $976–$11,905) are sometimes referred to as developing countries.

Once considered like a foreboding swamp for modern multinational enterprises (MNEs), developing markets now seem to offer some of the best prospects for economic growth in the coming years. For example, *The Economist* has presented the comparative prospects for developing markets as follows:

> The rich world will continue to suffer from anemic growth for years to come. The emerging world, by contrast, will be a whirling hub of dynamism and creativity. Over the next decade it will account for more than 50% of global growth. It will see 700 million people enter the middle class. And it will account for a disproportionate share of business innovations. (The Economist, 2010a, p. 1)

This change of view toward business investment in developing markets is nothing short of remarkable. The BRIC countries of Brazil, Russia, India, and China currently receive the most attention from businesses in the developed world (The Economist, 2010a, pp. 1–2). But problems for business exist in the developing world. For example, the Chinese government remains committed to authoritarian ways and not holding elections. Russia's government is corrupt and capricious, although it is blessed with plentiful oil and gas reserves. India remains chaotic to those from outside India. Although Brazil has made economic gains in recent years, the poor continue to proliferate in the slums of its biggest cities.

Other developing countries might be sorted into "overlooked" countries, such as African ones like South Africa, Egypt, Algeria, Botswana, Mauritius, Morocco, and Tunisia (The Economist, 2010a, p. 2). However, the Arab Spring presents uncertainties for Egypt and Tunisia as the civil unrest that toppled the regimes there in 2011 may return. Alternatively, "frontier" economies pose more risks and come with more poverty. Sri Lanka, Bangladesh, Pakistan, Kenya, Nigeria, and Rwanda are examples of countries with such frontier economies.

After summarizing current perspectives about the success and failure of economic development across countries, this chapter will review macro factors for developing markets (Shultz et al., 2011). Six important dimensions of developing countries will be explained, including (a) culture, (b) population, (c) geography and climate, (d) economy, (e) political system, and (f) infrastructure. Institutions of society will also be featured in the final dimension of developing countries as they are proposed to be "soft" infrastructure (Khanna & Palepu, 2011).

The poor in developing countries deserve special attention for marketers and leaders of business because of the larger share of the population they comprise in developing countries. Before his death in 2010, University of Michigan business professor C. K. Prahalad called the developed world's businesses to wake up to the fortune they could obtain by marketing to the very poorest consumers in countries, such as India (Prahalad, 2005). Among many, the MNEs that have responded to Prahalad's justifications for pursing the "fortune at the bottom of the pyramid" (BOP) have been consumer packaged goods companies like Unilever and Procter & Gamble. However, skeptics assert that this fortune resulting from BOP marketing is a mirage (Karnani, 2007). This chapter will include a review of this debate about BOP marketing.

Finally, studies of female entrepreneurs in the Middle East and North Africa (MENA) identify three challenges for women pursuing ventures in this region (World Bank, 2007). First, attitudes toward women and working outside the home are less favorable in MENA than in other regions. Second, cumbersome and costly procedures character- ize the opening or closing of a business in countries of the region. Women (who are typically more risk averse) perceive launching a venture as being more risky in such environments because of the accompanying expectation of bribe-paying needed to make the system work. Third, despite gender-neutral laws in MENA, conservative judges and lawyers often perceive women as "legal minors" and make decisions pref- erential to men, who are perceived to be "legal adults" and more trusted to carry out the wishes of society. Despite such challenges, one Egyptian woman who has achieved success in the technology field is Hanan Abdel Meguid, this chapter's Maverick Who Made It.

After this chapter, you should be able to answer the following questions:

- Is global development succeeding? Explain.
- What does the rise of "emerging giants" say about business in developing countries today?
- What are six important macro factors for understanding developing market contexts?
- Why might there be a fortune at the bottom of the pyramid by marketing to poor consumers in developing countries?
- Why might a fortune at the bottom of the pyramid be a mirage?

## WHAT WE KNOW ABOUT COUNTRY DEVELOPMENT

### Challenges in Explaining Economic Development

When considering developing countries, it is encouraging to remember that some of these countries actually become developed countries. The "Four Asian Tigers"— Singapore, Hong Kong, Taiwan, and South Korea—began serious economic growth in the 1960s and became developed countries as a result of rapid economic growth in the 1980s and the 1990s (Cateora, Gilly, & Graham, 2011, p. 313). Notably, each of these countries has earned rankings in the top 30 for quality of life (Economist Intelligence Unit, 2005).

This rise is remarkable when remembering that South Korea and Taiwan were no larger economically than sub-Saharan African countries in the 1950s (Rodrik, 2011, p. 146). Each of these "tigers" really did not have natural resources of which to speak, so this forced them to emphasize human development—primarily education and entrepreneurship—in their rise (Friedman, 2012). Governments in these countries also improved their investment climate by (a) keeping taxes low, (b) controlling inflation, (c) bringing discipline to the operation of their bureaucracies, and (d) investing in infrastructure development (Rodrik, 2011, p. 147). In sum, a variety of factors contributed to the development success of these countries.

**Figure 13.1**   The "Four Asian Tigers" from South to North—Singapore, Hong Kong, Taiwan, and South Korea

*Source:* http://en.wikipedia.org/wiki/Four_Asian_Tigers

Despite the remarkable stories of the Four Asian Tigers, few other developing countries have had similar records of growth and prosperity. Accordingly, understanding why some countries grow and generally improve people's living standards and why others do not remains a perplexing question for macromarketers and developmental economists (Dapice, 2008). The transnational entity charged with assisting long-term development of countries, the World Bank, acknowledges that it still does not know the sufficient conditions for growth. "We can characterize the successful economies of the postwar period, but we cannot name with certainty the factors that sealed their success, or the factors they could have succeeded without. It would be preferable if it were otherwise," the World Bank Commission on Growth and Development said (World Bank, 2008, p. 33).

Using the narrow view of development as growth in GDP per capita, macromarketing research suggests that rich countries grow about 2% per year (Dapice, 2008, p. 414). For poor nations to catch up over a long period spanning decades would require at least a 3% growth rate each year. Since 1975, only 11 countries that are not rich have grown this fast. Most of these are Asian: China, India, Indonesia, Laos, Sri Lanka, Thailand Viet Nam, Botswana, Chile, Lebanon, and Poland.

Importantly, it is not easy to identify a "silver bullet"—a seemingly magical solution to a complicated problem—for development across these countries. For example, a closer examination of this set of countries shows that the government's ability to deliver services and create a stable environment for investment is not the only explanation for growth. India receives good ratings for its governance, but it has grown more slowly than China or Viet Nam, which receive less favorable ratings for governance (Dapice, 2008, p. 414).

For those who encourage an unleashing of the market with minimum interference by government as the avenue for economic growth, evidence suggests some sobering findings. For example, the Heritage Foundation's Index of Economic Freedom (that focuses on the economic policies and laws of countries) ranks most fast-growing nations in the bottom of their list of countries based on economic freedom (Dapice, 2008, pp. 414–415). It seems that nations with restrictions on economic freedom can grow fast—at least for a decade or two. A question remains about how long such growth can be sustained because growth rates can be very volatile over two decades or more (Kenny, 2011, p. 33).

## The Complexity, Heterogeneity, and Unintended Consequences of Aggregate Marketing Systems

### Complex

As discussed in Chapter 3, the aggregate marketing system is the collection of all marketing systems in society (Wilkie & Moore, 1999). Macromarketing scholarship offers three primary generalizations about aggregate marketing systems that offer some insight into the difficulty researchers have in explaining economic growth for countries. First, aggregate marketing systems are highly complex (Mittelstaedt, Kilbourne, & Mittelstaedt, 2006, p. 133). They are made up of thousands of firms, nongovernmental organizations (NGOs), and regulators, along with millions of households. As a result, it is not surprising that one variable cannot explain economic growth or lack of it.

### Heterogeneous

Second, aggregate marketing systems are heterogeneous (Mittelstaedt et al., 2006, p. 134). In other words, they are different. Countries have different geographies (including climates) and natural resource endowments. These starting conditions for countries affect the types of markets and the resulting economic system that develops. For example, snow plows are not needed in Saudi Arabia, which is uniquely endowed with oil reserves on the eastern side of the country. Not surprisingly, marketing systems have developed in Saudi Arabia that are focused on the export of oil and the importation of food and manufactured goods.

In addition to country geographies contributing to the heterogeneity of aggregate marketing systems, macromarketing researchers have identified five preconditions for markets that make markets heterogeneous (Klein & Nason, 2000, p. 270). These are (a) a legal system to establish and protect property rights, contract rights, and choice; (b) adequate information systems; (c) physical infrastructure to facilitate transportation and communication; (d) regard for social aspects of marketing (such as environmental protection, food safety, and cultural enhancement); and (e) a reliable financial system.

A country's history influences these preconditions. For example, Namibia (northwest of South Africa) and Java (an island part of Indonesia) have differences in their aggregate marketing systems because each had a different colonizer (Shultz et al., 2011). Germany colonized Namibia, while Holland colonized Java. Each colonizer brought different ideas, administrative practices, and technologies. Additionally, each colonizer built on a different cultural foundation. Tribal groups lived at subsistence levels in Namibia prior to the Germans colonizing in 1884. For this reason, German colonizers strongly influenced the market preconditions of Namibia. In contrast, Java was a center of Hindu/Buddhist Empires and then Islamic Sultanates prior to the arrival of the Dutch. Accordingly, Java's aggregate marketing system carries the imprint of multiple cultures from Asia that traded extensively throughout the region, as well as Dutch influence.

### Unintended Consequences

Third, macromarketing scholarship recognizes that choices of marketplace actors have consequences far beyond themselves, for better or worse (Mittelstaedt et al., 2006, p. 135). These can be in the form of externalities (uncalculated costs or benefits of exchange) or social consequences (any unforeseen effect to those involved in a transaction or to those not involved in a transaction). For example, Vietnamese environmental police had to disguise themselves as night fishermen on the Thi Vai River to investigate allegations that the Taiwanese food-additive and chemical manufacturer Vedan had constructed an elaborate underground system from one of its factories (Nguyen & Pham, 2011). During this 2009 investigation, the environmental police discovered an 800-meter pipe of Vedan's that had been discharging untreated wastewater directly into the river for 14 years. The Vietnamese government responded slowly over the next two years as a result of conflicting purposes of government agencies, as well as of delays engendered by a vast bureaucracy. Distrust for foreign direct investment increased among farmers, consumers, and government officials as a result of the Vedan scandal. The implication is that such externalities and social consequences may bedevil attempts to boost economic development.

A social consequence of marketing in developing countries can be discerned in Slater's framing of the developing country problem in this way:

> The trend in most underdeveloped societies is for the expanding population in traditional sectors to gradually drift into urban slums and create a proletariat.

Meanwhile, the upper income elite continue to consume imported luxuries so that the nation has a high requirement for foreign exchange and limited demand for internal production. Foreign exchange can usually be most easily earned by maintaining labor intensive plantations for export commodities which delay the education and industrialization changes need for takeoff. (Slater, 1977, p. 120)

Here, elites want luxuries unavailable in the home country. Cheap labor is used to export agricultural commodities. With this cash, the elites buy the imported luxuries or invest overseas—and the cycle repeats itself year after year. By purchasing imported luxuries or investing overseas, a social consequence results from these transactions. Development lags and the only opportunities remain low-paying jobs on the farms of the elite. As a result, farm laborers and their children have few prospects for developing themselves as wage earners over the course of their lives.

For the country to break out of this cycle, growth must be a serious priority for those who govern the country (Dapice, 2008, p. 416). In the end, economic growth is a political choice and often a difficult one to make and sustain over time. Most elites and interest groups are more concerned about their relative share of power and/or wealth than they are about the rate of overall economic growth for their country. Those who would be hurt by new policies resist the adoption and implementation of such policies—at least at first, but possibly longer.

In sum, economic development results from many factors. The first 30 years of macro-marketing scholarship offers three primary generalizations that help understand the challenge of explaining economic development. First, aggregate marketing systems are highly complex. Second, aggregate marketing systems are heterogeneous. Third, market transactions frequently have consequences for those not involved in them.

## Gains for Developing Countries

Although discussions about developing countries often turn to the poverty in these countries (poor consumers will be given treatment later in this chapter, too), there actually is much development to report: "Despite counterclaims and hand wringing, things are getting better, everywhere," senior fellow at the Center for Global Development Charles Kenny said. He continued:

Rich countries may be getting richer faster than poor countries, and we may be unsure how to improve that situation, but poor countries and poor people aren't stuck in the nightmare of an ever-growing and unsupportable population, living on bare subsistence. Instead, those countries with the lowest quality of life are making the fastest progress in improving it—across a range of measure including health, education and civil and political liberties. (Kenny, 2011, p. x)

Progress in developing countries has resulted from the spread of technologies (such as vaccinations), as well as from the spread of ideas (such as sending one's daughter to school). Although Africa and many other parts of the world have lagged in income growth, they have made marked improvement in health, education, gender equality, security, and human rights (Kenny, 2011, p. 4). By broadening one's view of developing countries from income growth to quality of life or well-being, many of the gains for developing countries become evident. In education, the best measure of a country's human capital—average number of years of schooling for adults—increased from around two years to seven years from 1900 to 2000. Today, 80% of the global population of adults can read (in 1950, only half could read). In health, global average infant mortality has declined by more than half since 1960.

Looking only at developing countries, it is hard to believe gains in quality of life that can be seen. In the Middle East and North Africa, life expectancy has increased from 48 to 69 years from 1962 to 2002 (Kenny, 2011). Much of this can be attributed to a reduction in infant mortality. Notably, this gain for the region occurred when per capita economic growth averaged only a grim 0.5% each year.

Businesses of the developing countries have also posted striking gains. Some of these firms (referred to as "emerging giants" in the business press) have globalized their businesses with much success. For example, Kuwait-based Zain has become one of the world's largest telecommunication firms by targeting developing countries, such as those in Africa (Khanna & Palepu, 2011, p. 170). When operating in sub-Saharan African countries, Zain discovered that it needed to fill voids in the infrastructure by generating its own power with thousands of small generators. With such agility, Zain went from a government-controlled monopoly with just 600,000 customers in Kuwait in 2002 to becoming the world's fastest-growing telecommunications provider with 32 million customers in 22 countries in the Middle East and Africa in 2008.

Emerging giants are not limiting themselves to the developing world, however. They now compete with MNEs in the home markets of the MNEs in developed countries. After Indian laws changed in 2007 to allow total overseas direct investment by Indian firms to rise from 100% of an Indian firm's net worth to 400%, India's Tata Motors purchased the Jaguar and Land Rover brands then owned by Ford Motor Company (Khanna, Palepu, & Bullock, 2009). Not limited to mergers and acquisitions for its worldwide expansion, Tata produces its own brand of cars, trucks, and busses for worldwide markets. It is the fifth largest producer of commercial vehicles in the world and the second largest producer of busses (Tata Group, 2011).

Tata Motors is part of the Tata Group comprising more than 90 operating companies in seven business sectors: (a) communications and information technology, (b) engineering, (c) materials, (d) services, (e) energy, (f) consumer products, and (g) chemicals. The group has operations in more than 80 countries across six continents, and its companies export products and services to 85 countries. The total revenue of Tata companies, taken together, was $83.3 billion in 2010–2011, with 58% of this coming from business outside India. Because the Tata trusts (philanthropic entities dedicated to education and poverty alleviation in India) own 65.8% of the shares of Tata Sons, and because of Tata Group's commitment to ethical and sustainable business, Tata Group is regarded as pursuing Conscious Capitalism (presented in Chapter 5) similar to firms such as Whole Foods, Patagonia, Interface, and Starbucks (O'Toole & Vogel, 2011, p. 60).

Another emerging giant is China's Lenovo, which overtook Dell in 2011 to become the second-largest PC firm in the world (Lenovo, 2011). Lenovo serves customers in more than 160 countries, and as a result, its advertising can be found in major media and sports sponsorships across these countries. Formed by Lenovo Group's acquisition of the former IBM Personal Computing Division, its product lines include ThinkPad PCs, as well as servers, workstations, and mobile Internet devices, such as tablets and smartphones. Lenovo is a global Fortune 500 company and has major research centers in Yamato, Japan; Beijing, Shanghai and Shenzhen, China; and Raleigh, North Carolina.

## Macro Factors for Understanding the Context of Developing Markets

Developing market researchers have identified six important dimensions of developing country contexts for business practitioners, public policy makers, NGOs, and scholars (Shultz et al., 2012). These are (a) culture, (b) population, (c) geography and climate, (d) economy, (e) political system, and (f) infrastructure. Institutions of society are included in the final dimension of developing countries because they are proposed to be "soft" infrastructure (Khanna & Palepu, 2011).

When comparing the lowest income countries of the world with the highest income countries of the world, marked differences become evident. Figure 13.2 depicts such differences in eight social indicators. The inner ring represents the low-income countries, while the outer ring signifies the high-income countries on these indicators using a 0–10 scale with 10 signifying the most favorable rating on these indicators and 0 representing the worst rating. The culture macro factor is represented by the gender development index at the nine o'clock position. This index covers demography, education, health, labor force and employment, and political participation for women.

The variables at the top (human development index of income, health, and education) and the bottom (average years of schooling for adults) represent the population macro factor. The geography and climate macro factor is not represented because these are natural endowments and not the result of man-made efforts as the other social indicators are. Employment in services (lower left part of graph) is an indicator for the economy macro factor. Regulatory quality (three o'clock position on the graph) and days to start a business (upper right part of the graph) represent the political system macro factor. Finally, Internet users per 1,000 people (upper left of graph) and total expenditure for research and development expenditures as a percentage of GDP (lower right of graph) represent the infrastructure macro factor. As can be seen by comparing the two rings of the graph, the low-income and high-income countries are very different on these social indicators. Some of the poorest of poor consumers are in these low-income countries. (These will be discussed later in this chapter.)

### Culture

Culture is the learned meaning system of a people group that provides a guide for those in the group about how to think and behave (Cateora, Gilly, & Graham, 2011, p. 102). Values, beliefs, and attitudes are commonly shared by members of a cultural group (Harrison,

**Figure 13.2**  Comparison of Low- and High-Income Countries on Eight Social Indicators

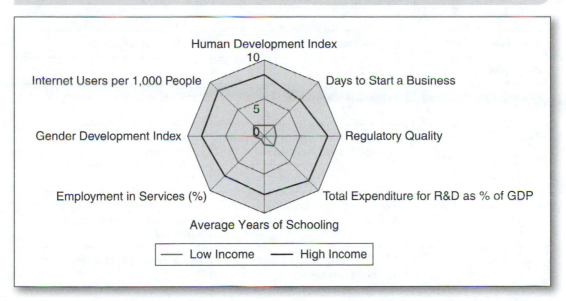

*Source:* World Bank (2011).

2006, p. 6). These can support and promote prosperity because they strongly affect perceptions of individuals and organizations about the way to win (Porter, 2000).

Table 13.11 presents the framework proposed by Argentine lawyer and political essayist Mariano Grondona to explain the differences between what he terms progress-prone cultures and progress-resistant cultures. A worldview of progress-prone cultures includes personal agency for the individual, as compared with fatalism for the progress-resistant culture. The expandability of wealth characterizes progress-prone cultures, as opposed to a peasant mentality that wealth is finite. (If someone gains, someone else must lose.) In terms of values and virtues, progress-prone cultures reinforce trust in public or commercial activities with lesser values like punctuality being important. By comparison, progress-resistant cultures reinforce mistrust and give little emphasis to lesser values, such as punctuality.

Economic behavior in progress-prone cultures is influenced by regard given to entrepreneurial effort in competitive markets. Progress-resistant cultures see rent-seeking (taking advantage of what their position allows for self-gain) by cultural elites in government as the privilege granted to those who attain power.

Social behavior in progress-prone cultures can be characterized by a self-governing citizenry in which half the population (women) are able to function as the equals of the other half (men). Progress-resistant cultures tend to carry patriarchal hierarchy in which male chiefs or strong men dominate others because of their place in the tribe or kinship group. Women might run the home but usually not business, government, or civic organizations.

**Table 13.1**  Condensed Typology of Progress-Prone and Progress-Resistant Cultures (Harrison, 2006; Grondona, 2000)

| Dimension | Progress-Prone Culture | Progress-Resistant Culture |
|---|---|---|
| **World View** | | |
| Destiny | I can influence my destiny for the better | Fatalism, resignation, sorcery |
| Wealth | Product of human creativity is wealth expandable (positive sum) | What exists (zero-sum) is wealth; not expandable |
| **Values, Virtues** | | |
| Ethical Code | Rigorous within realistic norms; feeds trust | Elastic, wide gap twixt utopian norms and behavior. Mistrust reinforced |
| The lesser values | A job well done, tidiness, and punctuality matter | Lesser virtues unimportant |
| **Economic Behavior** | | |
| Entrepreneurship | Investment and creativity | Rent seeking: income derives from government connections |
| Competition | Leads to excellence | Is a sign of aggression, and a threat to equality and privilege |
| Advancement | Based on merit, connections | Based on family and/or patron connections |
| **Social Behavior** | | |
| Rule of law/corruption | Reasonably law abiding; corruption is prosecuted | Money, connections matter; corruption is tolerated |
| Family | The idea of "family" extends to the broader society | The family is a fortress against the broader society |
| Gender relationships | If gender equality not a reality, at least not inconsistent with value system | Women subordinate to men in most dimensions of life |

## Population

Population characteristics contribute much to country development. Important aspects of a population for country are (a) urbanization, (b) health, and (c) education. As shown in

Figure 13.3, urbanization has risen steadily since 1950 (UN, 2011). It is predicted to continue its rise through 2050.

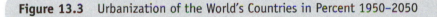

**Figure 13.3**   Urbanization of the World's Countries in Percent 1950–2050

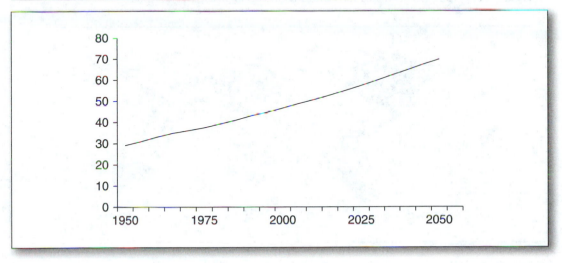

*Source:* UN (2011).

Although the concentration of people living in cities makes industrialization more of a possibility, in many countries, the move to the cities exacerbates housing shortages resulting in expansive slums. At the same time, towns and villages in rural areas have emptied leaving mostly the elderly in some (Batson, 2008). Those who remain rely economically on cash sent back from those who left. Currently in China, the largest migration in human history is under way. One hundred and fifty million people have already migrated internally in China in pursuit of jobs in the cities, and there are predictions that 300 million more people will eventually migrate to the Chinese cities over the next 30 years (The Economist, 2010b). China's urbanization matches the world's urbanization for the year 2000 in Figure 13.3. It will likely soon catch up with the world's urbanization percentage and continue along with it to 2050.

The health and education of a country's population contribute much to country development because they represent important elements of human capital (Baumol, Litan, & Schramm, 2007, p. 159). Figures 13.4 and 13.5 depict life expectancies for the world's countries and expected years of schooling, respectively (HDRO, 2011a, 2011b). Health and education indicators are important in development because they represent important aspects of human capital—the wellness and knowledge of a society. Notably, Figure 13.4 suggests that China has a higher life expectancy than either India or Russia. However,

Figure 13.5 suggests that China only outperforms India in expected years of schooling while lagging behind Russia's relatively well-educated population that is on par with the expected years of schooling for developed countries.

**Figure 13.4** Life Expectancies for World's Countries Expressed as an Index

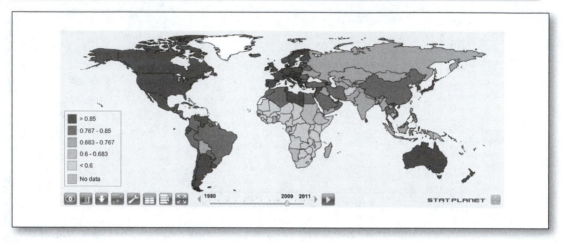

*Source:* HDRO (2011a).

**Figure 13.5** Expected Years of Schooling for Children

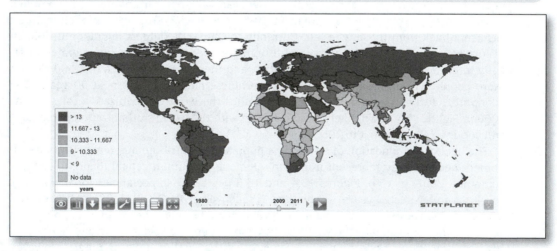

*Source:* HDRO (2011b).

## Geography and Climate

Temperate regions of the world are undeniably more developed than the tropical countries. Of the 24 countries classified as "industrial," not one lies between the tropics of Cancer and Capricorn (about 23 degrees North and South of the Equator), except a bit of Australia and the Hawaiian Islands (Hausmann, 2001). Figure 13.6 depicts the "Grand Canyon" of the tropics regarding GDP per capita for 1960, 1980, and 2007 on the left side. Figure 13.6 also depicts population density for 1960, 1980, and 2005 on the left side, as well as total population and urbanization percentage on the right side. Additionally, the bar charts on the bottom part of the left side depict a comparison for GDP per capita and population density for countries above the Equator (the North) and those below the Equator (the South).

**Figure 13.6**   Population and GDP Per Capita by Latitude

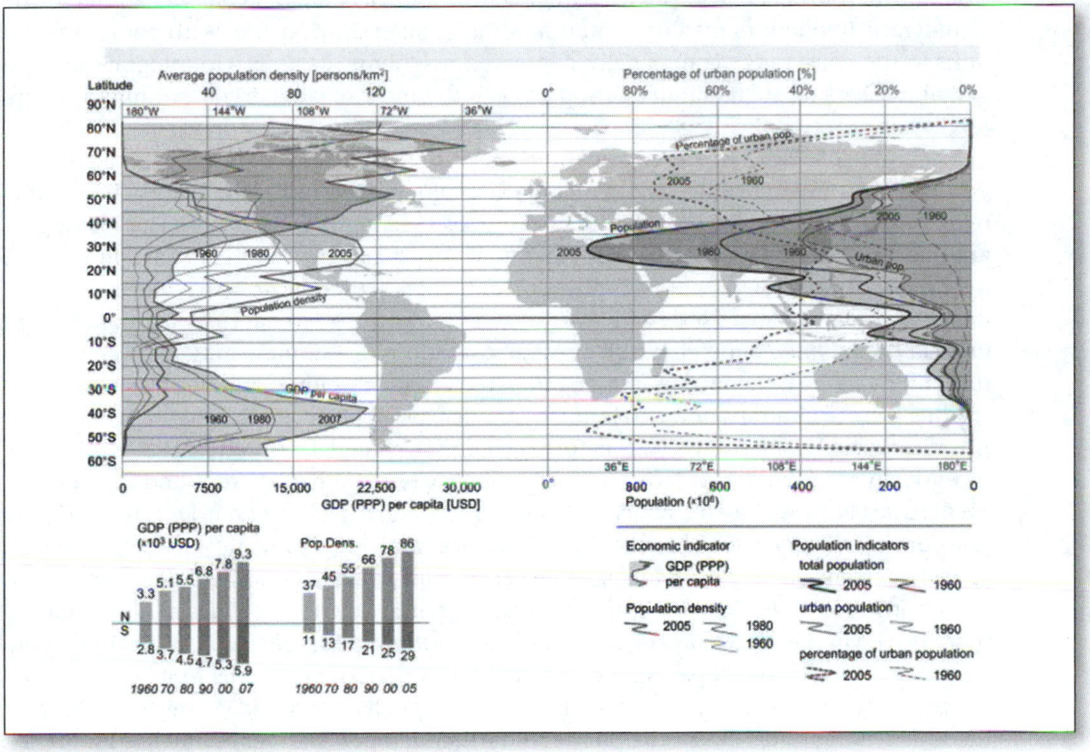

*Source:* Kummu & Varis (2011).

Philosophers and social scientists from previous centuries proposed simplistic explanations for such latitude differences. For example, Montesquieu believed climate might have a direct effect on human temperament, work effort, and social harmony (Mellinger, Sachs, & Gallup, 2000). During times of colonial rule, ideas such as Montesquieu's implied racial superiority for the ruling empires. Not surprisingly, these ideas became popular among imperialists.

Although rejecting notions from past eras regarding climate's links with race, work effort, or culture, new economic geographers view climate as one of many important influences on development. Some social scientists have argued that climate helps determine the means of production (small farming in the temperate regions and plantation farming in the tropics). With such profound effect on production, climate would thereby indirectly affect the organization of society and the possibilities for development.

Coastal location (which results in lower transportation costs and increased access to markets and new technological approaches and ideas) would be another dimension of geography critical to development. Being a landlocked country is a disadvantage because of the complications (risks) this adds to foreign trade (Wolf, 2004, p. 147). Although a landlocked country like Switzerland successfully oriented its economy to serve the markets of its neighbors in Europe, countries such as Uganda have neighbors that are economically troubled or burdened with civil strife, such as Kenya, Sudan, Rwanda, Somalia, the Democratic Republic of the Congo, and Tanzania (Collier, 2007, p. 55). With poor transport links to the coast, and economically depressed neighbors, its ability to integrate itself in global markets through manufacturing (to date the most reliable driver of rapid development) has proved difficult.

Recently, scholars have developed three reasons why tropical countries are consistently poorer than temperate ones. These include agricultural factors, health factors, and factors related to the mobilization of scientific resources (Sachs, 2000). Eurasia's east–west geographical layout and the north–south layout in Africa and the Americas have influenced historical patterns of agricultural innovation and, thus, economic growth (Diamond, 1997). Because climate changes little with longitude, but markedly with latitude, the countries of Eurasia happily had fairly common climatic conditions. Such uniformity allowed agricultural innovations developed in one region to travel long distances and be shared by many regions. On the contrary, new agricultural varieties developed in the tropics of Africa or the Americas could not travel very far before the climate changed dramatically.

Agriculture in the tropics faces reduced productivity of perennial crops and staple foods. This is true because of (a) weak soils, high soil erosion, and depletion of nutrients from tropical rain forest conditions; (b) water control difficulties and risk of drought in wet-dry tropics; (c) high incidence of pests; and (d) high rate of spoilage for food in storage (Sachs, 2000).

The incidence of infectious disease is also higher in the tropics. Flies and mosquitoes that flourish in the warm climate carry major vector-borne diseases, such as malaria, hookworm, schistasomiasis (a parasitic worm that feeds on red blood cells in its victims contracted through exposure to contaminated water), river blindness, and yellow fever. Because the afflicted countries tend to be poor and underdeveloped with respect to the temperate countries, tropical diseases do not receive research-and-development (R&D) investments that instead might be directed to cures for baldness in Western markets (Hausmann, 2001). In sum, changes in latitude have a profound inhibiting effect on the diffusion of technological innovations to the tropics in crucial sectors for development, such as agriculture, health, and construction (Sachs, 2000). Overcoming distance to developed markets through increased globalization in these economic sectors could help overcome what has been called "the tyranny of geography" in the tropics.

## Economy

Economies of countries can be described in several ways, such as level of development, or percentage of the labor force working in the agricultural, manufacturing, or service sectors. For example, 41% of the labor force in the United States worked on farms in 1900. However, by 2000, only 1.9% of the labor force worked on farms (Dimitri, Effland, & Conklin, 2005). In the early part of the 20th century, the United States industrialized. But after 1950, it entered a postindustrialization phase in which the service sector (such as healthcare, education, financial services, government, media, entertainment, hospitality, and tourism) became dominant (Lee & Mather, 2008, p. 7).

Figure 13.7 presents a comparison of a postindustrial economy (the United States), an industrializing economy (China), and an agricultural economy (Ethiopia) based on the percentage of the labor force in each country working in service, industry, and agriculture (CIA, 2011). As shown, the most workers in the United States are in the services sector (83%), while the most in China are in agriculture (38.1%), and the most in Ethiopia are in agriculture (85%).

**Figure 13.7**   Comparison of Labor Sector Percentages for the United States, China, and Ethiopia

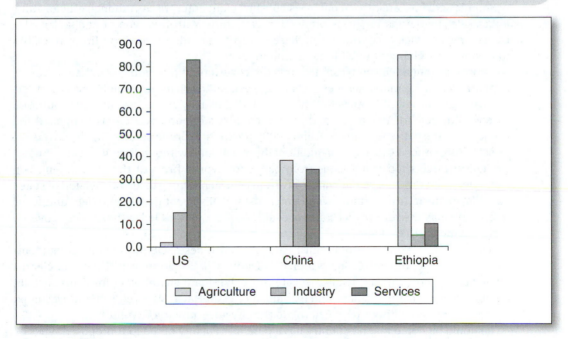

*Source:* CIA (2011).

Economies can also be classified by the type of capitalism they have adopted in their societies. Aside from communist stalwarts Cuba and North Korea, the rest of the world uses some form of capitalism in which the means of production are owned privately. Table 13.2 presents a proposed framework for four types of capitalism (Baumol et al., 2007, pp. 60–61). First, entrepreneurial capitalism allows small, innovative firms to play a significant role in markets. The benefit of this for society is that research suggests that most radical innovations come from entrepreneurs, rather than from large firms. With the changes coming as a result of firms and businesses adopting innovations (such as the PC in the 1980s and the accompanying rise of the software industry), outmoded technologies and brands cannot be sustained in the marketplace. With this comes job losses for many (typewriters and their manufacturers). The United States and Canada are examples of countries where entrepreneurial capitalism bloomed before big-firm capitalism took root and displaced much of entrepreneurial capitalism there.

Second, oligarchic capitalism exists in much of the developing world still, such as Latin America, the countries of the Former Soviet Union, much of the Arabic Middle East, and much of Africa (Baumol et al., 2007, p. 71). Here, the bulk of the power and wealth are held by a few individuals and families. Oligarchic capitalism brings with it (a) a high degree of income inequality across society, (b) corruption, (c) much informal business activity done without the licenses required by the state, and (d) an excessive focus on resource extraction. Such a focus diverts talent away from starting successful businesses either purposely (those who favor the status quo usually resent the changes brought about by entrepreneurs) or inadvertently.

Third, big-firm capitalism in continental Europe and Japan exists when most significant economic activities are carried out by established giant enterprises. Although efficient and large-scale operations for mass production can come with this type of capitalism, the bureaucracy needed to control one of these enterprises renders these large firms inflexible to respond to a changing environment around them.

Fourth, state-guided capitalism features the government trying to guide the market by supporting favorite industries it expects to prosper. Although it can result in the export-led growth seen in the 21st century for China and India, usually consumers in these countries receive little regard. When demand for the country's exports decline (as happened for China's exports to the West in 2008 and 2009), prosperity for the country can be adversely affected (Bremmer, 2010, p. 139). Additionally, when done without discipline, state-guided capitalism directs too many loans from banks to favored firms of the government. For example, when China began moving away from central planning to its own version of state-guided capitalism, many state-owned enterprises (SOEs) went deeply into debt and were unable to repay the state banks (Baumol et al., 2007, p. 60). This led to the Chinese government paying for these losses.

The guidance from the Communist Party that a Chinese SOE in China receives today varies. The oil company, China National Offshore Oil Corporation (CNOOC), is clearly owned by the government, while the state is the dominant shareholder for firms such as computer-manufacturer Lenovo and for appliance giant Haier (Woetzel, 2008). Most shares in the auto manufacturer Chery belongs to the city government of Wuhu.

It should be noted that no country has a pure form of any of the four proposed types of capitalism, but instead it borrows some features from the other types. For example, the

United States can be characterized as a hybrid of entrepreneurial and big-firm capitalism. However, when the U.S. government intervened in the automobile industry and the financial services industry in 2008 to bail out privately held firms (such as GM, Chrysler, many large banks, and insurer AIG), the form of capitalism in the United States took on more elements of state-guided capitalism.

## Political Stability

*Civil War*

Working political systems are often taken for granted in developed countries. For example, when Al Gore lost to George W. Bush in the 2000 presidential election, the election was very close. It was so close that it took three weeks of recounting votes in Florida and a trip to the U.S. Supreme Court to resolve the issue with a 5-4 vote by the Supreme Court justices

**Table 13.2**    Four Types of Capitalism (Baumol et al., 2007)

| Type of Capitalism | Characteristics | Advantages | Disadvantages | Examples |
|---|---|---|---|---|
| Entrepreneurial Capitalism | Significant role played by small, innovative firms | 1. Radical innovations tend to come from entrepreneurs, rather than large firms | 1. Creative destruction of innovations can be disruptive for society due to job losses | 1. Canada & United States in the 1800s 2. Europe soon after WW II |
| Oligarchic Capitalism | Bulk of the power & wealth held by a few individuals and families | 1. Many plusses for a few wealthy families and government elites | 1. High degree of income inequality 2. Corruption 3. Much unlicensed business activity 4. Excessive focus on resource extraction | 1. Much of Latin America 2. Many countries of Former Soviet Union 3. Most of Arabic Middle East 4. Much of Africa |
| Big-Firm Capitalism | Most significant economic activities are carried out by established giant enterprises | 1. Above average profits for large corporations 2. Efficient manufacturing and incremental innovations | 1. Drive for continued improvement wanes 2. Firm's bureaucracy slows & even impedes adaptation to change | 1. Continental Europe 2. Japan |

*(Continued)*

| Type of Capitalism | Characteristics | Advantages | Disadvantages | Examples |
|---|---|---|---|---|
| State-Guided Capitalism | Government tries to guide the market by supporting favorite industries it expects to prosper | Export-led growth possible | 1. Consumers given little regard<br>2. Banks guided to loan too much to favored firms of government | 1. China<br>2. India |

favoring the case put forward by Bush's attorneys that recounting in Florida should stop. Although many in the United States grimaced at the arcane workings of the Electoral College (Gore polled more votes in the popular vote, but fewer in the Electoral College), both men were on the podium at the inauguration of Bush in January 2001. The important point here is that power changed hands peacefully—as expected by the citizens of the United States.

By comparison, 1,200 people died and more than 500,000 Kenyans fled their homes in violence that took on an ethnic dimension after the 2007 elections in Kenya (BBC, 2011). Although calm eventually returned to Kenya, the eruption of violence after the 2007 elections suggests that societies often have enormous pent-up tensions that can be triggered by such events as an election.

It must be remembered that when the United States was a developing country in 1860, the election of Abraham Lincoln (who did not advocate the termination of slavery—just its restriction to states where slavery currently existed) was so disagreeable to many living in the southern United States, they took up arms as rebels and initiated a civil war that lasted four years. Three percent of the entire population died as soldiers in the U.S. Civil War— 620,000 (however, a new study asserts that 750,000 actually died as soldiers [Glover, 2011].) This was by far the bloodiest war in human history up to that time. These numbers put the violence in Kenya in better perspective, but they also highlight the cost a society pays when its political system ruptures into civil war.

Slow growth, stagnation, or economic depression makes a country prone to civil war (Collier, 2007, p. 20). When looking toward the countries where the poorest billion people on the planet dwell, 73% of these countries have recently had a civil war or are currently in one (Collier, 2007). Half of these civil wars are resumptions of earlier civil wars.

The costs of civil war are many. It is like development in reverse—shrinking economic output by 2.3% each year on average (Collier, 2007). A country enduring a seven-year civil war will have an economy 15% smaller than when it began. Surprisingly, most who die in civil wars are not victims of bullets or shrapnel but of disease. This is, in part, a result of the sudden migrations of refugees to safer areas. Refugees are exposed to disease vectors during their treks when they are weakened. They later infect humans in the safer areas.

Sadly, the economic losses and disease do not stop at the end of the civil war. Government of postconflict countries typically double military spending over what it was before conflict began (Collier, 2007, p. 27). Kalashnikov rifles (the weapon of choice for developing country rebels) flood countries during times of conflict. After conflicts, such weapons remain cheap. Not surprisingly, homicide rates spike as the culture of violence and extortion cannot be suddenly terminated after formal cessation of hostilities.

The problems of civil war spill over to neighboring countries. Weapons smuggled from Libya at the end of the Libyan civil war apparently flowed into the surrounding region. "Arms were stolen in Libya and are being disseminated all over the region," President Mahamadou Issoufou of Niger (Libya's neighbor to the south) said. "Saharan countries are facing terrorist threats, arms and criminal trafficking. The Libya crisis is amplifying those crises" (Maylie & Hinshaw, 2011, p. 1).

Neighboring countries must also endure (a) lost trading opportunities with the country experiencing civil war, (b) an influx of refugees that strain social services and infrastructure, and (c) the rise of criminal activities emanating from the civil war. All of this tends to destabilize neighboring countries. For example, 95% of global production of hard drugs comes from conflict countries (Collier, 2007, p. 31). In this way, conflict creates territory beyond the control of a recognized government—a good match for illegal activities. Osama Bin Laden chose to set up Al Qaeda operations in Afghanistan for this reason.

*Coups*

Another violent challenge to government can take the form of a *coup d'état*. Usually leadership in the military forces takes over the country in such a coup. A script for a coup might include capturing the current leader and cabinet members, securing communication centers (television, radio, newspapers) to broadcast programming favorable to the coup, and declaring martial law because of the national emergency that the deposed leaders thrust the country into because of their incompetence or illegal activities. Under martial law, the army is now responsible for governmental activities. The new military rulers usually suspend most civil rights (such as the state having to give reasons for jailing citizens) and impose curfews to restrict public activity. Later, a new constitution might be introduced and martial law rescinded.

As a 27-year-old army captain, Libya's Muammar al-Qaddafi led a bloodless coup that deposed King Idris I of Libya on September 1, 1969 (History.com, 2011) (The king had left the country to seek medical treatment at a Turkish spa). Qaddafi ruled with an iron hand for 42 years. However, as unrest spread through much of the Arab world during February 2011, massive street protests against the Qaddafi regime initiated a civil war between revolutionaries and loyalists. In March, an international coalition began conducting airstrikes against Qaddafi strongholds under the authority of a UN Security Council resolution. On October 20th, Qaddafi died at the hands of a mob who administered vigilante street justice after capturing him near his hometown of Sirte.

Libya's victorious National Transitional Council estimates that 25,000 of Libya's five million citizens died during the eight-month civil war with 3,000 maimed and 60,000 wounded (Mulholland & Deshmukh, 2011). The International Monetary Fund estimated that the financial cost of the Libyan civil war will come to more than $35 billion—half of its 2010 GDP (MENAFN, 2011).

Aon Corporation is a global firm with offices in more than 120 countries focused on providing research on political risk, as well as offering insurance and management consulting to businesses. Figure 13.8 depicts its 2011 terrorism and political violence map. As shown, countries with high or severe levels of terrorism and political violence include most of Africa, Southern Asia, and Indonesia, as well as Mexico, Honduras, Colombia, and Ecuador.

---

**Figure 13.8**   Terrorism and Political Violence Map

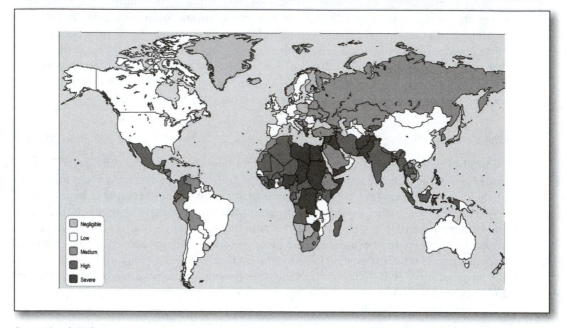

*Source:* Aon (2011).

## Infrastructure

*Physical and Institutional Infrastructure*

In developed markets, a range of intermediaries provide the information and contract enforcement needed to make commercial transactions (Khanna & Palepu, 2011, p. 14). Most developing countries lack the infrastructure—both physical and institutional—needed for the smooth running of markets. Physical infrastructure includes publicly owned goods, such as ports, harbors, airports, miles of railroads and highways, bridges, ferries, and water and sewer systems. In some countries, private companies operate other physical infrastructure, such as electrical utilities, communication systems (telephone, cell phone, Internet service providers, television, and radio), warehouses, refrigerated warehouses, and banks. Institutional infrastructure includes government-run courts and judicial systems, advertising agencies, media outlets, marketing research companies, logistics consultants, credit-rating agencies, and online clearinghouses for goods and services (for example, eBay and Orbitz).

Legal systems are of utmost importance to countries and the conduct of business. The legal system can take four forms: (a) common law evolving over time based on judicial rulings—in the United Kingdom and its former colonies, (b) civil law made by legislative action or official edict—in most of the rest of the world, (c) Islamic law where Sharia law is in effect, or (d) Marxist-Socialist tenets in communist countries, such as North Korea, Cuba, and China (Cateora et al., 2011, pp. 187–190). Although common law proves to be the most flexible for businesses, what is important is that the legal system is viewed widely by residents and foreign investors as trustworthy, stable, and effective (Baumol et al., 2007, p. 155). In this way, all parties to exchanges can reasonably expect to know what the rules are when they conduct business or lead their private lives.

Because of thin budgeting for governmental services in many developing countries, judicial systems can become ineffective. For example, because of a huge backlog of cases, resolving disputes in Indian courts can take 5 to 15 years (Khanna & Palepu, 2011, p. 14). Family or clan patriarchs might be used if the dispute is between two parties from the developing country, but this typically strikes foreign businesses as disadvantageous. The end result frequently is that deals are not initiated as a result of such institutional voids that increase risk to intolerable levels for MNEs.

Researchers of productive entrepreneurship propose that governmental institutions can create conditions that will promote the kind of entrepreneurial activity leading to economic growth for a society (Sobel, 2008). Governments can facilitate the operation of markets through an effective legal system (Forbes & Ames, 2009, pp. 313–316). First, the rule of law must be established and respected within a country. This means that government leaders, government agencies, and any other individuals (mafia chieftains) cannot act arbitrarily toward businesses and private individuals. This implies that government limits itself in its ability to tax and regulate businesses. Additionally, the judicial system must be fair and balanced, so that contracts can be enforced without bias. Second, property rights must be respected (Carman, 1982). When this happens, land, buildings, and equipment can be used as collateral for growing a business. Without this ability, stagnation occurs (de Soto, 2003). When ownership of property is respected in a society, entrepreneurs will take the necessary risks to conceive, launch, and implement their business plans. This includes intellectual property, such as inventions, new software, new music, and creative works.

### Corruption

Corruption is the abuse of public power or authority for private benefit (Anokhin & Schulze, 2009). It comes in two forms: (a) petty corruption (low-level government officials seeking relatively small amounts of money), and (b) grand corruption (high-ranking government officials seeking huge sums of money).

*Petty Corruption.* Petty corruption contributes to the delays in distributing products in the marketing system of a country (The Economist, 2002). In a 500-km trip from the capital city of Douala to Bertoua, a small town in Cameroon's southeastern rainforest, a

Guinness beer truck encountered 47 roadblocks manned by off-duty policeman set up for the seeking of bribes to allow motorists to continue their journeys. That is one roadblock every 8 km. Instead of a 20-hour journey, the trip took four days.

Bridges and roads had washed out in the heavy seasonal rains and these added to delays. The impact on any business is that just-in-time inventory management is out of the question. Consequently, Guinness Cameroon has to keep 40 days of inventory in the factory along with the crates, drums of malt, hops, and bottle caps to continue operations. Inventory, along with its storage, security, and insurance, costs money. Out in distant corners of Cameroon, wholesalers have to carry as much as five months of inventory at the beginning of the rainy season when roads become most subject to flooding and damage from hard rains.

Table 13.3 depicts the results of Transparency International's interviews with more than 91,500 respondents across 86 countries asking about bribes paid to service providers in the last 12 months (Transparency International, 2010, p. 14). As shown, regions with developing countries (the Middle East, sub-Saharan Africa, Latin America, and the Newly Independent States (NIS) of the Former Soviet Union) report the most bribe paying. Importantly, no region remains free of bribery.

**Table 13.3**  Bribe Paying to Service Providers in the Past 12 Months by Region

| | Education System | Judiciary | Medical Services | Police | Registry & Permit Services | Utilities | Tax Revenue | Land Services | Customs |
|---|---|---|---|---|---|---|---|---|---|
| GLOBAL | 11% | 23% | 12% | 29% | 17% | 10% | 10% | 20% | 23% |
| Asia-Pacific | 7% | 11% | 8% | 13% | 9% | 5% | 8% | 11% | 14% |
| Central & South Asia | 20% | 35% | 21% | 43% | 33% | 21% | 30% | 34% | 34% |
| EU+ | 3% | 4% | 7% | 4% | 4% | 3% | 2% | 5% | 4% |
| Latin America | 5% | 18% | 5% | 27% | 14% | 5% | 4% | 8% | 17% |
| Turkey, Middle East & North Africa | 26% | 32% | 22% | 37% | 36% | 24% | 29% | 34% | 42% |
| Newly Independent States | 18% | 24% | 27% | 34% | 16% | 4% | 9% | 22% | 24% |
| North America | 6% | 20% | 5% | 20% | 11% | 6% | 6% | 7% | 11% |
| Sub-Saharan Africa | 30% | 40% | 26% | 55% | 37% | 27% | 26% | 32% | 44% |
| Balkans | 5% | 11% | 12% | 13% | 6% | 2% | 2% | 6% | 12% |

*Source:* Transparency International (2010), http://www.transparency.org/policy_research/surveys_indices/gcb/2010/results

When asked about paying a bribe to someone from any of the nine institutions presented in Table 13.3 in their country in the last 12 months, those in the lowest 20% income bracket reported a higher incidence of bribing eight of the nine institutions when compared with those in the highest 20% income bracket (Transparency International, 2010, p. 15). By comparison, the rich had a higher incidence of bribery with the institution of the judiciary (the courts).

Given that any bribe would represent a larger chunk of the poor's income, the burden of bribery is relatively heavier for the poor. Nearly half of all respondents reported that the last bribe was paid "to avoid a problem with the authorities." In these regions with developing countries, the police are the service provider with the highest frequency of receiving bribes. Almost one quarter of respondents cited "speeding things up" as the reason for the bribe, followed by "to receive a service they were entitled to" (Transparency International, 2010, p. 19).

*Grand Corruption.* Grand corruption is perpetrated by those in high-ranking leadership positions for a country. After the end of the Libyan civil war, Libya's National Transitional Council estimated former Libyan leader Muammar al-Qaddafi had hidden more than $220 billion in bank accounts and investments around the world—an amount representing $30,000 for every Libyan (Richter, 2011). About one third of Libyans live in poverty. Most of the money was under the name of government institutions such as the Central Bank of Libya, the Libyan Investment Authority, the Libyan Foreign Bank, the Libyan National Oil Corp, and the Libya Africa Investment Portfolio. Qaddafi and his family members had access to these accounts.

Researchers estimate that, on average, dictators take about 3% of their nations' incomes in the form of excessive taxation (Mulligan, 2011). Judging from Qaddafi's share of Libya's national wealth, that is about what he was taking. However, other costs accrued to the Libyan people because the Qaddafi regime's security services included torturing and executing political enemies, making exiles living overseas disappear, as well as blocking unfavorable websites outside of the country (MacFarquhar, 2009, p. 32).

### No Institutions and Weak Institutions

Under Qaddafi's rule, Libya had no parliament, political parties, unions, NGOs, and independent newspapers or media outlets (MacFarquhar, 2009, p. 25). Because he had led a coup as an army officer, Qadaffi never trusted the military and frequently moved around its commanders and would not allow coordination across Libya's military units. This later proved fateful to Qaddafi himself, as his military forces could not unify their actions to stop the uprising against him that began in February 2011 and ended with his lynching in October of the same year.

During the last years of his 42 years of despotic rule, the official Libyan television news ended each night with dated video clips of rioting and civil unrest in cities of the West with the announcer intoning that it was only a matter of time before the decaying West came to adopt Libya's Popular Committees as the way of societal organization. Government-run newspapers typically filled themselves with songs, poems, and salutes to Qaddafi penned by Africans from the many countries where he directed foreign aid.

For writing about the Popular Committee meetings and how they showed Libyans as being discouraged with the incompetence of their rulers and their low quality of life, *New York Times* Cairo bureau chief Neil MacFarquhar never again received a visa to visit the country under Qaddafi's rule after his two-week visa expired in 2001. Keep in mind that MacFarquhar's writings were never published inside Libya but outside of it in the West.

A free press is an important ingredient in checking corruption in a society. In developed countries, the press is regarded as the "fourth estate," meaning it is the unofficial fourth branch of government that exposes government corruption, bad business practices, and the criminal activity of individuals (Quelch & Jocz, 2007, p. 208). The journalistic press enables freedom of speech. It consists of newspapers and magazines, television and radio broadcasters, book publishers, cable operators, and the blogosphere. An informed citizenry results from a strong and active journalism. This enables democratic processes to be more effective.

Chapter 9 related the story of Peter Eigen and the NGO he founded, Transparency International (TI). An examination of Figure 9.6 in chapter 9 suggests how developing countries in particular carry a burden of corruption. Researchers have found that increasing the corruption level in a country from that of Singapore (9.5 on a 10-point scale for lack of corruption) to Mexico's (3.1 on the same scale) is equivalent to raising the tax rate by more than 20 percentage points (Eigen, 2002). Not surprisingly, global investors tend to stay away from countries with high corruption levels.

Although TI has focused in the past on those taking bribes in the public sector, in recent years, it has broadened its focus to bribe payers. The 2011 Bribe Payers Survey for the first time also asked more than 3,000 business executives from 28 of the leading economies about the frequency of bribes being paid from one private firm to another when doing business abroad (Transparency International, 2011). Surprising to many, respondents perceived the likelihood of this form of bribery is almost as high as bribery of public officials across all sectors.

Companies may bribe employees in other firms to secure business and facilitate the functioning of hidden cartels seeking to control supplies of products. Employees from large firms can exploit their influence by demanding bribes or kickbacks from potential suppliers. Bribery can also be disguised through offering clients gifts and corporate hospitality that are inappropriate in value.

The effects of this particular form of bribery can be felt through the entire supply chain, distorting markets and competition, increasing costs to firms, harming smaller companies that cannot afford to compete on these terms, and firms with high integrity that refuse to do so. This not only prevents a fair and efficient private sector but also reduces the quality of products and services to the consumer.

## Summary of Macro Factors for Developing Country Contexts

In sum, the physical and institutional infrastructure for a country matters much to a society and its proper functioning. To repair or overhaul such infrastructure can be costly in terms of time and financial resources.

After reviewing the six macro factors for countries, one should gain an appreciation for the challenges confronting many developing countries across these six dimensions. Some countries might have (a) cultures characterized as progress-resistant, (b) low levels of health and education, (c) poor natural resources and a harsh climate, (d) an economy based on agriculture or extractive industries (such as mining or oil production), (e) civil war in recent years, and (f) weak institutions afflicted by corruption. Most of the countries with high or severe levels of terrorism and political violence face such disadvantages in development. Despite similar challenges across these six dimensions, some developing countries have managed to show promise for developing themselves in recent years. These countries have been described as "emerging markets" (Khanna & Palepu, 2011).

## Emerging Markets

Although a variety of lists have appeared in recent years to label the most promising developing countries as "emerging markets," there is no consensus definition of emerging markets. Table 13.4 presents Dow Jones's list of 30 developed and 35 emerging market countries. This set of countries is valuable because it represents 98% of the investments across stock markets of the world.

**Table 13.4**   A Listing of Developed and Emerging Markets

| DEVELOPED MARKETS | | | EMERGING MARKETS | | |
|---|---|---|---|---|---|
| AMERICAS | | | | | |
| CANADA | U.S | | ARGENTINA | CHILE | MEXICO |
| | | | BRAZIL | COLOMBIA | PERU |
| ASIA/PACIFIC | | | | | |
| AUSTRALIA | NEW ZEALAND | TAIWAN | CHINA OFFSHORE* | MALAYSIA | |
| HONG KONG | SINGAPORE | | INDIA | PAKISTAN | SRI LANKA |
| JAPAN | SOUTH KOREA | | INDONESIA | PHILIPPINES | THAILAND |
| EUROPE | | | | | |
| AUSTRIA | GREECE | PORTUGAL | BULGARIA | POLAND | |
| BELGIUM | ICELAND | SLOVENIA | CZECH REPUBLIC | ROMANIA | |
| CYPRUS | IRELAND | SPAIN | ESTONIA | RUSSIA | |
| DENMARK | ITALY | SWEDEN | HUNGARY | SLOVAKIA | |
| FINLAND | MALTA | SWITZERLAND | LATVIA | TURKEY | |
| FRANCE | NETHERLANDS | U.K. | LITHUANIA | | |
| GERMANY | NORWAY | | | | |

*(Continued)*

(Continued)

| DEVELOPED MARKETS | | | EMERGING MARKETS | | |
|---|---|---|---|---|---|
| MIDDLE EAST | | | | | |
| ISRAEL | | | JORDAN | BAHRAIN | KUWAIT |
| | | | OMAN | QATAR | UAE |
| AFRICA | | | | | |
| | | | EGYPT | | |
| | | | SOUTH AFRICA | MAURITIUS | MOROCCO |

*Source:* Dow Jones (2011).

In general, emerging markets can be characterized by (a) poverty (low-middle income and not industrialized), (b) capital markets (low market capitalization relative to GDP and low sovereign debt ratings), and (c) growth potential (economic liberalization, openness to foreign direct investment, and recent economic growth) (Khanna & Palepu, 2011, p. 4). In short, emerging markets offer attractive investment opportunities for MNEs to acquire firms in these markets or to introduce their own brands there. MNEs expect to find 70% of their future growth in emerging markets—40 % in China and India, alone (Eyring, Johnson, & Nair, 2011).

The future looks bright for such countries—although volatility will remain a part of the risk in doing business in emerging markets. In 2003, Wall Street investment bank Goldman Sachs forecasted that before 2050 the BRIC countries of Brazil, Russia, India, and China would grow to be collectively larger than the G-6 countries (United States, Japan, United Kingdom, Germany, France, and Italy) (Wilson & Purushothaman, 2003).

Not surprisingly, MNEs have taken increased interest in emerging markets in recent years. For example, a few years ago, consumer packaged goods manufacturer H. J. Heinz Company had less than 5% of its sales come from emerging markets. In 2011, 20% of its revenues came from emerging markets (Johnson, 2011).

In evaluating possible acquisitions in emerging markets, Heinz looks at several of the same aspects of businesses as in developed countries, such as operating metrics of the business, recent and forecasted growth, as well as how the business fits with Heinz's core business. But Heinz also uses an entire set of biggest M issues when evaluating acquisitions in emerging markets. "We look at how the company goes to market, the tax system, the regulatory environment, currency trends, and the political climate, comparing them with what exists in the United States," Johnson, Heinz's CEO, said. He continues:

> We take these things for granted in developed economies, but they're a big consideration in emerging markets, where governments are often much more active. This process may take a lot of time, and the companies we're considering as acquisitions are sometimes frustrated by that, But these issues are very important. We have walked away from deals in Ukraine, Vietnam and other markets because our due diligence told us there were considerable risks involved in trying to generate acceptable returns on the businesses. (Johnson, 2011, p. 49)

Firms from developed countries like Heinz's have learned that they need to make adaptations to their marketing mixture of product, place, price, and promotion when they go to the emerging markets. Products frequently need to be adapted to the tastes of the host culture if consumers have intimate involvement with them. For example, ketchup in the Philippines is made from bananas and tastes differently from ketchup in the West. Places of distribution also have to be relevant for host cultures. Supermarket chains only cover about 15% of the market in India, whereas in the United States, they cover virtually 100% of the market. In emerging markets, corner stores and open-air markets comprise a majority of food retailing. Prices need to be kept relevant for consumers in emerging markets. Often, this is done by offering different sizes, such as packets of soy sauce, instead of bottles of soy sauce. Finally, the promotion of brands must be done with an understanding of how host-country consumers live. If they are not likely to have refrigerators, then it is useless to sell them quantities that must be stored in refrigerated places. Having local managers in place addresses many of these issues in better ways than having expatriate staff members of the MNE there to run the business in the host country.

"We have learned that to succeed in emerging markets, you need to be risk aware but not risk averse," Johnson said. He continues:

> Indonesia provides a great example of that. We bought a big business there in 1999. The country was just starting to democratize and have elections: it wasn't especially stable. Frankly, some people wondered if it was a good place for an American company. Today that's a $400 million business for us, versus $80 million when we bought it. Generally, we focus on the long term. Our Indian business took seven or eight years to get right. You have to be patient, flexible, and open to ideas from local management. (Johnson, 2011, p. 50)

## THE POOR OF DEVELOPING MARKETS

### Living on $2-a-Day

Developing countries accounted for 20% of consumer-packaged goods manufacturer Procter & Gamble's (P&G) sales in 2000, but in 2011, they accounted for 33% of sales (Reingold, 2011). By 2020, the firm wants to have 50% of its sales coming from developing countries. Although P&G's current strategy across 180 countries emphasizes providing "mass prestige" to middle- and upper-class consumers by selling high-quality brands, such as Olay, Crest, Tide, and Pampers at premium prices, the future market segment for P&G and companies like it will be poor consumers in developing countries. P&G refers to these consumers as the "$2-a-day" consumer based on their average income.

To understand these consumers better, a newly created special unit within P&G now spends days or weeks in field settings across countries such as Brazil, India, and China. "Our innovation strategy is not just diluting the top-tier product for the lower-end consumer," CEO Robert McDonald said. "You have to discretely innovate for every one of those consumers on that economic curve, and if you don't do that, you'll fail" (Reingold, 2011, p. 88).

On one field research outing in China, one research team made a bumpy two-hour drive into the treeless hills of red clay on the Yellow River in the midsection of China. In the village of Shahe, the team visited a tiny cinder-block house where a 29-year-old corn and potato farmer named Wei Xiao Yan would show how she washed her hair.

Because of water shortages, the fully dressed Wei only used three cups of water in a basin for washing her waist length hair with Rejoice—P&G's cheapest local offering (costing approximately $1.50 a bottle). Previously, Wei had used laundry soap flakes to wash her hair—which left her hair oily. One female researcher from the West made the mistake of asking Wei whether it might be more practical to cut her hair. Wei fired a disdainful look at the researcher before declaring, "As a woman, you should have long hair," Wei said. "And my husband likes it" (Reingold, 2011, p. 88).

The research team has identified several misconceptions about poor consumers. For example, researchers had believed that poor consumers always wanted the simplest product. This is not true (Reingold, 2011, p. 91). Additionally, researchers had believed that function alone drove poor consumer purchases. They have since found evidence suggesting that poor consumers would buy personal care products based on the image such products offered that they might come closer to attaining (for example, movie star looks). Additionally, researchers with $2-a-day consumers need more skin-care products because they spend so much time outdoors. Surprisingly, the research team discovered poor consumers would like to buy hair dye. "We say, 'Why would they buy that? It's not like food, clothing, and shelter,'" P&G principal research scientist Cindy Graulty said. "But to get a good job, to be presentable, they have to have beauty" (Reingold, 2011, p. 91). Not surprisingly, P&G is now developing an inexpensive colorant that uses little water.

## The Bottom of the Pyramid

In his landmark book, *The Fortune at the Bottom of the Pyramid*, C. K. Prahalad argued that MNEs could make money selling to the world's poorest customers (Prahalad, 2005). Prahalad used $2-per-day at purchasing power parity (PPP) rates in 1990 prices to classify those at the bottom of the pyramid (BOP) of consumers in the world. The World Resources Institute, a global think-tank, has updated the 1990 figures to equal PPP in 2005, which can be seen in Figure 13.9. The point remains the same that 4 billion consumers (two thirds of the world's population) live in survival markets on subsistence income.

Prahalad's initial premise for BOP marketing was that the poor should not be viewed as victims or a burden, but as resilient and creative entrepreneurs, and as value-conscious consumers (Prahalad, 2005, p. 1). According to Prahalad's poverty alleviation framework, a new world of opportunity would open up when the West and MNEs, in particular, adopted this positive view of the poor.

His arguments influenced transnational institutions to encourage the involvement of firms in country development (Knowledge@Wharton, 2009). Some of these transnational institutions include the World Bank (offering grants and low-interest loans to developing countries for building physical infrastructure projects), the United Nations Development Fund (the UN's global development network), the International Finance Corporation (financing private sector projects and companies in developing countries), and USAid (the U.S. government agency providing economic and humanitarian assistance worldwide). But

**Figure 13.9**   The World Economic Pyramid

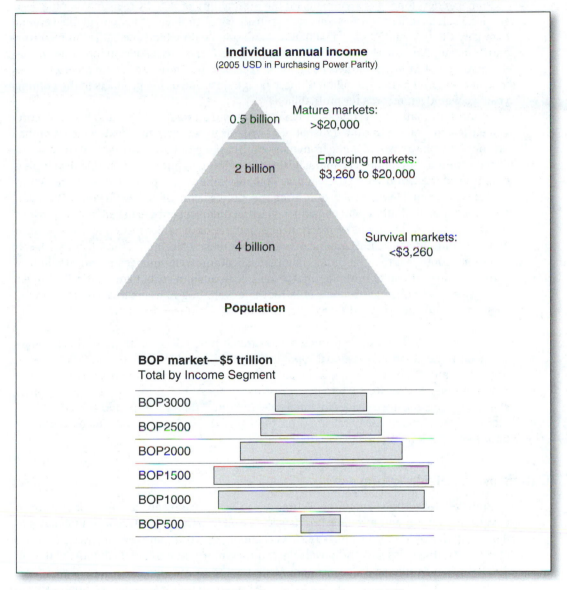

*Source:* World Resources Institute (2011). http://www.wri.org/publication/the-next-4-billion

more importantly, influential MNEs (such as Microsoft, healthcare giants GlaxoSmithKline from the United Kingdom and DSM from the Netherlands, Unilever, and Procter & Gamble) changed the way they approach marketing in the developing world. Within these MNEs, poor consumers became targets of corporate strategy.

Prahalad developed his arguments for the profitability of BOP by focusing on nine case studies, such as India's Hindustan Lever (a subsidiary of Unilever), Mexico's global cement company CEMEX, and Casas Bahia (a Brazilian retail chain which specializes in furniture and home appliances). His persuasive writing engaged business leaders in the same way as the potential of Chinese markets has done in recent years. Here, the exciting realization is that "if every one of the 1.2 billion Chinese bought just one of my products in the coming year, we would set records for profitability."

In short, Prahalad's prestige as a management and strategy scholar and his book convinced leaders of MNEs and transnational organizations that the next stage of global business prosperity would come from marketing to the 4 billion consumers at the bottom of the economic pyramid. Fortuitously, the rise of the cell phone industry in developing countries of the world seemed to validate Prahalad's main idea that the poor of the world would buy from MNEs. Five years after the publication of his BOP book, Prahalad explained that 2.5 billion BOP consumers had become subscribers to cell phone services in places thought to be out of reach of high-technology services, such as sub-Saharan Africa, South Africa, Latin America, India, Southeast Asia, and China (Knowledge@ Wharton, 2009). All the cell phone companies in these regions became profitable in a very short time. Despite illiteracy, masses of poor consumers had adopted cell phones. In doing so, new business models took root in developing markets to serve consumers, such as pay-per-use prepaid cards, and transfers of cash from banks via text messaging services like M-PESA in Kenya.

The success of India's Jaipur Rugs demonstrated how telecommunication technology allowed for the creation of a global supply chain. Here, wool from Australia, New Zealand, Argentina, and China came into India to be blended with wool from India. Jaipur would then send the wool to 40,000 weavers across five states of India, collect the rugs, and later ship them to the United States for final sale. In sum, Prahalad imparted a vision of the future in which inclusive capitalism would offer growth, profits, and incalculable contributions to humankind (Prahalad & Hart, 2002).

## Criticisms of BOP Marketing

Prahalad's assertions about the fortune at the BOP have received some criticism from poverty-alleviation entrepreneur Paul Polak, as well as a fellow professor of Prahalad's at the University of Michigan's Ross Business School, Aneel Karnani. Polak asserts that the idea that big business will end poverty is "nothing more than a tantalizing myth" (Polak, 2008, p. 41). According to Polak, very few MNEs know how to make a profit serving customers who survive on less than a dollar a day, who may be illiterate, and who do not have access to mass media. According to Karnani, there is little glory or fortune at the BOP, but rather "it is (almost) all a mirage" (Karnani, 2007, p. 91).

Karnani believes that the size of the BOP market is grossly overstated. Instead of being about $14 trillion, Karnani estimates that using the revised numbers in Figure 13.9, the BOP market is only $0.36 trillion (Karnani, 2009, p. 6). Karnani asserts that BOP advocates confuse the emerging middle class with the poor. Being without many financial resources, the poor have low savings rates and little "untapped" purchasing power. They spend 80% of their incomes on food, clothing, and fuel alone. There is not much left over for anything else according to Karnani. MNEs have yet to figure out how to reduce prices without reducing quality. Selling in smaller units cannot be done with every product. Finally, entrepreneurship is demanding and requires human capital acquired through learning and sustained effort in the marketplace.

At this point in the development of BOP marketing, most attempts to harness the BOP market have failed (Ringold, 2011, p. 88). What remains to be seen is whether MNEs and entrepreneurs can learn enough in the coming years to include it effectively in marketing efforts. MNEs such as P&G see developing markets growing at 6% to 8% compared with 1% to 2% in the developed world. To take advantage of such market growth, P&G is shifting its emphasis from the West to Asia and Africa. Whether firms like P&G sell to the poorest of the poor in Asia and Africa or an emerging middle class, they will not be disparaged by many. The fact that they are committing themselves to overcome challenges in the developing world will be enough to suggest that a new era in country development has arrived.

## CONCLUSION

This chapter examined country development. Undeniably, quality of life has improved for millions all over the world during the last 50 years. Health and education have improved markedly in many regions. Today, several firms from developing countries now challenge MNEs from developed countries in markets of the world. Such emerging giants include India's Tata Motors, China's PC-maker Lenovo, and Kuwait's rising telecommunications company Zain. Despite these successes, researchers estimate that 4 billion people exist on $2-a-day. A review of six important dimensions of developing countries suggests some of the complexities in country development. These six macro factors of developing country contexts include (a) culture, (b) population, (c) geography and climate, (d) economy, (e) political system, and (f) infrastructure. Institutions of society were included in this final dimension of developing countries as they represent "soft" infrastructure (Khanna & Palepu, 2011).

Emerging markets such as those listed in Table 13.4 have captured the imagination of MNE leaders around the world. The opportunities to win millions of new customers are now proving to be very attractive when compared with the forecasted sluggish growth in developed markets.

BOP marketing has caught the attention of leaders of MNEs and transnational organizations in recent years. Before his death in 2010, University of Michigan business professor C. K. Prahalad called the developed world's businesses to find their fortune by marketing to the very poorest consumers in countries, such as India (Prahalad, 2005). At this time, few firms have had an easy time in figuring out how to market to the poorest of the poor. It seems that some firms might be having success with the emerging middle-class consumers in developing markets. Nevertheless, many MNEs see their future in developing markets and succeeding with poor consumers there.

## QUESTIONS

- How can macromarketing's three primary generalizations help explain country development?
- What are the six macro factors of developing country contexts?
- Which of these six macro factors do you believe is the most critical to achieving an improved quality of life for citizens of developing countries?
- Compare and contrast progress-prone cultures and progress-resistant cultures.
- What can be said about what is happening in the world today regarding the three important population dimensions presented in this chapter?
- What are the advantages and disadvantages of each of the four types of capitalism?
- What are the types of costs civil war imposes on a country and its neighbors?
- What are the two types of infrastructure presented in the chapter?
- Name emerging market countries you were surprised to see included in Table 13.4.
- In your view, will MNEs find a fortune at the bottom of the pyramid?

## MAVERICKS WHO MADE IT

### Hanan Abdel Meguid

COMPARED WITH OTHER regions, attitudes toward women working outside the home are less favorable in the Middle East and North Africa than in other regions (World Bank, 2007). Here, a woman working outside the home is a signal to many that her male kin cannot provide sufficiently for her. Additionally, the region's high unemployment rate leads to feelings among many that men are more deserving of scarce jobs. Hanan Abdel Meguid, a mother of two, has achieved success in Egypt's technology field despite the unfavorable attitudes of many in society toward woman working outside the home and despite the bias of MNE executives against locating technology development in the region.

Hanan Abdel Meguid launched her first Cairo-based technology firm before the Web became publicly available and before many technology MNEs, such as Microsoft, operated in the Middle East (Hamdan, 2011). As one who has launched several firms, she is a serial entrepreneur who has learned important lessons about growing a business in a developing country, such as Egypt.

In the early 1990s as a student at the American University in Cairo, Meguid decided to major in computer science although she had never seen a computer. She later switched her major to economics to avoid the late nights doing computer programming, but a year later, she returned to the male-dominated field of computer science. The idea for her first venture, Microlabs, came to Meguid when she was playing squash with a classmate, Khaled Bichara, during a trip to Sharm el

Sheik, an Egyptian resort on the Red Sea. Both Meguid and Bichara wanted to work as programmers, but technology MNEs such as IBM that were in Egypt then only had sales offices that did no programming.

"I started my first company with friends right after university because our dreams and our capabilities were much bigger than the opportunities in the market," Meguid said. "By graduation, we were all so inspired we decided to create our own lab to develop applications on Windows. And we were good" (Hamdan, 2011, p. B7).

With only $3,500 and three computers when it began in 1993, Microlabs earned income by creating accounting systems for big firms and won a competition to design time-management software for the Egyptian government. But Microlabs became ridden with problems the next year after it merged with another software company, Pie Practical Solutions. Before the merger, Meguid and her partner Bichara deferred completing legal paperwork formalizing the merger because the newly merged firms needed to tackle a major project of rewriting a software program for the Windows platform. When the business took off, everything remained in the name of Pie Practical while Microlabs and its founders were not entitled to any of the success. Meguid and Bichara would be forced out of the merged firm soon after success came. "We learned the hard way from this experience," Bichara said (Hamdan, 2011, p. B7).

Meguid had registered Microlabs in her name, so she had to wind down its operations in a complicated process as a result of the vague or contradictory writing of Egyptian laws then regarding liquidating a business and settling debt. Six years after closing Microlabs, Meguid received letters from government authorities requesting taxes these authorities believed were still outstanding.

In 1996, Meguid joined the Egyptian government herself to help develop websites for the government. She would eventually receive appointment to run Web development for the government. However, it took her former Microlabs partner Bichara six months to convince Meguid to return to entrepreneurial endeavors with him. They helped launch a venture affiliated with Orascom Telecom (now an Egyptian-based MNE operating across Northern Africa, the Middle East, Bangladesh, South Korea, Canada, and sub-Saharan Africa). The new venture—Link Development—offered the opportunity for develop "dream Web sites and services" for Meguid (Hamdan, 2011, p. B7). At Link Development, Meguid became CEO and began developing cultural websites, such as yallabina.com. Link Development began working with Microsoft at the end of 1997.

Meguid learned from her earlier mistakes. When Link merged with InTouch Communications in 2000 to form LinkdotNet, Meguid scrutinized the legal documents to make sure ownership and roles in the merged firm were clearly delineated. LinkdotNet became one of Egypt's star companies serving as the largest Internet solutions provider in Egypt (American University in Cairo, 2011). Two years later, LinkdotNet acquired eight established Internet companies in Egypt. In 2010, Link sold part of the business to Mobinil for $130 million. Meguid became CEO of the spin-off firm—OTVentures—with different subsidiaries operating in the sectors of finance, telecom, advertising, data management, and software development.

*(Continued)*

(Continued)

Although the Egyptian revolution that began in early 2011 led many clients to cut their spending on services OTVentures would supply, the way the revolution unfolded has heightened the awareness of social media and entrepreneurship—two key elements for the technology industry in the Middle East. "The revolution turned out to be a validation of our vision," Meguid said. "I.T. is becoming a catalyst for change, not just a platform or business tool" (Hamdan, 2011, p. B7).

As OTVentures CEO, Meguid oversees operations across 17 countries and maintains exclusive partnerships with Facebook and Microsoft. "She is one of very few Egyptian women who has a good knowledge of technology and of business, so she is a great inspiration to mentees," Google's head of Egyptian operations Wael Fakharany said. "She's an icon in Egypt's Internet world" (Hamdan, 2011, p. B7).

Meguid is an advocate of home-grown entrepreneurship in Egypt. When she took the reins of OTVentures, she said she wanted "to build a new wave of success and prove to the world that with our local hands and expertise we will define the digital future of our country and region" (LinkdotNet, 2010). To promote and nurture Egyptian entrepreneurship, she serves as an advisor for three different organizations devoted to developing young entrepreneurs in Egypt. These include Tahrir2 (an effort in venture incubation), Flat6Labs (venture incubation affiliated with American University in Cairo), and Google's Ebda2—a venture creation competition for Egyptian entrepreneurs.

"There are a lot of depressed young people in Egypt today not finding the right work opportunities, but we have to move away from this idea that when you graduate you must find a job with a multinational company to succeed," Meguid said. "You can have a dream, build on it and become a major contributor to your economy without being an employee" (Hamdan, 2011, p. B7).

## Questions

- What episodes across the career of Hanan Abdel Meguid mark her as a visionary?
- What role do relationships have in Meguid's story?
- How effective do you think Meguid will be as a mentor and coach to those thinking about starting ventures in Egypt, and later implementing the plan for their ventures? Explain.
- Discuss Meguid's success as an entrepreneur in Egypt in terms of Egypt's (a) culture, (b) population, (c) geography and climate, (d) economy, (e) political system, and (f) infrastructure. How does knowledge of these six macro factors for the context of a developing country like Egypt make Meguid's accomplishments more special?

## REFERENCES

35th Infantry Division Association. (2011). Major General Paul William Baade. Retrieved from http://www.35thinfdivassoc.com/GeneralBaade/

American University in Cairo. (2011). *Career conference, session leaders.* Retrieved from http://www.caps.aucegypt.edu/careerconference2011/speakers.htm

Anokhin, S., & Schulze, W. S. (2009). Entrepreneurship, innovation, and corruption. *Journal of Business Venturing, 24*(5), 465–476.

Aon. (2011). *2011 terrorism and political violence map.* Retrieved from http://www.aon.com

Batson, A. (2008, April 12). On the move. *The Wall Street Journal.* Retrieved from http://online.wsj.com

BBC. (2011, September 21). Kenya election violence: Uhuru Kenyatta at The Hague. *BBC News Africa.* Retrieved from http://www.bbc.co.uk

Baumol, W. J., Litan, R. E., & Schramm, C. J. (2007). *Good capitalism, bad capitalism and the economics of growth and prosperity.* New Haven, CT: Yale University Press.

Bremmer, I. (2010). *The end of the free market: Who wins the war between states and corporations?* New York, NY: Portfolio.

Carman, J. (1982, Spring). Private property and the regulation of vertical channel systems. *Journal of Macromarketing, 2*(1), 20–26.

Cateora, P. R., Gilly, M. C., & Graham, J. L. (2011). *International marketing* (15th ed.). New York, NY: McGraw-Hill Irwin.

CIA. (2011). CIA factbook. Guide to country comparisons. Retrieved from https://www.cia.gov/library/publications/the-world-factbook/

Collier, P. (2007). *The bottom billion: Why the poorest countries are failing and what can be done about it.* New York, NY: Oxford University Press.

Dapice, D. (2008). What do we know about economic development? *Journal of Macromarketing, 28*(4), 413–417.

de Soto, H. (2003). *The mystery of capital: Why capitalism triumphs in the West and fails everywhere else.* New York, NY: Basic Books.

Diamond, J. (1997). *Guns, germs, and steel: The fates of human societies.* New York, NY: W.W. Norton.

Dimitri, C., Effland, A., & Conklin, N. (2005, June). *The 20th century transformation of U.S. agriculture and farm policy.* USDA Electronic Information Bulletin Number 3. Retrieved from http://www.ers.usda.gov/publications/eib3/eib3.htm

Dow Jones. (2011). *Dow Jones total stock market indexes.* Retrieved from http://www.djindexes.com

Economist Intelligence Unit. (2005). The Economist Intelligence Unit's quality of life index. *The Economist.* Retrieved from http://www.economist.com/media/pdf/QUALITY_OF_LIFE.pdf

Eigen, P. (2002). Controlling corruption: A key to development-oriented trade. *Trade, Equity and Development, 4,* 1–8. Retrieved from http://www.ceip.org

Eyring, M. J., Johnson, M. W., & Nair, H. (2011, January–February). New business models in emerging markets. *Harvard Business Review*, pp. 89–95.

Forbes, S., and Ames, E. (2009). *How capitalism will save us: Why free people and free markets are the best answer in today's economy.* New York, NY: Crown Business.

Friedman, T. L. (2012, March 10). Pass the books. Hold the oil. *The New York Times.* Retrieved from http://www.nytimes.com

Glover, G. (2011, September 21). New analysis suggests Civil War took bigger toll than previously estimated. Binghamton University Press Release. Retrieved from http://www.eurekalert.org/pub_releases/2011-09/bu-nas092111.php

Grondona, M. (2000). A cultural typology of economic development. In L. E. Harrison and S. P. Huntington (Eds.), *Culture matters: How values shape human progress* (pp. 44–55). New York, NY: Basic Books.

Hamdan, S. (2011, November 3). Egyptian entrepreneur shares lessons from her playbook. *The New York Times*, p. B7.

Harrison, L. E. (2006). *The central liberal truth: How politics can change a culture and save it from itself.* New York, NY: Oxford University Press.

Hausmann, R. (2001, January–February). Prisoners of geography. *Foreign Policy.* Retrieved from http://www.jstor.org/stable/3183225

HDRO. (2011a). Human development report office. Retrieved from http://hdrstats.undp.org/en/indicators/72206.html

HDRO. (2011b). Human development report office. Retrieved from http://hdr.undp.org/en/data/map/

History.com. (2011). Qaddafi leads coup in Libya: September 1, 1969. This day in history. Retrieved from http://www.history.com/this-day-in-history/qaddafi-leads-coup-in-libya

Johnson, B. (2011, October). The CEO of Heinz on powering growth in emerging markets. *Harvard Business Review, 89*(10), 47–50.

Karnani, A. (2007, Summer). The mirage of marketing to the bottom of the pyramid: How the private sector can help alleviate poverty. *California Management Review, 49*(4), 90–111.

Karnani, A. (2009, August). The bottom of the pyramid strategy for reducing poverty: A failed promise. United Nations Department of Economic and Social Affairs. DESA Working Paper No. 80. Retrieved from http://www.un.org/esa/desa/papers/2009/wp80_2009.pdf

Kenny, C. (2011). *Getting better: Why global development is succeeding—and how we can improve the world even more.* New York, NY: Basic Books.

Khanna, T., & Palepu, K. G. (2011). *Winning in emerging markets: A road map for strategy and execution.* Boston, MA: Harvard Business Press.

Khanna, T., Palepu, K. G., & Bullock, R. J. (2009). *House of Tata: Acquiring a global footprint* (Harvard Business School case 9-708-446). Boston, MA: Harvard Business School.

Klein, T. A., & Nason, R. W. (2000). Marketing and development: Macromarketing perspectives. In P. N. Bloom & G. T. Gundlach (Eds.), *Handbook of marketing and society* (pp. 263–297). Thousand Oaks, CA: Sage.

Knowledge@Wharton. (2009, October 14). New approaches to new markets: How C. K. Prahalad's bottom of the pyramid strategies are paying off. *Knowledge@Wharton.* Retrieved from http://knowledge.wharton.upenn.edu

Kummu, M., & Varis, O. (2011, April). The world by latitudes: A global analysis of human population, development level and environment across the north–south axis over the past half century. *Applied Geography, 31*(2), 495–507.

Layton, R., & Grossbart, S. (2006, December). Macromarketing: Past, present, and possible future. *Journal of Macromarketing, 26*(2), 193–213.

Lee, M. A., & Mather, M. (2008, June). U.S. labor force trends. *Population Bulletin, 63*(2).

Lenovo. (2011). Lenovo statement on becoming the world's second largest PC company. Retrieved from http://news.lenovo.com/article_display.cfm?article_id=1516

LinkdotNet. (2011). OTVentures a new company of Orascom Telecom, Hanan Abdel Meguid designated as its CEO. Retrieved from http://www.link.net/English/Linkcorp/News + and + Events/OTVentures.htm

MacFarquhar, N. (2009). *The media relations department of Hizbollah wishes you a happy birthday: Unexpected encounters in the changing Middle East.* New York, NY: PublicAffairs.

Maylie, D., & Hinshaw, D. (2011, November 12). Alarm over smuggled Libyan arms. *The Wall Street Journal.* Retrieved from http://online.wsj.com

Mellinger, A. D., Sachs, J. D., Gallup, J. L. (2000). Climate, coastal proximity, and development. In G. L. Clark, M. P. Feldman, & M. S. Gertler (Eds.), *The Oxford handbook of economic geography* (pp. 169–194). Oxford, UK: Oxford University Press.

MENAFN. (2011). Libya's civil war to cost economy around USD35b. Middle East North Africa Financial Network, October 27th. Retrieved from http://menafn.com/qn_news_story_s.asp?storyid=1093453256

Mittelstaedt, J. D., Kilbourne, W. E., & Mittelstaedt, R. A. (2006). Macromarketing as agorology: Macromarketing theory and the study of the agora. *Journal of Macromarketing, 26*(2), 131–142.

Mulholland, R., & Deshmukh, J. (2011, October 3). Residents flee Gaddafi hometown. *The Sydney Morning Herald*. Retrieved from http://news.smh.com.au

Mulligan, C. B. (2011, October 26). Was Qaddafi Overpaid? *The New York Times*. Retrieved from http://economix.blogs.nytimes.com/2011/10/26/was-qaddafi-overpaid/

Nason, R. W. (2010). The legacy of Charles C. Slater. *Journal of Macromarketing, 30*(3), 287–292.

Nason, R. W., & White, P. D. (1981). The visions of Charles C. Slater: Social consequences of marketing. *Journal of Macromarketing, 1*(1), 4–18.

Nguyen, H. P., & Pham, H. T. (2011). The dark side of development in Vietnam: Lessons from the killing of the Thi Vai River. *Journal of Macromarketing*. In press.

O'Toole, J., & Vogel, D. (2011). Two and a half cheers for conscious capitalism. *California Management Review, 53*(3), 60–76.

Peterson, M. (2006). Focusing the future of macromarketing. *Journal of Macromarketing, 26*(2), 245–249.

Polak, P. (2008). *Out of poverty: What works when traditional approaches fail*. San Francisco, CA: Berrett-Koehler.

Porter, M. (2000). Attitudes, values, beliefs, and the microeconomics of prosperity. In L. E. Harrison and S. P. Huntington (Eds.) *Culture matters: How values shape human progress* (pp. 14–28). New York, NY: Basic Books.

Prahalad, C. K. (2005). *The fortune at the bottom of the pyramid: Eradicating poverty through profits*. Upper Saddle River, NJ: Wharton School.

Prahalad, C. K., & Hart, S. L. (2002, January 10). The fortune at the bottom of the pyramid. *Strategy + Business, 26*, 1–13.

Quelch, J. A., & Jocz, K. E. (2007). *Greater good: How good marketing makes for better democracy*. Boston, MA: Harvard Business Press.

Reingold, J. (2011, January 17). Can P&G make money in places where people earn $2 a day? *Fortune*, pp. 86–91.

Richter, P. (2011, October 22). Gaddafi salted away about $200 billion. *The Age*. Retrieved from http://www.theage.com.au

Rodrik, D. (2011). *The globalization paradox: Democracy and the future of the world economy*. New York, NY: W. W. Norton.

Sachs, J. (2000). Notes on a new sociology of economic development. In L. E. Harrison & S. P. Huntington (Eds.), *Culture matters: How values shape human progress* (pp. 29–43). New York, NY: Basic Books.

Shultz, C. J. II, Deshpande, R., Cornwell, T. B., Ekici, A., Kothandaraman, P., Peterson, M., Shapiro, S., Taulkdar, D., & Veeck, A. (2011). Marketing and public policy: Transformative research in developing markets. *Journal of Public Policy & Marketing*. In press.

Slater, C. C. (1977). A theory of market process. In C. C. Slater (Ed.), *Macro-Marketing: Distributive processes from a societal perspective* (pp. 117–140). Boulder, CO: Graduate School of Business, University of Colorado.

Sobel, R. S. (2008). Testing Baumol: Institutional quality and the productivity of entrepreneurship. *Journal of Business Venturing, 23*(6), 641–655.

Tata Group. (2011). Tata Group. Retrieved from http://www.tata.com

The Economist. (2002, December 21). The road to hell is unpaved. *The Economist*. Retrieved from http://www.economist.com/node/1487583

The Economist. (2010a, November 22). The emerging markets: Businesses will learn to look beyond the BRICs. *The Economist*. Retrieved from http://www.economist.com

The Economist. (2010b, May 6). Migration in China: Invisible and heavy shackles. *The Economist*. Retrieved from http://www.economist.com

Transparency International. (2010). *Global corruption barometer 2010*. Retrieved from http://www .transparency.org

Transparency International. (2011). Bribe payers index 2011. Retrieved from http://www.transparency .org

UN. (2011). World urbanization prospects. The 2007 revision population database. Retrieved from http://esa.un.org/unup/

Wilkie, W. L., & Moore, E. S. (1999). Marketing's contributions to society. *Journal of Marketing, 63*, 198–218.

Wilson, D., & Purushothaman, R. (2003, October 1). *Dreaming with BRICs: The path to 2050*. Goldman Sachs Economics Paper No. 99.

Woetzel, J. R. (2008, July). Reassessing China's state-owned enterprises. *McKinsey Quarterly*. Retrieved from http://www.mckinseyquarterly.com

Wolf, M. (2004). *Why globalization works*. New Haven, CT: Yale University Press.

World Bank. (2007). *The Environment for women's entrepreneurship in the Middle East and North Africa Region*. Washington, DC: World Bank. Retrieved from http://web.worldbank.org

World Bank. (2008). The growth report: Strategies for sustained growth and inclusive development. Commission on growth and development. Retrieved from http://www.growthcommission.org

World Bank (2010). *Data and statistics: Country classification*. Washington, DC: World Bank. Retrieved from http://web.worldbank.org/WBSITE/EXTERNAL/DATASTATISTICS/0,,contentMDK:20420458 ~ menuPK:64133156 ~ pagePK:64133150 ~ piPK:64133175 ~ theSitePK:239419,00.html

World Bank. (2011). Data. Retrieved from http://data.worldbank.org

## CHAPTER 14

# Poverty Alleviation

## DARING TO LEARN ABOUT MARKETING GAPS IN POOR, RURAL AREAS

### Paul Polak—Applying His Life's Lessons to Alleviate Poverty

Although he looks like someone's retired grandfather (he is), Paul Polak might be one of the most effective alleviators of poverty to ever live. As an outsider to government, development agencies, and corporate business, Polak has achieved what few have done—helping millions of the rural poor earn more money (Polak, 2008). The nongovernmental organization (NGO) he founded, International Development Enterprises (IDE), claims to have helped more than 19 million—mostly rural farmers—increase their incomes (IDE, 2011). This is especially noteworthy as the United Nations (UN), governments, aid agencies, NGOs, and corporate philanthropy programs have difficulty measuring the impact of their poverty alleviation programs or sustaining results of these programs for more than a few years.

As an outsider, Polak has avoided many biases and flawed thinking about poverty swirling in the subculture of those desiring to alleviate poverty. For example, in the 1980s when Polak began working with poor people, many in developing agencies considered business or solutions to poverty that included business as tainted or undesirable. Polak said:

> In the first twenty years of my work with IDE, development leaders were outraged by my notion that you can and should sell things to poor people at a fair market price instead of giving things to them for nothing. "Business" was a dirty word to development organizations. I'm happy to say that all this is now changing. With the abject failure of central planning in socialist countries, there is a new awareness in development circles that unleashing the energy of the marketplace is the best help we can give to poor people in their efforts to escape poverty permanently. (Polak, 2008, pp. 39–40)

When he began his work with the poor, Polak did not bring any predetermined model of poverty alleviation. Instead, he dared to bring much of himself and his previous life experiences to his work with the poor. In his life, Polak had been a refugee, farmer, psychiatrist, businessperson (in real-estate rehabilitation), inventor (in the oil and gas industry), and entrepreneur. Polak would draw on learning in each of these realms of his life as he moved ahead as a social entrepreneur set to alleviate poverty.

Polak began life in 1933 in Czechoslovakia (McNeill, 2011). His family came from a line of peasants. In 1938, Jewish refugees with wounds and physical injuries began streaming across the border from Germany. Being Jewish himself, Polak's father decided to escape. Polak explained as follows:

> Pretty much anybody could see what was coming. My dad said, "There's going to be hell to pay soon," and made plans to escape. But when he tried to tell our family and friends, they said things like "But what would we do with the furniture?" Most of them stayed in Czechoslovakia and died. I got from him an eye for seeing the obvious. (McNeill, 2011, p. D4)

Polak credits his father for teaching him to see the obvious. Polak's father sold the thriving plant nursery he had started at a 90% discount and escaped with his family to Canada before British Prime Minister Neville Chamberlain gave Czechoslovakia to Hitler (McNeill, 2011).

## Pursuing Opportunity

Polak's father inherited an entrepreneur's instincts for starting ventures from his father. As a 15-year-old living near Hamilton, Ontario, Polak enlisted the assistance of two local farmers who provided seven acres on which the three of them planted, fertilized, and harvested strawberries. Polak made an agreement with a large grocery and food distributor Loblaw's and became the principal supplier of strawberries for half of the 195,000 living in Hamilton at the time. At the end of two summers, Polak had earned $700—equivalent to $7,000 now—and it seemed like a lot of money to him.

Polak's success as a teenage farmer gave him a deep appreciation for what it takes to run a small farm and make money. "The challenges, opportunities, and hard work I experienced in the strawberry business mirror the challenges one-acre farmers face every day as they try to make a living from their scattered quarter-acre plots," Polak said (Polak, 2008, p. 4).

The horse-drawn plows, cultivators, and manure spreaders Polak used as a teenager in 1948 offered him a significant advantage over the farming methods used on one-acre farms all over the world today. On these tiny farms across the developing world, the work has to be done by hand without mechanization and without animals. Despite the advantages Polak had as a farmer, the lessons he learned about himself proved to be invaluable to him. "I learned that learning new things every day brought me more pleasure and happiness than anything else I could do with my life," Polak said (Polak, 2008, p. 4).

Polak followed his interest in learning new things all the way to medical school, where he earned a degree in psychiatry (McNeill, 2011). He moved to Denver, Colorado, and obtained a job working at the Fort Logan Mental Health Center.

In his work as a psychiatrist, Polak learned that he could be more influential in the lives of his patients if he understood the context in which they lived. "I was one of the pioneers in treating people more effectively in real-life settings," Polak said. He continued:

> The conventional assumption is that patients are admitted to psychiatric institutions because a therapist or family member says they're mentally ill. But I talked to a lot of our patients as if they were customers, and they defined something going on in their family or workplace as the primary reason they were there. So I started going into patients' homes or workplaces. (McNeill, 2011, p. D4)

In Polak's spare time as a psychiatrist, he began investing in real estate. "I bought mismanaged apartment buildings," Polak said. He continued:

> I also owned a small oil company drilling stripper wells [in oil fields coming to the end of their useful lives]. I invented a pump jack for the oil-field industry—I've always knocked around in that kind of stuff. By 1981, I'd worked for 22 years as a psychiatrist, and I'd cleared about three million bucks, mostly in real estate. (McNeill, 2011, p. D4)

Polak's instincts to consider his patients holistically and to treat them as a businessperson would—as customers with important perspectives—led him to recognize that many of his patients were very poor. This led to his interest in poverty and his first overseas trip to investigate poverty in 1981.

"My wife's a Mennonite, and they had programs in Bangladesh," Polak said. "It had hit me between the eyes that homeless people in Denver were living on $500 a month, but there were people overseas living on $30 a month. So I took a trip to Bangladesh" (McNeill, 2011, p. D4).

### Doing What He Knows—Overseas

"I learned quickly that the best way to satisfy my curiosity about poverty is to have long conversations with poor people in the places where they live and work and dream, and to listen to what they have to say," Polak said (Polak, 2008, p. 27). He continued:

> Over 28 years, I've interviewed over 3,000 families. I spend about six hours with each one—walking with them through their fields, asking what they had for breakfast, how far their kids walk to school, what they feed their dog, what all their sources of income are. This is not rocket science. Any businessman knows this: You've got to talk to your customers. (Polak, 2008, p. 27)

Polak has distilled four simple points from his interviews of poor people (Polak, 2008, p. 10). First, the biggest reason people are poor is because they do not have enough money. Second, most of the extremely poor people in the world earn their current income from one-acre farms. Third, these one-acre farmers can earn much more if they find a way to grow and sell high-value, labor-intensive crops, such as off-season fruits and vegetables. Fourth, to do this, they need access to cheap, small-farm irrigation, good seeds and fertilizer, and markets (buyers) where they can sell these crops at a profit. Notably, each of these four points deals with business.

Each year since 1981, Polak has interviewed at least 100 of IDE's small-acreage customers. "All my ideas for projects that worked, and even some that didn't work, came from what I learned from these small-acreage farmers, and now all the people who work for IDE talk to and learn from these farmers every day," Polak said (Polak, 2008, p. 23).

Over the years, Polak and his IDE team have invented devices to help small-acreage farmers, such as drip-irrigation systems (a hose with small holes that leaks water slowly across an area) and a treadle pump (similar to a stair-climber apparatus for exercise, but one that pumps water from a well for irrigation). Polak and his team not only emphasize invention to assist in farming but also distribution and promotion. In the case of treadle pumps in Bangladesh, IDE created a private sector supply chain by energizing 75 small-scale manufacturers, more than 2,000 village dealers, and 3,000 well-drillers, all earning a living by making, selling, and installing treadle pumps at an unsubsidized, fair-market price of $25 each. Although told by development experts in 1985 that treadle pumps could never make a significant impact (because they irrigate only half an acre of land), more than 1.5 million treadle pumps now irrigate 750,000 acres at a fraction of the cost a dam/canal system would require to do the same thing.

Promotion is a key ingredient in IDE's approach. "We hired troubadours to write songs about treadle pumps, and we'd pass out leaflets when they performed," Polak said (McNeill, 2011, p. D4). Because people in these villages could not read or write, IDE even produced a 90-minute Bollywood movie that played from a van with a video screen. IDE hired the top director in Bangladesh and two top actors.

The movie cost $25,000 to make and featured a love story frustrated by the girl's father not being able to pay a dowry. The movie included lots of singing and dancing, as well as dowry bandits and a near-suicide. At the climactic moment of the movie, IDE's dealers stop the movie and explain just what the treadle pumps they sell can actually do. "The movie resumes, the father buys a pump, makes enough for the dowry, they live happily ever after," Polak said (McNeill, 2011, p. D4). Typical open-air audiences numbered between 2,000 and 5,000 persons.

Since its beginning in 1982, IDE and its donors have directed $78 million to end rural poverty (Polak, 2008, p. 47). During the same time period, dollar-a-day/small-acreage farmers have invested $139 million in income-generating tools, such as the treadle pumps and drip-irrigation systems promoted by IDE. On these combined investments of $217 million, these small-acreage farmers have realized $288 million per year in permanent new net income.

"This is only a drop in the bucket in the context of 1.1 billion dollar-a-day people in the world," Polak said. "The good news is that potentially this approach can be scaled up to move 500 million or more rural dollar-a-day people out of poverty (Polak, 2008, p. 47).

---

### Your Thoughts?

- What elements in Polak's life have contributed to his success in poverty alleviation? Be specific. Explain how each of these might influence his entrepreneur's story.
- Why do you think Polak and IDE have had success in poverty alleviation in Asia and Africa when others with more resources have failed?
- How important is learning for Polak? How do you see evidence of this across his life?
- If you could ask Polak one question, what would it be?

---

## CHAPTER OVERVIEW AND LEARNING OBJECTIVES

This chapter will highlight social innovation in poverty alleviation. Paul Polak's story highlights how an NGO can use a simple approach when applying business principles to produce meaningful gains for the poor. Polak's immersion approach to understanding poverty in field settings sets him apart from most others in government, transnational organizations (such as the UN), nonprofits, and business. "In 1981, I said, 'I'm going to interview 100 $1-a-day families every year, come rain or shine, and learn from them first," Polak said (McNeill, 2011, p. D4). Because of his rich experiences with the poor and where they live and work, his ideas about poverty alleviation will frame much of this chapter.

Surprising to some, interventions on behalf of the poor or disadvantaged might sometimes do more harm than good. This chapter will review controversies regarding aid to alleviate poverty. The chapter will also provide an overview of interventions by governments, development agencies, and NGOs.

Social entrepreneurship occurs when an entrepreneur with a social vision creates a venture intending to result in social consequences (Yunus & Weber, 2010, p. 4). New forms of social entrepreneurship manifesting themselves in philanthropy, in hybrid organizational structures combining for-profit and nonprofit structures, and in for-profit businesses seeking to earn profits by serving poor consumers will be presented in this chapter.

Finally, Costco supplier Rwanda Partners had a humble beginning in 2004 when Tracy Stone of Bellevue, Washington, visited Rwanda ten years after the horrific civil war had engulfed the country with 17 members of her church. A year later, Tracy became a reluctant entrepreneur by launching Rwanda Partners with her husband Greg to help meet some of the many needs in Rwanda. Tracy and Greg Stone will be featured as Mavericks Who Made It.

After this chapter, you should be able to answer the following questions:

- How can charitable actions actually hurt recipients of charity?
- How effective have government and transnational organizations' poverty alleviation efforts been over the years?
- What is social entrepreneurship?
- What are four possible structures for social enterprises today?
- What is a B Corporation?

# PUTTING POVERTY ALLEVIATION INTO PERSPECTIVE

## Wisdom From a Longtime Poverty Alleviator

Paul Polak came to poverty alleviation as a result of his desire to help the clients of his psychiatry practice in Denver, Colorado. As a skilled interviewer and listener, Polak inductively developed his own views on poverty from the hundreds of interviews he conducted with the poor on their small farms in countries like Nepal, India, Ethiopia, and Zambia.

Although he does not present his thoughts on addressing social problems with a business approach, Polak's steps to practical problem solving for any social problem all relate to business. First, Polak believes that field interviewing of poor people is a must. This is in the finest traditions of social science and contemporary business. Importantly, Polak notes that the knowledge from interviewing accumulates over time. Simply put, the more interviewing, the more knowledge one will have to draw on when attempting to solve social problems. Second, the process of innovation matters. Just as successful innovators in business, social innovators also must use their research to address the needs of a targeted group of customers. Polak's targeted group comprises small-acreage farmers in Asia and Africa.

Third, the marketing mixture (the 4 Ps of product, price, place of distribution, and promotion) must be composed correctly. A worthy invention to assist poor farmers must be combined with effective distribution and promotion of the invention at an affordable price for rural farmers. Fourth, planning and the implementation of plans must be done in a vigorous manner. Polak recommends three-year plans. "If you can't come up with a specific plan for the next three-year period, you'll never get anywhere," Polak said (Polak,

2008, p. 22). He also recommends adapting any plan to the specific demands of the local environment when the plan does not play out as expected. The final ingredient is tenacity, which all entrepreneurs must bring to any venture. It will likely look hopeless at several points during the journey of any venture. Hanging on until success is achieved cannot be understated.

## Three Poverty Eradication Myths

Polak also asserts that three great poverty eradication myths exist today (Polak, 2008, p. 27). The first myth is that we can donate people out of poverty. Polak says:

> "It's exactly the multinational corporations that use the business approach you advocate who have caused the problem of poverty in the first place," they would say. "Poor people simply can't afford to buy the things they need, and they need these things very badly. The only way to make a real difference is to donate these things to them." And the development organizations continued to donate mountains of food, free village hand pumps that broke down with a year and were never fixed, and thousands of free tractors that continue to rust under the African sun. Most importantly, more and more people are beginning to realize that making it possible for very poor people to invest their own time and money in attractive, affordable opportunities to increase their income is the only realistic path out of poverty for most of them." (Polak, 2008, p. 34)

According to Polak, the second myth is that national economic growth will end poverty (Polak, 2008, p. 40). From 1950 to 2001, the world's per capita GDP increased by a factor of 2.87 (Maddison, 2007, p. 234). However, bottom-of-the-pyramid approaches to poverty alleviation (previously discussed in Chapter 13) propose that 4 billion people still live on less than $2 per day (Prahalad, 2005, p. 4).

Although countries such as China and India have posted sustained economic growth of 8% and 6%, respectively, for many years, more than 575 million across these two countries live in extreme poverty on less than $1 per day (Polak, 2008, p. 40). Most of the poor in the world live in remote rural areas, so urban-centered growth continues to bypass them. Accordingly, growth in remote rural areas is needed to impact most of the poor.

**Table 14.1** Polak's Three Myths of Poverty Alleviation

| |
|---|
| 1. We can donate people out of poverty. |
| 2. National economic growth will end poverty. |
| 3. Big business will end poverty. |

*Source:* Polak (2008).

The third myth of poverty alleviation concerns big business ending poverty (Polak, 2008, p. 41). Although the move of multinational enterprises (MNEs) to develop their operations in developing countries will likely continue, Polak views most MNEs as currently not knowing how to make a profit serving illiterate customers living in remote areas with no mass media. A challenge for MNEs will be fielding products and services designed to reach price points affordable to those who earn less than one or two dollars a day when sold at an unsubsidized fair market price.

Even in a developed country like the United States with all the MNEs operating, the U.S. Census Bureau reports that 15.1% of the population (46.2 million citizens) lived below the poverty line in 2010 (the poverty line for a family of four was $22,314 in 2010) (Tavernise, 2011). This was the highest poverty line since the Census Bureau began tracking poverty statistics since 1959. The continuing economic recession contributed to the relatively high percentage of those living in poverty.

## The Role of Aid

Macromarketing researchers have categorized 50 solutions to poverty, which can be seen in Table 14.2 (Kotler, Roberto, & Leisner, 2006). In the 1980s, international aid agencies introduced interventions or safety nets in developing countries hit by natural disasters. The first five solutions to poverty represent these relief interventions to protect the poor—especially the extreme poor living on $1 per day or less. As shown, these solutions focus on cash, food, or public works. The sixth through the eighth poverty solutions in Table 14.2 represent the "triple R framework" of relief, rehabilitation, and reconciliation in postconflict situations. The ninth through the fifteenth solutions focus on social safety net programs intended to provide protection from deteriorated conditions of life the poor often experience. Healthcare for vulnerable populations complete the set of solutions that became popular in the 1980s.

In the 1990s, social protection services became popular as poverty solutions. These included social safety net measures but also covered longer term solutions. Toward the end of the last century and in the first decade of the current century, empowerment solutions rose in prominence. These sought to expand individual freedom of choice for the poor in their lives. The World Bank made empowerment its primary strategy in "attacking poverty." Many of these empowerment solutions focused on improving the poor's ability to interact with institutions (such as business and government) that affect their lives and to hold these institutions accountable.

Overall, these 50 solutions (and hundreds more) have posted a spotty record of success around the world since 1980 (Kotler et al., 2006, pp. 237–238; Karlan & Appel, 2011, p. 5). Some have worked in some places but not in others. The ones that have worked have not always sustained success.

Macromarketing researchers have offered several reasons for the uneven outcomes of these 50 poverty solutions. First, the poor are a heterogeneous group. This implies that segments characterize the population of the poor, and that field research where the poor live and work is needed to understand these subgroups of the poor effectively. For example, those living on $4 to $5 a day might belong to the middle-class in some countries (Polak,

**Table 14.2** Fifty Solutions to Poverty

| 1980s—Interventions | 1990s—Social Protection Services | 2000s—Empowerment Solutions |
|---|---|---|
| *Postdisaster Relief* | *Social Assistance (old-style social welfare)* | *Social Equity Services* |
| 1. cash transfers | 21. disability benefits | 32. victims of domestic violence or sexual abuse |
| 2. direct feeding programs | 22. single-parent allowances | 33. marginalized minorities |
| 3. free food distribution | 23. social pensions for the elderly poor | 34. stigmatized groups |
| 4. price subsidies | **Social Insurance Schemes** | **Material-asset Building Assistance** |
| 5. public works programs | 24. pensions | 35. expanding financial assets: working capital |
| **Post-conflict Rehabilitation** | 25. health insurance | 36. expanding physical assets, for example, land, housing, or livestock |
| 6. relief institutions & services | 26. maternity benefits | **Human Capability-Building Assistance** |
| 7. rehabilitation assistance | 27. unemployment benefits | 37. education |
| 8. reconciliation & peace-building | 28. funeral societies | 38. good health |
| **Social Safety Net Programs** | **Social Service for the Poor - Special Care** | 39. production |
| 9. social security for informal workers | 29. orphanages for abandoned kids | 40. other life-enhancing skills |
| 10. services for school dropouts & street kids | 30. care for those unable to provide | **Social Capability-Building Assistance** |
| 11. workfare (emergency work relief) | 31. refugee & displaced-person camps | 41. collective problem solving |
| 12. microfinance and self-employment | | 42. collective action |
| 13. maternal and child health services | | 43. creating "bridging" to other groups |

*(Continued)*

(Continued)

| 1980s—Interventions | 1990s—Social Protection Services | 2000s—Empowerment Solutions |
|---|---|---|
| *Postdisaster Relief* | *Social Assistance (old-style social welfare)* | *Social Equity Services* |
| 14. psychosocial care for affected families | | **Empowerment Support Services** |
| 15. assistance for the elderly and disabled | | 44. boosting community-driven development |
| **Healthcare for Vulnerable Populations** | | 45. citizen report cards on gov't services |
| 16. ambulatory care | | 46. promoting pro-poor regulatory change |
| 17. hospital emergency room & inpatient care | | 47. new linkages with mkts. & banks |
| 18. drug abuse, disability & mental illness | | 48. increasing access to IT for market access |
| 19. assistive care for daily living | | 49. strengthening networks of the poor |
| 20. medication assistance & health support | | 50. supporting reforms for access to justice |

*Source:* Kotler et al. (2006).

2008, p. 42). By comparison, extreme poverty would characterize those living on $1 a day or less who would likely regularly suffer hunger and malnutrition. Second, poverty alleviation encounters a surprising degree of complexity. For example, poverty can come and go. Natural disasters and civil unrest can disrupt conditions where one lives, or alternatively, poor decisions, sickness or injury can degrade a person's ability to earn a living. Third, rising from poverty might require accessing many institutions that function with varying degrees of effectiveness or corruption, such as governments, schools, international development agencies, and businesses.

## Complexities of Aid

Almost all of the 50 solutions to poverty presented in Table 14.2 invariably structure an unbalanced power arrangement between donors (the helpers) and receivers of aid (the helped). However, this power imbalance often creates problems if sustained over time for relief and rehabilitation (humanitarian aid) to development situations (Corbett & Fikkert, 2009, p. 104). Following natural disasters or societal trauma, the provision of material assistance constitutes relief to reduce immediate suffering. Poverty solutions 1 through 5 in Table 14.2 represent such relief intended to "stop the bleeding." Such solutions end after days or weeks. Rehabilitation begins after "the bleeding stops" with the goal of restoring people and their communities to positive aspects of their pre-crisis conditions. Poverty solutions 6 through 8 in Table 14.2 often involve working *with* those afflicted (rather than doing things *for* or *to* the poor). Such solutions end after months or a few years. However, there are exceptions. The Canadian government estimated that returning Haiti to its precrisis conditions prior to its devastating January 2010 earthquake in which 200,000 died (including one third of all senior civil servants) will take ten years (Chung, 2010, p. 1; Wroughton, 2010, p. 1).

Development between helpers and the helped represents longer term projects extending for years. Here, the power imbalance between the helper and the helped can create serious problems. A "Samaritan's dilemma" emerges where the help offered by the helper results in a reduced effort of the helped activity participating in their own development (Gibson, Andersson, Ostrom, & Shivakumar, 2005). Although helpers receive a "warm glow" from helping, the helped receive more perceived value when they expend less effort to receive the aid they know will be forthcoming.

Paternalism characterizes such imbalanced relationships, as the helpers do for the helped what the helped could do for themselves (Corbett & Fikkert, 2009, p. 115). The helpers have their feelings of goodness and superiority reinforced, while the helped have their feelings of inferiority underlined to them and to those in their communities. "NGOs flatter themselves into thinking that they save lives," former Zambian Agriculture Minister Guy Scott said. "It is arrogant of the West to think that without whites, without pop stars, Africans would all be dead" (Astier, 2006, p. 2).

The helped may actually lose skills and motivation over time (Gibson et al., 2005, p. 39). In the remote, central-Sudanese region of the Nuba mountains, Yousif Kowa led an insurrection against the Sudanese government that began in the 1980s and lasted until a tenuous peace agreement in 2005. Kowa made it clear that unchecked humanitarianism was a threat to the self-reliant spirit of the Nuba tribe numbering more than one million

(Fisher, 2011). According to Kowa, food relief—when continued—distorted farmer incentives and created dependence. Kowa recalled a trip he made in 1993 to an area in southern Sudan that had received much food aid from the United Nations. "The people of the area are great farmers," Kowa said. "But because there is this relief food, they did not farm for three years. I could see the difficulty. It was spoiling people. They just sleep and have food. It is very bad" (Fisher, 2011, p. 3).

"It is axiomatic that flooding the market with food drives down the price for local farmers," economist William Easterly said (Astier, 2006, p. 2).

Because of the problems that develop in long-term development, the poverty solutions on the right side of Table 14.2 emphasize empowerment of the poor. Despite this new emphasis, aid agencies—not the poor themselves—still decide how aid is given and in what form (goods, services, information, awareness-raising, and skills training). "Today, only a tiny amount of aid (almost certainly less than 10 percent) is given directly to poor people and poor communities for them to choose how to use it," foreign-aid expert Roger C. Riddell said. "Even recipients who are committed to using aid effectively are not equal partners. They remain junior partners who have to struggle to make use of funds over which they have and retain limited control" (Riddell, 2007, p. 387).

### Aid in the Context of Total Overseas Economic Engagement

Since 1950, support for aid has gone up and down. But since 9/11, support for aid has surged as governments of developed countries became keen to stabilize the development of poor countries during the fight against global terrorism (Riddell, 2007, p. 5). The total aid given by developed country governments to developing countries doubled from $52 billion in 2001 to $100 billion in 2005.

But government aid is just one part of the total economic engagement of developed countries with developing countries. Figure 14.1 depicts private investment, official flows, remittances, and private philanthropy of Organisation for Economic Co-operation and Development (OECD) countries to developing countries from 1999 to 2009 (Hudson Institute, 2011, p. 15). As shown, official flows to developing countries was the top component in overall economic engagement in 1991, but in 2009, it was only the third-leading element in overall economic engagement at $120 billion. Private investment (foreign direct investment by firms) topped all elements in 2009 at $228 billion, while remittances (money sent back home from expatriates working overseas) came in second at $174 billion. Private philanthropy came in fourth at $53 billion in 2009 using the more complete data of the Hudson Institute's Center for Global Prosperity (CGP).

The character of economic engagement of developed countries with developing countries can be better understood by examining the case of the United States. Table 14.3 presents the sources of net economic engagement with developing countries in 2009. U.S. official development assistance (government flows) for 2009 accounted for 13% of total economic engagement with developing countries. The remaining 87% of economic engagement with developing countries came from private sources. Private philanthropy in all its forms accounted for 17%, while remittances (going mostly to Latin America) accounted for the largest portion at 40%, followed by private capital flows at 31%. Behind the increase in private philanthropy was the proliferation and strengthening of NGOs.

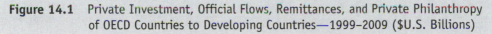

**Figure 14.1**   Private Investment, Official Flows, Remittances, and Private Philanthropy of OECD Countries to Developing Countries—1999–2009 ($U.S. Billions)

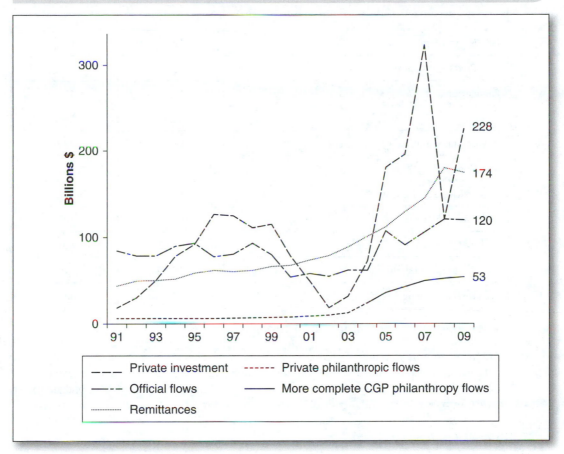

Notably, giant aid agencies, such as Save the Children, Oxfam, the Red Cross, CARE, and Catholic Relief Services have budgets in the hundreds of millions of dollars each year (Riddell, 2007, p. 9).

Currently, less than 1% of the U.S. budget goes to helping the world's poor (Easton, 2011, p. 164). Table 14.4 presents the elements of economic and military assistance the United States provided to foreign countries in 2010 (USAID, 2011). As shown, the U.S. Agency for International Development (USAID) accounted for the largest portion of assistance the United States gave at more than $14 billion. Food aid came to more than $2.3 billion, while State Department programs accounted for the second-largest portion at more than $12.2 billion.

**Table 14.3** U.S. Economic Engagement with Developing Countries in 2009

|  | Billions of $ | % |
|---|---|---|
| U.S. Official Development Assistance | $28.8 | 13% |
| U.S. Private Philanthropy | $37.5 | 17% |
| Foundations | $4.6 | 12% |
| Corporations | $8.9 | 24% |
| Private and Voluntary Organizations | $12.0 | 32% |
| Volunteerism | $3.0 | 8% |
| Universities and Colleges | $1.8 | 5% |
| Religious Organizations | $7.2 | 19% |
| U.S. Remittances | $90.7 | 40% |
| U.S. Private Capital Flows | $69.2 | 31% |
| U.S. Total Economic Engagement | $226.2 | 100%* |

*Source:* Hudson Institute (2011), http://gpr.hudson.org/

Other economic assistance included the Millennium Challenge Corporation (discussed below), the Peace Corps, and voluntary contributions to multilateral organizations, such as the UN and the World Bank. More recently, the United States directly funded 22% of the UN's budget (Better World Campaign, 2011), and provided $2.3 billion to the World Bank in 2011 (Reddy, 2011).

### Innovation in Aid

"I couldn't defend a lot of foreign aid over the past years, much of which disappeared into the pockets of corrupt foreign leaders," former U.S. Secretary of State Condoleeza Rice said. "But foreign aid is one of the most important parts of diplomacy. We need countries that are responsible. A stable society is not going to become a failed state. But every tax-payer ought to be asking is it working?" (Easton, 2011, p. 164).

A critic of "big push" plans to alleviate poverty is economist William Easterly who dared to criticize the effectiveness of World Bank programs when he worked there. He lost his job for speaking out against the World Bank programs and agreeing with Rice's assertion that aid should be scrutinized by those funding it (Postrel, 2006). "This is the tragedy in which the West spent $2.3 trillion on foreign aid over the last five decades and still had not managed to get 12-cent medicines to children to prevent half of all malaria deaths," Easterly

**Table 14.4** 2010 U.S. Overseas Economic and Military Assistance ($U.S. millions)

| | *2010* |
|---|---|
| **I. Table Economic Assistance** | **37,670.6** |
| A. USAID and Predecessor | 14,068.6 |
|    Economic Support Fund/Security Support Assistance | 7,190.0 |
|    Development Assistance | 2,345.3 |
|    Child Survival & Health | 5.3 |
|    Other USAID Assistance | 4,527.9 |
| B. Department of Agriculture | 2,637.9 |
|    Food Aid Total | 2,335.3 |
|      Title I | 91.2 |
|      Title II (USAID Implemented) | 2,146.4 |
|      Food for Education | 74.0 |
|      Other Food Aid programs | 23.8 |
|    Other USDA Assistance | 302.6 |
| C. State Department | 12,224.3 |
|    Global Health and Child Survival | 6,436.1 |
|    Global HIV/AIDS Initiative | 54.9 |
|    Narcotics Control | 2,887.7 |
|    Migration and Refugee Assistance | 1,830.8 |
|    Nonproliferation, Anti-Terrorism, Demining & Related | 705.7 |
|    Other State Assistance | 309.2 |
| D. Other Economic Assistance | 5,836.2 |
|    Millennium Challenge Corporation | 1,617.3 |
|    Peace Corps | 353.7 |
|    Department of Defense Security Assistance | 1,277.7 |
|    Other Active Grant Programs | 2,587.5 |
|    Inactive Programs | |
| E. Voluntary Contributions to Multilateral organizations | 2,903.7 |
| **II. Total Military Assistance** | **15,057.6** |
| **III. Total Economic & Military Assistance** | **52,728.2** |
| Non-Concessional U.S. Loans | 6,085.9 |
|    Export-Import Bank Loans | 4,260.6 |
|    OPIC & Other Non-Concessional U.S. Loans | 1,825.3 |
| Annual Obligations to International Organizations (Assessed) | 3,780.5 |

*Source:* Summary of All Countries, "Fiscal Year 2010, US Overseas Loans and Grants" on p. 19 of USAID (2011).

said. "The West spent $2.3 trillion and still had not managed to get $4 bed nets to poor families. The West spent $2.3 trillion and still had not managed to get $3 to each new mother to prevent five million child deaths" (Easterly, 2006, p. 4).

Before 1982, USAID sent less than 15% of its annual spending through local and international NGOs and universities (Natsios, 2009). Facing the reality that sending aid during the Cold War to foreign governments, such as Zaire's anti-communist regime led by Mobutu Sese Seko, resulted in no public services or reform, USAID's leaders decided to pursue different ways to send aid to foreign countries. USAID began directing grants and contracts to NGOs, universities, and businesses. As a result, transparency, accountability, and performance of aid programs increased. Today, donor government aid agencies increasingly work with corporations and NGOs to encourage development in poor countries. Figure 14.2 depicts the different channels for aid delivery by obligations, as well as by disbursements (what was actually paid) in 2010. As shown, the U.S. government accounts for the largest channel itself. Disbursements to foreign governments (third set of bars from the left) represent the smallest channel (tied with foreign businesses) now at $0.9 billion in disbursements. Multilateral organizations, U.S. businesses, U.S. NGOs, foreign NGOs, and other channels all account for more aid disbursements than foreign governments now.

**Figure 14.2**   Implementing Partner Types for U.S. Economic Assistance 2010 ($U.S. billions)

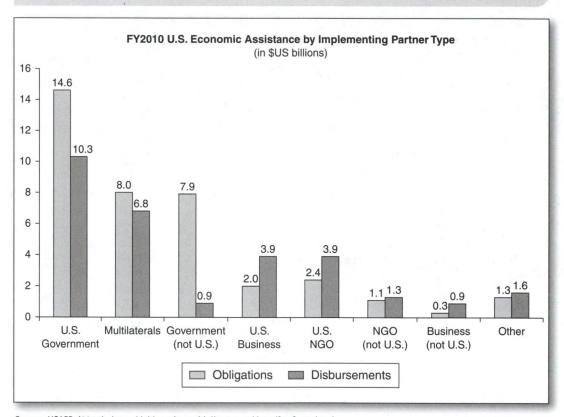

*Source:* USAID (2011), http://gbk.eads.usaidallnet.gov/data/fst-facts.html

The UN's Millennium Development Goals—the first being cutting in half the number of the poor living in extreme poverty by 2015 from 1990 levels—provide a useful frame for the aid efforts of both governments and NGOs in continuing their "big push" approach featuring aid. One different kind of government aid program is the Millennium Challenge Corporation (MCC), which U.S. President George W. Bush jointly announced at the White House with U2 star Bono in 2002 (Easton, 2011, p. 158). The focus of the MCC is funding private enterprises in developing countries that must have a democratic government, economic freedom, and lack of corruption. The MCC evaluates countries on 24 criteria using third-party social indicators to qualify them for large grants that would go to private business ventures or social enterprises in these countries (MCC, 2011). Table 14.5 presents these criteria that come under the headings of (a) ruling justly, (b) economic freedom, and (c) investing in people. With such criteria for society's performance in the public, private, and social sectors, the MCC approach resonates with research suggesting donors and international NGOs move "toward thinking about how they can support progressive forces of change, so that local NGOs can call their own governments to account," the Institute of Development Studies' Andy Sumner said (Ruvinsky, 2011, p. 9).

**Table 14.5**   The Millennium Challenge Corporation's Criteria for Country Eligibility

| Ruling Justly | Economic Freedom | Investing in People |
|---|---|---|
| 1. Civil Liberties | 1. Inflation | 1. Public Expenditure—Health |
| 2. Political Rights | 2. Fiscal Policy | 2. Public Expenditure—Primary Education |
| 3. Freedom of Information | 3. Business Start-Up | 3. Immunization Rates |
| 4. Government | 4. Trade Policy | 4. Girls' Education |
| **Effectiveness** | 5. Regulatory Quality | 5. Primary Education Completion |
| 5. Rule of Law | 6. Land Rights and Access | 6. Secondary Education Enrollment (lower middle-income countries) |
| 6. Control of Corruption | 7. Access to Credit | 7. Child Health |
|  | 8. Gender in the Economy | 8. Natural Resource Protection |

*Source:* Millennium Challenge Corporation, http://www.mcc.gov

Developing countries have to compete for MCC funding of projects, so government leaders gain the impetus for curbing their anti-democratic impulses, as well as for fighting corruption. More than $8 billion in MCC aid has gone to countries, such as the Philippines, Georgia, and El Salvador. When Nicaragua suppressed the political opposition in local elections in 2008, it lost a $62 million MCC grant. Likewise, when Malawi in southern Africa used violence to quell demonstrations there, it lost a $350 million MCC grant.

The MCC takes a different approach than other aid agencies such as USAID or the World Bank that establish sizable staffs of expatriates in countries receiving aid. By comparison, MCC posts only two expatriates in a country, but these are backed by a team of engineers and auditors in Washington, DC. Projects are designed and administered by a coalition of host-country government officials, business and labor leaders, along with environmentalists. The coalition engages in hot debates about projects and funding in its own exercise of democracy.

Unlike other aid, the funding is designed to end. "My goal is to replace our money with private sector money," MCC Director Daniel Yohannes said (Easton, 2011, p. 156).

In Ghana in western Africa, more than half a billion dollars has funded the training of 65,000 farmers, the construction of storage facilities, and the paving of gutted dirt roads to enable fresh produce to arrive to distant markets in a timely way (Easton, 2011, p. 156). Such accomplishments have enabled Ghanaian farmer Tony Botchway to develop a pine-apple and mango processing plant in the central town of Nsorbi that pays 750 workers more than the minimum wage. Botchway's firm, called Bomarts, is profitable, exports to Spain and Switzerland, and now serves as a supplier for MNE Dole. "We're ready to compete with Costa Rican producers," Botchway said (Easton, 2011, p. 156).

The MCC is daring because it promotes that economic growth is the best antipoverty tool making the MCC at odds with much of the donor community (composed of governments, multilateral organizations, and NGOs), which views the marketplace with suspicions. "All humans need money—they need it to buy food and water every day," UN deputy special envoy Haiti Paul Farmer said. "And no matter how hard the government or the aid industry tries, people will want for all three things until they are employed" (Easton, 2011, p. 164).

# SOCIAL ENTREPRENEURSHIP

## Creating Social Value

Social entrepreneurship is a process in which citizens launch ventures or transform existing institutions to advance solutions for social or environmental problems (Bornstein & Davis, 2010. p. 1). Although many think of nonprofit ventures as comprising the domain of social entrepreneurship, for-profit ventures fall in this domain as well (Yunus, 2010, p. 4). Chapter 1 introduced Fábio Rosa and his Project Light in Brazil as a prototypical social entrepreneur. Rosa's mission of bringing electrification to the rural poor of Brazil's south-ernmost state of Rio Grande do Sul using steel wire brought enormous social value to hundreds of poor families (Bornstein, 2004). Chapter 1 also introduced Tom Szaky and his privately owned TerraCycle that manufactures fashion accessories, such as over-the-shoul-der handbags and backpacks made from juice packs that are stitched together (Szaky, 2009). With more than 14 million people in 11 countries collecting waste for TerraCycle, TerraCycle's re-cycling has created more than 280 different products sold at major retailers, such as Wal-Mart and Whole Foods Market.

Like traditional entrepreneurs, Rosa and Szaky pursue the accumulation of physical and financial capital. However, by explicitly addressing social or environmental problems in the missions of their ventures, they can be considered social entrepreneurs. The biggest advantage social entrepreneurs have is an authentic voice that is their own, as well as the authentic voices from user testimonials of their products and services (McGee, 2007). In other words, their persistence and effectiveness in addressing social problems makes their words about the solution to these problems persuasive and compelling to others.

Social entrepreneurs play the role of change agents (Dees, 1998). They adopt a mission to create and sustain social value for society. They often are intrepid in this pursuit overcoming formidable obstacles and the initial lack of interest of others. They frequently must act boldly without being limited by the resources they currently control.

Some of the most exciting accomplishments of social entrepreneurs in recent years have come from enabling poor people to function more effectively in the marketplace. Finding buyers for high-quality produce or artisan crafts characterize some of the ways the poor have earned more income in markets. For example, Paul Polak and his International Development Enterprises have worked with more than 3.8 million households in ten countries to provide low-cost access to water and effective markets. The work of IDE has helped increase the average family's annual income by $250 within the first year (IDE, 2011).

Another example of social entrepreneurship can be seen in the story of alternative trade organizations (known as fair trade). Fairtrade International has led a movement whose objective is to ensure the ethical treatment of workers (Clark, 2011). By bringing together retailers and other marketers in wealthy countries with small-scale producers of foods, such as tea, coffee, fruits, flowers, and vegetables, these small-scale producers receive a larger portion of the final sale price to the customer. For example, Fairtrade only certifies coffee if it does not come from estate farms or agribusiness and is grown in sustainable ways, ensuring that coffee will not be bought at a lower than a fair-trade price, which prevents price fluctuations in the market from working against a small-farmer cooperative's farm (Haight, 2011; see Figure 14.3). Additionally, a fair-trade premium (about $.20 per pound of coffee) will be paid into a communal fund at the cooperative so that workers and farmers can improve their social, economic, and environmental conditions. In 2010, $6 billion of Fairtrade-approved goods sold around the world—up 27% from 2009 (Clark, 2011, p. 15). Eight percent of the coffee used in Starbucks's global operations came from fair-trade farms in 2010, or about 21 million pounds. "Companies like Wal-Mart, Costco, Green Mountain, Starbucks and Ben & Jerry's are expanding their offerings in terms of fair-trade products," Fair Trade USA CEO Paul Rice said (Clark, 2011, p. 15).

Reports have surfaced about a recurring unevenness in the receipt of benefits for buyers (not always obtaining the top-grade coffee for the fair market price when the market price for top-grade coffee is higher) or for sellers (the fair-trade premium goes to the farmers' democratically governed farmers' cooperative and not to the farmers themselves). However, macromarketing researchers have found evidence suggesting that Latin American coffee producers supplying one alternative trade organization, Fair Trade USA, reported a greater overall sense of well-being and a more positive outlook for their future when compared with nonmembers of such an alternative trade organization (Geiger-Oneto & Arnould, 2011).

**Figure 14.3** Fair Trade Certified Logo

*Source:* Fair Trade USA, http://www.fairtradeusa.org

Fair trade is an example of a social innovation that is distinct from commercial innovations. Social innovations provide novel solutions to a social problem (that are more effective, efficient, and sustainable than existing solutions) in which the value created accrues primarily to society as a whole rather than to private individuals, such as entrepreneurs, investors, or ordinary consumers (Phills, Deiglmeier & Miller, 2008). Other examples of social innovations include the following:

- Individual development accounts
  - where every dollar a poor person saves for a college education, buying a home, or starting a business is matched by philanthropic, government, or corporate sponsors with two dollars on average.

- Microfinance
  - where groups of people (usually poor people) hold each other accountable for the repayment of small amounts for their businesses (Discussed later in this chapter with examples, such as India's SKS Microfinance and the Internet's Kiva).

- Supported employment
  - programs that help disabled or otherwise disadvantaged workers find and retain good jobs.

## Structures for Social Enterprises

Social entrepreneurship (focused on entrepreneurs) and social enterprise (focused on organizations) have their roots in the nonprofit sector where the creation of social value—benefit to the public or society as a whole—is the underlying objective of NGOs (Phills et al., 2008). Toward the end of creating social value, NGOs have applied marketing principles in their social marketing campaigns.

Social marketing involves the marketing of behaviors that benefit society, as well as the target audience (Kotler & Lee, 2009, p. 53). Society can benefit through improved public health, development, safety, environment, and communities. For example, if an anti-smoking campaign is effective, then public health will improve as a result of fewer respiratory illnesses and smoking-related cancer cases. In development, NGOs such as IDE have used social marketing to impart better farming practices to the rural poor.

As some social problems have proved difficult to eliminate and have actually increased in size and scope in many countries (such as poverty, malnutrition, energy resource depletion, environmental degradation, the trafficking of contraband, and HIV/AIDS and flu pandemics), the limits of the nonprofit—or citizen sector—to complement government fully in stemming these social problems has become evident. Business leaders have begun to realize that their businesses can have a role to play in addressing social problems. With the rise of corporate social responsibility in the late 1980s, founders of firms such as Patagonia, the Body Shop, and Ben & Jerry's have viewed their businesses both as a vehicle to make money and as a means to improve society (Vogel, 2005).

Today, the boundaries between the nonprofit, government, and business sectors have become diffused and semipermeable as ideas, values, roles, relationships, and capital flow more freely across these sectors (Phills et al., 2008). In recent years, nonprofit and government leaders have looked to businesses to learn about management, entrepreneurship, and performance measurement. Government and business leaders increasingly turn to nonprofit leaders to understand social and environmental issues better, and how to succeed in bottom-of-the-pyramid settings of developing countries. Finally, business and nonprofit leaders both engage governments to shape public policy regarding social issues that affect their missions or their customers. For example, six national sales directors for cosmetics firm Mary Kay drove their pink Cadillacs to the U.S. Capitol in June 2005 to advocate for the continuation of the Violence Against Women Act that included $500 million in additional federal funds for combating domestic violence, sexual assault, and stalking (Peterson & Pfitzer, 2009). Their efforts paid off as U.S. President George W. Bush signed the reauthorization into law in January 2006.

As a result of the increased interplay among nonprofits, government, and business, a variety of structures have emerged in recent years for social enterprises (Kelly, 2009). Current U.S. law does not currently recognize any single legal entity that would allow receiving (a) charitable contributions that would be tax-deductible for donors, (b) invested equity capital that would produce capital gains to be taken by investors, or (c) quasi-invested capital such as loans from foundations that do not expect a market rate of return (Bromberger, 2011). Some social entrepreneurs have found ways to integrate aspects of the for-profit and nonprofit models for structuring their enterprises. Figure 14.4 depicts a matrix for these structures based on the upside potential for profit or social benefit, as well as the legal aspect of being a for-profit or a nonprofit entity.

**Figure 14.4** Profit/Social Value Potential for Social Enterprise Structures

| | | Social Enterprise Structure | |
| --- | --- | --- | --- |
| | | For-Profit Structure | Nonprofit Structure |
| **Upside Potential For** | **Profits** | **For-Profit** ex: SKS Microfinance (foundation-owned) ex: Salesforce.com (business philanthropy) | **Nonprofit** With a Mission-Related **Enterprise** ex: Rwanda Partners (surplus revenues) ex: Fair Trade USA (revenue shortage) |
| | **Social Value** | **For-Profit With a Social Overlay** ex: Equal Exchange (worker co-op) ex: Organic Valley (producer co-op) ex: Grameen Bank (customer co-op) | **Nonprofit** ex: Acumen Fund Kiva Ashoka |

## For-Profit

In the upper-left quadrant is the traditional for-profit model. Advantages for the for-profit model include the relative ease for raising money as equity or debt, and the ease of selling or shutting down (as long as creditors receive their due) (Fruchterman, 2011). Disadvantages for the for-profit model include being required by law to put the interests of the shareholders first, meaning making money for them. Taxes on income and property must also be paid to governments, and for-profit companies cannot accept foundation grants or nontaxable contributions.

An example of a for-profit corporation focused on alleviating poverty is SKS Microfinance of India. SKS distributes small loans that begin at Rs. 2,000 to Rs. 12,000 (about $44–$260) to poor women so they can start and expand simple businesses and increase their incomes (SKS Microfinance, 2011). The microenterprises of these poor women range from raising cows and goats in order to sell their milk to opening a village tea stall. A major challenge for social enterprises is scaling up their operations to influence more than just a locale or a region. SKS switched from a nonprofit model to a for-profit model early in its existence in order to gain access to the financial resources that could come from being listed on the Bombay Stock Exchange, as well as on the New York Stock Exchange. Although this move resulted in millions of more dollars as a base from which to lend to poor consumers, the idea of profiting from poor people poses an ethical dilemma in macromarketing research (Laczniak & Santos, 2011). The story of SKS Microfinance and its founder Vikram Akula will be discussed more fully later in this chapter.

Creative business persons have tweaked the for-profit model to pursue different forms of philanthropy. For example, sales-support-software firm Salesforce.com's founder and

CEO Marc Benioff developed a "1-1-1 rule" in which 1% of the firm's equity, 1% of its profit, and 1% of employees' time went into a nonprofit (a 501(c)(3) public charity (Rose, 2011). Benioff said:

> We run 10,000 non-profits for free. We do not charge universities for our services. We will deliver hundreds of thousands of hours of community service. Google copied our 1-1-1 model, and others have, too. That's been probably our most successful part of our business, far more than our business success—our ability to inspire others to do philanthropy. It's been a huge missing part of Silicon Valley. (Rose, 2011, p. 52)

Google's philanthropy is not structured as a charitable foundation but as a division of the firm itself. In this way, Google declines a tax-exempt status for its "for-profit philanthropy" but gains full access to the Google's staff, technology, and products in the process (Kelly, 2009).

Large publicly traded companies have integrated a social priority with their imperative for generating ongoing profits in several ways worth noting (Kelly, 2009). A dual-class governance structure at carpet-tile manufacturer Interface, Inc. (featured in Chapter 1) put supervoting shares in the hands of Chairman Ray Anderson and a few other top executives, giving them control of 72% of votes for the board—although they own far less than a majority of publicly traded shares. As a result, Interface has stayed focused on its drive toward sustainability. Google also adopted a similar dual-class stock configuration when it went public in 2004 that vested power with its founders. The New York Times Company is controlled by the Sulzberger family, which has allowed *The New York Times* to stay focused on its mission of serving an informed electorate. A foundation controls Novo Nordisk, a Danish pharmaceutical company. This has enabled the firm to remain committed to its mission of defeating diabetes. Companies like these are termed mission-controlled companies.

## For-Profit With a Social Overlay

The lower-left quadrant of Figure 14.4 represents the hybrid forms that have a for-profit legal structure with upside potential for social value rather than profits (Bromberger, 2011). These are for-profits with a social overlay (Fruchterman, 2011). Some of these structures have existed for decades. These include stakeholder-owned firms in the form of cooperatives. Such cooperatives might be formed by workers as in the case of Equal Exchange—a fair-trade food company—based in West Bridgewater, Massachusetts (www.equalexchange.coop). Alternatively, a cooperative might be formed by producers as in the case of Cooperative Regions of Organic Producers Pool (CROPP), better known by its brand name in grocery stores—Organic Valley—based in La Farge, Wisconsin. CROPP is owned by the 1,200 organic family farms that produce the dairy, eggs, and meat it distributes. "We don't have any need for profits much over 2 percent," CROPP CEO George Siemon said. "We'd just pay taxes on it. We'd rather give it to the farmers" (Kelly, 2009, p. 6). Finally, a cooperative can be owned by customers as in the case of Bangladesh's Grameen Bank that is owned by the poor people who are its depositors and customers (Yunus, 2010, p. 2).

For-profits with a social overlay now include new structures approved in some states that are being adopted elsewhere. Instead of being either for-profit or nonprofit, these new structures allow an enterprise to be "for-benefit" (Sabeti, 2011).

States such as California, Illinois, Michigan, Utah, Vermont, and Wyoming have enacted statutes allowing for the creation of for-profit corporations with a primary charitable purpose called benefit corporations. A branded form of a benefit corporation is the beneficial corporation—"B Corporation, or B Corp"—a new type of corporation that uses a business structure to solve social and environmental problems. B Lab, a nonprofit organization, certifies B Corporations the same way TransFair certifies Fair Trade coffee or USGBC certifies LEED buildings. Annual scores on the legal structure of firms for the more than 400 B Corps expands corporate accountability so they are required to make decisions that are good for society, not just their shareholders. States such as Vermont, Maryland, New Jersey, and Virginia have passed laws backing B Corps. Seventh Generation is the nation's most recognized brand of natural household and personal care products. It became a founding B Corporation in 1991 because the firm believes it is critical that there be a standard for corporate responsibility in the United States (B Lab, 2011).

Figure 14.5 depicts Agora Management's B Corp rating page. Agora helps businesses in developing countries grow and prosper through business consulting and arranging financial assistance. As shown, five dimensions comprise the B Corp score card: (a) accountability, (b) employees, (c) consumers, (d) community, and (e) environment. Firms become certified as a B Corp when they achieve 80 points or more. Agora Management earned 105.2 points in 2010. It attained levels of excellence in accountability and consumers. Such ratings can be useful in demonstrating to employees, clients, and investors the firm's success in creating social value.

In October 2011, California added the Flexible Purpose Corporation (FPC)—a new corporate form similar to a benefit corporation that allows a corporation to integrate the for-profit philosophy of the traditional corporation with a *special purpose* mission that is similar to a charitable purpose (Salceda, 2011). This special purpose might be promoting or minimizing short or long-term effects on (a) the FPC's employees, suppliers, customers, and creditors; (b) the environment; or (c) the community and society.

A low-profit limited liability company (L3C) is another version of the for-profit with a social overlay. For example, Maine's Own Organic Milk Company was created by family farmers and investors to sell the farmers' organic milk (Fruchterman, 2011). Because there were other owners than the producers' themselves, the L3C proved to be the best structure for this social enterprise.

In settings outside the United States, an analog to the L3C would be what Nobel Peace Prize winner Muhammad Yunus calls a social business—a nonloss, nondividend company with an owner and social objectives (Yunus, 2010, p. 4). "The existing company law in most countries is enough to create a social business," Yunus said. "That's the beauty of the concept. The only thing is, it must be specified in the charter that the owners cannot take dividends. They only get back their investment" (Wimmer, 2012, p. 194).

Yunus sees social businesses as allowing owners to express their selflessness, and to attract investors—a feature unavailable to nonprofits. In sum, the social business is run like a business with long-term planning. It generates income from business activities and

**Figure 14.5** Agora Management's B Corp Rating Page

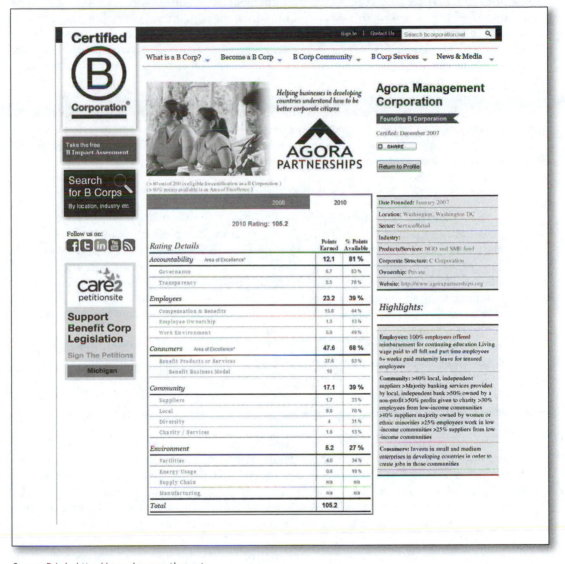

*Source:* B Lab, http://www. bcorporation.net

focuses on long-term impact—rather than on chasing donations year to year (Wimmer, 2012, p. 195).

Yunus's Grameen Danone is an example of a social business. It is a joint venture with French MNE Groupe Danone that attacks the problem of malnutrition by selling affordable yogurt fortified with micronutrients in rural areas of Bangladesh (Yunus, 2010, p. 1). The joint venture, founded in 2006, produces a yogurt enriched with crucial nutrients at a price of 6 BDT (= 0.06 EUR), which even the poorest can afford. Grameen Danone Foods improves the lives of poor people not only by improving their health, but also benefits accrue to those manning the whole value chain. For example, the milk for the yogurt is purchased from small farmers. The production is designed in such a way as to give as many people as possible a job. Finally, sales ladies distribute the yogurt door-to-door and receive a 10% commission.

In sum, for-profits with a social overlay have the same advantages as a standard for-profit. However, they have additional options for raising capital as it is easier for foundations to invest in an L3C. A disadvantage of for-profits with a social overlay is that investors may not want to invest in such a form without strong social motivations. In other words, investment financing may be limited.

## Nonprofits With a Mission-Related Enterprise

The upper-right quadrant of Figure 14.4 depicts nonprofits with a mission-related enterprise. Tax-exempt nonprofits that have earned income that is clearly related to their social mission are nonprofits with a mission-related enterprise (Fruchterman, 2011). Although many types of nonprofits earn income from selling goods and services (theaters, museums, colleges, and used-goods stores), income cannot be distributed to investors or shareholders (but it can be used to repay loans for the nonprofit).

Fair Trade USA is a nonprofit, but it obtains most of its revenues from service fees charged to retailers when they buy shipments of Fair Trade goods such as coffee, chocolate, and fruits. For example, 70% of the goods it sells are coffee, and ten cents of every pound of Fair Trade coffee goes to Fair Trade USA to help promote its brand (Haight, 2011, p. 77). In 2009, Fair Trade USA had a budget of $10 million, and certification fees funded 70% of it. The remaining 30% came from philanthropic contributions—mostly from grants and private donors. In this way, Fair Trade USA is a revenue-shortage nonprofit with a mission-related enterprise.

Seattle-based Rwanda Partners is a nonprofit organization committed to fighting poverty and restoring hope to the poor and marginalized through economic and educational opportunities (Rwanda Partners, 2011). In a country impacted by genocide, Rwanda Partners grounds its work in the healing and reconciliation of the Rwandan people. Through its website (www.rwandapartners.org) and basket parties, this nonprofit sells multicolored, hand-woven baskets made by women artisans in Rwanda. These baskets are also sold at Costco stores.

In effect, the Rwanda Basket Co. is an international enterprise that employs more than 2,000 rural women in Rwanda by providing a market for their strikingly beautiful, hand-crafted baskets in the United States. Since one of the principal aims of this faith-based NGO is reducing poverty, the enterprise is mission-related because the weavers receive a steady income, as well as reconciliation training and leadership opportunities. The Mavericks Who Made It section at the end of this chapter profiles the founders of Rwanda Partners Tracy and Greg Stone.

Nonprofits with mission-related enterprises face no taxation on mission-related income (Fruchterman, 2011, p. 47). They also have the ability to raise philanthropic funds for any of their programs. Because of the charitable nature of the enterprise, the products and services offered by the mission-related enterprise usually have a selling advantage. However, nonprofits with mission-related enterprises cannot raise capital in financial markets because of their status as a nonprofit. Philanthropists and debt stand as the only sources for funding.

## Nonprofits

The lower right quadrant of Figure 14.4 depicts nonprofits. The social mission of nonprofits is their most distinguishing characteristic. All resources for nonprofits come from donations of money, products, or time (Fruchterman, 2011, p. 47). Nonprofits do not have any earned-income enterprises. In the United States, traditional nonprofits carry the tax classification of a 501(c)(3) charity or a 501(c)(3) foundation.

The Red Cross and the Red Crescent are nonprofits that provide relief after natural disasters (Red Crescent, 2011; Red Cross, 2011). Habitat for Humanity is a faith-based nonprofit that seeks to eliminate poverty housing and homelessness from the world (Habitat for Humanity, 2011). Habitat for Humanity has helped build more than 500,000 decent, affordable houses around the world that now house more than two million people.

Jacqueline Novogratz founded the nonprofit Acumen Fund as a venture capital fund for the poor in developing countries (Novogratz, 2011). Investors in developed countries avoid placing long-term bets in troubled regions of the world. They seek a quicker payback and less risk. By comparison, the Acumen Fund scours the world to identify worthy ventures that would benefit the poor in developing countries using "patient capital" that will allow up to 15 years for payback. Investments have included International Development Enterprises India (a subsidiary of Paul Polak's IDE) and its water-saving drip irrigation system, WaterHealth International of Irvine, California's water purification system, as well as d.light Design, a privately held, San Francisco-based company that sells affordable solar-powered LED lights in the developing world. Ten years after its founding in 2001, the Acumen Fund had invested $68.5 million in 65 businesses (Coster, 2011). Three have bought back their shares from Acumen, 11 have repaid loans, and 10 are profitable. Five companies have been written off versus the 50% a typical venture capitalist will bury.

Kiva is a nonprofit organization that connects people through microfinance lending to alleviate poverty (Kiva, 2012; see Figure 14.6). Using the Internet and a worldwide network of microfinance institutions, Kiva lets individuals lend as little as $25 to help create opportunity around the world. Since its founding in 2005, Kiva has helped hundreds of thousands lenders make $293 million in loans. To date, the repayment rate for these loans exceeds 98.9%. Kiva operates in more than 60 countries in conjunction with 147 partnering organizations in these countries. These partnering organizations identify and qualify potential borrowers for Kiva loans.

Some of the most exciting social innovations in recent years have resulted from social entrepreneurs sponsored early in their ventures by the educational foundation Ashoka, which was founded by Bill Drayton. Ashoka searches the world for social entrepreneurs

**Figure 14.6**   Kiva's Website Helps Lenders Identify Worthy Borrowers for Microfinance Loans

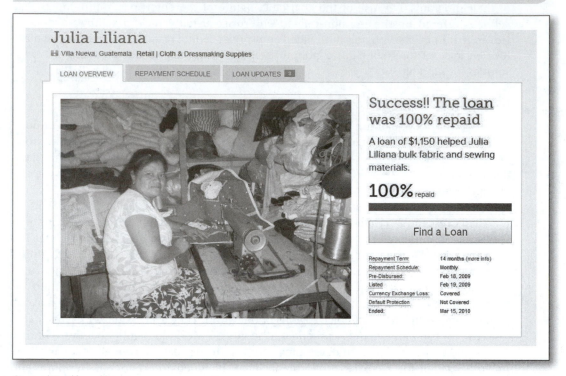

*Source:* http://www.kiva.org

gearing up to launch a social venture and then sponsors them for three years with a salary as Ashoka Fellows (Ashoka, 2011). Ashoka Fellows receive coaching to boost the success of their ventures. Being an Ashoka Fellow helped Rakhee Choudhury launch her venture to teach women in India's far-northeastern Assam Valley the traditional weaving skills they need to earn income at the same time they deepen their pride in the Asasamese culture.

Nonprofits do not have a conflict between the venture and the social objectives like a for-profit enterprise might. Importantly, donors to nonprofits receive a tax deduction for their donations in the United States. A drawback to the nonprofit model is that traditional fundraising is the only way to raise financial resources. Social business advocate Muhammad Yunus said:

> Relying on charitable donations is not a sustainable way of running an organization. It forces NGO leaders to spend a lot of time, energy, and money on fund-raising efforts. Even when these are successful, most NGOs are perennially strapped for cash and unable to sustain, let alone expand, their most effective programs. (Yunus, 2010, p. 6)

## Vikram Akula—Founder of SKS Microfinance

Indian American Vikram Akula founded SKS Microfinance in 1997 as an NGO, but later he converted it to a for-profit business. SKS distributes small loans that begin at about $44–$260 to poor women so they can start and expand simple businesses and increase their incomes (SKS Microfinance, 2011). Their microenterprises range from raising cows and goats in order to sell their milk, to opening a tea stall in their village.

SKS uses a group-lending model in which poor women guarantee each other's loans. Those who borrow from SKS undergo financial literacy training and must pass a test before they are allowed to take out loans. Weekly meetings with borrowers follow a highly ordered approach. Repayment rates on SKS' collateral-free loans are more than 99% because of this systematic process.

### Early Influences

Although born in the southern Indian city of Hyderabad, Akula moved to Schenectady, New York, when he was two years old. On return visits to relatives living in middle-class neighborhoods in Hyderabad as a young boy, Akula witnessed the poor collecting a few fallen grains of rice lying on the ground. He also saw them scavenging food from tables being cleared at wedding celebrations. The desperation of the poor he saw affected him deeply. He became taken with the idea of returning to India someday to help alleviate poverty.

Akula completed his undergraduate degree at Tufts University in the Boston area, and a masters' degree later at Yale University. Akula returned to India with the nonprofit Deccan Development Society (DDS) (Akula, 2011, p.1). In his second stint with DSS as a Fulbright Scholar, Akula became involved with microfinance. He managed agricultural lending for 30 villages motoring down dirt roads on his Indian-made Honda motorbike to disburse loans and collect repayments. Akula recalls:

> Working in these villages was incredibly gratifying, though there were definitely hardships to living in remote villages: sleeping on a straw mat on the floor in a small room, fetching drinking water from a distant well, and seeing the effects of poor nutrition and hygienic conditions all around me was certainly a far cry from the middle-class comfort of Schenectady, New York, where I had grown up. But I felt like I was really making a difference, really helping to end poverty in India. (Akula, 2011, pp. 2–3)

But DSS could not lend as much money as the poor wanted for their development projects. In this way, Akula became aware of the limits of a nonprofit's approach to reducing a social problem; it could not attract enough money to lend to the poor because it did not pay dividends to investors.

### The Founding of SKS Microfinance

Vikram Akula founded SKS Microfinance in 1997 as a nonprofit organization (after taking a two-week Grameen Bank training program in Bangladesh). He led the organization until 2004, when he joined McKinsey & Co. in Chicago as a management consultant. In 2005, he returned to SKS when it converted to a for-profit company (Acharya & Virk, 2011). Under the leadership of Akula, SKS became the largest micro lender in India (Bajaj, 2011). In August 2010, SKS Microfinance began selling shares of the company on the Bombay Stock Exchange as well as on the New York Stock Exchange. Its initial public offering (IPO) of shares brought $350 million to the firm.

"If you look at most microfinance institutions, they're structured as NGOs," Akula said. "They're small, they think about a thousand clients, or maybe 10,000 clients. In contrast, a business, whether it's Starbucks or Coke or McDonald's, thinks about millions or tens of millions of customers. We've looked at those types of companies and adopted the techniques that they've used within microfinance. That has given us an extremely fast growth rate." (Knowledge@Wharton, 2008, p. 1). By the end of 2010, SKS had served more than 7.8 million borrowers across India (Bamzai, 2010).

SKS Microfinance charges an average interest rate of 24%. Akula puts this in context this way:

> Informally the village money lender, the loan sharks, will charge anywhere from 50% to as high as 1,000% interest. So, we are charging much less than what they charge. I also submit that our interest rate is actually the lowest cost financing available to the poor. Even though a retail bank might charge, let's say, 12%, or a subsidized government loan might cost 7%, if you actually talk with borrowers and ask them how many trips they are making to a bank branch, what are the lost wages, the bus fares, the brokers fees, and sometimes bribes are paid to access that 7% loan, they actually end up paying much higher than 30%. (Knowledge@ Wharton, 2008, p. 4)

Akula's story combines the heart of a social worker with the savvy of a financier. His effort with SKS Microfinance found a way markets can be used to enable the poor to develop their own entrepreneurial ventures—on an enormous scale. The promise of SKS's success since 2005 lifted Akula out of obscurity to fame. *Time* magazine named Akula one of the 100 most influential people in the world in 2006 (The Economic Times, 2011). Also in 2006, the World Economic Forum named him the Social Entrepreneur of the Year at its meeting in Delhi (Knowledge@Wharton, 2010). The *Harvard Business Review* featured his story (Akula, 2008), and later published his book, *A Fistful of Rice* (Akula, 2011). He gave talks at the Wharton Business School at the University of Pennsylvania (Knowledge@ Wharton, 2008). However, his story is a cautionary tale about the hazards of venturing into developing markets as a foreigner and as an innovator.

## Controversy Surrounding SKS

Although Akula obtained a doctorate from the University of Chicago in political science, managing the political environment proved to be the biggest challenge for Akula and SKS since its move to a for-profit model of business. "The fact is that microfinance is still very much misunderstood by politicians and bureaucrats," Akula said. "People hear the interest rates, and they don't understand the context, and they feel something exploitative is going on" (Knowledge@Wharton, 2008, p. 3).

In 2010, Indian lawmakers in Andhra Pradesh (in southeastern India where Hyderabad is located) passed a law that severely restricted new micro lending and made it more difficult for lenders to collect loan repayments (Bajaj, 2011). The lawmakers cited the public offering of stock in SKS Microfinance as a sign that financiers were profiting on the financial struggles of the poor and cited 31 suicides by borrowers of micro-lending institutions (17 of them SKS Microfinance borrowers) as reasons for the change in the law (Bamzai, 2010).

As a result of these changes, large losses ensued for SKS Microfinance as 90% of its borrowers in Andhra Pradesh (where one third of SKS' borrowers lived) stopped repaying loans in late 2010 (Bajaj, 2011). The stock price of the firm dropped to 10% of its high the previous year.

Despite growing SKS to 2,032 branches across 19 states in India that serve 6.4 million customers, controversy continued to dog Akula in 2011 (Acharya & Virk, 2011). It seemed to outsiders that he wanted more power within SKS. It seemed that Akula wanted board governance to become narrower and focused on the financial returns of SKS (deemphasizing the social cause of SKS) (Sriram, 2010, p. 72). Two board members resigned in the months prior to the IPO as a result of SKS's intention to steer proceeds from the IPO to Akula's original nonprofit group rather than to many charitable entities (Strom & Bajaj, 2010). In 2007, the SKS board granted Akula a $308,000 interest-free loan at the same time it allowed the purchase of shares for the same amount in SKS. Eighteen months later, these were sold for a $2.9 million gain. Then, the SKS board fired the CEO just after the IPO—raising concerns in the investment community about SKS's intentions to diversify into businesses like selling life insurance (Akula, 2011).

Another oddity of SKS finances was the stake sold to Unitus, a Seattle-based microfinance supporting nonprofit. The IPO provided a gain of $70–$80 million for this nonprofit putting it into a position of having to increase the scale of its operations in micro lending or lose its nonprofit status. Unitus stunned many of its donors by choosing to shut down its micro-lending efforts entirely (Strom & Bajaj, 2010). This meant terminating 40 employees in its Seattle headquarters and in its offices in Bangalore, India, and Nairobi, Kenya (Unitus, 2010). Unitus CEO Joseph Grenny explained that market-based microfinance was displacing the need for Unitus's involvement in micro lending. He further said that Unitus intended to use the money for other charitable purposes.

Although it posted $15.6 million in 2010, SKS posted losses of more than $189 million in the first three quarters of 2011 (Acharya & Virk, 2011; Associated Press, 2011). Amid mounting pressure, Akula resigned as executive chairman on November 23, 2011 severing his ties to SKS Microfinance with no compensation package—although it is believed that Akula sold all of his shares in SKS prior to the IPO of SKS in 2010 for $13 million.

## Other Microfinance Endeavors

Although it has existed for centuries, microfinance became one of the most exciting models of lending to the poor in recent decades (Khavul, Chavez, & Bruton, 2011). In the past 30 years, micro lending has spread all over the world and has benefited more than 100 million families (Yunus Center, 2011). Muhammad Yunus pioneered the nonprofit Grameen Bank in 1974 in Bangladesh and received the Nobel Peace Prize in 2006 for using microfinance to create economic and social development from below.

"Microfinance is mission-driven banking," Yunus said. He continued:

When you float an IPO you are telling your investors there is a good opportunity to make money off poor people. The message is wrong, the direction is wrong. Staunch believers of market forces keep saying competition will bring business to people who are now unreached. Over centuries, this has not happened. Competition never brought credit to the poor; it only took it to richer people. That is the route the IPO will take them (SKS). (Knowledge@Wharton, 2010, p. 1)

Despite being a well-loved figure as an advocate of poverty alleviation around the world, Yunus encountered his own political problems in 2011. Bangladesh Prime Minister Sheikh Hasina did not like it when Yunus tried to create his own political party in 2007 dedicated to opposing corruption (OneIndiaNews, 2011). Because Yunus had allowed the government of Bangladesh to appoint the managing director of Grameen Bank when he established it in 1976, the Prime Minister forced him to resign in 2011 because he was 11 years past retirement age. In sum, the role for-profit businesses and nonprofit NGOs will play in poverty alleviation remains a hotly contested issue in many countries. Although some regard for-profit approaches to microfinance as "sucking blood from the poor," Akula estimates that poor households in India need close to $50 billion in credit but only 15% of this can be met because of lack of access to large amounts of capital. "It is precisely where that US $50 billion will come from," Akula said. "It is the only place it can come from. That is why we did this IPO" (Knowledge@Wharton, 2010, p. 2).

The end of the stories for both SKS and Grameen Bank put in high relief the political risk involved in tackling poverty alleviation in developing countries. The actions of lawmakers in India derailed Akula, while the actions of the government in Bangladesh led to Yunus's ouster from the NGO he founded. In both cases, politicians separated these men from the organizations they founded. In so doing, the political potential of both men became clouded. "You have to understand—every loan is a future vote," Akula's ex-wife Malini Byanna said (Strom & Bajaj, 2010, p. 4). Akula has denied political ambitions and remains a U.S. citizen.

## CONCLUSION

This chapter considered poverty alleviation and its related issues. Poverty makes itself present in almost all countries today. In 1990, 93% of poor people lived in poor countries (Ruvinksy, 2011). However, 75% of those who live on $1.25 per day today live in middle-income countries, such as India and Nigeria. The implication is that ameliorating poverty used to be more straightforward with aid and resource transfers. Today, a more comprehensive approach is needed to impact poverty that would include government, NGOs, and businesses.

Macromarketing researchers have listed 50 solutions to poverty that have been pursued since the end of World War II, but the record of success for these solutions is weak overall when these are applied outside of relief situations (after natural disaster or war) to development projects. Part of this is a result of the contextual factors that have to be considered to understand poverty in each locale.

Social entrepreneurs such as Paul Polak have done extensive field research in the contexts of the poor in many Asian and African countries. He perceives commonality across the rural poor he has interviewed—poor farmers need more income. Toward this end, his International Development Enterprises have sought to boost the marketing effectiveness of poor farmers. Importantly, his market-based approach avoids the trap of paternalism (doing for others what they could do for themselves), as well as side-stepping corrupt government officials. Polak's wisdom about poverty alleviation approaches should encourage those taking the "biggest M" approach to marketing and to poverty alleviation. In light of business' leading role in cross-border financial flows from developed to developing countries—it seems that market-based approaches to poverty alleviation will grow in importance in the coming years. Evidence for this can be seen in the U.S.-based Millennium Challenge Corporation's new version of foreign aid that directs aid to private enterprises in qualifying countries rather than to foreign governments.

Social entrepreneurs offer many reasons to be hopeful about poverty alleviation efforts in the future. Because of the increasing interplay among governments, NGOs, and businesses in poverty alleviation, new hybrid forms combining aspects of for-profit and nonprofit have become more important in recent years. For-profits with a social overlay include cooperatives, benefit corporations, beneficial corporations (B corps), flexible purpose corporations, and low-profit limited-liability companies (L3C). Nonprofits with mission-related enterprises have businesses as subsidiaries that contribute to the budget of the nonprofit or, in some cases, provide surplus funds that are then reinvested in the programs of the nonprofits.

The story of Vikram Akula's SKS Microfinance sheds light on how complicated things can become in poverty alleviation when a for-profit model is applied in a developing country. Discord among board members for SKS involved priorities for funding charities to which SKS had committed support. However, the threat a powerful organization such as SKS posed to politicians in one state of India led to a crackdown on lending practices to poor people that previously seemed to be working.

## QUESTIONS

- Why do you think poverty alleviation has become a concern for business in recent years?
- What are the three poverty eradication myths proposed by Paul Polak?

- After examining the empowerment solutions on the right side of Table 14.2's Fifty Solutions to Poverty, which one do you think would have the most potential for poverty alleviation in the city or region in which you live? The least potential?
- What is the most surprising aspect of foreign aid that you learned in this chapter? Explain. What are the implications of this for business in the future? For NGOs? For governments?
- What are three aspects of the Millennium Challenge Corporation's approach to awarding and administering foreign aid that distinguish it from traditional approaches to foreign aid?
- Reviewing Figure 14.4, what is the most intriguing version of structure for social enterprises to you? If you started a venture with a social dimension, which one would appeal to you the most? Explain.
- How did the success of SKS Microfinance become complicated?
- What are reasons for a developing country to regulate lightly microfinance to the poor?
- What are reasons for a developing country to regulate heavily microfinance to the poor?
- Think about the SKS Microfinance story. On a scale of 1 to 10, with 1 representing "villain" and 10 representing "hero," how would you rate the following: (a) Vikram Akula, (b) the lawmakers of Andhra Pradesh, (c) Muhammad Yunus, (d) the government of Bangladesh, and (e) Unitus CEO Joseph Grenny. Explain your reasoning for each of these ratings.

## MAVERICKS WHO MADE IT

### A More Perfect Union

### Tracy and Greg Stone - Rwanda Partners

### Rwanda Partners strives to weave a torn country back together

#### By T. Foster Jones

In 1994, THE WORLD watched in horror as the impoverished Republic of Rwanda was convulsed in a civil war, one that led to one of the most brutal genocides in human history.

The ruling Hutu majority of the tiny central African country implemented the mass slaughter of the Tutsi minority, brutally murdering—over the course of approximately 100 days—at least 1 million Tutsi men, women and children. Hundreds of thousands of Rwandese were forced to flee, leaving behind their homes or their families in the ensuing chaos.

The Tutsi fought back, defeating the government army and seizing control of the country. They organized a coalition government and eventually elected Paul Kagame as president.

But the genocide left the nation in need of healing: caring for orphans and widows and rape victims left behind, and providing opportunities for Rwanda's 11 million citizens to find a way out of the devastation and poverty.

### A Call to Help

Enter Costco member Tracy Stone.

In 2004, Stone, a Bellevue, Washington, mother of two, and self-described "risk-averse and unadventurous person," felt called to help in Rwanda. She led 17 members from her church on a visit to the country. There, she met women who had endured rape and the murders of their family, yet who survived and even forgave their assailants.

"Over the years, I had heard stories of these courageous women. I wanted to go there and thank them," says Stone, explaining that their stories helped her through some of her own personal struggles.

Compelled by the Rwandan widows stories of survival, Stone felt, upon returning home, that thanks weren't nearly enough. With her husband, Greg, she created the non-profit Rwanda Partners to help address the country's many needs.

"Greg had extensive experience running nonprofits," says Stone, "and both of us had experience working in missions."

They made contacts in Rwanda and hired employees. Eventually, the needs of the organization and the enormous amounts of travel (Tracy has made 13 trips to Rwanda; Greg has made 16) made it obvious that Rwanda Partners was growing beyond Tracy's ability to manage. Greg came on full time in 2008 and in 2010 took over as the executive director.

Rwanda Partners has gone on to become an international organization, raising more than $2 million since its inception and helping thousands of people every year. The organization provides trauma counseling to rape victims, assistance to households headed by orphans, educational support for the poorest children, loans for small businesses, and training and supplies to basket weaving women.

---

### Supplier Profile

**Name:** Rwanda Partners

**Principals:** Tracy and Greg Stone

**Founded:** 2004

**Number of employees:** 15

**Contact at:** 159 Western Ave. W., Suite 455, Seattle, WA 98119 (206) 588-8029; www. rwandapartners.org

**Products at Costco:** Rwandan baskets and handbags

**Comments about Costco:** "Our weavers' lives have been transformed. Costco has definitely been instrumental in this transformation, enabling us to reach more customers than we ever have before." *–Greg Stone*

---

*(Continued)*

(Continued)

## Reconciling and Healing

Perhaps Rwanda Partners' most dramatic program involves the "healing and reconciliation" teams that bring together genocide survivors and perpetrators.

"Forgiveness is a terribly challenging concept for people to grasp, particularly in such a horrific scenario as Rwanda's genocide," says Stone. "However, for the country to heal, the past has to be confronted."

About 400,000 survivors of the genocide still live in Rwanda. More than 80,000 genocide perpetrators have been released from prison back into their communities.

"Rwanda's situation is unique in that the perpetrators are being released from prison and are returning to their communities in which they did their killing" says Stone. "The survivors are terrified of the perpetrators coming after them and the perpetrators are terrified of the survivors retaliating. The situation is one that is filled with fear, terror, extreme anxiety."

Through multiday sessions, reconciliation team members, themselves survivors of the genocide who have forgiven the perpetrators, speak to both groups about their need to reconcile and move on in order to heal. Survivors confront the perpetrators about how the violence has impacted their lives. The perpetrators own up to their actions, apologize and ask for forgiveness.

Innocent Matata, a Hutu, acknowledges that he killed his Tutsi neighbors. "Those victims, they forgave us, and now we live together," Matata says.

"I forgave those I know and even those that I don't know yet," says Elena Nytrakibibi, a Tutsi widow whose husband and nine children were killed. "Nothing will bring my children back. That's why I have already forgiven them."

The healing among Rwandans is a lesson for the world, Stone says.

With that act, "the changes we see in the lives of participants are amazing," she adds.

"Victims and perpetrators are finally able to move on, to stop hating, and are able to see hope for their future."

## Rebirth in a Basket

HANDCRAFTED BASKETS have been a part of the Rwandan culture for centuries. Rwanda's women learn to weave the baskets, woven from natural fibers and grasses, at the hands of their mothers and grandmothers, passing the tradition down from generation to generation.

The intricately woven baskets are used as containers for grain and food products, as packages for small gifts, and for events such as weddings and baby christenings.

So, when Rwanda Partners was looking for ways to help Rwandans gain more financial freedom, baskets were a natural choice.

"The seeds for the basket program were planted during our first trip to Rwanda in 2004," says Greg Stone, who oversees the basket program. "We saw how unique and beautiful they were, and when we learned that the women had only a very small domestic market that could only sustain a handful of weavers, we started to put a plan together for marketing the baskets in the U.S.

"In 2005 we placed out first order of baskets for $3,000," he continues.

"This was a large financial risk for Rwanda Partners. But the bet paid off and we quickly sold out of the baskets. We knew at that point that there was a much bigger market for us to access."

In 2009, Costco began carrying the baskets in the Northwest. The response was so positive that the baskets are now sold at Costco locations across the country. Greg and Tracy recently introduced sewn fabric handbags as well.

Rwanda Partners works directly with the basket weavers through their Rwanda-based staff, providing the women with skills training and weaving materials, as well as opening up markets for their baskets outside Rwanda.

"By working directly with the weavers, we are able to pay the weavers the highest wage for their baskets," says Stone. With the proceeds from their baskets, the women can provide their families with health insurance, school fees, additional food and clothing. Many of the weavers are able to pay someone to work their farmland so they can continue to weave–a more profitable source of income. In addition, many of the weavers have been able to purchase a cow–a valuable commodity–for their families.–*TFJ*

Source: *The Costco Connection* (September, 2011).

## Questions

- How does Rwanda Partners manifest important traits of a social business?
- How would Rwanda Partners's story be different if it was a for-profit organization? Explain.
- Would Rwanda Partners benefit from becoming a "B Corporation?" Explain.
- How important is Rwanda Partners's involvement in reconciliation in Rwanda to the buyers of its woven baskets at Costco Wholesale stores?
- What does Tracy Stone's story suggest about what might happen to someone who becomes personally involved in the problems of others overseas?
- What needed to happen for meaningful impact to result?
- What did Tracy bring to her work that Hutus or Tutsis in Rwanda could not?

# REFERENCES

Acharya, N., & Virk, S. G. (2011, November 23). A microlending star moves on. *The Wall Street Journal*. Retrieved from http://online.wsj.com

Akula, V. (2008, June). Business basics at the base of the pyramid. *Harvard Business Review, 53*, 53–57.

Akula, V. (2011). *A fistful of rice: My unexpected quest to end poverty through profitability*. Boston, MA: Harvard Business Review Press.

Ashoka. (2011). About us. Retrieved from http://ashoka.org/about

Associated Press. (2011, November 23). SKS founder and chairman Vikram Akula steps down as microlender struggles to revive itself. *The Washington Post*. Retrieved from http://www.washingtonpost.com

Astier, H. (2006, February 1). Can aid do more harm than good? *BBC News*. Retrieved from http://newsvote.bbc.co.uk

B Lab. (2011). What is a B corp? Retrieved from http://www.bcorporation.net/about

Bajaj, V. (2011, November 23). Amid scandal, chairman of troubled lender will quit. *The New York Times*. Retrieved from http://www.nytimes.com

Bamzai, S. (2010, November 6). Vikram Akula: The loan ranger. *India Today*. Retrieved from http://indiatoday.intoday.in

Better World Campaign. (2011). U.S. funding for the UN. Retrieved from http://www.betterworldcampaign.org/issues/funding/

Bornstein, D. (2004). *How to change the world: Social entrepreneurs and the power of new ideas*. New York, NY: Oxford University Press.

Bornstein, D., & Davis, S. (2010). *Social entrepreneurship: What everyone needs to know*. New York, NY: Oxford University Press.

Bromberger, A. R. (2011, Spring). A new type of hybrid. *Stanford Social Innovation Review, 9*(3), 49–53.

Chung, A. (2010, January 26). Haiti: 10 years and $10 billion in aid? *The Toronto Star*. Retrieved from http://www.thestar.com/news/world/article/755860--haiti-10-years-and-10-billion-in-aid

Clark, S. (2011, November 7–13). An American rebel roils ethical commerce. *Bloomberg BusinessWeek*, p. 15.

Corbett, S., & Fikkert, B. (2009). *When helping hurts: How to alleviate poverty without hurting the poor and yourself*. Chicago, IL: Moody.

Coster, H. (2011, November 30). Can venture capital save the world? *Forbes*. Retrieved from http://www.forbes.com/sites/helencoster/2011/11/30/novogratz/4/

Dees, J. G. (1998). The meaning of social entrepreneurship. Retrieved from http://www.caseatduke.org/documents/dees_SE.pdf

Easterly, W. (2006). *The white man's burden: Why the West's efforts to aid the rest have done so much ill and so little good*. New York, NY: Penguin Books.

Easton, N. (2011, November 21). Foreign aid, capitalist style. *Fortune*, pp. 154–164.

Fisher, I. (2011, February 11). Can international aid do more good than harm? *The New York Times*. Retrieved from http://www.nytimes.com

Fruchterman, J. (2011, Spring). For love or lucre. *Stanford Social Innovation Review*, pp. 42–47.

Geiger-Oneto, S., & Arnould, E. J. (2011). Alternative trade organization and subjective quality of life: The case of Latin American coffee producers. *Journal of Macromarketing, 31*(3), 276–290.

Gibson, C. C., Andersson, K., Ostrom, E., & Shivakumar, S. (2005). *The Samaritan's dilemma: The political economy of development aid*. New York, NY: Oxford University Press.

Habitat for Humanity. (2011). Habitat for Humanity fact sheet. Retrieved from http://www.habitat.org/how/factsheet.aspx

Haight, C. (2011, Summer). The problem with fair trade coffee. *Stanford Social Innovation Review*, pp. 74–79.

Hudson Institute. (2011). *The index of global philanthropy and remittances 2011*. Washington, DC: Center for Global Prosperity.

IDE. (2011). Our results. Retrieved from http://www.ideorg.org/OurResults/iQ.aspx#iq

Jones, T. F. (2011.) A more perfect union: Rwanda Partners strives to weave a torn country back together. *Costco Connection, 26*(9), 25–26.

Karlan, D., & Appel, J. (2011). *More than good intentions: How a new economics is helping to solve global poverty*. New York, NY: Dutton.

Kelly, M. (2009). Not just for profit. *strategy + business, 54*, 1–10.

Khavul, S., Chavez, H., & Bruton, G. D. (2011). When institutional change outruns the change agent: The contested terrain of entrepreneurial microfinance for the poor. Working paper.

Kiva. (2012). Kiva website. Retrieved from http://www.Kiva.org/

Knowledge@Wharton. (2010, October 7). Capitalism vs. altruism: SKS rekindles the microfinance debate. Retrieved from http://knowledge.wharton.upenn.edu/india/article.cfm?articleid = 4533

Knowledge@Wharton. (2008, May 1). SKS Microfinance's Vikram Akula: Mobile banking could be the future of microfinance. *Knowledge@Wharton*. Retrieved from http://knowledge.wharton.upenn.edu/india/article.cfm?articleid = 4284

Kotler, P., Roberto, N., & Leisner, T. (2006). Alleviating poverty: A macro/micro marketing perspective. *Journal of Macromarketing, 26*(2), 233–239.

Kotler, P., & Lee, N. R. (2009). *Up and out of poverty: The social marketing solution*. Upper Saddle River, NJ: Wharton School.

Laczniak, G. R., & Santos, J. N. C. (2011). The integrative justice model for marketing to the poor: An extension of S-D logic to distributive justice and macromarketing. *Journal of Macromarketing, 31*(2), 135–147.

Maddison, A. (2007). *The world economy: Historical statistics*. Paris, France: OECD. Retrieved from http://www.ggdc.net/maddison/other_books/new_HS-7.pdf

MCC. (2011). Millennium Challenge Corporation. Retrieved from http://www.mcc.gov

McGee, L. (2007, June). Social entrepreneurship and macromarketing. Paper presented by Senior Marketing Officer – Ashoka. Macromarketing Society Conference, Washington, DC.

McNeill, D. G., Jr. (2011, September 27). An entrepreneur creating chances at a better life. *The New York Times*, p. D4.

Natsios, A. S. (2009, Fall). Public/private alliances transform aid. *Stanford Social Innovation Review*, 42–47.

Novogratz, J. (2011, October 24–30). Making a case for patient capital. *Bloomberg BusinessWeek*, p. 62.

OneIndiaNews.com. (2011). 'Friends of Grameen Bank' defend Nobel Laureate Yunus from aggressive govt attacks. *One India News*. Retrieved from http://news.oneindia.in

Peterson, K., & Pfitzer, M. (2009, Winter). Lobbying for good. *Stanford Social Innovation Review*, pp. 44–49.

Phills, J. A., Jr., Deiglmeier, K., & Miller, T. D. (2008, Fall). Rediscovering social innovation. *Stanford Social Innovation Review*, pp. 34–43.

Polak, P. (2008). *Out of poverty: What works when traditional approaches fail*. San Francisco, CA: Berrett-Koehler.

Postrel, V. (2006, March 19). The poverty puzzle. *The New York Times*. Retrieved from http://www.nytimes.com

Prahalad, C. K. (2005). *The fortune at the bottom of the pyramid: Eradicating poverty through profits*. Upper Saddle River, NJ: Wharton School.

Red Crescent. (2011). Red Crescent. Retrieved from http://www.redcrescent.org

Red Cross. (2011). American Red Cross. Retrieved from http://www.redcross.org

Reddy, S. (2011, August 4). U.S. House Targets World Bank Funds, *The Wall Street Journal*. Retrieved from http://online.wsj.com

Riddell, R. C. (2007). *Does foreign aid really work?* New York, NY: Oxford University Press.

Rose, C. (2011, December 5–11). Charlie Rose talks to Marc Benioff. *Bloomberg BusinessWeek*, p. 52.

Ruvinsky, J. (2011, Summer). The new bottom billion. *Stanford Social Innovation Review*, p. 9.

Rwanda Partners. (2011). Mission and values. Retrieved from http://www.rwandapartners.org

Sabeti, H. (2011, November). The for-benefit enterprise. *Harvard Business Review*, pp. 98–104.

Salceda, A. (2011). Flexible purpose corporation: California's new corporate form. The Network. *BerkeleyLaw*. Retrieved from http://thenetwork.berkeleylawblogs.org/2011/12/13/flexible-purpose-corporation-california%E2%80%80%99s-new-corporate-form/

SKS Microfinance. (2011). Know SKS. Retrieved from http://www.sksindia.com/know_sks.php

Szaky, T. (2009). *Revolution in a bottle*. New York, NY: Penguin Group.

Sriram, M. S. (2010, June 12). Commercialization of microfinance in India: A discussion of the emperor's apparel. *Economic & Political Weekly*, XLV(24), 65–73.

Strom, S., & Bajaj, V. (2010, July 29). Rich I.P.O. brings controversy to SKS Microfinance. *The New York Times*. Retrieved from http://www.nytimes.com

Tavernise, S. (2011, September 13). Soaring poverty casts spotlight on "lost decade." *The New York Times*. Retrieved from http://www.nytimes.com

The Economic Times. (2011, November 28). India's microfinance pioneer faces flak, uncertain future. *The Economic Times*. Retrieved from http://economictimes.indiatimes.com

Unitus. (2010, July 2). Unitus, Inc. redirects efforts. Press release. Retrieved from http://unituslabs.org

USAID. (2011). [US Loans and Grants Overseas]. *US overseas loans and grants, obligations and loan authorizations, July 1, 1945–September 30, 2010*. Retrieved from http://gbk.eads.usaidallnet.gov/

Vogel, D. (2005). *The market for virtue: The potential and limits of corporate social responsibility*. Washington, DC: Brookings Institution Press.

Wimmer, N. (2012). *Green energy for a billion poor: How Grameen Shakti created a winning model for social business*. Vaterstetten, Germany: MCRE Verlag.

Wroughton, L. (2010, February 10). World Bank maps out Haiti recovery plan. *The Vancouver Sun*. Retrieved from http://www.vancouversun.com

Yunus, M., & Weber, K. (2010). *Building a social business: The new kind of capitalism that serves humanity's most pressing needs*. New York, NY: PublicAffairs.

Yunus Center. (2011). About the Yunus Centre. Retrieved from http://www.muhammadyunus.org/

# PART V

# The Future of Marketing Is Macromarketing

## CHAPTER 15

# Venturing Into the Future of Market-Based Sustainability

# HOW TO MAKE MONEY AND SAVE THE WORLD

## Gary Hirshberg—CE-Yo of Stonyfield Farm

In 1982 at the age of 28, environmental activist Gary Hirshberg visited Disney's Epcot Center in Orlando, Florida (Hirshberg, 2008, p. 2). While there, he saw in the Land Pavilion how MNE Kraft Foods projected a future of plants grown hydroponically in plastic tubes in rivers of chemical fertilizers, herbicides, and pesticides washing their naked roots. Hirshberg was aghast.

"Natural farming is all about creating great dirt, rich with nutrients," Hirshberg said. "This was a cartoon scene of chemistry gone mad. As I saw it, nothing grown the Kraft way would sustainably nourish a laboratory rat, much less soil itself" (Hirshberg, 2008, p. 2).

Hirshberg knew what he was talking about regarding natural ways to grow food. In the late 1970s, he had become executive director of the New Alchemy Institute—an ecological research and education center on Cape Cod, Massachusetts (Hirshberg, 2008, p. 2). Hirshberg's center had built a solar-heated greenhouse that used no fossil fuels, herbicides, pesticides, or chemical fertilizers. Yet, this greenhouse produced enough food to feed ten people three meals each day every day for a year. Wind systems provided electrical and mechanical power to the greenhouse. Tanks of water with fish absorbed sunlight by day and radiated heat by night.

Yet, Hirshberg had to admit that every day 25,000 people paid to enter Epcot and see the Kraft Foods presentation—more than visited his New Alchemy Institute in a year. He viewed the Kraft-sponsored pavilion twice on his trip to Epcot and came away deeply disturbed.

During his second trip to Epcot, he was accompanied by his mother. After ruminating about what he had experienced at the Kraft Foods exhibit, he had an epiphany and suddenly blurted out to his mother: "I have to become Kraft!" (Hirshberg, 2008, p. 3).

What Hirshberg had realized was that people like himself were unheard voices preaching to other like-minded people in an uncaring world. "To change anything, we needed the leverage of powerful businesses like Kraft," Hirshberg said. He continued:

> If we had their cash and clout, people would listen and begin to make changes, which led to my key point: To persuade business to adopt sustainable practices, I would have to prove they were profitable. Ever since, the challenge of proving that sustainability pays—and hugely—has driven my career." (Hirshberg, 2008, p. 3)

Realizing that the nonprofit New Alchemy was not going to be the vehicle for attaining success in the marketplace, Hirshberg needed to legitimize sustainability, so he returned home to New Hampshire and joined his friend Samuel Kaymen and fellow idealist in what seemed to most as a quixotic endeavor in yogurt production. In 1983, Hirshberg and Kaymen opened Stonyfield Farm in New Hampshire. The organic dairy farm had a fitful four-year start, but it survived. With no supply or demand for organic yogurt at the beginning, Hirshberg led a small, organic-farming school to become a $360 million sales company in 2010. Stonyfield Farm is now the third-largest seller of yogurt in the United States behind Dannon and Yoplait (Stanford Daily, 2011).

Although Hirshberg did his share of manual labor on Stonyfield Farm in the early years, his real talent was in brinksmanship. Hirshberg kept Stonyfield out of bankruptcy despite the debt-ridden conditions for the business when he arrived. He called on friends and family to make loans and invest in the enterprise. Hirshberg's wife Meg—an organic farmer before marrying Hirshberg in 1986—remembers the farm as cold, crowded, and having a road so muddy that many semi-truck drivers picking up and delivering products refused to drive it (Brady, 2006). Meg's mother, Doris Cadoux, loaned the business tens of thousands of dollars in the early years. "Every time Gary would come to me for money, Meg would call to say 'Mama, don't do it,'" Cadoux said (Brady, 2006, p. 1).

Later, Hirshberg's talent as a leader became evident as he focused on introducing organic yogurt to the greater public. His workers and the few organic farmers in New England did their part by farming without insecticides and fertilizers. They managed manure and soil fertility carefully. They tended sick cows without antibiotics, but they found that the cows would likely be healthier in the first place. However, it took a lightning strike in November 1984 and the resulting inoperability of the farm's milking machines for Hirschberg and his team to realize that other dairy farmers should supply the milk and let Hirshberg and his team focus on the development of the Stonyfield Farm brand (Hirshberg, 2009).

Hirshberg soon realized that "organic"—doing things nature's way—was a powerful concept when applied to business. Rich nutrients and no artificial fertilizer led to trees and animals thriving with no waste, as one part of the ecosystem fed on the waste of the other parts of the ecosystem.

Although it seemed nutty to other business people, Stonyfield made a practice of paying its organic milk suppliers as much as twice for what the firm could have acquired for ordinary milk. It also did very little advertising because Hirshberg viewed it to be analogous to chemical fertilizers in the growing of plants—expensive and unnatural. Instead, Stonyfield opted to make its containers attractive with the soft colors of the dairy farm (greens, blue, and brown) and to offer samples to consumers to introduce them to its products.

Hirshberg became the firm's animated pitch-man, convincing the public to buy organic products like Stonyfield's. Sampling events doubled as lectures on eating healthy and protecting the environment were given by Hirshberg (Reveries, 2002). Environmental facts went on the lids of yogurt containers. Hirshberg and his team built mailing lists and published their own "Moosletter." In these ways, it became evident that Hirshberg viewed the marketing challenge for Stonyfield as an educator for a nonprofit organization—the job he held before coming to Stonyfield Farm.

Hirshberg learned early in his time at Stonyfield that product sampling proved to be effective. "But our idea of sampling was to drive our truck right into the middle of anti-nuke rallies," Hirshberg said. He continued:

> There we'd be, in a field with 4,000 protestors, handing out cups of yogurt. . . . There was always an environmental edge to it. . . . More recently, we came up with the idea of sampling people who ride mass transit, because they're doing something good for the environment. So we went to the Chicago Transit Authority and told them we'd like to stand on their train platforms, hand people cups of yogurt and thank them for riding the trains. They said, *excuse me? You want to do what?* They

had never before allowed food to be served on their platforms. But we reached 85,000 people in three days and bumped our market share three points. (Reveries, 2002, p. 2)

"Now, I confess that our gross margins are nowhere near that of our competitors," Hirshberg said. He continued:

But here's the beauty part: Our net profit margins are better than theirs. It costs significantly more to produce Stonyfield yogurt than, say, Yoplait, our primary competitor. We can't pass all those costs on to the consumer, only some of them. So we had to find a different way to make a profit. In our high-cost, low-margin model, we minimize advertising while assuring customers that they're buying superb yogurt and being part of a planet-saving mission. (Hirshberg, 2008, pp. 11–12)

Perhaps more than anyone, Hirshberg has acted as organic food's leader by lobbying governments, winning over consumers, helping farmers switch to organic, and giving 10% of profits to environmental causes (Brady, 2006, p. 4). Yet, between 2001 and 2003, Stonyfield sold 85% of its company shares to French MNE Groupe Danone (Stonyfield Farm, 2011a). The sale of the shares let his original investors cash out, but also it tapped into the financial and distribution power of a $17 billion in sales industry giant. Although advocates of purist approaches to organic food production decried Stonyfield's "selling out," Hirshberg countered that his firm intends to accomplish its goal of making organic more than a niche of the U.S. food market. "Our kids don't have time for us to sit on our high horses and say we're not going to do this because it's not ecologically perfect," Hirshberg said. "The only way to influence the powerful forces in this industry is to become a powerful force" (Brady, 2006, p. 4).

Hirshberg continues to parry with organic supporters who advocate small-scale (correct-scale) and local commodity chains and who disfavor Stonyfield's "big organic" global sourcing of fruit for its yogurt. "It would be great to get all of our food within a 10-mile radius of our house," Hirshberg said. "But once you're in organic, you have to source globally" (Brady, 2006, p. 1).

Joel Salatin of Polyface Farms in Virginia's Shenandoah Valley would advocate for supporting local food and embracing seasonality through community-supported agriculture (CSA), as well as personal gardening (Salatin, 2011). But this implies small-scale operations and a dramatic shift in consumer supermarket preferences.

"Organics right now is just 3.5% of US food," Hirshberg said. "The good news is that's $23.5 billion of sales, but 3.5% of total food. What that means is, we're still a rounding error, we're still at the starting line. And price is the impediment there" (Schomer, 2010, p. 2).

Although many assume that it is impossible to be a big business and have a minimal environmental footprint, Hirshberg disagrees. Hirshberg offers examples of how Stonyfield Farms has zero sludge from its wastewater facility since it invested $600,000 to install an anaerobic facility where microbes feed on the water used to clean the ingredients from the yogurt-making equipment and thereby clean the water (Heimbuch, 2010). On this project, Stonyfield Farm earned back its investment after only nine months and gained the benefit of drastically reducing the waste that has to be hauled offsite to be managed. As an added benefit, the anaerobic digester makes some of its own energy (Stonyfield Farm, 2011b). Stonyfield expects to save $3.5 million over the first 10 years of operation.

Additionally, the firm supports 1,750 organic farmers through milk-buying and boosts fair-wage coops through its banana and sugar purchases (Heimbuch, 2010). Although every one of their nonorganic competitors had to lay off workers during the recession that began in 2008, Stonyfield has added 46 new jobs. In these ways, Stonyfield continues to make the case that sustainable practices are profitable for both business and nature.

## Your Thoughts?

- Before Hirshberg came to Stonyfield Farm, he was an educator as an environmentalist and director of the New Alchemy Institute. To what degree did Hirshberg continue as an educator in the domain of business? Explain.
- In what ways did Hirshberg apply an organic approach to business?
- Why would Hirshberg call his approach to business at Stonyfield Farm "win-win-win capitalism?"
- Why did Stonyfield Farm decide to sell most of its shares to Groupe Danone?
- Why did this prove to be controversial?

## CHAPTER OVERVIEW AND LEARNING OBJECTIVES

This chapter will consider the promise of marketing in the future with a macromarketing approach. Toward this end, the possibilities and pitfalls of businesses with social intent will be featured. First, the chapter asks again what business can accomplish in solving the problems of the world. Thinking about both positive and negative views on this question offers some valuable perspective for those attracted to integrating social value into the operations and outcomes of a business. The chapter will also offer perspective on what it takes to sustain oneself as an entrepreneur and business leader for society through one's career. Finally, Heath Van Eaton of Agri Fibers Inc. will be featured as this chapter's Maverick Who Made It. The appendix to the chapter features a business plan for one of Van Eaton's previous entrepreneurial endeavors with a sustainability focus WyoComposites—maker of composite building materials using recycled consumer plastic and biomass (wheat straw). The appendix to this chapter can be accessed at the supporting website for *Sustainable Enterprise: A Macromarketing Approach*, www.sagepub.com/peterson.

After this chapter, you should be able to answer the following questions:

- What United Nations (UN)-sponsored report serves as the backdrop for most recent sustainability scholarship?
- What is the difference between corporate social responsibility and market-based sustainability?
- What are the three skeptical assertions emerging from doubts expressed about taking a holistic approach to stakeholders and integrating environmental and social issues into the purposes of firms?
- What are responses to these skeptical assertions?
- What are two dimensions of risk that virtuous ventures carry that established firms using a conventional approach to business do not?
- What are three reasons sustainable entrepreneurs can be considered controversial by some?

## CURRENT THINKING ABOUT FIRMS AND THE "BIGGEST M"

### Market-based Sustainability

In 2011, one of the leading scholarly journals in marketing—*The Journal of the Academy of Marketing Science*—published a special issue on sustainability. In reviewing the contributions of the ten papers comprising the special issue, editor Tomas Hult perceived some important convergences in thinking about sustainability by marketers.

First, the 1987 Bruntland Report of the World Commission on Environment and Development (WCED) serves as a unifying focus for today's thinking about sustainability (Hult, 2011). The Bruntland Report defined sustainability as "meeting the needs of the present without compromising the ability of future generations to meet their own needs" (United Nations, 1987). In Figure 4.1 of Chapter 4, future generations and the environment can be seen as one of the secondary stakeholders for business. In this way, the futurity underlined in the Bruntland Report's definition of sustainability should be woven into the stakeholder thinking of sustainability-minded firms.

Second, a strategically based marketing view of sustainability is different from one that stops at corporate social responsibility (CSR) (Hult, 2011). CSR efforts that might include a triple-bottom-line framework (environmental integrity, economic prosperity, and social justice) might ignore primary and secondary stakeholders (with the exception of investors, future generations and the environment, and society and communities). In this way, primary stakeholders (such as customers, employees, and partners) as well as secondary stakeholders (such as nongovernmental organizations [NGOs], competitors, media, and the government) might not be considered in strategy development for the firm.

At their worst, CSR efforts provide only a veneer of social value to current firm operations. At their best, CSR efforts would likely not offer competitive advantage in the marketplace of the future as new product development and other value-creating activities of the firm would not provide the social value and core benefits customers would seek at affordable prices. By comparison, firms that stress market-focused sustainability, by integrating the customer and other important stakeholders, stand to gain a marketing strategy that is valuable, rare, and difficult to replicate (Hult, 2011, p. 2). Additionally, sustainability efforts can engage the organization's employees and become part of the cultural fabric of the firm's values, beliefs, and norms of the organization (Crittenden, Crittenden, Ferrell, Ferrell, & Pinney, 2011). This can be seen in many firm stories presented in the chapters of this book, such as carpet-tile manufacturer Interface, Inc., New Belgium Brewing Company, and Stonyfield Farm, to name a few.

Many organizations today realize that paying attention to the "big picture" of doing business can have direct and indirect advantages for the organization. Hult proposes firms take a "marketing orientation plus" for elevating market orientation beyond a narrow focus on customers to incorporate a wider set of stakeholders and triple-bottom-line issues in firm strategy (Hult, 2011, p. 2). In this way, market-based sustainability would be achieved to the extent that a firm would align itself with the product needs and wants of customers and the interests of multiple stakeholders concerned about social responsibility issues involving economic, environmental, and social dimensions (Hult, 2011, p. 1). In other words, market-based sustainability can be achieved by taking the "biggest M" approach of macromarketing.

*Sustainable Enterprise: A Macromarketing Approach* has underlined the importance for taking the biggest M approach to business so that the firm and its stakeholders could benefit as much as possible in the future. In this way, the book is about how to think about and pursue market-focused sustainability with a market orientation plus.

## Addressing Doubts

With such a potentially transformative approach to business as the biggest M, it is not surprising that some have voiced skepticism about taking a holistic approach to stakeholders and then integrating environmental and social issues into the purposes of firms. In general, these doubts are summarized by the following three assertions: (a) it will not work; (b) if it does work, it will not last; and (c) business, by itself, cannot solve the problems of the world.

### It Will Work

First, market-based sustainability *does* work. The business press now carries their stories regularly. Success stories of entrepreneurs and leaders of multinational enterprises (MNEs) who have led their firms to success in the market fill the chapters of this book. These stories include Ray Anderson's story of Interface, Inc.'s transformation in Chapter 1 to Gary Hirshberg's story of creating and growing the for-profit social enterprise Stonyfield Farm in this chapter.

### It Will Last

Second, market-based sustainability is proving that it can last. Of course, this takes time, but environmentally oriented businesses, such as Patagonia, have existed for well over 30 years. Early reports from firms, such as Stonyfield Farm and other firms employing the biggest M in their approach to market-based sustainability, show that such firms have better net profit margin percentages than their competitor companies—even though these competitors register better gross-profit-margin percentages (Sisodia, 2011, p. 101). (Although gross profits have only the cost of goods sold subtracted from revenues, net profits would begin with gross profits and additionally subtract operating expenses, as well as interest and taxes.)

Firms, such as retailer Trader Joe's, spend much less than their peer companies on marketing expenses, such as advertising. Research suggests that they spend 10% to 25% of the industry average on marketing expenses. They rely on word-of-mouth endorsements from satisfied or delighted customers to win new customers. Employees tend to like working at these firms because many of the employees resonate with the higher purposes of the firm, such as caring for the planet and its people. With lower turnover rates for employees, these firms spend less money on employee recruitment and training. Additionally, these firms have lower managerial expenses, legal fees, and executive compensation. In the end, environmentally and socially conscious firms run their businesses with lower operating expenses.

Such firms as Whole Foods Market apply what is said to be Conscious Capitalism (discussed in Chapter 5 as capitalism that views a business as a community of people working together to create value for other people and all the stakeholders). To the uninformed, it might seem that moral reasons or higher prices to customers allow these firms to approach the marketplace differently. By comparison, conventional competitors continuously try to lower input prices (to achieve higher gross profits) often resulting in cheapening the quality of their product and service offerings. However, with lower operating expenses, firms achieving market-based sustainability offer higher quality products and capture higher profits than conventional competitors. These results bode well for enduring marketplace success.

## Business, by Itself, Cannot Solve the Problems of the World

The third doubt about market-based sustainability is that business cannot solve the world's problems by itself. Granted, to a certain extent, this is true. Hitler was not defeated by a business. However, it is difficult to imagine making much progress in solving or reducing the world's problems without business. According to Clifford J. Shultz II of Loyola University Chicago's Marketing Department, such problems include (a) environmental degradation, (b) poverty, (c) public health crises, (d) immigration and refugee flows, as well as (e) the trafficking of contraband, such as humans, illegal drugs, counterfeit pharmaceutical products, and arms (Shultz, 2007, p. 294). In sum, a concerted effort to solve problems like these must involve business, government, and NGOs (O'Toole & Vogel, 2011, p. 73).

"Creative entrepreneurs of all types are essential to create the innovations necessary to solve the world's problems," Whole Foods Market co-founder and co-CEO John Mackey said. "These include not just business entrepreneurs, but also social entrepreneurs, educational entrepreneurs, medical entrepreneurs, environmental entrepreneurs, and political entrepreneurs. In addition, some problems will likely only be solved through international government cooperation" (Mackey, 2011, p. 89).

Social entrepreneurs are increasingly adopting for-profit business models and tailoring these models for their purposes. Alternative forms of structuring a social enterprise, such as the B Corporation, are now emerging that allow firms to institutionalize their pursuit of social value. The social business (a nonloss, nondividend company) whose products and services reduce or eliminate a social ill is a hybrid organization combining important features of the for-profit and nonprofit models. For example, Grameen Danone in Bangladesh makes yogurt locally and sells it cheaply to the rural poor through a sales force of the poor working on commission. The purpose of this social business is to provide the rural poor with much needed nutrients for their diet.

## Coping With Failure

### Virtuous Big Firms

Behind doubts about the feasibility of using the biggest M approach to market-based sustainability is an assumption about competitive market forces demanding profits. Such demands imply that when trade-offs occur across the multiple stakeholder groups of the firm, the owners'/investors' interests in profits and dividends must remain paramount. One example of this is jeans manufacturer Levi Strauss, Inc. deciding to off-shore its production facilities from the United States to foreign countries (O'Toole & Vogel, 2011). Levi Strauss had an admirable record of managing with multiple stakeholders in mind, but market forces beyond its control forced this move for its survival.

At the factories that Levi Strauss closed over a period of years, the firm committed teams to the shuttered plants up to two years afterward for the purpose of assisting former employees with outplacement services, lay-off payments, and health insurance (beyond the time period required by law) (Thigpen, 2011). The important point here is that off-shoring was the last resort.

When plants closed, employees received care from Levi Strauss. At the San Antonio plant, 76% of those laid off were either in training or re-employed two years later. These results suggest that only about one in four of the employees experienced long-term dislocation from the closing of the San Antonio plant. However, Levi Strauss's ability to know what happened to their former employees two years after a plant closing shows that the firm's regard for employees persisted long after other firms would have abandoned the relationship. In this way, Levi Strauss proved the firm regarded its employees as autonomous and free human beings deserving of respect and dignity. This matches the moral imperative of Immanuel Kant for treating people as the ends and not merely as the means for accomplishing something (Kant, 1785).

### Virtuous Ventures

*Venture Activity*

Because of the marketplace challenges in launching and maintaining a venture, it is not surprising that ventures can experience high rates of failure. Ventures are entrepreneurial startup business that have the potential for above average growth. Research about venture failures in U.S. metropolitan areas from 1990 to 1995 reported that 69% of ventures failed in the San Francisco area. By comparison, 32% of ventures failed in the New York City area (Cardon, Stevens, & Potter, 2011, p. 85). However, as a result of Silicon Valley and the high-tech sector in the south Bay area, San Francisco generated almost 50% more ventures. Overall, entrepreneurs in San Francisco saw 7,293 of their ventures continue after five years, while New York entrepreneurs saw 10,640 do the same. When considering that the New York City metropolitan area had more than three times the population of the metropolitan San Francisco Bay area in 1995, one gains a better perspective on what was accomplished among San Francisco's entrepreneurship community. There was more venture activity per capita in San Francisco—more than twice the rate of what would have been expected using New York's rate.

*Views on Venture Failures*

In a place such as San Francisco with vibrant venture activity, researchers have noted that failure is more tolerated and more commonly attributed to misfortune, rather than to the mistake of the entrepreneur or business leader (Cardon et al., 2011, p. 89). In metropolitan areas with lower venture activity, such as New York or Washington, DC, research suggests less tolerance for failure and more frequent blame attributed to entrepreneurial mistakes rather than to misfortune. At the national level, half of media accounts of venture failure attribute the failure to mistakes of venture leaders while the other half attribute failure to misfortune external to the ventures (Cardon et al., 2011, p. 86).

The point here is that business failure is part of the landscape that most entrepreneurs will travel in their careers. Perspective on failure is important. In the United States, bankruptcy laws favor those who borrow money. Entrepreneurs can form limited liability corporations (LLCs) that shield their personal wealth from that of their businesses. These legal arrangements encourage risk taking for entrepreneurs.

Failure may be functional in that it provides an opportunity for the entrepreneur to learn and improve their abilities as entrepreneurs (Cardon et al., 2011, p. 81). Important learning can be obtained about oneself by having a much better sense of oneself in the entrepreneurship process. Learning about one's venture and its demise is also valuable. Venture-related learning might include (a) issues of timing, (b) the need to develop more funding at the outset for avoiding financial stress later when investors do not want to fund debt-ridden firms, and (c) how failure often does not result from one cataclysmic event but from a series of minor crises. In future venturing, learning about networks and relationships can prove to be indispensable. Such learning might include (a) learning about leadership as well as (b) building collaborations with external investors and internal talent. Finally, serial entrepreneurs report the benefit of venture management because it leads to the skill of seeing the warning signs of trouble in future venturing.

Rebounding from failure leads to resiliency and a sense of confidence in one's abilities to succeed—both essential components of entrepreneurship. Surprising to some, research on entrepreneurs who experienced venture failure suggested no difference between this group and those still managing their ventures with regard to keenness about pursuing venturing (Cardon et al., 2011, p. 81). In fact many of those who experienced venture failure regarded it as an entrance fee for entrepreneurship.

*Socially and Environmentally Minded Ventures*

For the entrepreneur pursuing an environmentally and/or socially minded venture, the imperative to have an ethical grounding is more pressing than for a traditional venture. The reason for this is that without an articulation of a transcendent purpose for the venture (such as eliminating diabetes or increasing bicycle commuting by 20% each year), the default reasoning for decisions in the firm will be to earn more profits by reducing expenses and/or increasing revenues. This logic is difficult to argue against without a moral framework that is part of the culture of the firm that would strongly direct decisions to be made with a different logic than dollars and cents.

"To achieve most corporate operating goals, the direct link to profit is usually clear, making management decisions relatively straightforward," Rice University management professor Marc Epstein said. He continued:

> To achieve the goal of sustainability, however, requires a more complex decision-making process. Often, it's unclear how trade-offs between financial and social performance should be made. Sometimes there are no additional costs or even savings to be achieved by being a good corporate citizen—such as reducing the amount of packaging that improves both the environment and reduces the use of raw materials. Even when a company thinks that sustainability is providing financial benefits, the benefits can, at best, be measured over long time-horizons only. This makes it difficult to measure the impact of social and environmental performance and to quantify the resulting benefits. (Epstein, 2010, p. 52)

In sum, the virtuous venture might carry two extra dimensions of risk that an established business would not. First, making sustainability decisions is relatively new, so such ventures are "out there on their own" inventing the future without the body of knowledge available on other dimensions of business. For example, the source of much squabbling among the board members of Vikram Akula's SKS Microfinance (featured in Chapter 14) had to do with disagreements resulting from Akula steering funds to his original nonprofit rather than granting these funds to many charitable entities (Strom & Bajaj, 2010, p. 1). Second, ventures are usually resource-constrained and energetically pursuing sales to keep cash flow moving. There is "unparalleled excitement" with a startup (Cardon et al., 2011, p. 89), but there is not much room for mistakes—much like flying an airplane at high speed fifty meters above the ground for long distances.

# CONTROVERSIES RELATED TO SUSTAINABLE ENTREPRENEURSHIP

## Growth

Although feted as heroes in many cultures, entrepreneurs are not without controversy, and this goes for sustainable entrepreneurs as well. Controversies related to (a) growth, (b) institutional change, and c) social change swirl around entrepreneurs of all types. However, sustainable entrepreneurs, such as Patagonia's Yvon Chouinard featured in Chapter 11, raise their own special controversies (see Figure 15.1).

**Figure 15.1** Don't Buy This Jacket

It's Black Friday, the day in the year retail turns from red to black and starts to make real money. But Black Friday, and the culture of consumption it reflects, puts the economy of natural systems that support all life firmly in the red. We're now using the resources of one-and-a-half planets on our one and only planet.

Because Patagonia wants to be in business for a good long time – and leave a world inhabitable for our kids – we want to do the opposite of every other business today. We ask you to buy less and to reflect before you spend a dime on this jacket or anything else.

Environmental bankruptcy, as with corporate bankruptcy, can happen very slowly, then all of a sudden. This is what we face unless we slow down, then reverse the damage. We're running short on fresh water, topsoil, fisheries, wetlands – all our planet's natural systems and resources that support business, and life, including our own.

The environmental cost of everything we make is astonishing. Consider the R2® Jacket shown, one of our best sellers. To make it required 135 liters of

**COMMON THREADS INITIATIVE**

**REDUCE**
WE make useful gear that lasts a long time
YOU don't buy what you don't need

**REPAIR**
WE help you repair your Patagonia gear
YOU pledge to fix what's broken

**REUSE**
WE help find a home for Patagonia gear you no longer need
YOU sell or pass it on*

**RECYCLE**
WE will take back your Patagonia gear that is worn out
YOU pledge to keep your stuff out of the landfill and incinerator

**REIMAGINE**
TOGETHER we reimagine a world where we take only what nature can replace

water, enough to meet the daily needs (three glasses a day) of 45 people. Its journey from its origin as 60% recycled polyester to our Reno warehouse generated nearly 20 pounds of carbon dioxide, 24 times the weight of the finished product. This jacket left behind, on its way to Reno, two-thirds its weight in waste.

And this is a 60% recycled polyester jacket, knit and sewn to a high standard; it is exceptionally durable, so you won't have to replace it as often. And when it comes to the end of its useful life we'll take it back to recycle into a product of equal value. But, as is true of all the things we can make and you can buy, this jacket comes with an environmental cost higher than its price.

There is much to be done and plenty for us all to do. Don't buy what you don't need. Think twice before you buy anything. Go to patagonia.com/CommonThreads or scan the QR code below. Take the Common Threads Initiative pledge, and join us in the fifth "R," to reimagine a world where we take only what nature can replace.

patagonia.com

*If you sell your used Patagonia product on eBay® and take the Common Threads Initiative pledge, we will co-list your product on patagonia.com for no additional charge.

TAKE THE PLEDGE

*Source:* Patagonia, http://www.thecleanestline.com/2011/11/dont-buy-this-jacket-black-friday-and-the-new-york-times.html. Property of Patagonia, Inc. Used with permission.

First, a differentiating dimension of entrepreneurs (when compared with small business people) is the focus of the entrepreneur on growing his or her ventures. Yet, too much growth can bring risks to any firm. Patagonia's sales grew fast but erratically during the 1980s and 1990s, and profit margins fluctuated much from year to year (Reinhardt, Casadesus-Masanell, & Freier, 2004, p. 3). In 1991, Patagonia had grown too fast and had become overly dependent on a growing line of credit from a bank that experienced difficulties during the savings-and-loan crisis. When Patagonia's sales faltered in a recession, it could not meet the repayment schedule demanded by the struggling bank. Chouinard had to reduce his staff by 20%.

Chouinard saw growth as the culprit and sent a letter to Patagonia's dealers informing them that Patagonia was curtailing domestic growth for economic and moral reasons (Sirico, 2001). In the difficult year of 1991 for Patagonia, Chouinard seemed unable to reconcile his idealism about the environment with growing a business that carried with it a degree of harm to the environment. He said he could convince the president of any company that growth was evil.

Chouinard's stance against growth at this time suggests that he was caught in an internal struggle similar to the one between the critical and developmental schools of macromarketing thought presented in Chapter 10. (The critical school sees markets and marketing as moving societies away from sustainability, while the developmental school sees markets and marketing as part of the solution for moving societies toward sustainability.) His "no growth" declaration fit with the critical school's demands for a radical change in society's attitude toward consumption of resources (Kilbourne & Mittelstaedt, 2011). Despite the prescriptions of the critical school, research links entrepreneurship with what modern society seems to want the most—rising material standards of living and the elimination of poverty (Whaples, 2011). This tension between "no growth" and having a healthy business persists today for many sustainable entrepreneurs.

However, Chouinard tempered his stance toward growth over time and now Patagonia espouses a "slow growth" approach. In this way, Chouinard's approach is now more in line with the developmental school of macromarketing thought that proposes that solutions to current problems caused by marketing can be solved. It seems that Chouinard realized that the world needs a thriving business pioneering ways to better outcomes for the environment more than it needs a "no growth" business. Such a no growth business would likely be stifled from affecting social change because of being too small and too concerned with its own economic survival.

## Political Action

Patagonia has stayed clear of lobbying governments to intervene in markets in which it operates. However, the firm has historically supported grassroots activism for the environment. Targets of citizen action have been other companies, as well as governments. In 1990, Patagonia paid to bail out a number of its workers arrested at a protest of the Pacific Lumber Company's clear-cutting of ancient redwood trees (Chouinard, 2005).

The firm also serves as a trainer of activists intending to mobilize advocates for the natural world. It has covered all expenses for those who attend its Tools for Grassroots Activists Conference held every other year (Patagonia, 2011). At these conferences, seasoned activists help employees of Patagonia train members of the environmental groups Patagonia supports. Since the first Tools conference in 1990, the leaders of the firm realized that the concepts and techniques environmental activists need to market their ideas and programs are very similar to those Patagonia uses every day to sell outdoor clothing. So in short, Patagonia imparts marketing knowledge and skills at these conferences that have trained more than 1,000 activists. Patagonia staffers who participate report leaving exhilarated and more excited about their own work.

Patagonia educates readers of its seasonal catalogues, visitors to its website, and its retail outlets about thematic issues of the environment. For example, "Our Common Waters" is a campaign and includes links to organizations supported by Patagonia for the protection of American rivers, international rivers, and specific projects, such as saving Bristol Bay in Alaska from the expansion of the Pebble Mine—already 54 square miles in size.

In 2010, Patagonia's thematic campaign was "Vote the Environment in 2010." Although such a campaign might imply favor for the Democrats in the United States, Patagonia has not explicitly made a connection with one political party. "The environment is not exclusively a Democrat issue," Patagonia's Director of Environmental Grants Lisa Myers said. She continued:

> The environment is not a political issue. It is a human issue that goes beyond politics. We have Republicans working at Patagonia and there are a lot of amazing Republicans out there who care about the environment. In fact, the biggest environmental breakthroughs came under a Republican president. Richard Nixon put forth the "Big Three" of the environmental movement—1) the Clean Air Act, 2) the Clean Water Act, and 3) the Endangered Species Act. He also founded the Environmental Protection Agency in the 1970s when the environmental movement began. The environment didn't use to be a Republican or Democrat issue. (Myers, personal communication, 2011)

Other environmentally oriented firms have pursued a different kind of political action than Patagonia. For example, activist entrepreneurs in the U.S. solar energy industry sought government intervention in recent years to receive tax credits, subsidies, and solar energy production requirements among other benefits (Pacheco, Dean, & Payne, 2010). Using the industry's leading trade association—the Solar Energy Industries Association (SEIA)—firms such as Namasté Solar actively lobbied for the passage of Amendment 37 in Colorado. This amendment mandates power generators to obtain 4% of the total electricity of the state from solar energy sources. In this way, Namasté Solar improved its competitive position.

To the embarrassment of many, Solyndra—a maker of solar panels based in Fremont, California—declared bankruptcy in August 2011 (Mosk & Greene, 2011). Solyndra received a $535 million loan guarantee from the Department of Energy in 2009 for its manufacturing of solar panels in the United States (Friedman, 2011). Upon bankruptcy, taxpayers must pay for these loans, and 1,100 employees must lose their jobs.

## Focus of Social Change

As discussed in Chapter 6, the role of government in society is resolved through a political process. In a similar way, the priorities for society receive attention in a public discourse conducted in the media and among citizens. Gatekeepers in the media and interested citizens move individual issues related to the environment toward center stage for public consideration. Public attention is not limitless. Therefore, to a certain degree, as one issue rises, another weakens or is pushed toward the side.

Most sustainability startups tend to take a single-issue focus in their campaign for the environment because the issue has captured the imagination of the entrepreneur leading the venture and/or because of resource constraints (Hockerts & Wüsterhagen, 2010). Patagonia is unusual among environmentally oriented firms in that it has focused on a wide range of environmental issues. However, the issues it champions may not be the ones others would choose to put at the top of the list for social change. For example, when advocating to preserve Bristol Bay in Alaska from being despoiled by the expansion of the Pebble Mine, Patagonia cannot give as much support for environmental causes that might have higher importance to other activists. Additionally, an Alaskan hoping to move off the unemployment rolls and take a job at the Pebble Mine would likely not favor the Southern California–based Patagonia opposing the expansion of the Pebble Mine. In sum, one set of priorities for social change are likely not to be universally shared.

Although Patagonia's story of environmental advocacy continues to unfold, observers have noted that Patagonia's focus on wilderness preservation and reclamation are not the most important environmental issues of the day (Holt & Cameron, 2010, p. 128). Climate change, infiltration of chemicals into the food supply, and the impact of Western consumerism on the environments of the developing countries of the world receive little or no mention in Patagonia's marketing. Environmental problems that have no relation to the wilderness have been downplayed.

In research with consumers, Douglas Holt and Douglas Cameron (2010, p. 128) report that mass-market fans of Patagonia viewed the firm as an advocate for wilderness conservation—a very popular kind of environmentalism across a broad political spectrum. These consumers reported having little idea that Patagonia's environmentalism is focused on the ills of industrialization and consumer society. Holt and Cameron further assert that Patagonia succeeded in developing a broad appeal for its brand because it presented its brand as one for sophisticated wilderness adventure. Perhaps, partly as a result of Patagonia's branding efforts, upper-middle-class consumers in urban areas developed a craving for wilderness experiences in the 1980s and afterward as a way to express their cultural status. In sum, as a first-mover in environmental entrepreneurship, Patagonia was able to position its outdoor gear as the tools for sophisticated experiences in the wilderness. Firms that followed Patagonia would be left to focus on less palatable issues about the environment to brand themselves.

## CONCLUSION

This chapter considered the promise of marketing in the future tense with macromarketing. Pursuing market-based sustainability in business is not for the faint of heart, but increasingly more firms adopt such a focus and succeed in creating social value, as well as financial value for investors and owners of such firms.

The story of Gary Hirshberg and Stonyfield Farm showcased valuable aspects of intending to create value in one's venture. Hirshberg clearly intends for Stonyfield Farm to increase the scale of operations for his firm in order to win over more converts to healthy food, such as the organic yogurt his firm makes and sells. However, the sale of Stonyfield Farm to Groupe Danone raised questions about whether Stonyfield's commitment to environmental principles would be adversely affected by becoming another subsidiary of an MNE. So far, it seems that Hirshberg and Stonyfield are retaining their original values of caring for the Earth and for healthier living.

In addition to the recent growth of sustainable ventures, scholars also have begun focusing on market-based sustainability. Most all of them use the Bruntland Report's definition of sustainability as not impeding future generations' ability to provide for themselves (United Nations, 1987). Marketing scholars note that triple-bottom-line formulations connected with CSR efforts do not explicitly integrate customers (or a complete set of stakeholders) into such thinking for firm strategists. This implies that such CSR approaches will likely prove to lag market-based sustainability approaches that would use a "market orientation plus" for including a more complete set of stakeholders and triple-bottom-line concerns into new product development and into the relationships managed by the firm.

Despite the successes of firms taking a holistic approach to stakeholders and integrating environmental and social issues into the purposes of the firm, skeptics still voice doubts about such a new approach to business. Doubts about the financial viability and durability of firms pursuing market-based sustainability top the list of doubts. Additionally, mischaracterization of business as the only solution to the world's problems develops occasionally. A combined effort from business, government, and NGOs will likely be the most effective in reducing the scale and scope of these problems for the world.

Finally, the need for more nuanced understanding of failure in business is needed by those who would seek to use business as a vehicle to address environmental and social concerns. Business is one of the few endeavors where competition is allowed in a strong form. If someone broke in and took the office equipment and furnishings of a business, one would hear cries to send the thief to jail. But if a competing business comes into the market and takes a firm's customers, there would not be similar cries for justice.

Where more is risked, there should be more acceptance of failure in entrepreneurial endeavors. "In high-tech, failure isn't a stigma," said one former leader of a failed venture from Austin, Texas (Cardon et al., 2011, p. 89). Virtuous ventures carry two additional risks in that (a) they are developing sustainability concepts for business operations as they are operating, and (b) like most new ventures, they have limited financial resources. As in high-tech, if the leader of an environmentally and/or socially oriented firm has not lied, cheated, or stolen, such a leader remains viable for leading future ventures in the eyes of stakeholders.

Sustainable entrepreneurs, like all entrepreneurs, are agents of change. Not surprisingly, sustainable entrepreneurs find themselves embroiled in controversy because (a) opponents of growth see them as bringing more consumption and material depletion of the Earth's resources, (b) political action is part of what some of them do, and (c) their successes with their own causes sometimes move other causes lower in priority in public discourse.

## QUESTIONS

- If a conventional firm sells 85% of its shares to an MNE, there is little controversy. However, if Gary Hirshberg does the same, there is controversy. Explain why is this so?
- What does the biggest M of macromarketing offer firm leaders who want to integrate environmental and social issues into the purposes of their firms?
- What is market orientation plus?
- What is the most surprising thing you learned about firms pursuing market-based sustainability in this chapter? Explain. What are the implications of this for business in the future? For NGOs? For governments?
- Jeffrey Hollender founded the Seventh Generation brand of household products in 1987. The firm had $150 million in sales in 2010. *Fast Company* cited him as a model green business innovator. Yet, Hollender was fired in October 2010 by the company's board as a result of a disagreement about expansion plans for the firm (Schwartz, 2010). To what degree has Hollender failed? What would you want to know before investing in his next venture?
- What types of learning can an entrepreneur gain from a venture that falls short of meeting its goals?
- Which of the three sources of controversy surrounding sustainable entrepreneurs such as Yvon Chouinard bothers you the most? The least? Explain.

## MAVERICKS WHO MADE IT

### Heath Van Eaton—Agri Fibers, Inc.

GROWING UP, Heath Van Eaton's family farmed wheat and other small grains in northwestern Kansas on a family farm, so it is not surprising that he obtained a bachelors' degree in agribusiness management (WyoComposites, 2009). But rather than return to the family farm, Van Eaton saw his future in business, which explains the minor in accounting he earned as an undergraduate. When he dreamed about his future, he dreamed he would combine major elements of his life, such as wheat farming and business, in the launch of an agriculturally related business.

"I was going to be a hard worker no matter [what]," Van Eaton said. "So, I wanted to do something I had more control over (Van Eaton, personal communication, April 13, 2009).

After graduation, Van Eaton thought much about entrepreneurship. During his 20s, Van Eaton purposely chose jobs in restaurant management to not only pay the bills but also to develop his

*(Continued)*

(Continued)

abilities in managing and leading workers. He felt these skills would be important to him in his future venture.

"In the 1990s, I heard of a New Jersey-based company called Trex creating composite lumber out of recycled plastic and sawdust," Van Eaton said. He continued:

> I felt that substituting wheat straw for the sawdust would be better for the environment and create a much needed secondary income to farmers for their by-products (stalks and straw). At the time in the late 1990s, recycling was a giggle. But I cared about the environment and as a restaurant manager I found ways to recycle. So, based on my ag background and my passion for green, I decided to pursue composite lumber using wheat straw as the focus for my venture. (Van Eaton, personal communication, April 13, 2009)

Van Eaton eventually returned to the University of Wyoming where he applied himself in masters-level courses culminating in obtaining his masters' in agriculture and applied economics (WyoComposites, 2009). During his masters' studies, he learned more about processing agricultural products into wood-alternatives. He also spent some time at a Wyoming saw mill shadowing the manager to understand better the wood products that would compete against the products he hoped his venture would someday begin to manufacture.

"What I wanted to get out of it was not so much the money," Van Eaton said. "In 20 to 40 years, I wanted to know I had made a difference at a time when industry needed it. My real goal is to show how agriculture can supply and add more sustainability to issues of industry," Van Eaton said (Van Eaton, personal communication, December 20, 2011).

Van Eaton engaged the public sector prior to launching his venture. "The University of Wyoming led me to the Small Business Innovation Research program," Van Eaton said. He continued:

> My research project was sponsored by the US Department of Agriculture because I intended to produce a substitute for lumber. When finalizing my business planning, Wyoming Senator Mike Enzi met with me and challenged me to do a feasibility study for locating the plant in Wyoming. I am glad he did this. Later, the state of Wyoming gave me a Community Development Block Grant to locate my proposed manufacturing facility in Wyoming. Local government interest paid off. The local folks in the eastern Wyoming town of Torrington went to the federal Economic Development Agency and obtained funds for locating in Torrington as the town hadn't had any positive changes in the last ten years or more plus Torrington was already the "agri-business" hub in terms of Wyoming. (Van Eaton, personal communication, April 13, 2009)

Van Eaton did much planning prior to the eventual launch of Heartland Biocomposites in 2006. "Planning is the toughest part," Van Eaton said. "When you are in the market, it is real. If things go bad, it is on you" (Van Eaton, personal communication, April 13, 2009).

After launch in October 2006 with 27 employees, the firm succeeded in obtaining orders for the composite lumber intended to be used in decking and fencing (LeMahieu, 2010). Heartland

Biocomposites's claim for being a green product derived from its using wheat straw (annually renewable) instead of lumber (which takes 2 to 40 years for harvesting another crop). The firm's products also emphasized using reclaimed plastic with no chemical additives rather than using virgin plastics, which is the material used by most firms in the industry at that time. Additionally, Heartland Biocomposites focused on being a zero-waste facility where all staff involved themselves in energy reduction.

The composite lumber made by Heartland Biocomposites had superior qualities to competitors' products by being stronger, having less water absorption, and having very low fading as a result of sun exposure and weather. Additionally, Heartland Biocomposite guaranteed its product for 25 years while wood products offered no guarantee.

In 2007, Van Eaton's factory employed 40 workers. The firm's sales grew about 50% each year until it happened—the economic crisis of 2008. "The economic crisis brought uncertainty," Van Eaton said. He continued:

> Distributors like retailers quit carrying inventory. Manufacturers like me had depended on them to do this to have product in stock at their locations. They began taking a few jobs, then ordering a few more the next month. For us, it became spot manufacturing. We lost our economy of scale as our volumes declined, the inputs from our suppliers increased in price. At Home Depot, the end-customer would take that other product, instead of waiting for delivery of products that now had extended lead times for ordering. (Van Eaton, personal communication, December 20, 2011)

After years of 70-hour work weeks, and after much anguish in the final months, Van Eaton was not able to keep Heartland Biocomposites from bankruptcy in July 2009 as Pinnacle Bank foreclosed on its operating and equipment loan. Heartland Biocomposites owed creditors $5.13 million (LeMahieu, 2010). "It was taken over by a hedge fund group in late 2007 even though its sales were growing 50% a year," Van Eaton said. "But it had quit paying vendors, me and taxes" (Van Eaton, personal communication, 2011).

In the aftermath, representatives of Pinnacle Bank came to Van Eaton and enlisted his help in pulling together new investors to revive a business using the equipment and facilities that Heartland Biocomposites had used in Torrington. As the bank held these currently unproductive assets, they stood a better chance of recovering their losses if a viable firm purchased them, rather than having the assets sold at an auction.

Under the banner of WyoComposites, Van Eaton went to one of Heartland's original 20 investors and proposed relaunching another venture using Heartland's assets. Van Eaton felt this former investor of Heartland from Mexico was trustworthy. A new firm, Natures Composites, opened in April 2010 (LeMahieu, 2010). Van Eaton became a Vice President of the firm. "I was fired up and super-charged," Van Eaton said. "I formed and trained my management team and got the plant running. We began with retained customers. Many of these customers had waited eight months for more product. In 2010, 95% of sales were attributed to me from keeping former Heartland customers in place" (Van Eaton, personal communication, 2011).

*(Continued)*

(Continued)

Despite this promising start of another related business, the lead investors of Nature's Composites and Van Eaton ended their working relationship in July 2010, thus freeing Van Eaton for his next venture—Agri Fibers, Inc. This time, Van Eaton's firm will give more emphasis to a broader range of agri fibers (wheat straw, rice hauls, flax, corn, among others) in a wider variety of uses and applications. In addition to composite lumber, some of these other uses include particle board, concrete fillers, paper and cardboard fillers, as well as bioenergy products.

"Ag growers have all been very supportive and trusting of me over the years and are willing to sell to me," Van Eaton said. He continued:

Previously, I would have one truckload of straw to use in processing each week. In the future, I believe I will have ten or up to twenty deliveries per week with more agricultural suppliers from Canada and the southern plains states. There is no firm out there doing things like this that have the true potential of helping to address society's concerns related to natural resource sustainability issues. (Van Eaton, personal communication, 2011)

## Questions

- What does Heath Van Eaton's story say about long-term planning? About commitment to sustainable business practices? About the ups and downs of the marketplace? About the ups and downs of a career?
- Why would Heath Van Eaton be called a sustainable entrepreneur?
- What social value has Van Eaton created in his career to date?
- Thinking about what you learned about B Corporations in Chapter 14, would Agri Fibers qualify as a B Corp if it chose to apply for this certification?
- What are the similarities and differences of Heath Van Eaton's story with that of Gary Hirshberg's?

## REFERENCES

Brady, D. (2006, October 16). The organic myth. *BusinessWeek*. Retrieved from http://www.business week.com

Cardon, M. S., Stevens, C. E., & Potter, D. R. (2011). Misfortunes or mistakes? Cultural sensemaking of entrepreneurial failure. *Journal of Business Venturing, 26*(1), 79–92.

Chouinard, Y. (2005). *Let my people go surfing: The education of a reluctant businessman*. New York, NY: Penguin Books.

Crittenden, V. L., Crittenden, W. F., Ferrell, L. K., Ferrell, O. C., & Pinney, C. (2011). Market-oriented sustainability: A conceptual framework and propositions. *Journal of the Academy of Marketing Science, 39*(1), 71–85.

Epstein, M. J. (2010, Summer). Thinking straight about sustainability. *Stanford Social Innovation Review*, pp. 50–55.

Friedman, T. L. (2011, September 14). Is it weird enough yet? *The New York Times*, p. A29.

Heimbuch, J. (2010, October 18). Bioneers 2010: Gary Hirshberg explains how to scale up sustainable Foods. *Treehugger*. Retrieved from http://www.treehugger.com

Hirshberg, G. (2008). *Stirring it up: How to make money and save the world*. New York, NY: Hyperion.

Hirshberg, M. C. (2009). The full story. Retrieved from http://www.stonyfield.com

Hockerts, K., & Wüsterhagen, R. (2010). Greening Goliaths versus emerging Davids—Theorizing about the role of incumbents and new entrants in sustainable entrepreneurship. *Journal of Business Venturing, 25*(5), 481–492.

Holt, D., & Cameron, D. (2010). *Cultural strategy: Using innovative ideologies to build breakthrough brands*. Oxford, UK: Oxford University Press.

Hult, T. M. (2011). Market-focused sustainability: Market orientation plus! *Journal of the Academy of Marketing Science, 39*, 1–6.

Kant, I. (1785). *Fundamental principles of the metaphysic of morals* (T. K. Abbott, Trans.). Retrieved from http://ebooks.adelaide.edu.au/k/kant/immanuel/k16prm/

Kilbourne, W., & Mittelstaedt, J. (2011). From profligacy to sustainability: Can we get there from here? In D. G. Mick, S. Pettigrew, C. Pechmann, & J. L. Ozanne (Eds.), *Transformative consumer research for personal and collective well-being* (pp. 283–300). London, UK: Routledge Academic.

LeMahieu, C. (2010, April 14). Natures composites takes over Heartland BioComposites building. *The Torrington Telegram*. Retrieved from http://www.torringtontelegram.com

Mackey, J. (2011, Spring). What conscious capitalism really is. *California Management Review, 53*(3), 83–90.

Mosk, M., & Greene, R. (2011, August 31). White House-Backed Solar Energy Company Collapses. *ABC News*. Retrieved from http://www. abcnews.com

O'Toole, J., &Vogel, D. (2011, Spring). Two and a half cheers for conscious capitalism. *California Management Review, 53*(3), 60–76.

Pacheco, D., Dean, T. J., & Payne, D. S. (2010). Escaping the green prison: Entrepreneurship and the creation of opportunities for sustainable development. *Journal of Business Venturing, 25*(5), 464–480.

Patagonia. (2011). Patagonia's Mission Statement. Retrieved from http://www.patagonia.com

Rauch, D. (2011, Spring). Conscious capitalism: A better road map. *California Management Review, 53*(3), 91–97.

Reinhard, F., Casadesus-Mansanell, R., & Freier, D. (2004, December 14). Patagonia. *Harvard Business School*.

Reveries. (2002, June). Everybody must get Stonyfield. *Reveries Magazine*. Retrieved from http://www .reveries.com

Salatin, J. (2011). *Folks, this ain't normal: A farmer's advice for happier hens, healthier people, and a better world*. New York, NY: Center Street.

Schomer, S. (2010, February 9). Eat-onomics with Gary Hirshberg, CEO of Stonyfield Farm. *Fast Company*. Retrieved from http://www.fastcompany.com

Schwartz, A. (2010, November 2). Seventh Generation co-founder Jeffrey Hollender fired by company board. *Fast Company*. Retrieved from http://www.fascompany.com

Shultz, C. J. II. (2007). Marketing as constructive engagement. *Journal of Public Policy & Marketing, 26*(2), 293–301.

Sirico, R. A. (2001). *The entrepreneurial vocation*. Grand Rapids, MI: Acton Institute.

Sisodia, R. (2011, Spring). Conscious capitalism: A better way to win. *California Management Review, 53*(3), 98–108.

Stanford Daily. (2011, April 20). Stonyfield Farm CEO lights up about sustainability. *Stanford Daily.* Retrieved from http://stanfordaily.com

Stonyfield Farm. (2011a). About us: Our story in a nutshell. Retrieved from http://www.stonyfield.com/about-us/our-story-nutshell/our-extended-family

Stonyfield Farm. (2011b). Our yogurt works facility: Wastewater. Retrieved from http://www.stonyfield.com

Strom, S., & Bajaj, V. (2010, July 29). Rich I.P.O. brings controversy to SKS Microfinance. *The New York Times.* Retrieved from http://www.nytimes.com

Thigpen, P. (2011, Spring). Can we find another half a cheer? *California Management Review, 53*(3), 118–123.

United Nations. (1987, December 11). Report of the World Commission on Environment and Development. General Assembly 42/187. Retrieved from http://www.un-documents.net/a42r187.htm

Whaples, R. (2011, July/August). Cool capitalism. *Books & culture.* Retrieved from http://www.booksandculture.com/articles/2011/julaug/coolcapitalism.html

WyoComposites. (2009, October 23). WyoComposites, LLC business plan. Retrieved from http://www.sagepub.com/peterson

# Photo Credits

# Index

# About the Author

Dr. Peterson received his PhD in marketing from Georgia Tech in 1994 and joined the University of Wyoming faculty in Fall 2007 where he teaches doctoral, MBA, and undergraduate students. He previously taught at the University of Texas at Arlington. His research interests include marketing and society issues, research methods, as well as international marketing. He is an associate editor for the *Journal of Macromarketing*, and has served as Secretary/Treasurer of the Macromarketing Society. He currently serves on the board of directors for the Macromarketing Society, and the International Society for Quality of Life Studies (ISQOLS). His research has been published in such outlets as *Journal of Macromarketing, Journal of Academy of Marketing Science, Journal of Public Policy & Marketing, Journal of Advertising, Journal of Advertising Research, Entrepreneurship Theory & Practice, Journal of International Marketing, Journal of Business Research*. Dr. Peterson was a Fulbright Scholar at Bilkent University in Ankara, Turkey in 2006.

# ⑤SAGE researchmethods

The essential online tool for researchers from the world's leading methods publisher

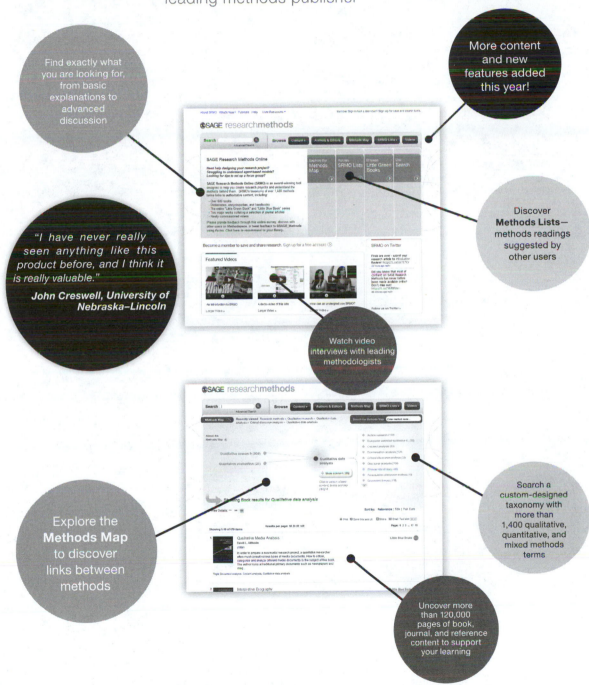

**Find exactly what you are looking for, from basic explanations to advanced discussion**

**More content and new features added this year!**

*"I have never really seen anything like this product before, and I think it is really valuable."*

**John Creswell, University of Nebraska–Lincoln**

Discover **Methods Lists**— methods readings suggested by other users

Watch video interviews with leading methodologists

Explore the **Methods Map** to discover links between methods

Search a custom-designed taxonomy with more than 1,400 qualitative, quantitative, and mixed methods terms

Uncover more than 120,000 pages of book, journal, and reference content to support your learning

# Find out more at
# www.sageresearchmethods.com